Managing International Trade and Investment

Casebook

Managing International Trade and Investment

Casebook

Debora L. Spar

Harvard Business School

Imperial College Press

Published by

Imperial College Press
57 Shelton Street
Covent Garden
London WC2H 9HE,
UK

Distributed by

World Scientific Publishing Co. Pte. Ltd.
5 Toh Tuck Link, Singapore 596224
USA office: Suite 202, 1060 Main Street, River Edge, NJ 07661
UK office: 57 Shelton Street, Covent Garden, London WC2H 9HE

British Library Cataloguing-in-Publication Data
A catalogue record for this book is available from the British Library.

MANAGING INTERNATIONAL TRADE AND INVESTMENT (Casebook)

by Debora L. Spar

ISBN 1-86094-281-X
ISBN 1-86094-294-6 (pbk)

This book is printed on acid-free paper.

Printed in Singapore by Mainland Press

LIST OF NOTES AND CASES

Part IV. International Trade in the Age of Information

MANAGING INTERNATIONAL TRADE AND INVESTMENT
COURSE OVERVIEW

Despite the ease with which it is often conducted, doing business across borders is not the same as doing it at home. Rather, it entails a whole new set of managerial challenges: reassessing competitive advantage; evaluating diverse political environments and legal structures; considering the impact of currency fluctuations and trading regimes; and understanding widely disparate cultures and business norms. The purpose of MITI is to build a framework of analysis that enables managers to understand the challenges of international trade and investment and to master the opportunities they represent.

In contrast to many other courses on international business, MITI does not concentrate on the internal administration of the multinational enterprise. It focuses instead on the external environment of trade and investment. Specifically, it explores the interaction between firms and the international economy. It examines how macroeconomic and political forces shape the environment in which firms compete and how firms, in turn, influence the political and economic conditions that surround them. MITI is more about politics than most courses in international business, more about institutions and the legal constructs of trade.

The course consists of four inter-related modules. It begins with a brief series of cases designed to illustrate how the basic elements of competitiveness can shift and alter as firms cross national boundaries. Factors that define a firm's strategy and success in one market may prove illusive or ill-fitting in another. Perceptions of a product's value may vary; so can industrial structures, relations with suppliers, terms of competition, and the interests of would-be customers. To operate successfully in new markets, firms must analyze these changes and respond effectively to them.

The second module expands our level of analysis to the state, examining how national policies shape and constrain the climate for international business. Using a series of company-based cases, we will investigate how firms feel the impact of foreign governments' policies and what tools are available for predicting, or avoiding, or even employing the long arm of government policy. The third module then extends this analysis to the international system, exploring how international arrangements and institutions — such as GATT and NAFTA — can affect industrial structures and change the opportunities for international business. It also considers how more subtle international pressures such as environmental and human rights concerns may shape firm options and strategy.

MITI ends with a capstone module on trade and investment in information-based industries. These industries are amongst the fastest growing segment of international trade. But the trade they entail is new, since the product — information — is invisible and relies heavily on systems of property rights and professional licensing that vary widely across national borders. Using both cases and selected articles, we will consider how firms can best manage these uncertainties to gain a comparative and sustainable advantage in the international marketplace for information-based goods and services.

Part I

FIRMS IN THE GLOBAL ECONOMY:
THE FUNDAMENTALS OF TRADE AND INVESTMENT

Lenzing AG: Expanding in Indonesia

In the mid-1990s, Lenzing AG was quietly going global. The world's largest manufacturer of rayon fiber, Lenzing was an Austrian company that historically had not ventured far from its base, a small company town about 70 kilometers from Salzburg. For decades, the firm had prospered in the comfortable European market for textiles, concentrating its sales on the 60 large spinning and weaving concerns that formed the bulk of its customer base. But in 1978, an unexpected phone call had awakened Lenzing to the possibility of international expansion. The call came from Ashok Birla, an Indian entrepreneur who had struck upon the idea of developing a rayon industry in Indonesia. Without prior experience in either overseas investments or joint ventures, Lenzing's management initially rejected Birla's approach. But eventually, enticed by the prospect of Indonesia's vast and untapped textile market, Lenzing's Chairman agreed to join Birla in an Indonesian joint venture. The resulting firm, South Pacific Viscose (SPV), became Lenzing's first overseas affiliate.

Within several years, SPV had become tremendously profitable, selling rayon fiber to Indonesia's booming textile industry and expanding its revenues by roughly 15% a year. In 1988, Lenzing was so pleased with the Indonesian operation that it decided to create a second production line, boosting the plant's capacity from 32,000 tons a year to 73,000.[1] It also began to invest elsewhere outside of Europe, using the experience gained at SPV to launch a small string of new projects. In 1992, it purchased a third rayon staple plant in Lowland, Tennessee and in 1994 it moved tentatively into China, signing a $36 million contract with an arm of the Chinese government to construct a new rayon production plant northeast of Beijing. These investments made Lenzing the only rayon company in the world with a truly global presence.

By 1994, Lenzing's Indonesian affiliate was operating so successfully that the company was considering a further expansion, a third line that would increase capacity to 109,000 tons and concentrate on production of the highest-quality rayon fibers. If this line were added, SPV would become one of the largest rayon facilities in the world, second only to Lenzing's Austrian plant. There was much to recommend the expansion: SPV had firmly established relationships with its

---

[1] The plant initially produced 17,000 tons a year. A series of design modifications subsequently boosted its capacity to 32,000 tons.

Research Associates Lygeia Ricciardi and Laura Bures prepared this case under the supervision of Professor Debora Spar as the basis for class discussion rather than to illustrate either effective or ineffective handling of an administrative situation.

downstream customers in Indonesia and an excellent working relationship with its local partner. As the most profitable of Lenzing's several operations, SPV was also located in a country that could well become a powerhouse in the global textile industry. But as the site for a major capital investment, the Indonesian operation also had its drawbacks. First, because rayon production is intimately tied to the downstream production of garments and apparel, expanding in Indonesia effectively entailed a bet that Lenzing's downstream customers would also remain, and indeed concentrate, in Indonesia. This was a good bet in 1994 but, with the emergence of major textile centers in China and India, by no means a sure one. Second, despite being located in one of the world's largest tropical forests, the Indonesian plant had no local access to wood pulp, its most critical and cost-sensitive input. Instead, SPV imported its pulp from Brazil and South Africa, adding considerably to its costs and, potentially at least, putting it at a serious disadvantage vis-a-vis any local competitor that managed to integrate backwards into pulp production. Finally, with the third line, Lenzing would be increasing its exposure in a country that remained politically and economically uncertain. Before investing another $100 million for a third line, Lenzing's management needed to consider whether the expansion made sense, and if Indonesia was an appropriate base for its growing international business.

The Rayon Production Process

Rayon, the world's leading "man-made" fiber, was first developed as an inexpensive substitute for silk. For centuries, scientists had tried to duplicate the complex production of silk, which involved unraveling the cocoons of silk worms fed exclusively on mulberry leaves. In the 1920s two English chemists, Charles F. Cross and E.J. Bevan, finally perfected the means to replicate the worms' spinning process. Essentially, their patented "viscose process" took the same raw material—trees—dissolved it chemically, and then spun the dissolved solution into a delicate thread. Though refined somewhat over the subsequent decades, the viscose process is still the core of modern rayon production.

Like the silkworm, the rayon production process relies on the chemical breakdown and realignment of wood fiber. In the first stage, sheets of wood pulp are mixed in a caustic soda solution that dissolves the weaker portion of the wood fiber.[2] The remaining portion is then pressed to wring out the chemicals, shredded into small pieces or "crumbs," aged, and blended with carbon bisulphide to form a spongy mixture called xanthate. The xanthate is then dissolved in a chemical solution to produce the molasses-like liquid that is viscose. In the final stages of the process, the liquid viscose is forced through spinnerets and into an acid bath that gels the liquid into a nearly invisible thread. The threads, or "filaments," are stretched and cut into "staples," and then drained, bleached, washed, and pressed into bales for shipment.[3]

With small changes in the production process, rayon plants can vary the size, brightness, or thickness of the final product. All types of rayon, however, depend on the same essential input: wood pulp. To ensure quality and consistency, they all also require an uninterrupted and unchanging production line. Wherever they are located, therefore, rayon plants share the same basic characteristics. They are technologically complex, operate continuously, and rely on a steady and predictable supply of dissolving grade wood pulp. While workers, both technical and lower-skilled, are involved in each stage of the process, the plants are still basically capital-intensive, with a greenfield facility with 32,000 tons of capacity costing roughly $100 million to construct in 1995.

---

[2] Sodium hydroxide, also known as caustic soda, is a corrosive chemical.

[3] Rayon staples account for roughly 70% of total rayon production. The other 30% is left uncut, and sold as rayon filament. Because the filament produces a rougher texture than rayon staple, it is used primarily in non-garment products such as tire cord.

Output varies with the quality of technology and number of lines, but most plants produce roughly 60,000 tons a year. This rayon output, in turn, becomes the raw material for a wide range of industrial and consumer products. About 15% of the world's rayon staple production goes into non-woven products such as bandages and tampons; another 15% is used in the manufacture of home furnishings such as drapery and upholstery; and rayon filament, made from uncut rayon strands, provides material for light bulbs and the inner lining of tires. What drives the rayon industry, however, and accounts for the bulk of its consumption is its use in the garment industry. In the garment trade, rayon serves as a basic input, a raw material fiber that competes with other natural and synthetic fibers such as cotton, wool, nylon, and polyester. Like these other fibers, rayon has certain defining traits that differentiate its usage in fabric and garments. It holds bright colors well and "breathes," traits that make it particularly practical for traveling and casual clothes. In the high-end segment of the garment trade, rayon's adaptability and "luxurious drape," as the industry describes it, also makes it appealing to designers such as Calvin Klein, who once claimed that "Rayon is sexy in a way silk can't be."[4]

Still, for more mundane and extensive uses such as T-shirts and socks, rayon fiber effectively competes in the market with the full range of natural and synthetic fibers. While some buyers demand rayon to suit particular fashion needs, many buy just "fiber," choosing competitively among the various alternatives and taking advantage of changing price differentials. Rayon's ultimate demand, therefore, is determined by one of the world's largest and most important industrial sectors, the textile and apparel industry.

The Textile Production Pyramid

In structure, the textile industry is comparable to a tremendous pyramid, with fiber manufacturers at the top and producers of a vast array of finished goods stretching across the bottom. Because each of the levels is distinct and complex, no one company spans its entirety. Rather, each is composed of very different sorts of firms and marked by very different patterns of production and competition.

At the pinnacle of the pyramid are the producers of rayon and other fibers such as polyester, nylon, cotton, and wool. Customarily, producers are grouped by fiber into two main categories: natural fibers (wool, cotton and silk) and synthetics. Global production of roughly 40 million tons of fiber is split nearly evenly between these two groups. At the production level, the two fiber groups are radically different: synthetics are produced in large-scale, capital-intensive plants, while natural fibers are produced by clusters of small farmers spread across regions with appropriate geographic and climatic conditions. In terms of sales and marketing, however, the two groups of fibers bear strikingly similar characteristics. In most regions conducive to the production of natural fibers, sales and marketing are handled, not by the farmers themselves, but rather by large collectives that pool production from across the region. With their buying power and marketing clout, these associations usually dominate their particular regional market for natural fibers. On the synthetics side, meanwhile, production tends naturally towards oligopoly. Due to the capital intensity and scale economies of fiber, and particularly rayon, production, the industry is customarily highly concentrated, with just a handful of firms clustered at the top of the textile pyramid. The level and intensity of rivalry among these producers varies widely across regions, with some firms competing much more ferociously than others. In all regions, though, the industry's concentration tends to create a high degree of familiarity among the producers and a relatively stable pattern of competition.

---

[4]Quoted in Lenzing presentation.

Demand patterns for all fibers, by contrast, are more volatile, since they fluctuate both with the global and regional demand for garments, and with the garment industry's demand for specific types of fibers. Some producers, such as DuPont (nylon), and some marketing associations, such as Cotton Incorporated, actively attempt to shape demand for their particular fiber by appealing directly to the public. Others, including rayon manufacturers, generally eschew advertising of any sort and instead base their marketing almost entirely on the acquisition and maintenance of relationships with their direct customers.

These customers, spinning mills, form the next tier of the textile pyramid. Much more numerous than fiber producers, they are also smaller in size and capital-intensity, with a typical plant requiring an initial investment of around $4 million. Using an almost entirely mechanized process, spinners twist and blend the fiber staples to convert them into yarn. Most spinning plants can spin any sort of fiber but require several months to switch from one type to another. Even mixing the same type of fiber from more than one producer is considered unwise, since blended yarn can result in fabric imperfections further down the line. As a result, spinners tend to maintain close relations with a relatively small number of fiber producers, minimizing the costs of switching.

The spinners in turn sell the completed yarns to weaving or knitting mills. On this third tier of the textile pyramid, firms are still more numerous and disparate. Most compete almost exclusively in their local markets and perform a fairly wide range of functions. Some weavers, for example, dye their own material, while others sell only in a "greige," or undyed, form. Often, firms will specialize in specific dyeing, printing, or finishing techniques and target their production to a particular segment of the fashion industry. Even here, though, the relationships between buyer and seller are considerably more fluid than those that prevail at the upper levels of the pyramid. Weavers and dyers sell generally to a wide range of customers and fabric prices are determined in a large, even if still primarily domestic, market.

Finally, at the base of the pyramid are thousands of garment makers, located in virtually every country of the world. Although there are a growing number of giant apparel manufacturers such as Burlington Industries and Springs Industries, the bulk of the industry is composed of small and mobile firms, requiring little more than some sewing machines and a handful of low-skilled workers to enter the industry. In contrast to the capital-intensity of fiber production, garment manufacture is exceedingly labor-intensive and global prices generally follow the trends of prevailing wage rates in the world's lowest-wage labor markets. At the base, vertical relations are also much weaker than they are higher up on the pyramid. Switching costs are low and styles easy to reproduce, giving garment makers little reason to invest in long-term relationships with their fabric suppliers. Instead, most garment firms are very sensitive to price, tend to purchase their fabric on a short-term contractual basis, and generally like to retain the flexibility to buy from a large and fluid base of suppliers.

This bottom tier of the textile pyramid thus bears very little resemblance to the fiber industry at its summit. Whereas fiber production is the province of a small number of capital-intensive firms engaged in stable, long-term trading relationships, garment manufacturing is a chaotic and volatile industry, filled with thousands of small, mobile firms and entrepreneurs. Despite these sharp differences, though, the two industries work essentially in tandem, with garment manufacturers reliant on fiber as their key input and fiber manufacturers selling primarily to the garment trade. The effect of this reliance is to tie all of the seemingly disparate tiers in the textile industry into one and to force them all, eventually, to follow the direction established at the bottom. Thus, as garment makers migrate in response to labor costs and productivity differentials, they compel fabric suppliers to accompany them, or lose out to lower-cost suppliers located near to the new garment center. The fabric producers then induce the yarn producers and so on up the pyramid until even rayon producers, with their huge capital investments and stable trading relationships, ultimately need to locate their production facilities as close as possible to the downstream industry in order to save their customers time and shipping costs. In the 1990s, this push for proximity was becoming even more critical, as garment makers increasingly employed information technologies to allow their customers immediate shipment and even customer-designed clothing.[5] The advent of mega-chains such as Benetton and Walmart only heightened this pressure, since buyers for those chains demanded the flexibility and speed to re-create high fashion trends for the mass market. They also bought in sufficient quantity and on narrow enough margins to influence the movement of wide swatches of the textile pyramid. If The Limited, for instance, decided to purchase the bulk of its T-shirts in China, the weight of its purchasing power would compel upstream suppliers to the T-shirt trade to shift to China as well, using proximity to provide the T-shirt makers with the speed and price that The Limited demanded.

Traditionally, rayon producers had solved the problem of proximity by serving just a single regional market and locating themselves at the heart of its garment-manufacturing district. Thus, U.S. producers clustered around the textile mills of the Southeast and Lenzing supplied Europe from its Austrian base. As garment makers moved in search of ever-lower wage rates, however, the single-market strategy became correspondingly risky. Once the bottom tiers of the textile pyramid ventured to lower wage countries, fiber producers had to locate themselves close to their newly-global downstream customers.

But making these moves was not always simple. To begin, the very mobility of the garment makers made it difficult to determine in advance where the industry was likely to concentrate. Since the 1960s, the newest producers had clustered in low-cost, labor-intensive countries such as Hong Kong and Korea. Yet the very success of these countries, brought on in large part by textile exports, had also put pressure on labor rates; by the 1990s, even firms from Hong Kong and Korea themselves were beginning to flee to lower-cost countries such as Sri Lanka, Indonesia, and Bangladesh. Just how far this migration would go, and where, if anywhere, it would end, remained unclear.

Adding to the uncertainty was the impending demise of the Multi-Fiber Arrangement (MFA), set to expire in 2004. Since 1974, the MFA had essentially regulated all international trade in textiles and apparel, providing a framework by which individual states could impose country-specific quotas on imported textiles.[6] The MFA was a vast and unwieldy system which served primarily to protect expensive producers in the industrialized world from their lower-cost competitors. But, as messy and inefficient as it was, the MFA had at least created a certain stability and predictability in the industry, since the quotas in effect determined the size and direction of trade flows. Once the quotas were removed, no one really knew which firms and countries would prove most competitive in a truly free market. Moreover, no one in the industry could really be sure that the international marketplace would remain free for long, since domestic lobbies around the world might well succeed in raising new, possibly more onerous, barriers to imports.

For rayon producers, uncertainty in the bottom tiers of the pyramid created a particularly expensive quandary. To remain competitive in a global textile market, they had to follow the garment makers. But, because rayon production demands such extensive up-front investments in training and relationship-building as well as in plant and equipment, producers like Lenzing had to determine in advance where the international textile industry was likely to concentrate. With the elimination of the MFA, they also had to assess how trade patterns were likely to evolve and whether that evolution would occur primarily in an open or regulated marketplace.

---

[5]See Janice H. Hammond, "Quick Response in the Apparel Industry," Harvard Business School Note No. 690-038.

[6]For more information on the structure of the Multi-Fiber Arrangement, see David B. Yoffie and Jane Kenney Austin, "Textiles and the Multi-Fiber Arrangement," Harvard Business School Case No. 383-164.

Finally, the rayon producers also needed to balance these downstream pressures against their own input constraints, and particularly their dependence on a predictable and nearby source of pulp. For rayon producers, pulp is the single most important input, dominating the production process and effectively setting the price of rayon fiber. Each ton of rayon demands a ton of wood pulp; there are no close substitutes and no known means of reducing the ratio of pulp to fiber.[7] There is also no easy way for rayon producers to control either the price or supply of this key input, since the rayon industry is but a tiny player in the global pulp market. The vast bulk of pulp, around 98%, goes into the production of various forms of paper. Dwarfed by comparison, rayon production accounts for just 2% of consumption and requires the highest quality pulp: bleached, "dissolving grade" pulp made from hardwoods, such as acacia or eucalyptus, or softwoods, such as northern pine. Because the process that makes pulp for rayon is technically similar to that which makes pulp for high-end paper users, most mills that sell to the rayon industry also produce paper-grade pulp, switching from one to another to meet demand conditions. As a result of this switching, rayon producers find themselves at the mercy of the paper market, since it is this market that determines the availability and price of dissolving grade pulp. As demand for paper increases, so too does the price of pulp, regardless of conditions in the textile industry. Rayon producers thus act almost purely as price-takers, captive to the highly volatile and cyclical paper market. To remain profitable throughout these inevitable cycles, they need to pass along increases in pulp prices to their own downstream customers. Beyond a certain point, however, price increases become unfeasible, since consumers will simply substitute wool, or cotton, or polyester if rayon becomes too expensive. All that the rayon producers can do to minimize this substitution is to build long-term relations with their spinning and weaving customers, relying on the strength of these relationships and the consistent quality of their fiber to pull them through periods of high pulp prices. They also try whenever possible to locate near the source of their wood pulp, thereby reducing the transportation costs which can account for 5 to 10% of total pulp costs.

A company like Lenzing, therefore, was constantly torn between two competing geographical pulls: the need to follow its customers and the need to remain close to its supply base. Getting the balance right was critical, since miscalculations could leave the company vulnerable on either the supply or the sales side of its operations. Given the up-front investment amounts in the rayon industry, mistakes were also exceedingly expensive.

It was against this backdrop that Lenzing's management considered the proposed line expansion at South Pacific Viscose. Before investing an additional $100 million in the plant, they needed to consider how the complex dynamics of the rayon market were liable to play out in Indonesia and whether, over the long run, an expanded facility at SPV represented the best possible use of their capital.

South Pacific Viscose

The decision to invest   By 1994, SPV had grown so successful that it was difficult for anyone at Lenzing to recall just how risky the operation had seemed at the outset or how radically it had altered the company's traditional modes of business. Prior to 1978, Lenzing had focused almost exclusively on the European market. From its Austrian facility, Lenzing catered to the fashion industry clustered around France and Italy and profited from a post-war surge in demand for synthetic fabrics. Because demand was strong and rayon fiber so bulky to transport, Lenzing saw little reason to expand its operations beyond Europe. Instead, it nurtured relations with its established customer base and

---

[7]In some markets, cotton lintner pulp is used as a substitute for wood pulp, but since it produces a much lower-quality fiber, most producers will not consider it as a viable alternative.

dedicated the company's resources to perfecting the technology and efficiency of rayon production. All non-European business was handled by a small network of private agents, who purchased occasional lots of Lenzing fiber to sell to buyers in Asia and the Middle East. To leverage its technological edge, Lenzing also sold rayon-making machinery to companies around the world.

It was Europe, though, that stayed the focus of Lenzing's operations and Europe that provided the base for the company's growth. Unlike its local competitors, Lenzing had the distinct advantage of backwards integration; indeed the rayon facility had been developed in the 1930s to make use of an existing pulp mill at Lenzing. Thus, even when pulp prices in Europe rose, Lenzing was protected by its internal source of supply; and when segments of the European garment industry fell prey to emerging low-wage competition, Lenzing was able to protect its customers by supplying them with the highest quality fibers at a competitive price. As of the late 1970s, Lenzing was well-entrenched and well-positioned, with no intention of changing its business operations or its primarily European focus.

Then came Birla's call, forcing Lenzing's management to at least consider the possibility of an overseas expansion. At the outset, Indonesia seemed a highly improbable target. In 1978, the country was poor and isolated, with a government that remained hostile to foreign business activity and sharply regulated all foreign investment in the country. The domestic economy was firmly under the authoritarian control of President Suharto, who had created a series of industrial monopolies and bestowed them (and purportedly much of their revenues) upon his friends and relatives. Tariff barriers were high, foreign exchange restricted and the entire economy subject to a barrage of regulation—hardly an attractive spot for foreign investment.

Yet, Lenzing's Chairman at the time, Dr. Hans Winter, had grown increasingly intrigued by the prospect of investing in Indonesia's fledgling rayon industry. For a country like Indonesia, rayon made sense: it was cheap, it was light and, unlike cotton or wool, rayon did not depend on natural conditions unsuited to Indonesia's tropical climate. Moreover, if Indonesia could develop a domestic rayon industry, it could break its traditional reliance on imported cotton and clothe its 140 million people without having to draw upon its heavily-protected foreign reserves. With its vast pool of low-wage labor, Indonesia might even be able to develop an export trade in rayon or some of its downstream products. Recognizing this potential, the Indonesians had already begun to encourage investment in rayon production, relaxing some restrictions on foreign investments and hinting that the industry would likely receive long-term protection from foreign competition. With these inducements in mind, plus the sheer size of the untapped Indonesian market, Lenzing eventually decided to join Birla in an Indonesian joint venture and the two partners each took 42.5% of the newly-created South Pacific Viscose. Because Indonesian law required a local partner, the remaining 15% of SPV's stock was split between Ali Noor Luddin, a local entrepreneur, and PT Pura Golden Lion, a subsidiary of Indonesia's most influential business conglomerate, the Salim Group. [8]

The plant at Purwakarta   From the start, SPV was a risk and a challenge. The partners decided to locate the new plant in Purwakarta, a remote town in Western Java that offered a plentiful source of water, a nearby electrical company, and government tax breaks for development. Situated halfway between Java and Bandung, it was within a day's drive of 80% of Indonesia's spinning, weaving, and garment manufacturing companies. It was also in the middle of a jungle, with no roads, buildings, or other infrastructure. For many months, SPV's main office consisted of an umbrella and a table; even after an extensive housing colony was built, it had to be surrounded by a ditch with acid to keep the jungle's animals from wandering in.

---

[8]Salim is the single most important business entity in Indonesia, with earnings amounting to roughly 5% of the country's GDP.

Despite the physical hardships, construction proceeded quickly, and SPV's first rayon line came on stream in 1982 with an annual capacity of 17,000 tons. During the next few years, the plant's engineers raised production to 32,000 tons. By this point, however, relations between Birla and Lenzing had deteriorated as Lenzing's management grew increasingly concerned about Birla's ability to manage SPV. During a 1983 liquidity crunch, the partners agreed that, in exchange for refinancing assistance, Lenzing would formally assume managerial responsibility for SPV. Daily control over the plant's operations passed to Leopold Fermüller, the Austrian-born technical director who had spearheaded SPV's creation. In the plant's early days, Fermüller had become famous for his hands-on exploits -- clearing lizards from the machinery and diving into flooded rivers to repair corroded pipes. In 1983, he became SPV's President Director. In return for its new oversight responsibilities, Lenzing was to receive a 4.7% commission based on SPV's total turnover.

The new arrangement proved a windfall for Lenzing as rayon consumption in Indonesia skyrocketed in the mid-1980s. Under President Suharto's "New Order" regime, Indonesia's economy finally improved, achieving GDP growth rates of roughly 7% in the 1980s and substantially decreasing the percentage of people living below the poverty line.[9] As these people began to consume, the demand for clothing exploded, as did the corresponding demand for fiber, and particularly rayon. From a base of 45,000 tons in 1984, Indonesian rayon demand grew to 82,000 tons by 1990. SPV and its local competitor, PT Indo Bharat Rayon, were unable to keep up with local demand. To address this imbalance and leverage what was by the late 1980s an extremely profitable investment, Lenzing decided in 1988 to construct a second rayon line at SPV. Although Lenzing management was initially concerned about reports of impending political turmoil in Indonesia, they ultimately decided to go ahead with the $92 million expansion which increased yearly production at SPV to 73,000 tons. When the second line began production in 1992, its new President Director, Ram Goyal exclaimed, "Everything is looking green: shareholders are happy, management is pleased, and we are proud of doing something in the country."

The third line   Even with this expanded capacity, SPV found itself unable to meet Indonesia's continuing demand for rayon. Because of the difficulties of investing in Indonesia, only one other firm, Indo Bharat, had entered the rayon market since 1983. Located just down the road in Purwakarta, Indo Bharat had an annual capacity of 21,900 tons, just over SPV's initial capacity of 17,000. With SPV's second line in place, the two new firms together still produced only around 100,000 tons, considerably under Indonesia's 1992 consumption of 132,000 tons. Tariff levels of roughly 20% only heightened the imbalance, effectively eliminating any threat of import competition and assuring SPV and Indo Bharat of a virtually captive market.[10] Meanwhile, the downstream textile industry in Indonesia continued to grow, with yarn-spinning capacity already the largest in ASEAN and expected to account for a full 50% of ASEAN's total by 1997. In 1993, SPV's sales increased by 18%.

Faced with such propitious market conditions, Lenzing's management began to examine the possibility of a third expansion at SPV, adding a new, cutting-edge production line that would push the plant's total capacity to 109,000 tons. Unlike the existing lines, the new line would also produce a particularly high-quality rayon fiber that had not yet been introduced into the Indonesian market. Although Fermüller had since left SPV to join Lenzing's Management Board in Austria, he remained intimately connected to SPV and strongly supportive of its expansion. In the summer of 1993, he formally proposed the third line to Lenzing's Chairman and CEO, Dr. Heinrich Stepniczka.

---

[9]In 1970, 60% of Indonesians lived in official poverty. By 1994, that figure had been reduced to 14%. See *Financial Post*, August 17, 1994.

[10]Twenty percent is the average and unweighted tariff level for 1992.

Stepniczka was basically receptive to the idea, since he trusted Fermüller's judgment and Lenzing's Board of Management was extremely pleased with SPV's performance to date. Stepniczka and the Board also wondered, though, whether the timing and location of the investment really made sense. While SPV had proposed a feasible plan for funding the expansion through a combination of outside bank loans and its own internal proceeds, the questions Lenzing now had to consider were fundamentally strategic: was Purwakarta the right plant and Indonesia the right country to account for such a large share of Lenzing's overall operations? Before proceeding with the expansion, the Board wanted to evaluate these issues in greater detail. And so, in December of 1993, they sent Mikel Dodd, President of Lenzing's U.S. subsidiary, to investigate the situation in Indonesia. Dodd was to report back to the Board by June 1994.

Once in Indonesia, Dodd quickly realized that the long-term success of SPV depended heavily on the evolution of Indonesia's textile industry. Until this point, SPV had produced rayon almost entirely for the domestic yarn and fabric market; it had succeeded largely because the government had chosen to nurture and protect the textile sector just as the economy finally began to develop. By the mid-1990s, however, the situation had begun to evolve. After nearly a decade of explosive growth, the Indonesian rayon and textile markets appeared to be hitting a plateau. In 1994, the growth of Indonesian rayon consumption had slowed to 8%, and some industry experts predicted that the country would become a net rayon exporter. Already SPV exported between 5 and 15% of its product, mostly to developing markets in Pakistan, India and China. A similar trend was underway in the spinning market, and SPV management estimated that roughly 30% of their domestic rayon sales eventually became exports, mostly in the form of greige fabrics. By itself this trend toward exports was scarcely threatening; indeed, it gave evidence of Indonesia's growing strength in the international textiles market. But Dodd was nevertheless concerned about a possible slowdown in Indonesia's domestic consumption of clothes. He worried, too, about the longer-term movements of the industry's "food chain whip." If exploding markets or cheaper labor in India and China drew garment makers away from Indonesia, then the rest of the pyramid would eventually have to follow. In 1994, some evidence of this movement had already begun to emerge, as Indonesia's textile and garments exports decreased by nearly 8%. Pushing this trend, apparently, were widening differentials between the productivity levels in Indonesian garment and textile plants compared to those of low-wage competitors such as China and Sri Lanka.[11]   So long as the MFA remained intact, these differentials would be muted by the Arrangement's intricate quota system; if the MFA expired as projected in 2004, however, price competition in the international apparel market would presumably run rampant.

Simultaneously, a new breed of competitors had also begun slowly to encroach upon SPV's comfortable Indonesian position. Indo Bharat had added a second production line in 1992 and was constructing a third, designed to expand its capacity to 75,000 tons by the end of 1995. SPV was not particularly worried about this new capacity, since Lenzing's superior technology allowed SPV to produce a better quality product at lower cost. Still, it was not clear just what this quality advantage was worth in the Indonesian market, especially if the government began to lower the existing tariff barriers and facilitate the entry of imported, possibly even cheaper, fibers, fabrics and garments. Meanwhile, other competitors had also entered directly into the Indonesian field and three new firms had already applied for licenses to produce a total of 115,000 tons of rayon. One of these, PT Inti Indo Rayon, had already constructed a 54,000 ton plant on Sumatra, the large island to the west of Java. In the process, the company had also lured away 90 of SPV's skilled technical workers with promises of significantly higher salaries. To date, the new plant had apparently been stymied by a series of technical problems that prevented it from supplying its full capacity to the market. But it also had two tremendous advantages. First, because it was controlled by one of Indonesia's major

---

[11]According to industry insiders, Hong Kong investors claimed that workers in their Indonesian plants produced just over half as much output by volume as their counterparts in the investors' Chinese plants.

industrial conglomerates, it was intimately connected to the Indonesian government and its power elite. Second, located directly in the vast Sumatran rain forest, it had an immediate access to domestic pulp. When and if it managed to solve its technical problems, PT Inti Indo Rayon would be the only backward integrated rayon plant in Indonesia. [12]

By comparison, SPV still imported all of the pulp used at Purwakarta. Although Indonesian regulation permitted them to import this pulp free of duty, the company nevertheless still bore the costs of shipping the pulp from foreign suppliers, mostly in South Africa, all the way to Indonesia. While the cost was not prohibitive given SPV's position in the Indonesian market, it did nevertheless account for 5-10% of its total pulp costs. In addition, purchasing pulp on the open market left SPV with all the vulnerabilities of a non-integrated rayon producer. Unlike its new competitor, SPV's cost position was determined in large part by the inevitable fluctuations of the pulp and paper market.

To avoid the risks of this dependence, Lenzing's management had seriously considered either integrating Purwakarta backwards into pulp production, or at least forging alliances with local pulp producers. In many ways, Indonesia offered an unparalleled opportunity for this backwards integration, since it had an ideal climate for growing eucalyptus trees and already supported 14 pulp producers. None of the existing pulp producers, though, had yet invested in the technology needed to switch from paper grade pulp to dissolving grade. They might, of course, be persuaded to invest in the necessary technology but the switch was potentially risky, since the value of their investment would depend on the permanence of a domestic rayon industry.

An even more subtle yet important constraint was that all of the pulp producers, and indeed most of Indonesia's forests, were controlled by a few military leaders linked to Suharto's immediate family. To invest in the forest products industry, all private investors had to collaborate with state-owned forestry firms; most of the private firms, moreover, were the province of those closely connected to Suharto.[13] Given the political sensitivity of the forests, as well as the huge but undisclosed revenues they generated, Lenzing had just not felt comfortable approaching the people who controlled them.

Instead, Lenzing had sought to cover its supply side risks by other means. Most dramatically, in 1994 the company had purchased 37.4% of a new pulp factory in Bahia, Brazil. The factory, called Bacell Ltda., was to be a joint venture between Lenzing and the Brazilian firm Klabin Fabricadora de Papil e Celulose, South America's largest pulp and paper manufacturer. Located in the heart of Brazil's vast eucalyptus plantations, Bacell would specialize in dissolving grade pulp, selling 60 to 70% of its annual capacity of 100,000 tons directly to either SPV or Lenzing's U.S. subsidiary, Lenzing Fibers Corporation. Once Bacell came on line at the end of 1995, SPV would presumably be able to protect itself against the vagaries of the pulp market and the possibility of a pulp shortage. But it still could not compensate for the cost of shipping pulp from Brazil to Indonesia, the time entailed in shipping, or the uncertainties of relying on a raw material whose local supply was controlled by Indonesia's ruling elite.

The subtle uncertainties that surrounded this elite infused other aspects of the Indonesian plant as well. Since SPV's inception in 1978, the Indonesian economy had done remarkably well, disproving nearly all analysts' predictions about the country's potential and Suharto's rule. In fact, with annual growth rates averaging 6.5% between 1980 and 1992, Indonesia's economic performance

---

[12]"Report & Analysis: Textile Chemicals, Fibers & Rayons," *P.T. CAPRICORN Indonesia Consult, Inc.*, No. 74, March 23, 1991. p. 13.

[13]See, for instance, "Pulp Investors Should Collaborate with Government," *Jakarta Post*, June 29, 1995, p.4; and "Pulp and Paper Chase," *Indonesia Business Weekly*, vol. III, No. 14, March 20, 1995, p.12.

during this period was among the most successful of developing countries.[14] Beneath the numbers, though, lay some disturbing notes. All political power in Indonesia lay still with Suharto and the military clique that surrounded him. To get nearly anything done in the country meant gaining some access to this inner circle and—usually—paying for the privilege. These sorts of deals became even trickier once they approached Indonesia's industrial core, since most of the country's key industries were controlled directly by Suharto's children and closest friends. Not only did this arrangement make business dealings inherently political, but it also raised the prospect of significant political backlash as economic liberalization proceeded.

By the 1990s, Suharto and his advisors were proclaiming their commitment to opening both the economy and the political system to new players. Following the course set by several of their Asian neighbors, they were relaxing trade barriers, privatizing state enterprises, and allowing for the development of a more fluid capital market. Most critically, Suharto had pledged to relinquish power in 1996 or 1998, letting the country's ostensibly democratic political system function freely for the first time. All of these changes promised to put Indonesia on the appropriate path to economic and political development. But they also threatened to be de-stabilizing and perhaps even violent. Demographically, Indonesia was an awkward patchwork of several hundred religious and ethnic groups, spread over 13,000 islands in a 3,000 mile archipelago. Since gaining its independence in 1949, the country had been ruled by only two men—Sukarno (1957-1965) and Suharto—both of whom had tightly controlled all levers of power. Under both leaders, the government had responded to dissent with force, using the military to squelch the uprisings that periodically gripped the country. On several occasions, these clashes had raised the ire of the international human rights community, particularly in the United States; more importantly, they had created large and violent pockets of ethnic and political opposition in Indonesia. As liberalization proceeded, this opposition to the central government might well become a de-stabilizing force, or even an excuse for the government to resort to its traditional, authoritarian ways. What either of these developments would mean for business in Indonesia was unclear; but because the Indonesian economy was tied so tightly and personally to the political structure, any change in this structure would doubtless carry strong ramifications for the business community. Complicating matters even further was a potentially explosive split between the ethnic Chinese who dominated the Indonesian business elite and the larger, but much poorer, Muslim community. In 1995, this tension, like many in Indonesia, was hidden mostly by a veneer of political calm. But once let loose, it had a devastating potential.

Remote as this possibility was, it highlighted the risks that Lenzing might take by concentrating its resources in Purwakarta. If Indonesia continued on its recent course of political and economic liberalization, it could well become a major center for the international textile trade. If the country became mired in internal politicking, however, or even if it grew so rapidly that its wage-levels outpaced those of neighboring countries, it could be abandoned by the more mobile tiers of the textile pyramid. In that case, investment in the Indonesian rayon industry would fail to provide the long-term rewards that Lenzing's management envisaged. Moreover, despite the upstream protection that Bacell offered, South Pacific Viscose still did not have the geographical and cost advantages of a fully integrated producer. Thus far, the lack of a nearby supply source had not hampered the plant's profits or competitive position. As other producers entered the market however, the situation was liable to change.

Bearing these possibilities in mind, Dodd prepared to make his recommendation to Lenzing's Board of Directors.

---

[14] International Monetary Fund, *International Financial Statistics Yearbook: 1993*, p. 413.

Exhibit 1   The Rayon Production Process

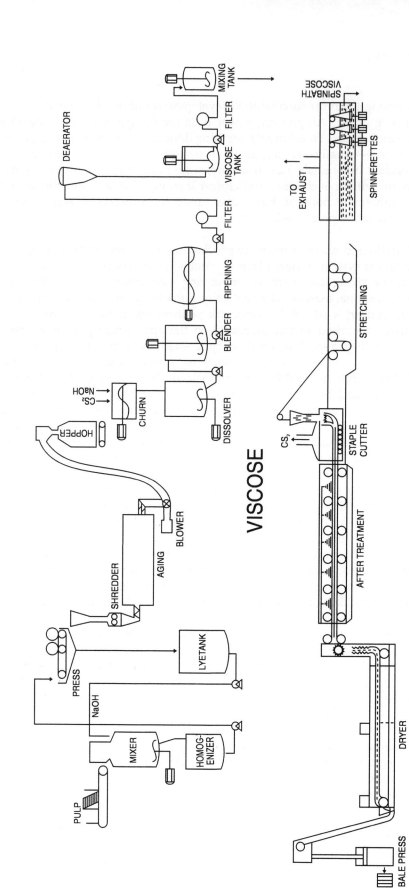

VISCOSE

SPINNING

Source: Lenzing Fibers Corporation

Exhibit 2 World Fiber Demand, 1990-1994 (thousands of metric tons[a])

	1990	1991	1992	1993	1994
Rayon fibers[b]	2,758	2,443	2,327	2,283	2,325
Synthetic fibers	14,894	15,273	15,911	16,084	17,718
Natural fibers					
Raw cotton	18,587	18,409	18,715	18,494	18,600
Raw wool	1,965	1,928	1,725	1,682	1,634
Raw silk	66	67	67	68	69
World total	38,270	38,120	38,745	38,611	40,346

Source: *Fiber Organon*, vol. 66, no. 6, June 1995, p. 122.

[a]One metric ton equals 2,204 pounds, or roughly 1.1 tons.
[b]Demand figures for rayon include acetate, a related cellulosic fiber. Generally, acetate comprises roughly 10% of total cellulosic production.

Exhibit 3 Rayon Staple World Market, 1970 and 1993 (thousands of tons)

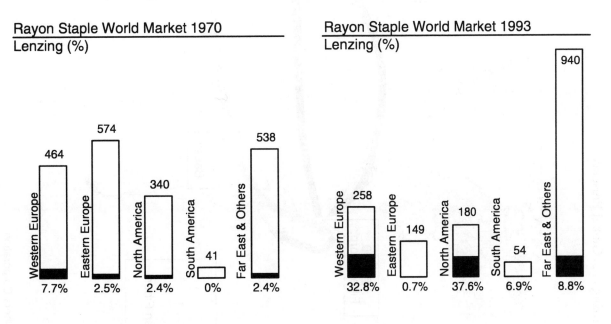

Source: Lenzing Fibers Corporation

Exhibit 4   Lenzing AG, Global Presence

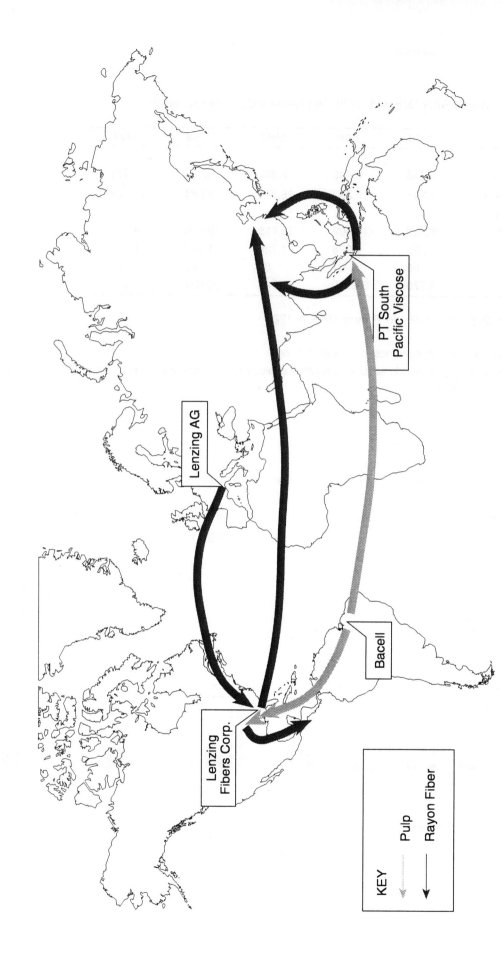

Source: Lenzing Fibers Corporation

Exhibit 5   Indonesia's Production, Import, Export and Consumption of Rayon, 1984-1992

Year	Production (tons)	Import (tons)	Export (tons)	Consumption (tons)	Growth (%)
1984	40,026	5,404	---	45,430	---
1985	40,655	7,231	—	47,886	5.40
1986	47,091	474	—	47,565	(0.67)
1987	52,844	574	192	53,226	11.90
1988	65,820	2,908	3,161	65,567	23.19
1989	66,055	3,340	1,961	67,434	2.85
1990	70,437	12,579	598	82,418	22.22
1991	90,251	9,182	7,684	91,749	11.32
1992	116,465	18,520	2,806	132,179	44.73

Source: *Indonesian Commercial Newsletter*, various issues.

Exhibit 6   Projected Supply and Demand of Rayon Fiber in Indonesia, 1995-1999 (thousands of metric tons)

	1995	1996	1997	1998	1999
Production	190	211	234	234	234
Net exports	20	27	36	20	3
Local demand	170	184	198	214	231
Export % total	11	13	15	9	1

Source: SPV marketing

Exhibit 7   Indonesia's Textile Trade, 1984-1993 (metric tons)

		Fiber	Yarn	Fabric	Garment	Others	Total
1984	Export	27.6	6,979.2	33,627.9	58,438.1	13,820.2	112,892.9
	Import	179,995.6	13,788.6	2,591.0	327.5	42,548.6	239,251.2
1985	Export	40.1	5,136.7	37,193.4	44,036.8	18,234.7	104,641.7
	Import	196,264.8	13,292.7	3,506.2	119.7	39,754.0	252,937.5
1986	Export	1,520.5	7,072.5	50,597.0	54,588.5	14,602.6	128,381.1
	Import	212,167.3	28,045.6	6,125.1	22.6	54,690.3	301,050.8
1987	Export	713.4	25,641.5	65,778.6	52,396.3	14,516.8	159,046.5
	Import	264,479.8	27,750.0	10,962.5	96.4	44,617.9	347,906.7
1988	Export	11,385.5	33,372.0	72,365.0	61,363.9	26,806.6	205,293.0
	Import	240,151.5	26,676.8	14,185.2	244.4	39,485.1	320,743.1
1989	Export	9,024.8	26,365.3	87,178.9	84,897.0	40,194.3	247,660.4
	Import	318,217.4	50,859.2	28,402.8	381.1	94,366.1	492,226.7
1990	Export	6,506.7	30,499.4	115,846.3	120,288.0	35,663.1	308,804.3
	Import	401,293.8	79,906.1	44,425.4	815.3	119,075.9	645,516.6
1991	Export	13,702.3	59,872.0	146,480.0	146,678.9	40,774.6	407,507.9
	Import	441,070.7	48,631.8	55,329.1	1,097.6	103,859.3	649,988.4
1992	Export	21,654.7	100,064.7	193,279.9	172,980.8	89,525.6	577,505.7
	Import	564,096.9	91,949.6	64,620.9	988.3	131,423.6	853,079.2
1993	Export	31,582.4	143,239.4	297,275.8	187,033.8	11,105.1	670,236.6
	Import	579,494.2	46,826.3	154,776.5	1,959.4	4,288.9	787,345.2

Source: Asosiasi Perteskstilan Indonesia

Note: Numbers may not add due to rounding.

Exhibit 8   The World's Ten Leading Garment Exporters, 1980 and 1993

Exports	1980 Value (US$ bn)	1980 Share of World Trade (%)	1993 Value (US$ bn)	1993 Share of World Trade (%)
Hong Kong	5.0	12.3	21.0	15.8
domestic exports	4.7	11.5	9.3	7.0
re-exports	0.3	0.8	11.7	8.8
China[a]	1.6	4.0	18.4	13.9
Italy	4.6	11.3	11.8	8.9
Germany	2.9	7.1	6.7	5.1
South Korea	2.9	7.3	6.2	4.6
USA	1.3	3.1	5.0	3.7
France	2.3	5.7	4.6	3.4
Turkey	0.1	0.3	4.3	3.3
Thailand	0.3	0.7	4.2	3.1
Portugal	0.6	1.6	3.1	2.4

Source: Textiles Intelligence Limited, *Textile Outlook International*, July 1995, p. 26.

[a]Includes exports from processing zones.

Exhibit 9   Comparative Labor Costs in Spinning and Weaving, 1980-1994 (US$/hour)

	1980	1990	1993	1994	Average annual % change		
					1980-94	1990-94	1993-94
Hong Kong	1.91	3.05	3.85	4.40	6.1	9.6	14.3
Thailand	0.33	0.92	1.04	1.41	10.9	11.3	35.6
Malaysia	n/a	0.86	1.18	n/a	7.8	11.1	n/a
Egypt	0.39	0.45	0.57	0.64	3.6	9.2	12.3
India	0.60	0.72	0.56	0.58	(0.2)	(5.3)	3.6
China	n/a	0.37	0.36	0.48	6.3	6.7	33.3
Indonesia	n/a	0.25	0.43	0.46	7.2	16.5	7.0
Pakistan	0.34	0.39	0.44	0.45	2.0	3.6	2.3
Sri Lanka	n/a	0.24	0.39	0.42	4.1	15.0	7.7
Vietnam	n/a	n/a	0.37	0.39	n/a	n/a	5.4
Bangladesh	n/a	n/a	0.23	0.26	n/a	n/a	13.0

Source: Textiles Intelligence Limited, *Textile Outlook International,* July 1995, pp. 33-34.

Exhibit 10   Structure of the Forest Products Industry

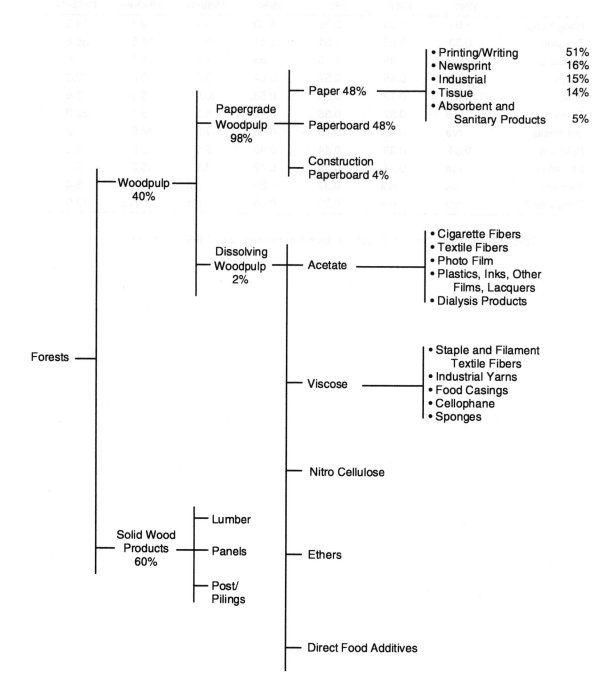

Exhibit 11   Rayon Fiber and Pulp Prices, 1986-1994 (Rupiah per kg)

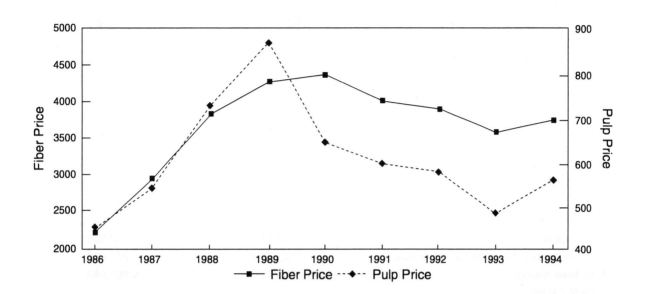

Source: PT South Pacific Viscose

Exhibit 12   Lenzing AG: Balance Sheet, 1992-1993 (thousands of Austrian schillings)

	1992	1993
Assets		
Fixed Assets		
Intangible assets	385,316	360,668
Tangible assets		
Land with buildings and buildings on third-party land	781,979	908,418
Undeveloped land	16,205	15,606
Plant and machinery	1,718,195	1,764,882
Tools, plant, and office equipment	183,356	157,330
Tangible assets under construction	422,252	176,520
Payments on account	1,725	8,935
Financial assets		
Affiliated undertakings	978,748	906,979
Other undertakings	44,794	41,059
Loans	11,517	82,536
Investments held as current assets	216,653	247,050
Total fixed assets	4,760,740	4,669,983
Current Assets		
Stocks		
Raw materials and consumables	266,306	256,560
Work in progress	180,181	125,044
Finished goods	447,108	284,413
Performances prior to invoicing minus payments received on account	135,528	50,800
Payments on account	3,218	5,843
Debtors and other assets		
Trade debtors	1,148,145	1,012,318
Amounts owed by affiliated undertakings	99,023	267,622
Other amounts owed	17,723	8,544
Other debtors and assets	249,221	239,886
Investments		
Other investments	0	105,242
Cash at bank and in hand	100,051	431,144
Total current assets	2,646,504	2,787,416
Prepayments and accrued income	14,132	19,562
Total Assets	7,421,376	7,476,961

Exhibit 12   Lenzing AG: Balance Sheet, 1992-1993 (thousands of Austrian schillings)
              (continued)

	1992	1993
Liabilities		
Capital and Reserves		
Share capital	367,500	367,500
Capital reserves committed	875,149	875,149
Revenue reserves uncommitted	268,343	240,396
Balance sheet profit	59,891	19,537
Public-Sector Investment Grants	77,999	120,469
Untaxed Reserves		
Valuation reserve (under 1988 Income Tax Act)	722,289	539,672
Other untaxed reserves	593,555	597,363
Provisions		
Severance payments	362,288	381,760
Pension obligations	961,994	964,883
Taxation	52,588	52,588
Other provisions	370,294	503,681
Liabilities		
Amounts owed to non-banks	119,121	228,454
Amounts owed to banks	1,821,162	2,015,396
Payments received on account of orders	64,702	32,514
Trade creditors	505,375	371,033
Amounts owed to affiliated undertakings	16,837	9,801
Amounts owed by other undertakings	0	263
Other creditors	157,726	138,937
Accruals and Deferred Income	24,563	17,561
Total Liabilities	7,421,376	7,476,957
Exchange rate (schillings/US$)	11.3	12.1

Source: Lenzing Annual Report 1993

Note: Numbers may not add due to rounding.

Exhibit 13   PT South Pacific Viscose: Balance Sheet, 1992-1993 (millions of Rupiah)

	1992	1993
Assets		
Current Assets		
Cash and cash equivalents	1,742.6	2,551.3
Time deposits	50,769.4	62,664.2
Trade accounts receivable	35,065.8	30,433.4
Other accounts receivable	1,573.1	2,032.8
Inventories	45,651.9	54,020.7
Prepaid expenses	827.5	898.4
Claim for tax refund	2,193.8	---
Total Current Assets	137,824.1	152,600.8
Property, Plant and Equipment	133,952.6	145,669.9
Total Assets	271,776.7	298,270.7
Liabilities and Stockholders' Equity		
Current Liabilities		
Trade accounts payable	15,343.0	25,888.8
Other accounts payable	6,013.9	6,435.1
Taxes payable	1,149.9	5,046.0
Accrued expenses	8,072.4	11,314.8
Current maturities of long-term debt	4,938.6	12,533.4
Total Current Liabilities	35,517.8	61,218.1
Long-term debt	108,255.0	88,113.6
Stockholders' equity and retained earnings	128,004.0	148,939.2
Total Liabilities and Stockholders' Equity	271,776.8	298,270.9
Exchange rate (Rupiah/US$)	2,029.9	2,087.1

Source: PT South Pacific Viscose Annual Report, 1993, and International Monetary Fund, *International Financial Statistics,* August 1995, p. 300.

Exhibit 14 PT South Pacific Viscose: Income Statement, 1992-1993 (millions of Rupiah)

	1992	1993
Net sales	186,056.3	219,877.0
Cost of goods sold	144,797.7	166,406.1
Gross profit	41,258.6	53,470.9
Operating expenses	13,091.0	12,957.5
Operating income	28,167.6	40,513.4
Deductions from operating income:		
Interest and financing charges, net	2,993.8	2,962.5
Tax expenses	---	527.6
Loss (gain) on foreign exchange, net	(1,586.9)	442.2
Loss (gain) on sale of properties	(65.9)	(10.8)
Insurance claims	(538.6)	---
Miscellaneous	---	(484.7)
Total deductions	802.4	3,436.9
Income before provision for income tax	27,365.2	37,076.5
Provision for income tax	4,602.7	9,107.4
Net income	22,762.5	27,969.0
Retained earnings at beginning of year	44,506.4	64,038.4
Cash dividends	(3,230.6)	(7,033.8)
Retained earnings at end of year	64,038.3	84,973.6
Exchange rate (Rupiah/US$)	2,029.9	2,087.1

Source: PT South Pacific Viscose Annual Report, 1993, and International Monetary Fund, *International Financial Statistics,* August 1995, p. 300.

Microsoft in the People's Republic of China, 1993

Richard Fade, vice president in charge of Microsoft's Far East Operations, pondered Microsoft's planned introduction of products in the People's Republic of China (PRC). Experience in Japan and in other Asian countries had unambiguously pointed to the importance of localizing the product to suit the Chinese language and culture. However, as the country underwent a period of transition from a socialist to a market economy, localization was proving to be a bigger challenge in the PRC than initially anticipated. Especially on Fade's mind was the localization of Microsoft's widely successful English version of Windows 3.1.

Fade realized that his decisions regarding whether and how to deal with the local Chinese software vendors represented a delicate balancing between political and economic considerations. It could play an important role not only in influencing the current structure of the personal computer (PC) software industry in the PRC but also its structure in the years to come. Given the burgeoning importance of software in Asia (**Exhibit 1**), the decision was an important one.

The PC Software Industry

Kinds of Software

Three layers of software lay between the PC's microprocessor and most users. The operating system was the layer closest to the microprocessor, and was responsible for performing the basic "housekeeping" functions (like file creation and maintenance, printing).

The next layer above was a graphical user interface (GUI) which assisted communication between the operating system and the application programs (the layer closest to the user). Among other things, GUIs allowed the user to use a mouse to point and shoot, made it easier to use programs, and generally made the computer much more user friendly. GUIs had been around since the Macintosh GUI helped Apple differentiate its products from the existing personal computers. However, it was only with the third release of Microsoft's Windows in May 1990 (in the United States) that such interfaces became very popular. Microsoft's Windows was the first GUI written for DOS and was by far the most popular. By 1993, GUIs for major operating systems were fully integrated into the operating system software.

Applications constituted the third layer. The most commonly used applications included spreadsheets, word processors, and database managers.[1] Separate versions of each application were written for specific GUIs and operating systems. In fact, the popularity of a GUI or an operating system depended on the availability of applications that could be used in conjunction with it. Similarly, the likelihood of applications being written to run with a particular GUI or operating system depended on the popularity of the latter.

Localization

Localization was the term given to the adaptation of software to specific locales. It was a complicated process that involved several tasks. These tasks included, but were not limited to (1) supporting local character sets that were different from the conventional character sets developed for the English language, (2) making software compatible with different formatting conventions, (3) adapting various functions to be used with the new character set (for example, a standard sorting function would have to be re-coded to sort in Chinese), (4) translating the interface to a form that was familiar to the local user,[2] (5) configuring the software so that it could support other locally available software and hardware, (6) translating all documentation and promotional literature into the local language, (7) providing local customer service. Many of the tasks grouped under localization could involve substantial and costly reengineering of the software's underlying computer code.

Asian languages required representing non-Roman characters. The ideographic[3] script used in the PRC, referred to as the "simplified" Chinese character set, had over 7,000 commonly used characters,[4] originally created with brush and ink. Taiwan and Hong Kong used the "traditional" Chinese character set with 13,000 characters. Thus, product had to be localized separately for the PRC on the one hand, and for Taiwan and Hong Kong on the other. Software used in Japan had to support three distinct writing scripts, Hiragana, Kanji and Katakana.[5] Going hand-in-hand with the more complex character sets was the need for developing several creative ways of entering information, since the standard Western keyboard was clearly inadequate. These included the use of sequences of key-strokes and of menu-driven systems to choose characters.

In addition to reengineering the code to take into account the changes needed to represent the more complicated character sets, localization required sensitivity to differences in the visual presentation of information. For example, some concepts that appeared standard to the Western user of word processors like tabs, cursors, and margins, stemmed from a typewriter culture that was absent in parts of Asia. In Japan, documents (before computers were extensively used) were typically formatted using writing pads that used a carefully constructed grid for each character. Thus, Japanese users were initially unfamiliar with the concept of cursor movements in word processors. Further, Japanese text was traditionally written from top to bottom rather than from left to right. A typical paragraph translated into Japanese took about 60% of the space used by the corresponding English paragraph.[6]

---

[1] Suites, which bundled together a single manufacturer's most commonly used applications (often a spreadsheet program, a word-processing program, and a presentation manager), were becoming increasingly popular in the United States.

[2] For example, all screen displays visible to the end user, such as prompts, menus and error messages, had to be put into a familiar form. The user had to be able to edit and print horizontally and vertically.

[3] An ideographic character script uses pictures or symbols to depict a thing or an idea.

[4] The most common PC character set was the extended ASCII character set which could support up to 256 characters. Character sets that had more than 256 characters were particularly difficult to localize, especially if the original code had not taken into account the possibility that such a localization might be needed later on.

[5] Text typically contained an average of 55% Hiragana, 35% Kanji and 10% Katakana.

[6] Cultural differences played a role as well. For example, software with animated characters that appealed to children in the West did not always do well in Asian countries. The average Japanese consumer thinks that the nose on cartoon characters used in the United States is too big!

Certainly, localization was not a zero-one affair. The software vendor could choose the extent to which it wished to localize software—and hence the cost it incurred in doing so—by its decisions on the number of features that it chose to adapt to the local context, and by the attention paid to the quality of localization of the individual features. Localization required considerable attention to detail. Even a simple translation could run into problems if the vendor performing the localization did not pay sufficient attention to detail and was not a very competent programmer.

There were two ways in which localization could be carried out. One way was to create a software layer that lay between the program being localized and the user. This required relatively little input from the software producer and could be done independently by any third party. If the program thus localized was an operating system or a GUI, then application programs would have to interface with the newly added layer, in addition to the operating system or GUI. If the program being localized was an application, then the new layer determined the look and feel of the application to the user.

The more refined method of localization required the involvement of the original software producer in the localization process. This involved rewriting some of the internals of the code that allowed it to, among other things, create an internal representation system for the vastly greater number of characters in the Chinese character set than in the English character set. In this method, there was no additional software shell sitting in between the software and the user. While Western software companies had not traditionally taken into account the need for localization into Chinese (and other Asian languages), the expectation was that new product releases would be written in a way that facilitated localization for the booming Asian market.

The People's Republic of China

China's 3.7 million square miles (**Exhibit 2**) were divided into 22 provinces, 3 municipalities (Beijing, Shanghai, and Tianjin), and 5 autonomous regions (Guangxi, Zhuang, Nei Mongol, Ningxia Hui, Xinjiang Uygur, and Tibet). The country's population, at 1.1 billion people in 1992, was expected to grow to 1.5 billion by the year 2020. The vast majority of the people lived in the eastern half of the country. Trends toward increased urbanization (roughly 28% of the population were urban dwellers) and a move from the agricultural to the service sector were evident in the early 1990s and expected to continue. The late 1980s also saw the emergence of a higher-income middle class with very substantial savings rates. Goods were available easily in the major cities, and new products were adopted swiftly. The opening of a large number of private enterprises largely accounted for the increase in the number of retail outlets from 2 million to 12 million in the 12 years leading to 1992.

The transition to what the Chinese called a "socialist market economy" arguably began with Premier Deng Xiaoping's reforms initiated after Mao Zedong's death in 1976. Agriculture, science and technology, industry, and defense were the four areas targeted for modernization. In 1978, diplomatic relations were reestablished with the United States after 30 years.

The passage of the first joint venture law in 1979 was a departure from the previous policy of self-reliance. Joint ventures were usually with a state-owned enterprise as the Chinese partner. Traditionally, profits were split according to a contractual agreement; the Chinese managed domestic sales while the foreign entity managed exports. The first joint venture involving American and Chinese companies formed in 1980. It involved the International Data Group (the world's largest supplier of information on information technology) and the Technical Information Research Center, a division of China's Ministry of Machinery and Electronics Industry (MEI). MEI was the ministry that had primary responsibility for the development of the electronics and computer industry in the PRC.

The Chinese leadership also devised an experiment in market economics by loosening all restrictions in designated Special Economic Zones and Coastal Open Cities, and in larger areas called

Open Economic Zones. Collectively, these special areas, constituting the second "system" in the "one country, two systems" approach pursued by Deng, accounted for a significant portion of total investment.

The reform process was interrupted by the clash between conservative members of the Chinese Communist Party and the reformers. Student protestors were suppressed in the events at Tiananmen Square in June 1989. Despite these events, from 1978 to 1992, China's GNP grew at 9% per year. Coastal areas grew much faster (for example, Guangdong province grew at 30% in 1992). Exports grew at 12% a year during this period. The domestic market was surging, fueled primarily by the population in the coastal areas and Beijing; $58 billion in contracted investment were pledged in 1992, largely by overseas Chinese who were anxious to participate in the resurgence of what came to be called "Greater China."

Diplomatic relationships with Taiwan remained on edge. Neither country's government acknowledged the right of the other to exist. The PRC government regarded Taiwan as a province of the PRC.

The Computer Industry in the PRC

An estimated 1 million PCs had been installed in the PRC by the end of 1992. The number of PCs being installed annually had grown rapidly with the economy, which had grown at a robust 13% in 1992: 250,000 PCs were expected to be shipped in 1993, with annual shipments rising to over 1 million by the year 2000—a CAGR of over 22%. Installed base in the year 2000 was expected to be about 5.6 million PCs. Many industry observers thought these numbers conservative.

Fully 22% of the 1992 installed base was in the South China region. The northwest and southwest parts of the country were less developed than the northeast and southeast and had a correspondingly smaller share of the installed base (see **Exhibit 3**). The installed base was spread among a reasonably diverse set of industries (see **Exhibit 4**).

Computer Hardware

Over 95% of the PCs shipped in the PRC in 1992 used Intel chips for their central processing units (CPUs). By far the most common PCs were based on Intel's 286 chip. However, the more advanced 386 and 486 chip-based PCs were increasingly accounting for a larger share of the PCs shipped. As more and more computer companies entered the growing computer market in the PRC, prices of the PCs fell, and user demand surged.

Unlike the West, where the more advanced chips had essentially displaced the 286 chips, there was a demand for the latter in China. First, cheap 286-based machines had cut into the traditional market for Chinese word processors. Most users that needed only a Chinese word processor found that 286-based machines were adequate for their needs. Small enterprises were similarly quite content with minimal functionality. Last, it appeared that PCs were increasingly penetrating the home use market as the general standard of living rose. While the overall PC market in the PRC had grown at 32%, 386- and 486-based machines had grown at 102%, and 286-based machines had grown at 9%.

In 1992, 5 of 36 domestic vendors (Great Wall Group, Legend Computer Group, Langchao Group, Changjiang Group, and Yunnan Electronic Equipment Factory (YEEF)) accounted for 82% of the units of domestically manufactured PCs (see **Exhibit 5**). Domestic manufacturers sold PCs directly to large accounts (including SOEs) as well as through a retailer channel spread across the PRC. Great Wall, Legend, Langchao, and YEEF sold over 40% (by value) of their PCs to large accounts—a slightly larger percentage than the other domestic manufacturers. Many manufacturers, including some of the major ones, did have a geographic focus to their distribution. Thus, Langchao had a virtual stranglehold on PC distribution in Shandong, its home province. Changjiang focused on Shanghai and East China provinces. Others, like Great Wall and Legend, had nationwide networks.

In contrast to the domestic PC manufacturers, the foreign manufacturers sold only 5% (by value) of their PCs directly to large accounts. They relied primarily on supporting authorized distributors (who had their own dealer networks) rather than expending resources to create a direct presence. Thus, Legend distributed products of IBM, Hewlett-Packard, Digital Equipment Corporation, Sun Microsystems, AST, and other Western manufacturers. The Beijing Stone Group company acted as a distributor for both local and foreign manufacturers.[7] The foreign vendors usually bundled their hardware with software to attract more customers.

AST's position as market leader had been weakened somewhat following late arrival Compaq's adoption of an aggressive pricing strategy in mid 1992. Legend had also started producing highly acclaimed Legend brand 386- and 486-based PCs. Meanwhile, Great Wall's unit shipments and sales had declined despite its approach of lowering prices. Nonetheless, it had substantial excess capacity and planned to expand production. IBM had declined from its position of dominance in the early 1980s, and its attempt to introduce a new hardware platform into the PRC had been unsuccessful (see **Exhibit 6**).

Software in the PRC

The most prevalent application on the PCs were databases. Almost 50% of PCs installed in the PRC were thought to have a database program installed. Because of the lack of standard methods of data input, word processing use was not as significant as it might otherwise have been.

Buyers and Suppliers

State-owned enterprises   At the top of each sector of economic activity (for example, banking and finance, electronics and computers), there was typically a state-owned enterprise (SOE) answerable to the national government. Additionally, other enterprises reported to provincial authorities or to even smaller administrative units. Prior to 1978, there were extremely few private businesses. The SOEs all shared two characteristics that distinguished them from similar large industrial firms in other economies. First, they had a societal mandate, including the provision of education, housing, and health care for all their employees—who could number in the hundreds of thousands for some SOEs. Second, they enjoyed little autonomy in the command economy, where the state dictated the prices of all the goods (raw materials and finished products) and the quantities that the SOE was to produce.

In keeping with the general tenor of Deng's reforms, the SOEs acquired some autonomy in the early 1980s under the Contract Responsibility System, whereby they could negotiate targets with their controlling ministry. Once the targets were met, they could run their businesses like any Western free enterprise system. A dual price system resulted. Dealings with the state were at state-fixed prices, while other dealings were at market-determined prices. A significant side effect was that cheap fixed-price inputs were used to make goods sold at market prices.

---

[7] The *Wall Street Journal* (June 3, 1988) called the Beijing Stone Group Company "the biggest corporate success story in the Communist government's decade-long flirtation with capitalism." Its president, Wan Runnan, aspired to become the "IBM of China."

Of the 420,000 SOEs in the PRC, 71% were found in just 4 sectors (light industries, building materials, machinery, and metal processing) with the remainder scattered over a number of disparate sectors; 13,500 of the SOEs were classified as large or medium-sized; and 40% of these were more or less computerized, including all of the 500 key SOEs.

Provincial and national governments   Traditionally, all revenues from SOEs accrued directly to the national government. However, granting SOEs some autonomy automatically meant collecting some money through a normal taxation system that relied on the provincial governments for its administration. Inevitably, the provincial governments acquired some power vis-à-vis the national government. This was augmented by the rising importance of the SEZs whose administration also involved the provincial government. Finally, provinces like Guangzhou which had attracted numerous foreign corporations tended to remain less tied to Beijing than others. To all intents and purposes, many Chinese had taken Deng's 1978 exhortation—"To get rich is glorious!"—to heart and had established private enterprises that took less direction from Beijing.

Selling software to the ministries and SOEs could be a very complicated process. Traditionally, the central ministry in Beijing exercised a lot of influence over all the businesses in the PRC that it supervised. Thus, the Ministry of Coal Mines managed all coal-related businesses and had roughly 7 million employees reporting to it through a complex structure. A coal mine in a province might report to the provincial government and to the representative of the central ministry stationed in the province. Additionally, there might be separate functions within the coal mine that reported to separate central ministries that supervised that particular function.

One Western executive had explained it thus: "Different departments in a Chinese company have more allegiance to—and ties with—their counterparts in the planning and government bureaucracy than they have to other departments in their own organization. A Chinese state enterprise is subject to a supervising bureau that is roughly analogous to the parent company of a conglomerate. In addition, a series of local functional bureaus oversee each function within a company. That means that the company's labor, materials, engineering, production, and finance departments report not only to the general manager of the plant but also to their respective municipal functional bureaus, which supervise all corresponding departments of all the companies in the city. Each local bureau reports to its corresponding ministry in Beijing." The Chinese term for the locally autonomous fiefdoms created within a company was "shanto juyi," or "mountain peakism."[8] There was no consistency in reporting structure across companies or industries.

The central ministry bought software in a variety of ways. Sometimes they requested a proposal and bought the software directly and rolled it out to their subsidiaries. At other times, they crafted the specifications of the software that they wanted and directed their subsidiaries to adopt similar specs, while giving them budgetary control over exactly what to buy. Occasionally, the specs might be part of the needs for a larger initiative. Sometimes the specs were incredibly detailed; at other times they only provided the broadest outline of the requirements. Provincial authorities—in government or those in charge of the SOEs—traditionally complied with the directives, but had increasingly begun to challenge them in many instances. Particularly for an outside observer, it was very difficult to tell what the de facto hierarchy was. While institutional buyers paid software vendors for their purchases, there was no way to tell whether the buyers copied software freely after purchase for distribution throughout the institution.

Original equipment manufacturers   Several major local PC manufacturers were at least partially government run, or had significant ties with the government. It was not always clear exactly what the decision-making procedures were in these firms, or to what extent the government was involved on a daily operating basis. Software bundling agreements (for nonlocalized versions of software products)

---

[8]Steven R. Hendryx, "The China Trade: Making the Deal Work," *Harvard Business Review* (Reprint No. 86404).

with the Western PC manufacturers were usually governed by worldwide agreements signed in the West.

Software vendors (SV)   SVs were the principal suppliers to the software industry, in the sense of being available to localize software products. In the PRC, the technically competent SVs were few in number, often associated with ministries or universities or both, and varied in size from 5 to 100 people. For example, a vendor named Beijing High Tech was an offshoot of Beijing University. Several firms in the PC industry were affiliated with MEI, as was a firm named SunTendy. Sometimes the MIS department of a ministry acted as a VAR (value-added reseller) to the industries that the ministry operated, providing them with a common solution and services to install those solutions. As was the case with the local hardware manufacturers, the extent of the government involvement in the daily operations of the large SVs was sometimes thought to be substantial, and was very often unclear to outsiders.

The SVs were, by and large, very technically competent.[9] However, widespread piracy (see below) had led them to shy away from providing packaged software, which could be pirated more easily than software that required more after-sales service and maintenance. Independent SVs were thus reluctant to enter the PC software development market. The cumulative experience base was not geared toward user-friendly software development.

The government assigned a high priority to developing software as an industry and wanted to encourage entrepreneurial activity in software. In July 1992, the Chinese government decided to establish a software industry district in Shanghai and planned to attract 30 software firms to set up shop there. The Chinese government intended this to be used as a way to get more advanced technology from the West. It also thought that the software industry was a good way to obtain foreign capital. Finally, it intended to become a supplier of software to the entire East Asia region.

Localization

Western software companies had not historically introduced localized versions of software in the PRC. Nonetheless, several Chinese SVs had written overlaying shells for the popular operating system, DOS, that allowed the program to be used in the PRC. There were more than 100 different shells (5 of which had significant market share) and 20 different input methods, with no clear standard emerging. Since each shell had its own idiosyncracies, DOS applications written taking into account the features of one of the shells often displayed behavioral incompatibilities when run with another. Thus, to capture a large fraction of the market, SVs would have to customize the applications that they created for each different localized version of DOS. This was another deterrent to entry by independent SVs. While the rest of the world used DOS version 5, the earlier DOS version 3.3 was being used in the PRC because Chinese shells had been created only for version 3.3.

Within the Greater China region, the PRC used a simplified character set that differed from the one used in Taiwan and Hong Kong. Thus, products had to be localized separately for the PRC. However, some features, like the keyboard unfriendliness of the Asian languages, were common to the different Asian markets (China, Japan, Korea, Hong Kong, Taiwan).

---

[9] More than 30 universities offered computer science programs, with Beijing University, Qinghua University, and Jiaotong University being the most acclaimed. Because the acceptance rate into all universities was very low (only 0.2% of the population attended university, compared with the over 65% of Americans receiving some form of tertiary education), the quality of the technically trained graduates was very high.

Entry of Foreign Firms

In February 1989, Ashton-Tate signed an agreement with a research institute of MEI to create a Chinese version of its DOS-based database application. Following the signing of the Sino-U.S. memorandum on intellectual property protection in early 1992, several Western firms had been striking agreements with major state-run enterprises. In August 1992, Borland, maker of database products and spreadsheets, announced distribution agreements with China Computer Systems Engineering Corporation, an arm of MEI, and with an affiliate of the Chinese Academy of Sciences. DEC signed a contract to sell software to Taiji Computer Corp, another MEI offshoot. In November, Unix Systems Laboratory and a Hong Kong-based firm formed a software joint venture, sponsored by MEI, with six partners in the PRC—including the Great Wall Corporation, the largest indigenous PC supplier. The 28-year venture was aimed at popularizing the Unix operating system, which would compete with those operating systems introduced by other firms, and producing software for both the domestic and international markets.

Piracy

The Berne Convention for the Protection of Literary and Artistic Works extended copyright protection to books, movies, music, and software. However, the PRC's 1990 copyright law did not afford copyright protection to U.S. computer software as a literary work. A prominent Western analyst had commented that the Chinese "believe that knowledge should belong to everyone . . . they don't appreciate how much it costs to produce technologies."[10] In response to huge piracy problems in the Far East, several U.S. software manufacturers (Aldus, Apple Computer, Autodesk, Borland International, Lotus Development, Microsoft, Novell, and WordPerfect) had banded together to form the Business Software Alliance (BSA), dedicated to fight software theft in overseas markets. Application software was especially susceptible to software theft. Experts estimated that overall losses due to piracy of computer programs in the PRC was over $300 million a year.

However, there was some evidence that things were improving. In January 1992, a memorandum of understanding (MOU) was signed between the United States and the PRC under which the Chinese government agreed to provide copyright protection to all foreign works by joining the Berne Convention effective October 1992. The MOU also undertook to protect all U.S. copyrighted works created prior to the date of signing of the agreement as long as those works were copyrighted in the United States.

In May 1992, a major international software pirate ring, specializing in counterfeiting Microsoft's Windows and MS-DOS operating system software, was broken with arrests all over Asia, including the PRC. Microsoft's attempt to protect its software with a hard-to-imitate hologram sticker proved quite ineffective. The ring apparently made copies of the software in several languages for distribution throughout the world.

The Regulations for Computer Software Copyright Registration were adopted in the PRC in May 1992 and provided for the establishment of a Software Registration Office in Beijing. U.S. firms hoped that this would increase awareness about the illegality of software piracy among the Chinese. The first case was to be brought to trial later in 1993 between the Beijing Weihong Software Research Institute, a small firm that had copyrighted software to protect databank programs, against the Yuanwang Technology Company, an affiliate of the very powerful Chinese Academy of Sciences.

Ultimately, despite several steps taken to limit piracy, it remained a huge problem in the PRC. A survey in early 1993 showed that though Microsoft's FoxPro program accounted for 65% of its class of programs in the PRC, Microsoft had not sold a single legal copy of Foxpro in the PRC.

---

[10] Lucian Pye, "The China Trade: Making the Deal," *Harvard Business Review* (Reprint Article #86410).

Because of the continuing piracy problem, SVs found it difficult to earn a return on their investment in writing application software. Consequently, it was difficult to get SV interest in writing application software in the PRC (see **Exhibit 7**). It was sometimes speculated that charging lower prices for software might give people an incentive to avoid buying pirated software.

Japan

Japan's PC industry had a peculiar history. When the PC was introduced, it did not have enough power to manipulate the numerous Japanese "kanji" characters fast enough to make a localized product, in the current sense of the term, feasible. So different manufacturers came up with their own innovative solutions to the problem, including developing different video and keyboard approaches. Accordingly, the Japanese PC market evolved into one having 5 incompatible PC platforms, one sponsored by each of NEC, Fujitsu, Apple, IBM-Japan, and Toshiba. Fierce competition had set in following aggressive strategies by Compaq and Dell. Nonetheless, in 1993, NEC still had over 50% of the market.

SVs had to write separate versions of application programs to get them to run with each of the hardware platforms. This stunted the development of the retail software products market. Additionally, escalating price wars between other providers of shrink-wrapped[11] software (like Lotus, Borland and Microsoft) had shrunk margins in the business and had deterred entry by SVs who would otherwise write application software programs. All the PC suppliers bundled software products with their PCs. Another effect of the fragmented market was high support costs; indeed Microsoft estimated that, while 260 of its personnel in Japan were engaged in product development (most related to localization), close to 90 were engaged in product support activities. At a cost of roughly $100,000 per employee, support did not come cheap.

The 1992 year-end installed base was 12 million PCs, in a country with a population of 124 million. In 1992, there were approximately 1.8 million 386 or 486-based PCs in Japan, expected to rise to about 2.3 million in 1993 and 2.6 million in 1994. The penetration rate of Windows was 18% in 1993 and expected to rise to 41% in 1994 as more Windows-based application products became available and as a localized Kanji version of Windows 3.1 became available later in 1993. In general, research had shown that the sales of operating systems/GUIs were highly correlated with those of applications designed to run on them. The peak sales of applications occurred about 6 months after the peak sales of the operating system/GUI.

In Japan, localization had posed a significant challenge, and much of the software had not found ready acceptance until localized versions were available. The word processing software market provided a good example of the discretion available to firms in localizing products. Both Microsoft Word and Lotus's AmiPro had been positively reviewed by the press and both had strong local followings. However, there were differences in the way Japanese write and enter text that neither localized program addressed. The local vendor's (Justsystems) product, called Ichitaro, provided free cursor movement on the blank screen (where Word and AmiPro offered only left to right placement), vertical writing, and a large number of box and line functions that were used extensively when the Japanese created documents. On the other hand, the products from the Western vendors were better integrated with other software offerings. Ichitaro, Word, and AmiPro had street prices of 39,800 yen, 38,900 yen, and 36,900 yen (see **Exhibit 8** for purchase criteria and brand loyalty).

In 1993, piracy was still a problem in Japan. Annual losses due to piracy were estimated to be approximately $1.2 billion a year. Experts opined that, in Japan's manufacturing-oriented culture, software was considered an adjunct that one was entitled to have along with hardware, and not

---

[11] Software available in stand-alone form (i.e., not bundled with an original purchase of a computer).

worth paying for in its own right. An official of the American Electronics Association's Japan office said, "There's a lack of separation in their minds between software and hardware."[12] Microsoft had taken the lead in trying to reduce piracy by trying to shame large companies into paying for software through an aggressive public relations campaign and direct mail to these companies. It had pointed out that, whereas the Japanese hardware market was 18% of the world market, its software market was only 5% of the world market.

The Japanese spreadsheets market was dominated by Microsoft and Lotus, with competition expected from Justsystems. Price wars were common, with prices generally following U.S. price levels. Both Lotus and Microsoft delivered their most up-to-date products in the Japanese market. Lotus's 1-2-3 product dominated the spreadsheets market for DOS, while Microsoft's Excel dominated that for Windows. Justsystems' Ichitaro word processor had 65% share in the DOS word-processing market. In the Windows wordprocessing market, Microsoft Word was the leader with 52% share, followed by Lotus's AmiPro with 27% share; 59% of the overall market was DOS based, 26% Windows based, with the rest accounted for by Macintosh-based products. WordPerfect had introduced a localized version of WordPerfect for DOS with English manuals only, and a localized version of WordPerfect for the Macintosh. It expected to deliver a Windows localized version soon. As for database products sold in Japan, 97% were DOS based, and this market was dominated by local products. The leading foreign vendor was Borland with 11% share, which it obtained through localized versions of its product for both DOS and Windows. However, its Japanese product range was not its most advanced.

The importance of localization was clear from the fact that Microsoft's English language products accounted for only 5% of its total sales in Japan.

Microsoft

Company Overview

Started in 1975 by Bill Gates and his high school friend, Paul Allen, Microsoft had become the dominant PC software company in the world. Revenues at Microsoft grew by 60% per year in the 1980s—double the software industry's growth. By 1992, Microsoft had $3.2 billion in sales, of which 55% were derived from international sales (see **Exhibit 9**).

Microsoft's first overseas subsidiary opened in the United Kingdom in 1982. It subsequently opened offices in over 40 other countries. Though Microsoft's presence in Asia went back to a profitable partnership started in Japan in 1978, it did not open its first Asian subsidiary until 1986 in Tokyo.

Microsoft began distributing product in Korea in 1984 and opened an office in Seoul in 1988 when a large chaebol[13] committed to buying large quantities of customized software. In 1984, Microsoft signed its first OEM agreement in Taiwan, home of over 3,000 PC systems and component manufacturers, before opening an office there in 1989. Microsoft initially supplied the Hong Kong market through two distributors, but opened an office there in 1989 in order to signal a greater commitment to the region. Finally, Microsoft opened an office in the PRC in 1993. Microsoft's best in-house Chinese language programming capability was located in Taiwan.

The PRC office was part of the Greater China administrative unit, established in 1992 with its headquarters in Taiwan. In addition, Microsoft established an administrative unit called the Far East

---

[12] *Wall Street Journal*, March 4, 1993, page A10.

[13] *Chaebol* is the name given to large Korean conglomerates.

Region in 1993, with headquarters in Tokyo. Country managers for Taiwan, Hong Kong, and the PRC reported to the general manager of the Greater China Region. Country managers for Japan, Korea, and the Greater China region reported to the vice president of the Far East Region, Richard Fade. Additionally, Far East Product Strategy and Far East Redmond-based marketing also reported into Far East Regional Management. As of 1993, Microsoft employed approximately 690 people in the Far East Region. Revenues in the Greater China region had grown 33% and 62% in 1991 and 1992 and were expected to grow 97% in 1993 (see **Exhibit 10**).

Microsoft's Activities in the PRC

It was estimated that 95% of PCs in the PRC had the (mostly pirated) English version of Microsoft DOS installed together with one of the many Chinese shells. Windows version 3.0 had been introduced in the United States in 1989. Though there had been no explicit product release of English version or localized Windows 3.0 in the PRC, Chinese SVs had already created a shell that overlay the Windows program and allowed it to be used by the Chinese market. Windows 3.1 was released in 1991 in the United States and again several Chinese SVs had created shells that overlay this systems program. Two of these shells had survived. The dominant shell being used in conjunction with Windows 3.1 was called Chinese Star and was produced by the SV SunTendy, a firm with close links to MEI. Several local and foreign hardware manufacturers had licensed Chinese Star to bundle with their computers which already included English Windows.

In early 1993, all Microsoft's Chinese products used the traditional character set and targeted the market in Taiwan. Microsoft intended to introduce products localized in the simplified character set for the PRC by the end of the year. Specifically, it planned to introduce Windows 3.1 in October 1993, followed by localized versions of its spreadsheet and word-processing programs, Excel and Word.

Microsoft had also decided to launch a unilateral effort to bring together the three most popular versions of Chinese DOS into something the company named the PRC-DOS or P-DOS. Microsoft announced that it would support P-DOS in its forthcoming system software releases in the PRC. Management thought that promoting a standardized version of DOS was easier and cheaper than providing support for multiple DOS versions and ensuring that future systems software releases were backwards compatible with multiple incompatible releases of older localized software. Having worked with the SV Legend on a smaller project recently, Microsoft agreed to work with them on the P-DOS project. In addition to its past relationship with the SV Legend, Microsoft signed a licensing agreement in November 1992 with Beijing-based China Great Wall company which it hoped would allow it to spread legitimate copies of MS-DOS. Great Wall oversaw licensing of software to several major government-run PC makers.

Based on their experiences with large and complicated software development exercises, Fade knew that it was very difficult to parcel out a particular major software localization task to more than one SV. The ability and inclination of the SVs to deliver quality product on time also was in some question. Overall, there were only a handful of Chinese SVs that had the capability to participate in a localization exercise of the kind that might be satisfactory to the major foreign software producers. It was unclear whether these SVs would remain committed to only one foreign software producer.

Working with an SV involved training its personnel in some aspects of the Microsoft development methodology and the project management structure, both of which were new to vendors in the PRC. Past experience suggested that it would take the SV about 6 months to get used to some of the tools that Microsoft made available to them (for example, editing tools). To some extent, the time taken for the vendor to get used to the arrangement depended on its willingness to invest in the relationship.

Microsoft had found it difficult to recruit people with the requisite marketing skills in the PRC. It had begun hosting software seminars at which it announced job openings. Part of the problem was that it could not match the job benefits that employees received at state-run enterprises. These benefits usually covered housing and children's education and other expenses. However, when developers could be found, they cost only 20%-40% of their counterparts in Taiwan.

Microsoft personnel also worked directly with the central ministries in developing the specifications for their programs whenever they could. They also participated in internal training programs to train the organization to use Microsoft software. Often, Microsoft was asked to develop specific applications for use in a particular ministry. However, Microsoft did not see itself in the business of writing such "vertical" programming applications.

Regional Competition

Lotus, a maker of application software, was Microsoft's only regional competitor in the sense that both companies maintained a presence in several major Asian markets. Lotus delivered localized DOS and Window's versions of its best-selling 1-2-3 spreadsheet in Japan, Korea, and Taiwan and localized versions of its AmiPro wordprocessor product to Taiwan and Japan. Lotus planned to enter the PRC with localized applications shortly. Japan was the only Asian country where Lotus delivered its most current product. Lotus's general approach was to start with product in Japan and follow later on in other countries. Generally, it emphasized time-to-market even if it involved poorer localization. Correspondingly, Lotus spent considerably less than Microsoft in localizing its product. Typically, it added few local features, and limited its localization to providing a basic translation of the English software version. For example, a comparison of Lotus's 1-2-3 for Windows and Microsoft's Excel for Windows in Japan revealed that 1-2-3 had 6 disks and 2 manuals (378 pages), while Excel had 5 disks, 7 manuals (2,172 pages) and a more elegant package. Microsoft estimated that Lotus's unit product cost was approximately 40% of that of Microsoft. Similarly, Lotus's AmiPro for Windows had 11 disks compared with 14 for Microsoft's Word for Windows, and had 22% of the manual pages, at an estimated 60% of the unit cost of Microsoft's product. Similar comparisons extended to the two firms' suites of products. Lotus's Smartsuite unit cost was about 66% of that of Microsoft's Office for Windows. Microsoft also estimated that, on average, it spent about 40% more on overall localization efforts for a particular product than did Lotus.

The Decision

Richard Fade pondered Microsoft's experiences in Asia, particularly in the PRC and Japan, and knew that localization was a necessary step to succeeding in the PRC. Fade was immediately concerned with decisions regarding the localization of Windows 3.1 for the PRC. He expected that, with time, Windows could become established as the standard operating system for PCs in the PRC. However, its acceptance as a standard hinged on some of the decisions he made now. In particular, he wondered whether and how to involve the Chinese SVs, or whether to use Microsoft's well established software development infrastructure in Taiwan to create localized products for the PRC. He knew that his decisions could set the tone for future dealings between the Chinese and Microsoft, and that it could play a pivotal role in determining the shape of the software industry in the PRC. Additionally, Microsoft's experience in Japan had shown that sales of operating systems were quite correlated with sales of application software. As such, Fade wondered what Lotus's inevitable product introductions in the PRC would look like, and how that should impact his decision on the issue of the extent to which Microsoft's products should be localized.

Exhibit 1   World Computer Software and Programming Services Market by Region, 1980-1995 (in current billion US$)

Year	North America	Europe	Asia	South America	Rest of World	Total World
1980	19.6	1.5	4.8	0.8	0.8	37.5
1985	44.4	27.1	13.1	2.0	1.7	88.3
1990	80.0	47.5	25.8	2.7	2.7	158.7
1995 (est.)	145.0	87.0	47.6	5.2	5.2	290.0
CAGR 1980-1995	14.3%	14.4%	16.5%	13.3%	13.3%	14.6%

Source: CBEMA, Industry Statistics Program

Exhibit 2   Map of China

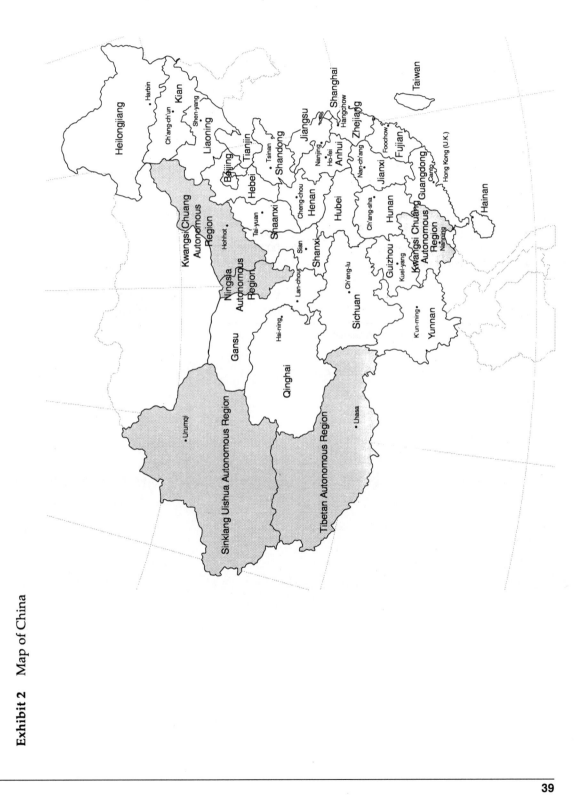

Exhibit 3   PC Installed Base by Geographic Distribution

Geographical Region	1992 Unit Shipments	1992 Year-End Installed Base
North China	39,000	185,000
Northeast China	24,000	125,000
Central China	23,000	120,000
East China	31,000	165,000
South China	37,500	220,000
Northwest China	14,500	85,000
Southwest China	21,000	100,000
Total	190,000	1,000,000

Source: IDC China/Hong Kong, February/March 1993.

Exhibit 4   PC Installed Base by Industry

Economic/Sector Industry	1992 Unit Shipments	1992 Year-End Installed Base
Banking/finance	29,500	186,000
Manufacturing	22,000	130,000
Energy	17,000	90,000
Government sector	34,000	170,000
Science, technology, and education	31,000	159,000
Telcom and transportation	17,500	125,000
Commerce	11,000	65,000
Other	28,000	75,000
Total	190,000	1,000,000

Source: IDC China/Hong Kong, February/March 1993.

Exhibit 5 Market Shares of Leading PC Hardware Vendors in PRC, 1992

Yunnan Electronic Factory	Unit Shipments	Vendor Units/ Total Units	Direct Unit Sales/Total Unit Sales	Shipments (US$MM)	Vendor $ Sales/ Total $ Sales	Direct $ Sales/ Total $ Sales
Great Wall Group	20,500	10.8%	44.9%	49.0	11.2%	46.0%
Legend Computer Group	12,000	6.3	42.3	28.7	6.5	47.0
Langchao Group	8,500	4.5	41.5	19.0	4.3	44.2
Changjiang Group	7,000	3.7	35.0	15.4	3.5	38.3
Yunnan Electronic Factory	5,000	2.6	39.0	12.2	2.8	45.1
Other Domestic Vendors	11,600	6.1	32.1	24.5	5.6	35.9
Total Domestic Vendors	64,600	34.0%	40.1%	148.8	33.9%	43.4%
AST	55,700	29.3%	0.0%	118.0	26.9%	0.0%
Compaq	31,000	16.3	0.0	81.0	18.4	0.0
Acer & Other Taiwan	15,000	7.9	0.0	26.0	5.9	0.0
IBM	7,800	4.1	23.1	23.0	5.2	25.0
Olivetti	4,500	2.4	25.0	12.8	2.9	29.7
Other Foreign Vendors	11,400	6.0	16.1	29.5	6.7	18.3
Total Foreign Vendors	125,400	66.0%	3.8%	290.3	66.1%	5.2%
Grand Total	190,000	100.0%	16.2%	439.1	100.0%	18.1%

Source: IDC China/Hong Kong, February/March 1993.

Exhibit 6 Activities of Western Hardware Manufacturers

Vendor	Date of Initial Presence	Sales and Other Agreements	Other Activities
Olivetti	1970	20 distributors in the PRC. Beijing and Shanghai offices. Joint venture software support center planned in mid 1993 in Shenzhen.	
IBM	Early 1980s	Direct presence. Joint venture agreement signed in 1989.	
AST	1986	28 distributors in the PRC (including Legend). 6 distributors in Hong Kong. Beijing office.	Donation of PC to influential organization. Participation in exhibitions.
Compaq	1989	1 distributor in the PRC. 3 distributors in Hong Kong. Beijing representative office planned.	Established Compaq/Tsinghua training center.
ACER and other Taiwan manufacturers	(?)	Mainland or Hong Kong based distributors. No direct presence.	

Exhibit 7 Application Software in PRC, January 1993

	Estimated Copies Installed	Share	Fiscal Year 92 Sold (Legal)
DATABASE MANAGERS			
Microsoft	100,000	66.7%	None
Dbase	10,000	6.7	500
Oracle	40,000	26.7	10,000
Total	150,000	100.0%	
LOCAL AREA NETWORKS			
3COM	2,500	19.8%	None
Novell	10,000	79.4	500
LaMan	100	0.8	35
Total	12,600	100.0%	
OFFICE APPLICATIONS			
Lotus	< 100	NA	None
Excel	< 500	NA	None
Total			
PROGRAMMING LANGUAGES			
Borland C	15,000	83.3%	100
Microsoft C	3,000	16.7	50
Total	18,000	100.0%	

Source: Microsoft estimates

Exhibit 8 PC Software Buying Criteria, Japan-1992

	Microsoft Office	Lotus Office	Ichitaro Word Processor	WordPerfect Word Processor
Price	76%	73%	56%	82%
Coupon	65	55	16	24
Components	41	55	NA	NA
Features	35	27	44	59
Ease of use	24	36	67	29
Support	12	9	18	0
Brand image	15	0	8	6

Brand Loyalty, Japan–1992

	Buyers of			
	Microsoft Office	Lotus Office	Ichitaro Word Processor	WordPerfect Word Processor
Did you compare your purchase to other products before buying?	47	36	65	53
Had you already determined what to buy before coming?	94	64	97	76

Source: Microsoft Far East Survey

Exhibit 9   Microsoft and Lotus Financials (in $ millions)

	1985	1986	1987	1988	1989	1990	1991	1992	1993
Microsoft[a]									
Net revenue	$140	$198	$346	$591	$804	$1,183	$1,843	$2,759	$3,753
Cost of revenue	30	41	74	148	204	253	363	466	633
Research and development	17	21	38	70	110	181	234	352	470
Sales and marketing	43	58	85	162	219	318	537	855	1,205
General and administrative	9	18	22	24	28	39	62	90	119
Operating income	41	61	127	187	242	393	650	996	1,326
Net income	24	39	72	124	171	279	463	708	953
Working capital	41	118	164	227	310	533	736	1,323	2,289
Shareholder's equity	54	139	239	375	562	919	1,351	2,193	3,242
Total assets	65	171	288	493	721	1,105	1,644	2,640	3,805
Lotus									
Net revenue	226	283	396	467	556	685	829	900	981
Cost of revenue	43	53	69	91	105	142	174	20	202
Research and development	21	33	58	84	94	157	117	118	127
Sales and marketing	73	82	129	171	222	276	371	424	463
General and administrative	27	51	47	54	61	62	70	69	70
Operating income	70	84	123	106	106	147	154	151	181
Net income	38	48	72	59	68	23	43	80	55
Working capital	94	81	139	225	300	226	207	296	417
Shareholder's equity	139	115	202	232	278	309	333	399	528
Total assets	186	209	318	422	604	657	726	763	905

Source: Corporate Annual Reports
[a]Microsoft's fiscal year ends June 30.

Exhibit 10   Asian Market Characteristics

	Japan	Korea	Taiwan	Hong Kong	PRC
Population (millions)	125	44	21	6	1,150
PC installed base	12	2	?	?	1
Windows penetration[a]	18%	40%	18%	40%	?
Microsoft FY 1993 sales ($MM)	155	37	57	8	1
Microsoft subsidiary established in	1986	1988	1989	1989	1993
Microsoft personnel	569	70	30	17	5

[a]Microsoft estimates.

Japan's Automakers Face *Endaka*

Give me 180/dollar yen and I'll show you how to compete.

— Lee Iacocca, chairman of Chrysler, March 1986[1]

You can't be a slave to exchange rate movements. The only certainty is that things are going to change. This puts a premium on foresight, flexibility, and luck.

— John F. Device, general manager of Ford Motors, Asia, December, 1986[2]

The question is not how to avoid endaka hell, but which hell to choose.

— Kazuo Inamori, chairman of Kyocera Corp., June 1995[3]

In the spring of 1995, the Japanese yen hit a post-World War II high against the U.S. dollar. After appreciating 12% over the course of 1994, the yen had continued its relentless climb in 1995. In April, it briefly rose as high as ¥81 to the dollar; just ten years earlier it had hovered consistently between ¥200 and ¥250 to the dollar. Japan had entered "Super *Endaka*."

While the rise of the yen spoke to Japan's astounding record of economic and financial development, it also entailed significant costs for Japanese manufacturers. By mid-1995, these costs appeared to have reached a breaking point. For over a decade, Japan's exporters had adjusted to the rising yen by skimping on wage increases, squeezing suppliers, and turning off the lights. Now the heightened value of the yen was forcing them to consider far more drastic maneuvers. According to a survey conducted by *Nihon Keizai Shimbun*, Japan's leading business daily, 59% of the country's manufacturers were seriously considering moving their production facilities abroad. If

---

[1] *Forbes*, March 24, 1986, p. 144.
[2] *Wall Street Journal*, December 15, 1986, p. 18.
[3] *Tokyo Business Today*, June 1995, p. 26.

Professor Debora Spar prepared this case with the assistance of Research Associates Julia Kou and Elizabeth Stein and Karen Gordon, MBA Class of 1996, as the basis for class discussion rather than to illustrate either effective or ineffective handling of an administrative situation.

even a portion of these manufacturers actually made the move, they would radically transform Japan's industrial landscape. But if they stayed, they would have to continue battling against the yen.

The Birth of *Endaka*

First coined in 1986, the term *endaka* translates literally as "high yen." It entered popular discourse after the 1985 Plaza Accord, the inter-governmental arrangement that had launched the yen's meteoric rise. During the first half of the 1980s, the dollar had continuously strengthened against the yen. Pulled up by the high interest rates of the early Reagan years, the dollar appreciated 30% between 1981 and 1985. Its rise, in turn, led to massive increases in the U.S. trade deficit and sudden inflows of foreign capital. In the United States, many also blamed the high dollar for declining employment levels in core manufacturing sectors such as steel, textiles, and automobiles. By mid-1985, with protectionist sentiment in the United States running strong, business and labor leaders were loudly demanding that the U.S. government take action to lower the dollar's value. As Ford Motor Company executive John V. Deaver explained, "[a] strong dollar got us into this fix and a weak dollar will help get us out."[4] Facing such strong and concerted demands, Republicans and Democrats united in a rare protectionist coalition and rallied around legislation to restore a "healthy" trade balance.

The upshot of this concern was the Plaza Accord. In September 1985 the finance ministers of the world's largest capitalist economies—Britain, France, West Germany, Japan, and the United States—met at New York's Plaza Hotel to coordinate an intervention into their respective foreign exchange markets. The meeting occurred under the auspices of the United States, but all the participants shared an interest in lowering the value of the dollar relative to the yen. If the dollar were depreciated enough, they expected, the persistent and growing U.S. trade imbalance would reverse itself. As a result, protectionist demands in the United States would almost certainly lessen.

In an obliquely worded statement issued from the Plaza, the world's most powerful financial officials asserted that the dollar was overvalued because currency traders had given too little weight to "economic fundamentals."[5] As a result, they claimed, the underlying conditions of the world's economies "had not been reflected fully in exchange markets."[6] To address these imbalances the government of Japan agreed to pursue "flexible management of monetary policy with due attention to the yen rate." The next day, the U.S. Federal Reserve Bank sold massive quantities of dollars, and the Bank of Japan reportedly dumped $3 billion in the New York and Tokyo markets in exchange for yen.

The economic impact of the Plaza Accord was sudden and strong. Prior to the Accord, the dollar had traded at ¥240; one year later it was down to ¥150. Many large companies that had failed to sell dollars forward quickly enough suffered huge exchange losses; Japan Airlines, for example, reported a ¥10 billion ($70 million) currency exchange loss in fiscal 1986.[7] But it was exporters, especially small- and medium-sized exporters, who suffered the real brunt of *endaka*.

---

[4]Julia Horn, "General Motors and the Dollar," HBS Case Number 9-389-094, p. 4.

[5]*New York Times*, September 23, 1995, p. D12.

[6]U.S. Department of Treasury Press Release, September 22, 1985. Quoted in I. M. Destler and C. Randall Henning, *Dollar Politics: Exchange Rate Policymaking in the United States*, Washington, DC: Institute for International Economics, 1989, p. 42.

[7]The loss stemmed from exchange contracts the company concluded with foreign exchange banks in the summer of 1985 to buy $300 million each year from fiscal 1986 through fiscal 1996 at an average rate of ¥185.

Shoichiro Toyoda, president of the Toyota Motor Corporation, compared the first anniversary of the Plaza Accord to *isshuki*, the first anniversary of someone's death.[8] By 1986, most financial observers acknowledged that the strong yen was a market correction. *Endaka* had come to stay.

In response to this substantially stronger yen, Prime Minister Yasuhiro Nakasone called on the Japanese to begin to restructure their economy, giving exports less emphasis than they had been awarded in the past. Though it was an obvious strategy for dealing with *endaka*, Nakasone's call also represented a radical reversal of Japan's economic strategy. Since the end of World War II, exports had fueled Japan's growth and developed its powerful industrial sector. In 1985, net exports comprised 3.5% of Japan's GNP, making the country more dependent on trade than any other country in the world.[9]

If the Japanese were to heed Nakasone's advice, therefore, they would have to abandon many of their traditional practices, moving away from long-established export markets and key industrial lines. Over the long run, this shift was liable to be beneficial, since it promised to increase the purchasing power of Japan's citizens and push Japanese firms into higher value-added sectors. In the short run, though, change would be painful, especially for firms in the traditional export sectors. One such sector was automobiles.

Endaka and Japan's Auto Manufacturers

When *endaka* hit in 1985, Japanese automakers were enjoying an unprecedented and largely unexpected period of prosperity. Although Japan's powerful Ministry of International Trade and Investment (MITI) had never targeted passenger vehicles as a high priority sector for industrial development, Japan's automakers had nevertheless managed to create a domestic automobile industry. Gradually, they also began to introduce their products into the world market. After the global oil shocks of 1973 and 1979, Japan's small and fuel-efficient cars found ready acceptance with buyers in Europe and North America. Indeed, Japanese cars proved so competitive in these markets that, by the early 1980s, domestic manufacturers in Europe and the United States were already complaining bitterly of the "Japanese invasion." By 1985, imports from Japan accounted for a full 20% of passenger car sales in the United States and 10% of sales in Europe. In Japan, export sales accounted for 58% of total vehicle production, making the Japanese auto industry one of the most export-reliant manufacturing sectors in the world.

It is difficult to calculate precisely what constituted Japan's competitive advantage in automobile manufacturing. The vehicles that led Japan's export invasion were lighter, more fuel-efficient, and arguably better designed than their European and American competitors. They were also cheaper. Prior to the signing of the Plaza Accord, Japanese manufacturers had a reported cost advantage per similar vehicle of roughly $1,500 to $2,000. Part of this advantage was presumably due to labor differences and technical efficiencies — Japanese automakers, for example, used fewer people to build their cars, yet still took only 39 hours per car versus the Americans' 72.[10] Part of the advantage, though, was the lower exchange value of the yen. With *endaka*, this piece of Japan's cost advantage was largely obliterated.

---

[8]*New York Times*, September 22, 1986, p. D6.

[9]In fact, the only time that any country had ever attained a higher ratio was in 1946, when U.S. exports had poured into the devastated states of Europe. *Economist*, June 21, 1986, p. 44.

[10]According to *Ward's Automotive Yearbook*, a leading industry publication, one third of the advantage was attributed to cheaper labor and greater efficiencies; the remainder was due to the lower exchange value of the yen. *Ward's Automotive Yearbook*, 1984, p. 10.

To make matters even worse for the Japanese automakers, the advent of *endaka* did little to quell protectionist sentiment in the U.S. market. Instead, even as the value of the yen increased, U.S. dollar-denominated trade figures actually showed the trade deficit to be widening. Thus, cries for protectionism remained strong, particularly in the politically sensitive automobile sector. Since 1981, the Japanese had responded to these cries by "voluntarily" agreeing to limit their exports to the U.S. market — initially to 1.68 million units and then, in 1983, to 1.85 million. When *endaka* came, though, the automakers found themselves doubly constrained. Just as they were trying to cut their costs and maintain their hard-won position among the world's largest automakers, Japan's producers also had to limit their sales in the lucrative U.S. market.

The Japanese Response

To meet this complex challenge, the Big Four producers — Toyota, Nissan, Honda, and Mazda — resorted to a tough but imaginative combination of tactics. They started, not surprisingly, by cutting costs. Between 1985 and 1988, Japan's auto companies maintained an austerity program described by industry observers as "squeezing water out of a dry rag."[11] To tighten its belt, Toyota trimmed overtime in its plants and overhead in its offices. In some factories, the company declared Thursday and Friday the "weekend," so that work could continue on Saturday and Sunday, when the cost of electricity was lower. Less dramatically, the car makers were also able to use the strong yen to lower the price they paid for many foreign inputs.[12]

For Toyota, already considered the most cost efficient car manufacturer in the world, these cost-cutting measures allowed the company to remain profitable throughout the late 1980s. Lacking Toyota's efficiencies and $10 billion cash reserves, however, Japan's other major car manufacturers did not fare nearly as well. Or as a 1986 article in *Forbes* calculated:

> . . . A hypothetical Japanese car wholesaled to the United States for $10,000 at 220 yen to the dollar would bring the Japanese 2.2 million yen. Figure the car cost 1,870,000 yen to build plus 330,000 yen for profit. At 180 yen to the dollar, the same car when exported brings only 1.8 million yen, but it still costs 1,870,000 yen to build. Good-bye profit.[13]

To address this basic imbalance, therefore, the automakers had to adopt a more radical response. Rather than try to export from the higher-priced Japanese market, they began to move production facilities directly into the U.S. market.

Even before *endaka*, several Japanese auto firms had already opened overseas plants — or "transplants," as they became known — in the United States.[14] In October 1983, Honda opened an assembly plant at Marysville, Ohio with a projected capacity of 500,000 cars; Nissan followed suit with a 220,000-car plant in Smyrna, Tennessee. The following year, Toyota joined the fray, forming New United Motor Manufacturing, Inc. (NUMMI), an innovative joint venture with General Motors. The real rise of the transplants, however, came after 1985, as Mazda, Diamond-Star Motors, and Subaru/Isuzu all scrambled to gain a direct foothold in the suddenly less expensive U.S. market. Between 1980 and 1988, the stock of Japanese investment in the U.S. auto industry grew from $1.4 billion to $4.0 billion, and U.S. affiliates' automotive manufacturing sales increased from $6.7

---

[11]*Financial Times*, December 7, 1988, p. 111.

[12]Reportedly, cheaper input prices allowed Toyota to save at least ¥20 billion a year. See *Los Angeles Times*, February 23, 1988, p. 18.

[13]*Forbes*, March 24, 1986, p. 144.

[14] This section draws heavily on John B. Goodman, Debora Spar, and David B. Yoffie, "Foreign Direct Investment and the Demand for Protection," *International Organization*, 50, 4, Autumn 1996, pp. 565-91.

billion to $16 billion.[15] By the end of 1989, Japanese transplant facilities employed over 26,000 American workers and produced 30.6% of the total Japanese vehicles available in the U.S. market. At this point, the transplants had become a significant feature of the industrial landscape of the United States.[16] They were also a key component of the Japanese automakers' global operations.

The final two prongs of the automakers' strategy were diversification and price increases. Though obvious in some respects, both responses represented significant departures for the Japanese manufacturers. Until 1985, the automakers' success in foreign markets had come almost entirely from low-end, compact cars such as the Toyota Corolla and Honda Civic. Now, constrained by the high yen and voluntary restraints, as well as by new competition from low-cost Korean and East European entrants, the Japanese firms began to migrate into higher-margin segments. In 1986, Honda leapt from its low-end Civic to introduce the upscale Acura and Integra models into the United States. Nissan and Toyota soon followed suit with the introductions of their upgraded Maxima and Cressida models. By 1989, with the highly-publicized introduction of the Toyota Lexus and Nissan Infiniti, all of the major Japanese producers had offerings not only in the mid-range, but also at the very top of the luxury market.

Yet, even as they moved up-market, the Japanese manufacturers were loath to raise prices, especially in the highly competitive U.S. market. In 1986, for instance, despite the yen's 35% appreciation against the dollar, prices for Japanese cars sold in the United States rose only by 10%. As a result, Nissan alone saw its U.S. import income drop by 27%. Expressing his frustration, the president of Nissan USA, Kazutoshi Hagiwara, commented that "[d]espite what happened to the yen, we know that our prices have to remain competitive. We can't pass along all the appreciation of the yen if we want to maintain our sales level and market share."[17]

As the yen continued to appreciate, however, this resolve eventually broke down. Between 1985 and 1988, sticker prices for Japanese cars rose by 40%.[18]

Results

Despite these increases and a host of other inconveniences, though, the consensus by the late 1980s was that Japan's automakers had managed to survive, and perhaps even thrive on, the pangs of *endaka*. By 1990, 26% of all cars sold in the United States were imported, and another 15% came from Japanese transplant operations. Astonishingly, the Japanese firms had increased their share of the U.S. market even as the yen rose sharply against the dollar. Reflecting on this turn of events, Ford's Chairman Donald E. Petersen warned that "growing excess capacity in the global auto market during the early 1990s will cause competition to escalate from a fight for market share to a battle for survival." Chrysler's Lee Iacocca, as usual, was more blunt. "They're murdering us," he claimed.[19] In 1990, Japan's automakers collectively enjoyed record sales.

But then, just as the worst seemed over for Japan's Big Four, the auto industry was pummeled by a new round of challenges. In 1991 a global recession reduced demand for new cars, leaving the automakers with considerable excess capacity. Price pressures caused car dealers to sacrifice profits on each sale, while the last decade's proliferation of models and options weighed heavily on the manufacturers' formerly lean production systems. In 1991, all of Japan's automakers posted production and sales declines.

---

[15] Donald H. Dalton, "Foreign Direct Investment in the U.S. Automotive Industry," *Foreign Direct Investment in the United States* (Washington, D.C.: U.S. Department of Commerce, 1991) p. 53.

[16] *Ibid.*, p. 56.

[17] Charles Hart, "Japan Takes Aim at the Luxury End," *Focus*, May 21, 1986, p. 56.

[18] James Risen, "Detroit Still Sings the Blues," *Los Angeles Times*, May 25, 1988, Part 4, p. 1.

[19] Both quotes are taken from Goodman, Spar, and Yoffie.

In 1993, these problems were compounded by a second wave of exchange rate shifts. With the onset of "super *endaka*," a newly appreciating yen drove the dollar price of Japanese cars higher and higher. With over 40% of total capacity in Japan's auto industry still devoted to exports, super *endaka* led to continued sales declines, especially in the U.S. market. And in the European community, where the price effects of *endaka* were less severe, explicit trade barriers prevented Japanese manufacturers from expanding exports sufficiently to compensate for their U.S. losses. By the first quarter of 1995, Japan's auto assembly plants were operating at just 78% of capacity, with no recovery in sight.

Take Two: Responding To Super *Endaka*

On April 18, 1995, the yen hit a record level of ¥80.63 to the dollar. At this exchange rate, Japan's adjusted GDP came within one-fifth of a percentage point of the United States'. Considering that Japan had but one-half the population of the United States and one-twenty-fifth of its land mass, the comparison was stunning.

The impact on Japan's corporations, and particularly its automakers, was equally staggering. Even the all-powerful Toyota revealed that each one-point increase in the value of the yen erased ¥10 billion ($111 million) in dollar-dominated profits.[20] Industry analysts agreed that Toyota, like all of Japan's auto firms, would be squeezed almost unbearably by the financial impact of super *endaka* . According to one observer at Kleinwort Benson, a British merchant bank, "Toyota is looking at paper-thin margins and declining profits, and it's unlikely that there will be any resurgence."[21]

To combat the effects of the yen, Japan's car makers turned first to the strategies that had protected them in the late 1980s. They cut costs even further, raised prices selectively, and pressured their suppliers to reduce the cost of components. By pushing dramatically on these fronts, the manufacturers managed to forestall some of the harshest impact of super *endaka*. Honda, for instance, had already decided to design 50% of its new 1994 Accord model using parts directly from its 1991 generation. Aiming to break even at ¥80 to the dollar, Toyota had restructured its Notomachi plant in northern Japan and minimized its use of expensive robots. And firms across Japan were maintaining labor costs as a percent of sales close to their 1981 level.[22] But as the yen pushed higher, Japan's automakers realized that traditional cost-cutting measures would no longer suffice. If they were to prosper through super *endaka*, they had to consider far more radical changes.

Selective Price Increases

An obvious place for change was prices, since the first round of *endaka* had already demonstrated that the demand for Japanese cars allowed for some upward movement in prices. Accordingly, once super *endaka* hit, the Japanese automakers raised both wholesale and retail prices, pushing the bulk of the increase onto the wholesale level and leaving dealers with smaller profit margins and less opportunity for showroom bargaining. The price increases also fell heaviest on low-volume cars and trucks, leaving family sedans, the core segment of Japan's overseas car market, relatively unaffected. Toyota, for instance, raised the price of its popular Camry LE sedan

---

[20]*Automotive News*, March 13, 1995, p. 34.
[21]Henry Sender, "Nippon's Choice," *Far Eastern Economic Review*, June 8, 1995, p. 42.
[22]*Ibid*.

only 1.7%, from $21,508 to $21,878. Its Super Turbo, by contrast, jumped 8.2% to $47,800. Even with selective tinkering of its price levels, though, Toyota still lost an average of $45 on every vehicle sold.[23] Nissan, Honda, and Mazda showed a similar restraint with their sticker prices — and similar losses on their vehicle sales. Nissan actually reduced the price of its up-market Maxima sedan, for example — and lost an average of $374 on every vehicle sold in 1994. Chrysler, meanwhile, recorded per unit profits of $1,259.[24]

In an effort to boost sales volumes in the face of higher prices, Japan's Big Four supported their most popular vehicles with an array of new advertising and marketing strategies. Previously, with their plants operating close to capacity, the Big Four had avoided promotion programs. As capacity accumulated, however, increased sales volume became critical to maintaining production efficiencies. As a result, Japan's automakers filled 1994 with consumer rebates and dealer sales bonuses. Leasing became a central marketing tool, with low interest rates allowing the companies to keep monthly payments competitive with U.S. models. Despite continued pressure on profits, advertising budgets were also kept intact. "They never had used good, American-based marketing the way they are now," noted George Patterson, president of Auto Pacific Group, a Santa Ana auto industry research firm. "They've taken a page out of the domestics' book, and it's worked."[25]

Outsourcing and Domestic Shifts

As they adjusted their U.S. marketing efforts, Japan's automakers were also contemplating a more fundamental shift in their global strategy. Expanding upon their already successful programs of transplant production, several were thinking simply of leaving Japan. They were not alone. Indeed, even before the yen's peak in the spring of 1995, a trend toward outsourcing was already underway throughout Japan. According to a survey published by Japan's Export-Import Bank in January 1995, nearly all Japanese industries planned significant increases in their overseas production facilities. In 1993, overseas production had accounted for 16.1% of the total production of Japanese companies. By 1997, officials of the bank predicted, this level would rise to 21.7%.[26] Export data revealed a similar trend: whereas capital goods had accounted for 47% of total exports in 1995, they hit nearly 60% in 1994. Some of these exports were traditional goods, such as machines and machine tools, destined for countries such as South Korea. Increasingly, though, Japan's capital goods exports were comprised of components bound for the offshore subsidiaries of Japan's own manufacturing companies.

Whereas the first round of *endaka* had led Japanese firms, and particularly the auto firms, to invest directly in the U.S. and European markets, the second round led them instead to Asia. By 1994, as the yen climbed 16% against the dollar, Japan's investment in Asia climbed 47% to a record $9.7 billion — one-fourth of Japan's total overseas investment. Leading this surge were the automakers, who saw particular attractions in Asia's vast, low-wage, and untapped markets. During 1994, all of Japan's Big Four firms negotiated to build or expand production facilities in the region. Mazda, for example, which had an existing alliance with China's Fuzhou Solid Motors Corporation, planned to boost production of pickup trucks more than tenfold, to 30,000 units a year,[27] and Toyota announced plans to produce 150,000 passenger cars in China beginning in 1996. Honda

[23]*Financial Post*, May 19, 1995, p. 3.
[24]*Ibid.*
[25]Quoted in J. L. Sullivan, "Japanese Carmakers: We're Back," *Orange County Business Journal*, June 27, 1994, p. 5.
[26]"That Sinking Feeling," *Time*, March 20, 1995, p. 15.
[27]*Japan Economic Almanac 1995*, p. 94.

boosted its capacity in Thailand and the Philippines, and Nissan planned a series of expansions designed to triple its Asian-Pacific output between 1994 and 1997.[28]

As the automakers launched these aggressive Asian plans, however, the flip side of their overseas expansion became apparent. Expanding in Asia meant reducing production, and thus employment, back home in Japan. And this reduction would be traumatic, both for the automakers and for Japan.

In May 1995, the Japanese public learned that, for the first time ever, Toyota was considering cuts in its domestic production capacity. Representatives for the company tried to soften the blow. "We recognize we have responsibility to the domestic economy," explained one spokesperson. "In our company, we have huge arguments about this, and we haven't reached a conclusion yet. Logically, it's natural to decrease domestic production in the future."[29] To forestall its move from Japan, Toyota also described its efforts to develop a "world car," a new subcompact that could be produced competitively in Japan even if the yen stayed at ¥80-90 to the dollar. In the meantime, though, Japan's most successful auto company planned to boost its 1996 offshore production 60% above its 1993 level. Nissan also reduced its exports from Japan by 26% and correspondingly increased its overseas production by 22%.[30] And Honda announced that by 1996 all Honda Civics sold in the United States would come directly from its plant in Marysville, Ohio.

Japan's Dilemma

By 1995, Japan's auto manufacturers had been battling the effects of *endaka* for nearly a decade. Expecting the dollar to rise in 1993, the U.S. Federal Reserve Bank had doubled short-term interest rates. Yet the dollar continued its decline against both the yen and the German mark. Two years later, with low inflation and solid growth in the United States, Washington had little incentive to tinker any further with monetary policy. Moreover, as Robert Hormats, vice chairman of Goldman Sachs International explained, "Fiscal virtue in America won't solve Japan's yen problem."[31]

Most economists agreed that super *endaka* was the result of a complex interplay of variables. The U.S economy was marked by low savings rates and high government borrowing, while Japan's economy had long been geared to produce more than the Japanese people consumed. In addition, Japan's complicated domestic web of regulation, retail practices, and commercial customs served as a further impediment to import penetration of the domestic market.

None of these factors were liable to change very rapidly. Indeed, some seemed nearly permanent features of the international economy. And thus the carmakers, ten years into *endaka*, struggled to concoct a more permanent response. If they raised export prices along with the true exchange value of the yen, sales would inevitably fall. This would increase their excess capacity just as the Japanese economy remained mired in recession. If they only increased prices modestly, their losses would continue to mount. Even worse, low prices in the U.S. market were likely to incite the U.S. Big Three to challenge the Japanese producers with antidumping lawsuits.

---

[28] "A review of Japan's expanding presence in the Pacific Rim," *Japanese Motor Business*, 3rd quarter 1995, p. 14-33.
[29] Sender, p. 42.
[30] *Business Week*, November 15, 1993, p. 154.
[31] *New York Times*, April 21, 1995, p. A1.

Meanwhile, although shifting production to overseas facilities appeared an appropriate solution on economic grounds, it would inevitably be complicated by Japan's domestic politics. As with most Japanese companies, the Big Four Japanese automakers faced strong internal pressure to maintain domestic production levels and uphold their commitment to life time employment. When Nissan disclosed that it would shut its outdated production line at Zama and reduce its workforce by 8,000, the shock waves reverberated across Japan. The impact was magnified by the revelation that unemployment in Japan had hit 3% in 1995, a record by Japanese standards. Under these circumstances, Japanese companies that invested abroad were widely criticized for their disloyalty, and for seizing unfair advantages for themselves.

As of mid-1995, the cultural and political pressures of loyalty had prevented most Japanese companies, and particularly the automobile companies, from transferring significant production capacity out of Japan. Rather than lose market share or close factories, many seemed willing to let themselves bleed. Critics of this response, including Sony chairman Akio Morita, argued that Japanese corporations needed to shift their strategic focus from a policy of maintaining market share to one of boosting profit margins. "The situation is terrible," warned Smith Barney Tokyo's chief economist, "and there is no easy way out."[32]

---

[32]*Los Angeles Times*, August 8, 1994, p. D4.

Exhibit 1   Appreciation of the Japanese Yen

1874	Emperor Meiji sets the yen at parity with the U.S. dollar, both currencies being fixed at 1.5g. of gold.
1949	U.S. occupying forces set the yen at ¥360/dollar in the hope that a low exchange rate will help Japan's exporters and jump-start the economy.
1952	Japan enters the International Monetary Fund (IMF). The yen's value is pegged at ¥360 to the dollar.
1971	After President Nixon "closes the gold window," the yen is revalued to ¥308/dollar.
1973	After the final collapse of the Bretton Woods system of fixed exchange values, Japan moves to a floating exchange rate system
1978	The second oil crisis, stemming from the Islamic revolution in Iran, brings down the dollar's rate to ¥250.
1981-1985	U.S. dollar appreciates consistently against most major world currencies.
1985	Plaza Accord is reached in a meeting of finance ministers and central bank governors of the Group of Five (G-5) industrialized countries. The yen appreciates to ¥200 to the dollar.
February 1987	Meeting of the Group of Seven (G-5 plus Canada and Italy), known as the Louvre Accord, agrees to stabilize the dollar's rate.
October 1987	Black Monday affects global stock markets and pushes the yen up to ¥120 to the dollar
1992	After Britain secedes from the European Exchange Rate Mechanism, the dollar falls to ¥110.
1993	A coalition government is organized under the leadership of Prime Minister Morihiro Hosokawa. The yen rises briefly to ¥100/dollar in Tokyo.
June 1994	The yen rises to ¥99/dollar.
December 1994	The Mexican currency crisis triggers another fall of the dollar.
February 1995	The dollar's value drops agains major currencies after U.S. President Bill Clinton's Budget Message shows the federal deficit expanding for the first time in four years.
March 1995	The dollar falls below ¥90. Though the Bank of Japan tries to lower short-term money market rates, the dollar continues dropping to ¥86.
April 1995	The yen hits a new high of ¥80.63 to the dollar. The Japanese government announces measures to restrain the yen's further appreciation, while the Bank of Japan cuts the official discount rate to 1%.

Source: Compiled from *Japan Economic Newswire*, April 19, 1995; *Financial Times*, April 20, 1995, p. 4

Exhibit 2   Yen/Dollar Exchange Rate, 1973-1995

Source: Adapted from The Bloomberg online service

Exhibit 3   Japan's Balance of Payments, 1984-1994 (US$ billions)

	1984	1985	1986	1987	1988	1989	1990	1991	1992	1993	1994
Current Account	35.00	49.17	85.83	87.02	79.61	56.99	35.87	72.91	117.64	131.51	129.24
Exports	168.29	174.02	205.59	224.62	259.77	269.55	280.35	306.58	330.87	351.31	384.18
Imports	(124.03)	(118.03)	(112.77)	(128.20)	(164.77)	(192.66)	(216.77)	(203.49)	(198.47)	(209.74)	(238.25)
Trade balance	44.26	55.99	92.82	96.42	95.00	76.89	63.58	103.09	132.40	141.57	145.93
Net services	(7.75)	(5.17)	(4.93)	(5.72)	(11.27)	(15.62)	(22.19)	(17.69)	(10.14)	(3.97)	(9.21)
Net transfers	(1.51)	(1.65)	(2.06)	(3.68)	(4.12)	(4.28)	(5.52)	(12.49)	(4.62)	(6.09)	(7.48)
Capital Account											
Direct investment	(5.97)	(5.81)	(14.25)	(18.35)	(34.73)	(45.22)	(46.29)	(29.37)	(14.52)	(13.64)	(17.00)
Portfolio investment	(23.60)	(43.07)	(101.38)	(94.37)	(66.11)	(28.76)	(4.81)	39.66	(28.72)	(63.77)	(48.78)
Other capital	(7.00)	(4.65)	42.15	67.35	34.62	26.00	29.56	(82.14)	(63.31)	(26.19)	(20.33)
Change in reserves	(2.12)	0.58	(14.84)	(37.94)	(16.52)	12.76	6.59	6.62	(.63)	(27.66)	(25.28)
Errors and omissions	3.69	3.78	2.49	(3.71)	3.13	(21.82)	(20.91)	(7.67)	(10.47)	(0.28)	(17.77)

Source: Compiled from International Monetary Fund, *International Financial Statistics Yearbook*, various issues

Exhibit 4   U.S. Balance of Payments, 1984-1994 (US$ billions)

	1984	1985	1986	1987	1988	1989	1990	1991	1992	1993	1994
Current Account	(99.84)	(125.58)	(151.36)	(167.31)	(128.46)	(102.98)	(91.97)	(7.20)	(68.29)	(104.36)	(156.16)
Exports	219.93	215.91	223.35	250.21	320.23	362.13	389.31	416.92	440.36	456.87	502.73
Imports	(332.41)	(338.09)	(368.41)	(409.77)	(447.19)	(477.38)	(498.33)	(490.98)	(536.46)	(589.44)	(669.09)
Trade balance	(112.48)	(122.18)	(145.06)	(159.56)	(126.96)	(115.25)	(109.02)	(74.06)	(96.10)	(132.57)	(166.36)
Net services	33.39	19.74	18.05	15.51	23.71	38.55	50.98	60.48	60.28	60.80	44.78
Net transfers	(20.75)	(23.14)	(24.35)	(23.26)	(25.21)	(26.28)	(33.93)	6.38	(32.47)	(32.59)	(34.58)
Capital Account											
Direct Investment	13.82	6.61	18.52	31.04	41.82	30.90	17.97	(5.21)	(31.12)	(36.50)	1.63
Portfolio Investment	28.74	64.41	71.59	31.06	40.30	43.50	(33.00)	8.55	16.64	(17.55)	33.43
Other capital	37.24	36.80	(2.62)	52.56	22.44	(7.71)	36.99	21.52	57.34	68.21	112.12
Change in reserves	(.72)	(5.80)	33.78	56.86	36.27	(16.93)	29.81	21.78	42.20	68.65	41.75
Errors and omissions	20.59	23.39	29.89	(4.44)	(12.59)	52.97	39.96	(39.71)	(17.18)	21.09	(33.24)

Source: Compiled from International Monetary Fund, *International Financial Statistics Yearbook*, various issues

Exhibit 5   U.S. and Japanese Auto Companies: Net Return on Sales, 1981-1994[a]

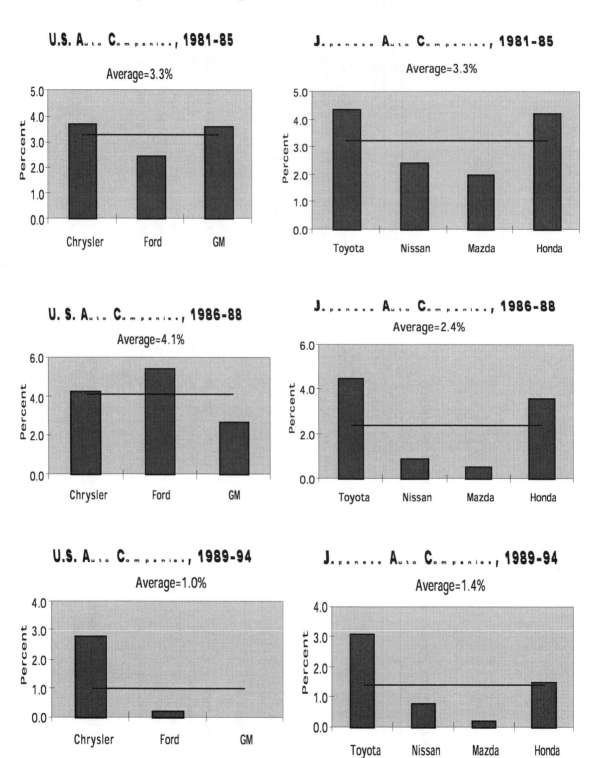

Source: Complied from "General Motors and the Dollar"; company reports

[a]GM data for 1992 do not include the cumulative effect of an accounting change enacted in that year.

Exhibit 6 Consolidated Financial Summary of Selected Japanese Automakers, 1984-1994 (¥ billions)

	1984	1985	1986	1987	1988	1989	1990	1991	1992	1993	1994
Net Sales											
Toyota	5,909	6,770	6,646	6,675	7,216	8,021	9,193	9,855	10,163	10,211	9,363
Nissan	4,308	4,626	4,628	4,273	4,244	4,812	5,645	5,965	6,418	6,198	5,801
Mazda	1,530	1,669	1,728	1,691	2,003	862[a]	2,402	2,714	2,722	2,593	2,188
Honda	2,374	2,740	3,009	2,961	3,499	3,489	3,853	4,300	4,392	4,132	3,863
Mitsubishi	NA	NA	NA	1,749	2,008	2,186	2,361	2,798	3,087	3,180	2,947
Cost of Sales											
Toyota	4,736	5,286	5,392	5,601	5,989	6,705	7,479	8,227	8,772	8,946	8,152
Nissan	3,328	3,516	3,672	3,547	3,424	3,782	4,219	4,670	5,023	4,960	4,747
Mazda	1,287	1,402	1,537	1,533	1,809	771[a]	2,122	2,358	2,377	2,270	1,970
Honda	1,459	1,736	1,917	2,111	2,547	2,544	2,764	3,134	3,199	2,988	2,820
Mitsubishi	NA	NA	NA	NA	1,668	1,816	1,918	2,798	3,087	2,672	2,474
Net Income											
Toyota	295	406	346	261	311	346	441	431	238	176	126
Nissan	74	82	36	20	65	115	116	49	101	(56)	(87)
Mazda	35	40	15	5	10	7[a]	23	27	9	1	(49)
Honda	96	129	147	84	108	97	82	76	60	37	24
Mitsubishi	NA	NA	NA	11	13	19	21	26	30	26	6
Capital Investment											
Toyota	189	265	409	369	360	428	526	804	768	556	339
Nissan	120	123	150	200	192	299	475	665	630	507	283
Mazda	71	109	188	135	95	49[a]	72	166	214	115	85
Honda	NA	148	281	224	211	279	333	261	238	168	122
Mitsubishi [b]	NA	NA	NA	NA	NA	120	140	160	164	140	100

Source: Company annual reports

[a] Mazda's fiscal 1989 year was abbreviated to five months from November-March 1989.

[b] Mitsubishi's non-consolidated capital investment estimates were obtained from *Japan Company Handbook*, various issues.

Exhibit 7   Japanese Passenger Car Industry, 1975-1994

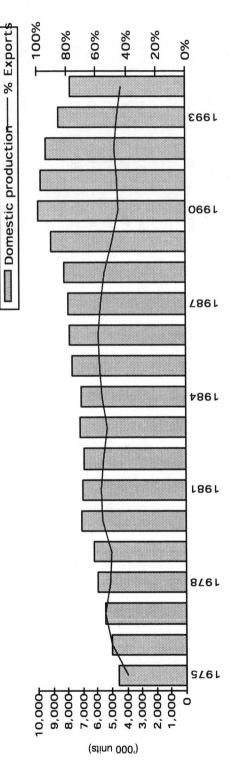

Source: Compiled from Japanese Automobile Manufacturers Association, *Motor Industry of Japan*, various years; Economist Intelligence Unit, *Japanese Motor Business*, 2nd quarter 1995

Exhibit 8   Motor Vehicle Exports from Japan by Destination, 1986-1995 (thousands of units)

	1986	1987	1988	1989	1990	1991	1992	1993	1994	1995[a]
Asia	456	473	474	513	569	566	633	744	594	302
Europe	1,564	1,643	1,705	1,709	1,750	1,709	1,608	1,281	1,053	455
Middle East	188	204	225	223	284	377	516	380	275	101
North America	3,719	3,380	2,979	2,725	2,522	2,363	2,049	1,792	1,758	775
Central America	184	150	105	98	110	113	140	128	115	58
South America	85	81	98	96	106	161	238	236	226	143
Africa	126	148	230	120	129	138	144	126	102	72
Oceania	261	195	265	382	344	309	325	318	328	145
Others	22	30	21	18	16	17	17	12	9	3
Total	6,605	6,305	6,102	5,884	5,830	5,753	5,670	5,017	4,460	2,054

Source: Compiled from *Japanese Motor Business*, various issues

[a] January-June 1995

Exhibit 9   Japanese Overseas Production of Motor Vehicles, 1989-1994 (thousands of units)

	1988	1989	1990	1991	1992	1993	1994
North America							
Honda	416	449	541	550	562	504	603
Mazda (including Ford-badged vehicles)	163	217	184	165	169	218	125
Nissan	307	359	372	408	473	572	636
Toyota	148	364	382	369	489	550	604
Europe							
Honda	5	4	26	36	35	48	52
Nissan	132	164	156	196	256	330	309
Suzuki	22	18	21	22	33	44	36
Toyota	—	—	4	6	7	37	85
Southeast Asia and Others							
Honda	73	77	79	86	96	NA	NA
Nissan	47	54	56	NA	NA	NA	130
Toyota	293	NA	NA	NA	NA	NA	392

Source: Compiled from *Japanese Motor Business*, various issues

Exhibit 10   New Car Sales in the United States, 1979-1994 (thousands of vehicles)

	Total	Import Sales	% Total	Transplant Sales	% Total	Big 3 Sales	% Total
1979	10,600	2,332	22	-	-	8,268	78
1980	8,976	2,397	27	-	-	6,579	73
1981	8,619	2,327	27	-	-	6,292	73
1982	7,939	2,223	28	-	-	5,716	72
1983	9,182	2,387	26	43	0.5	6,752	74
1984	10,390	2,439	23	293	3	7,658	74
1985	10,978	2,774	25	299	3	7,905	72
1986	11,404	3,189	28	540	5	7,675	67
1987	10,186	3,106	30	678	7	6,402	63
1988	10,543	3,004	28	804	8	6,735	64
1989	9,777	2,699	28	1,036	11	6,042	62
1990	9,300	2,403	26	1,415	15	5,482	59
1991	8,174	2,038	25	1,461	18	4,675	57
1992	8,213	1,944	24	1,460	18	4,816	58
1993	8,518	1,784	21	1,584	19	5,151	60
1994	8,991	1,750	19	1,841	21	5,414	60

Source: Compiled from *Ward's Automotive Yearbook*, various issues

Exhibit 11 Production of Passenger Cars in the United States (thousands of units)

Year	Chrysler	Ford	General Motors	Transplants
1979	936	2,043	5,092	173
1980	639	1,307	4,065	197
1981	749	1,320	3,904	168
1982	601	1,104	3,173	84
1983	904	1,548	3,975	154
1984	1248	1,775	4,345	213
1985	1266	1,636	4,887	286
1986	1298	1,764	4,316	401
1987	1109	1,830	3,603	556
1988	1073	1,806	3,501	733
1989	916	1,677	3,214	1,016
1990	727	1,377	2,755	1,218
1991	510	1,172	2,401	1,356
1992	523	1,334	2,393	1,417
1993	495	1,490	2,457	1,540
1994	551	1,661	2,601	1,787

Source: Compiled from *World Motor Vehicle Data*, 1992; *Ward's Automotive Yearbook*, 1995

Exhibit 12 Japanese Auto Assembly Plants in the United States

	Production Start-Up	1991 Production	1994 Production	1994 Production Capacity	1994 Number of Employees
Honda	1982	451,197	498,710	500,000[a]	10,100
Nissan	1985	133,504	312,654	450,000	6,000
NUMMI (Toyota/GM JV)	1985	206,634	229,327	370,000[b]	4,600
Mazda	1987	165,314	247,004	240,000	3,800
Toyota	1988	187,726	275,678	400,000[c]	6,000
Diamond-Star Motors	1988	153,936	169,829	240,000	3,900
Subaru/Isuzu	1989	57,945	54,002	170,000	2,220
Total		1,356,256	1,787,204	2,370,000	36,620

Source: Adapted from *Ward's Automotive Yearbook*, 1995

[a]Includes capacity for 120,000 motorcycles

[b]Includes 220,000 cars and 150,000 compact pickups

[c]Does not include capacity for an additional 500,000 engines

Exhibit 13 Selected New Car Prices by Year ($US)

	1984	1986	1988	1990	1992	1994
Pontiac Bonneville	9,545	10,663	14,579	16,279	19,154	20,999
Chevy Celebrity	8,304	9,345	11,450	12,845	NA	NA
Olds Cutlass Supreme	9,943	11,286	13,598	15,050	16,300	17,900
Olds 98 Regency	14,651	16,489	18,520	20,545	25,195	26,500
Buick LeSabre	10,615	13,026	14,885	16,555	19,250	21,435
Buick Century	9,697	10,642	12,218	13,700	14,295	16,020
Cadillac Deville	18,125	20,490	23,929	28,090	32,340	33,615
Ford Escort (Hatchback)	6,143	6,849	7,588	8,476	9,858	10,265
Ford Mustang	7,472	7,563	9,209	9,861	11,163	13,840
Lincoln Town Car	18,595	21,288	24,897	28,541	32,137	35,375
Toyota Corolla 4-door sedan	6,498	7,148	8,998	9,013	9,713	12,303
Toyota Camry	8,148	9,378	10,998	11,853	14,663	16,823
Honda Accord DX	8,549	9,299	11,175	12,590	13,515	14,680
Honda Civic 2-door hatch	5,249	5,479	8,635	8,940	9,940	NA
Nissan Sentra	6,549	6,899	8,659	8,549	9,850	10,979
Nissan Maxima	11,399	13,699	17,449	18,749	21,115	23,679

Source: Compiled from *Ward's Automotive Yearbook*, various years

Exhibit 14 Hourly Compensation in the U.S. and Japanese Auto Industries, 1982-1992

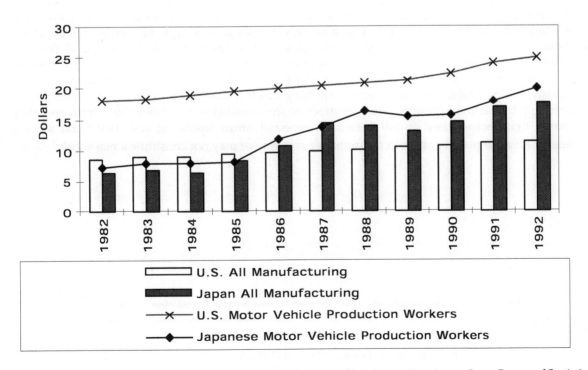

Source: Compiled from U.S. Bureau of Labor Statistics, *Employment and Earnings*, various issues; Japan Bureau of Statistics, *Monthly Statistics of Japan*, various issues; *Ward's Automotive Yearbook*, 1994

Note On Operating Exposure To Exchange-Rate Changes

This note examines operating exposure: the effect of a change in exchange rates on the expected value of a firm's future operating cash flows. It is useful to begin with a comparison of this phenomenon to another, similar one. Consider the oil shocks of the 1970s. When oil prices changed abruptly, the price of oil relative to other goods rose sharply. Many firms' expected future cash flows changed dramatically as a result, because manufacturing costs changed, consumption patterns changed, some technologies changed, etc. This change in the relative price of oil represented a real macroeconomic shock and most firms were exposed to it, some positively and others negatively, and each to a greater or lesser degree depending on many firm-specific factors. Similarly, large unexpected changes in exchange rates may represent real macroeconomic shocks and can result in changes in the value of firms' expected future operating cash flows. Operating exposure, sometimes referred to as "economic exposure," should be thought of as the response of operating cash flows to a real exchange-rate shock.

This definition of operating exposure immediately distinguishes it from two other types of foreign exchange exposures: contractual exposure (often referred to as "transaction exposure") and translation exposure. The former denotes the exposure of contracts *denominated* in a foreign currency; for example, firms may have cash deposits or debt obligations that carry a specified foreign currency denomination. With a few exceptions, it is easy to calculate the effect on these instruments of a change in the exchange rate. It is also easy to hedge this type of contractual exposure. Translation exposure, in contrast, denotes the change in a firm's reported results and financial condition brought about by changing exchange rates. For accounting purposes, it is necessary to express the firm's financial statements in a common currency, regardless of economic reality. Obviously, the particular rules adopted for effecting this translation will play an important part in determining translation exposure. Thus, contractual and translation exposures differ from operating exposure, first because they do not pertain to expected future operating cash flows and second, because the contemplated change in the exchange rate may or may not constitute a real shock.[1]

---

[1]For more on these other types of exposures, see "Note on Transition and Translation Exposure."

Professor Timothy A. Luehrman prepared this note as the basis for class discussion.

Purchasing Power Parity and Real Exchange Rates

The oil shock mentioned above was a real shock because oil prices rose *relative* to the prices of other goods. In the same way, a *real* change in exchange rates is one that changes the relative prices of the goods and services consumed and produced by firms. To see the importance of this distinction, suppose instead that oil prices rose no more or less than the prices of all goods and services. In such a case the general price level rises ("inflates"), but relative prices remain the same and firms and consumers have no reason to change their decisions about production and consumption. Similarly, if a change in a given exchange rate only reflects the difference in inflation rates associated with two currencies, then relative prices do not change and the shift in the exchange rate is said to be nominal rather than real.

To the extent that changes in exchange rates reflect only the differences in inflation rates among currencies, they are consistent with Purchasing Power Parity (PPP). PPP implies that the rate of change of an exchange rate should be equal to the difference between inflation rates for the two currencies. If PPP always held, changes in exchange rates would be nominal rather than real and would not give rise to operating exposure. However, empirical evidence indicates that PPP is not a good explanation of exchange rate movements, except in the very long run, and it has done especially poorly during the 1980s. Some of this evidence, for the specific case of the yen/dollar exchange rate, is presented in **Exhibit 1** and described in the Appendix to this Note.[2]

When PPP fails to hold, for whatever reason, changes in exchange rates may be associated with changes in relative prices. For example, the relative prices of manufacturing inputs, such as labor in the U.S. vs. labor in Japan, may change in response to a real change in the yen/dollar exchange rate. When this happens, cost structures change and firms may change their pricing and output decisions; as a result, expected future cash flows change.

Two final points should be noted. First, it is possible to have a real exchange-rate shock even if observed nominal exchange rates are constant. If two countries have different inflation rates, PPP says that the *nominal* exchange rate between their currencies should change. If it does not, then the *real* exchange rate does change; i.e. relative prices change and this will affect firms' cash flows (note this implies that firms have operating exposures even under fixed exchange-rate regimes). Second, it should be obvious that relative prices can change for reasons other than shifts in exchange rates (e.g., technological or demographic changes) and firms' operating cash flows are also exposed to these types of real phenomena.

The Responses of Operating Cash Flows

Estimating a firm's operating exposure requires an assessment of the responsiveness of operating cash flows to a given real change in exchange rates. The major categories of inflows and outflows are revenues and costs, respectively, and these are addressed first.

Consider a U.S. firm whose primary activity is manufacturing a product in the U.S. for sale in the U.S. and Germany. It imports none of its inputs, a large fraction of which is labor, and it exports roughly half of its output. Suppose now that the dollar unexpectedly appreciates against the mark and that this change is real; i.e., it represents a deviation from PPP. What happens to the cash flows of the U.S. firm?

---

[2]For more on PPP and why it breaks down, see "Note on Fundamental Parity Conditions," Harvard Business School note 288-016; or M. Levi, *International Finance*, 2nd ed., McGraw-Hill, New York, 1990.

First, a currency must be chosen to measure cash flows. Since the firm is from the U.S., the dollar is the likely candidate, though this is not required. Next, consider the effect on the dollar costs of the U.S. firm. Since inputs are all sourced in the U.S. their prices, measured in dollars, may be unaffected by the exchange-rate change. Assume for the moment that this is the case and that the firm need worry only about revenues. In particular, let dollar prices and unit volume remain the same in the U.S. and focus instead on revenues from the German market.

When the firm exports to Germany, it must set a price in DM for its products because the German consumers have DM cash to spend (even if the firm quoted prices in US$, consumers would have to sell their DM and buy US$ at the prevailing exchange rate, so the firm would still be exposed to the DM/US$ rate). When the dollar appreciates, the firm must decide what to do with the DM price it has quoted. To pick two extremes, it can either leave the DM price constant or it can raise the DM price to offset fully the DM depreciation.

In the first case, with DM prices constant, German consumers may continue to purchase the product as if nothing had happened: unit volume remains constant, as does DM revenue. But the firm's shareholders measure their returns in US$; because the DM has depreciated (the US$ has appreciated), the same DM revenue represents a lower US$ revenue and, because US$ costs are unchanged, lower US$ cash flow. In the second case, the firm raises DM prices in order to keep US$-equivalent prices the same as before the exchange-rate shock. German consumers are bound to notice the DM price rise and can be expected to either lower their consumption of the product or purchase it from other (presumably German) producers. Either way, the consequence is a drop in unit volume for the U.S. firm and hence, again, a drop in US$ cash flow.

In the simple example just described the US$ cash flow of the firm is *negatively exposed* to the real DM/US$ exchange rate. When the real DM/US$ rate goes up, corresponding to a US$ appreciation, the US$ cash flows of the firm decline, regardless of how the firm adjusts its DM prices. This illustrates the traditional view of operating exposure, namely that a real home currency appreciation reduces the cash flow of home country firms engaged in exporting or competing at home with imports. This is because a home currency appreciation makes exports from the home country relatively more expensive for consumers abroad while making imports into the home country relatively cheaper. While it is important to understand this fundamental concept, it is also important to realize that it is quite simplistic and therefore may be very misleading.

Important Extensions

To consider the factors that complicate the traditional view of operating exposure, it is helpful to return to the example of the oil shock. When the relative price of oil rose dramatically in the 1970s (and when it subsequently fell) many economic actors changed their behavior. Energy users changed their consumption habits, primarily by conserving. Consumers changed their buying habits, for example, by buying smaller cars instead of bigger ones. Firms designed new products, modified manufacturing processes, and developed new technologies. Governments introduced new taxes and new tax incentives. The business cycle changed; some economies expanded and others fell into recession, with important implications for inflation and interest rates.

While the oil shocks may seem an overly dramatic example of changes in economic behavior, they illustrate the important point that people respond, sometimes very quickly and dramatically, to real macroeconomic shocks. Further, the recent changes in exchange rates have also been very dramatic; since 1980 the ¥/US$ rate has been both over ¥270/US$ and under ¥140/US$. Changes of this magnitude can be expected to have great impact on the world economy, principally because consumers, managers, and government officials all react to them.

Consumer reactions   One aspect of the problem frequently overlooked is the direct effect of a real exchange-rate shock on consumers. Returning to the example above of a real appreciation of the US$ against the DM, note that because the change is real, the DM loses purchasing power relative to the US$. Consumers in both countries are affected directly by the change, regardless of what any particular firm decides to do. German consumers may cut back their purchases of many goods, including those of the U.S. exporter, even if the U.S. firm decides to keep DM prices constant. At the same time, U.S. consumers are better off because the relative purchasing power of the US$ has risen; they may demand more of many goods. So the firm may experience *both* an increase in U.S. demand and a decrease in German demand. How these effects net out depends on the behavior of German and U.S. consumers and on the relative importance to the firm of the two markets. If the U.S. market contributes significantly more to the firm's cash flow, the dollar appreciation may help the firm more than hurt it.

An example of this phenomenon is the rise of the US$ in the early 1980s. The traditional view is that such a rise is bad for U.S. producers who have to compete with imports. However, by 1984 the real increase in the dollar's value had put such purchasing power in the hands of the huge pool of U.S. consumers that the general economic expansion in the U.S. may have helped many firms more than imports hurt them. While the rise of the dollar should not be viewed as the sole cause of the expansion, such currency movements can clearly be good for consumers and at least some firms will benefit from this direct effect on their customers.

Competitor reactions   Another important determinant of operating exposure is the nature of a firm's competition. Just as consumers respond to exchange-rate changes, so do competitors. A U.S. firm's exposure to the depreciation of the DM described above may be very different if its competitors in Germany are other U.S. exporters as opposed to German firms. If they are German, the competition may find themselves with a new cost advantage (e.g., German labor may have become relatively cheaper than U.S. labor). If competition is price-based, they may exploit this cost advantage to increase market share; alternatively, they may choose to keep DM prices and margins up, thereby increasing DM profits. On the other hand, if the competition comes from other U.S.-based exporters, it may be that none of them will obtain a relative cost advantage from the DM/US$ shift.

Note that even the U.S. business of a U.S. firm is exposed if it faces competition from non-U.S. producers. In the present example, the U.S. firm may find US$ prices changing in the U.S. market as (foreign) competitors react to the new level of the DM/US$ exchange rate. Other good examples of this sort of competitive exposure are the steel, textile, and machine tool industries in the U.S. Producers in these industries have found themselves significantly exposed to real exchange rates even though they may have no foreign operations themselves, because they compete with firms producing abroad.

Supplier reactions   A third complication is the behavior of a firm's suppliers in the face of an exchange-rate shock. In general, they also are exposed to changes in relative prices and their reactions to an exchange-rate shock will be felt by firms using their products as inputs. An obvious example is imported inputs. If two U.S. firms are competing with each other and one imports more raw materials than the other, then a shift in the real value of the US$ may give one or the other a relative cost advantage, even if neither of them exports and neither faces product market competition from imports. How large an advantage is realized by which firm depends on how the firms' suppliers react to the exchange-rate change.

The nature of competition among suppliers also must be examined. For example, suppliers competing on the basis of price will respond differently to an exchange-rate change than if they competed on quality, service, or delivery. In general, the location of suppliers, their cost structures, and the types of demand they face will affect their customers' exposures. This is clearly true for traded inputs such as steel or energy, and it may be true for non-traded ones as well, such as labor. Recall from above that a real appreciation of the US$ relative to the DM appeared to make German labor relatively cheaper than U.S. labor. However, this simple conclusion ignores the fact that laborers are affected directly by the exchange-rate shock; i.e., it ignores the impact of the suppliers' (laborers') exposures. If a lower real DM lowers the relative cost of German labor, both employers and employees feel the effect of this, and the latter may be expected to demand higher pay if they are in a position to do so. Once again, the nature of the relationship between the firm and its suppliers and between competing suppliers will help determine the outcome.

Public sector reactions   Finally, politicians and governments react to real macroeconomic shocks and this is no less true for exchange-rate changes than for oil price changes. Following the oil shocks, governments taxed "windfall" profits on "old" oil, introduced incentives for exploration and conservation, and invested in the development of alternative energy sources. These actions had significant effects on firms' expected cash flows. Similarly, real changes in exchange rates induce governments to contemplate protectionist trade legislation, to offer tax breaks as incentives to new (possibly foreign) investment, to control currency flows and capital transactions, etc. While the timing of governmental policy changes may be difficult to predict, it is often easy to observe a political consensus developing for one action or another as real exchange rates change. For example, during 1985-86 the value of the US$ against a number of currencies, primarily the yen, was widely regarded as a barometer of the likelihood of protectionist trade legislation in the U.S. While it may be argued that changes in expected cash flows resulting from shifts in government policies is really "political exposure" more than exchange-rate exposure, this distinction seems academic if the policy changes were motivated by the exchange-rate shock and were, to some degree, predictable.

So far, two basic points have been made about the responsiveness of operating cash flows to real exchange-rate changes. First is the fundamental notion that, all other things equal, a real appreciation of the "home" currency makes exports from the home country more expensive for consumers abroad and makes goods from abroad relatively cheaper for consumers in the home country. This characteristic of relative prices is at the root of changes in corporate cash flows. Second, the traditional view that a home currency depreciation helps home country firms is complicated by changes in behavior by consumers, suppliers, competitors, governments, and the firm itself. Thus, understanding operating exposure requires a thorough understanding of how a business works; namely, where output is produced and sold; where competitors produce and sell; where suppliers produce and sell; and how each of these actors will respond to a real exchange-rate shock.

Some Further Extensions

In addition to the considerations described above, there are some which may be less obvious. First among these are the macroeconomic relationships among interest rates, inflation rates and exchange rates. Recent empirical evidence from the U.S. and Japan suggests that changes in real exchange rates tend to be accompanied by changes in real interest rates. This implies that while a real exchange-rate shock changes expected future operating cash flows, a concurrent shift in real interest rates changes the discount rate applicable to those cash flows. To the extent that real exchange rates and real interest rates move together, effects on cash flows should not be viewed in isolation; some decisions are made on the basis of present values rather than cash flows per se, so discount rates need to be examined.

Though there are no hard and fast rules, existing evidence indicates that if currency A is appreciating (in real terms) relative to currency B, then A's real interest rate tends to decline relative to B's real interest rate. For example, suppose the U.S. exporter described above realizes a decrease in its expected US$ cash flows following a real rise in the US$ vs. the DM. It may also be the case that the real US$ interest rate has declined relative to the real DM interest rate, and that the discount rate applicable to future US$ cash flows has decreased. If so, then the decrease in cash flows is offset to some extent (perhaps even more than offset) by the decrease in the discount rate. In this sense, the exposure of the *value* of the cash flows depends on their timing and on the relationship between real interest and exchange rates in addition to the factors outlined above.

Next, as the foregoing discussion made clear, the reactions of various economic actors are important determinants of a firm's exposure. Such reactions are often very difficult to anticipate. It is usually helpful to bear in mind that the response of say, a competitor, to an exchange-rate shock depends not on the exposure of the competitor's *total* cash flows, but rather on the exposure of its *marginal* cash flows. The distinction is an important one because total exposure and marginal exposure can have opposite signs. For example, revenues may be slightly positively exposed to a given exchange rate and costs highly negatively exposed, resulting in an overall negative exposure; however, if a substantial portion of costs are fixed, marginal cash flows may be positively exposed. The firm will respond differently depending on whether marginal cash flows are positively or negatively exposed. In short, to determine the effect of an exchange-rate shock on a firm's value (its operating cash flows), one looks at (total) operating exposure; to anticipate what the firm will do about it, i.e., what actions it will take in response to the shock, one looks at the exposure of marginal cash flows. Note that as a result, a given firm's total operating exposure depends on its *competitors'* (and suppliers') *marginal* exposures.

These competitive relationships are especially important and difficult to analyze in a setting of global competition. Global competitors pursue business strategies designed to coordinate and optimally exploit interdependent positions in multiple markets. As a result, actions taken by a firm in one market have significant spillover effects on both its own and its competitors' operations in other markets. Hence, a U.S. firm exporting to Germany and facing global competitors will find that the exposure of its US$ cash flows depends on the exposure of its suppliers and competitors' marginal cash flows, not only in Germany, but also in the U.S. and other markets.

Finally, it should be pointed out that by focussing on revenues and costs, the foregoing discussion has largely neglected another type of cash flow, namely investment. While capital budgeting analyses may take into account changes in net working capital and net fixed assets when computing a project's free cash flows, these types of investments are not typically considered cash flows from operations. Nevertheless, they affect future operating cash flows. A firm's expected future operating cash flows may be thought of as follows:

$$\text{Total operating cash flows} = \text{Operating cash flows from assets already in place} + \text{Operating cash flows from future discretionary investments}$$

"Operating cash flows from future discretionary investments" refers to cash flows the firm is expected to realize, but for which the necessary investments have not yet been made. For example, IBM is expected to have access in the future to projects that have positive net present values. Access to such projects is valuable and comprises part of IBM's value now. The access may arise from IBM's position as a market leader, from new technologies in the computer business, etc. Essentially, IBM owns a call option on some operating assets. At some future date, the option may be exercised by making the necessary investment, in return for which IBM would receive the assets, which then have a value equal to the present value of the cash flows they are expected to produce. Alternatively, the option may never be exercised, but it is still valuable until it expires.

A real exchange-rate shock may change the terms on which a firm can make such investments in the future; i.e., the terms on which the "option" may be exercised. This may affect the firm's decision about when or even whether to exercise the option. Thus, operating cash flows from assets not yet in place, i.e., from future discretionary investments, are subject to this additional effect of the exchange-rate change, and it forms part of their exposure.

Once again, competition further complicates the possibilities. Just as competitors' pricing and output behavior affects exposure, so does their investment behavior. Many investments have a competitive aspect to them; for example if one firm invests in a new technology, its competitor may be forced to follow or, alternatively, may be prohibited from following by patents. Either way, one firm's investment expenditures affect another's. A shift in real exchange rates changes the terms on which firms compete for some kinds of investments. When a firm's home currency appreciates, it may be able to make investments (exercise options) on more favorable terms than a particular competitor because the relative purchasing power of its currency has increased. This can be so even if cash flows from assets already in place are reduced, and even if the future cash flows from newly acquired assets are reduced. The same exchange-rate shock may also speed up or slow down investment plans and it may cause some investments to be undertaken which previously seemed unattractive. A good recent example of this phenomenon is the greatly increased pace of investment by Japanese firms following the rapid appreciation of the yen in 1985-86.

Managing Operating Exposure

There are three steps to managing operating exposure: understanding how it works; estimating its signs and magnitudes; and doing something about it. This Note has emphasized the first of these and has comparatively little to say about the other two. Estimating exposures is very difficult, because they are complex, because they may change from year to year or even quarter to quarter, and because they depend on variables that are largely unobservable.

One approach to the estimation problem is strictly qualitative and takes the form of an exposure "audit". An audit consists of a careful examination of the separate elements of a firm's operating cash flows, and an attempt to anticipate the effects of a particular type of real exchange-rate change. This exercise is especially useful to line managers whose responsibility it will be to respond to an exchange-rate shock when it arrives.

A second approach is to appeal to the judgement of the capital markets. When exchange rates change, investors are faced with the task of assessing the effects on the value of firms' public securities. A regression of changes in firm value on changes in exchange rates gives a statistical estimate of operating exposure. The advantages of this approach are that all the necessary variables are observable, the data are of reasonably high quality for many firms, and securities prices respond very quickly to shocks which makes it unnecessary to worry about the nature of the lag between an exchange-rate change and its effect on cash flows. The primary drawback of this statistical approach is that it measures aggregate exposure and so does not afford a view of the different elements of operating exposure the way an audit does.

Once a firm has an estimate of its operating exposure, what should be done about it? This is a question on which there is little agreement among either academics or managers. Much of the debate concerns whether or not exposures should be hedged, and if so, by whom. On the one hand, such exposures are very difficult to measure and hedge and, in any event, could be hedged by investors rather than firms to the extent that hedging is desirable. On the other hand, firms should have much better information about their operations and hence, about the nature of the exposure, than do individual investors. Firms also may be able to hedge at a lower cost than investors could.

By comparison, there is less debate about how a firm should respond internally to an exchange-rate shock. In short, it should continue to maximize value. This requires certain operating responses, including, for example, changes in pricing, sourcing, and product mix. One way to train managers to take such actions in a timely fashion is to conduct "rehearsals". This involves asking line managers to walk through the specific steps they would expect to take in response to a hypothetical exchange-rate change. It provides potentially valuable information about how the organization as a whole is likely to perform, and where bottlenecks and misunderstandings are most likely to appear. The direct involvement of line, as opposed to staff, managers makes such rehearsals a useful training exercise within firms that have significant operating exposures.

Summary

Operating exposure should be thought of as the response of a firm's expected future operating cash flows to a real macroeconomic shock, i.e., a real change in exchange rates. Real exchange rates change when changes in nominal exchange rates fail to reflect Purchasing Power Parity. As a result, the relative prices of goods and services change, and consequently, so do firms' operating cash flows.

A real change in exchange rates leads to the following fundamental type of change in relative prices: the real appreciation of a currency, say the US$ vs. the DM, makes exports from the U.S. to Germany relatively more expensive for German consumers and imports from Germany to the U.S. relatively less expensive for U.S. consumers. Under many plausible scenarios, this results in a reduction of US$ cash flows to a firm producing goods in the U.S. for sale in Germany. The US$ operating cash flows of the firm are said to be negatively exposed to the DM/US$ exchange rate. The magnitude of the exposure is equal to the amount by which the value of the cash flows changes following a given shift in the exchange rate, and it is typically measured in the foreign (DM) currency. This simple relationship underlies the traditional view of operating exposure, namely that a home currency appreciation reduces the cash flows of home country firms engaged in exporting or competing with imports.

There are many complicating factors which can make this traditional conclusion misleading. A significant change in relative prices represents a real macroeconomic shock to which many people will respond. It is important to examine the reactions of consumers, suppliers, competitors, and governments and to assess the impact of these reactions on the particular firm's operating cash flows. It is also necessary to consider possible changes in the investment behavior of a firm and its competitors in addition to the more obvious changes in production and consumption decisions. Finally, the effects of real exchange-rate changes should not be taken out of their proper macroeconomic context. In particular, if real interest rates change simultaneously, the appropriate discount rate for future operating cash flows may change as well. The complications just described are capable, separately or together, of either offsetting or reinforcing the firm's basic operating exposure. Note that if they completely offset it, the traditional view predicts both the wrong sign and the wrong magnitude of actual operating exposure.

Appendix

Purchasing Power Parity and Real Exchange-Rate Changes

The term "real exchange rate" is widely used in business and economics, but unfortunately is not very precise. It typically refers to a nominal exchange rate that has been adjusted to reflect deviations from Purchasing Power Parity (PPP). However, this still leaves some doubt about its meaning.

PPP can be stated in two forms: absolute and relative. Its absolute form is given by:

$$S = P_f/P_d$$

where S denotes an equilibrium exchange rate stated in terms of foreign currency per unit of domestic currency and P_f and P_d denote price levels in the foreign and domestic country, respectively. The condition simply states that a given unit of currency should have the same purchasing power around the world. If a certain value for an exchange rate is accepted as an "equilibrium" or "parity" value, then subsequent changes in price levels in the two countries imply a new level for the exchange rate in accordance with PPP. To the extent that this level is not realized, PPP is violated and the *real* exchange rate is said to change. Note that this conception of a real exchange rate depends on the particular value chosen to represent parity.

Exhibit 1 presents data from the period 1974-90 for the ¥/US$ exchange rate and for consumer prices in the U.S. and Japan. The exchange rates predicted by PPP and the price level data are shown in Columns 5 and 6 of the exhibit, using base ("parity") years of 1974 and 1984-I, respectively. For example, using the 1974 value of ¥300.95/US$ as a base, absolute PPP suggests that the dollar was undervalued for most of the decade 1974-83, returned to parity in mid-1984, was briefly overvalued in 1985, and has been undervalued since. By comparison, if 1984-I is deemed to represent equilibrium for the ¥/US$ rate, a somewhat different story emerges (Column 6): the dollar appears to have been overvalued until the third quarter of 1985, and has been undervalued since, though less seriously than if 1974 is used as a base.

A real exchange rate may be formally defined and computed as the ratio of the actual exchange rate and the rate predicted by absolute PPP for a given base value. So for example, if Column 4 is divided by Column 6, the result is a "real" exchange rate, which is equal to 1.0 when PPP holds. If it is greater than 1.0, the dollar is overvalued (the actual ¥/US$ is higher than PPP predicts); if less than 1.0, the dollar is said to be undervalued.

Because it is difficult to decide whether a given level of the exchange rate represents parity, a *relative* form of PPP is commonly used. Relative PPP applies to changes in the exchange rate rather than absolute levels of the rate. It states that regardless of the level of the exchange rate, changes in the rate should be driven by differences in inflation rates. This can be expressed as:

$$S_{t+1}/S_t = (P_{f,t+1}/P_{f,t})/(P_{d,t+1}/P_{d,t})$$

where the subscripts t and t+1 refer to time periods t and t+1. In words, the fractional change (from t to t+1) in the exchange rate is equal to the fractional change in foreign prices divided by the fractional change in domestic prices. Note that numerator and denominator of the right hand side of this expression are just: {1 + inflation rate} for the foreign and domestic countries, respectively.

The exchange rates predicted by relative PPP are given in Column 7 of **Exhibit 1** and they tell yet a different story about real movements in the ¥/US$ rate. In particular, they suggest that the dollar was mostly overvalued from 1981 through 1985-I, but since then it has not deviated from relative PPP one way or the other for more than three quarters in a row. Note that the 1990-IV level of ¥133.55/US$ is close to the level predicted by relative PPP and that, in general, all of the figures in Column 7 are closer to actual exchange rates than are the predictions in Columns 5 and 6. This is because relative PPP does not rely on a particular base as an equilibrium value for the exchange rate.

It is not possible to state with confidence that any one of these conflicting sets of predictions is "right." It depends on what version of PPP (if any) is deemed most appropriate and what level of the exchange rate is adopted as an equilibrium value. The conflicting data clearly illustrate the difficulty of defining "the real exchange rate" in a useful way.

Fortunately, for the purpose of analyzing operating exposure, it is not necessary, and may even be misleading to focus on "the real exchange rate". Firms cannot observe a real exchange rate per se; they can observe changes in currency values and try to determine whether these have effected changes in relative prices of goods and services. "The real exchange rate" as conventionally defined is an artificial construct devised by economists to measure the extent to which PPP holds. This does not make it a perfect way to determine the extent to which relative prices have changed for a given firm.

As stated in the text of this Note, operating exposure should be thought of as the response of operating cash flows to a real exchange-rate shock, where "real" refers more properly to "shock" than to "exchange rate". In other words, cash flows are exposed to real macroeconomic shocks, meaning shocks that change relative prices. Sometimes, changes in exchange rates are "real" in this sense. Violations of PPP give an indication of whether a given change in exchange rates merely reflects changes in price levels or whether relative prices have changed as well. It is still necessary for the firm to understand which relative prices have changed, how they have changed, and how the changes affect expected cash flows.

Exhibit 1   The Yen/Dollar Exchange Rate and Violations of PPP

1	2	3	4	5	6	7
					Exchange Rate Predicted by:	
			Actual Exchange	Absolute PPP		Relative PPP
Year/ Quarter	Japan CPI	U.S. CPI	Rate (¥/US$)	1974 base	1984-I base	
1974	100.00	100.00	300.95	300.95		300.95
1975	111.85	109.14	305.15	308.42		308.42
1976	122.23	115.44	292.80	318.66		315.28
1977	132.07	122.88	240.00	323.43		297.19
1978	137.12	132.30	194.60	311.92		231.46
1979	142.01	147.19	240.30	290.36		181.15
1980	153.42	167.10	203.00	276.33		228.69
1981	160.98	184.43	219.90	262.68		192.98
1982	165.27	195.73	235.00	254.11		212.72
1983	168.32	202.03	232.20	250.73		231.87
1984-I	172.01	210.63	224.70	245.77	224.70	227.61
1984-II	173.40	213.01	237.50	244.99	223.99	223.99
1984-III	173.25	215.38	245.50	242.07	221.32	234.67
1984-IV	175.25	216.91	251.10	243.15	222.31	246.60
1985-I	175.56	218.27	252.50	242.07	221.32	249.98
1985-II	177.11	220.98	248.95	241.20	220.52	251.59
1985-III	177.42	222.51	217.00	239.96	219.39	247.67
1985-IV	178.03	224.55	200.50	238.61	218.15	215.78
1986-I	178.19	225.06	179.60	238.28	217.85	200.22
1986-II	178.65	224.55	165.00	239.44	218.91	180.48
1986-III	177.72	226.24	153.60	236.41	216.14	162.91
1986-IV	177.72	227.43	159.10	235.17	215.01	152.80
1987-I	176.18	229.98	145.80	230.55	210.78	155.97
1987-II	178.96	233.03	147.00	231.12	211.30	146.16
1987-III	178.61	235.69	146.35	228.07	208.51	145.06
1987-IV	178.96	237.69	123.50	226.59	207.16	145.40
1988-I	178.07	239.24	125.40	224.00	204.80	122.09
1988-II	179.31	242.12	132.40	222.88	203.77	124.77
1988-III	179.67	245.45	134.55	220.30	201.41	130.87
1988-IV	180.91	247.89	125.85	219.63	200.80	134.15
1989-I	180.02	250.77	132.05	216.04	197.52	123.79
1989-II	184.27	254.76	144.10	217.68	199.02	133.05
1989-III	184.45	256.98	139.30	216.01	197.49	142.99
1989-IV	185.69	259.41	143.45	215.43	196.90	138.92
1990-I	186.04	263.85	157.20	212.20	194.01	141.30
1990-II	188.70	266.51	152.90	213.08	194.32	157.86
1990-III	189.53	271.17	137.80	210.40	192.36	150.97
1990-IV	189.08	271.17	133.55	209.84	191.86	137.44

Source: *International Financial Statistics* (Washington, D.C.:
International Monetary Fund, 1978, 1982, 1987, 1991)

Part II

THE RULES OF THE GAME:
NATIONAL POLICY AND FIRM RESPONSE

Layton Canada

In 1993, Veronica Bronson suddenly found herself facing an intractable dilemma. As President of Layton Canada, a major manufacturer of electrical systems, she had just completed a massive restructuring of her company's Canadian operations. Early results of the reorganization were positive. But a new, almost laughable, problem had emerged. If Layton Canada proceeded with its normal business practices, it would be liable for criminal prosecution under U.S. law. If the company changed its operations to comply with U.S. law, it would be liable under prevailing Canadian statutes. For reasons that had very little to do with Layton's own business practices, Bronson was stuck.

The Cuban Democracy Act of 1992

The source of Bronson's conundrum was the Cuban Democracy Act of 1992, a measure signed by President George Bush on October 23, 1992 to condemn the long-standing regime of Fidel Castro. Under the terms of the Act, U.S. companies were forbidden to engage in any form of trade with Cuba. To prevent U.S. firms from routing their transactions through third countries, the Act extended its prohibitions to include all foreign-based subsidiaries of U.S. firms.

Background: The United States and Cuba

Located only 90 miles south of Florida, Cuba had a history of strained relations with the United States. Though for centuries the island was officially ruled by its Spanish "discoverers," its proximity to the United States made it rely heavily on access to the U.S. market and friendship with the U.S. government. In the 1930s, an army sergeant named Fulgencio Batista wrested control of the island from its elected government and ruled through a succession of puppet presidents. During Batista's rule, the United States remained one of Cuba's main trading partners and political supporters. Then in 1953 a young lawyer named Fidel Castro launched an open campaign against the oppression of Batista and organized a prolonged series of guerrilla attacks on the government.

Research Associates Lygeia Ricciardi and Laura Bures prepared this case under the supervision of Professor Debora Spar as the basis for class discussion rather than to illustrate either effective or ineffective handling of an administrative situation.

In 1959, Batista was finally forced to flee, leaving Castro to organize the first staunchly Marxist-Leninist government in the Western hemisphere.

Under Castro's iron-handed rule, Cuba nationalized banks, farms, and industries and, to the great dismay of the United States, received ongoing support from the Soviet Union. Castro also redirected the island's sugar trade, its economic mainstay, entirely away from the United States and toward the Soviets. As a result, trade between the United States and Cuba dropped dramatically, plunging 80% between 1959 and 1963.[1] Political relations also deteriorated as Cuba drew closer to its Soviet protector and the United States grew increasingly wary of a Soviet outpost just 90 miles off its coast. By 1961, the two countries were in a virtual state of war. That year, President Kennedy launched the Bay of Pigs invasion, an ill-fated attempt to re-take the island by force.

When Castro's army overwhelmingly defeated the invading forces, Kennedy retreated, but tightened his resolve against Castro even further. The following year, tensions between the two countries erupted in the Cuban Missile Crisis, an incident that marked the height of the Cold War and brought the United States and the Soviet Union perilously close to nuclear conflict. The crisis developed after U.S. reconnaissance planes discovered Soviet-built missile sites capable of supporting massive nuclear warheads. Fearing an imminent attack, U.S. forces launched a naval blockade of Cuba, demanding that the missiles be removed. After a week of treacherous negotiation, the Soviet Union's Nikita Khrushchev finally "blinked," pulling the missiles from Cuba and averting further confrontation.[2]

Still, the link between the Soviet Union and Cuba stood strong throughout the duration of the Cold War. During the 1970s and 1980s, Cuba contributed troops to the Soviet Union, while the Soviet Union supplied Cuba with trade and economic aid. But despite this help, Cuba's standard of living remained low, declining an estimated 9% between 1959 and 1970.[3] When the USSR crumbled in 1989, Cuba's conditions became even worse. The country experienced severe energy shortages, and supplies of critical food and medical imports dropped to record low levels. In 1992, the first full year in which Cuba received no Soviet bloc aid, the country experienced the worst depression since Castro's rise to power.[4]

The declining economy hastened a long-term trend of emigration from Cuba to the nearby coast of Florida. Since Castro's rise to power, Cubans had periodically escaped the country's Communist regime—by raft, boat or plane—and, over the years, established powerful and relatively prosperous communities in Miami and other southern cities. This flow of refugees peaked in 1980 when Castro suddenly lifted emigration restrictions. In what became known as the Mariel Boatlift, an estimated 118,000 Cubans, some with criminal records, set sail for Florida.[5] After this massive exodus, Castro closed the island to prevent others from following. But after several years of economic deprivation in the early 1990s, Cubans were once again clamoring for emigration. In August and September of 1994, the demand turned feverish, as more than 30,000 Cubans took to the seas in a desperate attempt to float or paddle to the United States. As U.S. Coast Guard ships plucked thousands of refugees from the straits of Florida, President Clinton

---

[1] United States Department of Commerce, *United States Commercial Relations with Cuba: A Survey* (Washington, DC: U.S. Government Printing Office, 1975), p. 7.
[2] Just how close they were to war has been the subject of substantial academic debate. For two of the most important examinations, see Graham T. Allison, *Essence of Decision* (Boston: Little, Brown and Company, 1971), and James G. Blight and David A. Welch, *On the Brink* (New York: The Noonday Press, 1990).
[3] *Random House Encyclopedia*, electronic version (New York: Random House, Inc., 1990).
[4] Jeremy Morgan, "Lenin's Labours Lost," *Energy Economist*, January 1993.
[5] The influx was so great that it increased the Miami labor force by 7%. See David Card, The Impact of the Mariel Boatlift on the Miami Labor Market," *Industrial & Labor Relations Review*, January 1990, vol. 34, no.2, pp. 245-257.

announced the end of a 28-year policy that had allowed unlimited immigration from Cuba. Thousands of refugees were held or returned to the U.S. base at Guantanamo Bay and Clinton deployed two warships to monitor the waters between the two countries.

The Record of Export Restrictions

Despite the tensions of the Bay of Pigs and the Cuban Missile Crisis, hostility between Cuba and the United States has primarily been expressed through economic rather than military actions. Indeed, by the 1990s, the United States had already imposed export restrictions, or sanctions, on Cuba for more than three decades.

As a policy tool, sanctions have a long and checkered history. With documented use extending back to the fifth century B.C., states employ sanctions for a number of reasons.[6] Generally, sanctions serve as a "middle-of-the-road" policy, a way for states to express their disapproval, or even influence another state's actions, without engaging in actual combat. Insofar as the "sending" nation sells critical materials to the "target," sanctions promise to weaken the target and thus compel it to comply with the sender's wishes. Even when the sender's embargo does not seriously affect the target's economy, sanctions are a potentially powerful symbol, signaling the sender's disapproval and resolve.

Whether sanctions actually work has been a subject of great academic and foreign policy debate. While sanctions seem to have played some role in loosening South African apartheid, for example, they were notoriously ineffective in blocking the Soviet occupation of Afghanistan or stemming the conflict in former Yugoslavia. Often, they have appeared doomed from the start by a lack of cooperation among would-be senders: if the target state can receive the blocked goods from other sources, the physical and economic impact of sanctions is minimal.[7] In these cases, sanctions can even undermine the goals of the sending country, galvanizing the target's allies or causing permanent shifts in trade patterns.

Recognizing these risks, senders usually try to organize sanctions under the auspices of an international organization such as the United Nations. Since the start of the Cold War, the United States and its industrial allies have also participated in CoCom (the Coordinating Committee of the Consultative Group), an informal alliance which reviews and regulates the export of materials and technology related to military capability.[8] Although established as a committee of equals, CoCom has often functioned as a veritable tool of U.S. foreign policy. Because the United States had until 1989 a particular animosity toward communism—and a preponderance of military and economic power—it was often able to use CoCom as a means of convincing its allies to enforce trade restrictions that might otherwise have been ignored.

Such was the case with Cuba. In 1962, President John F. Kennedy made a formal proclamation forbidding trade between the island and the United States.[9] For the next 30 years, U.S. policy toward Cuba maintained a variety of bans and embargoes, changing with the

---

[6] For a full historical review, see Gary Clyde Hufbauer and Jeffrey J. Schott, *Economic Sanctions in Support of Foreign Policy Goals* (Washington, DC: Institute for International Economics, 1983).

[7] For more on the role of alliances in enforcing sanctions, see Lisa L. Martin, *Coercive Cooperation: Explaining Multilateral Economic Sanctions* (Princeton, New Jersey: Princeton University Press, 1992).

[8] The original members of CoCom, which was formed in 1949, included the United States, the United Kingdom, France, Italy, the Netherlands, Belgium, and Luxembourg. Australia, Canada, Denmark, Germany, Greece, Japan, Norway, Portugal, Turkey, and Greece subsequently joined.

[9] Presidential Proclamation No. 3447. In Jason S. Bell, "Violation of International Law and Doomed U.S. Policy: An Analysis of the Cuban Democracy Act," *University of Miami Inter-American Law Review*, Fall 1993, vol. 25, no. 1.

sentiments of U.S.-Soviet relations, but aiming always to isolate Cuba and encourage it to adopt a more democratic system of government.[10]

With the rapid decline of communism in the late 1980s, many had expected this hard-line position to change. Instead, U.S. policy became more confrontational, even as Cuba was abandoned by its Soviet patron. In 1989, Senator Connie Mack of Florida introduced an amendment to tighten the existing U.S. boycott of Cuba. Until this point, foreign-based subsidiaries of U.S. firms were allowed to trade with Cuba as long as they obtained specific licenses from the Treasury Department. The Mack Amendment, however, which was attached to the Cuban Democracy Act of 1992 (CDA), forbade even this circuitous corporate route, prohibiting "any corporation, partnership, or other organization organized under the laws of the United States" from trading with Cuba.[11]

Initially, U.S. President George Bush opposed the amendment, arguing that it imposed an "extraterritorial application of U.S. law that could force foreign subsidiaries of U.S. firms to choose between violating U.S. or host country laws."[12] In an election year, however, political pressures gradually changed the president's position. Republican presidential candidates had solidly won every election in Florida since 1980, but in the fall of 1992 Bush and his Democratic opponent, Bill Clinton, were closely tied in that state's popularity ratings. While Democrats generally ridiculed the Mack Amendment in private, many leading Democratic contenders rallied around the boycott and its influential supporter, the Cuban American National Foundation. At a widely publicized fund-raising event in Miami, Clinton warmly endorsed the amendment, arguing that "[the Bush] Administration has missed a big opportunity to put the hammer down on Fidel Castro and Cuba."[13] A short time later, Bush signed the bill at a Republican rally in Miami.

Stipulations and Debate

The stated objective of the Cuban Democracy Act of 1992 was to "seek a peaceful transition to democracy and a resumption of economic growth in Cuba through the careful application of sanctions directed at the Castro government and support for the Cuban people."[14] To implement this policy, the Act prohibited all trade between U.S. firms or their subsidiaries and Cuba. It also required that any company trading U.S. goods with Cuba obtain a license from the U.S. government. An item was considered "of American origin" if 10% or more of its total value came from parts manufactured in the United States. If foreign companies failed to comply with this requirement, the U.S. Department of Commerce could cut the firms off from any further supply of U.S. goods or technologies. The "officers, directors, or agents" of violating companies were subject to fines of up to $100,000 and prison sentences of up to 10 years.[15]

With such stringent provisions, the Act received considerable criticism, both at home and abroad. Many Americans publicly argued that the CDA would never achieve its goals and that the sanctions hurt the beleaguered Cuban people far more than they harmed the Castro government. Others stressed the positive value of eliminating sanctions, reasoning that the benefits of free enterprise would lessen Cubans' loyalty to Castro.[16] U.S. firms were also particularly opposed to

---

[10] Bell, *op. cit.*, p.79.

[11] Section 11, "Definition," Cuban Democracy Act of 1992, S. 9523, H.R. 5323.

[12] Memorandum of Disapproval for the Omnibus Export Amendments Act of 1990 (H.R. 4653), quoted in Bell, *op. cit.*, p. 96.

[13] Larry Rohter, "The 1992 Campaign: Florida; Clinton Sees Opportunity to Break G.O.P. Grip on Cuban-Americans," *New York Times*, October 31, 1992, p. A6.

[14] Section 1703, "Statement of Policy," Cuban Democracy Act of 1992.

[15] *Federal Register*, Vol. 58, No. 123, June 29, 1993.

[16] "Cuba: Trade Must Wait," *Advertising Age*, September 5, 1994, p. 16.

the Act since it closed off the potentially lucrative Cuban market just as the country was beginning to make sizable purchases from abroad. Already, Canadian, Chilean, Spanish, and Greek firms had established serious trading relationships with Cuba, and in June 1994 Castro sold 49% of the country's phone system to Mexico's Grupo Domos Internacional.[17] With more big deals clearly in the wings, U.S. firms were reluctant to be forced out of the market.

Abroad, meanwhile, many of the United States' allies also expressed their disapproval of the Cuban Democracy Act. With communism in clear decline, they saw little reason to worry about Castro and even less to follow a decidedly American policy. The United Nations even joined the fray, condemning the Act as a violation of international law insofar as it sought to apply U.S. legislation to foreign companies.[18]

Despite these objections, Congress and the Clinton administration stood reluctantly behind the embargo. Indeed, making any implicit threat more transparent, the Act underlined its supporters' intent to "make clear to other countries that, in determining its relations with them, the United States [would] take into account their willingness to cooperate in such a policy."[19] Thus, foreign countries and foreign subsidiaries of U.S. corporations were put on notice that the U.S. government did not want them doing business with Cuba and was prepared to stop them.

The Canadian Response

The provisions of the Cuban Democracy Act applied equally to all countries, but they had a particularly strong and immediate impact in Canada, where passage of the Act incited a small storm of opposition. After living for decades aside their huge southern neighbor, many Canadians resented what they perceived as the undue interference of U.S. corporations and American foreign policy. Because U.S. firms held such a disproportionate position in the Canadian economy, Canadians had periodically tried to restrict these firms' activities or at least sever their political allegiance to the U.S. government.[20] Overall, these efforts had proven inconclusive, and relations between Canada and the United States remained close and harmonious. Still, U.S. foreign direct investment in Canada formed a backdrop of tension and many Canadians retained a deep suspicion of any U.S. policy that appeared to interfere with Canada's political or economic autonomy.

Cuba was a particularly sore point. Although Canada had always joined the United States in opposing communism and the Soviet bloc countries, it had never shared America's ideological hatred for Fidel Castro and his Cuban regime. Instead, while Canada's formal foreign policy stance opposed Castro, Canadians had been free for years to trade with Cuba, travel to Cuba, and vacation there. In recent years Canadians had invested heavily in Cuban industries such as gold mining and tourism, and the majority of visitors to Cuba were Canadian—120,000 in 1992 alone. Although Cuba did not figure prominently in Canada's foreign relations, it was an increasingly large market for Canadian exports, and Castro was specifically wooing new joint-venture opportunities with Canadian partners.[21] With both business and pride at stake, therefore, Canada's leaders were determined not to yield to U.S. policy towards Cuba—especially when that policy seemed motivated more by electoral politics than by ideological considerations.

---

[17] Geri Smith, "Salinas' Sweet Deal with Castro is a Bitter Pill for the U.S.," *Business Week,* June 27, 1994, p. 47.
[18] The U.N. voted on the Act on November 24, 1992. Bell, *op. cit.*, p. 80.
[19] Section 1703, "Statement of Policy," Cuban Democracy Act of 1992.
[20] For more on the background of Canada's response to U.S. foreign investment, see Debora Spar and Allegra Young, *Foreign Investment and Free Trade: Canada in the 1990s,* Harvard Business School (No. 793-032).
[21] Larry Luxner, "Cuba: Welcome Canadians," *Business Latin America,* October 11, 1993.

Accordingly, even before the actual passage of the CDA, the Canadian government had formalized a response: the Foreign Extraterritorial Measures Act, known as the "Order," issued by the Attorney General of Canada on October 9, 1992. Under the Order, Americans able to "direct or influence" the actions of Canadian companies with respect to the trade embargo of Cuba were prohibited from doing so. Should an American company deliver such "directives, instructions, intimations of policy or other communications" to a Canadian affiliate, the Canadian company was instructed to inform the Attorney General of Canada and continue business as usual. Thus, any communication by an American company to a Canadian one to the effect that the Canadian company was in violation of a U.S. law put Canadian subsidiaries of U.S. firms in an immediate quandary. If they changed their behavior to comply with U.S. law—that is, if they halted exports to Cuba—they would violate the Canadian Order. But if they did not halt their exports, they remained in violation of the CDA. A violation of the Canadian law could result in sanctions and fines against the company or imprisonment of its officers.[22]

Layton N.V.

Timing made Layton Canada's position particularly ironic. Prior to 1993, the company's parent corporation, Layton N.V., had no corporate links to the United States. Layton was instead a Dutch corporation whose Canadian assets were but one portion of its overall global holdings. As a result of corporate restructuring carried out in part by Veronica Bronson, however, Layton Canada had fallen suddenly under the jurisdiction of U.S. law.

Layton Canada's $10.5 billion parent company, Layton N.V., was one of the 500 largest industrial corporations in the world. Layton N.V. operated in 104 countries and employed 88,000 people. Founded in 1854 in Apeldoorn, Gelderland in the Kingdom of the Netherlands, it was one of the oldest companies in the country. At first it specialized in steel, later diversifying into mining, shipyards, and cannon manufacturing. After World War I, the company expanded its expertise to include electrical engineering. By the 1990s, it had become one of the world's leading manufacturers of electrical components.

In 1983, Maarten Kouwenhoven became Layton N.V.'s CEO and instantly set out to tighten the focus of what he deemed an "incoherent conglomerate." Under Kouwenhoven's leadership, the company sold its steel, mechanics, shipbuilding, kayak equipment, fashion, kitchen utensil, and travel agency divisions and focused exclusively on its core business: electrical control systems. Once this focus was firmly established, the company intended to upgrade and modernize its products.

Central to Kouwenhoven's vision was his intention to extend the company's global network, making Layton a fully international company. Thus in 1991 Layton acquired Circlectric, a large American manufacturer of industrial-control and electrical-distribution products. Following the acquisition, Kouwenhoven hoped to increase Layton's American stockholders from four or five percent to 20%. The company also planned to expand in Europe, South America, and China. In June of 1994, Layton announced a proposed joint venture with the Austrian Lindner Industrie A.G. that would give the joint company a significant share—12.9%—of the world programmable logic controller market. By the year 2000, Layton also planned to move seriously into Asia, investing $650 million in the region.

To streamline this increasingly global structure, in 1993 Kouwenhoven divided Layton's operations into four geographical regions: the Netherlands, Europe, North America, and

---

[22] Gardner, Carton, and Douglas, *International Trade and Technology Transfer*, September 19, 1994.

"International," which comprised the rest of the world. In North America, which accounted for 15% of the company's activities, the Tennessee-based Circlectric was to serve as the regional center of operations.

In the several years previous to this re-grouping, Layton had expanded its Canadian operations significantly, acquiring the Canadian-based Frontier Technologies in 1990 and then purchasing Circlectric Canada in 1991, along with its U.S. parent, Circlectric. In 1992, Layton changed the name of Circlectric Canada to Layton Canada and in 1993 it merged Frontier Technologies into Layton Canada. Finally, to complete its North American consolidation, Layton Canada was grouped with other Layton holdings to become units of Layton North America. At the center of the regional group was Circlectric which, as of October 1993, owned 90% of Layton Canada. The remaining 10% belonged to Layton N.V.

Thus, as soon as the legal reorganization was complete, Layton Canada found itself in potential violation of U.S. law. For years, Frontier Technologies had maintained a trading relationship with Cuba. Although this Cuban business constituted only 2% of Layton Canada's total business, the acquisition of Frontier Technologies had given Layton a significant installed base in Cuba. The components, originally sold by Frontier Technologies, still required compatible parts, and Cubans were so desperate to get them that they had already suggested that Layton Canada set up a manufacturing facility in Cuba.

Further complicating matters was Layton Canada's relationship with its distributors. As was the case in nearly all of its operations, Layton sold its products in Cuba primarily through independent distributors. In Cuba these distributors happened to be Canadian firms that also distributed Layton Canada's products in countries such as Argentina and Mexico. If Layton Canada were suddenly·to refuse to supply these distributors, it risked losing valuable partnerships. Moreover, because the distributors were Canadian, they could easily bring the matter to Canadian courts, which were likely to judge Layton Canada's change of business practice as a—now illegal—compliance with U.S. law.

Meanwhile, Layton Canada had already received an order from one of its largest Canadian distributors operating in Cuba. The goods were boxed, marked, and ready to ship. Sending them would violate U.S. law. Canceling the order would violate Canadian law.[23]

Bronson and the Lawyers

Veronica Bronson was not by nature a fainthearted woman. She played semi-pro tennis, piloted small planes, drove Formula racing cars, and liked to spend her vacations camping on deserted Arctic islands. But the legal situation concerned her. She knew that Circlectric's lawyers might be able to give her advice, but she was also aware that even speaking with these lawyers put her at some legal risk, since following their advice technically entailed violating the Canadian prohibition against receiving instructions from an American parent company. She was, of course, allowed to confer with representatives of Housman-Gilmore, Layton's Canadian law firm, but they were not in a position to advise her of anything short of full compliance with Canadian

---

[23] Similar policies influenced U.S. companies trading in other parts of the world. In the spring of 1995 the Clinton administration forbade Conoco, Inc. from developing two oil fields in Sirri, Iran, through a Dutch subsidiary. Senator Alfonse D'Amato (R-NY) introduced a bill that would ban all U.S. firms and their subsidiaries from trading oil with Iran in order to "stop . . . [providing] terrorists with hard currency." See "Conoco: U.S. Killed Iranian Deal at Last Minute," *Oil and Gas Journal*, March 27, 1995, p. 25.

law. Personally, Bronson was particularly vulnerable since she was a U.S. citizen residing in Canada and crossed the border frequently to see her husband in Buffalo.

Bronson was also aware that the stipulations of the CDA extended even beyond Layton Canada. Most of Layton N.V.'s products contained parts made in several countries, including the United States. Indeed, as Kouwenhoven had described in a recent interview:

> Ninety percent of our products fit local requirements, and they really are global products. We make global component products such as circuit breakers, and then we modify them in each local region to fit that area's requirements. For example, we designed a circuit breaker that can be used globally, but which requires minor adaptation of the shell to make it work in Mexico or Egypt or the U.S.

Under these circumstances, virtually all of Layton's global production could potentially be subject to the terms of the CDA. Against this backdrop, Bronson was eager to keep her company away from any legal mishaps. She just was not sure how.

Exhibit 1   Layton N.V.: Balance Sheet (millions of $US)

	1993	1992
Current assets:		
Cash and equivalents	1,069	901
Accounts receivable - trade	2,040	2,643
Other receivables and prepaid expenses	1,156	1,344
Deferred taxes	133	88
Inventories and work in process	1,031	1,326
Total current assets	**5,429**	**6,302**
Noncurrent assets:		
Property, plant and equipment - net	1,764	1,978
Total investments	559	640
Intangible assets - net	49	63
Goodwill - net	2,695	2,824
Total assets	**10,496**	**11,807**
Current liabilities:		
Accounts payable - trade	1,951	1,713
Taxes and benefits payable	844	977
Other payables and accrued liabilities	807	1,021
Short-term debt and current position	1,079	1,353
Customer prepayments	399	557
Total current liabilities	**5,080**	**5,621**
Other liabilities:		
Perpetual subordinated bonds	355	398
Long-term debt	1,157	2,301
Provisions for contingencies	878	886
Provisions for pensions	442	194
Total other liabilities	**2,832**	**3,779**
Capital stock	211	50
Retained earnings	2,269	1,054
Minority interests	104	1,303
Total liabilities and shareholders' equity	**10,496**	**11,807**

Exhibit 2   Layton N.V.: Sales by Geographic Region (millions of $US)

	1988	1989	1990	1991	1992	1993
Netherlands	1,048	1,293	1,770	2,092	2,260	1,952
EC	3,762	3,951	5,208	5,306	5,221	4,173
Americas	590	881	1,025	1,763	2,124	2,040
Middle East	170	172	157	89	182	181
Asia	283	261	293	340	477	449
Africa	558	365	355	464	826	672
Other	338	128	429	486	535	424
Total	6,749	7,051	9,237	10,540	11,625	9,891

Exhibit 3   Trade Between the United States, Canada, and Cuba 1990-1993
(millions of U.S. dollars)

CANADA	1990	1991	1992	1993
Exports to Cuba	136	114	94	103
Exports to United States	95,388	95,574	103,860	114,448
Total exports	$126,447	$126,160	$133,447	$140,748
Imports from Cuba	123	147	233	145
Imports from United States	75,252	75,025	79,294	87,759
Total imports	$119,673	$120,452	$124,830	$134,914

CUBA	1990	1991	1992	1993
Exports to Canada	89	133	212	132
Exports to United States	0	0	0	0
Total exports	$1,351	$1,064	$1,149	$777
Imports from Canada	150	125	103	113
Imports from United States	2	1	1	3
Total imports	$2,945	$2,387	$1,571	$1,574

UNITED STATES	1990	1991	1992	1993
Exports to Canada	82,959	85,146	90,156	100,177
Exports to Cuba	1	1	1	3
Total exports	$393,106	$421,743	$447,366	$464,827
Imports from Canada	93,780	93,736	101,292	113,617
Imports from Cuba	0	0	0	0
Total imports	$517,018	$509,299	$552,599	$603,306

Source: International Monetary Fund, *Direction of Trade Statistics Yearbook*, 1994.

Exhibit 4   North America

Exhibit 5   Selective List of International Economic Sanctions, 1914-1984

Principal Sender	Target Country	Active Years	Success[a]	Goals of Sender Country
United Kingdom	Germany	1914-18	12	Military victory
United States	Japan	1917	4	(1) Contain Japanese influence in Asia (2) Persuade Japan to divert shipping to Atlantic
United Kingdom	Russia	1918-20	2	(1) Renew support for Allies in World War I (2) Destabilize Bolshevik regime
League of Nations	Yugoslavia	1921	16	Block Yugoslav attempts to wrest territory from Albania; retain 1913 borders
League of Nations	Greece	1925	16	Withdraw from occupation of Bulgarian border territory
United Kingdom & League of Nations	Italy	1935-36	1	Withdraw Italian troops from Abyssinia
United Kingdom & United States	Mexico	1938-47	9	Settle expropriation claims
United States	Japan	1940-41	1	Withdraw from Southeast Asia
United States	Argentina	1944-47	4	(1) Remove Nazi influence (2) Destabilize Perón government
Arab League	Israel	1946-	4	Create a homeland for Palestinians
United States	Netherlands	1948-49	16	Recognize Republic of Indonesia
United States & COCOM	USSR & COMECON	1948-	4	(1) Deny strategic materials (2) Impair Soviet military potential
United States & CHINCOM	China	1949-70	1	(1) Retaliation for Communist takeover and assistance to North Korea (2) Deny materials
United States & United Nations	North Korea	1950-	2	Withdraw attack on South Korea
United Kingdom & United States	Iran	1951-53	12	(1) Reverse the nationalization of oil facilities (2) Destabilize Mossadeq government
United States & South Vietnam	North Vietnam	1954-	1	(1) Impede military effectiveness of North Vietnam (2) Retribution for aggression in South Vietnam
United Kingdom, France & United States	Egypt	1956	9	(1) Ensure free passage through Suez Canal (2) Compensate for nationalization
France	Tunisia	1957-63	1	Halt support for Algerian rebels
USSR	Finland	1958-59	16	Adopt pro-USSR policies
United States	Dominican Republic	1960-62	16	(1) Cease subversion in Venezuela (2) Destabilize Trujillo government
USSR	China	1960-70	4	(1) Retaliation for break with Soviet policy (2) Destabilize Mao government
United States	Cuba	1960-	1	(1) Settle expropriation claims (2) Destabilize Castro government (3) Discourage Cuba from foreign military adventures
United States	Ceylon	1961-65	16	Settle expropriation claims
USSR	Albania	1961-65	1	(1) Retaliation for alliance with China (2) Destabilize Hoxha government
Western Allies	East Germany	1961-62	1	Berlin Wall
United Nations	Brazil	1962-64	12	(1) Settle expropriation claims (2) Destabilize Goulart government
United Nations	South Africa	1962-	1	(1) End apartheid (2) Grant independence to Namibia
Indonesia	Malaysia	1963-66	1	Promote "Crush Malaysia" campaign
United States	Indonesia	1963-66	8	(1) Cease "Crush Malaysia" campaign (2) Destabilize Sukarno government
United States	South Vietnam	1963	12	(1) Ease repression (2) Remove Nhu (3) Destabilize Diem
United Nations & Organization for African Unity	Portugal	1963-74	8	Free African colonies
France	Tunisia	1964-66	9	Settle expropriation claims

Source: Gary Clyde Hufbauer and Jeffrey J. Schott, assisted by Kimberly Ann Elliott, *Economic Sanctions Reconsidered: History and Current Policy* (Washington, DC: Institute for International Economics, 1985).
a A Success is rated on a scale of 1 (outright failure) to 16 (significant success).

Exhibit 5   Selective List of International Economic Sanctions, 1914-1984 (continued)

Principal Sender	Target Country	Active Years	Success[a]	Goals of Sender Country
United Kingdom & United Nations	Rhodesia	1965-79	12	Majority rule by Black Africans
United States	Arab League	1965-	6	Stop U.S. firms from implementing Arab boycott of Israel
United States	Chile	1970-73	12	(1) Settle expropriation claims (2) Destabilize Allende government
United States	India & Pakistan	1971	2	Cease fighting in East Pakistan (Bangladesh)
United Kingdom and United States	Uganda	1972-79	12	(1) Retaliation for expelling Asians (2) Improve human rights (3) Destabilize Amin government
Arab League	United States & Netherlands	1973-74	9	(1) Retaliation for supporting Israel in October war (2) Restore pre-1967 Israeli boarders
United States	South Korea	1973-77	4	Improve human rights
United States	Chile	1973-	6	Improve human rights
United States	Turkey	1974-78	1	Withdraw Turkish troops from Cyprus
Canada	India	1974-76	4	(1) Deter further nuclear explosions (2) Apply stricter nuclear safeguards
Canada	Pakistan	1974-76	4	(1) Apply stricter safeguards to nuclear power plant (2) Forego nuclear reprocessing
United States	USSR	1975-	4	Liberalize Jewish emigration
United States	Eastern Europe	1975-	12	Liberalize Jewish emigration
United States	South African	1975-82	4	(1) Adhere to nuclear safeguards (2) Avert explosion of nuclear device
United States	Kampuchea	1975-79	1	(1) Improve human rights (2) Deter Vietnamese expansionism
United States	El Salvador	1977-81	6	Improve human rights
China	Albania	1978-83	1	Retaliation for anti-Chinese rhetoric
Arab League	Egypt	1978-83	1	Withdraw from Camp David process
China	Vietnam	1978-79	1	Withdraw troops from Kampuchea
United States	Libya	1978-	4	(1) Terminate support of international terrorism (2) Destabilize Qaddafi government
United States	Iran	1979-81	12	(1) Release hostages (2) Settle expropriation claims
Arab League	Canada	1979	12	Retaliation for planned move of Canadian Embassy in Israel from Tel Aviv to Jerusalem
United States	Bolivia	1979-82	6	(1) Improve human rights (2) Deter drug trafficking
United States	USSR	1980-81	1	(1) Withdraw Soviet troops from Afghanistan (2) Impair Soviet military potential
United States	Iraq	1980-82	4	Terminate support of international terrorism
United States	Nicaragua	1981-	4	(1) End support for El Salvador rebels (2) Destabilize Sandinista government
United States	Poland	1981-84	6	(1) Lift martial law (2) Free dissidents (3) Resume talks with Solidarity
United States	USSR	1981-82	1	(1) Lift martial law in Poland (2) Cancel USSR-Europe pipeline project (3) Impair Soviet economic/military potential
European Community	Turkey	1981-82	6	Restore democracy
United Kingdom	Argentina	1982	12	Withdraw troops from Falkland Islands
United States & Organization of Eastern Caribbean States	Grenada	1983	8	Destabilize Bishop/Austin regime

Source: Gary Clyde Hufbauer and Jeffrey J. Schott, assisted by Kimberly Ann Elliott, *Economic Sanctions Reconsidered: History and Current Policy* (Washington, DC: Institute for International Economics, 1985).

[a] Success is rated on a scale of 1 (outright failure) to 16 (significant success).

Export Controls

Restrictions on exports have long been a familiar tool of war. But as Table 1 illustrates, export controls have been applied in a broad array of peacetime circumstances in the post-World War II period. One purpose has been to protect the domestic economy from the effects of inflation. When foreign demand for a product is high, domestic prices might rise. Export controls can limit excessive foreign demand by preventing companies from seeking higher profits abroad. Another objective has been to support foreign policy goals. A 1983 survey of economic sanctions used for political reasons revealed that between 1914 and 1982 there were 81 cases, worldwide, of politically motivated export controls; 52 of these were American and over half of the U.S. embargoes had been implemented since 1970.[1] The main goals of foreign policy export controls have been to: (1) restrict the military capability or commercial competitiveness of an adversary; and (2) influence the domestic or international policy of another nation.

Immediately after World War II, most American export controls fell into the first category; the goal was to limit the military capability of the Soviet Union. Since 1949, the U.S. and most of its industrial allies participated in CoCom (Coordinating Committee), an informal organization which regulated exports of armaments, strategic materials and military technology. CoCom maintained secret lists of embargoed products; to export any item on the list, approval of all parties was required. Enforcement was difficult since each member country decided for itself whether a particular product should be approved. The U.S. was more rigorous in its embargo than were its allies, giving rise to disagreements. In the 1980s some American legislators were advocating the formalization of CoCom's policies and the tightening of enforcement.

Limiting strategic exports has not been the only rationale for export embargoes. The U.S. has also employed export restrictions to destabilize governments (Iran, 1951-53; Chile, 1970–73); to punish human rights violations (Argentina, 1978–81); to pressure countries to adopt nuclear safeguards (Pakistan, 1978–80); and to punish aggressive behavior (the Soviet invasion of Afghanistan, 1980–81).

---

[1] Gary C. Hufbauer and Jeffrey J. Schott, "Economic Sanctions for Foreign Policy Goals," Institute for International Economics. Unpublished manuscript, 1983.

This note was prepared by Research Assistant Sigrid Bergenstein and Assistant Professor David Yoffie as a basis for class discussion.

Table 1   Purposes and Methods of Government Export Controls
(some country and product   examples)

Purpose \ Method	Quantitative Restrictions on Exports[1]	Taxes on Exports	Quantitative Restrictions on Domestic Production[2]	Taxes on Domestic Production[2]
1. Retrain domestic prices	**U.S.**–soybeans, 1973 **U.S.**–logs, 1973[3]		NA	NA
2. Reinforce domestic price controls	**U.S.**–fertilizers, 1973–74[4] **EEC**–wheat and rice, 1973	**EEC**–various agricultural products (sugar, rice, cereals, etc.) 1973.		NA
3. Increase export earnings from the controlled product	**Philippines**–coconut oil, 1974	**Panama, Honduras, Costa Rica**–bananas, 1974	**Kuwait, Libya, Venezuela**–oil, 1974	**Jamaica**–bauxite, 1974
4. Seize earnings generated by other countries' import controls	**Several European countries,** 1930s	**Netherlands**–several products, 1932		
5. Conserve limited resources	(requires massive stockpiling)	(requires massive stockpiling)	**Kuwait**–oil, 1971	
6. Promote domestic processing of the controlled product	**Pakistan**–leather, 1962 **Canada**–amendment to Export and Import Permits Act, 1974	**Brazil**–coffee, 1965		
7. Avoid shortages	**U.K.**–copper scrap, periodic		NA	NA
8. Raise government revenue	NA	**Thailand**–rice, longstanding	NA	**Several oil producers**– longstanding
9. Limit other countries' military and economic potential	**U.S. and COCOM**–to communist countries, 1949 **U.K.**–textile machinery, 1930s to mid 1950s			
10. Change other countries' foreign policies	**Several oil exporters,** 1973–74		**Several oil exporters,** 1973–74	
11. Reduce balance of payments surpluses	**Japan**–20 industries, 1971	**Germany**–all products subject to export rebates, 1968–69		
12. Head off import controls ("voluntary" export restraints)	**Japan**–textiles, 1956			

NA - Not Applicable.

[1]including embargoes.

[2]Not strictly and "export control".

[3]Implemented by Japanese "voluntary" import restraints.

[4]Export controls were informal.

Source: C. Fred Bergsten, *Completing the GATT: Toward New International Rules to Govern Export Controls* (Washington: The British–North American Committee, National Planning Association, 1974). Reprinted by permission.

Measuring Effectiveness

Whatever the goal, policy makers must consider two fundamental questions in considering the effectiveness of export controls: (1) Will restrictions yield the intended response? and (2) What will be the costs of the controls, not only to the target nation, but also to the sender nation? Although precise answers to these questions are difficult, some of the relevant factors are outlined in Table 2.

Table 2   Variables Affecting Costs and Effectiveness of Export Restrictions

Sender	Target
Market Power	*Demand Elasticity*
• market share of exports to target	• availability of other suppliers
• market share of world exports	• domestic production capacity
• availability of substitute product	• price sensitivity
Enforcement	*Ability to Retaliate*
• possibilities of circumvention	• trade (import or export controls)
• equality of costs and benefits	• diplomacy
• sanctions for violations	• military
• domestic opposition	
Administrative Costs	*Ability to Endure*
• unemployment	• political cohesiveness
• foregone sales	• control mechanisms
• displaced resources	• political or strategic importance
• terms of trade gains	of policy goal

Using the above variables, a number of hypotheses have been suggested about the effectiveness of export controls. For example, export controls are more *likely to be successful* if: (1) the sender has a large market share of the embargoed product; (2) bilateral trade is more important to the target country than to the sender; and (3) few substitutes exist for the restricted export. Export controls applied forcefully and for a limited period of time are usually most effective because the longer controls are applied, the greater the likelihood of circumvention.

Similar hypotheses can be generated about the failure of export controls. For example, an embargo is *unlikely to succeed* if: (1) the sender nation demands that the target nation change fundamental policy objectives (e.g., ceasing apartheid; withdrawing troops from occupied territory); (2) the target nation can retaliate at low cost to itself; and (3) the target economy can fill demand for the embargoed product with domestic production.

Centrally planned economies (CPEs) have special features that can inhibit the successful application of export controls.[2] In most cases, export controls are designed to affect the target country by imposing higher costs. In a CPE, however, resources are allocated administratively rather than by price signals. This means that a CPE is less price sensitive than a market economy. The decision to import is based on its perceived contribution to economic plans. Even if export controls result in a price increase, planners can compensate for the higher costs by shifting resources from one sector to another. And even if shortages appear, rationing is a readily available policy option that forces the civilian population to bear the brunt of shortages.

---

[2] See *China: Central Economic Planning*, Harvard Business School case #0-383-089.

The Role of Business

The stated purpose of U.S. laws regarding export controls has been to prevent U.S. firms from selling to restricted markets. But effective implementation of the laws has not been easy. Some companies have complied with the letter of the law and adhered to export restrictions, regardless of the costs. Others have avoided export restrictions through legal and illegal means. Under certain conditions, for example, the U.S. government has permitted American firms to violate embargoes. Legal precedents support the right of foreign governments to regulate commerce in their own countries, including multinationals domiciled there. So-called foreign compulsion has been upheld as a legitimate reason for failing to comply with U.S. law, provided that American firms exhaust *all* alternative options. During the 1960s, for example, when the UN sponsored an oil embargo against Rhodesia, subsidiaries of major oil companies operating in South Africa were obliged by South African laws to continue oil shipments. Under these circumstances, the U.S. government did not enforce penalties.[3]

Not all companies, however, have abided by the letter of the law. Some firms have been known to transship their goods through third countries while others have set up dummy corporations that purchase on behalf of the restricted nation. Still others have gambled that the authorities would fail to detect illegal shipments. Occasionally the U.S. government has cracked down on such offenders. When the government tightened surveillance over exports of critical technology to the USSR in 1982, Customs officials seized 765 shipments valued at $56 million.[4] Authorities conceded that many more shipments went undetected, due to inadequate staff. The cost of such crackdowns, however, was expensive delays for legitimate exporters.

---

[3] Another legal response to export controls has been to redirect exports to competitors' markets. During the 1980 American grain embargo of the USSR, other countries increased their sales to the Soviets while U.S. exporters increased shipments to their competitors' traditional markets.

[4]"Technology and East-West Trade," Office of Technology Assessment, Washington, 1983, p. 40.

Chiquita Brands International (A)

"For many years, world trade has been characterized by multilateral arrangements that reduce or eliminate restrictions on the international flow of goods and services. In direct contrast to this trend, the European Union has imposed an increasingly restrictive and discriminatory trade policy on the Latin American banana industry in the last several years. This has been the primary cause of the significant losses Chiquita Brands International has posted since 1992, following a long record of profitable growth."[1]

With these words, Keith E. Lindner, President and Chief Operating Officer of Chiquita Brands International, began his 1994 annual report to shareholders. Lindner's pointed language, like the situation facing Chiquita, was stark: the world's largest distributor of bananas was in the midst of a serious and unprecedented downturn. From a net income of $128 million on sales of $2.6 billion in 1991, the company had suffered three consecutive years of losses. By year-end 1994, Chiquita's stock was trading at $13.63, down from $40 at the close of 1991.

These setbacks had come during a crucial stage for the 35 year-old Lindner. Along with his father, Carl, a financier who had acquired Chiquita in 1984 and served the company as Chairman of the Board and Chief Executive Officer, the younger Lindner had been attempting to implement a new strategy for the Cincinnati-based fruit colossus. In 1992 he had launched an ambitious plan to shed underperforming assets, cut costs, focus on the company's core fruit businesses, and restructure Chiquita's debt commitments. By the end of 1994, these efforts had begun to produce positive results for the company's balance sheet.

But, as Lindner pointed out in Chiquita's 1994 annual report, the company had suddenly found itself under siege from a powerful, if unlikely, source. As the European Union (EU) neared completion of its single market, member states had adopted a series of import restrictions that threatened to topple Chiquita from its leading position in the $3 billion EU banana market. Indeed, in the time that had elapsed between the July 1, 1993 effective date of the EU banana import regime and the last days of 1994, Lindner had seen Chiquita's market share in Europe slide significantly. This eroding market share, combined with mounting annual losses, called for swift action on the part

---

[1]Chiquita Brands International, *Annual Report 1994*, p. 2.

Terence Mulligan, MBA Class of 1996, prepared this case under the supervision of Professor Debora Spar and with the assistance of Research Associate Laura Bures as the basis of class discussion rather than to illustrate either effective or ineffective handling of an administrative situation.

of senior management. Just what Chiquita could do to respond to the EU's banana policy, however, was unclear.

"La Pulpa": The History of Chiquita and United Fruit

In 1870, Captain Lorenzo Baker, commander of the fishing boat *Telegraph*, sailed into Jersey City, New Jersey with 160 bunches of bananas aboard his schooner and proceeded to introduce a rather improbable tropical fruit to North American consumers. Eleven days earlier, Baker had purchased the bananas in Port Antonio, Jamaica for one shilling per bunch.[2] When he sold them upon his arrival for $2 per bunch, he realized that he had stumbled upon a potentially lucrative trade. And so Captain Baker began to carry bananas on all his trips from Jamaica, unloading them for sale at the larger port of Boston.[3]

In Boston, Andrew Preston, an agent of the produce firm Seaverns & Co., sold the fruit on commission. After more than a decade of profitable sales, Baker convinced Preston and several of his partners to form an independent fruit company; in 1885, the new partners established the Boston Fruit Company (BFC) to sell imported bananas throughout New England. Over the next ten years, BFC expanded its sourcing and distribution operations and eventually merged with a New Orleans-based competitor to form the United Fruit Company in 1899. Business was conducted under this name for more than 70 years. Then, in 1970, Eli Black bought UFC and changed its name to United Brands; in 1989, Carl Lindner changed the company's name once more, to Chiquita Brands International.

In the 91 years that preceded the creation of Chiquita Brands, the United Fruit Company grew to dominate the international banana trade and to affect profoundly the economic and social conditions of the Caribbean and Latin American countries that grew and shipped its bananas. Although United Fruit never reached the enormous size of U.S.-based producers of oil, steel, or automobiles, it was nevertheless a giant in the eyes of the banana producing nations, where it played a central and unprecedented role throughout the first half of the twentieth century.

Deemed *la pulpa*, or the octopus, by those who saw the company as a highly visible extension of U.S. political and economic hegemony in the region, UFC was indeed an enterprise that reached deeply into the countries where it owned plantations and sourced fruit. It owned vast tracts of land in Jamaica, Cuba, Costa Rica, Panama, Colombia, and Nicaragua, as well as the equally vast transportation networks that it needed to move its bananas quickly and across long distances. It also developed extensive political connections over time, working closely with the governments of its producing regions, and helping them earn the infamous label of "banana republics." In many of the countries in which it operated, the United Fruit Company wielded disproportionate power, blending its control of bananas, railroads, and politicians into a legendary, often incendiary, mix. Minor Keith, vice-president of UFC at the turn of the century, came to be known as "the uncrowned king of Central America," the "Green Pope," and the "Cecil Rhodes of Central America." In 1962, Miguel Angel Asturias, a Guatemalan novelist and winner of the Nobel Prize in Literature, echoed the sentiments of many Latin intellectuals in his complaint that, "the Green Pope . . . lifts a finger and a ship starts or stops. He says a word and a republic is bought. He sneezes and a president, whether general or

---

[2]In 1870, the exchange rate was fixed at $4.86 per pound sterling. Thus Baker bought each bunch of bananas for 24¢.

[3]This section and the next borrow heavily from Stacy May and Galo Plaza, *The United Fruit Company in Latin America*, (Washington, DC: National Planning Association, 1958).

lawyer, falls. . . . He rubs his behind on a chair and a revolution breaks out."[4]   While clearly an overstatement of United Fruit's influence, Asturias's description finds some support from the historical record.   In 1911 and 1912, U.S. President Taft sent the marines into Honduras to protect investments which UFC claimed to be threatened by the country's political instability.   Also in 1911, UFC and Samuel Zemurray, founder of a rival fruit company and later president of UFC, were implicated in a conspiracy to break U.S. neutrality laws and overthrow the Honduran government.[5]

To its supporters, the power of UFC was merely an extension of the benefits that the company had brought, at tremendous cost, to the region.   As an organization, UFC made unparalleled contributions to the development of transportation and communications infrastructure in Latin America.   It employed thousands of workers at wages that exceeded local rates; it furnished them with housing, medical care, education, and recreational activities; and it came to represent a major source of foreign exchange earnings for governments in Costa Rica, Honduras, Panama, Guatemala, Ecuador, and Colombia.   To its detractors, however, the company remained an extractor of value, a runaway multinational with shady connections to unstable governments, and an agent of the status quo that locked the developing economies of the region into a state of dependence on U.S. capital and commodity agriculture.[6]

In all likelihood, the long history of the United Fruit Company in Latin America is complicated enough to support the opinions of detractors and supporters alike.   But while the long-term effects of the company's operations remain the subject of debate, the vast scope of UFC's banana empire is a matter of historical record.   At the time of its incorporation in 1899, the newly consolidated company controlled 112 miles of railroad, 212 thousand acres of land and $11 million in capital.   By 1930, UFC's capital stock had grown to $215 million; by 1955, it crested $390 million.[7]   By the mid-1950s, UFC was the largest single landowner, the largest single business, and the largest

---

[4] Miguel Angel Asturias, *Strong Wind,* trans. Gregory Rabassa (New York: Delacorte Press, 1968), p. 112.

[5]When UFC and Samuel Zemurray realized that their companies would not receive certain concessions including a transoceanic line, a port, and the surrounding banana lands from the President of Honduras, Miguel Dávila, Zemurray forged a personal friendship with the former president of Honduras, Manuel Bonilla, who was plotting to stage a revolution and overthrow Dávila. Zemurray lent Bonilla money to buy a yacht which the former president then rigged for military operations and loaded with arms. Bonilla recruited a small army and in January of 1911 invaded Honduras, taking Trujillo and Tegucigalpa. Bonilla then ousted Dávila and took the presidency. Paul J. Dosal, *Doing Business with the Dictators: A Political History of United Fruit in Guatemala, 1899-1944* (Wilmington, Delaware: SR Books, 1993), pp. 79-81. See also Charles David Kepner, Jr. and Jay Henry Soothill, *The Banana Empire: A Case Study of Economic Imperialism* (New York: Russell & Russell, 1967), pp. 107-112.

[6]In some Latin American countries where UFC conducted business, the company has been described as an enclave, defined as an extractive enterprise with few links to the host economy. In some of UFC's divisions, for example, the company farmed coastal plantations that were far removed from the rest of the country, built wharves in the Caribbean Sea, and laid railroads only to transport its bananas to port. Dosal, p. 8. A number of prominent Latin American authors have written eloquently about the problematic issues surrounding the operations of UFC. See, for example, the treatment of the banana company and its railroads in Gabriel Garcia Marquez, *One Hundred Years of Solitude,* or Pablo Neruda's "United Fruit Company" in his work, *Canto General,* included as Exhibit 3.

[7]Descriptions of the United Fruit Company's activities abound and make for fascinating reading. See, for example, May and Plaza *The United Fruit Company in Latin America*; Dosal, *Doing Business with the Dictators*; Kepner and Soothill, *The Banana Empire*; Robert Thompson, *Green Gold: Bananas and Dependency in the Eastern Caribbean* (London: Latin America Bureau, 1987); Eduardo Galeano, *Open Veins of Latin America: Five Centuries of the Pillage of a Continent,* trans. Cedric Belfrage (New York: Monthly Review Press, 1973); Aviva Chomsky, *West Indian Workers and the United Fruit Company in Costa Rica, 1870-1940,* (Baton Rouge, LA: Louisiana State University Press, 1996); and Diane K. Stanley, *For the Record: The United Fruit Company's Sixty-six Years in Guatemala,* (Centro Impresor Piedra Santa, 1994).

corporate employer of labor in Guatemala, Honduras, and Costa Rica. In Panama, the company was second in size only to the Panama Canal and its adjuncts. In Costa Rica, Panama, and Honduras, where central government revenues in 1955 amounted to $47 million, $44 million, and $30 million, respectively, UFC accumulated a $330 million gross profit, $33 million in profits after taxes, and $26 million for dividend payments.[8] In the same year, the United Fruit Company owned more than 1.7 million acres of land in Guatemala, Honduras, Costa Rica, Panama, Colombia, and Ecuador and a total of 85% of the land suitable for banana cultivation in the American tropics.

Structure of the Banana Industry

It was not entirely by accident that UFC grew to such mammoth dimensions. Indeed, commercial banana production and distribution are by nature capital intensive and inclined to support very large firms. First, land must be purchased, cleared, drained, and irrigated to grow the fruit. At the turn of the century, when UFC was establishing a beachhead for itself in the lowland jungles of Central and South America, setting up plantations was dangerous, and sometimes deadly, work. Productive acreage had to be captured from the tangled vegetation of the jungle, and progress was hampered by tropical storms, poor infrastructure, and frequent outbreaks of malaria and yellow fever. Because bananas grow only in the equatorial climates of the Caribbean, Latin America, Africa, and the Pacific Rim, banana companies had no choice but to operate there and to accept the high costs of doing so.

Second, because bananas are extremely vulnerable to bad weather and disease, multiple sources and systematic crop management techniques are needed to ensure a steady flow of product. Excess land is often held for cultivation on an as-needed basis, and significant investments are required to repair acreage damaged by floods and other natural disasters.[9] Large capital outlays are also needed to support modern disease control, creating a key barrier to entry for small growers attempting to achieve competitive scale. In addition, banana companies frequently purchase property not just for cultivation, but also to house workers, to build power plants, packing stations, and warehouses, and to make way for transportation and communication facilities.

These investments in transportation and communications are also sizable and represent the third driver behind the capital intensive nature of the banana business. To support each banana plantation, and to ensure a steady flow of fruit from producing regions to the major markets of North America, Europe, and Asia, banana companies need to develop complex logistical systems. Plantations are crisscrossed with a network of roads, tramways, and rail lines, each of which plays a role in moving harvested fruit to port facilities, where the product is shipped in refrigerated cargo vessels to overseas markets. Since production and consumption are separated by vast distances, and because bananas are harvested several times a year and can not be stored for long periods of time (indeed, bananas are uniquely perishable, and cannot be processed readily by freezing or canning), coordination of production and distribution has always been essential. Communications infrastructure, therefore, has always been a key component of the banana industry; and capital has historically been required not only for transportation assets like rail lines and cargo ships, but for telegraph, telephone, and computer information systems as well. Both kinds of investments are needed to strike a balance between supply and demand.

---

[8]May and Plaza, p. 117.

[9]Bananas are usually grown year-round, with 10-12 months between planting and harvest. Most plants typically produce only for two to three growing cycles.

It was precisely this need for balance—combined with the asset intensity of large scale production, transportation, and distribution—that caused the global banana industry to integrate vertically. From the earliest days of the banana trade, companies needed to supply their rapidly growing consumer markets with fruit on a timely basis, and thus to structure and control their operations to ensure consistent delivery of a quality product. These needs led them to combine production and distribution in one firm, controlling the process all the way from the banana-growing fields of Latin America to the wholesale distribution networks in major developed country markets. Once established, combined producer/distributors like the United Fruit Company faced little threat of entry in either the upstream or downstream segments of their value chain: capital costs to achieve competitive scale were high, and existing players had already formed strong relationships in all of the major producing regions.[10] In this competitive landscape, the global banana industry grew to support a handful of large, vertically integrated companies.[11]

The Banana Industry in the 1990s

In 1994, just six of these large firms dominated the global banana industry. They included U.S.-based Chiquita and Dole, by far the largest of the major producer/distributors, as well as the Fresh Produce division of Del Monte, which had been spun off from its corporate parent in 1989. Geest PLC and Fyffes PLC, both based in the European Community (EC)[12], were smaller than the two U.S. industry leaders, but still competed vigorously for market share, especially in the European market. Noboa, a private company based in Ecuador, was also a major player. Together, these six companies controlled almost all of the global banana market, valued in 1991 at approximately $5.1 billion.[13]

Although these companies' production was still located primarily in the equatorial plantations of Latin America, the Caribbean, Africa, and the Philippines, their sales were overwhelmingly concentrated in the developed country markets of North America, the EC, and Asia. The EC was the largest of these markets, accounting for roughly 40% of world imports by volume, 60% of which came from Latin America. North America was the second largest consumer with approximately 35% of world imports; Japan and other Asian countries absorbed another 15% of global banana shipments; and the remaining 10% supplied the rest of the world.

---

[10]Although UFC/Chiquita has always turned to non-owned plantations to supply some of its product, about two-thirds of the company's bananas has historically been sourced from its own subsidiaries in Latin America. This figure has been fairly consistent over time and is probably the result of two factors: the unpredictability of growing conditions; and the high costs associated with adding marginal capacity in a commodity industry, where excess supply leads quickly to downward pressure on prices.

[11]The development of such large and vertically-integrated companies also eventually drew charges of unfair competition. In 1954, the U.S. Department of Justice filed an antitrust suit against the United Fruit Company, concluding that the firm "adopted and pursued a consistent policy of absorbing or excluding competitors in all phases of the industry." Memorandum, Milton A. Kallis to Victor H. Kramer and W. Perry Epes, "Banana Investigation," December 20, 1952, U.S. Department of Justice, Antitrust Division, *United States v. United Fruit Co.*, Civil No. 4560, File 60-166-56, 3-4.

[12] In the discussion that follows, "EC" and "EU" will be used interchangeably to describe the European countries that now comprise the EU. The European Community became the European Union after the Maastricht Treaty, or the Treaty of the European Union, took effect on November 1, 1993.

[13]Petition of Chiquita Brands International, Inc. and the Hawaii Banana Industry Association before the Section 301 Committee Office of the United States Trade Representative, September 2, 1994, p. 10.

High transportation costs and perishability were crucial in determining the pattern of supply across the world's markets.   Thus, bananas from the Philippines and other Asian sources were shipped to Japan, while exports from Latin America, the Caribbean, and Africa went primarily to the North American and European markets.   Latin America, the heart of United Fruit's operations, was still the largest banana producing region in the world, accounting for roughly 75% of global shipments by volume.   The Philippines accounted for an additional 10%; bananas from Africa, the Caribbean, and the Pacific (the "ACP" region) represented another 10%; and a handful of other countries supplied the balance of world banana shipments.[14]

As a traded foodstuff, bananas were second in value only to coffee.   But despite the large size of the global market, the concentration of power within the industry, and efforts on the part of major distributors to differentiate their products through branding, bananas in the 1990s were still traded essentially as commodities.   As such, they tended to experience wide swings in price, as even powerful producers found themselves essentially at the mercy of forces beyond their companies' control.   Hurricanes and tropical storms, for instance, could easily destroy large portions of a crop in one or more countries in any given year, creating a situation of short supply.[15] Likewise, periodic outbreaks of fruit disease could reduce annual yields dramatically, causing prices to spike upwards. Labor unrest on the companies' plantations was also an occasional contributor to supply shortages.

In most cases, such shortages of supply did not cause the producers any great difficulty, since they were happy to ride prices upwards, or to bolster supply by expanding production on some of their reserve acreage.   What did cause significant problems for the producers, however, were periodic surpluses.   Typically, this situation arose when demand fell during a recession, or when over-investment flooded the world market with too much product, driving prices and profit margins downward.   In these situations, downward pressure on prices was further exacerbated by the perishability of bananas and the high fixed costs associated with their production, transportation, and distribution. Even when they recognize that larger volumes of banana shipments will sharply reduce margins, therefore, banana companies have tended to unload product.[16]   Periodic attempts by producers to manage their supply have consistently been thwarted by the problem inherent in bananas: with no effective means of long-term storage, there is little incentive to keep production from reaching the market.

Going Bananas: Chiquita and the European Union

When Keith Lindner and his father Carl acquired a controlling share of United Brands in 1984, the company had already spent nearly a century dealing profitably with the vicissitudes of the global banana market. While there were some concerns at the time about growing global supplies of bananas, United Brands was nevertheless enjoying record levels of sales and earnings. The good times persisted for several years. Throughout the late 1980s, United Brands remained the industry leader, boosting global sales of bananas and increasing promotion of the "Chiquita" brand name. In 1989, Lindner changed the corporation's name to Chiquita Brands International and plotted an aggressive strategy of global expansion, focusing in particular on the EU, Eastern Europe, and Asia. In 1991, following eight years of continued growth in earnings, Chiquita planned to invest in

---

[14]The ACP countries include Belize, Jamaica, Suriname, the Windward Islands (Dominica, Grenada, St. Lucia, and St. Vincent) Somalia, Cameroon, and the Ivory Coast.

[15]For instance, a 1991 earthquake in Costa Rica cut world banana production by roughly 10%.

[16]In 1994, a banana glut sent prices plunging to their lowest level in six years, from $13-15 for an 18 kg crate in the U.S. market in 1992 to only $4 per crate in 1994.

increased banana production, acquiring new acreage in Latin America and new ships for its transportation fleet. This decision reversed the company's strategy during the 1980s, which had been to decrease banana production and convert some fields to the production of other crops. In 1990 and 1991, Chiquita's sales of fresh foods grew by a rather remarkable 18%.

In 1992, however, the company's net income plummeted, and Chiquita lost $284 million after having earned $128 million and $93 million in 1991 and 1990, respectively. Losses continued to accumulate in 1993 and 1994. By the end of 1994, Chiquita's cash balances had fallen to $179 million, down from $712 million in 1991. A staggering $1.3 billion in value had been destroyed, an amount which represented 66% of the firm's 1991 net worth.

As his letter to shareholders indicated, Keith Lindner believed that the European Union was principally to blame for his company's alarming decline. On July 1, 1993, the EC had adopted a new banana import regime that established a Community-wide quota on bananas imported from the Latin American countries where Chiquita sourced most of the fruit it sold in the EC. Under the terms of the new regime, Latin American banana imports above a two million metric ton ceiling would face tariffs so onerous that no firm, including Chiquita, could afford to exceed the quota. Moreover, to administer the quota, the EC established a complex licensing system that would grant Chiquita's EU-based competitors the right to import a significant percentage of the two million metric tons permissible under the scheme.

From Lindner's perspective, the EC banana regime was a devastating blow. To the implementing countries, however, it was a political and economic necessity, the culmination of a long and complex attempt to regulate Europe's banana trade.

Europe's Banana Policies

Beginning in 1975, with the adoption of the ACP-EEC Convention of Lomé, most members of the EC provided preferential access to banana imports from developing countries in the ACP region. These countries, which were essentially the former colonies of Britain and France, were granted tariff-free access to the EC market, while banana imports from other regions, including Latin America, faced a variety of restraints that differed widely across each of the countries in the Community. Imports from EC territories (Martinique, Guadeloupe, the Canary Islands, Crete, and Madeira), like imports from ACP countries, were given duty-free access to all markets within the Community.

Because Germany lacked any banana producing former colonies of its own, it gave no preferential treatment to country-specific bananas and thus became over time the only free market for bananas in the European Community. It was also by far the largest market in Europe, accounting for roughly one-third of all EC banana imports. While other members of the Community imposed a common external tariff of 20% *ad valorem* on imports of bananas, Germany accorded duty-free access to imports from all sources at the level of estimated consumption, resulting in entry that was effectively free. In 1991, Germans consumed 16.6 kilograms of bananas on a per capita basis, with an average price per ton at customs of 438 ECU. In France, by contrast, per capita consumption was only 8 kilograms, and the comparable price at import was 604 ECU.[17]

With the exception of Germany, all of the other EC member states maintained a variety of restrictions on imported bananas. Some states, such as Belgium, Denmark, Ireland, Luxembourg, the Netherlands, and Greece limited their protectionist policies to a fairly straightforward 20% a.v. tariff on banana imports from "non-preferred" countries. Others, such as France, the United Kingdom,

---

[17]Chiquita Section 301 Petition, pp. 12-18.

Italy, Portugal, and Spain paired the tariffs with a number of less transparent, non-tariff barriers, including quantitative restrictions, import licensing requirements, and import bans.

In the countries where banana imports were most limited, the stated purpose of these trade barriers was to support producers in former colonies and territories. Explicitly, import barriers served as an indirect form of aid, allowing smaller, less efficient growers in these regions to compete with the U.S.-based multinationals, who sourced most of their product from the giant plantations of Latin America. Although there was undoubtedly an element of company-specific protection involved in the most restrictive EC import policies (Geest, a British multinational, controlled almost all of the production of the Windward Islands, while Fyffes, based in Ireland, controlled almost all the production of Belize and Suriname, along with some of the output of Jamaica), the principal beneficiaries of the EC's trade barriers—the former colonies of the ACP region—would almost certainly have been forced out of the global banana business without preferential access to a protected European market.

In most of the beneficiary countries, bananas played a crucial economic role. In the Windward Islands (Dominica, St. Lucia, St. Vincent, and Grenada), for example, bananas were the predominant export and thus the largest earner of foreign exchange. In 1991, bananas accounted for more than 75% of all agricultural exports, over half the value of total exports, and 15% of GDP. Approximately 57,000 people, or 31% of the active labor force, were involved either directly or indirectly in banana production. For roughly 60% of the households involved in the banana industry, the crop represented their sole source of income. There were roughly 27,000 small farmers cultivating bananas on the islands, and most of these crops were raised on less than five acres of land. At this minuscule scale, average production costs were more than double the comparative costs faced by growers in Latin America, where plantations often exceeded 20,000 acres.[18] Without preferential access to the large EC market, the banana industry in the Windward Islands would have collapsed, taking the entire economy down with it.

The same was true for most of the ACP/EC territory countries. However, while the implications of banana market liberalization were understood by all members of the EC, the Community had always been sharply divided on the issue. Germany, with free banana imports and no colonial connection to the preferred suppliers, had struggled continuously with the UK and France to maintain an open market. In fact, conflict over banana imports had delayed the 1957 signing of the Treaty of Rome, the document which laid the groundwork for European integration. Only after Germany received a special dispensation from the common external tariff on bananas did it consent to join the move toward a single market.[19]

As the single market approached the full economic integration promised by 1992, the debate about bananas had emerged again. Once more, Germany was pitted against the other members of the Community. And once more the debate centered on the relative merits of preferential treatment and economic liberalization.

The EU's New Regime

Inherent in the movement towards a full-fledged European Union was an agreement to harmonize external tariffs and import policies among all the member states. Accordingly, bureaucrats within the EC had begun to work on a common banana policy as early as 1988. But

---

[18] Anita van de Vliet, "Banana Wars," *World Link*, March/April 1994, p. 36.
[19] Ibid., p. 35.

because member states disagreed so strenuously, consensus proved exceedingly difficult to reach, and the new regime, agreed to in principal in early 1992, was not finalized until 1993. The resulting common banana import policy, Council Regulation (EEC) 404/93, became effective on July 1, 1993, four months prior to the official integration of the European Union.   Titles I, II, and III of the Regulation were relatively innocuous, providing for the establishment of common quality and marketing standards, producer "concentration" mechanisms, and assistance for EC producers. Title IV, however, provided for significant changes in banana import patterns. Under its terms, the EC would henceforth divide banana imports into four categories: Latin American and non-ACP sources, called "third country imports"; "traditional" ACP imports; "non-traditional" ACP imports (ACP imports exceeding the "traditional quota amounts"); and EC imports. Separate import policies would apply to each banana source. "Third country" imports were restricted to a two million ton quota, with in-quota volumes dutiable at 100 ECU/mt (approximately 30% a.v.). Imports in excess of the quota were dutiable at 850 ECU/mt (approximately 250% a.v.). By contrast, "traditional" ACP imports were granted duty free access to the European market. "Non-traditional" ACP imports were subject to the two million ton quota free of duty, and imports above the quota were dutiable at 750 ECU/mt. In addition, "third country" and "non-traditional" ACP banana sources were restricted by a licensing provision, while "traditional" sources were given automatic, non-restrictive licenses. "Category A" licenses restricted operators that had historically marketed "third country" and/or "non-traditional" bananas (U.S. multinationals) to 66.5% of the total "third country" quota. Companies that historically marketed EC and "traditional" ACP bananas (such as Geest and Fyffes) were given a 30% share of the "third country" quota amount under "Category B" licenses. Companies which started marketing bananas other than EC or "traditional" bananas as of 1992 were allotted 3.5% of the quota amount under "Category C" licenses.

As soon as the broad outlines of the common banana policy became clear, parties that would be adversely affected by the new regime sprang into action. Late in 1992, Colombia, Costa Rica, Guatemala, Nicaragua, and Venezuela, major Latin American producers, filed a GATT (General Agreement on Tariffs and Trade) complaint against the existing EU import policies. Honduras, Panama, and Ecuador, which were also heavily dependent on the EU banana market, supported the GATT petition, but could not file an official complaint as they were not Contracting Parties to the General Agreement on Tariffs and Trade. Once the common banana policy came into effect in July, 1993, the original Latin petitioners also brought a second complaint to the GATT. In both instances, Chiquita and other U.S.-based banana companies provided assistance to the Latin governments in drafting and executing their petitions. And in each case, a GATT dispute resolution panel ruled against the EC's policies, first with respect to the pre-integration regimes, and second with reference to the common banana rule adopted on July 1, 1993.

However, because the GATT operated on the basis of consensus, any Contracting Party could block the formal adoption of a panel ruling.[20] Thus, the EC used its position in GATT to stand in the way of multilateral reform, and continued to move forward with the new banana import regime, despite the criticisms of the Latins and strong evidence from various World Bank reports that the EC's policy was seriously flawed.[21]

Between October 1993 and March 1994, in a series of negotiations conducted mostly with Costa Rica and Colombia, the EU attempted to split the Latin American producers by offering certain

---

[20]Under the World Trade Organization (WTO), the successor to the GATT established in 1995, the principle of consensus was substantially diluted.

[21]EU consumers, the World Bank noted, spent $1.6 billion every year to transfer $300 million to the 11 beneficiary countries of the common banana regime. Transferring one dollar cost consumers $5.30 because nearly 60% of the $1.6 billion —$917 million —was paid to protected EU importers and wholesalers in the form of excessive marketing margins. *Development Brief No. 50* (World Bank: Washington, DC), 1995, p. 1.

countries preferential access to the EU market under the common banana policy.   The strategy worked. In March of 1994, Costa Rica, Colombia, Nicaragua, and Venezuela signed a Framework Agreement with the EU that raised the quota on Latin American imports from 2 million to 2.1 million metric tons, and allocated a specific and substantial portion (49.4%) of the overall quota for Latin American banana imports to each of the four countries involved in the agreement. As part of the settlement, these Latin countries agreed to forgo the adoption of the GATT panel report which ruled against the common import regime. The Framework was to be implemented on October 1, 1994.[22]

Chiquita's Response

Chiquita had watched the formation of the EU's common import regime with mounting indignation, but took particular offense at the combination of the new banana policy and the Framework Agreement. Together, the EU banana scheme and the Framework represented a direct threat to the company's position in the EU. First, by placing an artificial cap on Latin American imports, the common banana policy would constrain growth opportunities in the world's largest market. In 1992, Latin American countries had shipped more than 2.4 million metric tons of bananas to the EU; Chiquita's sales accounted for 40% of this amount. Although the EU banana quota was slated to rise from 2 million metric tons in 1993 to 2.2 million metric tons in 1995, the import policy and the Framework Agreement together would significantly shrink the market for Latin American exports.[23]

Furthermore, the import licensing system established by the common banana policy and expanded by the Framework was almost certain to undermine Chiquita's market share and sharply increase its operating costs. Under the banana scheme's licensing provisions, the quota on Latin American imports was to be shared among several categories of operators, only one of which, the "Category A" operators, included the U.S. multinationals which had traditionally sourced product from Latin American countries. Shipments not covered explicitly by Category A licenses would need to be imported using licenses purchased on the open market from Chiquita's European competitors at inflated prices—assuming they were willing to sell. The Framework Agreement further complicated matters by allocating a certain percentage of these Category A licenses to specific Latin American countries. Costa Rica received licenses representing 23.4% of the overall quota on Latin American banana imports; Colombia's share was 21%; Nicaragua received 3%; and Venezuela got 2%. The balance was to be divided among the Latin American countries not party to the Framework Agreement. Because Chiquita owned significant banana operations in such non-Framework Latin American countries as Honduras and Panama, and because Chiquita's access to the European market had already been limited by the original distribution of Category A licenses, the slice of the Category A pie, which allowed Chiquita to export bananas to Europe, grew even slimmer.

Never before had U.S. banana companies been subject to geographic restrictions in fulfilling EU demand, and Chiquita anticipated that the Framework Agreement would, at a minimum, raise the company's operating costs by disrupting its traditional sourcing patterns in Latin America. Chiquita would probably need to purchase fruit from higher cost producers and lose efficiencies in the use of its transportation assets. In addition, compliance with the common banana policy and the Framework would require the company to incur a new set of administrative costs.

---

[22]Chiquita Section 301 Petition, September 2, 1994, p. 49-53. The Framework Agreement did not actually take effect until January 1, 1995.

[23]Ibid., p. 19

In 1993, the EU accounted for 45% of Chiquita's total banana sales—the largest market by far for the company's production.[24]   Clearly, something had to be done to protect the interests of the company from the effects of the restrictive EU banana policies.

The Section 301 Petition

On September 2, 1994, one month before the Framework Agreement was scheduled to take effect, Chiquita filed a Section 301 Petition with the Office of the U.S. Trade Representative (USTR). By this time, according to industry analysts, Chiquita had lost between 20% and 50% of its EU market share. Even though the common banana policy had created an artificial shortage in the EU, which drove up prices, Chiquita was continuing to lose money.[25]

Chiquita's 301 Petition, filed jointly with the Hawaii Banana Industry Association, called on USTR to take action against the EU and the Latin signatories to the Framework Agreement. In more than 100 pages of text, the Petition laid out a detailed case against the discriminatory provisions of the common banana policy and the Framework Agreement. USTR accepted the Petition and launched a formal investigation of EU and Latin American policies in October 1994.

Section 301 of the 1974 Trade Act, as amended, allows American companies to petition the U.S. government for relief from foreign acts and practices that burden or restrict U.S. commerce. The statute requires USTR to accept or reject a petition within 45 days and establishes a number of other deadlines by which time specific actions must be taken by USTR pursuant to an investigation. One of these actions, in the case of an affirmative finding of injury, is the imposition of trade sanctions. Although the Trade Representative can always exercise discretion with respect to the deadlines and actions stipulated by the statute, Section 301 has become a powerful tool for focusing public attention and executive branch resources on particular trade barriers overseas. More than anything, Section 301 provides the U.S. government with leverage in negotiations to remove foreign trade barriers, since sanctions are always a possibility—even if they are seldom used.[26]

The Other Dole

While its Section 301 Petition worked its way through the U.S. executive branch, Chiquita was also exploring other political options. As part of an all-out assault on the EU banana regime and the Framework Agreement, Carl Lindner approached Kansas Senator Bob Dole and asked him to put pressure directly on the Latin American governments involved in the Framework.   Lindner's assumption in this approach was that the Latin countries, by virtue of their developing country status and smaller economic size, would ultimately prove far more susceptible to U.S. negotiating power than would the European Union.

Reportedly, Senator Dole went to bat vigorously for Lindner and Chiquita, attempting on several occasions to sway the Latin governments most actively involved in implementing the

---

[24]The North American market, by contrast, accounted for 34% of Chiquita's sales, and Asia and the Middle East for 21%.

[25]Casewriter interview with Tim Ramey, equity analyst, Deutsche Morgan Grenfell Inc., April 24, 1996. Mr. Ramey's estimates with respect to lost market share were echoed in separate interviews with John Maggs at the *Journal of Commerce* and Jeff Harrington at the *Cincinnati Inquirer*.

[26]In a survey of the 91 Section 301 cases initiated between 1974 and 1994, Bayard and Elliott found only 15 instances in which trade sanctions were ultimately employed.   Thomas Bayard and Kimberly Ann Elliott, *Reciprocity and Retaliation in US Trade Policy* (Washington, DC: IIE), 1994, p. 66.

Framework Agreement. Among the measures Dole sought were legal provisions that would have stripped Colombia of the aid it receives under U.S. programs designed to reduce the international flow of illicit drugs and a bill that would have required Colombia and Costa Rica to undo the Framework Agreement or lose preferential access to the U.S. market.[27] The Senator was also active in keeping the banana issue on the front burner at USTR.[28] Late in 1994 he attended a private meeting with U.S. Trade Representative Mickey Kantor and Carl Lindner, some weeks after Chiquita had submitted its Section 301 Petition to the Administration. At the time, the Uruguay Round implementing legislation was being considered in Congress, and Dole reportedly sought to link passage of the GATT bill with action on behalf of Chiquita. [29]

Dole's campaign on behalf of Chiquita ultimately brought both the Senator and the company a good deal of unwanted attention. Common Cause, a non-profit advocacy group based in Washington, noted that Lindner and his companies were the second-largest contributors of "soft-money" to both political parties in the 1993-1994 campaign cycle, with donations of $525,000 and $430,000 going to Democratic and Republican coffers, respectively.[30] Dole, for his part, fielded questions about his frequent use of Lindner's private jet, and was asked to explain why he had acted so aggressively for a company with only 7,000 U.S. employees and no appreciable U.S. exports.[31] His aides, however, maintained that Senator Dole had played a leading role in the banana case because it was "right for America."[32] In late 1995, as the 1996 presidential campaign drew nearer, Dole drew back from his plan to impose trade sanctions on Costa Rica and Colombia for their cooperation in the Framework Agreement.[33]

Next Steps

By early 1995, Chiquita's position appeared to be only slightly better than it had been at the outset of 1994, when the company's zealous lobbying efforts had begun in earnest. On January 9, USTR issued an announcement stating that the EU import regime discriminated against U.S.-based banana companies and requested public comment by February 10 on what actions, including trade sanctions, should be taken next. At the same time, a separate Section 301 investigation was launched by USTR into the banana policies of Colombia and Costa Rica, the only signatories of the Framework Agreement actively implementing the accord.[34]

While these policy developments gave Chiquita hope, the company's management also realized that the 301 process, even if successful, could only produce results in the medium to long term. And the company needed to do something immediately to counter the effects of trade restrictions and improve Chiquita's financial performance.

---

[27]Steve Watkins, "Trade Expert Decries Deals for Chiquita," *Greater Cincinnati Business Record*, November 27, 1995; "Banana Republican," *The Economist*, November 18, 1995.

[28]James Pressley, "Banana Quotas by EU Draw U.S. Complaints," *Wall Street Journal*, September 7, 1994.

[29]Jeff Harrington, "Kantor Denies Deal Involving Chiquita," *Cincinnati Inquirer*, May 4, 1995, p. 13.

[30]Paul Blustein and Thomas W. Lippman, "The Riled Bunch," *The Washington Post*, October 20, 1995.

[31]Afshin Molavi, "Dole Puts Banana Campaign on Hold," *Financial Times*, December 13, 1995.

[32]Ibid.

[33]Ibid.

[34]Jeff Harrington, "US Will Challenge European Banana Quotas," *Cincinnati Inquirer*, January 11, 1995, p. 6.

Unfortunately, there were not many options.   Despite efforts to unlever its balance sheet, Chiquita still bore the weight of high debt payments and had very little cash on hand going into 1995. Without cash, Chiquita would find it difficult to follow the lead of its U.S.-based competitors, Del Monte and Dole, which were both seeking to increase their investments in ACP production as a hedge against market restrictions in the EU.   Dole was also acquiring smaller EU distributors in order to obtain import licenses, a move that would allow the company to sell more product into Europe. Chiquita was in the process of pursuing similar strategies, but its depressed stock had not proven attractive to acquisition candidates, and a cash purchase was out of the question.[35]

Shifting output to less restricted markets in North America and Asia was another possibility, but there was already too much product being diverted there from the EU, and prices outside of Europe were flat.   Other markets in the former Soviet Union and Eastern Europe were attractive, but not yet sufficiently developed to absorb a significant share of Chiquita's Latin American output.

Sitting in his office on a bitterly cold January evening in 1995, Keith Lindner pondered Chiquita's difficult situation and wondered what could be done to restore the century-old company to profitability. He couldn't help himself from thinking that the current problems would pass, and that Chiquita would soon return to its customary mode of doing business. At least that's what he wanted to believe.

---

[35]Casewriter interview with Tim Ramey, Deutsche Morgan Grenfell Inc.

Exhibit 1   Chiquita Brands International Consolidated Statements of Income, 1991-1994

	1994[a]	1993	1992	1991
($000s)				
Net sales	3,961,720	2,532,925	2,723,250	2,604,128
Cost of goods sold	3,293,341	1,993,552	2,309,425	2,027,669
Gross profit	668,379	539,373	413,825	576,459
SG&A	442,780	332,934	368,675	324,240
Depreciation and				
amortization	115,816	102,591	80,438	54,401
Restructuring	NA	NA	61,300	NA
Operating income	109,783	103,848	(96,588)	197,818
Interest expense	(169,521)	(169,789)	(155,036)	88,406
Non-operating income	24,538	26,860	34,916	50,597
Profit before taxes	(35,200)	(39,081)	(216,708)	160,009
Income taxes	(13,500)	(12,000)	(5,000)	(49,100)
Income from continuing				
operations	(48,700)	(51,081)	(221,708)	110,909
Discontinued operations	NA	NA	(62,332)	17,586
Extraordinary items	(22,840)[b]	NA	NA	NA
Net income	(71,540)	(51,081)	(284,040)	128,495
Shares outstanding	49,301	48,510	48,164	49,926
Market value equity	671,973	557,865	830,829	1,997,040
Closing stock price	13.63	11.5	17.25	40
Earnings per share	-1.45	-1.05	-5.90	2.57
Dividends per share	0.20	0.44	0.68	0.55
Interest coverage	0.79	0.78	-0.74	2.81

Source: Company annual reports and Value Line reports.

[a]All statements are from December 31.

[b] Extraordinary loss from prepayment of debt.

Exhibit 2   Chiquita Brands International Consolidated Balance Sheets, 1991-1994
($000s)

	1994[a]	1993	1992	1991
Cash	178,855	151,226	387,969	712,005
Marketable securities	0	0	25,212	113,442
Receivables	353,725	273,106	199,684	214,835
Inventories	351,730	307,073	350,578	311,984
Other current assets	33,932	39,054	107,280	156,318
Total current assets	918,242	770,459	1,070,723	1,508,584
Net PP&E	1,433,858	1,427,191	1,374,913	977,310
Investments and				
other assets	309,721	282,914	252,439	269,507
Other non-current	75,030	93,430	0	0
Intangibles	165,170	166,759	182,549	181,943
Total Assets	2,902,021	2,740,753	2,880,624	2,937,344
Notes payable	130,163	112,796	136,765	146,756
Accounts payable	270,033	202,923	226,860	256,125
Long term debt,				
current portion	91,032	79,411	92,521	41,065
Accrued expenses	162,589	108,536	132,239	104,545
Total current liabilities	653,817	503,666	588,385	548,491
Long term debt	1,364,877	1,438,378	1,411,319	1,202,839
Other long term				
liabilities	238,518	196,711	206,033	218,089
Total Liabilities	2,257,212	2,138,755	2,205,737	1,969,419
Preferred stock	190,639	52,270	52,270	NA
Common stock, net	16,434	16,170	16,055	16,642
Capital surplus	505,800	494,240	490,369	533,627
Retained earnings	(52,940)	39,318	116,193	417,656
Other equities	(15,124)	NA	NA	NA
Total shareholders'				
equity	644,809	601,998	674,887	967,925
Total liabilities and				
net worth	2,902,021	2,740,753	2,880,624	2,937,344

Source: Company annual reports.

[a]All statements are from December 31.

Exhibit 3   "United Fruit Co." by Pablo Neruda

La United Fruit Co.
Cuando sonó la trompeta, estuvo
todo preparado en la tierra
y Jehová repartió el mundo
a Coca-Cola Inc., Anaconda,
Ford Motors, y otras entidades:
la Compañía Frutera Inc.
se reservó lo más jugoso,
la costa central de mi tierra,
la dulce cintura de América.
Bautizó de nuevo sus tierras
como "Repúblicas Bananas",
y sobre los muertos dormidos,
sobre los héroes inquietos
que conquistaron la grandeza,
la libertad y las banderas,
estableció la ópera bufa:
enajenó los albedríos,
regaló coronas de César,
desenvainó la envidia, atrajo
la dictadura de las moscas,
moscas Trujillos, moscas Tachos,
moscas Carías, moscas Martínez,
moscas Ubico, moscas húmedas
de sangre humilde y mermelada,
moscas borrachas que zumban
sobre las tumbas populares,
moscas de circo, sabias moscas
entendidas en tiranía.

Entre las moscas sanguinarias
la Frutera desembarca,
arrasando el café y las frutas,
en sus barcos que deslizaron
como bandejas el tesoro
de nuestras tierras sumergidas.

Mientras tanto, por los abismos
azucarados de los puertos,
caían indios sepultados
en el vapor de la mañana:
un cuerpo rueda, una cosa
sin nombre, un número caído,
un racimo de fruta muerta
derramada en el pudridero.

United Fruit Co.
When the trumpet blared everything
on earth was prepared
and Jehovah distributed the world
to Coca-Cola Inc., Anaconda,
Ford Motors and other entities:
United Fruit Inc.
reserved for itself the juiciest,
the central seaboard of my land,
America's sweet waist.
It rebaptized its lands
the "Banana Republics,"
and upon the slumbering corpses,
upon the restless heroes
who conquered renown,
freedom and flags,
it established the comic opera:
it alienated self-destiny,
regaled Caesar's crowns,
unsheathed envy, drew
the dictatorship of flies:
Trujillo flies, Tacho flies,
Carías flies, Martínez flies,
Ubico flies*, flies soaked
in humble blood and jam,
drunk flies that drone
over the common graves,
circus flies, clever flies
versed in tyranny.

Among the bloodthirsty flies
the Fruit Co. disembarks,
ravaging coffee and fruits
for its ships that spirit away
our submerged lands' treasures
like serving trays.

Meanwhile, in the seaports'
sugary abysses,
Indians collapsed, buried
in the morning mist:
a body rolls down, a nameless
thing, a fallen number,
a bunch of lifeless fruit
dumped in the rubbish heap.

Source: Pablo Neruda, *Canto General*, ed. Fernando Alegria (Biblioteca Ayacucho, 1976), p. 67; English translation by Jack Schmitt, *Canto General* (Berkeley: University of California Press, 1990), p. 179.

*Note: Trujillo refers to Rafael L. Trujillo, a dictator in the Dominican Republic; Tacho to Anastasio Somoza in Nicaragua; Carías to Tiburcio Carías Andino in Honduras; Martínez to Maximiliano Hernández Martínez in El Salvador; and Ubico to Jorge Ubico Castañeda in Guatemala.

Exhibit 4   Global Banana Companies, 1994, ($000s)

	Total Sales	Sales of Bananas	Net Income
Chiquita	3,961,720	2,377,032	(71,540)
Dole	3,841,566	960,400	67,883
Fyffes	1,408,309	563,324	39,398
Geest	1,057,437	528,719	14,867
Noboa	700,000	280,000	21,000
Del Monte Produce	600,000	240,000	18,000

Source: Company financial reports and casewriter estimates.

Exhibit 5   World Trade in Bananas: Imports 1991-1992

Region	Volume (000s Metric Tons)				Value (Millions $)			
	1991	% Total	1992	% Total	1991	% Total	1992	% Total
World	10,095	100	10,443	100	5,229	100	5,132	100
United States	3,382	34	3,690	35	1,234	24	1,339	26
EU	3,798	38	3,976	38	2,571	49	2,487	48
Germany	1,355	13	1,378	13	853	16	784	15
UK	489	5	545	5	384	7	418	8
France	503	5	533	5	424	8	418	8
Italy	574	6	475	5	370	7	273	5
Belgium-Lux.	206	2	302	3	107	2	144	3
Netherlands	148	1	201	2	77	1	109	2
Other Europe	523	5	542	5	356	7	341	7
Japan	803	8	777	7	466	9	523	10
Other Asia	687	7	618	6	347	7	249	5
Latin America	317	3	377	4	63	1	83	2
All Other	1,108	11	1,005	10	548	10	451	9

Source: *UNCTAD Commodity Yearbook, 1994.*

Note: Percentage figures may not add to 100% due to rounding.

Exhibit 6   World Trade in Bananas: Exports 1991-1992

Region	Volume (000s Metric Tons)				Value (Millions $)			
	1991	% Total	1992	% Total	1991	% Total	1992	% Total
World	10,513	100	10,765	100	3,110	100	3,122	100
Latin America	8,036	76	8,188	76	2,132	69	2,089	67
Ecuador	2,714	26	2,557	24	716	23	655	21
Costa Rica	1,550	15	1,769	16	384	12	495	16
Colombia	1,473	14	1,500	14	405	13	400	13
Honduras	727	7	800	7	315	10	203	7
Panama	707	7	719	7	87	3	91	3
Guatemala	378	4	446	4	85	3	113	4
Mexico	238	2	180	2	81	3	84	3
Other Latin	249	2	217	2	59	2	48	2
ACP	612	6	715	7	291	9	312	10
EU	176	2	210	2	121	4	139	4
EU Territories	241	2	301	3	117	4	165	5
United States	356	3	378	4	198	6	190	6
Asia (non-ACP)	1,087	10	970	9	250	8	226	7
All Other	5	0	3	0	1	0	1	0

Source: *UNCTAD Commodity Yearbook, 1994.*

Note: Percentage figures may not add to 100% due to rounding.

Exhibit 7   World Banana Prices, 1985-1996

Year	Current $/Metric Ton	Constant (1990) $/Metric Ton
1985	378	551
1986	382	472
1987	393	442
1988	478	502
1989	547	578
1990	541	541
1991	560	548
1992	473	444
1993	443	418
1994	440	399
1995	445	387
1996	542[a]	377[b]

Source: World Bank, *Price Prospects for Major Primary Commodities, 1990-2005, including Quarterly Review of Commodity Markets,* Third Quarter 1992 and Fourth Quarter 1992; *Commodity Markets and the Developing Countries: A World Bank Quarterly,* May 1996; *Commodity Price Data,* July 1996 (see also http://www.worldbank.org/html/ieccp/pink.html); and U.S. Bureau of Labor Statistics.

[a] Second quarter, 1996.

[b] Projected.

Note: Data refers to Central and South American first-class quality tropical pack of bananas, importer's price to jobber or processor, f.o.b. U.S. ports.

Exhibit 8A   Unit Cost of Banana Production (ECU per kilogram)

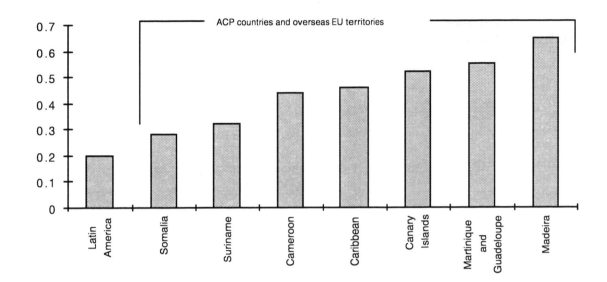

Note: Caribbean refers to Dominica, Grenada, Jamaica, St. Lucia, and St. Vincent.

Exhibit 8B   Average Retail Prices for Bananas, 1990 (US$ per metric ton)

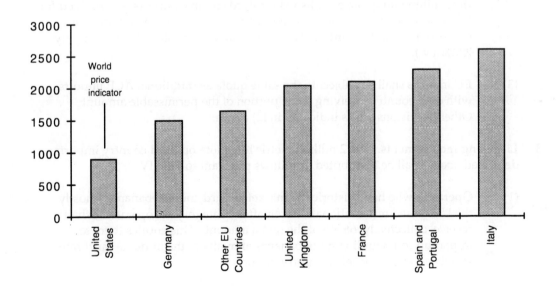

Note: The United States has no barriers to the entry of bananas, so world supply and demand determine U.S. retail prices.

Source: The World Bank, "Development Brief," No. 50, March 1995.

Exhibit 9   Key Provisions of the EU Banana Import Regime

1. **Classification of imports**. Title IV of Council Regulation 404/93 differentiates among four categories of imports:

(1)   "third country imports" are those from Latin America or any other non-ACP source;

(2)   "traditional" ACP imports are those ACP imports which fall under the limits fixed by the EU for each ACP country;

(3)   "non-traditional" ACP imports are ACP imports that exceed the "traditional" quota amounts provided for in (2) above;

(4)   EU imports are imports from EU territories overseas.

2. **Quotas and tariffs**. Title IV provides as follows:

(1)   Third country imports shall be restricted to 2 million metric tons, with in-quota volumes dutiable at 100 ECU/mt (roughly 30% on an *ad valorem* basis). Imports in excess of the quota amount shall be dutiable at 850 ECU/mt (roughly 250% a.v.).

(2)   Traditional ACP imports shall be restricted to a total of 857,700 metric tons, with each country receiving some portion of the permissible amount. In-quota volumes shall enter the EU duty free. Non traditional imports (imports in excess of the 857,700 quota) may enter the EU duty-free under the 2 million mt quota established for third country imports, as provided for in the licensing requirements section below. Non traditional imports in excess of the 2 million mt quota shall be dutiable at 750 ECU/mt (roughly 222% a.v.).

(3)   EU imports shall be subject to the same quota as traditional ACP imports, with each country receiving some portion of the permissable amount. Other provisions are as indicated in (2) above.

3. **Licensing requirements**. The 2 million metric ton quota on third country imports described above shall be distributed as follows pursuant to Title IV:

(1)   Operators who have historically marketed third country bananas (mostly the U.S.-based multinationals, hereinafter "Category A" operators) shall receive, collectively, 66.5% of the quota amount. This entitles them to import up to 1.3 million mt of bananas annually at the in-quota tariff rate stipulated above for third country imports.

Exhibit 9 (continued)

(2)   Operators who have historically marketed traditional ACP or EU territory bananas (mostly Geest and Fyffes, hereinafter "Category B" operators) shall receive, collectively, 30% of the quota amount. This entitles them to import up to 600,000 mt of bananas annually at the in-quota tariff rate stipulated above for third country imports.

(3)   Operators who began to market third country bananas as of 1992 (new entrants, hereinafter "Category C" operators), shall receive, collectively, 3.5% of the quota amount. This entitles them to import up to 70,000 mt of bananas annually at the in-quota tariff rate stipulated above for third country imports.

4. **The activity function rule.**   Commission Regulation 1442/93, which provides guidance for the implementation of the import licensing scheme in 3 above as it applies to Category A operators, establishes a series of activity weighting coefficients for subdividing the 66.5% Category A quota allocation among firms at different points in the value chain.

(1)   Operators that produce (or purchase from the producer), consign and sell bananas in the EU ("primary importers") shall receive a 57% coefficient.

(2)   Operators that own, supply and release bananas for free circulation in the EU (essentially, customs clearers or "secondary importers"), shall receive a 15% coefficient.

(3)   Operators that own and ripen bananas within the EU ("ripeners") shall receive a 28% coefficient.

(4)   The coefficients outlined in (1), (2), and (3) above shall be applied to shipment volumes to determine a "reference quantity" for the purposes of distributing import licenses to Category A operators. For example, an operator that conducted both the primary and secondary importer functions for 1,000 mt of bananas would be required to submit a license application that reflected a reference quantity of 720 mt [$(.57 + .15) \times 1,000 = 720$].

Source: Adapted from Chiquita 301 Petition and other public sources.

Toys "R" Us Japan

I do not believe the Japanese have chosen freely to have these limitations. All we would have to do is open a large retail store where prices were 40% less and choices were very broad. If the Japanese consumer didn't like products offered in that fashion, then the store would not be a success. . . .

—Carla Hills, United States Trade Representative, February 1990

In early 1991, Toys "R" Us seemed poised on the brink of a high profile entry into the world's second largest toy market. A "category killer" that enjoyed phenomenal success in the United States and Europe, Toys "R" Us had tried for several years to crack the lucrative but forbidding Japanese market. At every step, the U.S. company had faced difficulty and opposition. Japanese retailers had tried repeatedly to block the chain's entrance, as had small shopkeepers from the area around Niigata, site of the first Toys "R" Us store. The Japanese media had loudly denounced Toys "R" Us as the "black ship of Kawasaki," and a host of Japanese toy manufacturers, including Nintendo, had refused to deal directly with the U.S. retailer.[1] The very structure of Japan's multilayered distribution system also seemed to conspire against Toys "R" Us, thwarting the company's attempts and perpetuating Japan's infamously high consumer prices.

Despite this litany of problems, though, success seemed finally within reach. Toys "R" Us had found an influential local partner, Den Fujita, and won approval from Japan's powerful Ministry of International Trade and Industry (MITI). Management also felt confident that some of the more restrictive aspects of Japanese retail regulation were about to change. But still some basic questions remained: Would Japanese customers, accustomed to small shops and personal service, ever accept a self-service discount warehouse? Would Japanese manufacturers risk damaging long-standing relationships with wholesalers and retailers by dealing directly with Toys "R" Us? And how quickly and efficiently could the chain hope to expand in the face of protracted local opposition?

---

[1]The epithet referred to Commodore Matthew C. Perry's four black warships that sailed into the harbor at Edo (now Tokyo) in 1854, forcing the Shogun's government to end three centuries of self-imposed Japanese isolation. "Black ships" thus became symbolic of the opening of Japanese culture to Western influence. *Reuters,* December 19, 1991, and *The Toronto Star,* December 23, 1991.

Professor Debora Spar prepared this case with the assistance of Jacqueline MacKenzie, MBA '95, and Research Associate Laura Bures as the basis for class discussion rather than to illustrate either effective or ineffective handling of an administrative situation.

The Toys "R" Us Company

Toys "R" Us was the brainchild of Charles Lazarus, a shop owner who founded the chain in 1957. Born in Washington, D.C., in 1923, Lazarus had learned about the retail business from his father, who rebuilt bicycles and sold them at the family store. When Lazarus asked why the store did not sell new bicycles, his father explained that the big chain stores could sell them much cheaper—a comment Lazarus would clearly recall later in his career.[2]

After a wartime career as a cryptographer, Lazarus inherited the family shop and turned to selling children's furniture in a market boosted by the post-war baby boom. Over time, he began to realize that because baby furniture did not wear out, repeat purchases of items such as cribs were rare.[3] Toys, by contrast, were frequently requested. Toys, he therefore decided, created a far superior business opportunity. After studying the U.S. discounter Korvettes, Lazarus decided to experiment with a self-service, supermarket-style format. In his new Children's Supermarket, he vowed to undercut competition and have a bigger, better selection than any single toy store. Discounting had arrived in the toy business.

Children's Supermarket quickly grew into a thriving chain of four stores, renamed Toys "R" Us after Lazarus decided he needed better signs with "shorter words, bigger letters."[4] He sold the chain to Interstate Stores in 1966 for $7.5 million, retaining a seat on the company's Board. When Interstate folded in 1978, Lazarus rescued his company, determined to build it into a nationwide chain. Over the next decade, Toys "R" Us sales compounded by 26% per year, with sales productivity per square foot double that of the retailer's nearest competitor.[5] By 1988, Toys "R" Us had captured 20% of the U.S. toy market, with sales surpassing the $4 billion mark.[6] Sourcing directly from manufacturers, the chain used its huge buying clout to offer goods at 10-20% discounts compared to smaller toy retailers. Year-round advertising campaigns encouraged consumers to buy toys at any time, instead of just at Christmas.

A typical Toys "R" Us store brought together 8-15,000 SKUs (stockkeeping units) of toys and children's products in a warehouse-sized (54,000 sq. ft.) self-service outlet. The presentation was simple and colorful, based on a "cookie cutter conformity" where stores resembled each other down to the layout of each aisle. Central control was a key feature of the organization, and extensive computer networks ensured almost automatic replacement of every toy sold once inventories dropped below pre-determined levels. The key to the sales and inventory formula, according to Lazarus, was that "No decisions are made in the field."[7]

In 1984, the company took its retailing concept global, opening its first international outlet in Canada and then moving quickly into Europe, Hong Kong, and Singapore. As it had in the United States, the discount formula quickly proved popular with customers who flocked to the new Toys "R" Us outlets. Whenever the chain expanded abroad, however, it drew the ire of local retailers, who feared (correctly in many cases) that the giant discount stores would drive them out of business. German manufacturers, for example, refused to sell to Toys "R" Us in 1987 for fear of damaging their relationships with the thousands of small retailers and wholesalers who dominated toy distribution.

---

[2] David Owen, *The Man Who Invented Saturday Morning*, Villard, 1988.

[3] Ibid.

[4] *Newsmakers*, October 1992.

[5] *Business Quarterly*, June 22, 1989, and *Newsmakers*, October 1992.

[6] *Tokyo Business Today*, February 1990.

[7] *Newsweek*, November 11, 1991.

And in the United Kingdom, retailers also protested, noting that the number of British toy stores had declined from 3,500 to 2,000 in the five years after Toys "R" Us first arrived.[8]

But Toys "R" Us regularly overcame the protests and its foreign outlets flourished. By 1991, the chain operated 97 stores abroad, with international operations accounting for 14% of the chain's total sales. Commenting on this spectacular growth, Larry Bouts, president of the chain's international division since 1991, suggested that the expansion of Toys "R" Us actually benefited foreign retailers as well as consumers. "Initially I think there was a fair amount of consternation from competitors," he acknowledged, "but now the industry has grown so much, there's really a lot warmer feeling. From the consumer's point of view, they're very happy . . . coming to us in droves.... People said it wouldn't work, but consumers want value today."[9] Confident that this formula applied broadly, Toys "R" Us management began to contemplate an entry into one of the world's toughest retail markets: Japan.

The Japanese Market for Toys

By any measure, Japan was an extremely attractive market for toys. Throughout the 1980s, the entire retail market in Japan had expanded dramatically, propelled by the economy's continued strength and a long-awaited increase in consumer spending. According to the Bank of Japan, annual retail sales grew 94% during the 1980s, while Japan's GDP grew at an average annual rate of 7%.[10] Japan's children were particularly strong beneficiaries of this boom. Despite a rigorous education system that left children with little time for play, children's products accounted for a significant proportion of consumer spending in Japan. Perhaps to compensate for the constant pressure to excel in school, parents lavished expensive toys and clothes on their offspring.[11] Japan's falling birthrate also allowed parents and grandparents to focus their spending on fewer children; and fewer mouths to feed enabled families to spend less money on food and more on toys.[12]

Thus Japan's toy market had become the second largest in the world, lagging only behind the United States'. In 1991, the Japanese toy market was worth Y932 billion ($7.1 billion), up Y26 billion from the previous year. Responding to this boom, large retailers designed special formats to appeal to children. In October of 1990, Isetan opened a special section called "Dr. Kids Town" within one of its Tokyo department stores, while Seibu's flagship store opened a "Kids Farm," complete with a hollow miniature mountain amidst clothing racks and toy shelves.[13] A Sesame Street theme park was opened outside of Tokyo in 1990.

On the surface, these developments suggested that the Japanese toy market was ripe for Toys "R" Us. But as the chain's management quickly discovered, the structure of Japan's retail industry made it very difficult for new retailers—particularly foreign discount retailers—to establish a market position. Despite the rapid growth it had experienced, Japan's toy industry remained highly fragmented and locally-focused. Though some estimates claimed that the number of toy stores had fallen from 8,000 in 1980, at least 6,000 remained in 1990.[14] A typical toy store was less than 3,200

---

[8]*Wall Street Journal*, September 10, 1990.

[9]*Europe*, September 1992.

[10]*Business Tokyo*, May 1992, and *International Marketing Data and Statistics 1995*, p. 183.

[11]*The Washington Post*, February 11, 1991.

[12]The average number of children per family had fallen from four in the early post-war years to just two by the early 1990s. *Washington Post*, February 11, 1991.

[13]Ibid.

[14]*Nihon Keizai Shimbun*, February 10, 1990.

square feet in area and sold 1-2,000 SKUs. Display areas were customarily cramped, inventories turned slowly, and most stores stocked very similar merchandise. Nearly all retail shops were domestically owned and bought their toys from local wholesalers, usually for 75-80% of the manufacturer's "suggested price."[15] Retailers then sold the toys for the "suggested price," deviating from it only rarely.[16] In exchange for maintaining prices, retailers were able to return their unsold goods to the wholesaler or manufacturer for full credit. In this tightly-knit system, only two national players existed: Chiyoda, which sold through the Hello Mac and Ace formats; and Marutomi, which operated a traditional toy chain, Banban, as well as a discount format, Toy Ryutsu Center. With a combined 700-800 stores, the two chains accounted for over Y100 billion in annual sales.[17]

At the wholesale level, the Japanese toy industry was again marked by its characteristic pattern of fragmentation and long-standing relationships. Even such giants as Nintendo, the Kyoto-based maker of Gameboy and other popular electronic games, distributed its products through a sprawling network of 70 affiliated distributors.[18] These distributors served as the key link between manufacturers and retailers, cementing long-term relationships based on personal commitments rather than competitive terms. They also served as a barrier to foreign firms, making it difficult for foreigners to achieve sufficient scale in either manufacturing or retailing to cover the costs of their investment. As a result, foreign firms were almost entirely absent from the Japanese domestic toy industry, and even imports accounted for only 9.2% of sales.[19]

Potentially, Toys "R" Us had the ability to change the Japanese toy industry and profit handsomely in the process. Merely by undercutting the "suggested price" it could capture the entire discount market. All it needed to do was to mimic precisely what it had done elsewhere: establish large-scale stores and use the buying power created by these stores to negotiate lower prices from toy manufacturers. Since 1987, the chain's management had been trying to implement this strategy. But in Japan, they came to realize, the very structure of the retail sector made their customary strategy almost inconceivable.

The Structure of Japanese Retail

A "Nation of Shops"

For years, Japan had been aptly described as a nation of small shopkeepers. Though the population of the four islands was approximately half that of the United States, the number of retail outlets in Japan was almost the same, resulting in twice as many outlets per capita.[20] Many of these outlets were the country's famous "mom and pop" stores. In 1988, over half of all retail outlets in Japan employed just one or two people; less than 15% of outlets employed more than five people.[21]

---

[15]*Nikkei Weekly*, February 22, 1993.

[16]In 1989, 70% of toy retailers priced at the manufacturer's "suggested price," according to figures from Japan's Fair Trade Commission.

[17]*Nikkei Weekly*, February 22, 1993.

[18]*Nikkei Weekly*, June 29, 1991.

[19]*Nikkei Weekly*, June 20, 1992.

[20]Jack G. Kaikati, "Don't crack the Japanese distribution system - just circumvent it," *Columbia Journal of Business*, Summer 1993.

[21] MITI survey.

In the early 1980s, such small stores accounted for a full 75% of retail spending. Nearly half of these outlets sold food, compared with 20% in the United States.[22]

The fragmentation of the retailers was matched by the fragmentation of the wholesalers who served them. Of the 436,421 wholesalers operating in 1988, less than half employed more than five people, and nearly all sold their products through a complex distribution system that typically involved between three and five layers of intermediaries. The primary wholesaler was often a subsidiary, or close affiliate, of the manufacturer. The secondary wholesaler was a regional distributor, while the tertiary wholesaler operated on the local level. As in the toy industry, prices of goods were effectively controlled by the manufacturers, who sold to wholesalers at a pre-arranged discount of the "manufacturers' suggested price." With the added inducements of credit and generous payment terms, manufacturers throughout the Japanese system gained guaranteed distribution of their products, while wholesalers and retailers gained some measure of protection against economic swings and fluctuations in demand.

While Western observers tended to mock the Japanese retail system as cumbersome and archaic, most Japanese consumers genuinely seemed to enjoy and appreciate its benefits. As an article in *The Economist* explained, "The Japanese are as sentimental about their tiny shops as the French are about their peasants and the British about their old industries. Small Japanese shops are the centers of village neighborhoods in big cities. Small stores flourished before the rest of Japan modernized because merchants were restricted by law to their local patch, and retailers were encouraged to mop up labor from the land."[23]

In addition to its commercial function, small store retailing thus served a valuable social purpose. Described directly by some as a "social service," the retail sector was "filled with under-employed workers who in other societies might well be unemployed."[24] All together, the Japanese distribution system accounted for 18% of the nation's employees and 13% of its GNP.[25] In a 1980s survey, 26% of shopkeepers reported "security in old age" as a reason for opening a shop, and 10% said they opened a shop because their husbands would soon retire.[26] One quarter of owner-operators of stores were over 60. In a country with few pension provisions, small scale retailing offered a safety net for retirement.

Supporters of the Japanese system further argued that small stores were a natural reflection of the Japanese way of life, that Japanese consumers preferred to shop every day for small quantities of fresh goods.[27] Small homes and kitchens allowed no space for storing large amounts of goods, and use of automobiles was impractical in Japan's congested streets.[28] High quality and personalized service, many claimed, were expected by Japanese consumers, who were willing to pay for the privilege.

Detractors, though, argued that small stores continued to exist simply because they were protected from more efficient competitors by laws restricting the construction of large stores and by

---

[22]*The Economist*, September 19, 1981.

[23]Ibid.

[24]Ibid, and Hugh T. Patrick and Thomas P. Rohlen, "Small-Scale Family Enterprises," *The Political Economy of Japan: The Domestic Transformation*, Vol. 1, Stanford University Press, 1987, p. 350.

[25]*Business Asia*, January 4, 1993.

[26]Patrick and Rohlen, "Small-Scale Family Enterprises," p. 350.

[27]Takatoshi Ito, *The Japanese Economy*, MIT Press, 1992, p. 392.

[28]Japanese typically had 60% of the living space enjoyed by their U.S. counterparts. *Business Review Weekly* January 12, 1990.

tacit non-competition arrangements. Japanese consumers *would* accept less service in exchange for lower prices, they asserted, but by 1991, they had rarely been offered the choice.

Keiretsu Stores

In fact, choice of retail goods in some sectors was actively restricted by the activities of diversified conglomerates such as Matsushita and Toshiba. Working through their own distribution keiretsu (related groups of companies), these giant firms supported tens of thousands of small affiliate stores that stocked only "their" manufacturer's brand at manufacturer-specified prices. Where these stores prevailed, customers found no benefit in comparison-shopping, since price uniformity was nearly absolute. What they did get however, and what many Japanese reportedly preferred over low prices, was personal attention from the shop-owner and guaranteed repair or replacement service for the life of their purchase.

The operators of the small keiretsu stores also effectively made a trade-off between prices and personal loyalty. Simply by becoming a store owner, one gained a position of some visibility in the community, a position symbolized by the store-front pairing of the proprietor's name with that of a well-known manufacturer. Through the manufacturers' many affiliates, store operators also received financial and marketing advice and even information about their competitors' activities. In exchange for this assistance, they implicitly agreed to tie themselves closely to the keiretsu's lead manufacturer. Storekeepers who dared to meddle with the manufacturer's "suggested price" faced expulsion from the network and blacklisting by other manufacturers. In 1979, Yoshio Terada, a National (Matsushita) retailer in Tokyo, incurred the wrath of his supplier by discounting batteries by 20%. When he refused to remove the discount, a truck arrived instead to remove the National sign from his store and with it, his entire business.[29] Terada subsequently set up a no-service discount electrical appliance business called STEP and, despite Japanese consumers' alleged preferences for full-service stores, built a $100 million business in ten years. Yet, few keiretsu retailers at the time would have dared to defy the might of Matsushita. In 1991, over 20,000 keiretsu stores still existed, and the principle of loyalty to manufacturers remained strong in both retailing and wholesaling.

The Role of Regulation

In addition to customers' habits and personal loyalties, Japan's retail structure was also bolstered by a series of laws restricting the spread of larger retail stores. By sheer force of numbers, the country's 1.4 million store owners wielded considerable voting power. For decades, they had used this power to extract concessions and explicit protection from Japan's reigning political party, the Liberal Democratic Party (LDP). In 1990, the Chairman of the National Shopkeepers Promotion Association described the political situation succinctly: "The big stores stuff the politicians with money, but we have the power of 20 million votes."[30]

The small store owners won their first victory in 1956, just after the LDP came to power. The 1956 Department Store Law required that a permit be obtained for each new department store, effectively allowing department store construction to be blocked by smaller retailers. By 1990, there were still only about 1,600 department stores in Japan—one for every 75,000 people. With the growth of department stores so severely limited, most innovation in Japanese retailing came through the emerging supermarkets—large, non-specialized, low-price stores with large grocery sections. But just as the supermarkets were starting to gain ground, they, too, encountered the shopkeepers' force.

---

[29]Kenichi Miyashita and David W. Russell, *Keiretsu*, McGraw-Hill, 1994, pp. 203-4.

[30]*East Asian Executive Reports*, May 15, 1990.

In 1973, Japan's Ministry of International Trade and Industry (MITI) responded to the small retailers' demands by introducing the Large Scale Retail Law, legislation that subjected all would-be large retailers to a rigorous screening process. Before building any stores over 1,500 sq. m. (16,000 sq. ft.), retailers had to submit detailed plans to MITI and then allow these plans to be passed on to a local review board composed of consumers and retailers. In 1982, the law was made even more stringent, requiring large store operators to "explain" their plans to local retailers directly, even before notifying MITI. With this provision in place, small store owners could effectively delay the construction of large stores for years, simply by boycotting "explanation meetings" or raising objections to a myriad of small details. As a result, even powerful supermarket chains such as Daiei found themselves entangled for years in local negotiations.[31]

Innovations

If Japan's fragmented and hierarchical retail sector had remained unchanged in the 1980s, it is unlikely that even so powerful a force as Toys "R" Us would have dared enter the market. But as the Japanese economy expanded and developed in the late 1980s, several cracks in the retail structure began to appear.

The Rise of Convenience Stores

The first major change in Japan's retail structure came from a quiet and unlikely source: convenience stores. Usually occupying no more than 1100 sq. ft., convenience stores were small enough to slip past restrictive laws and establish themselves in the very heart of Japan's towns and villages. By 1982, Japan had 23,235 convenience stores, accounting for 2.3% of total retail sales.[32] Between 1982 and 1985, convenience store sales rose faster than any other form of retailing sales;[33] and by 1992, they accounted for nearly 8% of Japan's total retail sales.[34]

The most successful convenience store was the 7-Eleven chain, licensed from its U.S. parent Southland in 1974 by Ito-Yokado. At first glance a 7-Eleven Japan store fit the profile of many Japanese stores: small, locally-focused, and "open all hours." At the core of this business, however, was an information-oriented strategy unlike anything dreamed of by its "mom and pop" competitors. The key to 7-Eleven's strategy was close inventory control facilitated by early and comprehensive adoption of information technology. In the late 1970s, 7-Eleven cut its wholesale suppliers from 80 to 40 by closely supervising their inventory and eliminating goods which did not generate adequate sales. From 1985 onwards, the chain used point of sales equipment to track sales of each item and ensure timely replenishment. Employees also entered specific information about shoppers with each sale to predict product-specific shopping habits. Ito-Yokado used this information to refine product offerings and inventory replacement schedules to the point of providing fresh *o nigiri* (rice balls popular as lunch snacks) at lunch time in every store as well as adequate supplies of soft drinks for children on their way home from school in the afternoon. The information was also used as a

---

[31]*Business Week*, December 9, 1991.

[32]*The Economist*, January 31, 1987.

[33]Frank Upsham, "Privatizing Regulation: The Implementation of the Large-Scale Retail Stores Law," in Gary D. Allison and Yasunori Sone, eds., *Political Dynamics in Contemporary Japan*, Ithaca, 1993, p. 265. Cited in Jeff Bernstein and Thomas K. McCraw, "Convenience-Store Retailing in Two Countries: Southland and Seven-Eleven Japan," HBS Case Number N9-395-092.

[34]Cited in Jeffrey Rayport, "Japanese Retailing System: Tokugawa Period to the Present," HBS Industry Note prepared for Professor Thomas K. McCraw, April 1991.

bargaining chip with manufacturers, who could be persuaded to deliver according to 7-Eleven's precise requirements.

By 1990, almost 85% of goods in the chain's 94 wholly owned and 4,140 franchised stores throughout Japan were distributed through the chain's own elaborate regional distribution system, and 7-Eleven Japan had been described as one of the most efficient retailers in the world. As 7-Eleven grew, it also spawned a series of imitators, stores hoping to make similar use of information technologies and catering to the demands of Japan's aging population and increasing numbers of women in the workforce.

MITI's "Vision for the 1990s"

Just as the convenience stores were demonstrating the commercial potential of new retailing formats, the established format was also coming under pressure from Japan's changing demographics. Increasingly, young Japanese balked at the idea of taking over their parents' small shops and wanted instead to experiment with bolder ventures. With significantly greater international exposure than their parents, the younger generation also realized that they were paying highly inflated prices for many consumer goods. Slowly, their demands for fewer commercial restrictions and lower prices began to influence the political process.

In 1989, MITI quietly advocated reform of Japan's retailing sector. In a public document on Japan's distribution system, it first defended the existing retail structure, arguing that:

1. It cannot necessarily be said that our distribution system is inefficient; however, there is room for further rationalization as respects costs.

2. Though our country's distribution system is as a whole highly competitive, there are some factors which mitigate competition.

3. Due to unfamiliarity with commercial customs in Japan, foreign firms may feel difficulty attempting to gain access to the Japanese distribution sector; however, this system does not fundamentally discriminate against either domestic or foreign firms, and there are a large variety of distribution channels available to importing firms.

4. There are a variety of reasons for the gap in domestic and foreign prices, and some of them lie in the nature of the distribution system.[35]

MITI's document proceeded, though, to propose significant changes to the Large Scale Retail Stores Law, including limits on the amount of time each stage in the notification process could take. The law would remain in force, MITI explained, "since Japan still has a large number of retail stores and a limited amount of land, [and] giving large stores free rein to set up business would cause serious problems for regional communities."[36] Yet MITI did commit to "amending the system … to reflect recent changes in socio-economic circumstances" and to removing "all practices which deviate from the original intent of the system," noting in particular that "the purpose of [the "explanation" of store plans to relevant constituencies] is not to obtain the approval of local retailers."[37]

---

[35]*News from MITI*, September 1989.
[36]Ibid.
[37]Ibid.

Accordingly, MITI proposed reducing the permissible time between pre-notification and approval to as little as 18 months. It even promised to re-examine restrictions on opening hours, which required large stores to close at 6pm and for at least one full day per month. If MITI succeeded in implementing these proposed changes, small store owners would at last lose their power to hold back a tidal wave of space-hungry domestic retailers.

The Structural Impediments Initiative[38]

At the same time that MITI launched its re-evaluation of the retail system, it also began to respond to demands that Japan open its market to foreign investors. Even after half a decade of dramatically increased global investment flows, Japan's stock of foreign direct investment remained low. In manufacturing, for example, which attracted 65% of total foreign investment flows, foreign affiliated companies accounted for 2.1% of total capitalization and 2.3% of sales in 1988. By comparison, FDI in the United States at the same time accounted for 14.7% of capitalization and 12.2% of sales.[39] In 1990, Japan was host to less accumulated U.S. direct investment than Canada, the United Kingdom, Germany, Switzerland, or the Netherlands.[40]

For many in the United States, the imbalance in investment levels was evidence that the Japanese market remained unfairly closed to U.S. investors. Consequently, in the fall of 1989, U.S. negotiators launched a series of discussions with their Japanese counterparts "to identify and solve structural problems in both countries that stand as impediments to trade and to balance of payments adjustment with the goal of contributing to the reduction of payments imbalances."[41] Dubbed the Structural Impediments Initiative, the talks theoretically covered "structural impediments" in both countries. The bulk of the negotiation, however, was devoted to the perennial problem of perceived trade barriers to U.S. imports and investment in Japan. In particular, U.S. negotiators pushed their Japanese counterparts to address the prevalence of keiretsu structures and other interlocked relationships which, they argued, prevented foreign firms from competing on equal terms. The U.S. team also suggested that consumer prices in Japan were higher than they should be, compared with prices in other markets, and that Japan's distribution system remained a major impediment to U.S. export sales.[42]

Toys "R" Us: The Move into Japan

For Toys "R" Us, both the Structural Impediments Initiative and MITI's changes to the Large Scale Retail Store Law came at a propitious time. Together with domestic developments in the retail sector, they seemed to indicate that the largest barriers to the chain's entry—the distribution sector and the legal restrictions on establishment—were at last about to change. And so long as they changed, Toys "R" Us felt confident that the chain could succeed in the Japanese market.

Because the Japanese market retained so many idiosyncracies, however, Toys "R" Us management decided to seek an alliance with a strong local partner. Initially, the chain followed the

---

[38]This section draws heavily on Ito, *The Japanese Economy*, Chapter 12.

[39]The retail sector was host to a tiny but growing fraction of foreign direct investment in Japan. Between 1985 and 1990 U.S. investment in Japanese retailing quadrupled to reach $340m. *Business Tokyo*, May, 1992.

[40]Mark Mason, "United States Direct Investment in Japan: Trends and Prospects," *California Management Review*, Fall 1992.

[41]*Final Report of Structural Impediments Initiative*.

[42]The Large Scale Retail Law, for example, impeded the distribution of foreign goods by supporting the 1.6 million small family-run stores which were less likely to carry imported goods than were large stores.

same strategy that most foreign retailers had adopted and launched negotiations with a major Japanese retailer. But once the negotiations were underway, the Toys "R" Us representatives realized that the two sides had fundamentally different assumptions of how to run a business. According to one Toys "R" Us executive, "they pushed traditional business practices on us, like using wholesalers. That would distort the basic principle of our business."[43] And so Toys "R" Us broke off the first round of talks and began to search for someone in Japan with a better grasp of U.S. retailing practices.

Den Fujita

In 1989, Joseph Baczko, then head of Toys "R" Us International, met Den Fujita, president of McDonalds Japan. Fujita, the son of an engineer, had grown up in Osaka, a city famous for its merchant tradition. He graduated from the Law Department of Tokyo University, the most prestigious university in Japan and traditional training ground for the country's political elite.[44] During the U.S. occupation of Japan, he had worked as a translator at McArthur's Headquarters in Tokyo, despite having lost his father and two sisters in U.S. bombing raids.

In 1950, he took the unusual step (for a Tokyo Law graduate) of starting his own trading venture, Fujita & Company, to import a range of items, such as Dior handbags, to a luxury-starved Japan.[45] Since post-war rationing and restrictions on imports had eliminated most other luxury goods, Fujita prospered, building one of Japan's strongest import businesses over the next two decades.

In 1971, McDonalds approached Fujita and asked him to join them in introducing U.S.-style fast food to Japan. Fujita agreed, arguing in public that McDonalds-style food would be good for Japan. As he later explained, "the Japanese are very hardworking, but very weak, very small . . . we had to strengthen ourselves."[46] Fellow retailers, though, were not amused—the Ginza Street Association was still attempting to evict the first McDonalds from its prestigious location more than 10 years after its establishment.[47] Fujita, undaunted, told Japanese teenagers that eating beef might give them the blond hair of their American counterparts.[48] Whatever the rationale, McDonalds' sales in Japan had topped Y50 billion by 1980 and reached Y208 billion ($1.6 billion) by 1991.

What Fujita had brought to McDonalds—retail experience, political influence, vision, and a unique understanding of both Japanese and American cultures—was equally attractive to Toys "R" Us. With strong links to influential government figures, Fujita also had unrivaled knowledge of real estate in Japan, boasting that "If you name a city, I can see the post office, the train station, everything."[49] Fujita's flamboyant style and frequent new ventures guaranteed publicity for each business. Often described as a heretic, he was quoted as wishing to "blow a hole in the under-developed structure of the Japanese retail industry."[50]

So impressed was Toys "R" Us with Fujita that Robert Nakasone, the American-born Vice Chairman of Toys "R" Us, described him as not only the first choice as a partner, but "our second, third, fourth, fifth, and so on. . . . We could see he was a bit of a maverick. He was not only bilingual,

---

[43]*Nikkei Weekly*, May 16, 1992.

[44]*New York Times*, March 22, 1992.

[45]Ibid.

[46]Ibid.

[47] *Nihon Keizai Shimbun*, October 11, 1983.

[48]*Reuters*, February 1, 1986.

[49]*Business Week*, December 9, 1991.

[50]*Nikkei Weekly*, May 16, 1992.

but bicultural."[51] Likewise Fujita regarded Toys "R" Us as a natural partner due to the similarities in the two companies' target markets. Soon after hearing of Toys "R" Us' plans, in fact, he began to think of ways to combine Toys "R" Us, McDonalds, and Blockbuster Entertainment, another foreign business seeking his help, in specially-developed family shopping malls. In the spring of 1989, Toys "R" Us formally asked Fujita to cooperate with the company in a Japanese joint venture. McDonalds Japan took a 20% stake in the new subsidiary: Toys "R" Us Japan.

Criticism and Opposition

Almost as soon as plans for the new venture were announced, other retailers and manufacturers claimed that Toys "R" Us Japan was doomed to failure. Consumers would check out the stores initially, they elaborated, but Japanese consumers would not like warehouse stores, and it was "unrealistic" to consider bypassing wholesalers.[52]

Explicit opposition to Toys "R" Us emerged rapidly from those most threatened by the chain's expansion. In January 1990, Toys "R" Us applied to the municipal government of Niigata, a city of 500,000 on the Japan Sea coast, for permission to open the first of its Japanese superstores. Local toy sellers were horrified. At 5,000 sq. m. (54,000 sq. ft), the proposed store would be over 50 times larger than the average Niigata toy shop; projected first year revenues of Y2 billion represented half the combined sales of the city's existing toy merchants.[53] Mobilizing quickly, the Niigata toy sellers warned publicly that, "If Toys "R" Us comes in, Japanese toy shops will be wiped out."[54] The group's spokesman, owner of eight Niigata toy shops further argued that, "Toys "R" Us is making this a political problem. But toys are more than that. Toys are culture."[55]

The Niigata application was just one of ten applications that Toys "R" Us filed across Japan, many of which sparked opposition of some kind. Toy retailers and wholesalers in Fukuoka submitted a petition to their local government demanding a one-year delay to the opening of a proposed Toys "R" Us. The toy industry in Sagamihara (near Tokyo) reacted with similar defensiveness. After Toys "R" Us announced its intentions to open seven stores by 1993, with an eventual target as high as 100, a group of 520 small toy retailers formed the Japan Association of Specialty Toy Shops to help small retailers develop ways to compete with Toys "R" Us and other foreign retailers.

Central to this concern was the effect Toys "R" Us would have on the long-standing ties between Japan's toy manufacturers and toy wholesalers. To leverage the economies of scale inherent in their large stores, Toys "R" Us would have to replicate in Japan the same buying structure that had worked so effectively elsewhere. That is, the chain would have to buy directly from the manufacturers, using the sheer size of its outlets to circumvent the wholesalers and win price concessions from the toy makers. If Toys "R" Us had to rely on Japan's cumbersome system of wholesale distribution, it would inevitably have to charge much higher retail prices, undermining its whole competitive strategy. If the chain did not use the wholesalers, though, it risked raising the ire of the manufacturers, who were tied so tightly to both the wholesalers and the small retail outlets. As one newspaper explained, "Japanese toy makers drool at the prospect of supplying Toys "R" Us, but worry they'll be locked out of their current distribution channels if they play ball with the U.S. company."[56] Accordingly, there were indications that toy manufacturers would resist, if not actually

---

[51]*New York Times*, March 22, 1992.

[52]Ibid.

[53]*The Economist*, June 16, 1990.

[54]*Wall Street Journal*, February 7, 1990.

[55]Ibid.

[56]*Japan Economic Journal*, February 16, 1991.

oppose, the U.S. discounter. Top toy manufacturers such as Bandai Co. refused to comment on whether they would deal directly with Toys "R" Us, insisting that anything they (Bandai) said could "have a great influence on toy wholesalers. . . . [E]ven the smallest comments cause concern."[57]

Meanwhile, like all foreign retailers hoping to invest in Japan, Toys "R" Us still faced major problems in obtaining suitable real estate. With a population density of 322 people per square kilometer and a land-mass filled 80% with mountains, Japan had very limited amounts of land suitable or desirable for retailing.[58] In the late 1980s, land prices around Tokyo were at an all time high, with a 540 sq. ft. shop in the exclusive Ginza area renting for about $11,500 per month.[59] Finding local workers also presented a serious and potentially expensive challenge. With the Japanese economy in a state of virtual full employment, competition for top male graduates was intense, particularly for foreign firms, which remained less prestigious employers than their Japanese counterparts.[60] Searching for something positive to say on the labor front, one report could only comment that "for flexible firms willing to hunt around, there is a strong supply of bright, well educated women."[61]

A final set of concerns centered on the company's choice of partner: the maverick Fujita had his detractors. In a letter to *The New York Times*, he was accused of anti-Semitism and of supporting Communism to provoke the Americans.[62] These criticisms stemmed from Fujita's well-known claim that Osaka-born Japanese (like himself) were more business-oriented than their Tokyo cousins because Jews had settled in Osaka hundreds of years ago. He had also written several books on "the Jewish way of doing business" and described himself as "the Ginza Jew."

As a result of all the resistance that Toys "R" Us Japan faced, the schedule of store openings began to slip steadily. Though initial publicity had suggested six stores by the end of 1991, subsequent plans slated only the first store to open in December 1991.[63] Without direct distribution deals, the high land prices and labor costs would render the cost structure of the superstores almost insurmountable.

---

[57]*Wall Street Journal*, September 10, 1990.

[58]The U.S. population density was only 26 people per square kilometer.

[59]*Business Tokyo*, May 1992.

[60]*Business Asia*, April 16, 1990.

[61]Ibid.

[62]Harold Solomon, "To the Editor: Beware the Agenda of Den Fujita," *New York Times*, April 12, 1992.

[63]*The Daily Yomiuri*, November 12, 1991.

Exhibit 1   Toys "R" Us Inc. Balance Sheet (millions of US$)

	January 1990	January 1991
Assets		
Cash and cash equivalents	40.9	35.0
Net receivables	53.1	73.2
Inventories	1,230.4	1,275.2
Prepaid expenses	14.0	21.0
Current assets – total	1,338.4	1,404.3
Net property, plant, and equipment	1,703.0	2,141.3
Other assets	33.4	36.8
Total assets	3,074.7	3,582.4
Liabilities		
Long term debt due within year	1.4	1.6
Notes payable	205.5	386.5
Accounts payable	517.9	483.9
Taxes payable	96.0	81.6
Other current liabilities	279.1	274.0
Total current liabilities	1,100.0	1,227.6
Long term debt	173.0	195.2
Deferred taxes	96.4	113.4
Equity		
Common stock	19.8	29.8
Capital surplus	322.7	352.6
Retained earnings	1,459.9	1,793.2
Less: treasury stock	97.0	129.3
Total equity	1,705.3	2,046.3
Total liabilities and equity	3,074.7	3,582.4

Source: *Standard & Poor's Compustat, Compustat PC Plus*

Note: Numbers may not add due to rounding.

Exhibit 2 Toys "R" Us Inc. Income Statement (millions of US$)

	January 1990	January 1991
Sales	4,787.8	5,510.0
Cost of goods sold	3,309.7	3,820.8
Gross profit	1,478.2	1,689.2
Selling, general, and administrative expense	866.4	1,024.8
Operating income before depreciation	611.8	664.4
Depreciation, depletion, and amortization	65.8	79.1
Operating profit	545.9	585.3
Interest expense	52.8	82.7
Non-operating income/expense	20.5	19.7
Special items	0.0	1.0
Pretax income	513.7	523.2
Total income taxes	192.6	197.2
Net income	321.1	326.0

Source: *Standard & Poor's Compustat, Compustat PC Plus*

Note: Numbers may not add due to rounding.

Exhibit 3 Toys "R" Stock Price (US$), 1979-1992

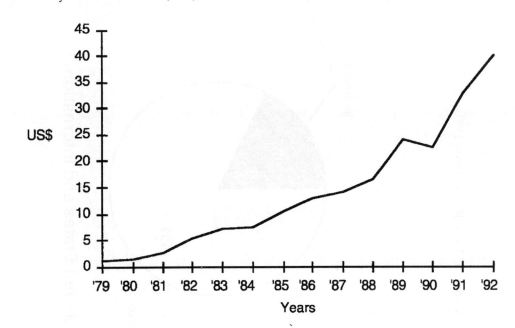

Source: *Standard & Poor's Compustat, Compustat PC Plus*

Exhibit 4   Distribution of Toys "R" Us Stores, 1991

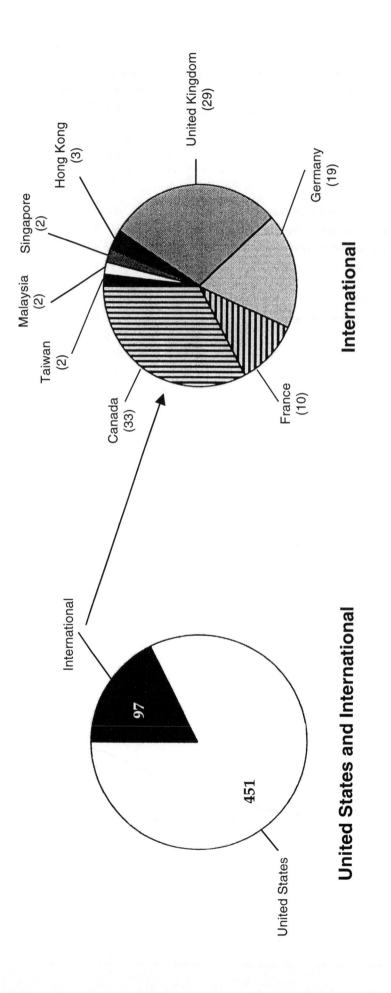

International

Canada
(33)

Taiwan
(2)

Malaysia
(2)

Singapore
(2)

Hong Kong
(3)

United Kingdom
(29)

Germany
(19)

France
(10)

International

International

97

United States

451

United States and International

Source: Toys "R" Us Annual Report, 1991

Exhibit 5   Total Retail Sales of Toys and Games, Selected Countries, 1992

Country	Sales of Toys & Games (Millions of US$)
Canada	1,033.0
China	140.0
Hong Kong	200.0
India	260.0
Japan	7,884.0
Malaysia	20.0
Mexico	220.0
Philippines	32.0
Singapore	55.0
South Korea	425.0
Taiwan	375.0
United States	20,684.0

Source: *International Marketing Data and Statistics 1994*

Exhibit 6   Index of Urban Land Prices in Japan, 1982-
1991 (end of March 1990 = 100)

	1982	1983	1984	1985	1986	1987	1988	1989	1990	1991
All urban land										
Total average	61.5	64.4	66.5	68.3	70.2	74.1	81.5	87.6	100.0	110.4
Commercial	55.6	58.0	59.8	61.7	64.2	69.2	78.4	86.3	100.0	111.5
Residential	64.6	68.3	70.7	72.7	74.2	77.6	84.0	88.7	100.0	109.7
Industrial	66.2	68.8	70.7	72.4	73.9	76.4	82.3	88.2	100.0	109.8
6 major cities										
Total average	28.4	29.7	31.3	33.6	38.4	48.3	61.8	76.9	100.0	103.0
Commercial	19.5	20.8	22.7	25.6	33.0	44.2	62.6	78.3	100.0	103.3
Residential	33.5	34.8	36.0	38.0	41.7	52.9	65.2	75.1	100.0	102.1
Industrial	35.7	37.0	38.2	39.6	41.6	48.7	58.1	77.2	100.0	103.8

Source: *Japan Statistical Yearbook 1995*

Exhibit 7   Monthly Living Expenditure per Average Household in Japan, 1980-1991
                (value in yen)

	1980	1985	1990	1991
Food	66,923	73,735	78,956	82,130
Medical care	5,865	6,931	8,866	9,016
Transportation/communication	18,416	24,754	29,469	30,533
Education	8,325	10,853	14,471	14,211
Reading/recreation	19,620	24,191	30,122	31,442
Housing	10,682	12,686	14,814	16,712
Fuel/light/water	13,225	17,724	17,147	17,981
Furniture/household items	9,875	11,665	12,396	13,401
Clothes/footwear	18,163	19,606	22,967	23,814
Miscellaneous/personal	12,411	15,589	17,207	19,173
Pocket money	21,002	24,345	27,569	28,502
Social expenses	21,504	25,573	29,830	32,543
Annual rate of inflation (% growth)	7.7	2.0	3.1	3.3

Source: *Japan Statistical Yearbook 1995, International Marketing Data and Statistics 1995*

Note: Numbers may not add due to rounding.

Exhibit 8   Employees and Establishments in Japan, 1970-1991

Year	Retail Establishments	Employees (000s)	Average/ Outlet	Wholesale Establishments	Employees (000s)	Average/ Business
1970	1,471,297	4,926	3.35	255,974	2,861	11.18
1972	1,495,510	5,141	3.44	259,163	3,008	11.61
1974	1,548,184	5,303	3.43	292,155	3,290	11.26
1976	1,614,067	5,580	3.46	340,249	3,513	10.32
1979	1,673,667	5,960	3.56	368,608	3,673	9.96
1982	1,721,465	6,369	3.70	428,858	4,091	9.54
1985	1,628,644	6,329	3.89	413,016	3,998	9.68
1988	1,619,752	6,851	4.23	436,421	4,332	9.93
1991	1,591,223	6,937	4.36	475,983	4,773	10.03

Source: Census of Commerce, MITI

Exhibit 9 Number of Outlets in Japan by Format, 1988 and 1991

Outlet Format	1988	1991
Department store	433	455
General supermarket	1,478	1,549
Other general supermarket	373	375
Specialty supermarket	6,397	7,130
Convenience store	34,550	41,847
Other supermarket	53,834	67,473
Specialty store	1,007,756	1,000,166
Miscellaneous retail stores	513,338	470,289
Others	1,593	1,939
Total	1,619,752	1,591,223

Source: *Retail Trade International*, Euromonitor 1995

Exhibit 10 Number of Outlets in Japan by Size, 1988 and 1991

Outlet Size (sq. m.)	1988	1991
Under 10	83,510	72,387
10-19	280,761	246,657
20-29	267,077	239,425
30-49	367,266	360,059
50-99	271,227	282,388
100-199	96,260	109,050
200-499	48,423	56,490
500-999	8,408	8,799
1,000-1,499	3,888	4,358
1,500-2,999	2,047	2,269
Over 3,000	2,107	2,371
Not reported	188,778	206,970
Total	1,619,752	1,591,223

Source: *Retail Trade International*, Euromonitor 1995

Note: 1 sq. m. = 0.092 sq. ft.

Exhibit 11   Comparison of Price Levels by Store Type in Japan (manufacturer's suggested retail price = 100)

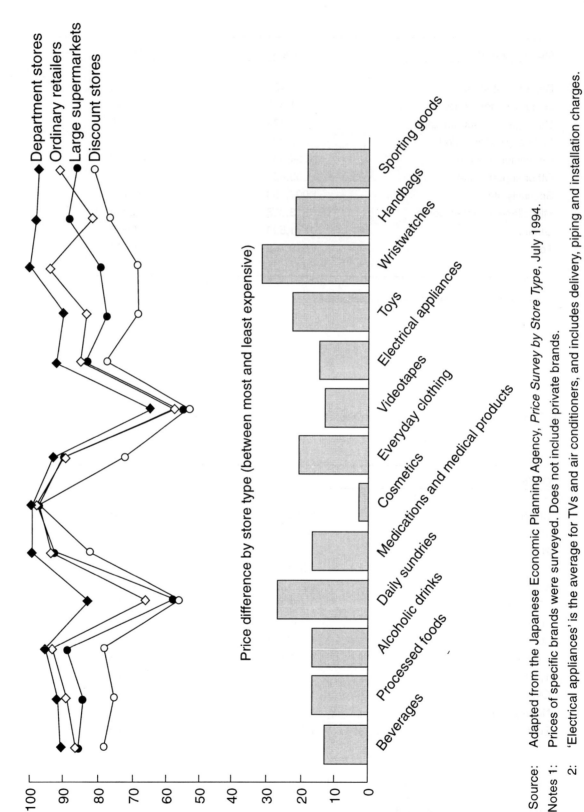

Price difference by store type (between most and least expensive)

Department stores
Ordinary retailers
Large supermarkets
Discount stores

Sporting goods
Handbags
Wristwatches
Toys
Electrical appliances
Videotapes
Everyday clothing
Cosmetics
Medications and medical products
Daily sundries
Alcoholic drinks
Processed foods
Beverages

Source: Adapted from the Japanese Economic Planning Agency, *Price Survey by Store Type*, July 1994.

Notes 1:   Prices of specific brands were surveyed. Does not include private brands.

2:    'Electrical appliances' is the average for TVs and air conditioners, and includes delivery, piping and installation charges.

Exhibit 12   Leading Foreign Retailers in Japan, 1991

Company	Year Opened	Number of Stores	Owners
Clothing/Accessories			
Brooks Brothers (Japan)	1979	3	Brooks Brothers Inc. (51%)
			Daidoh Ltd. (49%)
Hermes Japan Co.	1979	1	Hermes S.A. (50%)
			Seibu Department Stores Ltd. (50%)
Laura Ashley Japan	1986	12	Aeon Group (40%)
			Laura Ashley Group Plc. (40%)
Louis Vuitton Japan	1981	1	Louis Vuitton Malletier (99%)
Audio/Visual			
Blockbuster Japan	1990	1	Blockbuster Entertainment (50%)
			Fujita & Co. (50%)
HMV Japan	1990	3	HMV Group Ltd. (100%)
Tower Records	1980	14	MTS Inc. (100%)
Virgin Mega Stores Japan	1990	1	Virgin Group Ltd. (50%)
			Marui Co. (50%)
Others			
Tireplus	1990	3	Sears, Roebuck & Co. (50%)
			Saison Group (50%)
Toys "R" Us	1991	0	Toys "R" Us Inc. (80%)
			McDonald's Co. (Japan) (20%)

Source: *Nikkei Weekly*, November 16, 1991

Note: The first Toys "R" Us store in Japan opened on December 20, 1991.

Exhibit 13   Foreign Direct Investment in the United States and Japan, 1985 and 1991 (millions of US$)

	United States		Japan	
Year	Total Stock of Foreign Investment	Stock of Japanese-owned Foreign Investment	Total Stock of Foreign Investment	Stock of U.S.-owned Foreign Investment
1985	184,615	19,313	6,397	3,067
1991	414,358	92,896	22,771	9,907

Source: International Direct Investment Statistics Yearbook 1994

Harvard Business School

9-795-031
January 4, 1995

Note on Foreign Direct Investment

Between 1985 and 1990 the global economy witnessed an unprecedented surge in flows of foreign direct investment (FDI). According to U.N. estimates, world flows of FDI grew during this period at annual growth rates of close to 27%, while world income grew at less than 7% per annum and world trade at less than 9%.[1] By the end of the decade, analysts estimated that roughly $3.6 trillion of business assets had come under the control of foreign owners.[2]

In 1991, the surge subsided as quickly as it had begun, with global flows dropping roughly 25% from their 1990 level. The political and economic questions that surrounded FDI, however, remained, highlighted even by the speed and intensity of the shift in capital flows. What, analysts wondered, caused firms to contract and expand their purchase of foreign assets? How did patterns of foreign investment relate to world trade and development levels? And what impact if any did foreign owners have on the countries in which their assets were located?

Definition and Accounting

Roughly defined, FDI is simply all capital transferred between a non-banking firm and its new and established foreign affiliates. The investment itself can take any number of forms, ranging from a hostile takeover, to a joint venture, or a new, or "greenfield," operation. Conceptually, FDI is distinguished only by the control acquired by a foreign entity. Or as the International Monetary Fund defines it: [FDI] is "an investment that is made to acquire a lasting interest in an enterprise operating in an economy, other than that of the investor, the investor's purpose being to have an effective voice in the management of the enterprise."

Precisely what constitutes an "effective voice," though, is difficult to define. For reporting purposes, most governmental agencies classify a foreign investment as "direct" when a single investor acquires more than 10% of a foreign firm. From that point on, the controlled firm is generally considered a foreign affiliate or subsidiary of its overseas "parent." Often, however, the statistical

[1]Edward M. Graham and Paul R. Krugman, "The Surge in Foreign Investment in the 1980s," p.1. This note draws heavily on the excellent summary and analysis of this paper, much of which is reproduced in the authors' subsequent work, *Foreign Direct Investment in the United States* (Washington, D.C.: Institute for International Economics, 1991.)

[2]ibid.

Professor Debora L. Spar prepared this note with Research Associate Julia Kou as the basis for class discussion rather than to illustrate either effective or ineffective handling of an administrative situation.

relationship between subsidiaries and parents belies their relative position. For instance, because the Bronfman (Seagram) family of Canada owns 22.9% of DuPont, DuPont is classified in statistics as the U.S. subsidiary of a Canadian firm. But DuPont is widely considered a U.S. firm because foreign interests do not have managerial control over its operations.

Statistics on FDI can deceive in other ways as well, since the nature and intent of the investment is rarely evident in the numbers themselves. To begin, not all investment capital is captured in the measurement of FDI. In fact, under prevailing IMF guidelines, FDI consists only of the sum of 1) new equity purchased or acquired by parent companies in overseas firms they are considered to control; 2) reinvestment of earnings by controlled firms; and 3) intracompany loans from parent companies to controlled firms. Under these definitions, several increases in foreign control simply do not count. If a foreign parent funds its acquisition by borrowing in the local market, for instance, or if it increases its holding via a stock exchange with a local subsidiary, the investment is not officially registered as FDI. Thus, the element of FDI that is presumably of greatest interest—the increase in local assets under foreign control—is not easily discernable.

Likewise, calculating the total sum of foreign-controlled assets—the stock of FDI—is no easy task, since assets have customarily been computed on a historical cost basis.[3] That is, a plant or mine purchased in 1910 stays on the books at its original purchase price, regardless of the increase in its current, nominal, value. Capital gains and price increases are both systematically ignored, leading to a global understatement of FDI that varies significantly with the age of the investments. Countries like the United States, whose firms ventured abroad at the start of the twentieth century, thus appear to have fewer overseas assets than they actually do, whereas relative newcomers like Japan may seem to have an unrealistically large global presence. In either case, moreover, the size of accumulated assets is again only a proxy for the overriding questions mentioned above: why do firms invest abroad and how do they affect the countries in which they do business?

Motivations of Foreign Investment

The debate on the causes of foreign investment began most publicly with Vladimir Ilyich Lenin, who argued in 1916 that firms invested abroad to extend the monopoly rents and spheres of influence that they enjoyed already in their home markets. Although Lenin was primarily concerned with the effects of foreign investment (and particularly with the exploitation he saw as a result) he did nevertheless identify the crucial capitalist motivation of FDI. In broadest terms, firms venture abroad for the same reason they engage in most activities: to maximize expected returns.

But how do firms determine the most lucrative overseas sites? And what leads them to expect a higher return than that prevailing in their own domestic market? One obvious explanation is that firms venture abroad in search of lower factor costs. They move to foreign markets, quite simply, because they are cheaper. This explanation is particularly relevant with regard to basic inputs such as natural resources. Whenever resources are scarce or expensive in the local market, firms will have an incentive to acquire them abroad. Some of the earliest and most influential foreign investors, for example, were the great state-owned trading companies of Great Britain and the Netherlands, who established virtual colonies in Asia to harvest and produce the spices and teas that were prohibitively expensive in western Europe. They were followed by prospectors in Africa who built great empires from their control over the continent's diamonds, gold, and copper; and then by the emerging

---

[3]Recognizing these inconsistencies, the United States revised its valuation methods in 1991. In addition to the customary historical cost data, the Bureau of Economic Analysis (BEA) has subsequently included in its publications two other measures of FDI. The *current cost method* revalues investment by virtue of current costs and general price indices. The *market cost method* revalues the owners' equity portion using indices of stock market prices.

multinational oil firms, which chased each other around the world in a race to acquire petroleum fields. Currently, resource-based investment still describes a substantial portion of total investment flows, as resource-based companies continue to search for cheaper sources of supply and, increasingly, as manufacturing firms integrate backwards to assure a steady and secure supply of their most critical raw material inputs.

The search for accessible supply and low cost is also evident with regard to labor. For firms whose production relies heavily on unskilled or semi-skilled labor, investing in a low-wage overseas operation can be a powerful means of reducing factor costs. Industries like textiles and footwear, for instance, have seen a decades-long shift from the northern industrial states to Latin America and East Asia, where labor costs can be as much as 90% lower. The shift itself is a powerful cycle of trade and foreign investment: lower wages give states a comparative advantage in the production of certain labor-intensive products and thus an incentive to trade these goods on the international market. The resulting competition then forces firms in higher-wage states to either leave the industry, find some new means of differentiation, or move their own operations to the low-wage areas. In this cycle, FDI is thus both a response to trade and a generator of it, since the firms that venture abroad almost always re-export their product to their original markets.

In other cases, the motive for foreign investment lies squarely in the foreign, or "host," market. Sometimes firms invest overseas, not to lower costs for their domestic market, but instead to seek profits in new, often untapped, markets. The process fits squarely with Lenin's early description: as competition increases and profits decline in established markets, firms will need to find new ventures if they are to maintain the returns to which they have grown accustomed. Overseas markets provide an obvious target, especially if there are no local producers of the goods in question. IBM and Coca Cola for instance, became global giants largely by being the first to produce and sell their products in a host of foreign markets. Being first, they could act almost as monopolists, setting prices without fear of competitive pressures.

Moreover, even when local competitors are already established, foreign firms may have an incentive to invest in the local market. In many cases, the incentive lies in a technological or managerial innovation which simply makes them more competitive than the local firms. IBM, for instance, was for decades not only the first mover in foreign markets, but also technologically more advanced than its competitors. Or, as has long been the case with Coca-Cola, the brand-name or the very foreignness of a product may give the foreign investor an edge over local competitors.

But if foreign firms have this competitive edge, why would they invest directly instead of just serving their overseas markets through exports and distributorships? Again, the answers are numerous, and they vary by firm and industry. Sometimes, lower factor costs are an added incentive, especially when transportation costs are added to the equation. It makes little sense, for instance, for AT&T to export telephone answering systems to Mexico from Louisiana if Mexican workers cost one-tenth of their U.S. counterparts. In other cases, firms are wary of the arms-length transactions that characterize overseas trade and prefer to control their would-be dealers or distributors directly. To ensure this control they choose investment over trade, eliminating the risk of foreign intermediaries and instead internalizing their operations. Finally, and perhaps most frequently, firms have also turned to investment whenever tariff barriers prevented them from exporting their goods freely to foreign markets. Indeed for many decades, tariff jumping was a primary inducement for foreign direct investment. In countries such as Canada, Mexico, and Brazil, which explicitly chose development strategies based largely on import substitution, tariff levels were designed to keep exports out and thus foster the development of local (albeit often foreign-owned) manufacturing. Under these circumstances, outside firms had little choice but to invest directly. If they wanted to enter these large and relatively prosperous markets, their only option was to jump the tariff wall, setting up shop in the foreign market and becoming in effect a local or "national" enterprise. Thus, throughout the post-war period, tariff-jumping investment was a common phenomenon in the developing world, especially in countries with large populations and the high tariff levels that customarily accompanied a development strategy based on import-substitution.

As global tariff levels have gradually declined, however, the need to jump has become less pronounced. Increasingly, developing countries have abandoned import substitution and moved towards more liberal regimes of export promotion and open borders. Nevertheless, many firms continue to view direct investment as a way to hedge against the threat of future protectionism or avoid the subtle non-tariff barriers that can continue to thwart the success of imports. Japanese investment in the U.S. auto industry, for instance, is often seen as a reaction to the protectionist forces that struck the industry in the early 1980s, while U.S. investment in Japanese retailing is described as an attempt to get around domestic barriers in the Japanese market.

A final motive—one imputed most frequently by Marxist analysts of foreign investment—is simply the urge to dominate. Multinational firms enter foreign markets just because they are there. In this view, the decision to invest is not the result of a careful cost-benefit analysis but rather a basic response to a market opportunity. Taken to an extreme, of course, this explanation is nonsensical, since multinational firms are clearly not in the business of throwing capital randomly at emerging markets. A more moderate version, however, does seem to describe a not-uncommon phenomenon of business. Often, firms do rush into new markets, lured as much by the novelty of the country as by a rational calculation of financial opportunity. After the collapse of the Berlin Wall, for instance, Western firms scrambled to invest in the countries of the former Soviet bloc. Some of this investment was clearly motivated by the unprecedented opportunities inherent in these newly-liberalized states. But some, too, was motivated simply by the desire to be on the other side of the Wall and stand among the pioneers of eastern Europe's development. McDonald's famous Moscow franchise, for example, was never intended to generate particularly high returns. Instead, the Canadian-based management wanted a Russian store to symbolize Russia's opening to the West and McDonald's international scope.

Putting the Moscow McDonald's next to Mobil Oil or IBM reveals the wide range of reasons that prompt firms to invest abroad. In practice, of course, the motivations are even more varied and complex. They overlap and converge with one another, creating a whole web of reasoning that managers themselves can not always entangle or discern. For those who look further to the effects of their investment, the web becomes more complicated still.

The Effects of FDI

In the neoclassical view of capitalism, the establishment of a foreign firm in a local economy should affect little but the competitive structure of the market. Insofar as the foreign entrant is a new entrant, it will simply expand the field of competitors and increase the level of supply. If the foreign firm has organizational or technological advantages over the local firms, it may also put downward pressure on local prices. Eventually, it may even drive some local firms out of business. But the identity of the firm in this analysis is irrelevant. Its effects on the market stem from its size and competitive advantages, not from its foreignness.

Or so the theory goes. In practice, however, the expanding reach of multinational firms seems to carry wider consequences. Foreign investment in many cases changes the economic and political environment of host countries. When foreign firms bring capital, technology, and managerial expertise with them, they bring simultaneously the very tools of economic and industrial development. Often, they will be the only sources of capital a developing country can secure, and the only channel through which an isolated economy can begin to enter the international marketplace. It was, for instance, the British East India Company that launched India's industrialization and DeBeers that transformed Botswana into one of Africa's most prosperous economies. More recently, Western firms such as Alcatel and General Electric have helped revitalize the crumbling infrastructure of eastern Europe's formerly-socialist states. Especially in countries that lack the basic institutions and mechanisms of capitalism, foreign direct investment can be a powerful means of building the market from the bottom up, gradually creating the jobs, skills, and technological base that drive an advanced industrial economy.

Recognizing this potential many countries in recent years have warmly welcomed foreign firms, wooing them with tax incentives, special export zones, and other enticements. Especially since 1991, when global investment funds dipped, the competition among developing countries to attract potential investors has markedly increased, as countries from Lithuania to Tanzania race to secure the technology, capital, and managerial skills that only foreign investment can bring. Even in industrialized countries such as the United States and Great Britain, regions are vying with one another to attract the most promising investors, as evidenced in the competition among mid-western and southern states to draw Japanese investment in the automobile industry.

Such enthusiasm is new. For decades, the recipients of FDI viewed foreign firms primarily with suspicion, seeing their activities as an intrusion or even invasion. The criticisms against FDI were manifold, and focussed on the ill-effects that resulted from the establishment of a business entity that had no connection or loyalty to its new place of residence. Arguing against the neoclassical view, critics charged that foreign direct investment affected not only the structure of local markets but also the very fabric of the political and economic community.

To begin with, the impact of foreign competitors on local markets is not economically neutral. If foreign firms are more competitive they will drain profits from local firms, weakening the indigenous base of the economy. Moreover, if the foreign firm subsequently repatriates its profits in the form of dividends or salaries, it may actually act as a net exporter of capital from its host country. This export need not be significant for an advanced industrial economy, but could prove devastating for an underdeveloped economy with limited hard currency reserves.

If the capital benefits of foreign direct investment are thus illusory, critics have charged, so too are purported gains in technology and employment. Most multinationals, after all, do not transfer their highest-technology research or their corporate headquarters to their overseas subsidiaries. Instead, they tend to keep their core businesses at home, and establish manufacturing, or mining, or retail operations abroad. So they create jobs, but not necessarily the kind of highly-paid advanced positions that host countries would obviously prefer. Moreover, in many instances, multinationals bring older generation technologies with them, giving machinery and processes that were obsolete in one market a new life in another. To foreign investors, this practice is simply a logical use of resources and even a boost to the local economy, since older-generation technologies tend to be more labor-intensive. To some recipient states, however, import of these older processes and plants denies them the very technological edge that foreign investment was designed to bring.

Going further still, many investors have long insisted that foreign investment disrupts the political and cultural patterns of host states. Politically, it is easy to understand how the sheer financial magnitude of a foreign investor could give it an undue influence over local authorities. At the extreme, influence could even become control, as the very foundations of authority fall under the sway of foreign-owned enterprises. Though rare, instances of such control are dramatic and well-known. The first, of course, was the British East India Company, which came for spices and stayed to rule the subcontinent. The oil companies operated similarly in the Middle East, where, until the tables turned in the late 1960s, they supported the ruling families and virtually dictated policy. Mining companies in Africa, banana companies in the Caribbean, and Japanese financial services have all also been accused of using their economic clout to shape policies in line with their own demands. On a smaller scale, stories abound of foreign investors who have bought the favors of local officials or helped to preserve the rule of a particular party or military clique.

Political concerns also surface whenever foreign investors stray too close to the security interests of their host states. While the precise definition of these interests varies from state to state, the fear is always the same: that foreign firms will subvert national security by gaining control over key industrial or military assets. Even when the assets are immoveable and subject, potentially at least, to expropriation, worries about foreign ownership remain. States fear that the loyalties of foreign-owned firms will always tie them back to their home base and that, in a crisis, the investors may defect, dismantling the facilities they operate or refusing to supply the state with critical military or industrial components. Thus, many nations forbid foreign control in the defense sector and limit foreign ownership of strategic natural resources such as petroleum. Others aim wider, preventing foreign firms from "hollowing out" key industries. Even the United States moved in this direction in the mid-1980s, screening foreign acquisitions in sensitive industries like computers and semiconductors. Behind the move stood an inchoate but widespread belief that foreign owners might transfer core technologies and production to overseas locations, gradually weakening the industrial infrastructure—and thus the military might—of the United States.

In the cultural domain, the purported effects of FDI are subtler. When foreign firms establish themselves in new markets, they have the power to transform the local environment, often dramatically. By creating job opportunities and importing technologies, they may disrupt established patterns of work in the community, bringing more women into the work force, for instance, or driving less sophisticated businesses out of operation. Paradoxically, even higher wages can be disruptive insofar as they change social relations that may have existed for decades, or even centuries. New products can also have a serious impact, especially when introduced into relatively unsophisticated economies. Agrarian economies are forever changed by tractors and chemical fertilizers; rural communities transform themselves once motorcycles and cars arrive; and youth around the world have been affected by the sudden availability of Levis, Bart Simpson, and Madonna. Even Canada, one of the world's most sophisticated consumer markets, periodically rebels against the "cultural imperialism" many see as inherent in a reliance on goods produced by U.S.-owned firms.

To a large extent, such arguments can be dismissed as an inevitable reaction to globalization. As the world's economies draw closer, people may feel a nostalgia for the isolation of the past and a need to preserve the remnants of their own distinctive cultures. They lash out at foreign investors, not because of what they do so much as for what they represent. Nevertheless, there is still something in the critique of FDI that rings true. Foreign firms are different in some respects from local ones. They are owned by different people; they were raised on different laws; and they may have different loyalties, priorities, and operating styles. These distinctions are converging ever more rapidly as globalization progresses, but they are still there.

The critique of foreign direct investment that erupted in the 1960s and 1970s, however, has all but vanished in recent years, giving way to a new and virtually unanimous consensus on its merits. Few states limit investment flows any longer, or even regulate them to any great degree. Foreign investors are rarely screened, and expropriation hardly ever occurs. Even once-isolated nations such as China, Albania, Kazakhstan, and Cuba are rushing to attract foreign investors and make whatever legal or commercial adjustments entice them to stay.

But beneath the embrace the questions still lurk. Is the surge of foreign investment an undisputed good, either for firms or for states? How should managers and politicians decide which investments are wise and which too risky to attempt? And what will be the long-term effects on the international economy as firms increasingly do business beyond their own borders?

Exhibit 1   The OECD Declaration and Decisions on International Investment and Multinational
                Enterprises[1]

National governments have found it difficult to regulate MNEs. Multilateral regulation may be even more challenging, as demonstrated by the Organization for Economic Cooperation and Development (OECD) efforts to establish rules for MNEs and international investment.

In its 1976 Declaration and Decisions on International Investment and Multinational Enterprises, the OECD established two sets of rules, one governing the practices of MNEs and the other governing FDI.[2] To govern MNEs, the OECD established a voluntary code of corporate conduct that encourages MNEs to give their subsidiaries the autonomy to abide by national laws and to cooperate with local business and labor. The code of conduct advises MNEs to permit labor representation, contribute to technology transfer, and not obstruct competition or harm the environment. To govern FDI, the OECD recommended that all member countries extend national treatment to foreign MNEs. The influence of both sets of rules has been limited primarily because they rely on the good faith of MNEs and member nations.

For example, the code of conduct for MNEs has no quantitative means of measuring effectiveness and commitment. Instead, it promotes good corporate citizenship among MNEs, measured primarily by membership in national business federations that affiliate and consult with the OECD through the Business and Industry Advisory Committee (BIAC).[3] Individual firms have been reluctant to endorse the OECD's rules because of the political and legal implications of explicit commitment, especially in labor and environment disputes. Moreover, many MNEs reportedly feel that stronger, obligatory rules would be too intrusive.[4] The business community sees asymmetries in policies as the major impediments to foreign investment, and the BIAC has been pressing the OECD to enhance the International Investment and National Treatment portion of the Declaration.[5]

The OECD rules promoting national treatment allow exceptions based on concerns for national security and public order, particularly in regard to the natural resource, energy, and service sectors.[6] Given these exceptions, nations can impose tax obligations and investment controls on foreign controlled enterprises, restrict access to local bank credit and capital markets, and discriminate in government procurement contracts.[7] Concerned with an apparent trend towards excessive restrictions, the OECD recommended a standstill on further exceptions in 1988. In 1991, the OECD encouraged nations to make restrictive measures more transparent and to commit to eliminating them in the future.[8] At the same time, the OECD and the Committee on International

---

[1]This summary is taken from U.S. Congress, Office of Technology Assessment, *Multinationals and the National Interest: Playing by Different Rules* (Washington DC: Government Printing Office, 1993), pp. 70-71.

[2]Organization for Economic Cooperation and Development, *Declaration on International Investment and Multinational Enterprises*, (Paris: OECD, 1976).

[3]The Business and Industry Advisory Committee to the OECD is based in Paris.

[4]Confidential business federation interviews.

[5]Business and Industry Advisory Committee, *BIAC Statement on a Potential OECD Broader Investment Instrument*, Paris, December 3, 1992.

[6]OECD, The OECD Declaration and Decisions on International Investment and Multinational Enterprises: 1991 Review, (Paris: OECD, 1992), pp. 26-32.

[7]OECD, *National Treatment for Foreign-Controlled Enterprises*, (Paris: OECD, 1985), pp. 20-22.

[8]OECD, *The OECD Declaration and Decisions on International Investment and Multinational Enterprises: 1991 Review*, pp. 30-5; "National Treatment: Third Revised Decision of the Council," December 1991, revision of the Declaration by Governments of the OECD Member countries on International Investment and Multinational Enterprises.

Investment and Multinational Enterprises (CIME), which monitors use of the decisions by national governments and MNEs, expressed concern over a number of trends and activities in both private and government policies and practices, including sharp swings in investment flows, trade frictions, conflicting national requirements on MNCs, the marginal contributions of screwdriver assembly plants, preferential treatment in the private sector, the increase in bilateral investment agreements, and the use of reciprocity as a bargaining tool.[9] The OECD fears these conditions undermine the Declaration and Decisions and may impede future multilateral attempts to liberalize foreign investment rules.

In sum, the nonbinding nature of the OECD Declaration and Decisions and their institutionalized deference to national laws and prerogatives leave them inherently weak. Member countries often have different reactions to the effects of asymmetrical investment incentives, and while some wish to strengthen the national treatment decisions, others prefer to include more rights of exception.[10] These different views indicate that real progress towards further liberalization or enforcement of the Declaration and Decisions is unlikely.

---

[9]OECD, The OECD Declaration and Decisions on International Investment and Multinational Enterprises: 1991 Review, pp. 18-20.

[10]Confidential interviews.

Exhibit 2 Stock of Foreign-owned Assets in Selected Countries, 1975-1990 (in US$ billions)

	1975	1980	1985	1986	1987	1988	1989	1990
Germany	0.68	0.23	22.85	32.35	40.37	39.81	44.10	59.98
Japan[1]	0.23	0.29	4.74	6.51	9.02	10.42	9.16	9.85
United States	2.63	13.68	220.00	272.97	316.20	391.53	534.73	536.56

Source: International Monetary Fund, *Balance of Payments Statistics Yearbook*, 1983 and 1993.

[1]Japan's FDI stock data are recorded at historical cost, not market value.

Exhibit 3 Worldwide Distribution of FDI, by Recipient (1980-1990)

	1980	1985	1990
Total Inward FDI (US$ bil)	**$47**	**$51**	**$200**
European Community	37%	31%	39%
Developing Countries	22	25	19
United States	16	25	24
Canada	10	9	7
Other Developed	10	6	6
Other Europe	5	4	5

Source: International Monetary Fund, *Balance of Payments Statistics Yearbook*, various years; and U.S. Department of Commerce, *Foreign Direct Investment in the United States: An Update (June 1993)*, p. 13.

Exhibit 4 Worldwide Distribution of FDI, by Source (1980-1990)

	1980	1985	1990
Total Outward FDI (US$ bil)	**$46**	**$58**	**$237**
United States	43%	37%	26%
European Community	39	40	44
Other Europe	6	6	8
Canada	4	6	5
Japan	4	7	12
Others	5	5	6

Source: International Monetary Fund, *Balance of Payments Statistics Yearbook*, various years; and U.S. Department of Commerce, *Foreign Direct Investment in the United States: An Update (June 1993)*, p. 11.

Note: World outward and inward FDI are not equal because of differences between countries in FDI definition and data collection methodologies. FDI outflows are larger than FDI inflows because a larger proportion of outflows compared with inflows originate from a small number of developed countries which have relatively better data collection systems.

Exhibit 5   FDI Flows Into the Larger Industrial Countries (annual averages)

	1975-79	1980-84	1985-89	1990	1991	1992
Total inflows, $bn **% distribution**	**18**	**34**	**96**	**156**	**116**	**90**
United States	33	53	51	29	21	2
Larger EC countries	57	38	37	57	61	79
Belgium	6	3	3	6	8	12
France	10	7	6	8	13	24
Germany	7	2	2	2	6	8
Italy	3	3	3	4	2	3
Netherlands	4	3	4	7	5	6
Spain	4	5	5	9	9	9
United Kingdom	23	15	14	21	14	20
Australia	6	6	5	4	4	6
Canada	2	-1	1	5	6	9
Japan	1	1	0.4	1	0	3
Sweden	0.3	1	1	1	5	0
Switzerland	0	1	2	3	3	1

Source: "Where the rich countries do their shopping," *The Economist*, September 19, 1992, p. 17; and the International Monetary Fund, *Balance of Payments Statistics Yearbook 1993*, Part 2, pp. 66-67.

Note: Totals may not add to 100% due to rounding.

Exhibit 6   FDI Flows From the Larger Industrial Countries (annual averages)

	1975-79	1980-84	1985-89	1990	1991	1992
Total outflows, $bn **% distribution**	**34**	**40**	**126**	**214**	**170**	**153**
United States	47	24	19	15	17	23
Larger EC countries	40	53	48	50	52	59
Belgium	1	0.3	2	3	4	7
France	5	8	7	16	14	20
Germany	9	9	8	11	13	10
Italy	1	4	3	4	4	4
Netherlands	6	7	6	7	8	7
Spain	0.4	1	1	1	2	0
United Kingdom	18	24	21	8	9	10
Australia	1	2	3	1	1	0
Canada	4	7	4	0.2	4	4
Japan	6	11	17	22	18	11
Sweden	2	2	4	7	4	0
Switzerland	0	1	4	3	4	3

Source: "Where the rich countries do their shopping," *The Economist*, September 19, 1992, p. 17; and the International Monetary Fund, *Balance of Payments Statistics Yearbook 1993*, Part 2, pp. 66-67.

Note: Totals may not add to 100% due to rounding.

Exhibit 7   Developing Countries and Foreign Direct Investment

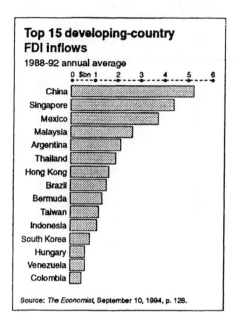

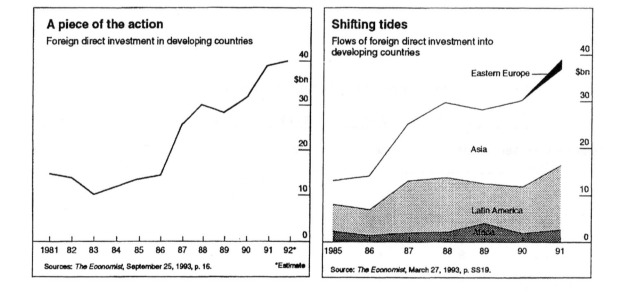

Exhibit 8   Trends in Foreign Direct Investment

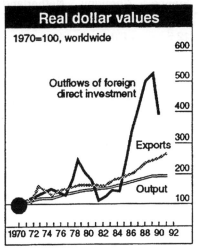

Sources: *The Economist*, March 27, 1993, p. 558.

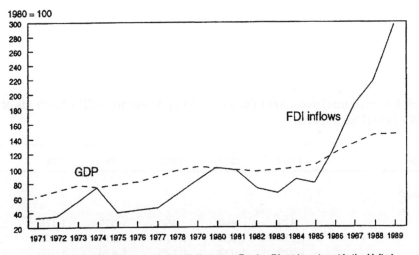

Sources: Edward M. Graham and Paul R. Krugman, Foreign Direct Investment in the United
States (Washington D.C.: Institute for International Economics, 1991), p. 51.

Exhibit 9   U.S. Employment by Foreign-owned Firms in Selected Industries, 1990 (in thousands of employees, by country of parent firm)

Industries	Canada	France	Germany	Netherlands	Switzerland	Britain	Japan
Food and kindred products	NA	12.5	2.9	17.4	NA	105.0	15.1
Chemicals and allied products	NA	22.8	94.4	41.5	60.4	129.2	23.7
Primary and fabricated metals	32.2	35.3	21.8	10.5	8.2	39.5	61.8
Machinery Of which:	41.3	34.5	59.9	NA	49.3	92.1	89.6
Computer and office equipment	0.7	NA	2.7	0.7	NA	10.3	25.2
Electric and electronic equipment	35.2	19.4	39.0	NA	NA	47.4	34.9
Other manufacturing	90.2	76.0	70.8	NA	NA	172.7	101.6
Total wholesale trade	20.7	43.4	65.6	16.2	14.9	59.9	152.9

Source: U.S. Department of Commerce, Bureau of Economic Analysis, *Foreign Direct Investment in the United States, Operations of U.S. Affiliates of Foreign Companies, Preliminary 1990 Estimates* (Washington, DC: U.S. Government Printing Office, August 1992), **Table F-3**.

Note: NA indicates data are not available.

Exhibit 10   U.S. International Investment Positions Using Alternative BEA Methods of Valuation, 1983-1989 (US$ billions)

Valuation Method	1983	1984	1985	1986	1987	1988	1989
U.S. assets abroad							
Historical cost	873	896	950	1,073	1,176	1,266	1,413
Current Cost	1,114	1,104	1,174	1,319	1,463	1,528	1,669
Market value	1,029	1,022	1,175	1,424	1,556	1,704	1,938
Foreign-owned assets in U.S.							
Historical cost	784	898	1,067	1,347	1,554	1,797	2,076
Current cost	829	941	1,110	1,393	1,605	1,852	2,133
Market value	805	911	1,110	1,410	1,605	1,865	2,219
International investment, net							
Historical cost	89	(2)	(117)	(274)	(378)	(531)	(664)
Current cost	285	164	64	(74)	(142)	(324)	(464)
Market value	224	111	64	15	(49)	(161)	(281)

Source: J. Steven Landefeld and Ann M. Lawson, "Valuation of the U.S. Net International Investment Position," *Survey of Current Business*, May 1991, p. 43.

White Nights and Polar Lights: Investing in the Russian Oil Industry

The basis of the economic revival of Russia and Western Siberia will not be some political laws. It will be the existence of strong companies. They will influence the new structure of the laws to be adopted. The oil companies are very active now. They should not wait. If they wait for political stabilization, it may take 1,000 years.

—Vladimir Spielman
Deputy Director of the Western
Siberian Geology Institute

In the second half of the 1980s the collapse of the Soviet empire created an unprecedented opportunity for Western businesses. With dizzying speed, nearly all of the world's communist states embarked upon radical programs of economic liberalization and declared themselves open for capital flows and foreign investment. Among the first to heed this call were Western oil firms, who rushed to investigate the vast petroleum reserves of what was once the Soviet Union. In many respects, investment in Russian oil seemed a perfect match between East and West. Western firms promised to bring to Russia the capital, technology, and managerial talent that the country so desperately needed. They also had the ability—and desire—to restore production levels in Russia's long neglected fields and provide the fledgling government with a valuable source of hard currency. For decades, oil sales had financed the Soviet Union's ambitious program of industrialization. Now, the continued capacity of the oil sector to generate tax revenues was vital to the success of political reform.

The potential for the Western oil firms was similarly vast. Even divorced from the other republics of the Soviet Union, Russia was still the world's largest single producer of crude petroleum. Its reserves of petroleum were the seventh largest in the world, and its reserves of natural gas the largest. Unlike many other oil rich countries, moreover, Russia was located directly next to the

---

Professor Debora L. Spar and William W. Jarosz, Esq., Associate, Debevoise & Plimpton, prepared this case with Research Associate Julia Kou as the basis for class discussion rather than to illustrate either effective or ineffective handling of an administrative situation.

lucrative European and Japanese markets, and boasted an existing network of pipelines and refineries capable of serving Western Europe. Finally, investment in Russian oil seemed relatively free of the currency constraints that dogged other potential investments, since oil exports could presumably be priced and sold in hard currency.

By the middle of the 1990s, however, a string of unforeseen events had significantly increased the risks of doing any business in Russia. The economy was in a shambles, the political situation remained unsettled, and, under nationalist pressure, the Yeltsin government had passed measures that taxed foreign-owned ventures nearly to the point of bankruptcy. The environment was particularly hostile for oil companies, which faced an onerous tax on export revenues. Still the sheer size of Russia's oil reserves and the oligopolistic structure of the international oil industry made it difficult for any Western firm to ignore Russia completely. Instead they ventured with varying degrees of caution, some anxious to grab the advantages of being first movers, others willing to exchange a smaller piece of the prize for a higher level of certainty. In all their calculations, though, the Western oil firms faced a common and generic, even if extreme, dilemma: how to balance the potential for very high reward with the possibility of very high risk. And in choosing their strategies, they all sought some means of defining and then hedging this risk.

The Russian Oil Industry

The petroleum industry in Russia dates from 1870, when the czarist regime recognized the market potential of the lands around the Caspian Sea and opened the entire area to competitive private enterprise. Because Russian industry at this time lagged significantly behind its Western counterparts, the first large-scale entrepreneurs were foreigners, who came to the region of Baku to develop the oil fields and export their production to serve a growing world demand. The Rothschilds and the Nobels built their fortunes in this way, as did Shell, which began as a trade and transportation company for Russian crude. By the turn of the century, Russian oil was a major factor in the world market. The state, however, remained largely aloof from the fields, intervening only to collect taxes from the foreign ventures.

This cozy relationship ended in 1905, when strikes in the Caucasus threw the oil fields into turmoil and launched the ill-fated Revolution of 1905. Subsequent discoveries in Kazakhstan and the Urals reignited Western interest in Russia but, for the most part, foreign investors began to pull out of the country, eager to cut their dependence on what was quickly becoming an unstable and uncertain supply. Between 1904 and 1913, Russia's share of world petroleum exports dropped from 31% to 9%.[1] By the time the Bolsheviks seized power in 1917, the foreigners were virtually gone, and Russian oil came under the sole direction of the state. It remained there for the next 70 years.

Oil in the Soviet Union

As with nearly all industries, oil in the Soviet Union was centrally controlled and hierarchically organized. Responsibility for the industry was divided among several ministries—Oil, Geology, and Pipelines—each of which handled its own segment of the production process and was rewarded on the basis of quantity. Thus, the Ministry of Geology and the regional geological

---

1. Daniel Yergin, *The Prize* (New York: Simon & Schuster, 1991), p. 133.

associations tried to maximize the volume of reserves discovered; while the Oil Ministry and its local subsidiaries, known as production associations, tried to maximize the production of crude petroleum. Costs and profits did not enter anywhere into the calculations, since inputs were allocated and prices set by the central planning agencies. Through yet another agency the Soviet state also controlled oil exports, which were critical to the country's balance of payments and its hard currency receipts. Throughout most of the post-war period, petroleum and gas accounted for roughly 90% of the Soviet Union's exports, and allowed the state to purchase the imported foodstuffs on which it increasingly depended.

The structure of this system—hierarchical authority, conflicting goals, and split responsibility—pushed the oil industry inevitably towards inefficiency and over-production. Since volume rather than efficiency was measured, officials tended to overestimate their output and stretch their resources to the breaking point. This tendency became even more pronounced whenever price shifts or bad harvests compelled the central authorities to sell more oil on world markets. Vast discoveries in western Siberia had eased this pressure somewhat in the mid-1960s, but by the 1970s a continuation of standard Soviet practices had reduced yields there as well. With an abandon unheard of in the West, Soviet managers would repeatedly drill new wells rather than repair existing ones, and flood oil fields with untreated water to push the oil flows as high and as fast as possible.[2] By the mid-1980s, the combined effect of these practices was evident in Soviet production and export figures. Production of crude petroleum, for example, fell from nearly 12 million barrels per day in 1983 to 8.4 million in 1992, while exports fell from 2.6 million to 1.4 million.[3]

Simultaneously, the political structure of the Soviet Union was also rapidly unravelling.[4] With the ascension of Mikhail Gorbachev to power in 1985 the Soviet state entered the transition that would lead, ultimately, to its demise. In the process, the centrally-planned economy was dismantled and industries such as oil were revamped and restructured. More importantly, they were also re-opened to the outside world and permitted again to woo foreign investment.

Russian Oil in Transition

During this transitional period the structure of the Russian oil industry remained fluid, changing shape with the changing political priorities of the new government. Basically, though, the Russian industry retained the broad outlines of its Soviet predecessor. The Ministry of Ecology and Natural Resources controlled exploration for petroleum; the Ministry of Fuel and Energy oversaw production, transportation, and refining; and 32 production associations (PAs) were established to manage oil operations at the provincial level. In a more radical departure from past practices, the Russian government also founded five new companies—LUKoil, YUKOS, Surgutneftegaz, Sidanco, and Rosneft—that were designed to mirror and behave like vertically-integrated multinational energy firms.

---

2. The technique of water-flooding involves injecting water into certain wells to increase the pressure and thus the yields of crude petroleum. If properly engineered and applied, water flooding will increase oil recovery. If performed incorrectly, however, there may be a short term increase in production, but it will be followed by reservoir damage and actual decrease in ultimate reserves recovery.

3. Oil exports to the West have remained fairly stable. Most of the decline in total exports has come from sales to the former Soviet bloc and CIS countries. U.S. International Trade Commission, "Trade and Investment Patterns in the Crude Petroleum and Natural Gas Sectors of the Energy-Producing States of the Former Soviet Union," Investigation No. 332-338, Publication 2656, pp. 2-5 and 2-9. (Hereinafter cited as USITC Report)

4. For a detailed description of the political and economic situation that prevailed in Russia at this time, see Alexander Dyck, *Russia 94: The Death of a System?*, HBS Case No. 794-107.

To facilitate investment, meanwhile, the Russian government passed a series of new and fairly radical foreign investment laws.[5] The 1991 Law on Foreign Investment explicitly allowed for foreign participation in the exploration of natural resources, granting a legal right for joint ventures with 30% or greater foreign participation to export 100% of their oil, stipulating only that exploration and extraction licenses be granted on the basis of public bid or auction. It also pledged the "full and unconditional legal protection" of foreign investments.[6] In 1992, the Law on Mineral Resources formally ended the state's monopoly on resource development and instead ceded to local governments the right to develop and exploit their own subsoil reserves. The Russian government, however, retained ownership of all resources. The Law on Mineral Resources also laid out in considerable detail the procedures for obtaining exploration and extraction licenses, and divided the responsibility for licensing between federal and local authorities.[7]

The weight of legislation, however, did little to change the underlying conditions for investment. Russia remained a perilous place by nearly all measures, with an inchoate political system and a rapidly deteriorating economy. Both the Soviet Union and the Soviet bloc had splintered into their component states, leaving Russia in the midst of a now-defunct trading and distribution network. Outside Russia's borders, many of the republics were embroiled in violent ethnic conflicts, while inside the Russian mafia was becoming a ubiquitous and ruthless presence. The ruble, pegged at 1.8/$1 during the communist days plunged to 150/$1 at the beginning of 1992, and then to roughly 3261/$1 by late 1994. The collapse of the communist system, moreover, had not been as clean as it had been elsewhere in eastern Europe, nor as controlled as it was in China. Instead, the system simply disintegrated, leaving little but the mafia and a handful of emerging private businesses to take its place. As price controls were gradually removed, inflation soared, letting loose a flood of popular discontent that often painted capitalism and foreigners as the source of Russia's woes. One of the few sectors that retained price controls, moreover, was energy, meaning that domestic fuel prices remained far below their international level, and even below the cost of production.

Most troubling of all for potential investors was the general uncertainty that surrounded any business venture in Russia. Despite rapid attempts to create a Western-style legal framework, Russia's legal system remained underdeveloped, lacking any serious foundation of contract, property, or corporate law. There were laws, to be sure, and courts, and jails, but no Western investor could be confident of how the laws would be interpreted, or on what grounds legal decisions would be made. Similarly, the pace of change in the country had tremendously complicated the old hierarchies of control, leaving investors—and oftentimes even officials—unclear about who had real power. This uncertainty was compounded in industries like oil, where finding the appropriate licensing agency was often critical. Even if the proper official was located, moreover, contracts for natural resource investments were notoriously difficult to implement, since the law required foreign firms to have domestic partners, and the partners were either the state or a state agency.

---

5. A full review of all of the Russian legislation which affects foreign investment in the petroleum sector is beyond the scope of this paper. See "Russian property law, privatization, and the right of "full economic control," 107 *Harvard Law Review* 1044 (1994).

6. See "Law on Foreign Investments in the RSFSR," 1991, at article 6.

7. The law provides for five types of licenses: 5-year exploration licenses; 20-year extraction licenses; licenses for nonextractive uses; licenses for the protection of geological features; and licenses for the collection of mineral samples. See USITC, p. 3-2; and "Law of the Russian Federation on Sub-soil Resources," dated February 21, 1992, effective May 5, 1992, as amended June 26, 1992.

Uncertainty also plagued the Russian tax code which, to investors at least, seemed driven by politics and arbitrary decisions rather than any economic motivations. Taxes in Russia, particularly in the oil and gas sectors, changed quickly and unpredictably, and included a number of overlapping components such as exports, production, profits, inputs, social costs, and repatriation. At times, the total tax burden on a venture was so high as to undermine any hope of profit—or even, in some cases, of recouping initial capital investments. In 1993, for example, officials from the Russian Subcommittee on Taxation acknowledged that taxes absorbed roughly 52% of the gross *revenues* of petroleum projects.[8] Price Waterhouse estimated the burden to be even higher, accounting for fully 75% of revenues and assuring a *loss* of $45 on each ton of petroleum produced in Russia.[9]

What made these taxes particularly ironic was that Russia was desperate for investment in its petroleum sector. The fields were in disrepair and the Russian production associations lacked access to the technology and expertise they needed to improve their yields. In 1993, 32,000 oil wells stood abandoned, even while the Russian government was critically short of hard currency and the Russian economy kept plummeting downwards. To bring Russia's energy sector back to the production levels of 1988-89, the industry needed an initial capital investment of $25 billion, and subsequent injections of around $6-7 billion a year.[10] The only realistic source for this capital was foreign investors, and particularly the large western energy firms with an obvious interest in Russia's vast oil and gas reserves. But before these investors would come, they needed some means to protect themselves against the financial, political, and physical risks of doing business in Russia.

Opportunities and Constraints

Nearly since its creation, the oil industry had been international in scope. The largest firms, known generally as the "majors", ventured across the globe in search of new fields and in the hopes of bringing these fields under their sole control. Through a fluke of geography and development, the majors tended to be Western, while the world's largest reserves of crude petroleum were located elsewhere, primarily in the Middle East, Latin America, and Russia. To bridge this gap, the majors had developed early into vast and diversified firms, bringing the exploration, production, refining, and transportation functions into a vertically-integrated whole. The size of these firms and the capital they required tended to reduce their number and drive the industry towards an oligopolistic structure. While the collusion that had marked the industry in its earlier days was gone, the big oil firms remained linked by their common interest in a global commodity that was still relatively hard to find and acquire. These links were made even stronger by the looming presence of the OPEC cartel which, even in its weaker periods, had a tremendous impact on petroleum supplies and prices.

Russia's position in the global industry was complex. Merely by virtue of the size of its reserves, it had been a player in the industry since the late 19th century. Once the early Western investors left, however, Russia's participation in international markets had been limited to the exports regularly channeled through its state trading agency. While this agency generally played by the rules

---

8. Sergey Gorbachev, First Deputy Minister of Finance, Second annual Russian Oil Conference, "The Russian Oil Industry: Foreign Investment Opportunities," London, February 11-12, 1993, cited in USITC, p. 3-3.
9. Byron Ratliff, Director of Petroleum Services, Price Waterhouse, Second Annual Russian Oil Conference, cited in ibid.
10. Deutsche Bank estimates, published in *Focus: Eastern Europe*, Jan. 6, 1993, No. 66, p. 4.

of the international markets, and indeed often mimicked OPEC's price behavior, it was never really part of the global industry, and had no direct contact with the Western majors or service providers.

Once liberalization re-opened Russia to the outside world, therefore, it was virtually virgin territory for the oil firms, comparable in many ways to the earlier great discoveries in the Middle East and Africa. As in these territories, there was a tremendous incentive for each of the major firms to establish itself quickly in Russia, gaining control over the fields before its competitors could do likewise. Given the size and reputed productivity of the Siberian fields, the stakes were particularly high. If a firm did not invest in Russia, it risked being permanently excluded from one of the world's largest single sources of crude petroleum. In the highly competitive oil industry, this exclusion could leave a firm with a serious disadvantage—especially since most of the other large sources of crude were located in the perpetually unstable Middle East.

Balancing these potentially high rewards, however, were correspondingly high risks. Under the conditions that existed in Russia, any investment was vulnerable to arbitrary taxation and possibly even expropriation. Soaring inflation and a plummeting ruble compounded exchange rate risk and operating exposure, while the tenuous state of Russia's legal system threatened to render any contract moot. Under these conditions, oil companies contemplating a Russian investment faced three major choices:

·   Should they venture early into Russia, with all of its concomitant risks, or should they wait until some of the country's uncertainties were resolved?

·   If they decided to go, what kinds of deals would best enable them to reduce risk to an acceptable level?

·   Once the deal was structured, how could they bind their various partners to the necessary contracts and commitments?

As of 1994, Western oil firms had responded to these questions in a wide range of ways. Some jumped eagerly in, confident that the advantages of being first mover would, over time, outweigh the risks. Others waited by the sideline, fearful of being left out of the Russian game, yet unwilling to accept the level of risk it entailed. Still others tried to manage the process more directly, attempting to craft institutions and sanctions to compensate for their absence in Russia.

The three companies and strategies described below reveal the range of decisions that Western firms made. Taken together, they begin to suggest how firms approach risk in highly unstable environments, and how they can manage it to their best advantage.

Phibro Energy: First Mover's Advantage?

Phibro Energy Production, Inc. is a wholly owned subsidiary of Salomon Inc, the New York-based investment firm. In late 1981, Phibro Corporation, a large international commodities trading group, joined with Salomon to create the firm Phibro/Salomon. The friendly merger was designed in part to consolidate trading activities under Salomon's roof and use Phibro's cash flow to fuel Salomon's growth.

The strategy appeared to make great sense in the 1980s, as Salomon rose to become the leading stock underwriter in the United States. In late 1983, Phibro Energy, Inc. was formed as Salomon's energy trading arm and subsequently purchased a series of refineries in Louisiana and Texas. Then, in 1990, Phibro Energy focused its sights on the newly-opened Russian market and established Phibro Energy Production, Inc. ("Phibro") specifically to develop opportunities in Russia. If Phibro could enter the Russian market quickly, management calculated the company would gain both a significant source of crude petroleum and a key advantage over its larger rivals. With Russian oil, Phibro and Salomon could together build a web of oil transactions that extended from extraction, to refining, to the sale of oil futures.

Thus in November 1990, Phibro took the plunge. Together with the Russian state-owned production association Varyeganneftegaz ("VNG"), it formed the White Nights Joint Enterprise, a 50/50 Russian/American joint venture. The project, based in the Tyumen Region of Western Siberia, was granted licenses by the then Soviet government to develop and produce oil and gas reserves in three fields: Tagrinsk, West Varyegan and Roslavl. As one of the first major foreign oil joint ventures in the Soviet Union, White Nights received tremendous publicity in the international oil community and compelled other firms to hasten their own Russian involvement.

Financially, White Nights was established as a three-way partnership: VNG (50%); Phibro (45%); and Anglo-Suisse, Inc., a small Texas-based company, (5%). Technically, White Nights was conceived as a field development project, with Phibro providing capital to fund the services and technology required to boost yields in the existing fields and VNG providing the fields and attendant infrastructure. The partners negotiated a "decline curve", which plotted the expected production from the existing wells. Under the terms of the joint venture agreement, all oil "under the curve," would go to VNG, which would sell the oil to its traditional Russian customers and use the proceeds to reimburse Phibro for the costs of producing this "under the curve" oil. All oil "above the curve" would be exported and remaining after-cost proceeds divided among the venture's partners in accordance with their ownership interest.

From the start, Phibro's management was well aware of the risks that faced their venture. Most critically, in 1990, the Soviet Union still lacked a comprehensive legal and fiscal framework for foreign investment. Phibro's management, however, determined that the rules and regulations already in place, while less than ideal, were sufficiently adequate to proceed. Company executives also felt reasonably confident that the investment climate would improve along with the fast-evolving political climate of the time. To secure Phibro's long-term interests, moreover, White Nights was consciously structured to maximize the incentives for cooperation among the partners. Since VNG's profits came from its share of production in excess of the decline curve, its natural objective would be to expand output as much as possible. To do this, it would need the Western technology and management skills that Phibro could provide. Indeed, central to the agreement was the $40 million in capital which Phibro was committed to put up as the Western party's share of the venture's $80 million charter fund. It was envisioned that this $40 million capital infusion would be used to provide the advanced oilfield technology, services, and management skills which VNG lacked and which would allow White Nights to remain a viable joint venture for its full 25 year duration. Thus, both VNG and Phibro conceived of White Nights not as a terminal project, but as a long term partnership. If VNG wanted continued access to western technology for future projects, it would have a real incentive to do whatever was necessary to ensure the success of White Nights.

With this assurance, during 1991, Phibro committed $40 million in cash and VNG contributed $40 million in wells and infrastructure to the White Nights venture.

Early Setbacks

Shortly after White Nights began field operations in April 1991, the project encountered unexpected difficulties. The biggest problem was increased taxation. When the venture was formed in November 1990, it was subject to four taxes. By early 1992, however, the number of taxes had soared to a dozen, many of which were revenue-based, as opposed to the more benign profit-based taxes in effect at the outset. As a result, by the spring of 1992, White Nights was paying approximately 70% of its *gross revenue* in taxes to the Russian government, reducing its remaining cash receipts to an amount below actual production costs. The worst tax from White Nights' perspective was the export tax, levied at the arbitrary rate of 30 ECUs ($35) per metric ton (or approximately $5 per barrel).[11] Ostensibly, in accordance with a decree issued in July 1992, any foreign venture established prior to January 1992 was eligible for exemption from the export tax until it recouped the full amount of its initial investment. But despite repeated pleas by the foreign investment community, promises by the Russian government, and high-level bargaining between the U.S. and Russian governments, no producing foreign joint enterprise received an exemption under the 1992 Decree.

In addition to these tax and fiscal concerns, White Nights also ran into technical difficulties. To begin with, once operations were commenced in 1991, White Nights' two producing fields (Tagrinsk and West Varyegan) proved to be far less productive than the Russian geological surveys had indicated. In particular, recoverable reserves proved to be much lower than Phibro had been led to believe due to a combination of complex geology, overly-optimistic Russian reserve projections, low well productivity, and years of poorly conceived reservoir management. As a result, Phibro's original strategy of boosting output with expensive, advanced imported equipment operated by western crews did not make economic sense; the well production rates and reserves were simply not high enough to cover the costs. A second problem concerned VNG's domestic sales. As the Russian economy disintegrated, the state-owned enterprises found themselves locked into a system that no longer functioned. VNG was required by the state to sell oil to its traditional customers, most of whom were large state-owned refineries. But because these refineries were not being paid by their customers, they could no longer afford to pay VNG for their purchases, even at the extremely low, state-mandated prices that still prevailed in the market. As a result of these and other factors, the White Nights venture began running significant deficits, and Phibro was compelled to loan the project an additional $60 million beginning in late 1991. By the middle of 1992, the company braced itself for a potential $116-million pre-tax loss from the White Nights project.[12]

Staying the Course

Despite all these troubles, Phibro and Salomon remained committed to their Russian venture. The venture also began to show some signs of emerging from the Siberian morass. In June of 1992, White Nights exported its first full cargo of crude oil, and by mid-1993, Phibro had succeeded in boosting production at the venture by a third to over 26,000 barrels per day. More importantly, by negotiating a reduction in the decline curve in March 1994, the venture's exports—and thus Phibro's

---

11. The Export Tax, initially imposed at a rate of 33.8 ECUs/ton on January 1, 1992, fluctuated broadly throughout 1992 between 21 ECUs/ton and 48 ECUs/ton before settling at 30 ECUs/ton for 1993 and 1994.

12. *Petroleum Intelligence Weekly*, May 11, 1992.

potential ability to recoup its investment—eventually began to rise. As part of the renegotiation, White Nights also assumed from VNG all responsibility for domestic sales of below decline curve oil. Because White Nights was not tied into the network of old contracts that had bound VNG to the state-owned refineries, the venture's management felt confident that they would begin to receive payment for their local sales and, thus, that they could begin to reduce some of White Nights' accumulated debts.

On the political front, Phibro had also joined with other U.S. oil companies to exert pressure for an official exemption from the export tax. Chairman and CEO Brian Lavers, who had been recruited in mid-1992 following his retirement as Chairman of Shell Nigeria to restructure White Nights and make it profitable, remained guardedly optimistic. Like others involved in the Russian oil industry, Lavers found reassurance in a May 1994 decree that established a new procedure for exempting foreign ventures from the onerous export tax. Lavers also believed strongly that high-level lobbying by the U.S. Departments of Commerce, Energy, Treasury, and State, through the medium of the newly-established Gore-Chernomyrdin commission, would convince the Russian government that it was in its own best interest to remove the tax.[13] This confidence was rewarded when, by Decree 1611R of October 11, 1994, the Russian government exempted six western joint ventures from the export tax, including Phibro's White Nights project.

Mobil: Waiting by the Side

Founded in the late 19th century as the Standard Oil Company of New York, Mobil was one of the oldest and most influential players in the international oil market. In the 1920s, Mobil had been one of the first U.S. firms to enter the newly discovered oil fields of Iraq and in the mid-1940s it joined the American charge into Saudi Arabia. Over the years the company had diversified, extending its operations into all segments of the energy sector. In addition to its estimated reserves of 5.8 billions of barrels of oil,[14] Mobil also had significant refining and transportation facilities, and an international chain of service stations. Even at the production stage it was diversified, with massive gas fields supplementing its oil holdings.

From this vantage point, Mobil's enthusiasm for Russia was mixed from the start with a certain degree of caution. In 1988, the company's overriding objective was to cut costs, rather than increase reserves, especially in the face of sharply declining oil prices. Like many of the other majors, Mobil had discovered that exploration in the post-OPEC world was a trickier prospect, since increased oil production was keeping prices hovering at the $11-17/barrel mark. Below that, many exploration and development projects simply could not break even.

Thus, while Mobil was attracted by the huge reserves of Russia, and the potentially low costs of production, company executives were also reluctant to make any high risk investment in oil that they really did not need. And so, unlike Phibro, Mobil approached the Russian oil market with great caution. It sent investigative teams to Siberia, it established contacts within the Russian oil

---

13. U.S. Vice President Albert Gore and Russian Prime Minister Viktor S. Chernomyrdin signed a series of agreements on June 23, 1994 that established a major oil and gas exploration project by U.S. companies and called for joint development of a space station. The two parties also agreed to work together on various economic and environmental issues.
14. The figure actually measures oil and its equivalents.

bureaucracy; and it tendered, and lost, bids for several projects. But as of the summer of 1994 it had not made any significant investments in the Russian petroleum sector.

What Mobil had done was to reorganize the way in which it approached uncertain but promising areas of the world. In 1992, the company formed a new organizational unit, the Strategic Ventures Group, and charged it with exploring and developing new activities in the former Soviet Union, eastern Europe, Mexico, and Venezuela. Explicitly, Mobil's management recognized that the scope of business in these areas and the impact they could have on the global oil market was too large either to be ignored or to be handled within the customary corporate structure. So the decisions about whether and how to proceed in these high-risk/high-reward markets were spun off, directed, as Mobil's chairman and CEO described, towards the "hot pursuit of opportunities that may materialize."[15]

In Russia, however, the group moved slowly. Early in 1992, the company bid for a major exploration and production contract on Sakhalin Island in Russia's far east, but lost to the "3M" consortium of Mitsui, McDermott Engineering, and Marathon Oil. Soon thereafter, the Russian government asked the 3M group to consider including Mobil in the $10 billion project, but Mobil seemed in no great hurry to participate. Instead company officials reported that they were generally quite pessimistic about options in Russia, categorizing it as "one of the most politically risky countries in the world." Thus, even while acknowledging that there already was "not enough of the pie left to divide up," Mobil was content to wait.

Conoco: Crafting the Venture

In several respects, Conoco holds the middle ground between Phibro and Mobil. Whereas Mobil is one of the original majors and Phibro a recent entrant to the market, Conoco is part of the second tier of so-called independent firms, with a significant presence in the international oil market, but not the clout or network of a Mobil or Exxon. In Russia, it also chose a middle course, entering the country early but cautiously and committing to large projects while simultaneously trying to minimize its own financial exposure.

Conoco's involvement in the Soviet Union began late in 1989, when the company acquired several detailed geological studies and began to choose the most interesting targets for potential investment. It soon narrowed its focus to three projects—Shtockman, West Siberia, and Timan Pechora—and attached an in-house task force to each. It also decided even at this early stage to structure the projects as separate "subsidiaries" with "headquarters support" provided by a single administrative staff.

Once this basic structure was established, Conoco's management tried to outline some basic strategies for dealing with the vast uncertainties of Russia. For instance, rather than just accepting the technical and geological information provided by the Russians, Conoco sent its own team to re-evaluate and test potential production sites. Likewise, to ward off the possibility of Russian expropriation or breach of contract, the company began to think about increasing their own leverage in any project by providing equipment—particularly pipeline—that would not be easily available to

---

15. Allen Murray, cited in *Energy Economist*, March 1992.

its partners. And finally, in a fairly radical departure, it started to investigate outside sources of financing.

In plotting its actual involvement in Russia, Conoco adopted a conscious strategy of sequential investment, striving to gain experience and contacts in Russia before making any major or irreversible commitments. It began, therefore, with the Shtockman project, a joint venture between Conoco, Norsk Hydro—three Finnish companies—and the Soviet Ministry of Oil & Gas. The project itself was straightforward, designed to produce gas from existing wells and then construct a pipeline to transport the gas to European export markets. Conoco's financial involvement in the deal was limited, as was its downside risk. In Western Siberia, its second project, Conoco also moved cautiously, launching major studies of the region's production potential and putting the project on a timetable of contingent approvals. First came a joint Conoco/Soviet feasibility study, then a six-month period for consideration, and only then the creation of an official joint venture.

Only after these initial forays did Conoco shift its attention to its largest and most significant venture. In June 1992, it signed an agreement with its Russian partner Archangelskgeologia to establish a new joint venture named "Polar Lights." Located at the Arctic edge of the Timan-Pechora Basin, Polar Lights was considerably more ambitious than Conoco's earlier ventures, and indeed more ambitious than nearly any previous investment in the Russian oil sector. Unlike most earlier projects, Polar Lights was established in an area without any existing production capacity. The venture thus planned to design, build, and operate the total infrastructure that production would demand, for an ultimate cost of roughly $3 billion. To get even the initial phases of the project underway, Conoco and its partner needed to develop 24 drilling wells, install a central processing facility, and build a 37-mile pipeline capable of transporting 40,000 barrels a day of Russian oil. All of this was to occur, moreover, in a sparsely populated region with virtually no infrastructure and where temperatures regularly dropped to - 40 Fahrenheit. Despite these obstacles, and despite the sheer magnitude of Polar Lights, Conoco's management continued to see the venture as an experimental foray. As the company's CEO, Constantine Nicandros, explained, "We chose to participate in developing this relatively small field with two goals in mind" to use the project as a test case to learn whether or not we could successfully do business in Russia and, if we could, to use it as a platform for future investments."[16]

The magnitude of the deal also forced Conoco to experiment with ways of reducing the company's financial and economic exposure. First, the number of middlemen involved with the project was sharply limited. Polar Lights would itself control the flow of oil from the well-head to the shipment point and would also operate and finance the pipeline.[17] This control, presumably, would allow the venture to increase its leverage with the Russian government even while maintaining a healthy distance between Polar Lights and the Oil Ministry in Moscow. To increase it financial leverage and reduce its exposure meanwhile, Conoco went to great lengths to bring outside partners into the venture. It sought the active involvement of multilateral and U.S. government lending institutions and successfully lobbied the European Bank for Reconstruction and Development (EBRD) for a $90 million loan. The International Finance Corporation put up another $60 million, and the Overseas Private Investment Corporation an additional $50 million. Under the terms of the agreement, all partners to the venture would receive cash through the declaration of dividends by the Board of Founders, composed of Conoco and Russian members. By using institutional funds, Conoco clearly increased the pressure for production and hard currency revenues. But it also subtly changed the

---

16. Constantine S. Nicandros, "The Russian Investment Dilemma," *Harvard Business Review*, May-June 1994, p. 40.
17. See D. Schlegel, "Joint Venture Gets $200 million in Loans to Develop Russian Oil Field" (1993).

stakes of the Russian game. Once the international institutions were involved, the costs of violation, or even excessive intervention, rose higher, since lending institutions have much greater clout than any individual company. Or as Randall Fischer of the EBRD described: "The Bank has certain rights, most importantly to close the window on further operations with that country."

Moving Ahead

In 1994, it was still too early to predict the ultimate fate of Conoco's Polar Lights venture. On one hand, Polar Lights was being heralded as one of the most exciting and well-conceived forays into post-communist Russia. On the other hand, though, the same problems that had plagued Phibro and other Western investors were beginning to loom.

The taxation issue, for instance, remained painfully unresolved. Although Conoco had ultimately negotiated a formal exemption from Russia's onerous export tax, it was not clear whether, and for how long, the exemption would prove acceptable to the Subcommittee on Taxation. Moreover any significant increase in other taxes—on revenues, wages, or the like—could also jeopardize the project's future, especially at a time when oil prices remained stubbornly fixed at $11-17 a barrel.

Meanwhile, even though production at Polar Lights had been slated to begin in 1994, Conoco's management was still wrestling with its partner and a host of Russian authorities over the details of its contractual terms. Negotiations were proceeding amicably for the most part, but many issues remained still unresolved. Export licenses, for instance, which were critical to the venture's commercial success, were being held up in Moscow, and the basic infrastructure at the fields remained wholly inadequate. Late in 1992, moreover, a little-known environmental group had brought suit against the Russian government, charging that it had undermined the national interest in approving the Polar Lights project. While the suit was subsequently dismissed, it created an air of uncertainty, and prompted even the chief engineer of Archangelskgeologia to complain that, "Patience is running out. If the Americans, after investing a bundle of money in the project, see that no work can be done this winter, they'll give up and go home."[18] Conoco had also suffered a blow in its Shtockman project: after the consortium had spent tens of millions of dollars surveying the region, the Russian government had summarily awarded the production concession to a hastily-assembled Russian group. Conoco and its partners received no compensation for their efforts.[19] In the summer of 1994, CEO Nicandros broke from his customary enthusiasm to characterize the Russian investment climate as "one of complete disarray."[20]

To settle this disarray, Nicandros and other investors continued to stress the importance of a strong and transparent legal framework. Along with representatives from Western governments and lending institutions, they lobbied Russia's fledgling government to pass legislation that would clearly define the financial and legal basis for investment in the petroleum sector and create some mechanism for resolving disputes. In the summer of 1994, many industry insiders thought the legislation was only months or weeks away from passage.

But then in August, Russian President Boris Yeltsin dismissed the draft law under consideration by the parliament, claiming that the document revealed an "anti-reform approach".

---

18. Quoted in Vasily Zakharko, "World 'Shark" is Near," *Izvestia*, December 17, 1992, p. 7. Reprinted in *The Current Digest*, vol XLIV, no. 50 (1992), p. 23.
19. *Economist*, "Russia's Cold Shoulder", March 13, 1993, pp. 73-74.
20. Nicandros, p. 40.

Yeltsin argued that the existing legislation on mineral resources was specific enough to make any new law redundant. In interpreting this unexpected move, the *Financial Times* wrote: "Mr. Yeltsin's dismissal of the draft law, and his evident reluctance to propose an alternative, suggests he would prefer this area, as others, to be regulated by his decree."[21]

---

21. John Lloyd, "Yeltsin Dismisses Draft Law to Build Up Oil Investment," *Financial Times*, August 5, 1994, p. 2.

Exhibit 1   Major Oil Fields in the former Soviet Union

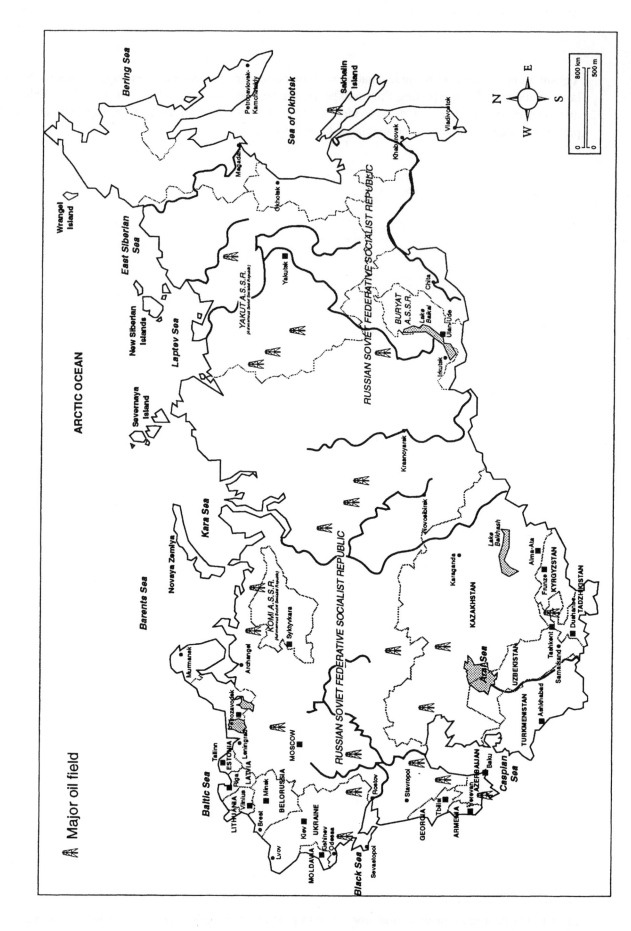

Exhibit 2   Structure of the former Soviet Union's Petroleum and Natural Gas Industries

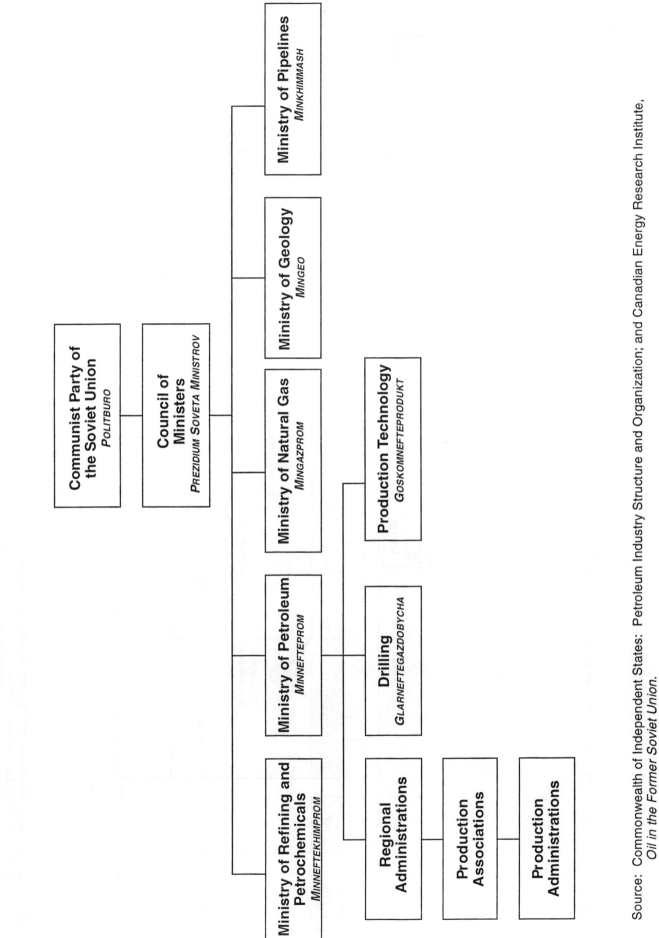

Source: Commonwealth of Independent States: Petroleum Industry Structure and Organization; and Canadian Energy Research Institute, *Oil in the Former Soviet Union.*

Exhibit 3   Structure of the Russian Petroleum and Natural Gas Industries

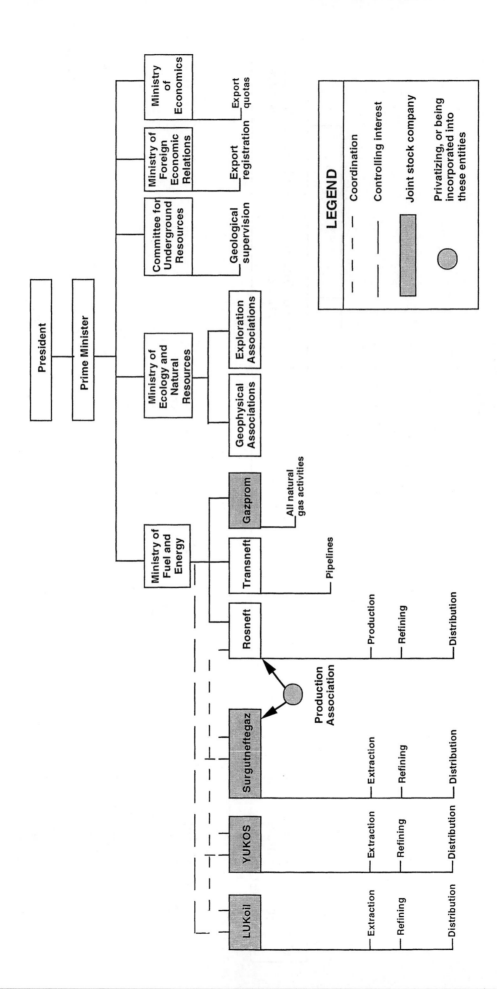

Source: Commonwealth of Independent States: Petroleum Industry Structure; Canadian Energy Research Institute, *Oil in the Former Soviet Union*; and Interfax-America. *Petroleum Report*.

Exhibit 4   World Crude Oil Production and Consumption, 1970-1992 (millions of barrels per day)

	1970	1975	1980	1985	1986	1987	1988	1989	1990	1991	1992
World Production	45.7	53.3	59.3	53.3	55.5	55.7	57.8	59.0	59.7	59.4	59.5
World Consumption	47.4	56.0	62.6	60.1	61.8	63.2	65.0	66.1	66.3	66.7	66.9

Source: Cambridge Energy Research Associates and Arthur Andersen & Co., World Oil Trends 1994, pp. 10, 24.

Exhibit 5   Average Prices of Crude Oil, 1970-1992 (US$ per barrel)

	Mideast Light		Brent	WII	U.S. Average
	Official	Spot	Spot	Spot	Wellhead
1970	1.35	1.21	NA	NA	3.18
1971	1.75	1.69	NA	NA	3.39
1972	1.90	1.82	NA	NA	3.39
1973	2.64	2.81	NA	NA	3.89
1974	9.56	10.98	NA	NA	6.87
1975	10.46	10.43	NA	NA	7.67
1976	11.51	11.63	NA	NA	8.19
1977	12.40	12.57	NA	NA	8.57
1978	12.70	12.91	NA	NA	9.00
1979	17.84	29.19	NA	NA	12.61
1980	29.38	36.01	NA	NA	21.61
1981	33.20	34.17	NA	NA	31.77
1982	33.77	31.76	NA	NA	28.52
1983	29.23	28.67	NA	NA	26.19
1984	28.75	28.10	NA	NA	25.88
1985	28.08	27.45	27.33	27.92	24.08
1986	28.00	13.33	14.56	15.14	12.60
1987	17.60	17.33	18.34	19.16	15.42
1988	17.52	13.40	14.94	16.01	12.57
1989	17.52	16.21	18.22	19.61	16.28
1990	17.52	20.71	23.39	24.30	19.98
1991	17.52	17.45	20.07	21.55	16.53
1992	17.52	17.86	19.28	20.52	16.00

Source: Cambridge Energy Research Associates and Arthur Andersen & Co., World Oil
          Trends 1994, p. 48.

Exhibit 6   Share of Crude Petroleum Production in the former Soviet Union, 1991

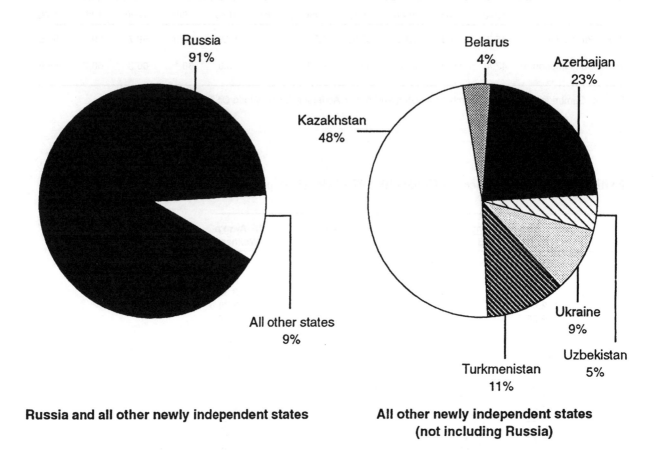

Russia and all other newly independent states   **All other newly independent states
(not including Russia)**

Source: U.S. Department of Energy, Policy Office

Exhibit 7 Comparison of Crude Petroleum Production in the United States, former Soviet Union, and World (1982–92) (1,000 barrels per day)

Year	United States	Former Soviet Union	World
1982	8,649	11,912	53,481
1983	8,688	11,972	53,255
1984	8,879	11,861	54,488
1985	8,971	11,585	53,981
1986	8,680	11,895	56,227
1987	8,349	11,985	56,601
1988	8,140	11,978	58,662
1989	7,613	11,625	59,773
1990	7,355	10,880	60,471
1991	7,417	9,887	60,221
1992	7,153	8,354	60,141

Source: U.S. Department of Energy, Policy Office.

Exhibit 8   Former Soviet Union Imports and Exports of Crude Petroleum and Natural Gas, 1982-92 (1,000 barrels per day)

Year	Crude Petroleum		Natural Gas	
	Imports	Exports	Imports	Exports
1982	100	2,500	80	2,240
1983	140	2,600	80	2,185
1984	264	2,509	80	2,312
1985	262	2,275	105	2,510
1986	240	2,450	105	2,778
1987	291	1,684	78	2,973
1988	396	2,826	78	3,140
1989	167	2,554	36	3,618
1990	271	2,170	54	3,935
1991	0	1,215	NA	3,677
1992	0	1,390	NA	3,500

Source: Official statistics of the U.S. Department of Energy, Interfax *Petroleum Report*, and *Petroleum Intelligence Weekly*.

Exhibit 9   Relationship of the former Soviet Union's Crude Petroleum Exports to Aggregate World Petroleum Prices, 1982-1992

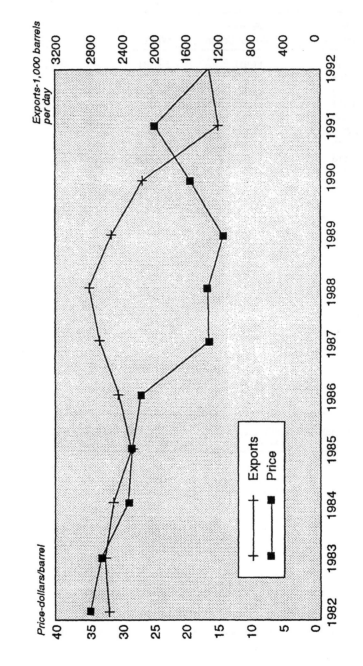

Source: U.S. Department of Energy

Exhibit 10   Development Cost Profile for Western Siberia, 1992

	10M Barrels	60M Barrels	350M Barrels	1,000M Barrels
Gross Cost (US$ millions)				
Drilling	34	67	146	232
Facilities	48	110	401	868
Pipeline	45	50	56	66
Operations	63	221	851	2,121
Tariffs	11	70	408	1,165
TOTAL	198	517	1,862	4,453
Per Barrel Cost (US$)				
Drilling	3.55	1.05	0.39	0.22
Facilities	4.77	1.73	1.08	0.82
Pipeline	4.69	0.78	0.15	0.06
Operations	6.54	3.49	2.30	2.00
Tariff	1.10	1.10	1.10	1.10
TOTAL	20.66	8.15	5.03	4.21

Source: Spears and Associates.

Exhibit 11   Location of White Night Fields

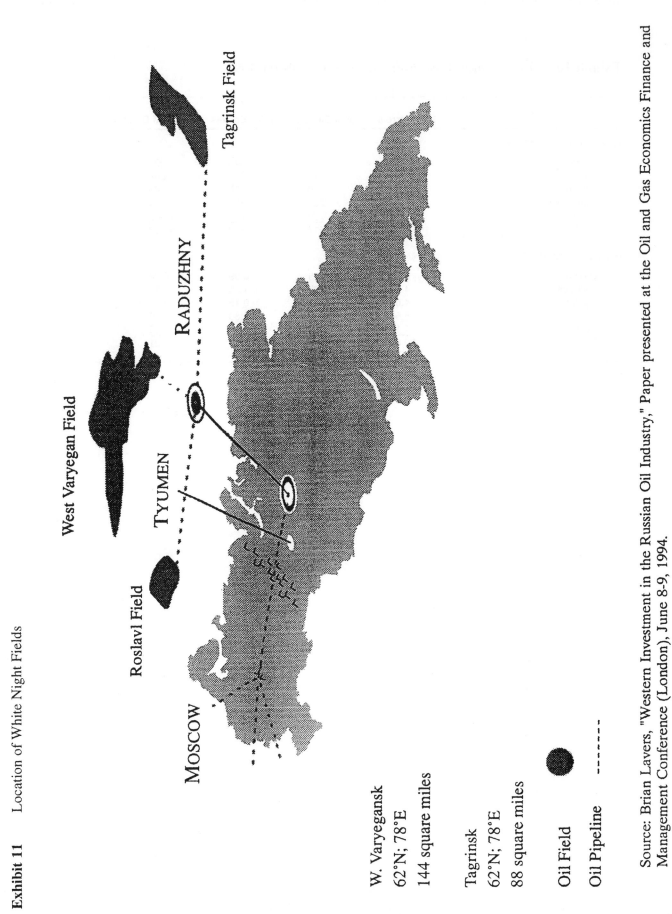

W. Varyegansk
62°N; 78°E
144 square miles

Tagrinsk
62°N; 78°E
88 square miles

Oil Field

Oil Pipeline   - - - - - - -

Source: Brian Lavers, "Western Investment in the Russian Oil Industry," Paper presented at the Oil and Gas Economics Finance and Management Conference (London), June 8-9, 1994.

Exhibit 12   White Nights Production

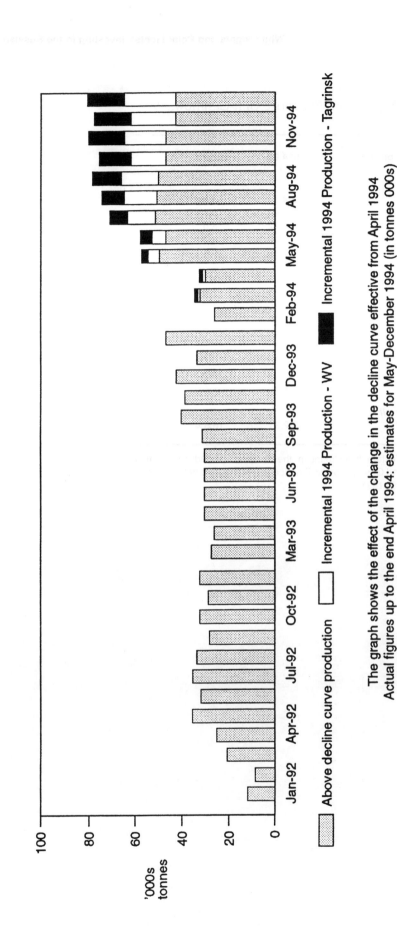

The graph shows the effect of the change in the decline curve effective from April 1994
Actual figures up to the end April 1994: estimates for May-December 1994 (in tonnes 000s)

Source: Brian Lavers, "Western Investment in the Russian Oil Industry," Paper presented at the Oil and Gas Economics Finance and Management Conference (London), June 8-9, 1994.

Exhibit 13   White Nights Joint Enterprise Unit Cashflow, 1994

Urals Blend (Revenue per barrel)	**$14.00**	**100.0%**
Taxes:		
Export tax	$ 4.74	33.9%
Excise tax	1.44	10.3
Mineral usage tax	1.12	8.0
Resource renewal tax	0.60	4.3
Road use tax	0.06	0.4
VAT on pipeline fees	0.58	4.1
Social and accommodation tax	0.21	1.5
Property and land tax (est.)	0.20	1.4
Payroll-related taxes (est.)	0.16	1.2
Excess payroll tax (est.)	0.09	0.7
Total taxes	$ 9.19	65.7%
Pipeline costs (est.)	$ 2.50	17.9
Sales commission (est.)	0.09	0.7
Net remaining revenue for _all_ operating and capital costs	**$ 2.31**	**16.5%**

Source: Brian Lavers, "Western Investment in the Russian Oil Industry," paper presented at Oil and Gas Economics Finance and Management Conference (London), June 8-9, 1994.

Exhibit 14   Financial Highlights, 1991-1994 (US$ millions)

	1991	1992	1993	1994
Mobil Corporation				
Revenues from sales and services	62,359	63,564	63,474	66,757
Crude oil, products & operating				
supplies and expenses	35,735	36,639	35,622	36,665
Exploration expense	779	507	405	516
SG&A expenses	4,944	5,324	5,483	5,453
Interest and related income (expense)	155	(280)	177	165
Net income (loss)	1,920	862	2,084	1,079
Total assets	42,187	40,561	40,733	41,542
Current liabilities	13,602	12,629	12,351	13,418
Total liabilities	24,653	24,021	23,496	24,396
E.I. du Pont and Company (Conoco)				
Revenues	38,695	37,799	37,098	39,333
Cost of goods sold	22,528	21,856	21,396	21,977
Exploration expense	602	416	361	357
Research & development expense	1,298	1,277	1,132	1,047
SG&A expenses	3,576	3,553	3,081	2,888
Interest and related income (expense)	76	(90)	149	367
Net income (loss)	1,403	(3,927)	555	2,727
Total assets	36,559	38,870	37,053	36,892
Current liabilities	7,935	10,226	9,439	7,565
Total liabilities	19,655	26,928	25,636	23,873
Salomon Inc				
Revenues	9,175	8,183	8,799	6,278
Interest expense	5,638	4,324	4,600	4,892
Total non-interest expenses	2,618	2,803	2,734	2,217
Net income (loss)	507	550	827	(399)
Total assets	97,402	159,459	184,835	172,732
Short-term borrowings	40,393	88,417	97,890	78,579
Total liabilities	93,387	155,151	179,589	168,240

Source: Company annual reports.

Harvard Business School

9-798-022
September 17, 1997

Note on Political Risk Analysis

Politics are almost as exciting as war and quite as dangerous. In war, you can only be killed once, but in politics many times.

—Winston Churchill

Political risk is a broad and diffuse concept that sits at the intersection of politics, economics, sociology, and finance. It refers, essentially, to the possibility that political decisions or events in a particular country will cause foreign investors there either to lose money or fail to capture their expected returns. Definitionally, political risk is held distinct from the more straightforward concept of economic risk. Whereas economic risk arises from the inability of a country or firm to meet its financial obligations, political risk arises from the vagaries of governmental action: from policy changes, leadership changes, nationalization of private property, expropriation of foreign holdings, civil strife, currency inconvertibility, or even war. Whenever policy decisions or political events can affect the profitability of foreign investments, political risk exists.

At some level, therefore, political risk always exists. Governments can always change tax policy, or investment regulation, or import restrictions. But some kinds of risk are inherently more dangerous. These are the risks -- of war, expropriation, nationalization and currency incovertibility·-- that have historically been most closely associated with political risk analysis and the political risk industry.[1]

Political Risk Analysis: Evolution of an Industry

Conceptually, the notion of political risk is nearly as old as the practice of international trade and investment.[2] Early traders were frequently caught by the political events that surrounded them, and early investors -- such as the Dutch or British East India Companies -- were constantly embroiled

---

[1]For a more complete description of these risks, see Jeffrey D. Simon, "A Theoretical Perspective on Political Risk," *Journal of International Business Studies*, Winter 1984.

[2]For more on the background and evolution of political risk, see Thomas L. Brewer, "Politics, Risks, and International Business," in Thomas L. Brewer, ed., *Political Risks in International Business: New Directions for Research, Management, and Public Policy* (New York: Praeger Publishers, 1985); Dan Haendel, *Foreign Investments and the Management of Political Risk* (Boulder, CO: Westview Press, 1979); James E. Austin and David B. Yoffie, "Political Forecasting as a Management Tool," *Journal of Forecasting*, no. 3, 1984; Jose de la Torre, "Forecasting Political Risks for International Operations," *International Journal of Forecasting*, no. 4, 1988; and Thomas E. Krayenbuehl, *Country Risk: Assessment and Monitoring* (Cambridge: Woodhead-Faulker, 1985).

Heidi Deringer MBA '97 and Jennifer Wang, MBA '97 prepared this note under the supervision of Professor Debora Spar. It draws in part on additional research conducted by Michelle Freyre, Joanne Lawrence, and Lider Sucre, all MBA '97.

in political conflict and outright violence. For centuries, indeed, international trade and investment were but subsets of international politics, and political risk dominated commercial activity.

In the modern era, however, the spheres of business and government have pulled further apart, leaving political risk as a separate area of commercial concern. No longer the dominant force in international business, it is instead a threat, or possibility, that impinges on certain aspects of international trade and investment. And firms have had to develop means for incorporating the analysis of such threats and possibilities into their core business functions.

Some of the first firms to deal explicitly with the modern practice of political risk were the oil multinationals. At the turn of the twentieth century, the scramble to discover new sources of oil led these firms to far-flung corners of the world -- to places like Saudi Arabia, Russia, Venezuela and Iran where the political environment was often raw and highly volatile. Because the extraction of oil was such an expensive enterprise and so crucial to these countries' economic livelihoods, the oil companies often found themselves hostage to dramatic political shifts: revolution and a communist takeover in the oil fields of the Caspian Sea; expropriation in Mexico; the growth of nationalism (and subsequent threat of nationalization) in Venezuela, Saudi Arabia and Iran.[3] Initially, the oil companies met these political risks with political responses. They enlisted the services of their home governments and lobbied for specific countermeasures, even occasionally including military force. Over time, however, the oil companies drew back from the use of such crude political tools. As they diversified operations around the world and watched the budding power of previously passive regimes, they began to focus on means of predicting political risk rather than just responding to it.

By the middle of the century, a host of new multinationals faced similar pressures and analytical demands. Feeling their way into unaccustomed markets, firms like Ford, General Electric and Unilever were eager to sidestep any political pitfalls that might await them. And so, like the oil companies, they began to develop in-house capabilities for risk analysis. They sent executives on reconnaissance missions, contacting local leaders and building ties with business and political elites. They asked specific questions and examined the particular aspects of a target market that were most likely to affect their own business prospects. This method of gathering information became known as the *Grand Tours* approach.[4] It gave managers hands-on exposure to the environment of their target markets and a focussed, high-level point of contact and inquiry. It was also an entirely subjective approach to risk, and a serious drain on management time.

In 1959, the efficacy of the *Grand Tours* approach was brought into sharp relief by the events following the Cuban revolution. After Fidel Castro seized control of the government, his communist regime nationalized all foreign investment. Few U.S. firms invested in Cuba had predicted this possible chain of events; not a single one had taken out insurance to protect its investments. Consequently, Castro's nationalization cost U.S. firms an estimated $1.5 billion in assets. In the aftermath, most firms argued that the events in Cuba were anomalous, a one-time episode that could not have been predicted or avoided. They defended their standard methods of risk analysis and their reliance on internal, subjective assessments.

In the 1960s and early 1970s, however, a wave of expropriations forced multinational firms to reconsider the magnitude of political risk and the methods of its assessment. Just as multinationals were expanding their presence across the developing world, governments in these countries turned increasingly towards authoritarian and strongly nationalistic regimes. Emerging often from decades or even centuries of colonial rule, many developing countries were wracked by political instability and sharp ideological shifts. Even in countries that had long been independent, political sentiment

---

[3]For more on the political history of the oil industry, see Debora L. Spar and Richard H. K. Vietor, "Controlling International Oil (A): The Seven Sisters," Harvard Business School case no. 9-795-065. The standard account is Daniel Yergin, *The Prize* (New York: Simon & Schuster, 1991).
[4]This label, along with the subsequent *Old Hands*, comes from R. J. Rummel and David A. Heenan, "How Multinationals Analyze Political Risk," *Harvard Business Review*, January/February 1978.

commonly reflected an antagonism toward the developed countries and their disproportionate hold over political and economic power. Foreign investors became a focus for much of these countries' discontent, and foreign assets were repeatedly subject to confiscations and nationalizations. When the oil shock of 1973 dramatically increased the value of foreign-owned extraction and refining operations, these assets became especially vulnerable to expropriation. In 1971, about 75 percent of the non-communist world's crude oil production was managed by the seven largest international oil companies, and the remaining 25 percent was split equally among other private oil firms and government entities. By 1980, the foreign governments' share had increased to over 50 percent.[5] A particularly painful chain of events occurred in Iran, where Islamic fundamentalists overthrew the Shah in 1979. U.S. businesses, which had long viewed the Shah as a powerful and tenacious ally, suffered almost $1 billion in losses. These losses capped what appeared to be a persistent and growing trend: between 1960 and 1979, governments in 79 countries had expropriated the property of 1,660 firms.[6] Casualties were particularly high in resource-intensive industries, as well as in newly-revolutionary states such as Nicaragua and El Salvador.

In the wake of these developments, managers at many multinational firms began to reconsider the means by which they evaluated political risk. Increasingly, they deemed the *Grand Tours* method insufficient for understanding the range of risks that surrounded them and turned to develop new analytical tools. One tool, dubbed the *Old Hands* approach, involved supplementing in-house scouts with outside "experts," such as former diplomats, consultants, academics, journalists and governmental officials. Some firms internalized these outsiders; Mobil Oil, for example, appointed former U.S. ambassador Christian Herter, Jr., as its Vice President of Governmental Affairs, and Citibank named Irving Friedman, formerly of the International Monetary Fund, as its senior advisor for international operations.[7] Most companies, though, employed these sources on a contract basis, hiring particular experts to review risk profiles for the countries they knew best.

Before long, the demand for these expert services blossomed into the new industry of political risk analysis. Bearing such names as Control Risks and International Reporting Information Systems, these firms sold formal political risk assessment (PRA) services to multinational clients. While packages varied, most PRA providers offered global rankings and some level of prediction. They summarized political developments around the world, highlighted political trends and sensitivities, and evaluated the relative stability of national governments. By the early 1980s, with firms sprouting rapidly around such obvious corporate centers as New York, London, and Washington, D.C., political risk analysis was a growth industry.

Models and Methods

During their heyday, PRA firms developed two distinct modes of analysis, quantitative and qualitative. Quantitative analysis was primarily the terrain of think tanks and academic groups, relative newcomers to the world of political risk. Qualitative analysis remained the purview of country experts, bolstered now by more sophisticated methods and a permanent corporate status.

Quantitative analyses of political risk assumed, essentially, that political events manifest themselves in a discernible pattern. By registering the frequency of various discrete events, analysts could calculate the political stability of a particular country and the likelihood that various destabilizing events -- such as demonstrations, strikes, armed insurgencies, or constitutional changes

---

[5]Emmett Dedmon, *Challenge and Response: A Modern History of Standard Oil Company (Indiana)* (Chicago: The Mobium Press, 1984) p. 226.
[6]Study done by Stephen Kobrin, cited in "Insuring Against Risk Abroad," *Business Week*, September 14, 1981, p. 62.
[7]R.J. Rummel and David A. Heenan, "How Multinationals Analyze Political Risk," *Harvard Business Review*, January - February 1978, p. 69.

-- would occur. One example of such an approach was the Political System Stability Index (PSSI), created in 1974 to provide an "empirical, indicator-based measure of political system stability." Using time-series data and wholly quantifiable indicators, PSSI analysts assessed a series of political factors, including ethnolinguistic fractionalization, irregular chief executive changes, and government crises. Relative levels were assigned to each of these factors and then used to create three equally-weighted indices: Socioeconomic Characteristics Index, Governmental Process Index, and Societal Conflict Index. These indices could then be compared across countries to judge relative degrees of political risk.[8]

By contrast, qualitative analyses of political risk generally included explicitly subjective assessments. Rather than counting events or other discretely quantifiable factors, qualitative approaches relied on the perceptions and judgments of country experts. Such assessments did not imply a lack of numbers; in fact, many qualitative risk services provided the same kind of numerical indices as their quantitative counterparts. They differed only in the methodology by which their indices and rankings were compiled. While specific approaches varied, most qualitative analyses were based on the Delphi technique, which used expert panels to generate forecasts. At Political Risk Services, for example, William Coplin and Michael O'Leary developed what became known as the Prince system, a political forecasting model that generated 18-month and 5-year risk forecasts for three different business models: financial transfer, direct investment, and export market. To compile these forecasts, PRS subjected each country in its survey to the analysis of three to seven country specialists, each of whom worked on a part-time basis and drew on previous experience in government, consulting, or academia. After each specialist had provided an independent response to a series of questions, PRS aggregated their answers into a common projection and assigned risk levels to each country or regime under consideration.[9] Other qualitative services, such as Henry Kissinger's Kissinger Associates or the British-based Control Risks, relied entirely on "expert" analyses, and drew many of their experts from either the diplomatic corps or intelligence agencies. Between 1977 and 1980, more than 20 retiring CIA agents reportedly took positions with political risk consulting firms.[10]

Both the qualitative and quantitative methods offered corporate managers what many had been seeking.   They offered tangible risk assessments and a purported ability to predict dangerous political developments.[11] According to one manager at Xerox, these outside assessments served as a "safety net" for internal managers, a way to corroborate their own political judgments and protect themselves against unforeseen occurrences.[12] With the heightened level of corporate concern about political risk, and an expanding multinational presence in overseas markets, the demand for PRA services multiplied rapidly in the late 1970s and early 1980s. The resulting proliferation of firms generated even more publicity for the industry, which further fueled management's awareness of the topic. Some corporations went so far as to develop discrete in-house PRA staffs and systems, specialized assessment processes that they typically used in conjunction with outside analyses. Dow Chemical, for example, established its own Economic, Social, and Political (ESP) Risk Assessment Program. Using the program, Dow managers would conduct a series of standardized interviews and analyses, determine the key issues that prevailed in a given country, and then develop scenarios and probabilities for a five-year time frame.[13] Likewise, to assist its managers in planning for international expansion, American Can developed an inhouse computer program known as PRISM

[8]Dan Haendel, Gerald T. West, and Robert G. Meadow, *Overseas Investment and Political Risk* (Philadelphia: The Foreign Policy Research Institute, 1975), pp. 61-72.
[9]Llewellyn Howell and Brad Chaddick, "Models of Political Risk in Foreign Investment," *Columbia Journal of World Business*, Fall 1994, pp. 84-89.
[10]See Peter H. Stone, "Boom Days for Political Risk Consultants," *New York Times*, August 7, 1983, p. 23.
[11]See Jeffrey Simon, "Political Risk Forecasting," *Futures*, April 1985, p. 134. For an excellent description of how managers at this time tended to employ political risk assessments, see Stephen J. Kobrin, *Managing Political Risk Assessment: Strategic Response to Environmental Change* (Berkeley: University of California Press, 1982).
[12]Cited in Stone, p. 23.
[13]See Stephen J. Kobrin, "Political Assessment by International Firms: Models or Methodologies?" *Journal of Policy Modeling*, vol. 3, no. 2, 1981, pp. 251-270.

(Primary Risk Investment Screening Matrix) which distilled 200 country variables into general ratings for economic desirability and political stability.[14]

Decline of Risk Analysis

For roughly 10 years, the political risk analysis industry flourished. But by the late 1980s, the fervor surrounding PRA had faded. Many multinational corporations disbanded their formal corporate political risk assessment functions and cut back significantly on their use of formal risk services.

Several factors contributed to this apparent, and rather sudden, decline. First, as corporate managers extended their use of political risk analysis, they increasingly realized the difficulties that were inherent in the exercise. No matter how they structured the information flow between the risk analysts and top management, serious gaps remained. The analysts (whether inside the firm or contracted externally) had limited information about the precise decisions and criteria facing the firm, and the decision makers were left floundering through material that was often too abstract, too general, and too far removed from their daily activities.[15] Over time, many senior managers came to view risk analysis as an "ivory tower exercise," rooted in academic theory rather than managerial practice.[16]

By the 1990s, the novelty of international expansion had faded as well. Most firms already had sizeable overseas operations and a growing familiarity with foreign markets. They were also, increasingly, making more subtle and diffuse decisions. Rather than choosing a single location for an overseas plant, or, like the oil companies, contemplating extremely expensive, in-the-ground investments, the new breed of multinational — diversified manufacturing firms or service providers — had to make decisions concerning a string of foreign affiliates and a less concentrated asset structure. Their concerns were different because their business models and levels of exposure were different. These firms were clearly still subject to political risk, but the diversity of their operations and the growing experience of their managers made the risks more familiar and somehow more palatable. Meanwhile, the wave of liberalization that swept the developing world in the early 1990s seemed to obliterate many of the old fears. Expropriation, long the bane of foreign investors, declined precipitously, and countries that for decades had challenged the power of the multinationals began, instead, to woo them.[17]

Finally, political risk analysis declined because, at some level, it had never lived up to its proponents' greatest expectations. The demand for risk analysis stemmed from firms' desire to predict key political events -- to figure out where the vulnerabilities lay in target markets, and how these vulnerabilities were likely to affect their own business prospects. Older approaches, such as the *Old Hands* and *Grand Tours* methods, had approximated some of these risks, but tended to miss big and devastating events: the fall of the Shah, the rise of Castro. It was to fill these gaps that firms had embraced the more scientific methodologies promised by formal risk analysis. But, as it turned out, the formal models did little to improve the accuracy of analysis. They still missed many of the big

---

[14]Louis Kraar, "The Multinationals Get Smarter About Political Risks," *Fortune*, March 24, 1980, p. 92.

[15]For more on these gaps, see Stephen J. Kobrin, "Global Strategy and National Politics: The Integration of Environmental Assessment and Strategic Planning," in Fariborz Ghadar, Stephen Kobrin, and Theodore H. Moran, eds., *Managing International Political Risk: Strategies and Techniques* (Washington, DC: Bond Publishing Company, 1983) pp. 142-152.

[16]For an analysis of the industry's decline, see Frederick Stapenhurst, *Political Risk Analysis Around the North Atlantic* (New York: St. Martin's Press, 1992): and Howell and Chaddick, p. 71.

[17]For a description of this trend, see Louis T. Wells, "God and Fair Competition: Does the Foreign Investor in Emerging Markets Face Still Other Risks?" (forthcoming, 1997). One recent study concluded that political risks in emerging markets have simply declined over the period from 1985-1995. See Robin L. Diamonte, John M. Liew, and Ross L. Stevens, "Political Risk in Emerging and Developed Markets," *Financial Analysts' Journal*, May/June 1996.

events and did a relatively poor job of linking political developments to commercial losses or industry-specific events. They also were not generally designed to capture the cumulative effects of smaller events or encroachments -- the "deaths by a thousand cuts" that could be just as hazardous as single political disasters. In 1992, a study published in the *Columbia Journal of World Business* evaluated the five-year performance of three political risk models. According to this analysis, only a small fraction of the variance in politically-driven losses was explained by any of the models, and aggregating political variables (as all of the models did) actually reduced predictive power.[18]

Anecdotally, similar problems were becoming apparent. As William W. Teeple, Treasurer of Monsanto Company, suggested, "Risk quantification, in my opinion, is very difficult. Quantification would be an exercise that involves a tremendous amount of administrative cost, and I am not sure of the end-use value.... It may be an exercise in futility."[19] Avars Krast, vice-president of coordination and planning at Conoco Inc., echoed these sentiments: "If you pretend to quantify things by your subjective judgment, it is not very helpful. You can't boil things down to numerical indices."[20]

By the mid-1990s, the political risk industry was in sharp decline. Two of the largest services, International Country Risk Guide and Political Risk Services, were consolidated under the same parent company. Others, such as Multi-National Strategies and International Reporting Information Systems, either shut down or substantially refocussed their offerings. In 1994, the Association of Political Risk Analysts, which had reached a membership of over 400 in 1982, was disbanded.

New Tactics

Unfortunately, the decline of the political risk industry did not entail the decline of political risk. It simply forced multinational corporations to find some other means for dealing with the political events and uncertainties that still surrounded their foreign operations. It forced them, in short, to learn to *manage* political risk.[21]

Having abandoned the quest for prediction, firms generally sought either to share the risks of foreign markets, to reduce them through contractual arrangements, or to insure against them. None of these responses was new or particularly novel; but the decline of political risk analysis provided new interest and impetus. Sharing in many instances came naturally, a logical byproduct of increased commitment to a variety of overseas locations. As firms expanded, and particularly as they expanded into newly-liberalized economies, they developed partnership tactics that effectively enabled them to share the risks of investment with local entities. Arrangements such as equity and contractual joint ventures, alliances, licensing, franchising, management contracts and countertrade all served to diffuse risk and transfer it away from nationalistic pressures.[22] Once local partners were involved in a "foreign" venture, it immediately became less "foreign" and more important to the local economy. Blessed with an innate knowledge of sensitivities in their home market, local partners could also be a potent source of political leverage and information. Particularly useful in this regard were strong private firms, since they tended to be deeply aware of local politics, without necessarily being dependent on local politicians.[23] A related and highly successful tactic was to create a

---

[18]See Howell and Chaddick, *passim*.
[19]William W. Teeple, "Integrating Political Risk Considerations into the Capital Budgeting Process," in Ghadar, Kobrin, and Moran, *Managing International Political Risk*, p. 154.
[20]Quoted in "Foreign Investment: The Post-Shah Surge in Political-Risk Studies," *Business Week*, December 1, 1980, p. 69.
[21]For detailed accounts of these evolving management techniques see Ghadar, Kobrin, and Moran, eds., *Managing International Political Risk*; and Wells, "God and Fair Competition."
[22]See Wenlee Ting, *Multinational Risk Assessment and Management* (New York: Quorum Books, 1988) p. 198.
[23]One study, for example, showed that independent companies were often the most effective partners for reducing the risk of nationalization. Firms that partnered with partially government-owned companies, by contrast, were more likely to be nationalized than either those that partnered with local private firms or those that remained 100% foreign owned. See Stephen J. Kobrin, "The Forced Divestment of Foreign Enterprise in the

dependence in the host country on the corporate parent. If, for example, the parent corporation continually transferred rapidly obsolescing technology to its foreign affiliate, it could essentially guarantee an ongoing need for its presence in the local economy. If it bound itself to performance requirements that mandated increased exports or local production over time, it raised the value of its operations to the host country and, potentially at least, reduced the likelihood of unwelcome political demands.[24]

Another powerful partner for foreign investors lay beyond the borders of the host country, in a financial community armed with increasingly sophisticated means for project financing and risk sharing. With project financing, companies could raise the capital required for their foreign investments from international capital markets, rather than from their own retained earnings. They could issue debt securities to cover the costs of specific investments and hedge the financial impact of political decisions through the use of forwards, futures, swaps, and other financial derivatives. By itself, project finance did little to minimize political risk; but by thrusting the investment into the global financial market, project finance spread the effects of risk across a much broader spectrum of participants. It also effectively raised the risks of political events *for the host country*. With project financing in place, more firms and institutions felt the impact of adverse decisions, and were likely to remember this impact when making subsequent investment or financing decisions.

Finally, by the mid-1990s, firms were increasingly able to insure themselves against the risks that they could not predict. While political risk insurance had existed in some form since the early days of mercantile trade, it expanded dramatically in the late 1980s and early 1990s -- prodded no doubt by the questionable performance of political risk assessment services. Like other forms of insurance, political risk insurance acts as a hedge against uncertainty. Firms purchase it to protect themselves against the potential (and unpredictable) impact of adverse political events. They purchase it as protection against currency inconvertibility, war, civil unrest, expropriation -- against, indeed, many of the contingencies that they formerly tried to predict. For decades, political risk insurance was issued mainly by governments. State-sponsored agencies such as OPIC (the U.S. Overseas Private Investment Corporation) supported the overseas ventures of their nationals by providing them insurance coverage against political risk. Because this coverage was backed by the full faith and credit of national governments, it carried a particular clout and even often helped to reduce the risk of the very events it was insuring against. It also occasionally became a tool of national policy, with governments using their insurance agencies to prod particular policy decisions in foreign countries. As of 1997, all of the G-7 nations had national insurance agencies offering similar forms of coverage against political risk. They were matched by multilateral agencies such as the World Bank's MIGA (Multilateral Investment Guarantee Agency), which provides insurance regardless of a firm's nationality and can assume particularly long term liabilities, such as 30-40 year infrastructure projects.

The final piece of the political risk insurance market belongs to private firms. Once focused solely on economic or commercial risk, these firms began in the 1970s to edge quietly into the political risk industry. Without the clout of national or multilateral agencies, and with no pretense at estimating the likelihood of the risks they cover, private firms simply offer insurance against political contingencies. In the process, they also offer an interesting, if implicit, twist on risk analysis. All of the older methods for dealing with political risk assumed, inherently, that political risk was somehow separate from the normal risks of commerce. Political risks were strange and enigmatic; they came, if not from acts of God, at least from acts of inexplicable social forces or apparently irrational leaders.

LDCs," *International Organization*, Winter 1980. Cited also in Theodore H. Moran, "International Political Risk Assessment, Corporate Planning and Strategies to Offset Political Risk," in Ghadar, Kobrin, and Moran, p. 165. For a classic account of the relative leverage enjoyed by investing firms and host governments, see Nathan Fagre and Louis T. Wells, Jr., "Bargaining Power of Multinationals and Host Governments," *Journal of International Business Studies*, Fall, 1982.
[24]According to Moran, this strategy has proven widely effective for manufacturing firms. See Moran, "International Political Risk Assessment," p. 163. He is drawing, in part, on LICIT, *Performance Requirements* (Labor-Industry Coalition for International Trade, 1981).

Political risks demanded special attention and a particular, often political response: sending Marines to the capital; dispatching top management to the countryside; or outsourcing the analysis to a politically-attuned band of experts. The shift towards insurance, particularly private insurance, suggests a wholly different approach. It suggests treating political risk as just another form of commercial risk, a risk akin to theft, or fire, or fraud. It implies removing political risk from its separate political category and integrating it with a more general commercial assessment.

As of the mid-1990s, the efficacy of this approach remained to be seen. With record levels of foreign direct investment, though, and unprecedented corporate interest in the world's emerging markets, the political risk insurance industry was clearly poised for expansion.[25]

---

[25]See, for instance, Russ Banham, "Firms' Demand at Record High for Political Risk Insurance," *Journal of Commerce*, December 6, 1996, p. 6A.; and Robert Svensk, "Underwriters Look Forward," *Project & Trade Finance*, October 1995, pp. 40-41.

Exhibit 1A Political System Stability Index (PSSI)

One approach to the quantitative assessment of political risk was the Political System Stability Index (PSSI), created in 1974 by Dan Haendel, Gerald West, and Robert Meadow. Using data from the period 1961-1966, the PSSI aggregated and weighted a series of country variables to generate an overall evaluation of political stability. The PSSI was composed of three equally-weighted indices:

Socioeconomic Characteristics Index:
- Ethnolinguistic fractionalization
- GNP growth per capita
- Energy consumption per capita

Governmental Process Index:
- Political competition index
- Legislative effectiveness
- Constitutional changes per year
- Irregular chief executive changes

Societal Conflict Indices:

Public Unrest Index (20%)
- Riots
- Demonstrations
- Government crises

Internal Violence Index (40%)
- Armed attacks
- Assassinations
- Coup d'etats
- Guerrilla warfare

Coercion Potential Index (40%)
- Internal security forces per 1000

Source: Adapted from Dan Haendel, Gerald T. West, and Robert Meadow, *Overseas Investment and Political Risk* (Philadelphia: The Foreign Policy Research Institute, 1975).

Exhibit 2   Sample Results of PSSI Index

PSSI was used to generate ordinal rankings of countries, based on their computed levels of stability. Higher PSSI scores reflected more stable environments. The index was created in 1974, and generally claimed to predict the underlying stability of the countries reviewed.

Country	PSSI Score
Israel	4.56
Trinidad	3.70
Venezuela	2.84
Zaire	(5.20)
Dominican Republic	(5.98)

For several years following the publication of this index, Zaire and the Dominican Republic were indeed among the world's least stable political systems. Zaire faced civil war and secessionist movements, while the Dominican Republic experienced persistent turmoil from civil war, border clashes with Haiti, and military intervention from the United States. Israel and Trinidad, on the other hand, experienced high levels of political stability and rapid economic growth. In 1974, Venezuela expropriated a number of foreign-owned oil fields.

Source: Adapted from Dan Haendel, Gerald T. West, and Robert Meadow, *Overseas Investment and Political Risk* (Philadelphia: The Foreign Policy Research Institute, 1975).

Exhibit 3 *The Economist* Rankings

In 1986, *The Economist* published a risk analysis of 50 countries entitled "Countries in Trouble." The analysis was based on an index of 100 points, with 33 assigned to economic factors, 50 to political ones, and 17 to societal. The following variables were included:

Politics (50 points)

- Being near a superpower or troublemaker (3)
- Authoritarianism (7)
- Longevity of regime (5)
- Illegitimacy (9)
- Generals in power (6)
- War/armed insurrection (20)

Economics (33 points)

- Falling GDP per capita (8)
- High inflation (5)
- Capital flight (4)
- High and rising foreign debt as a proportion of GDP (6)
- Decline in food production per capita (4)
- Raw materials as a high percent of exports (6)

Society (17 points)

- Pace of urbanization (3)
- Islamic fundamentalism (4)
- Corruption (6)
- Ethnic tension (4)

It is interesting to note that, along with its general analysis, *The Economist* suggested that "stability, at least in the medium term, is not just a matter of wealth, peace and democracy: the Soviet Union may be most non-Russians' idea of a terrible country, but it is probably going to be quite stable for many years." They were clearly not alone in this assessment.

Source: Adapted from "Who's on the Skids?" *The Economist*, December 20, 1986, pp. 69-72.

Exhibit 4   Business Environment Risk Intelligence (BERI) Political Risk Index

BERI's approach to political risk analysis was based on scores assigned to ten political variables. Each country was scored by one or two experts, who assigned ratings from 1 to 7, with 7 representing the lowest-risk environment. Up to 30 additional points could be assigned to a country's score, to reward especially favorable operating conditions. BERI's analysis was based on the following factors:

Internal Causes of Political Risk
- Political fractionalization
- Ethnic fractionalization
- Coercive measures required for retaining power
- Mentality, including xenophobia, nationalism, corruption, nepotism
- Social conditions, including population density and wealth distribution
- Radical left

External Causes of Political Risk
- Importance to hostile major power
- Negative regional influences

Symptoms of Political Risk
- Societal conflict involving demonstrations, strikes, and street violence
- Instability as perceived by non-constitutional changes, assassinations, and guerrilla wars

Source: Adapted from Llewellyn Howell and Brad Chaddick, "Models of Political Risk in Foreign Investment," *Columbia Journal of World Business*, Fall 1994.

Busang (A): River of Gold

We reckoned [in the fall of 1993] that we'd come up with a two-million ounce deposit, and be taken over by a major gold producer. We'd take our $4 or $5 a share. It would be a two year exercise.

—David Walsh
Chairman, Bre-X Minerals Ltd.

There is thy gold; Worse poison to men's soul.

—William Shakespeare, *Romeo and Juliet*

In November of 1996, David Walsh was trying, once again, to rescue his small company. If the situation hadn't been so dire, it would have seemed almost laughable. Walsh, the president of Canada's Bre-X Minerals Ltd., had claim to what many analysts believed was the largest gold deposit ever discovered. Yet, somehow, Walsh and Bre-X faced the very real possibility of losing control of all but a small fraction of the discovery. It wasn't obvious what the company should do to stave off this potentially disastrous turn of events.

Back in 1993, Bre-X had been just another junior mining exploration company, looking for mineral deposits in the jungles of Indonesia. With three properties scattered across the Indonesian archipelago, Bre-X had decided early on to concentrate its efforts on the Busang site, located in a remote corner of East Kalimantan[1] on the island of Borneo. Exploratory drill results had been encouraging, but Bre-X's lack of investment capital kept threatening to halt further testing. When a potential deal with Barrick Gold Corporation collapsed early in 1994, Bre-X had become desperate. Unable to find another partner or backer within the mining community, Walsh finally convinced a Canadian brokerage house to undertake a $4.5 million[2] private placement, the proceeds of which would be used to fund further exploration at the Busang site.

---

[1] In Indonesian, "Kalimantan" means "river of gold and diamonds."
[2] All figures are in Canadian dollars unless otherwise stated. The 1996 average exchange rate for the Canadian dollar was US $ .74.

Jeffrey Bell (MBA '97), Christine Dinh-Tan (MBA '97), and Philip Purnama (MBA '97) prepared this case under the supervision of Professor Debora Spar as the basis for class discussion rather than to illustrate either effective or ineffective handling of an administrative situation.

For the next year and a half, Bre-X engineers had drilled and sampled in their tiny pocket of the Borneo jungle, following an elusive trail of gold and finding increasingly impressive results. In July 1995, Bre-X announced that it had found a deep ore body in Busang's southeast zone. By December 1995, Bre-X pegged its reserves at 10 million ounces. Financial analysts in Canada talked about a potential deposit of 40 million ounces.

Bre-X's find was splashed across newswires worldwide. And as testing continued, reserves continued to grow. By the spring of 1996, mining analysts pegged the Busang reserves at 70 million ounces, and some even whispered reports that 100-200 million ounces were possible. At Bre-X's annual meeting, Walsh mentioned the possibility of selling a 25% stake in the company for $2 billion. This announcement came only two years after Walsh had tried, unsuccessfully, to peddle a 14% stake in Bre-X for only $500,000. Now, flush with good fortune, he was planning to hold an open auction to sell a minority stake to a major gold mine developer.

But in the summer of 1996, Bre-X found itself immersed in a new kind of trouble. Excitement over the Busang reserves had engendered resentment among some Indonesians, who questioned the right of foreigners to exploit such a valuable natural resource. Political forces within the country had begun to express their displeasure to the Indonesian authorities, pressuring them to restrict Bre-X's control over the Busang field. Meanwhile, some of the world's most influential gold mining houses were also actively courting the Indonesian government, eager to find local allies and plant a stake in Bre-X's claim. In the murky world of Indonesian politics, these political maneuverings could trump Bre-X's legal claim to Busang.

On November 12, 1996, the Indonesian government played this trump card. Walsh and other officers of Bre-X were called to a meeting with Indonesia's Minister of Mines and Energy, and instructed to complete a new deal. If Bre-X wanted to retain its claim to Busang, the company would have to give Barrick Gold a controlling stake in the project, and the Indonesian government an additional equity position. Though Bre-X was sitting, quite literally, on a gold mine, it was not clear how the company could make it pay.

Background: Doing Business in Indonesia

Indonesia in 1997 was a country in flux.[3] Since 1968, the country had been ruled by President Suharto, who largely controlled the country's economic and political direction, and doled out its industrial properties to a close circle of his family and friends.

Widely regarded as an authoritarian leader, Suharto had nevertheless presided over a substantial liberalization of Indonesia's economy and a remarkable surge of economic growth. Between 1980 and 1992, the country grew at an impressive average annual rate of 6.5%, boosting substantially the living standards of most of its 200 million citizens. Eager to join the ranks of the world's fastest growing economies, Suharto aggressively opened the economy in the early 1990s, loosening regulation and privatizing a number of formerly state-owned enterprises. He also reversed decades of commitment to an import substitution policy, and began instead to court foreign investors and the international capital markets.

Despite these aggressive moves towards the market, however, Indonesia remained enigmatic to many Western firms. Due in part to Suharto's personal handouts, and in part to the country's legacy of massive regulation, commercial activity was concentrated in a handful of exceedingly powerful conglomerates. These conglomerates, moreover, were split almost entirely along ethnic

---

[3] For more on the background of Indonesia, see the descriptions in *Lenzing AG: Expanding in Indonesia*, HBS Case No. 796-099, and *Indonesia (A)*, HBS Case No. 796-125.

lines: sixteen of the top twenty conglomerates were owned by ethnic Chinese, who had long dominated Indonesia's economy, despite constituting less than 5% of the country's population. The remaining four were considered *pribumi*, owned by indigenous Indonesians.

In Indonesia, a multi-racial nation of some 13,000 islands, the ethnic background of these groups mattered. Though the Chinese groups held a larger share of the nation's commercial assets, the *pribumi* conglomerates were much closer to the power circles surrounding Suharto. Together, these groups controlled much of the country's transportation, real estate, and basic commodity sectors. The Bimantara Group, for instance (owned by Suharto's second son) ran an extensive petrochemical business and owned the country's largest private television channel. Bob Hasan Group (owned by presidential confidante Bob Hasan) controlled Indonesia's largest forestry concession and wood processing industry. Humpuss (run by Suharto's third son) owned the largest private airline, in addition to having substantial interests in oil, transportation, and automobile manufacture. Since the mid-1990s, the country's fast-rising industrial star had been the Citra Lamtoro Gung Group, a major highway contractor owned by the president's eldest daughter.

In addition to this rather idiosyncratic pattern of industrial ownership, Indonesia in the 1990s was also characterized by persistent problems of corruption. Despite repeated pledges to wean the business sector and the bureaucracy away from their established patterns of "cooperation," scandals continued to erupt, frightening away foreign firms and costing the country billions of dollars in lost potential investments.

The firms that did enter Indonesia generally sought the advice, contacts, and comfort of a local partner -- usually one of the *pribumi* conglomerates. Korean Kia Motors and Hyundai, for instance, teamed up respectively with Humpuss and Bimantara. Freeport Indonesia began a joint venture with Bakrie, one of the few *pribumi* groups not linked to Suharto's family, and then shifted over to the Bob Hasan Group. Even the prestigious investment bank Morgan Stanley felt compelled to break with its standard pattern of independent entry, and formed an alliance with Suharto's daughter before launching its Indonesian operation. Not all foreign multinationals, of course, felt compelled to make these links: Citibank, Unilever, and IBM all entered Indonesia on their own, and thrived. But for most firms, political connections were still regarded in the mid-1990s as being crucial to success. Nowhere were these connections more important than in the politically sensitive mining industries.

The Indonesian Gold Industry

The Figures

Long before Bre-X had begun its exploration in East Kalimantan, Indonesia had been known for its mineral potential: for oil, tin, nickel, bauxite, coal, and gold. Gold mining in particular had been carried out for centuries, but only on a very small scale. In 1945, after gaining independence from the Netherlands, the newly-installed government of Indonesia nationalized its mines: one for tin; another for coal; and a third, PT Aneka Tambang, for a variety of metals including gold. Indonesia's first post-independence gold mine entered production in 1958 at Cikoto in west Java. It remained the country's sole gold mine until 1970, and between 1958 and 1970 produced only 32,000 ounces of gold.[4]

In the late 1960s, foreign multinationals and junior mining companies led a new push into Indonesia's gold mining sector. Encouraged by Suharto's liberalized foreign investment laws, these firms came to exploit the country's well-recognized geological potential. And Indonesia, hungry for

---

[3]Speech by Rozik B. Soetjipto, "Gold Supply Outlook in Indonesia," September 1996.

foreign capital and technology, readily let them in. One of the first successful entrants was Louisiana-based Freeport-McMoRan, which began production in 1973 at the Erstberg and Grasberg copper and gold deposits on the island of Irian Jaya. By 1995, these deposits were producing over 1.3 million ounces annually, and experts generally considered Grasberg to contain the largest single gold reserve in Indonesia, approximately 40 million ounces.[5] Based largely on Freeport's production, Indonesia had become by 1996 the world's seventh largest gold producing nation, with annual production of 44 tons. That same year, analysts estimated Indonesia's total gold reserves to stand at 2,663 tons, with over 90% of the reserves concentrated in just 23 deposits.[6]

The Rules (or, how to get a CoW)

Although Indonesia was anxious to attract foreign mining companies such as Freeport, it was also anxious to keep these companies on a relatively short tether, ensuring that some portion of the extracted wealth was returned to the country. Accordingly, foreign mining companies that ventured to Indonesia were subjected to an intricate, and occasionally baffling, barrage of regulations.

To explore gold deposits in Indonesia, foreign mining companies were required, first, to partner with a local Indonesian firm. Once a partnership was forged, the firms could begin application to the powerful Indonesian Ministry of Mines and Energy (MME). The initial permit, issued by the MME, was called a "KP" (Kuasa Pertambangan). It was essentially an exploration claim, allowing the foreign company and its partner(s) to undertake preliminary exploratory drilling and sampling within a small, defined geographic area.

If early results proved encouraging, the foreign company could subsequently apply for a Contract of Work (CoW), essentially a mining concession. In contrast to the KP, only foreign companies were permitted to apply for a CoW, which set timelines for further exploration, standards for environmental assessment and mine construction, and target production levels. Often, foreign mining companies in Indonesia also applied for a preliminary exploration permit (a "SIPP"), which served to keep their properties active while they waited for CoW approval. The SIPP essentially expanded the exploratory area allowed under the KP, but allowed only for minimal work, such as auguring or trenching, to be undertaken.

Explicitly, the Indonesian regulatory system was designed to recognize the long lead times and high risks associated with mineral exploitation. In Indonesia, a typical mining project may take up to three years to progress from exploration to the decision to mine; costs for this period run generally around US$20 million. To bring a mine to commercial production usually requires between US$260 million and US$1 billion.[7] Unless they have a reasonable degree of confidence that they will be able to exploit the deposits they discover, foreign firms are not going to engage in exploration. And thus the regulatory structure was intended to protect the financial interests of foreign firms that discovered mineral resources in Indonesia. Once a foreign firm received a CoW, it had the guaranteed right to proceed to development and production of its deposit. The CoW also included complete management control, the right to sell products on the international market, and the right to repatriate profits.

Administratively, the CoW belonged to several Indonesian institutions. Initial negotiations were conducted between the foreign firm and the Director General of Mines (DGM), which then passed the details of the specific project to the MME. Once the MME approved the particulars, it sent

---

[5] *Ibid.* Mr. Soetjipto, Indonesia's Director of Mining Industry Development, estimated Grasberg's gold reserves at 40 million ounces. Mr. Michael de Guzman estimated Grasberg's gold reserves at 82 million ounces during his July 1996 speech, "Potential of Bre-X Minerals to be the World's Largest Producer of Gold." See also *Freeport Indonesia*, HBS Case No. 796-124.

[6] Cesar Bacari and Keith Loveard, "Suharto's Man," *Asiaweek*, March 7, 1997.

[7] Jonathan Challis and Kim P. Wicks, "Special C. M. Oliver Research Report ," *Bull & Bear Financial Report*, June 1, 1996.

the CoW to the Parliament, which voted to give the contract the status of law. For CoWs of significant size, final approval often came from Suharto himself.

Not surprisingly, perhaps, getting a CoW in Indonesia was often an arduous and frustrating task, fraught with regulatory surprises and complex political maneuvers. Negotiations with the Director General of Mines could take years; and even then, approval of the permit was still subject to the approval of the MME.[8] In the 1980s, the MME turned particularly wary, worried that a number of Australian firms were using mineral exploration plays in Indonesia to sell and speculate on their own stock. As a result of this concern, it took nearly two and a half years for Freeport to receive its CoW for the Grasberg mine extension, even though Freeport had been the first foreign company to obtain a CoW (in 1969), and had already been operating the Erstberg mine for nearly 15 years.

Bre-X Minerals Ltd.

Walsh and Bre-X: The Early Years

David Walsh grew up in an affluent area of Montreal, Canada. After completing high school in 1963, he joined a small financial trust company, working the investment desk and taking finance and accounting classes at night. By 1969 he was head of the firm's investment department. Walsh stayed there until the mid-1970s, when he moved to Midland Walwyn Capital Inc., to become vice-president in the institutional equity sales department. By the early 1980s, Walsh was well established and making a very comfortable living. In 1982, Midland Walwyn asked Walsh to set up an institutional department in Calgary, so Walsh and his family moved to Western Canada. Unfortunately, though, Alberta's notoriously cyclical economy soon headed into one of its serious declines. By 1984, amidst disputes over compensation, Walsh left to start his own company.

Armed with a flair for promotion and good contacts in the investment community, Walsh first raised funds to invest in oil and gas properties in Louisiana. With the petroleum industry in a major downswing, however, the properties soon proved uneconomical. Not to be deterred, Walsh continued to look for properties with good mineral exploration potential. He next assembled claims in the goldfields of northern Quebec, but was again unable to get sufficient funding for exploration.

In early 1988, Walsh formed Bre-X Minerals Ltd., rolling the northern Quebec claims, as well as new claims in the Northwest Territories, into the company. He listed Bre-X on the Alberta Stock Exchange, and waited to raise the capital he needed for exploration. From 1989 to 1992 there was little activity in Bre-X — with no operational activity of note, the stock traded around $0.27 per share, going as low as $0.02.[9] In early 1993, Walsh and his wife declared personal bankruptcy.

Walsh was 47 years old, working out of his basement, driving a 1979 Buick, and the owner of a dormant penny stock mining company.[10] When Walsh placed a call in March 1993 to an old mining friend, John Felderhof, he had no idea the impact it would have on both their lives.

---

[8] Even the relevant authorities admitted to these delays. See, for example, speech by Kuntoro Mangkusubroto, "Modernizing the Indonesian Mineral Industry," March 1996.
[9] Brian Hutchinson, "The Prize," *Canadian Business*, March 1997, p. 30.
[10] *Ibid.*, p. 32.

Walsh and John Felderhof had first met in Australia in 1983. Felderhof, a native of the Netherlands, was a geologist who had been in the mining industry for over 20 years. He had spent time in Canada, Africa, and Australia, before moving to Papua New Guinea and co-discovering the giant Ok Tedi copper deposit. In 1980, Felderhof went to Indonesia, and worked his way across the island of Borneo, searching for gold deposits, assembling data, and testing his own geological theories.

In 1986 Felderhof met up with Michael de Guzman, a geology graduate from Manila's Adamson University. Intrigued by the prospect that gold deposits might accumulate at the junction of fault lines, de Guzman had headed to Indonesia to continue his research. For several years, Felderhof and de Guzman explored the East Kalimantan area of Borneo for various interested groups, but with little success. Part of the reason lay with the exceedingly arduous nature of the surveying and exploration: Borneo, covered in mountains and thick tropical rainforest, made for one of the least hospitable exploration environments in the world. It receives up to five feet of rainfall a year, and is swelteringly hot in the summer months. Roads are few, and malaria rampant. Felderhof reportedly contracted it thirteen times.[11]

The Busang Find

When Walsh contacted him in March of 1993, Felderhof was in the process of evaluating various properties in East Kalimantan for Montague Gold NL, an Australian mining company. One of the properties was a remote, hilly, 15,000 hectare site in the rain forest, 30 kilometers from the Mahakam River. Virtually untouched, the property was inhabited by a few hundred Dayak rice farmers, who called the area Busang.

Felderhof sent de Guzman to examine the property. Although Felderhof and de Guzman had walked the Busang Creek area of the property six years earlier, they knew little about the site's geology. There had been some exploration in the Busang area between 1987 and 1989, but the extent of mineralization there remained unclear. After a seven hour boat ride up the Mahakam River, and a week spent surveying the terrain and collecting gold samples, de Guzman wrote a favorable report on the property, estimating there could be up to 2-3 million ounces of gold. However, after scrambling for several years to raise exploration funds, Montague Gold decided it still wanted out. It offered the Busang property, along with two sites on the islands of Sumatra and Sulawesi, for sale. The three properties were available as a bundle, with an $80,000 option to purchase, and a $100,000 exercise price in one year.[12]

A number of companies looked at the Busang site and passed on its purchase. Felderhof, however, felt it was a good exploration site with interesting geological possibilities. After Walsh's phone call, they spent a week reviewing and discussing mineral prospects in the East Kalimantan rainforest. It seemed that mining companies were pulling out of Indonesia too quickly, and that it might be an opportune time for Bre-X to acquire claims on promising areas. After a week of evaluating properties with Felderhof, Walsh decided to purchase the bundle of properties that included Busang. The deal closed in July 1993, at which time Walsh had 45 days to come up with the $80,000 option price.[13]

The trip to Indonesia had cost Bre-X all of its remaining financial resources, so Walsh managed to convince friends and colleagues to purchase shares in Bre-X, telling them the money would go towards acquiring the three Indonesian properties. He managed to raise $200,000 at $0.40 per share, and acquired the properties from Montague Gold.[14] In the process, Bre-X

---

[11] Jennifer Wells, "Greed, Graft, Gold," *Maclean's*, March 3, 1997, p. 40.
[12] Hutchinson, "The Prize," p. 35.
[13] *Ibid.*
[14] *Ibid.*

acquired Montague Gold's Indonesian partners, PT Westralian Atan Minerals, and PT Askatindo Karya Mineral, each of which held a 10% interest in the Busang property.

Soon thereafter, Felderhof (whom Walsh hired as Bre-X's General Manager in Indonesia) and his team started mapping and sampling the three properties, but quickly began to focus on Busang. In September 1993, Bre-X drilled its first holes. Despite promising initial results, mineral exploration in the remote and inhospitable terrain of the Busang area was slow work, especially on a shoe-string budget. It meant covering the area on foot, hacking through dense jungle and edging along river banks.

Bre-X needed to be able to provide Felderhof with sufficient funds to continue to explore Busang. Therefore, when Barrick Gold Corporation, a Canadian gold mining company, and one of the biggest gold mining houses in the world, contacted Walsh in December 1993, it seemed that Bre-X's prayers for adequate exploration financing might have been answered.

Barrick Gold

Barrick Gold was controlled by Peter Munk, a Canadian entrepreneur who had previously built successful electronics and hotel enterprises. Munk entered the mining business relatively late in life, purchasing his first gold mine in Nevada in 1986. At the time, the Goldstrike Mine in Elko, Nevada had already been worked over by a major American mining house, and most gold analysts considered the viability of the project dubious at best. Munk proved them all wrong. Within a few years Goldstrike was producing 2 million ounces of gold annually. With this cash flow, Munk ventured further into the gold mining field. He puchased Lac Minerals Ltd. in 1994 and then Arequipa Resources' Peruvian properties. By 1996, Barrick was one of the largest gold producers in the world.

Barrick's preferred method of operation was to forge joint ventures with junior mining companies, funding their exploration efforts in return for a stake in any discoveries. This was a fairly common and extremely logical arrangement. In the mining industries, "junior" companies such as Bre-X filled a very specific niche. They raised funds strictly for the purpose of acquiring claims on property, and then explored these properties for minerals. Since the business was highly risky, junior mining companies rarely received debt financing. Instead, they relied almost exclusively on the issuance of share capital, either to individual investors or large mining companies. By definition, junior mining companies rarely had the size or expertise to build and operate a large scale mine. If they discovered gold, Barrick, or some other firm like Barrick, simply bought their operations.

Like most global mining firms, Barrick had long been aware of the mineral potential in Indonesia, and held interests in 22 million acres in Kalimantan and Irian Jaya.[15] Barrick geologists had visited the Busang site even before Bre-X had started drilling and recommended that Barrick strike a deal with Bre-X. Since Bre-X was short of cash as usual, the timing seemed opportune.

In December 1993, Walsh offered Barrick 14% of Bre-X for $500,000, or about $0.41 per share.[16] In January 1994, Barrick offered a different proposal, one that would have given Barrick majority control of the Busang property. Walsh refused to cede control, and began looking elsewhere for financing. Talks with another Canadian based mining company, Teck Corporation, also proved unsuccessful. Finally, in the spring of 1994, the Toronto brokerage house Loewan Ondaatje McCutcheon Ltd. became interested in Bre-X. Loewan handled a $4.5

[15] Jennifer Wells, "King of Gold," *Maclean's*, December 9, 1996, p. 33.
[16] Hutchinson, "The Prize," p. 34.

million private placement for the firm, giving Walsh at last the money he needed to continue exploration.

Bre-X spent the rest of 1994 drilling on the Busang property, following the gold in the ground. As Felderhof recalled "We stepped out one kilometre and drilled five holes 150 metres apart. Each time, [we] found traces of gold. We stepped out another 1.75 kilometres and drilled seven more holes. We got a hit each time."[17]

The trail led Bre-X to the western edge of the Busang property. And here they found the dome. It was de Guzman who had spotted the outcrop of yellowish, volcanic rock. Felderhof thought it might be just another mundane type of diatreme outcropping, but agreed it was worth examination. Subsequent exploration revealed that the dome ran northwest to southeast, in the shape of a cigar 12 kilometers long and six kilometers wide.[18]

The dome, however, lay almost entirely outside the property for which Bre-X had the necessary approval for exploration and drilling. It lay instead just southeast of the Busang property, on land abandoned by Australian interests after the 1987 stock market crash. In September 1994, Bre-X formed a new joint venture with PT Askantidno Karya Mineral to explore the site. They called the new Busang site the Southeast Zone (or Busang II), and the original Busang site the Central Zone (or Busang I). The only obstacle that remained was obtaining the necessary exploration approvals for Busang II.

The Golden Find

Luckily, Askatindo received its KP quickly, and Bre-X set off to explore the dome. When initial results looked promising, the company immediately applied for a CoW. In the interim it continued exploration under a SIPP. It also continued to engage in deep drilling, an activity that was expressly forbidden under the terms of the SIPP.

But the laws governing mineral exploration in the remote regions of Indonesia were not always uniformly interpreted. As Rozik Soetjipto, the director in charge of permitting at the time, explained, "In a certain way, to be honest, it's good for us that they are very aggressive in doing exploration, because when the contract is signed, in a few years they'll be ready to start production."[19]

By the summer of 1994 Felderhof was trying to piece together information from several drill results, searching for a geological structure to account for what appeared to be a large mineral concentration. It would be another five months before de Guzman found the answer to Felderhof's geological question. As reported by the *Far Eastern Economic Review*:

> Working alone at three o'clock one morning, it suddenly became crystal clear. Bounding upstairs, he woke Puspos [another Bre-X geologist] and explained his theory: that Busang, with its dome-like geological structure, lay at a fault-line crossroads. Together on that January 1995 morning, the two spent eight hours in "non-stop technical brain-storming" before Puspos was convinced. With Felderhof, it took half that time and four big mugs of coffee. Chuckled de Guzman: "It was like presenting my thesis to a professor."[20]

---

[17] Quoted in John McBeth, "The Golden Boys," *Far Eastern Economic Review*, March 6, 1997, p. 44.
[18] Hutchinson, "The Prize," p. 34.
[19] Wells, "Greed, Graft, Gold," p. 41.
[20] McBeth, "The Golden Boys," p. 44.

Armed with de Guzman's theory, Bre-X engineers continued to explore the Southeast Zone. Meanwhile, word of their find started to filter back to Canadian investors. In March 1995, Bre-X shares were trading at $2.05. In July, when Bre-X officially announced that it had identified a maar diatreme dome containing a very deep ore body, the stock leapt to over $14 a share.[21]

New results of drilling in the Southeast Zone continued throughout the fall. By December 1995 Bre-X was quoting reserves of 10 million ounces and talking about proving 30 million ounces within 12 months.[22] Analysts suggested that 40 million ounces was not out of the question.[23] Bre-X's stock price followed the estimates up.

By December 1995 the stock had risen to over $50 a share. In January 1996, when Felderhof announced drill results showing 30 million ounces of gold in the Southeast Zone, Bre-X's stock price shot to over $160. In February 1996, Bre-X raised $30 million in a private placement of just over 1% of its total stock.[24] At the annual Prospectors and Developers Convention in Toronto in March 1996, de Guzman said he would not rule out 50 million ounces; gossip running among the participants hinted that 100 million ounces was more likely.[25] In March, with a market capitalization of over $3 billion, Bre-X moved its offices out of Walsh's basement. By May 1996, a pre-stock split value of $286.50 was reached. At Bre-X's annual meeting that month, Walsh asserted that a 25% stake in Bre-X was worth roughly $2 billion.[26]

Preliminary samplings taken in July 1996, showed that Busang's Southeast Zone ore body could contain up to 47 million ounces of gold with a grade of up to 3.3 grams of gold per ton.[27] With exploration still a year away from completion, Busang had the potential to be the largest maar diatreme gold deposit in the world, surpassing Australia's Olympic Dam deposit of maar diatreme gold by a staggering 10 million ounces. Domestically, Busang already ranked second in total gold potential behind Freeport's Grasberg deposit, with 82 million ounces. Busang's gold would make Indonesia one of the five largest gold producing countries in the world.[28]

In addition to Busang's sheer size, its geological formation also allowed for open pit mining, which was much easier and cheaper to operate than an underground mine. An intermediate feasibility study indicated that an open pit mine at Busang could yield annual gold production of 2 million ounces, with scale up to 2.5 million of gold ounces annually after the year 2005.[29] Preliminary data indicated that up to US$1.5 billion dollars[30] in capital costs would be needed to achieve this scale of production. Once in production, cash mining costs at Busang were projected to be in the range of US$75-$96 an ounce, significantly lower than average world production costs of US$200 an ounce. Busang would be one of the lowest-cost gold mines in the world.[31]

---

[21] A maar diatreme dome is a volcanic crater containing fragmented rock. A maar is a crater caused by volcanic explosion. The maar explosion fractures rock (diatreme), scattering the fragments around and within the crater. A maar diatreme dome is formed when the fragmented rock is left in a concentrated area on the crater floor, often due to multiple eruptions.
[22] Hutchinson, "The Prize," p. 39.
[23] Ibid.
[24] Ibid.
[25] Wells, "Greed, Graft, Gold," p. 45.
[26] Ibid., p. 40.
[27] De Guzman, "Potential of Bre-X Minerals to be the World's Largest Producer of Gold"; Hutchinson, "The Prize," p. 39.
[28] De Guzman, "Potential of Bre-X Minerals to be the World's Largest Producer of Gold."
[29] Ibid.
[30] James Whyte, "Freeport-McMoRan to Develop Busang, Bre-X Retains 45% Interest," The Northern Miner, February 24, 1997, p. 2.
[31] Ibid.

Walsh and Felderhof were the toast of the gold mining industry and Canadian business alike. Investors who had signed on with the penny stock entrepreneurs had become multi-millionaires in a matter of months. In St. Paul, Alberta, a small farming community of 5,200, over 100 Bre-X investors had effectively hit the jackpot. [32]

Managing the Webs of Influence

As the size of the potential discovery grew, however, so did the scrutiny of the world's biggest mining houses and the Indonesian government. After failing to reach an agreement with Bre-X in early 1994, Barrick's apparent interest in Busang had waned, as major acquisitions in Mexico, Chile, the United States and Canada pulled the company's focus away from Indonesia. But by 1996 Busang had become too important for anyone in the mining industry to ignore. Munk wanted to make Barrick the largest gold producer in the world. Getting control of Busang had become a key piece of this goal.

Thus, as Walsh dealt with the ongoing logistics of Busang, Barrick began leveraging its own formidable resources. One of these was an international advisory board that Munk had established in 1995. The board included former Canadian Prime Minister Brian Mulroney and former U.S. President George Bush.

In June 1996, Ida Bagus Sudjana, Indonesia's Minister of Mines and Energy, and Kuntoro Mangkusubroto, the Ministry's top technocrat, were invited to Toronto to promote the Indonesian mining industry. During their visit, Sudjana received a letter outlining Barrick's interest in Busang. It was signed by Brian Mulroney. At a dinner hosted by the Indonesian consulate in Toronto, Barrick's executive vice president of development was seated on Sudjana's left. Walsh, sitting on the country's most promising discovery, was several places removed.[33]

Soon after the dinner, Barrick hired Erlangga Hartarto, the son of Indonesia's coordinating minister for production and distribution, to represent the firm in Indonesia. Hartarto then arranged for a meeting with Felderhof at the DGM offices in Jakarta. Felderhof admitted to being suprised at the request: "I mean, why would they [Barrick] use him [Hartarto]? [Barrick] had its own office in Jakarta."[34]

At another meeting later that month, Felderhof was made to understand that Barrick's Indonesian group would need to include Siti (Tutut) Hardijanti Rukmana, President Suharto's eldest daughter and one of the country's most influential power brokers. At a third meeting, Hartarto pushed for a joint venture agreement between Bre-X and Barrick. By this point, Felderhof was starting to get a sense of how widespread the pressure against him was, and how serious was its source.

Technocrats in the MME were also under attack. Although Parliament had recently approved Bre-X's CoW application for the Southeast Zone, reports indicated that Sudjana and Hartarto were attempting to have the CoW revoked. The obvious benefit to Barrick's negotiating position was lost on no one. Kuntoro, however, refused to reverse the approval, believing that to do so would be against the law. Kuntoro felt that the only legal option was to revoke Bre-X's SIPP, which would at least send a powerful signal to the company regarding the government's emerging opinion.

---

[32] Hutchinson, "The Prize," p. 39.
[33] *Ibid.*, p. 48.
[34] *Ibid.*

As the pressure in Indonesia mounted, Bre-X began to look for some way to let others into the Busang project without losing their own control. In August 1996 the company announced that it would consider selling a controlling interest in Busang to a major mining company. Bre-X hoped to hold an open auction process among the world's top mining houses, avoiding at least a forced merger with Barrick. Bre-X hired J.P. Morgan and Republic National Bank as financial advisors and launched discussions with two Canadian mining companies, Placer Dome and Teck Corp.

On September 22, former U.S. President Bush sent Indonesian President Suharto a letter outlining Barrick's abilities. Representatives of Barrick and Bre-X continued to talk, but failed to reach any agreement. Then, on October 17, Sudjana stripped Kuntoro's office of its responsibility for processing CoW applications, a duty it had carried out for thirty years. When asked by reporters why the change had occurred, Sudjana responded that outsiders were not entitled to know the reasons.[35]

By the end of October, Bre-X had negotiated a new, clearly strategic, alliance with PT Panutan Duta, a company controlled by President Suharto's eldest son, Sigit Harjojudanto. Under the terms of the hastily-signed agreement, Bre-X would pay Panutan US$1 million a month for 40 months for administrative, technical and other support functions in Indonesia.[36] Panutan would also receive a 10% interest in the Central and Southeast Zones of Busang. In Canada, the market responded positively to news of the agreement, pushing Bre-X shares up by another $3.45.[37]

Indonesian Reactions

In Indonesia, meanwhile, the Busang story was making very different kinds of headline news. The story of Bre-X's gold had galvanized the Indonesian public, and just about every Indonesian politician and public figure seemed to have their own perspective on the Busang find.

Initially, the debate was dominated by administrative agencies such as the MME, which had a strong interest in the project's success. With only a limited amount of funds at its disposal, the MME had realized long ago that Indonesia would have to rely on private sector firms, either local or foreign, to develop its vast stores of mineral wealth. MME officials were therefore anxious to find more stories like Freeport, stories of mining firms which had operated successfully in Indonesia, finding their gold (or iron, or copper) and enriching the country in the process.

Others in Indonesia, however, did not necessarily share MME's enthusiasm, nor its willingness to let foreign interests exploit Indonesia's mineral wealth. As word of the Busang deposit spread, their criticisms became louder and more pointed. The arguments of two prominent public figures, Dr. Amin Rais and Mr. Hartojo Wignjowinoto, typified these opposing views.

Amin Rais was the leader of Muhammadiyah Group, the backbone of Indonesia's largest Islamic group and its second largest political party (Partai Persatuan Pembangunan). His criticisms reflected a fairly standard form of nationalism, a deeply-felt sentiment that the resources of a country were to be bestowed only upon its citizens and used only for their benefit. His criticisms of Bre-X and other foreign mining companies appeared regularly in Indonesian newspapers and included explicit criticism of the Indonesian government -- a rare occurrence in Indonesia's heavily controlled press. Rais was direct in his condemnation of foreign firms and the bureaucrats that supported them: "We have to look to the future," he argued. "All the rich mines beneath Indonesian soil obviously

---

[35] *Ibid.*, p. 65.
[36] *Ibid.*
[37] *Ibid.*

belong to our nation, to our children. This [mine] is for Indonesian people, not for foreigners. It is not constitutional that Indonesia only gets 10% from whatever is mined from our soil."[38]

Hartojo Wignjowijoto was more subtle in his opposition. A prominent economist with a doctorate from Harvard, Wignjowijoto did not condemn all foreigners nor all foreign participation in Indonesia's mining economy. He was, instead, specifically opposed to Bre-X, which he criticized as being a short-term, high-flying stock player rather than a serious mining company with long-term intentions.[39] This kind of company, Hartojo argued, would do Indonesia no good. Instead, it would be a replay of the mid-1980s, when junior mining companies from Australia charged into Indonesia on a great and self-perpetuating gold rush. Sixty percent of the CoW applications prepared during that period had been subsequently abandoned. Hartojo worried that Bre-X would do the same. As he recalled: "They were 'irresponsible invesments' with 'rubbish technology.' Now, the Canadians are coming here. It's a repetition of history. It's not really a gold rush. It's rather a stock market rush."[40] Business executive Rachman Wiriosudarmo echoed these sentiments and complained publicly that, "The barriers of entry [for mining] are supposed to be high. When they are not, Indonesia gets burned."[41]

Hartojo continued, saying "I don't want to see Indonesia to be like Africa. The people are poor. They have uranium. They have minerals, but they have nothing to eat. I don't want that to happen to this country."[42] In addition, he emphatically blamed the Indonesian authorities for being weak, greedy, and short-sighted. "For politicians, it's always short term. If the foreign multinational brings cash, their eyes turn green, you know. They don't realize what they are doing has repercussions on international capital markets."[43]

Judgment Day

On November 12, 1996 Minister Sudjana summoned Walsh and his key executives to a meeting in Jakarta. Also present were Barrick executives, including Munk. Reading from a prepared statement, Sudjana announced that Barrick was to be given a 67.5% stake in Busang, and that Bre-X's share should be reduced to 22.5%. The goverment of Indonesia would itself take the remaining 10%.[44] Sudjana gave Barrick and Bre-X eight days to reach an agreement on the appropriate means of compensation and contractual terms.

The terms of this arrangement left Bre-X with only a fraction of its gold discovery. They also forced the company into one-on-one negotiations with Barrick, its long-time nemesis. Although the meeting between Bre-X, Barrick, and Sudjana had ostensibly been private, it would soon almost certainly become common knowledge.

Bre-X was in danger of losing control over its precious discovery. The company had only eight days to reach an agreement with Barrick Gold.

---

[38] *Kompas*, January 4, 1997, p. 1.
[39] Wells, "Greed, Graft, Gold," p. 44.
[40] *Ibid.*, p. 41.
[41] *Ibid.*
[42] *Ibid.*, p. 44.
[43] *Ibid.*
[44] Hutchinson, "The Prize," p. 65.

Exhibit 1   Indonesia's Gold Mines

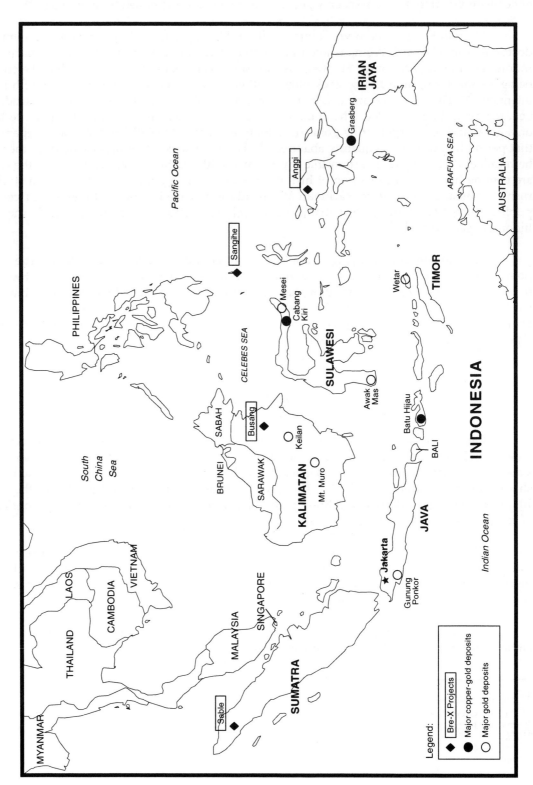

Source: Adapted from speech by Michael T. de Guzman, "Potential of Bre-X Minerals to be the World's Largest Producer of Gold," July 1996.

Exhibit 2a   Indonesian Economic Indicators

Indicators	1991	1992	1993	1994	1995
GDP at current market prices (Rp trillions)	227.9	260.5	329.8	377.4	445.4
Real GDP growth %	7.0	6.5	7.3	7.5	8.1
Consumer price inflation %	9.4	7.6	9.2	9.6	9.4
Population (millions)	182.8	186.3	189.7	193.1	196.6
Exports (US$ bn)	29.1	34.0	36.8	40.2	45.5
Imports (US$ bn)	25.9	27.3	28.3	32.0	39.8
Current account (US$ bn)	(4.26)	(2.78)	(2.02)	(2.79)	(7.22)
Reserves excluding gold (US$ bn)	9.26	10.45	11.26	12.13	13.71
Total external debt (US$ bn)	79.8	88.3	89.5	96.5	102.0
Total external debt-service ratio %	34.7	33.1	34.4	32.3	30.5
Average exchange rate Rp/US$	1,950	2,030	2,087	2,161	2,249

Note: 1995 figures are official estimates.

Source: Economist Intelligence Unit, *Country Report: Indonesia*, 4th quarter 1996.

Exhibit 2b   Indonesia's Principal Exports and Imports, 1995

Principal Exports	US$ (millions)	Principal Imports	US$ (millions)
Crude oil and related products	6,443	Machinery & transport equipment	16,290
Natural gas	4,002	Other manufactures	6,669
Plywood	3,462	Chemicals	6,251
Ready-made garments	3,388	Raw materials	3,643
Textiles	2,816	Food, drinks and tobacco	3,200
Rubber	2,233	Fuels and lubricants	3,007
Total exports (includes others)	**45,500**	**Total imports (includes others)**	**39,800**

Source: Economist Intelligence Unit, *Country Report: Indonesia*, 4th quarter 1996, and Exhibit 2a.

Exhibit 3 Indonesia's Largest Conglomerates [a]

Rank	Name	Main Owners	Main Business	Revenue (Rp. bn)[b]	Assets (Rp. bn)[b]	Number of Firms[b]	Number of Employees[b]
1	Salim	Liem Sioe Liong Family	Cement, finance, automotive, food	44,000	40,482	640	200,000
2	Astra	PT Delta Mustika, public	Automotive, agroindustry	16,300	15,617	342	51,000
3	Sinar Mas	Eka Tjipta Widjaja	Agroindustry, pulp paper, finance	15,200	39,292	205	75,000
4	Lippo	Mochtar Riady	Finance, property	7,900	12,697	78	21,000
5	Gudang Garam	Rachman Halim	Clove cigarette	7,700	4,493	16	60,000
6	Bimantara	Bambang Trihatmodjo	General trade, chemical	3,875	2,738	54	11,000
7	Bob Hasan	Bob Hasan	Wood, agroindustry	3,750	4,000	92	27,500
8	Gajah Tunggal	Sjamsul Nursalim	Tire, property	3,500	18,675	81	31,000
9	Ongko	Kaharuddin Ongko	Finance, property	3,462	6,946	59	8,500
10	Djarum	Robert Hartono	Clove cigarette	3,425	1,950	25	51,000
11	Rodamas	Tan Siong Kie	Chemical, glass	3,400	3,500	41	26,000
12	Argo Manuggal	The Ning King	Textile	3,200	1,754	54	22,000
13	Dharmala	S. Gondo-kusumo	Agroindustry, property	3,182	6,233	151	1,200
14	Kalbe Farma	FB Aryanto	Pharmacy, banking	2,976	18,675	62	7,400
15	Barito Pacific	Prayogo Pangestu	Wood	2,800	3,898	92	34,750
16	Panin	M. Ali Gunawan	Finance, property	2,150	5,751	43	4,800
17	Humpuss	Hutomo M. Putra	Transportation, oil	2,115	1,600	48	1,625
18	Jan Darmadi	Jan Darmadi	Property	2,115	3,452	60	11,540
19	CCM/Berca	Murdaya W. Poo	Electric, energy	2,100	1,150	32	25,000
20	Bakrie	Bakrie Family	Steel, agroindustry	1,972	4,610	37	7,800

[a]Based on 1995 revenues.
[b]Estimates.

Note: 1US$ = Rp. 2,249 in 1995.

Source: Adapted (and translated into English) from Indonesian *Warta Ekonomi* magazine, March 18, 1997.

Exhibit 4   "The Suharto Inc. Network: All the President's Men—and Women"

BY DESIGN OR BY coincidence, many Indonesians in big business are linked to the president. Some key components -- and cross-holdings -- of Suharto Inc.:

OLD FRIENDS

Liem Sioe Liong, 80. Has known the president since the 1950s. Controls Indonesia's largest conglomerate as well as a host of businesses regionwide. One of Asia's richest men.

Mohamed "Bob" Hasan, 65. Ties with Suharto and the army helped him secure a big chunk of the lucrative forestry sector. The president's weekly golfing buddy.

RELATIVES OF HIS OWN GENERATION

Suharto's half-brother, Probosutedjo, 66. Once commanded the clove import monopoly. Retains interests in glass and autos.

Sudwikatmoto, 61, the president's cousin. His Subentra group holds the monopoly in film import and distribution. Board member of Indocement and Indofood, two major Liem companies.

THE CHILDREN

Siti Hardyanti Rukmana (Tutut), 47, the eldest child. Controls listed Citra Lamtono, which is involved in a wide range of businesses at home and abroad. Shareholder in Liem's bank Central Asia, while husband Indra Rukmana has a sizable stake in the listed Bimantara group of Tutut's brother, Bambang.

Sigit Harjojudanto, at 44, the eldest son. Also holds slice of Bank Central Asia as well as 40% of brother Tommy's Humpuss group. Involved with British Petroleum.

Bambang Trihatmodjo, 43. His Bimantara group is strong in shipping, electronics, satellites and entertainment. Irked by national car project recently awarded to Tommy.

Hutomo Mandala Putra (Tommy), 34, major owner with brother Sigit. The company is in practically everything -- oil, gas, aviation, toll-road construction and agribusiness. Succeeded uncle Probusutedjo in the clove business as head of the Clove Marketing Board. Handed unprecedented waivers for national car project.

Siti Hediati Harijadi (Titiek), 37. Married to the fast-rising Brigadier-General Prabowo Subianto. Growing interests with brother-in-law Hashim Djojohadikusumo.

Siti Hutami Endang Adiningsih (Mamie), 31. Novice compared with her siblings. Only known contract -- so far -- is a North Jakarta land reclamation project.

AND A GRANDCHILD

Ari Sigit, 25, Sigit's son. In fertilizer and beer. Farmers say fertilizer prices have increased since he entered the business. Unsuccessfully tried to impose a levy on beer sales in Bali. His permit was withdrawn, but he retains distribution rights elsewhere in the country.

Source: "All the President's Men -- and Women," *Asia Week*, August 9, 1996, p. 20.

Exhibit 5   Gold Background

Gold: A (very) brief history in time....

Gold's history as a valuable metal dates back at least 6,000 years and outshines that of all other metals. Uniquely durable, malleable, and attractive, gold has been one of the most sought after materials on earth, and for centuries was the accepted currency used in the exchange of goods and services. Even though gold ceased to be the standard for setting international currency exchange rates after 1973, it is still a very important reserve asset for investors and central bankers alike: governments and central banks hold about 45% of the world's gold as reserve assets. Gold remains an accepted (though rarely used) international means of exchange.

Over the past 20 years, gold has been used by investors as a "hedging" commodity against inflation. Common wisdom says that gold will rise only if investors flock to it as a defense against a falling U.S. dollar. But just the opposite can be true as well, since an overly strong U.S. dollar can drive the gold market upward.

Source: "Gold," *The New Encyclopedia Britannica*, 1994, vol. 5, pp. 335-336; Brian Hutchinson, "The Prize," *Canadian Business*, March 1997, p. 46.

Comprehensive historical price fluctuations of gold, 1967-1996

GOLD

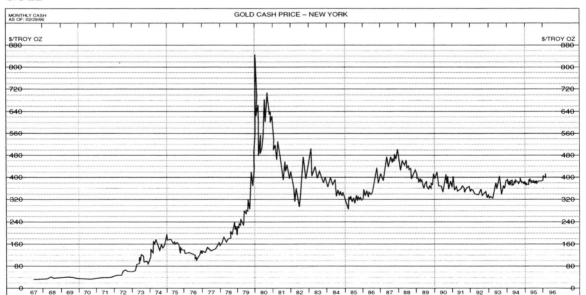

Source: *The CRB Commodity Yearbook*, John Wiley & Sons, Inc., 1996, p. 108.

Exhibit 6   Worldwide Mine Production of Gold and Maar Diatreme Gold Deposits

World Mine Production of Gold (Troy ounces[a])

Year	Australia	Brazil	Canada	Chile	China	Colom-bia	Ghana	Indonesia	Mexico	Papua New Guinea	Phillip-pines	Russia	South Africa	United States	Uzbeki-stan	World Total
1989	203,563	52,527	159,527	22,559	90,000	29,506	13,358	6,155	10,000	27,538	30,040	304,000	607,460	265,731	0	2,013,913
1990	244,137	101,913	169,412	27,503	100,000	29,352	16,840	11,158	9,682	31,938	24,591	302,000	605,100	294,189	0	2,180,000
1991	234,218	89,369	176,552	28,879	120,000	34,844	26,311	16,679	10,142	60,780	25,916	260,000	601,100	294,062	0	2,190,000
1992	243,400	85862	161,402	33,774	140,000	32,118	31,032	37,983	9,891	71,190	22,702	146,000	614,071	330,212	75,000	2,290,000
1993	247,196	74,200	152,299	33,600	160,000	27,500	39,235	42,097	11,100	60,587	15,826	149,500	619,201	331,013	75,000	2,310,000
1994	256,000	76,000	146,000	38,600	160,000	27,500	44,500	45,000	13,900	59,300	14,600	147,000	580,000	326,000	75,000	2,290,000

[a]1kg = 32.1507 Troy ounces

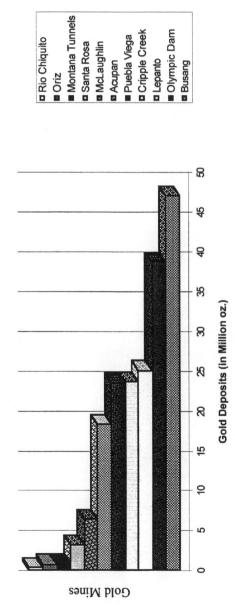

Worldwide Maar Diatreme Gold Deposits

Gold Mines

Gold Deposits (in Million oz.)

Legend:
- Rio Chiquito
- Oriz
- Montana Tunnels
- Santa Rosa
- McLaughlin
- Acupan
- Puebla Viega
- Cripple Creek
- Lepanto
- Olympic Dam
- Busang

Sources: *The CRB Commodity Yearbook*, John Wiley & Sons, Inc., 1996, p.108; Adapted from Michael T. de Guzman, "Potential of Bre-X Minerals to be the World's Largest Producer of Gold," July 1996.

Exhibit 7   Indonesia's Estimated Gold Reserves

Deposit	Resources (millions of tons)	Grade (gram/ton)	Gold (millions of ounces)
Grasberg	4,000.00	0.64	82.3
Busang[a]	622.4	2.34	46.9
Batu Hijau	919.5	0.51	15.1
Kelian	97.0	1.85	5.8
G.Pongkor	6.0	17.00	3.3
Cabang Kiri	136.0	0.58	2.5
Mesel	8.5	7.20	2.0
Mt. Muro	10.4	3.80	1.3
Awak Mas	14.9	1.75	0.8
Weter	5.4	4.2	0.7

[a]Resource evaluation incomplete.

Source: Adapted from Michael T. de Guzman, "Potential of Bre-X Minerals to be the World's Largest Producer of Gold," July 1996.

Exhibit 8   Gold Deposit Geology and Types of Gold Deposits in Indonesia

All igneous rocks[a] contain low concentrations of gold, which appears in about 0.005 parts per million in the earth's crust. Deposits of the metal are frequently found with deposits of copper and lead. There are two types of gold deposits: hydrothermal veins (in which gold exists alongside quartz and pyrite); and placer deposits (which result from the weathering of rocks containing concentrations of gold). Hydrothermal deposits formed beneath a boiling hot spring system are called "epithermal," the richest of which known as "epithermal bonanzas." Porphyry copper deposits (or copper-gold deposits) are another type of hydrothermal deposit. These are associated with porphyritic igneous rock (a rock which is a blend of coarse and fine mineral grains). Porphyry copper-gold deposits rank among the largest of hydrothermal deposits: some very large deposits hold billions of tons of ore and are therefore referred as "mega-deposits." Copper-gold deposits are often found in association with stratovolcanoes.

Two of the main types of gold deposits in Indonesia are the copper-gold porphyry and the epithermal. A full 60% of Indonesian gold deposits are copper-gold porphyry, the result of gold being carried up from great depths with other minerals and later precipitated. Geologists believe that mineralized fluids, such as gold deposits, are transported into the earth's surface at the junction of fault lines on the earth's crust. Indonesia's 13,000 volcanically formed islands -- stretching 5,200 km along the South Pacific's "Rim of Fire" -- lie exactly at the junction of these fault lines.

[a]Formed from molten magma.

One of the main types of gold deposit geology in Indonesia:

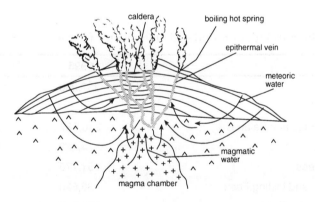

Example of an Epithermal Gold Deposit
This example shows the relationship between hot springs and epithermal veins. The magna chamber is the heat source for the hypothermal solutions (which contain both magnetic and meteoric matter) under the volcano.

Source: "Industries, Extraction and Processing," *The New Encyclopedia Britannica*, 1994, vol. 21, p. 389, and vol. 5, p. 336.

Exhibit 9a   Bre-X Minerals Ltd. Consolidated Balance Sheet, 1994-1995 ($Cdn.)

	1995	1994
ASSETS		
Current		
Cash	10,221,172	3,622,291
Deposits	430,859	n/a
Prepaid Mining Property Costs	470,796	n/a
Advances to Shareholder	1,178,613	279,647
Total Current Assets	12,301,440	3,901,938
Long-term Investment	505,000	25,000
Mining Properties	12,711,858	3,582,314
Total Assets	25,518,298	7,509,252
LIABILITIES AND SHAREHOLDERS' EQUITY		
Current		
Accounts Payable	1,707,420	173,107
Shareholders' Equity		
Share Capital	25,282,575	8,441,165
Deficit	(1,471,697)	(1,105,020)
Shareholders' Equity Total	23,810,878	7,336,145
Total Liabilities and Shareholders' Equity	25,518,298	7,509,252

Exhibit 9b   Bre-X Minerals Ltd. Consolidated Statements of Income, 1993-1995 ($Cdn.)

	1995	1994	1993
Revenue	237,260	116,004	33,000
Expenses			
Management Fees and Salaries	210,587	82,015	33,883
Office	74,439	65,611	39,140
Professional Fees	151,776	45,862	22,300
Transfer Agent and Listing Fees	36,620	15,273	9,104
Travel and Investor Relations	130,515	114,793	7,606
Total Expenses	606,937	323,554	112,033
Loss from Operations	(366,677)	(207,550)	(79,033)
Other	n/a	n/a	10,505
Net Loss for the Year	(366,677)	(207,550)	(68,528)
Deficit, beginning of year	(1,105,020)	(897,470)	(828,942)
Deficit, end of year	(1,471,697)	(1,105,020)	(897,470)
Shares outstanding, end of year	19,569,833	13,956,833	n/a

Note: Average 1996 Exchange Rate: 1 $Cdn. = 0.73 $US

Source: Bre-X Minerals Ltd., *Annual Report*, 1995.

Exhibit 10a   Barrick Gold Corp. Consolidated Balance Sheet, 1995-1996 (Millions $Cdn.)

	1996	1995
ASSETS		
Current		
Cash	245	284
Bullion Settlements & Other Receivables	107	116
Inventories	131	108
Total Current Assets	483	508
Property, Plant & Equipment, Net	3,991	3,004
Other	41	44
Total Assets	4,515	3,556
LIABILITIES AND SHAREHOLDERS' EQUITY		
Current		
Accounts Payable & Accrued Liabilities	167	172
Current Portion of Long-Term Debt	25	51
Total Current Liabilities	192	223
Long-Term Debt	500	100
Reclamation and Other Liabilities	135	112
Deferred Taxes	187	173
Shareholders' Equity		
Capital Stock	2,358	1,972
Retained Earnings	1,143	976
Shareholders' Equity Total	3,501	2,948
Total Liabilities and Shareholders' Equity	4,515	3,556

Exhibit 10b   Barrick Gold Corp. Consolidated Statements of Income, 1994-1996 (Millions $Cdn.)

	1996	1995	1994
Revenue	1,318	1,307	954
Expenses			
Operating	691	625	457
Depreciation & Amortization	183	181	106
Administration	33	31	23
Exploration	66	49	21
Interest on Long-Term Obligations	10	21	11
Write-off of Exploration Property	45	n/a	n/a
Total Expenses	1,028	917	607
Income before Taxes	290	390	347
Income Taxes	72	98	85
Net Income	218	292	262
Gold Reserves, End of year			
Millions of ounces (Proven & Probable)	51.1	36.5	37.6

Note: Average 1996 Exchange Rate: 1 $Cdn. = 0.73 $US

Source: Barrick Gold Corp., *Annual Report*, 1995.

Exhibit 11   Indonesian CoWs (Contracts of Work)

The CoW is the contractual basis of any gold exploration and development in Indonesia. In its 30 years of existence, the CoW has gone through six generations of revisions, with the seventh in the works. These revisions were gradually implemented and were *"aimed at attaining a balance between creating an attractive investment climate and satisfying the promotion of national interests."*[a] The formulation of CoWs centers around issues of "mineral resources ownership and rights, equitable distribution of benefits between the government and the contractors, the serving of all other national interests such as the maximizing of added-value by establishing downstream processing industries, environmental management, development of Indonesian personnel, divestiture, and regional and community development."[b] The CoWs also address issues such as tax rates (which have been reduced from 35% to 30% in an effort from the Indonesian government to promote its gold mining industry), more stringent controls, tighter production schedules in its implementation and stricter employment standards. CoWs are binding (often requiring companies to post million dollar bonds[c]) and grant mineral tenure to the mining company for up to 30 years, with the possibility of extensions to the mining company.

In exchange -- and in its efforts to attract "professional mining companies" -- the Indonesian MME has established a new regulation which requires applicants (the mining company) to submit a "commitment bond" of US$5.00 (10,000 Indonesian Rupiah) for every hectare of ground reserved for the (mining work) contracts; thus, "minimizing speculation by parties acting as a broker with the main objective of holding the reserved ground temporarily before transferring it to another party for a profit."[d] This principle, combined with protection of the on-going contracts from future changes in agreement terms and provisions, has been the main feature of the CoW system. Thus, reversing the earlier generations of CoWs in June 1994, the CoW's regulation 20 now permits: (i) foreign ownership of 100% of the shares in new Indonesian companies (previously, foreign ownership of a new company could not exceed 80%, requiring an Indonesian partner); and (ii) the elimination of the minimum investment requirement of at least US$1.25 million for each foreign investment.

[a]Jonathan Challis Senior and Kim P. Wicks, "Special C. M. Oliver Research Report," *Bull & Bear Financial Report*, June 1, 1996.

[b] Speech by Rozik B. Soetjipto, "Gold Supply Outlook in Indonesia," September 1996.

[c]Jennifer Wells, "Canadians find treasure in one of the world's most corrupt countries," *McLeans*, March 3, 1997, p. 41. Freeport-McMoRan had to post a $1-million bond to obtain its CoW for the Estberg cooper mine.

[d]Speech by Kuntoro Mangkusubroto, Director General of Mines, Ministry of Mines and Energy of Indonesia, "Modernizing the Indonesian Mineral Industry," given at The Prospectors and Developers Association of Canada 64th Annual Convention, Toronto, March 11-13, 1997.

Exhibit 12 Bre-X Stock Prices (US$)

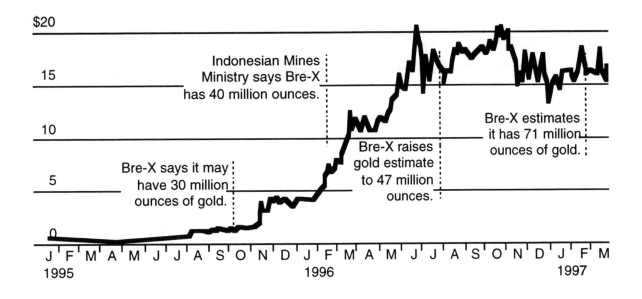

Note: Stock prices are adjusted for the 10 to 1 stock split in May 1996.
Source: *The New York Times*, March 27, 1997, p. D1.

Forever: De Beers and U.S. Antitrust Law

"As a worldwide dealer in enchanting illusions, Disney has nothing on De Beers."

- The Economist[1]

In 1999, a series of spectacular advertisements adorned the bus-sides and billboards of major American cities. Set against a lush black background, the ads displayed a perfect set of diamond earrings, or a single sparkling solitaire. The lettering, in white, was sparse and to the point: "What better time to celebrate the timelessness of love?" they asked. Or, "What are you waiting for, the year 3000?" Some were even more direct: "This wouldn't exactly be the year," they noted, "to give her a toaster oven."

Coyly, the ads captured a joint fascination with the new millennium and the enduring allure of diamonds. How better to capture time than with a diamond, they urged. How better to herald eternal love? Indeed. According to analysts, U.S. diamond sales (30% of which occurred during the Christmas season) were expected to surge by more than 10%, hitting a high of over $20 billion for 1999.[2] A significant portion of this windfall would flow to De Beers, one of the world's most successful corporations and the controlling force of the international diamond market.

There were many ironies behind De Beers's millennial campaign, not least of which was that diamonds — those eternal gifts — had only been sold on the mass market for a hundred years. And that their allure was largely a creation of advertising. There also, though, were many stories buried behind the campaign — stories which ran to the core of the global diamond market and De Beers's position within it. The millennial campaign, for example, was part of the company's first attempt to brand gems, to sell a "De Beers diamond" rather than a regular diamond. This was revolutionary in a market where stones had always been centrally mixed and distributed, where De Beers's power, in fact, stemmed from its ability to collect the world's rough diamonds and send them out again, anonymously and bereft of origin. The millennial campaign also occurred at a time of rapid change at the closely-held corporation. While the ads purred of luxury and langour, De Beers was facing turmoil on all fronts: in western Africa, where illicit diamonds were flowing from the war-torn fields of Sierra Leone and Angola; in Russia, where post-Soviet strongmen were carving out their own

---

[1] "Glass With Attitude," *The Economist*, December 20, 1997, p. 113.

[2] SG Frankel Pollak Securities, Ltd., *De Beers: Interim Forecasts*, March 1999, p.1; HSBC Simpson McKie, *Morning Meeting Notes: De Beers*, August 10, 1999, pp. 3-4.

Professor Debora L. Spar and Research Associate Jennifer L. Burns prepared this case as the basis for class discussion rather than to illustrate either effective or ineffective handling of an administrative situation.

diamond fiefdoms; and in their home state of South Africa, roiling with the impact of apartheid's end.

De Beers was accustomed to chaos. The company thrived on it, and had long ago learned to master it. But the millenium posed new challenges — serious challenges with the potential to undermine De Beers's legendary power and compel a rethinking of its strategy. The millennial campaign was the beginning of this change, an elegant tip-toe into a new kind of diamond market. It was also, though, an innovative legal and political move. For the millennial campaign was centered in the United States, a market that absorbed nearly half the world's diamond jewelry but also forbade the kind of selling practices upon which De Beers relied. Legally, the entire De Beers group — its officers, its operations, its marketing structure — was in violation of U.S. antitrust law. Legally, then, De Beers was prohibited from directly selling any diamonds at all in the U.S. market. De Beers executives, of course, were aware of this contradiction and had managed adroitly around it for decades. But now, for a host of intricate reasons, it appeared that all their maneuverings might not be sufficient. Either the law or De Beers would have to change.

History: De Beers and the Diamond Cartel[3]

For centuries, diamonds have been regarded as one of the most valuable commodities in the world. They have been the stuff of legend and the privilege of royalty, the symbol of romance and of greed. They have been treasured for their beauty, their hardness, and their unique ability to capture and transform light. Most of all, however, diamonds have been treasured because they are rare. In ancient times, this scarcity was real. Known to exist only in the riverbeds of India and jungles of Brazil, diamonds were the most exclusive of stones and only a tiny portion of the world's people had ever seen one, much less worn one. By the end of the nineteenth century, however, the discovery of the South African diamond mines had brought an avalanche of stones into the market. Suddenly diamonds were transformed from a privilege reserved for the elite into a commodity for the mass market. Surprisingly, though, after an initial period of adjustment, the vast change in the supply of diamonds had little effect on their price, or the way in which the public perceived them. The allure that had surrounded diamonds for centuries had not been tarnished at all.

Part of this allure was due, no doubt, to a deeply ingrained perception of scarcity that lingered even as diamonds were cascading into the markets of Europe. Most of it, though, was the result of a conscious effort by the new diamond producers to regulate the production of the stones and keep prices as high as possible. Realizing that South Africa's diamonds would be virtually worthless once they appeared commonplace, a young Englishman named Cecil Rhodes worked to consolidate the entire industry and keep the supply of gemstones sharply limited. Under his guidance, the international diamond cartel was born. Following his philosophy it became one of the world's most tenacious business operations and one of the most successful cartels of all time.

Since then, the international diamond cartel has regulated the market for diamond gemstones and maintained the fragile illusion of their scarcity. The cartel's reach is legendary. It controls a significant number of the world's diamond mines; it sorts and classifies a large percentage of the world's rough stones; and through its Central Selling Organization (CSO) in London, it determines

---

[3] The word "cartel" carries many complicated political, legal, and economic connotations. Economically speaking, a cartel cannot exist without the collaboration of three or more firms. Internally, members of the diamond trade do not consider themselves part of a cartel, but instead refer to the practice of maintaining "orderly marketing arrangements." While recognizing the complexity of the term, the authors of this Case have nonetheless chosen to rely upon the word "cartel" as a term of subjective description.

This section is a modified excerpt from Debora L. Spar, *The Cooperative Edge: The Internal Politics of International Cartels* (Ithaca: Cornell University Press, 1993), pp. 39-87.

who can buy which stones and how much each buyer must pay. Its tactics are varied and complex. Its strategy, though, is as simple now as it was in Rhodes's time: to balance the number of diamonds released into the market in any given year and thus to perpetuate the illusion of diamonds as a scarce and valuable commodity.

Cecil Rhodes and the Discovery of Diamonds in South Africa

In 1866 the accidental discovery of diamonds in South Africa changed the diamond industry forever. The first stone, picked up on the banks of the Gariep River[4] by a thirteen-year-old boy, was generally dismissed as a geological fluke; the second find, though, a stone of 83½ carats, was too tempting to ignore. By 1869, diamond fever had hit South Africa and some ten thousand diggers from around the world had rushed to the arid plains of the Cape Province to stake their claims and make their fortune.

By the end of 1872, five separate mines had been established in the Cape Province, producing an avalanche of gem-quality stones. Initially, the mines were rough-hewn affairs, agglomerations of individual prospectors, each scratching away at the yellow ground that lays atop most primary diamond deposits. As the diggers delved deeper and deeper into the kimberlite (diamond producing) ore they began to trip over each other's claims and tumble, quite literally, into the expanding chaos of the mines. At a certain level, the miners also tapped into underground water tables, flooding the claims and rendering them virtually unworkable. Fruitlessly, the diggers fought back the seepage with hand-held pumps. In 1874 a more effective steam-powered pump arrived at the Kimberley mine, hauled in and rented out by a sickly English youth named Cecil Rhodes. Within a year Rhodes was servicing all of the mines in the area. With this new-found wealth, he then started to buy small claims in the newly formed De Beers Mine and other holdings. In 1880, Rhodes formed the De Beers Mining Company to control his growing stake in the mine; by 1887 he had bought out all the other claim holders.

From the start, Rhodes realized that success in the diamond trade was contingent on the resolution of two serious problems. First, the very productivity of the South African diamond fields posed a threat to the long-term profitability of the diamond industry. If all the new South African gems were suddenly to sweep into Europe, the market would be flooded and prices would plummet. Secondly, there was an inherent conflict between buyers and sellers. The sellers (in this case, the diggers) have little control over the types and qualities of stones they produce; thus, they need to secure an indiscriminate buyer, one willing to purchase the smaller and less attractive stones as well as the large and flawless ones. The buyers, meanwhile, know that profitability rests with the ability to obtain a constant stream of stones and sell them at consistently high prices. The only relationship that serves both sides' interests is an ongoing arrangement between a single producer and a single distributor in which both benefit by keeping supplies low and prices high.

The solution Rhodes devised was ingenious. After having achieved full control over production at the De Beers Mine, he formed a coalition of merchants in Kimberley to whom he sold the full output of the mine. In 1890 this merchants' association was formalized as the "Diamond Syndicate," with all its members pledged to buy diamonds from Rhodes's mines and sell them in specific quantities and at set prices. By the end of the decade, Rhodes had completed his consolidation of the diamond industry by purchasing all the major South African mines. And just as he had predicted, diamond prices rose from eighteen shillings in 1889 to thirty-two shillings in 1890. The diamond cartel was in place.

---

[4] Formerly named the Vaal River.

Evolution of the Cartel

After Rhodes's death in 1902, his vision of a diamond empire was taken up by Ernest Oppenheimer, a German who had come to South Africa to work as a diamond buyer and quickly maneuvered himself into a position of power within the industry. Even more than his predecessor, Oppenheimer realized that control of the diamond trade entailed a monopoly of distribution as well as of supply. Unlike many commodities, diamonds vary tremendously in quality. Yet the diamond industry cannot survive on the top end of its market; it needs to sell the full range of stones, especially the lower-end goods that constitute the vast bulk of its production. Thus it needs to ensure that the diamond merchants will take the mediocre along with the spectacular and that all the links in the network commit themselves to selling the stones that together provide the mainstay of the industry. Similarly, because diamond prices bear no relation to the cost of production, Oppenheimer understood the necessity of ensuring uniform prices across the industry and straight down to the retail level. In an industry where mass perceptions of value and scarcity are critical, any undercutting would be disastrous.

With these concerns in mind, Oppenheimer worried that the Diamond Syndicate formed by Rhodes was too independent and that it might eventually be tempted to break away from the producers. Thus he resolved to create a "new syndicate," intimately linked to his own diamond interests and designed to exert unbearable pressure on the existing group of distributors. His scheme worked, and in 1925, Oppenheimer bought out the old syndicate and replaced it with a new one joined by corporate links to his own company, Anglo-American, and pledged to comply with the distribution levels desired by the diamond producers. At this point, the links between De Beers and the Diamond Corporation, between producers and distributors, had been permanently forged. By 1929, Oppenheimer was presiding as chairman of both organizations, positions he held until his death in 1957.

The Cartel in Action

In Rhodes's day, of course, the company could contain the supply of diamonds merely by regulating its own production; with the exception of several small outposts in Brazil, South Africa was the only source of diamonds in the world, and De Beers controlled all the diamonds in South Africa. In the mid-1950s, though, the yield from the once miraculous pipes at Kimberley, Dutoitspan, and Bultfontein began to decline, while discoveries in Siberia and different parts of Africa opened up rich new fields for exploration. De Beers was no longer alone in the market. By 1960, South African diamonds accounted for only 19 percent of the total world gemstone production and by 1999, 11 percent.[5]

To maintain its grip on the market, therefore, De Beers was obliged to reach out to the other major producers of rough diamonds, urging them to sell their production to De Beers. Generally, its entreaties were well received: realizing the benefits of cooperation and the dangers of oversupply, most diamond-producing states signed contracts with De Beers, agreeing to sell their rough diamonds solely to De Beers and its agents. While the precise terms of these contracts were highly secretive, most countries apparently agreed to a common set of arrangements. The country would promise to sell its rough diamonds only to De Beers, at a price that De Beers set. Although there were exceptions to this rule, countries generally also agreed to accept lower sales during times of slack demand and to refrain from polishing any of their own stones. In exchange for complying with these

---

[5] De Beers also handles the production from Debswana, a De Beers company in which the Botswana government has a 50% interest. The Debswana mines include three large kimberlite pipes that together produce 30% of the world's gem diamonds.

rather rigid restrictions, the other producers would reap the traditional returns of a cartel: stable prices, guaranteed purchases, and a buffer against the cold winds of competition.

The power of the cartel, however, did not rest simply with its control of diamond supplies; rather, it extended throughout the length of the "diamond pipeline" and into the distribution and marketing of rough diamonds. After De Beers obtained its diamonds — either from its own mines or purchased from outside sources — it sent them to the London office of the Central Selling Organization, known in the trade as the Syndicate. Located in a nondescript London office building, the CSO acted as the central distribution point for the world diamond trade.

Ten times a year, the CSO held diamond sales (known as "sights") to which only an elite group of diamond merchants (the "sightholders") were invited. About five weeks before each sight the sightholders would inform the CSO of their preferences — how many stones they wanted, what quality, what colors, and so forth. The CSO then tried to match these preferences with its own needs and supplies, determining what stones would be offered to which sightholder and how much the entire package would cost. After this analysis, it would divide the gem stones into individual parcels, place them in plain brown shoeboxes, and offer them to the predetermined distributors. No cherry picking was permitted: either the buyers took the entire contents of their allotted parcel or they turned the stones back. Generally they took the parcel. The effect of these policies was obvious: they enabled De Beers to regulate, down to the carat, exactly what stones entered the diamond market and at what price. It was a legendary level of market control, one that repeatedly astonished outsiders and confounded those who tried to fight against it.

Stockpiling

Not all of the cartel's benefits, however, redounded to De Beers. On the contrary, one of the cartel's strongest attributes was De Beers's ability to act as the buyer of last resort, using its own financial resources to stockpile excess diamonds during economic downturns. Thus whenever the market for luxury goods threatened suddenly to weaken, De Beers and the CSO would buy up the "excess" stones and add them to their stockpiles; whenever "outside" diamonds found their way to market, De Beers would buy again, always ensuring that the basic balance between supply and demand was not permitted to falter. Stockpiling was thus the final tool in De Beers's box, a last-ditch way to keep diamond prices high and convince the public that diamonds were indeed special and precious and scarce. But it could also be extremely costly. In 1981, for instance, the CSO responded to rising interest rates and slumping commodity prices with its normal strategy of witholding stones from the market. By the end of the year, the CSO's sales had slipped to 46% below their 1980 level, leaving De Beers with a stockpile estimated to equal a normal year's worth of sales. In the process, the company spent between $700 million and $1 billion of its own cash reserves to support diamond prices.

For most companies, that kind of financial blow would be devastating. Yet De Beers, clearly, wasn't like most companies. It had an exceedingly long-term view and a deep-seated commitment to market stability. It was also very much a family company, run by the Oppenheimers, their relatives and long-time associates. Even the shareholders were tightly interlocked, linked by a complex web to a series of firms that together composed the "Oppenheimer empire." De Beers was, to be sure, a publicly-owned corporation, but about half of its shares had historically been held by Anglo American, E. Oppenheimer and Son, and other friendly members of South Africa's commercial elite. They were an eminently patient lot, content to let De Beers sacrifice short-term financial gain in exchange for the long-term stability and prosperity of the international diamond trade.

For over a century, then, De Beers had presided over one of the world's most amazing commercial structures. In over a hundred years of operations, the corporation had only suffered two minor financial losses, in 1915 and 1932. It enjoyed absolute dominance in its market and an unparalleled reputation for quality and reliability. There was only one small downside: it was illegal in its largest market. Almost every single aspect of De Beers violated U.S. anti-trust laws, from its lion-sized market share to its unabashed price fixing scheme. In the United States, the company had been unsuccessfully prosecuted in 1945, 1974, and 1994, and was still under standing criminal indictment. Indeed, within the U.S. Justice Department, dislike of De Beers approached a religion: De Beers, government lawyers insisted, was in clear violation of U.S. law. It was a monopolist, a restraint on trade, a criminal entity. And it had gotten away with it.

U.S. Antitrust Law

History and Motivation

The U.S. antitrust laws that De Beers violated were not simple laws regulating commerce, but rather the fundamental underpinnings of capitalism as practiced in the United States. In a 1972 decision, the Supreme Court stated that, "The Antitrust laws... are the Magna Carta of free enterprise. They are as important to the preservation of economic freedom and our free enterprise system as the Bill of Rights is to the protection of our fundamental freedoms."[6]

The original legislation regulating the establishment of commercial monopolies was passed at the end of the nineteenth century, when the power of big businesses seemed to threaten American ideals of free enterprise and the small stakeholder. In 1890 the Sherman Act laid out the fundamental principles that would underpin antitrust law through the next century: it made illegal "every contract, combination in the form of trust or otherwise, or conspiracy, in restraint of trade or commerce."[7] Later, the 1914 Clayton Act strengthened antitrust laws even further, broadening the definition of unacceptable behavior and prohibiting any illegal behavior that might "[substantially lessen] competition or tend to create a monopoly in any line of commerce."[8] Thus even the apparent attempt to create a monopoly was deemed illegal.

Over the years, a series of decisions and interpretations developed a dual, and sometimes conflicting, focus to the antitrust legislation. The original Sherman Act contains language that seems to stress the well-being of the consumer as an important goal of anti-trust law, and subsequent court decisions have emphasized the loss in consumer welfare caused when monopolies or cartels eliminate competition. Some recent scholars have even argued that the sole purpose of antitrust law is to promote consumer well being. However, other interpretations of the same laws have given equal or greater weight to the social and political goods that result when monopolies are constrained. In this view, even if a monopoly is the most efficient means of production or distribution it still imposes unfair burdens on society. By preventing competition, for example, a monopoly may constrain technological innovation in an industry. It might also result in a dangerous concentration of power and wealth in the hands of a few, preventing opportunities for individual enterprise.

Depending on the national situation and the interests of those in political power, the Justice Department's enforcement efforts have ranged from fervent prosecution of monopolies and cartels to half-hearted exploration of anti-competitive behavior. During the Depression, principles fell by the wayside as the U.S. government allowed firms in the coal industry to collude in support of the

---

[6] As cited in John H. Shenefield and Irwin M. Stelzer, *The Antitrust Laws: A Primer* (Washington, D.C.; American Enterprise Institute Press, 1993), p. 1.

[7] *United States Code 1994 Edition, Vol. 6 Title 15,* (Washington: United States Government Printing Office, 1995), p. 114.

[8] Ibid., p. 119.

faltering economy.[9]   But only two decades earlier, the enforcement of antitrust laws had been a powerful campaign issue, giving birth to the iconography of Teddy Roosevelt and his trust-busters. Despite the controversy that surrounds antitrust laws and the occasional periods when the laws are laxly enforced, they remain philosophically vital to the American tradition. As legal analysts John Shenefield and Irwin Stelzer point out, even with all the various interpretations over the years, no one has ever doubted their importance: "Almost all agree that the antitrust laws are of central significance to our economy. They do no less than establish the economic framework within which most Americans and their businesses operate."[10]

Extraterritoriality

Despite the fact that De Beers retained no U.S. presence and was completely run by South African nationals, it was still subject to the reach of U.S. law. This is a tricky element of U.S. law and an infuriating one to many foreign nationals. It comes from the original wording of the Sherman and Clayton Acts, which make no reference to nationality and thus allows U.S. courts to extend their jurisdiction beyond U.S. companies and citizens. In a 1995 document, the Justice Department made its interpretation clear: "The reach of the U.S. antitrust laws is not limited, however, to conduct and transactions that occur within the boundaries of the United States. Anti-competitive conduct that affects U.S. domestic or foreign commerce may violate the U.S. antitrust laws regardless of where such conduct occurs or the nationality of the parties involved."[11]   Recent court decisions have supported this approach. In a 1993 case, for example, the Supreme Court ruled that, "The Sherman Act applies to foreign conduct that was meant to produce and did in fact produce some substantial effect in the United States."[12]

Armed with this rather broad legal infrastructure, the Justice Department had tried on several occasions to prosecute De Beers for violating U.S. antitrust law. In 1945, after a dispute over the wartime usage of De Beers's diamond stockpile, President Roosevelt's administration requested that the Justice Department investigate De Beers.[13]   The suit failed when the court found that De Beers's existing contacts with the United States, such as hiring an advertising agency, visits, making occasional sales, and maintaining a U.S. bank account did not constitute sufficient "doing of business" to warrant jurisdiction.[14]

Another attempt came in 1976, when the Department of Justice filed a civil and criminal suit against De Beers, ANCO Diamond Abrasives Corporation, and Diamond Abrasives Corporation for engaging in price fixing and customer and territorial allocation in the market for diamond "grit." ("Grit" is used primarily as an industrial abrasive.) Pleading no contest, De Beers Ireland (representing De Beers South Africa) and its co-defendants each paid a small fine and signed a consent degree agreeing to forego monopolistic practices. This settlement was the slim remains of an earlier and farther reaching action against the company. In 1973, acting off an anonymous tip, the Justice Department had discovered that De Beers held 50% of Christensen Diamond Products, an American company that made diamond drill bits for oil rigs and consistently received shipments of

---

[9] Shenefield and Stelzer, p. 12.

[10] Shenefield and Stelzer, p. 10.

[11] U.S. Department of Justice and the Federal Trade Commission, "Antitrust Enforcement Guidelines for International Operations," April 1995, http://www.udoj.gov/atr/public/guideline/internat.txt [accessed 10/21/99], p. 10.

[12] Ibid., p. 10.

[13] Stefan Kanfer, *The Last Empire*, (New York: Farrer Straus Giroux, 1993), pp. 227 – 230.

[14] James R. Atwood and Kingman Brewster, *Antitrust and American Business Abroad*, 2nd Edition, Volume 1 (Colorado Springs: Shepard's-McGraw Hill, 1981), p. 120.

De Beers's best industrial diamonds. Before the Justice Department could act on this discovery, though, De Beers swiftly divested itself of all holdings in Christensen.[15]

In 1994 the Justice Department tried again, filing a suit against De Beers and General Electric for price fixing in the industrial diamonds market. The lawsuit against GE went to trial and was dismissed in a scant *six weeks,* when the court ruled it was impossible to determine whether Phillippe Loitier, one of the individuals charged, had in fact acted in De Beers's interests. Loitier was the managing director of the Belgian company Diamant Boart, a customer of both GE and De Beers. Through other business dealings, he had allegedly been in repeated contact with De Beers board members. In the spring of 1992, both GE and De Beers raised their prices on industrial diamonds, the first increase in five years. Prior to that, Loitier had reportedly informed GE of De Beers's intended price increase, and GE had responded with information about its price increase. The government argued that this exchange was part of a conspiracy to fix prices, and that because Loitier's actions benefited De Beers, he had thus acted on behalf of the company. Disagreeing, the court ruled that this contact alone was not evidence of collusion, and what was alleged to be price fixing could merely have been legitimate information sharing between a firm and its customers. GE was acquitted. However, because De Beers had never appeared in court to defend itself, its criminal indictment remained outstanding.

These repeated failures did not dampen Justice's enthusiasm for prosecuting De Beers. In fact, they only reinforced the intolerable idea that the company was getting away with something, and had to be brought to heel. According to a government official close to the Justice Department, there was little the company could do, short of reinventing itself, that would make it legal in the United States. "Clearly, De Beers is a classic monopolist," said the official. "As long as De Beers continues to set the prices for both mined and rough stones, diamonds cannot be considered a legal, competitive market."

But if De Beers galled Justice with each day it continued to prosper, Justice was largely ignored at De Beers. Indeed, over the years, De Beers had simply come up with a series of ingenious strategies for remaining beyond the Department's grasp. It had no legal presence in the U.S. market, no U.S. directors, and — remarkably — no sales on U.S. soil. Instead, it sold all of its diamonds in London and then let its sightholders export them, perfectly legally, to the United States. By the time De Beers's diamonds reached the U.S. market they were no longer De Beers's diamonds — just an anonymous bundle of stones, mined and cut at some unknown location. With no direct U.S. presence, then, and no identifiable sales, De Beers remained at arms' length from the actual process of selling diamonds, dancing infuriatingly just beyond the grasp of U.S. law.

Challenges

Despite the diamond cartel's success, reports of its decline have endured nearly as long as the cartel itself. Indeed, throughout most of this century, reports have surfaced every few years that chart the assaults on the cartel's power and predict an immediate shake-out. In 1977 trouble came from the Israeli dealers, stunned by Israel's soaring inflation, who hoarded their diamonds and drove prices up. The company popped this speculative bubble through a combination of strong-arm tactics, including what may described as a "purge" of over 100 Israeli sightholders who were stripped of their sights.[16] In 1981 it was Zaire that threatened to destabilize the industry, when the cash-starved Zairian government struck a deal with three independent Belgian diamanataires for its small,

---

[15] Kanfer, pp. 317 – 318.

[16] According to De Beers, with the end of the speculative bubble, many of its sightholders went bankrupt and thus lost their sights.

industrial grade stones. De Beers retaliated by letting loose a storm of its own small, industrial grade stones, driving prices down and crippling Zaire's diamond industry. Next, it was the Soviets and then the Russians who threatened periodically to withdraw from the De Beers structure and establish one of their own. This was a bigger threat to De Beers (and remains so),[17] but De Beers nevertheless managed to pay the Russians enough to sate their appetite for defection. In 1990, just as the Soviet Union was breaking apart, De Beers struck a particularly sensational deal, loaning the tottering Gorbachev government $1 billion in hard currency and taking in exchange a significant chunk of the Russians' vast stockpile of diamonds. The sight of this transplanted stash was enough, reportedly, to squash the independent hopes of several other producers.[18]

In the late 1990s, however, De Beers found itself facing a new rash of problems. None of the problems was particularly dramatic; none suggested a direct threat to De Beers's power or an attack on its embedded business model. But together they began to hint at a very different structure for the world's diamond market and maybe even for De Beers. In retrospect, the problems really began in 1992, when De Beers suffered the double blow of Russian and Angolan defections. Caught in political turmoil, both countries began to leak diamonds on to the world market, Russia from its stockpile, Angola from its war-torn Cuango Valley. These flows came, moreover, right on the heels of a newly independent diamond development in Australia which had already forced De Beers to load diamonds into its stockpile. When the Russian and Angolan floods hit, De Beers loaded even more. The stockpile continued to grow.

Then, in 1997 the Asian crisis swept through the Far East, leading to a massive decline in consumer confidence and luxury purchases. Diamonds were among the hardest hit; between 1997 and 1998 De Beers watched diamond sales in Japan fall from 33% to 18% of the total world market. The impact of this fall was three-fold. First, it greatly enhanced the relative importance of the U.S. market, which grew from its customary level of 30%, to account, in 1998, for a full 46% of retail diamond sales.[19] Second, it depressed De Beers's sales and thus its share price. By the start of 1998, De Beers was selling at 98 Rand, down 45% from a high of 178 Rand achieved just six months earlier.[20] And third, it brought a new wave of value investors from the United States, who saw in De Beers's depressed share price a glimmering opportunity for financial gain.

By 1999, American investors held nearly 21% of De Beers's stock. This was a fundamental change for the closely-held De Beers, and would never have been possible during the long years of apartheid, when U.S. investors shied away from South African companies. But it was possible in 1999, and suddenly the company was faced with demanding shareholders, people who had little concern for the long-term stability of the diamond market or personal relations within the diamond trade. Suddenly accountants were prying into De Beers's financial management and scrutinizing the ever-growing weight of its stockpiles. For De Beers, of course, the stockpiles were a strategic asset, the final means by which supply and demand could be held in a perpetual delicate balance. For this new breed of investors, though, the stockpiles were a dead weight loss, a non-income producing asset that was actually destroying economic value.

Within De Beers, meanwhile, a new team of management was also pondering the company's strategic and financial position. In March 1998 De Beers and Anglo-American had ended their decades-long attachment, separating into two distinct firms. While the two companies would remain closely associated through cross holdings (Anglo-American and De Beers each owned 33-35% of the other, and the Oppenheimer family owned 8% of Anglo, and 3% of De Beers), this restructuring was described by company insiders as a significant step. Previously the bulk of De Beers management

---

[17] For more on the Russian threat, see Spar, pp. 64 – 73, 78 – 87.

[18] Spar, pp. 58-63, 83-85.

[19] Casewriter interview with Tim Capon, London, November 29, 1999.

[20] Andrew McNulty, "Investment," *Financial Mail Corporate Report: De Beers,* April 24, 1998.

had been paid by Anglo-American, and a typical De Beers career path started at Anglo-American. Yet according to Investor Relations Manager Mark Irvine, shareholders in both companies had grown dissatisfied with this arrangement during the late 1990s, worrying that the arrangement obscured accountability in both companies, and that De Beers's legal situation might impede Anglo-American's strategic objectives.[21] The changes, too, were an attempt to make both De Beers and Anglo-American into more transparent, modern companies. After the isolation of apartheid, De Beers was anxious to shed its image as a secret, sinister organization and instead move into the world as a cosmopolitan, world-class firm. Simultaneously, there was a turnover in De Beers's top management. Nicky Oppenheimer (Ernest's grandson) assumed the helm as chairman and Gary Ralfe became the firm's first managing director.

The Strategic Review

This changing of the guard brought significant changes to De Beers. In a move that seemed to signal an end to the company's secretive insiders-only style, Oppenheimer and Ralfe hired management consultants Bain and Company to conduct a wide-ranging strategic review. According to Financial Director Paddy Kell, "only a few years ago the use of external consultants would have been heresy."[22] But now, he recounted, there was a clear sense at De Beers that the company needed to refocus and decide why it was in business — for itself, or for the diamond industry as a whole? Oppenheimer himself seemed quite philosophical about the changes occurring in his family's business. "For any company that is long lived, there comes a time where you have to change, and cast your skin off," he said. "It seemed very natural to do this now, with all these personnel shifts. They were all new beginnings."[23]

The strategic review also highlighted concerns expressed by De Beers's new and aggressive American shareholders. Unaccustomed to dealing with either diamonds or South African firms, the new breed of investors lambasted De Beers with a litany of criticisms: its accounting methods could not be understood; it was "all cash and no dash," a stodgy company that refused to make bold acquisitions; it was far too heavily invested in Anglo-American; and it had significant legal issues in the United States. While such an outside perspective was new to De Beers, few company insiders could question the fact that the diamond market was changing rapidly. Although De Beers no longer controlled 80% of the world's rough production — generous estimates put the figure somewhere over 60% — the company continued to follow its traditional business model. As CSO Executive Director Tim Capon joked, "None of us have had to think for 100 years. It's been: 'what do we do? We control the diamond industry. How do we control it? We do what we've always done.' But clearly, the old model was creaking."[24]

Creaking loudest, of course, was the stockpile. Over ten years, the cost of these excess diamonds — with a book value of $4.8 billion at the end of 1998 — had eaten away at De Beers's profits. According to Bain, the company had consistently destroyed shareholder value throughout the 1990s, with returns on capital employed consistently below its weighted average cost of capital. Since so much of its profit was shared by other industry players, the company was only capturing a fraction of the very large diamond profit pool it had created. As a result, Bain argued, the company's stock price was undervalued.

However, Bain's analysis also revealed several nascent strengths within the company. Research revealed that De Beers was a tremendous brand name — one of the world's best recognized.

---

[21] Casewriter interview with Mark Irvine, Johannesburg, November 30, 1999.

[22] Casewriter interview with Paddy Kell, Johannesburg, December 2, 1999.

[23] Casewriter interview with Nicky Oppenheimer, Johannesburg, December 1, 1999.

[24] Casewriter interview with Tim Capon, London, November 29, 1999.

It also had a phenomenally strong slogan ("a diamond is forever") and a brilliant history of marketing.[25] Moreover, De Beers had achieved this prominence while spending only a fraction of the advertising money other luxury brands did. Bain's analysis stressed the fact that while other luxury goods makers, such as high-end whiskey manufacturers, spent 10% of consumer sales revenue on advertising, the diamond jewelry industry (and De Beers, by far its heaviest advertiser) spent less than 1%. Further, De Beers did not even advertise its own products. For all the 111 years of its existence, De Beers had shied away from its own name, preferring instead to advertise diamonds on behalf of the entire industry. Now, perhaps, it was time to change.

The Power of the Brand

With mounting excitement, De Beers managers began to contemplate an innovative branding strategy. They started to emphasize the De Beers name in advertisements, and even etched a microscopic logo onto some of their stones. In England, a small pilot project revealed that not only were customers interested in buying De Beers branded diamonds — they were willing to pay a 15% retail premium on jewelry bearing the De Beers name. And so, cautiously, the company began to raise its public profile. In honor of the approaching millenium, De Beers displayed in London a stunning 203-carat stone named the De Beers Millenium Star and crafted a high-end line of carefully-selected, limited edition "millenium" branded stones. The day they went on sale in Japan, one dealer found a line of waiting customers outside his shop; before lunch, he had sold 68 out of his available 72 branded diamonds.[26]

To De Beers, branding offered a seductive route out of its financial troubles. Analysts estimated that the De Beers brand could be worth anywhere from $175 million in rough stones up to $1.25 billion at the retail jewelry level.[27] By branding, De Beers could carve out a newly-lucrative niche in the diamond industry. It could capture the unquestionable cachet it had never exploited, and it could differentiate its diamonds from the Australian, Russian and Angolan stones that now haunted the market. Potentially, branding also promised to help reduce its stockpile. If the company could increase demand for this new tier of diamonds, it could begin at last to draw down some of its reserves. Over the long run, it might even be possible to extend the brand farther downstream, creating a De Beers luxury store or a line of high-end fashion accessories.

If De Beers had been nearly any other company, and diamonds nearly any other industry, the strategy would have been simple: brand the stones, exploit the name, forge retail alliances, and push the stock price to a more satisfactory level. But De Beers, of course, was not an average company and diamonds were hardly an ordinary business. As Finance Director and longterm employee Paddy Kell put it, "We could be an anachronism. Or, it could be that there is something different about diamonds."[28] What would happen to the firm if it moved away from the trade it had supported and controlled for over a century? What would happen to prices if De Beers started to compete instead of collaborate? And what would all of this turmoil do to the industry's carefully-nurtured vision of luxury and scarcity? No one knew.

Even more troubling were the potential legal ramifications. If De Beers was going to make branding a success, then it had to move aggressively into the U.S. market — the homeground of branding and the largest market by far for high-end diamonds. But each step closer to actually selling a product in consumer markets threatened to raise the ire of the Justice Department. A November 1999 report by Deutsche Bank Securities touched on this point, reminding readers that

---

[25] In 1999, the magazine *Advertising Age* voted De Beers's tagline the "Slogan of the Century."

[26] Casewriter interview with Capon.

[27] Andrew Jackson, "De Beers: 'Y' The Strategic Review?" Deutsche Bank Securities, November 11, 1999, p. 15.

[28] Casewriter interview with Kell.

"[the Antitrust] ruling is indeed a poison pill... The impact of a resolution of the Anti-Trust issue should not be underestimated." The report further surmised, "Given the significant limitations posed by the current stand-off with the U.S. Justice Department, we would find it surprising if De Beers had not formulated a plan to resolve the Anti-Trust problem."[29] For years, U.S. antitrust laws had just been a basic condition of reality for De Beers. But now, for the first time, they threatened to put a serious crimp in the company's business model.

In a remarkable March, 1999 speech to alumni of the Harvard Business School, De Beers chairman Nicky Oppenheimer directly addressed the conflict between his company and U.S. antitrust law. "We make no pretence that we are not seeking to manage the diamond market, to control supply, to manage prices and to act collusively with our partners in the business," he told the audience. But Oppenheimer argued that De Beers's "single channel marketing" also brought social goods and benefits to all involved in the diamond industry and in particular to the African continent, which continued to produce 75% of the world's diamonds. He continued boldly:

> It is always hard to argue that you are the exception to the rule but in the case of De Beers and the ultimate luxury – diamonds – I believe a review of U.S. anti-trust laws should form part of a new framework for engagement with Africa. Indeed it would be in line with the spirit of the African Growth and Opportunity Act, which reflects the fact that the U.S. is now trying to develop a policy towards Africa by recognizing its importance and the need to overcome Africa's image as a lost continent. De Beers supports any initiative that can break the mold of U.S.-Africa ties that were shackled historically by post-colonial and Cold War relations. We have a contribution to make in moving Africa from a past understanding based on aid and dependence, towards African trade, investment, sustainable prosperity and independence.

Perhaps. But as the millenium drew to a close it wasn't clear how Oppenheimer's argument would be greeted by U.S. policymakers and what, if anything, De Beers could do to affect the tone of debate.

---

[29]Jackson, p. 16.

Appendix: Nicky Oppenheimer's Speech at Harvard Business School Global Alumni Conference, March 1999

[This excerpt is from an off-the-record speech prepared for a closed audience of HBS alumni. Speaking as a private citizen, Mr. Oppenheimer made his opening remarks intentionally dramatic and provocative, as suitable for a keynote address. This speech should in no way be construed as an official statement of the De Beers Group.]

Ladies and Gentlemen,

It is with some surprise that I find myself addressing you today. In jest, but as with all good jests with a healthy serving of truth, I have always thought of American commercial life as being, in effect, a religion. There are certain fundamental beliefs and the Moses of that religion is Mr. Sherman, who in his act of 1890 set out some of the commandments:

1. Thou shalt not seek to monopolise.

2. Thou shalt not restrict competition.

3. Thou shalt not seek to fix prices.

4. Thou shalt not restrict production.

5. Thou shalt not divide markets.

6. Thou shalt not deny a competitor access to markets.

7. Thou shalt honor the consumer.

The torquemada of this religion is the head of the anti-trust division of the Department of Justice, who through Grand Juries conducts the equivalent of the Spanish Inquisition, routing out heresy wherever it may be found. No one is safe from the process, so that even the most successful and wealthy American businessman, Bill Gates, is going through trial by ordeal at this time.

I assume that you, as graduates of the Harvard Business School, have worshipped at the Temple of this religion and are no doubt fervent converts. Therefore in your eyes I must be the devil incarnate, the anti-Christ. For I am chairman of De Beers, a Company that likes to think of itself as the world's best known and longest running monopoly. We set out, as a matter of policy to break the commandments of Mr. Sherman. We make no pretence that we are not seeking to manage the diamond market, to control supply, to manage prices and to act collusively with our partners in the business. It seems that the only commandment of the ones I have set out that we do believe in is we do seek to honor the consumer. Despite all this we believe that what we do is not only good for us, and all producers of diamonds, but is also in the interests of the consumer.

How then am I bold enough to stand here before you and risk the rotten tomatoes? My confidence rests on two tenets. Firstly diamonds are unique; they are the ultimate luxury and yet they are desired and owned by a vast number of people. They are seen as the ultimate gift that lasts forever and has a store of value. But dealing in a complete luxury that lasts forever and has a store of value lays on some very firm disciplines. We at De Beers never dare forget that the material quality of a person's life would not be changed if they never bought a diamond. The purchase of a diamond at engagement, is a mixture of commitment, beauty and store of value — a heady cocktail of emotion and practicality. Certainly anyone who makes that investment becomes a supporter of the single channel marketing with its aim of preserving value.

The second factor is that for De Beers to continue to play its traditional role in the industry it must be able to clear the market of all rough diamond production. We do try (with some success) to even out the effects of economic cycles but we are not in a position to abandon economic reality. Indeed any company dealing in a total luxury cannot behave as an evil monopoly exploiting the masses because at the end of the day they do not have a compelling need to purchase.

The moment De Beers Consolidated Mines was incorporated by Cecil Rhodes some 110 years ago it became the largest and most successful diamond company in the world, and so it has remained. I always feel longevity must mean we are doing something right and fulfilling a need. What we have done is particularly important for growth and development in Africa. Diamonds have a special place in the economy of South Africa, and of many other African countries.

Until the discovery of diamonds along the Vaal River in the late 1860 South Africa was just another poor African colony with only Table Mountain and some grapes to attract the tourists. All that changed with diamonds — suddenly the country was full of young people heading for the diamond fields in order to make their fortunes, and with them came money, skills and capital. In today's politically correct atmosphere it can be argued that these newcomers paid no heed to the indigenous people and that the capital realised in the diamond fields was often lost to the emerging South Africa. But that is only part of the answer for from the diamond fields flowed the skills, expertise and wealth which enabled the gold fields of the Witwatersrand to be exploited. And on these two strong pillars, diamonds and gold, is built the modern South Africa, the economic powerhouse of the continent.

In the region diamonds have not only been important to South Africa. In 1908 deposits were discovered in what is now Namibia. Even today, 90 years later, diamonds account for 40% of the country's foreign exchange earnings.

The story in Botswana is even more dramatic. Prior to the discovery of diamonds by De Beers Botswana was one of the poorest countries in Africa with minimal infrastructure and a subsistence agricultural economy. The most important source of revenue was via remittances from Batswana working in South Africa as migrant labor. Once production of diamonds started there was a dramatic change — in the ten years immediately following the start up of the Orapa mine the economy grew at an average rate of 14.5% per annum and continued at an average of 11% for the next decade. The Government of Botswana has been careful to harbor the benefits flowing from their diamonds and their country is one of Africa's success stories. The only other country in Africa so endowed with a single mineral is Nigeria — there the product is oil. Interestingly the oil industry tries to regulate itself in much the same way as the diamond industry. One would have thought that OPEC had a major advantage over De Beers in that oil is an essential. But there can be little doubt which has worked the better!

Blackie Marole, Permanent Secretary in the Ministry of Mineral and Energy Affairs in the Government of Botswana and a director of De Beers said:

> "Diamonds have been the engine of our economic growth for a quarter of a century and through them our economy has become the envy of many in Africa .... Therefore our actions and role in the (diamond) market are always geared to promoting stability in the market. From the time we became part of this industry we have consistently subscribed to the concept of orderly marketing through a single channel system ...."

Currently South Africa, Botswana and Namibia account for 50% of the world's diamond production, by value. If you include Angola, Democratic Republic of the Congo, Tanzania and West African producers, then Africa produces 75% of the world's diamonds. Almost all diamonds produced in Africa are exported and the export earnings of these diamond mines are critical to the economies of many African countries.

Now it could be easy to say that all this is very fine and that no one could have an argument with De Beers and what it has done for Africa as a producer but that the argument would come over its marketing activities. But the production and marketing of diamonds are inextricably linked in a virtuous circle.

Cecil Rhodes first enunciated the need for a symbiotic relationship between production and sale. To attain the first objective of being the major producer he created De Beers Consolidated Mines, by amalgamating the major producing companies in Kimberley. To attain the second, he sold the output of the mines to a group of diamond merchants in Kimberley, which subsequently became the Diamond Syndicate...

This form of single channel marketing has exercised an extraordinary beneficial influence upon the whole of the diamond industry and particularly to many of the economies of Africa. This is best illustrated by how rough diamond prices, measured in dollars, have moved over time. Overall, between 1985 and 1996, the CSO's prices rose on average 5.4% per annum, compared with the average U.S. Consumer Price Index of 3.5% per annum, while production for the same years rose from 66 million to 109 million carats. In the past two decades, rough diamonds have out-performed commodities such as gold, oil and aluminium, all the more remarkable an achievement given that gem diamonds fulfil a purely emotional, rather than a practical need. It is no accident that diamond prices have been more stable when compared than other commodities. The positive trend in rough diamond prices is due to De Beers' marketing efforts. And this is an effort which is in the interest of both the producer and the consumer; a strange and illogical coming together of opposites.

The De Beers marketing strategy for diamonds is endorsed by our partners in Botswana and Namibia, and other major producers such as Russia, as well as those producers who do not sell through De Beers but are happy to shelter in its shadow. Stable prices are essential for the maintenance of confidence and the wellbeing of the industry...

It is ironic that 46% of the world's diamonds are sold in the United States, where De Beers cannot do business, although we do indirectly advertise there. In this case I believe the attitude of the Justice Department is at odds with American foreign policy which seeks to support the reconstruction and development of Africa and to contribute to the awakening of Africa and the African Renaissance. As President Clinton stated in his recent visit to South Africa: "America wants a strong South Africa; America needs a strong South Africa. And we are determined to work with you as you build a strong South Africa." This statement was further underlined by the President when he "borrowed" the word "Masakhane" or "building together," to characterise the relationship he would like to see emerge between the U.S. and South Africa. In fact the sub-theme of President Clinton's visit was "trade, not aid," and this is realised in the pending African Growth and Opportunity Act.

It is always hard to argue that you are the exception to the rule but in the case of De Beers and the ultimate luxury — diamonds — I believe a review of U.S. anti-trust laws should form part a new framework for engagement with Africa. Indeed it would be in line with the spirit of the African Growth and Opportunity Act, which reflects the fact that the U.S. is now trying to develop a policy towards Africa by recognising its importance and the need to overcome Africa's image as a lost continent. De Beers supports any initiative that can break the mould of U.S.-Africa ties that were shackled historically by post-colonial and Cold War relations. We have a contribution to make in moving Africa from a past understanding based on aid and dependence, towards African trade, investment, sustainable prosperity and independence.

Diamonds can have a key role to play in stopping Africa continuing to dig itself into a hole. Aid only increases the speed of the shovels, what is needed is trade and investment which will allow the digging to stop and the building to start. Two countries north of South Africa could particularly benefit from their diamond assets. These are Angola and the Congo. Both are currently meshed in violent conflict but both have considerable diamond deposits that should be used for their reconstruction and development. Both will need these assets to be used in the most efficient way possible.

De Beers, a truly African company, can and should be part of any effort involving by the USA to use diamonds to help the renaissance of Africa. To African countries endowed with diamond resources De Beers brings unparalleled mining expertise and a unique marketing mechanism. In countries like Botswana and Namibia, with democratic systems of government and an open economy, this partnership has proved its worth. In addition to a lasting skills and technology transfer, diamond mining has provided a revenue base for those countries to develop their economy.

Diamonds are a unique product and De Beers has, over the years, demonstrated how best to utilise this product in a way which enhances value to producers and consumers alike. I feel it deserves the support of the U.S. Government in its endeavours in Africa not their hindrance.

Source: De Beers

Exhibit 1 De Beers Financial Results

Rand millions			US$ millions	
1997	1998		1998	1997
29,280	24,845	**Turnover**	4,492	6,418
3,871	3,237	Diamond account	585	849
1,061	1,267	Investment income	229	233
279	158	Interest income	29	61
7	583	Other income	105	1
5,218	5,245		948	1,144
1,157	1,914	**Deduct:**	346	252
663	776	Prospecting and research	140	145
266	516	Interest payable	93	58
208	622	Other expenditure	113	45
20		Exceptional items		4
4,061	3,331	**Net income before taxation**	602	892
		Deduct:		
1,148	1,005	Taxation	182	252
2,913	2,326	**Net income after taxation**	420	640
94	256	**Deduct:**	46	21
92	254	Attributable to outside shareholders in subsidiaries	46	20
2	2	Dividends on preference shares		1
2,819	2,070	**Own earnings**	374	619
		Add:		
		Retained earnings of associated companies		
1,852	1,526	Current trading	276	405
936	(183)	Exceptional and non-trading	(33)	205
5,607	3,413	**Total net earnings**	617	1,229

Source: De Beers Annual Report 1998

Exhibit 2a   De Beers Financial Results

	1998	1997	1996	1995	1994	1993	1992	1991	1990	1989
Diamond stocks										
$ million	4,816	4,439	4,703	4,673	4,439	4,124	3,765	3,034	2,684	2,476
Rand millions	28,231	21,599	22,002	17,058	15,753	14,020	11,502	8,324	6,879	6,291
Investments outside the diamond industry										
Listed at market value										
$ millions	4,253	5,644	7,491	8,768	8,170	6,863	2,615	4,984	3,845	4,136
Rand millions	24,933	27,468	35,041	32,005	33,210	29,458	12,944	15,973	13,034	14,747

Source: De Beers Annual Report, 1998.

Exhibit 2b De Beers Share Price

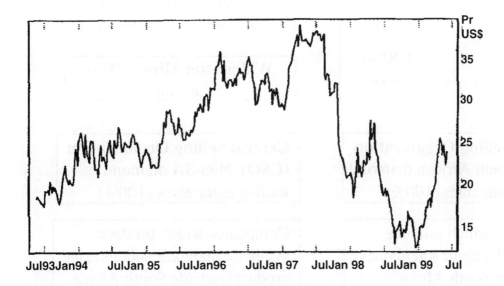

Source: CIBC World Markets

Exhibit 3   De Beers Corporate Structure

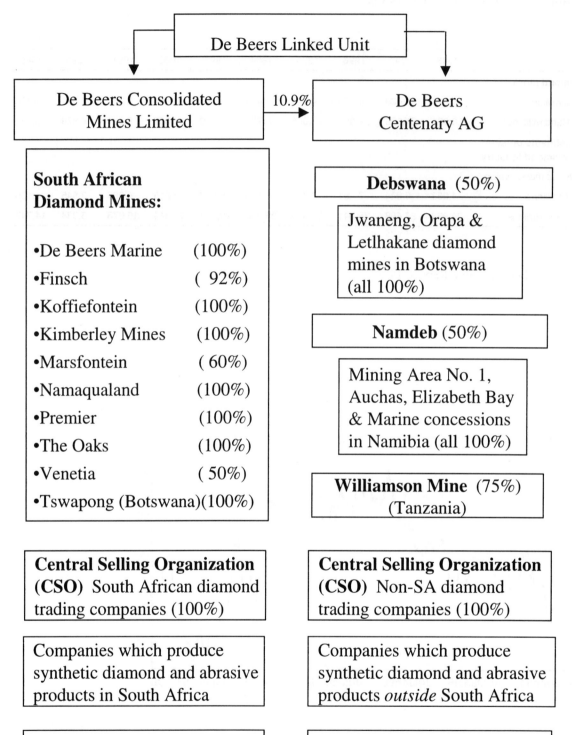

South: De Beers

Exhibit 4   Commodity Prices, 1980-1998

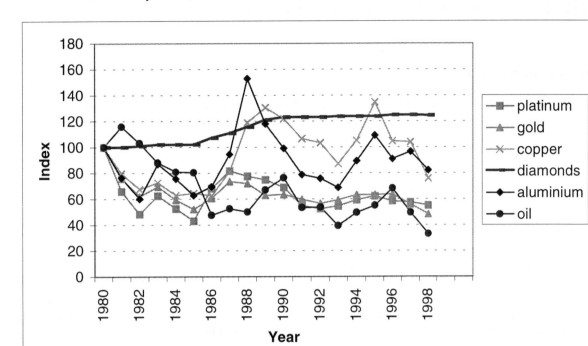

Source: De Beers

Exhibit 5 U.S. Antitrust Law: The Sherman and Clayton Acts

Sherman Act, Section 1.

Every contract, combination in the form of trust or otherwise, or conspiracy, in restraint of trade or commerce among the several States, or with foreign nations, is declared to be illegal.

Clayton Act.

It shall be unlawful for any person engaged in commerce, in the course of such commerce, either directly or indirectly, to discriminate in price between different purchasers of commodities of like grade and quality, where either or any of the purchases involved in such discrimination are in commerce, where such commodities are sold for use, consumption, or resale within the United States or any Territory thereof or the District of Columbia or any insular possession or other place under the jurisdiction of the United States, and where the effect of such discrimination may be substantially to lessen competition or tend to create a monopoly in any line of commerce...

Source: *United States Code 1994 Edition, Vol. 6 Title 15,* (Washington: United States Government Printing Office, 1995), p. 114, 119.

Exhibit 6   Diamond Industry Operating Profit, 1997 (Total = U.S.$8.5 billion)

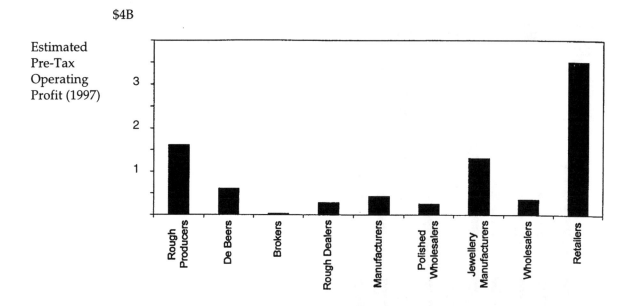

Exhibit 7   Value of De Beers's Rough Diamond Stockpile

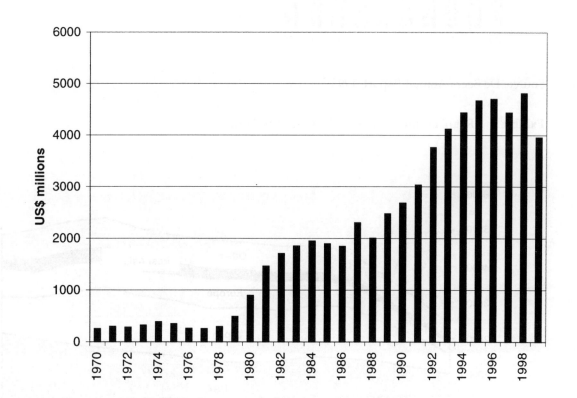

Source: De Beers

Exhibit 8 CSO Rough Diamond Sales, 1989-1998

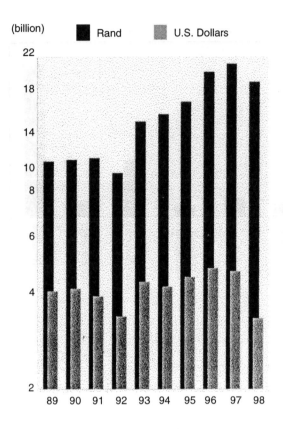

Source: De Beers Annual Report, 1998

Exhibit 9 Retail Diamond Sales by Region ($million)

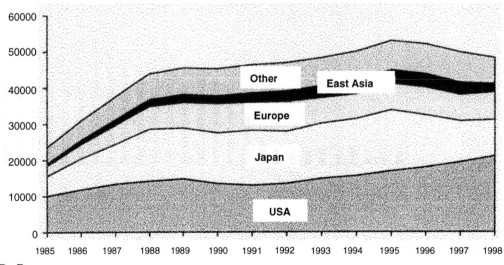

Source: De Beers

Exhibit 10   Diamond Jewelry Market in the United States, 1996 - 1998

Total Diamond Jewelry Market—by Pieces

Pieces (000)	1996		1997		1998		% Chg 1997-98
	# Pieces	% Pieces	# Pieces	% Pieces	# Pieces	% Pieces	
Total Women's	**23,367**	**75%**	**25,007**	**77%**	**26,415**	**78%**	**6%**
Married women	14,513	47%	15,368	47%	16,264	48%	6%
Single women	8,854	28%	9,639	30%	10,151	30%	5%
Bridal	**3,133**	**10%**	**3,051**	**9%**	**3,134**	**9%**	**3%**
Engagement Ring	1,675	5%	1,663	5%	1,659	5%	--
Wedding Band	977	3%	889	3%	963	3%	8%
Men's Wedding Band	481	2%	499	1%	512	1%	3%
Teens	**1,582**	**5%**	**1,736**	**5%**	**1,649**	**5%**	**-5%**
Men's	**3,046**	**10%**	**2,834**	**9%**	**2,697**	**8%**	**-5%**
Total	**31,128**	**100%**	**32,628**	**100%**	**33,895**	**100%**	**4%**

Total Diamond Jewelry Market—by Value

Value ($ million)	1996		1997		1998		% Chg 1997-98
	$ Value	% Value	$ Value	% Value	$ Value	% Value	
Total Women's	**$13,158**	**69%**	**$14,631**	**72%**	**$16,234**	**73%**	**11%**
Married women	$9,404	49%	$10,573	52%	$11,970	54%	13%
Single women	$3,754	20%	$4,058	20%	$4,263	19%	5%
Bridal	**$4,025**	**21%**	**$3,919**	**19%**	**$4,329**	**20%**	**10%**
Engagement Ring	$3,022	16%	$2,998	15%	$3,318	15%	11%
Wedding Band	$761	4%	$688	3%	$715	4%	4%
Men's Wedding Band	$242	1%	$233	1%	$296	1%	27%
Teen's	**$302**	**2%**	**$290**	**1%**	**$284**	**1%**	**-2%**
Men's	**$1,496**	**8%**	**$1,564**	**8%**	**$1,340**	**6%**	**-14%**
Total	**$18,981**	**100%**	**$20,405**	**100%**	**$22,186**	**100%**	**9%**

Total Diamond Jewelry Market—by Average Price

Average Price ($)	1996	1997	1998	% Chg 1997-98
Total Women's	**$563**	**$585**	**$615**	**5%**
Married women	$648	$688	$736	7%
Single women	$424	$421	$420	--
Bridal	**$1,285**	**$1,284**	**$1,381**	**8%**
Engagement Ring	$1,804	$1,803	$2,000	11%
Wedding Band	$779	$774	$742	-4%
Men's Wedding Band	$503	$467	$578	24%
Teen's	**$191**	**$167**	**$172**	**3%**
Men's	**$491**	**$552**	**$497**	**-10%**
Total	**$610**	**$625**	**$655**	**5%**

1 Diamond jewelry is defined as any jewelry piece with at least one real new diamond, regardless of the diamond's size or value.

Source: J. Walter Thompson, Inc.

Exhibit 11   De Beers Millennial Campaign Advertisement

Source: J. Walter Thompson, Inc.

Note on Rules

In religion, in politics, and indeed in nearly any form of social interaction, rule-making is the central act of governance. Rules define what is permissible and what is not. They specify standards of behavior for a given community, clarifying the terms of interaction and setting the norms of conduct. Although rules can emerge through a number of processes, they are essentially social constructs. That is, they are created by society and for society. They are the means by which societies govern their conduct and that of their members. To understand the rules of any group is to understand how that group functions: its goals, its prohibitions, its power brokers.

For business, and especially international business, rules are critical. Although managers frequently complain about rules, although they often pride themselves on bending the rules or succeeding despite them, business still operates – always and everywhere – in a world where rules apply. These rules may not necessarily have the public status of law; they may be formal in some cases, less formal in others. They will emerge through different processes and be enforced by agents with varying amounts of coercion or persuasion or force. But rules will always exist, defining the contours of any society and shaping the behavior of those who operate within it. Wherever business operates, it is affected – created, influenced, rewarded, punished, permitted – by rules.

The importance of rules applies equally to all business, in all countries. But understanding the rules is harder in some circumstances than in others. When firms do business in their own domestic market, they tend to know what the rules are and how they work. U.S. pharmaceutical firms, for example, are painstakingly aware of FDA approval procedures for new drugs and the political pressures that impinge on these procedures. German manufacturing firms understand the commitments that bind them to their unionized labor force. Chinese firms comprehend both the unspoken power of the state and the familial role of *guanxi*. When they grow up among a certain set of rules, managers tend to understand them, to the point where they simply become part of standard operating procedure.

When firms operate outside their home markets, by contrast, rules become less obvious – and more important to identify. In foreign markets, firms need to recognize broad stretches of an often unfamiliar landscape. They need to understand what is acceptable in a given society and what is not; what is rewarded and by whom; where the bases of power lie and how they exercise their control.

Professor Debora Spar prepared this Note as the basis for class discussion rather than to illustrate either effective or ineffective handling of an administrative situation.

Managers need, in short, to understand the rules of the game in a foreign market before they can start playing.

Frequently, the managerial response to unfamiliar terrain is simply to acknowledge the strangeness of a new environment and trudge ahead. Contemplating an investment in a complicated foreign market, managers may realize the depth of difference without having a sure sense of just what these differences are or how they are likely to affect the firm's commercial options. So managers revert to standard practice rather than trying to rearrange their strategies to fit what is often a wholly different political and social context. It is an understandable response but hardly an ideal one. Wherever the rules of the game are different, firms need to respond accordingly: to understand the rules that apply, analyze their likely impact, and plot a course that responds to these rules as effectively as possible. Where these rules collide with a firm's strategic objectives, managers should either leave the country or find some way to evade or change the rules they are about to confront.

The first step, though, is simply to understand the rules – which in itself is often a complicated task, but seldom an impossible one. For while rules may occasionally be slippery or tough to define, they are still amenable to systematic analysis. Managers can learn to read the rules of their target market and factor them into strategic calculations. They can directly assess how rules function and what drives their creation and enforcement. And then they can actually use the rules of the game to enhance their own competitive advantage.

A Typology

At a conceptual level rules are relatively easy to understand. They are the codes or principles that guide behavior in a particular society. By prescribing what is acceptable and what is not, rules enable the members of a society to order and regulate their interactions.

Broadly, rules can be defined as *normative codes that guide, control, or change the behavior of agents with decision-making capacities.*[1] Note the implications of this phrase. First, that rules (for present purposes at least) are normative. They *prescribe* behavior rather than *describe* it. Thus, "thou shalt not kill" is a rule but "the sun always rises in the east" is not. Second, rules serve a distinct social purpose. They seek to affect behavior and have the capacity to do so. Third, rules by this definition can only apply to those with the ability to follow them. To be ruled, one must be capable of obeying.

In practice, of course, rules are far more complex and diverse. While their *function* remains the same – to prescribe behavior upon those with the capacity to comply – their form is subject to almost infinite variation. Rules can be local, national, or international; they can be formal or informal; they can be mandated and enforced by the state, or settled by private associations. They can be general or highly specific, embedded in particular agencies or sanctioned by the norms of the community. Rules can mandate large things (thou shalt not steal) or small (all dogs must be on

---

[1] There is a tremendous body of scholarship within legal and philosophical circles about the meaning and definition of rules. See in particular Frederick Schauer, *Playing by the Rules* (Oxford: Clarendon Press, 1991). Schauer differentiates "prescriptive rules" (the subject of the analysis in this *Note*) from "descriptive rules," which seek to "describe the world rather than alter it" (p. 2). For more on the various legal and philosophical definition of rules, see H.L.A. Hart, "Definition and Theory in Jurisprudence," in *Essays in Jurisprudence and Philosophy* (Oxford: Clarendon Press, 1983); Max Black, "The Analysis of Rules," in *Models and Metaphors* (Ithaca: Cornell University Press, 1962); and John Rawls, "Two concepts of rules," *Philosophical Review* 64 (1955): 3-32.

leashes). They can be enforced by police forces and black helicopters, or the watchful eye of concerned neighbors. All are rules, but of sharply different types.

To understand both the variation that cuts across rules and the common function that binds them, it is useful to separate the universe of rules into a discrete set of categories. We can begin by differentiating three distinctive kinds of rules: norms, laws, and standards. All of these qualify as rules under the definition above. That is, all are prescriptive codes that seek to guide the behavior of those with the ability to comply. They provide this function in different ways, however, and appear in different forms.

Norms

Norms are rules that emerge from society. They are the *informal rules that define a society's members and bind them to one another.* As with rules in general, norms can cover both trivial and critical behavior patterns. In various national settings, shaking hands rather than bowing is a societal norm; so is wearing suits to business meetings, hiring a family member before a stranger, or cementing a business relationship with an elaborate round of toasts. Such norms structure interaction at its most basic level. Even though they are not ensconced in a formal document or upheld by the sanction of law, norms establish the underlying rules of a society, describing how this society operates and what it deems acceptable.

What separates norms from other types of rules is their informality and lack of official standing. Norms are cultural or societal creations, not legal or political ones.[2] They are rules that exist beyond the borders of the state, enabling societies to regulate themselves even when states are absent, or weak, or despised.

Consider, for example, *guanxi*, the complex network of personal and familial bonds that pervades China's business environment.[3] Often perceived by Western observers as simply bribery or corruption, *guanxi* is actually a far more complex system of relationships. It is a social construct, a set of norms that prescribe the terms of business and social interaction. Although it exists outside the legal realm, *guanxi* need not be a violation of law. Rather, to some extent, it is a replacement for law, a means of regulating society without making reference to the state.[4]

Other examples abound across the world of international business. All societies have general norms of interaction and particular norms that adhere to business. The relationships implied in India's caste system constitute a series of norms; so does the Muslim distaste for charging interest and

---

[2] The distinction between law and norms is often a contentious divide, especially among political philosophers. For the majority of legal scholars, the distinction is essential to an understanding of law; as John Austin, a prominent legal theorist of the 19th century, once complained, "the tendency to confound Law and Morals is one of the most prolific sources of jargon, darkness and perplexity." (John Austin, "The uses of the study of jurisprudence," in H.L.A. Hart, ed., *The Province of Jurisprudence* (New York, 1954), p. 371). Those writing in a more philosophical vein, however, argue that the distinctions are artificial, since law rests intimately on the norms and morals of a society. See, for instance, Shklar, *Legalism*.

While entirely sympathetic to this critique, the typology in this *Note* maintains this distinction for the sake of analytical simplicity. It is also in keeping with Shklar's own complaint that "playing with words has always been the favorite intramural sport of academicians." (*Legalism*, p. 24).

[3] Precise definitions of *guanxi* vary widely. See for instance Y. Bian, *Work and Inequality in Urban China* (Albany: SUNY Press, 1994); A.Y. King, "Kuan-hsi and network building: A sociological interpretation," *Daedalus*, Spring 1991, pp.63-84; and Yadong Luo, "Guanxi: Principles, philosophies, and implications." *Human Systems Management* 16(1): 43-51.

[4] For an interesting discussion of guanxi as a set of underlying interpersonal relationships, see Anne S. Tsui and Jiing-Lih Larry Farh, "Where guanxi matters," *Work and Occupations*, February 1997, pp. 56-79.

the American attachment to legalistic modes of transaction. Norms are often harder to identify than other types of rules. They are tougher to classify, define, and adapt to. Yet they are a critical aspect of rules and a dominant feature of any business environment.

Laws

Laws are the rules that states create. They are the codes that emanate directly from the political process. As the sections below describe, laws can derive from a number of sources. Though associated most often with the central authority of a nation state, laws can also be put forth by subnational authorities (state and local governments) or by international ones (the European Union or the World Trade Organization). What makes them laws is their issuance from a recognized public authority and the element of prohibition that accompanies them.[5]

By definition, laws are the rules that the state, in its many guises, proclaims and purports to enforce. Whereas norms are the codes that society constructs to regulate itself, laws are the codes that the state uses to govern society. These laws can take many forms – acts, executive orders, judicial decisions, military codes – but their function is always the same. Laws are mechanisms for political governance. They are the voice of public authority telling the people of a given territory what they can and cannot do. They are a force, moreover, that carries the distinctive threat of retribution. If laws are violated, the authority will punish the offender.

Note the several features that distinguish laws from norms (and also from standards, which are described below). First, laws are explicitly and overtly public. They are the pronouncements of authority. Unlike norms, which can percolate slowly from the core of society, laws must be trumpeted, usually loudly, from the top. Their promulgation is thus a public act. Second, laws emanate from a recognized public authority. They cannot come either from the broader authority of society or from a specific private entity. They come instead from the recognized rulers of a society: its legislators, or prime ministers, or dictators, or kings. Third, and perhaps most important, laws carry with them the implicit threat of force. In all political communities, what differentiates the rulers from the ruled is a monopoly on the legitimate use of force.[6] Thus the rules that the rulers put forth – the laws – bear always the mark of coercion. Breaking the law means risking the retaliation of the state.

Note also that laws are fundamentally territorial. Unlike some norms or standards, laws apply to and are confined by a particular geographical space. Because they are bound by definition to the rulers who pronounce them, their ambit extends only as far as the ruler's reach – a country in most instances; sometimes a city or province. Laws are political creations, linked to the state and its territorial lines.

Standards

Standards are different. While they retain the same basic function as laws, their form and origin are sharply dissimilar. In business, *standards are rules – either public or private – that govern specific aspects of commercial and industrial behavior.* They are rules that exist apart from the cultural bases of society and the coercive force of the state. Unlike norms, though, which emanate from

---

[5] Or as Kelsen argues in his classic treatment of the subject, law is created by a legislature and constitutes a coercive order. See Hans Kelsen, *General Theory of Law and State*, trans. by Anders Wedberg (Cambridge: Harvard University Press, 1945).

[6] See for instance Hedley Bull, *The Anarchical Society* (New York: Columbia University Press, 1977) p. 57.

---

society through a gradual and oblique process, standards are precise and often technical criteria issued by some recognized authority.[7]

By themselves, standards can appear mundane, even trivial. They include details such as the voltage for electrical appliances, the spacing of railroad rails, technical protocols for computer networking, the number of lines of resolution on a television screen. Note, though the force and impact of these standards: they prescribe behavior, delineating what is permissible and what is not. They function entirely as rules, even if they lack the imprimatur of law.

Sometimes, standards gain the force of law, particularly of the sort vested in regulatory acts and agencies. In the United States, for example, federal agencies such as the National Institute of Standards and Technology sets certain technical standards for product testing, measurement, and laboratory accreditation; the Federal Aviation Administration sets standards for airline safety and maintenance procedures; and the Federal Communications Commission generates the underlying standards for electronic communication. Similar functions are performed by many of the evolving agencies of the European Union.[8]

In other instances and areas, however, standards emanate wholly from private sources. The American Medical Association, for example, is a private organization. So are the National Association of Securities Dealers, the American Bar Association, the American National Standards Institute, and the Internet Engineering Task Force. These are private groups, creating private rules that shape and prescribe wide categories of behavior. They determine who can be a doctor, how a firm can offer shares or trade its stock, what voluntary standards U.S. industry will adhere to, and how the Internet's technical pathways will be laid and routed.[9] Such rules may exert a tremendous influence.

Unlike laws, private standards lack the power of the state and the force that, implicitly or explicitly, accompanies this power. Yet standards have a power all their own – the power, quite frequently, to shift markets and shape the contours of competition. As Arthur Levitt, Chairman of the U.S. Securities and Exchange Commission, once argued: "Standards are like a house we raise over our heads. They protect us. They define an area within which a person can function. Without them, civilized life is not possible. We live by the standards we set, and we dismantle them at our peril."[10]

Together, the three kinds of rules suggest a basic typology. In the world of business, we can divide the universe of rules into norms, laws, and standards, analyzing the structure of each in a target market and the forces behind its creation. We can also note, at a basic level, what differentiates the three kinds of rules. Norms are the rules that emanate directly from society; laws are rules that

---

[7] The International Organization for Standards (ISO), an international federation of national standards bodies, offers a similar definition of standards as: "documented agreements containing technical specifications or other precise criteria to be used consistently as rules, guidelines or definitions of characteristics, to ensure that materials, products, processes and services are fit for their purpose." Note here that standards are rules and are determined by "agreements," rather than by governmental dictate. Note, too, that the ISO prides itself as being a non-governmental (i.e., private) organization.

[8] See for example Michael A. Taverna, "Europe pushes broader oversight role for JAA," *Aviation Week and Space Technology* August 8, 1997, pp. 44-45; and Alan Pearce, "FCC will serve as regulatory model for European Union," *America's Network* January 15, 1996, p. 44.

[9] The creation of technical standards for the Internet has occurred largely through private, non-governmental bodies: the Internet Society, the Internet Architecture Board, the Internet Engineering Steering Group, and the Internet Engineering Task Force. See Ethan B. Kapstein, "Regulating the Internet: A Report to the President's Commission on Critical Infrastructure Protection," (Humphrey Institute of Public Affairs, University of Minnesota, June 1997).

[10] See Arthur Levitt, "The importance of standards," *Vital Speeches of the Day*, July 15, 1997, pp. 588-591.

emanate from the state; and standards are rules that emanate generally from particular private actors. As indicated in Figure 1, there will always be some overlap between the categories. Public law, for example, may enforce privately created standards, as is the case with the AMA, where state medical boards formally license physicians. It also describes the basic structure of contracts: private agreements that can be upheld, at least in the United States, by state and federal courts.[11] Similarly, public law often reinforces and codifies the existing norms of society. Laws against infanticide, for example, may not be completely necessary in order to stem what most societies already view as a reprehensible practice. And laws that stray too far from society's norms are generally either struck down (like the 18th amendment barring the sale of alcohol in the United States) or ignored (as are most state laws prohibiting homosexual practices). Thus the borders between the categories are fluid rather than fixed, reflecting the essential functionality that binds all rules together.[12]

Figure 1: A Typology of Rules

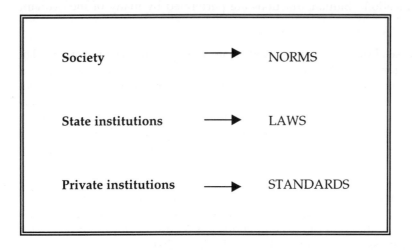

Rules of the International Sphere

Thus far we have spoken only of the rules that prevail within the borders of the traditional nation state. This is a natural focus, since the bulk of the rules that affect a particular country will tend to come from within that country: from its political system, its cultural traditions, its private firms. In a global economy, however, the rules that adhere to a particular state can also be generated outside that state, from a growing body of international and transnational forces.

To examine these forces and the kinds of rules they generate, we can extend the typology beyond the national level. That is, at the international level, we can also identify three analogous kinds of rules: international norms, international laws, and international standards.

---

[11] Note here that the court's role in contractual disputes is not generally to pass judgment on the provisions of the contract. It is to uphold the basic sanctity of contracts.

[12] In her classic account, *Legalism*, Judith Shklar argues that law is too often sealed off from the social context in which it occurs. She suggests considering law instead as a part of a social continuum, with legalistic institutions at one end and personal morality at the other. This continuum is reflected in the first two categories presented here, though they are handled discretely for simplicity's sake. Since she focuses on legalism, Shklar does not include a treatment of private rules. See Judith N. Shklar, *Legalism: Law, Morals, and Political Trials* (Cambridge, MA: Harvard University Press, 1986), especially pp. 1-28.

International norms are straightforward. They are *customs or traditions that extend across national boundaries to encompass a wide range of international behavior patterns.* Evolutionary by nature, they tend to migrate along with the predominant forces of the global economy. Thus English became the default language – the norm – of international business due to the successive expansion of British and American enterprise. And Chinese norms follow the trading patterns of Chinese capital. More fundamental norms – a prohibition against killing, a commitment to "do unto others" – can be traced either to the universal demands of all societies, or to the ancient missionary imprint of the world's major religions.[13]

International law encompasses a broader and more variegated range of rules. In the international system, there is no equivalent to the sovereign of the nation state. There is no central authority, no rule-making entity with either the might or the legitimacy to govern. Instead, the international system is composed of independent states and characterized, according to most scholars of international relations, by a permanent state of anarchy.[14] The law that exists, therefore, is different from that which prevails in the domestic realm. It is law by negotiation rather than dictate; law generated through negotiation and agreement by each of the participating states. The force behind this law rests with the sovereign power of each separate country, rather than with any almighty supranational entity.[15]

At the international level, law takes one of two principal forms. The first is *treaty law – codes and agreements to which states willfully bind themselves.* The North American Free Trade Agreement (NAFTA) is one example of a binding international treaty; the Single European Act is another. Historically, one of the most intriguing achievements of international law was the Law of the Sea, a protracted discussion launched in the 17th century that eventually produced a European consensus about the freedom of the open seas and a state's specific rights upon them.[16] According to some scholars, there are also laws of warfare (just cause; proportionality; discrimination) which constitute a form of international law, even if these laws are honored primarily in the breach.[17]

A second form of international law are the *codes and provisions that emanate from international organizations.* Often themselves the product of international treaties, international organizations are a proliferating feature of the international sphere. They include the United Nations and the World Bank, the World Trade Organization (WTO) and the International Atomic Energy Association, the International Telecommunications Union and the World Intellectual Property Organization. As with treaty law, the codes put forth by these groups have no independent force behind them. There is no sovereign power in the United Nations, no military to enforce the policies of the World Bank or the WTO. Rather, their power rests wholly with the member states that created and support them. But

---

[13] With the growth of international institutions described below, scholars have also begun to debate the possibility that norms emerge directly from the international system. See Andrew Cortell and James Davis, "How do international institutions matter? The domestic impact of international rules and norms," *International Studies Quarterly* 40 (December 1996).

[14] Representative works include Stanley Hoffmann, *The State of War: Essays in the Theory and Practice of International Politics* (New York: Praeger, 1954); and Friedrich V. Kratochwil, *Rules, Norms and Decisions* (New York: Cambridge University Press, 1990).

[15] See for example J.L. Brierly, *The Law of Nations* (Oxford: Oxford University Press, 1955) p. 95; and Hedley Bull, *The Anarchical Society* (New York: Columbia University Press, 1977) p. 71.

[16] See Brierly, *The Law of Nations*, pp. 304-316. More recently, a protracted international convention yielded an ambitious and formal agreement known as the United Nations Conference on the Law of the Sea. The agreement was never ratified by the United States, however, and is thus generally viewed as a disappointment among scholars of international relations. For the classic treatment of the negotiations that led to the Law of the Sea, see James K. Sebenius, *Negotiating the Law of the Sea* (Cambridge, MA: Harvard University Press, 1984).

[17] See William V. O' Brien, *The Conduct of Just and Limited War* (New York: Praeger Publishers, 1981); and Michael Walzer, *Just and Unjust Wars* (New York: Basic Books, 1977).

this is a considerable power in many cases, one which gives weight to their decisions and confirms their rule-making function. Once countries join an international organization, they generally comply with its rules and decisions, even when they run contrary to the national interest.

At the international level we can also see the impact and magnitude of *standards*. As in the domestic realm, standards are again private rules. They are *guidelines and procedures issued outside the formal structure of the state*, rules with a practical authority more than a legal one.

Typically, international standards are generated by private entities that span national borders. They tend, in particular, to migrate along with the activities of powerful multinational firms or industrial clusters. Consider, for example, the international expansion of U.S. accounting standards. Traditionally, countries have created their own systems for corporate accounting, and U.S. standards, created by the Financial Accounting Standard Board (FASB), are considered particularly stringent. Yet, as more and more non-U.S. firms seek to list their shares on U.S. stock exchanges, foreign accounting standards seem gradually to be shifting toward the U.S. model.[18] A similar dynamic is also well underway in the legal profession, where U.S.-style contracts for corporate transactions are rapidly becoming the international standard.

An even more dramatic example is ISO9000, an ambitious code of quality management standards promulgated in 1987 by the Geneva-based International Organization for Standards (ISO). As a private agreement between private parties, ISO9000 has absolutely no formal legal standing. Yet manufacturers increasingly feel compelled to follow its provisions, demonstrating explicitly that they perform at "world class" standards.[19] Reproductions of the ISO9000 process dot the global arena. ISO14000 is a series of environmental management standards; SA8000 is a code for monitoring labor conditions and other aspects of social accountability.[20] Like rules in general, these codes steer the behavior of affected firms. Their force lies in the marketplace rather than with any governmental body, but it is nevertheless a force, and often a very powerful one.

A second type of international standard is more subtle and ambiguous. It comes not from associations of private firms *per se*, but from the so-called non-governmental organizations (NGOs) that have recently proliferated across the international sphere. Essentially, NGOs are private non-profit groups that perform what their members consider a public or societal function. They tend to be watchdogs of one sort or another, pursuing environmental goals, or social, cultural, or health-related ones. Greenpeace, for example, is a vocal (sometimes even violent) advocate for environmental protection. Save the Children works for children's rights and opportunities; Médecins Sans Frontières provides emergency medical assistance.

Such groups create standards through the pressure they apply to other actors in the global arena. In a highly publicized 1995 incident, for instance, Shell Oil decided to abandon a $16 million plan to dump a disused oil rig on the bottom of the Atlantic Ocean because Greenpeace had succeeded in inciting a consumer boycott against the company. In Indonesia, both the government

---

[18] See Beth Simmons, "The international politics of harmonization: the case of capital market regulation," Mimeo, University of California, Berkeley, 1997.

[19] See S. Subba Rao, T.S. Ragu-Nathan, and Luis E. Solis, "Does ISO 9000 have an effect on quality management practices?" *Total Quality Management*, December 1997, pp. 335-346; and Sergio Mazza, "The significance of standards," *Plant Engineering*, January 1997, pp. 90-92.

[20] ISO 14000 is another "family" of standards, published by the ISO in 1996. SA8000 is the creation of the New York-based Council on Economic Priorities. For details of the ISO 14000 standard, see Chuck Pouliot, "ISO 14000: Beyond compliance to competitiveness," *Manufacturing Engineering*, May 1996, pp. 51-56. For more on the creation and intent of SA8000, see Debora L. Spar, "The spotlight and the bottom line: how U.S. multinationals export human rights," *Foreign Affairs*, March/April 1998.

and Freeport McMoran, the country's largest foreign investor, have scrambled to ward off environmentalist attacks on the vast Irian Jaya copper mine. China persistently revisits plans for its massive Three Gorges Dam at the behest of international pressure groups; so does India, with its own Sardar Sardovar Dam. Elsewhere, American and European chemical companies have been besieged by allegations of lax safety standards in some of their foreign facilities, and garment and footwear manufacturers have been accused of unfair and abusive labor practices in their Asian operations.[21] Such pressure constitutes an increasingly important feature of the global economy. Non-governmental organizations are demanding adherence to the standards they propose. Without any formal power, they are sometimes able to create standards for the international system.

Adding these three types of international rules to our previous diagram produces the modified version presented in Figure 2 below. We find three basic kinds of rules – norms, laws, and standards – occurring in the international sphere, as well as within nation states.

Figure 2: Rules of the International Sphere

In practice, once again, these rules will inevitably overlap. National laws find their way to the international system; private standards are often subsequently institutionalized as formal regulations. Still, dividing rules into these various categories provides a useful map of the political context in which firms operate. It depicts not just the legal backdrop – the formal rules that regulate firm behavior – but also the broader and more subtle rules of the game, the forces that shape the very nature of business but dwell beyond the normal scope of law or the reach of the nation state.

---

[21] See for example Ethan Kapstein, "Workers and the world economy," *Foreign Affairs*, May/June 1996, pp. 16-37; Terry Collingsworth, J. William Goold, and Phavis J. Harvey, "Labor and free trade," *Foreign Affairs*, January/February 1994, pp. 8-13; and J. Leonard, *Pollution and the Struggle for World Product* (Cambridge: Cambridge University Press, 1988).

To be complete, however, an analysis of the rules must go past even the six categories described above. Because rules are hardly ever static, the analysis should include a dynamic element as well, an exploration of *how rules emerge from a particular political or social context* and *how predictably and effectively these rules are implemented*. It must look at the sources and enforcement of rules.

Sources

Where do rules come from? It depends. Sometimes they bubble up from the deepest wells of a society's culture. Sometimes they are extended by private parties with an identifiable self-interest. Sometimes they are created by the formal structures of the state or the formal procedures of an international organization.

For simplicity's sake, these sources can be arranged to mirror the typology suggested above. Essentially, rules come from one of three primary places: from the culture and tradition of a particular society, from the state, or from private actors with the authority to impose their decisions upon others. Rules come, in other words, either from society, the state, or private groups. This pattern repeats at the international level, although the process of rule creation here will tend to be slower and less obvious.

Creating norms

When rules spring from society, the generation process is difficult to describe and track.[22] Societal evolution is by nature a gradual process, an iterative dialogue between past practices and current demand, between custom and change. Societies develop norms in response to some perceived need; they institutionalize norms through tradition and education, through complex social structures or internal divisions of power. As the economist Douglass North has described this intricate process: "[N]orms.. are derived from the constructions of reality (ideology) that individuals develop to contend with their environment... Consensus ideologies evolve when the individuals of a universe have similar experiences."[23]

Creating laws

Laws derive from a much clearer and more transparent process. This does not mean that the process is necessarily straightforward or even honest, or that it follows the same path in all countries. Laws emerge through very different means and can take radically different forms. All laws, however, are essentially political products. Their generation can be traced back to and through any country's political system.

---

[22] Recently, scholars from the fields of comparative politics and international relations have begun to track the process by which norms are institutionalized into more formal policies. See Peter Katzenstein, *Cultural Norms and National Security: Police and Military in Postwar Japan* (Ithaca: Cornell University Press, 1996); and Judith Goldstein, *Ideas, Interests and American Trade Policy* (Ithaca: Cornell University Press, 1993). As critics of this literature have been quick to point out, however, even scholars who work in this tradition have not yet explained how norms originate and why they change. See David Dessler, "What's at stake in the agent-structure debate?" *International Organization* 43 (Summer 1989).

[23] Douglass C. North, *Structure and Change in Economic History* (New York: W.W. Norton & Company, 1981) p. 205.

In some countries, rules emerge though a rational and predictable process of rent-seeking. Various interest groups express their preferences to a political system which arbitrates their interests and rewards those with the most votes, the greatest clout, or the staunchest coalition.[24] Though this view of the political process is stark and almost certainly oversimplified, it rings true in many cases, especially those concerning the formation of trade policy in democratic states. Consider, for instance, the United States' protracted embargo against trade with Cuba. Why does the United States persist in prohibiting trade with Cuba? Largely because there is a powerful domestic lobby in favor of the sanctions, and a relatively uncommitted and uncoordinated group of opponents. Precisely the reverse pattern characterizes U.S. trade policy towards China. Here, the strongly-held views of large and diverse domestic firms consistently overwhelm the more specific interests of human rights groups and (occasionally) labor groups. To track the likely outcome of trade policy in either of these cases, one would need only to follow the interest group politics that surround them.[25]

In other instances, laws spring much more directly from the will and power of the central leadership. For decades, policy in China was essentially the political desires of Chairman Mao; after his death, the mantle passed to Deng who, without Mao's monomaniacal fervor, nevertheless set the rules for China. Accordingly, analysts of China during this time focussed almost exclusively on the leader's pronouncements and the personal cohort that surrounded him. For these, they knew, were the source of China's rules. A similar relationship holds whenever power concentrates in a single personality or faction: Stalin's Russia; Qaddafi's Libya; Hussein's Iraq; Suharto's Indonesia. If firms want to understand what drives the business environment in these countries, they need to understand the interests and desires of the leadership. If they want to modify the rules to suit their own interests, they need to go directly to the leader.

Such excessive concentrations of power, however, are increasingly rare. In most countries, power is split among various groups and agencies, and laws emerge from a continuous bargaining among them. The outcomes of these struggles depend on the institutional structure of the various agencies and the relative weights of their power. In the United States, for instance, some rules are controlled almost entirely by particular agencies (the FCC for broadcast television; the Federal Reserve Board for reserve requirements), while others (particularly trade policy) are more susceptible to legislative and electoral politics. In Japan, by contrast, the lines of bureaucratic discretion are both broader and more clearly demarcated. Powerful agencies such as MITI (Ministry of International Trade and Industry) and MOF (Ministry of Finance) have been essentially removed from political vacillation and armed with rule-making and enforcement capabilities. For decades, therefore, firms that traded with or invested in Japan maintained the closest ties they could with these agencies, and watched carefully for any changes in their regulatory agendas.

---

[24] Standard works in this vein include Stephen P. Magee, William A. Brock, and Leslie Young, *Black Hole Tariffs and Endogenous Policy Theory* (Cambridge: Cambridge University Press, 1989); Giulio M. Gallarotti, "Toward a business–cycle model of tariffs," *International Organization*, Winter 1985, pp. 155-88; and James Cassing, Timothy McKeown, and Jack Ochs, "The political economy of the tariff cycle," *American Political Science Review* 80 (1986) pp. 843-62.

[25] The ability of special interest groups to affect the foreign policy making process seems particularly marked in the United States, and particularly strong with regard to trade policy. See for instance the comparative analyses in Peter Katzenstein, ed., *Between Power and Plenty: Foreign Economic Policies of Advanced Industrial States* (Madison: University of Wisconsin Press, 1978); and G. John Ikenberry, David A. Lake, and Michael Mastanduno, "Introduction: Approaches to explaining American foreign economic policy," in Ikenberry, Lake, and Mastanduno, eds., *The State and American Foreign Economic Policy* (Ithaca: Cornell University Press, 1988).

Creating standards

Though standards can emerge through a variety of channels, they typically develop through some sort of coordinated process – some arrangement that permits interested parties to arrive at a common set of specifications, or qualifications, or measurements. Often, standards are the work of expert committees or industry associations, groups bound by a common interest in developing an approved technical format before committing commercial funds to its development. Such arrangements are particularly appealing where large capital investments are involved, where several different kinds of technology must operate on a common platform, or when employment of the standard is likely to entail massive and expensive shifts in consumer behavior. Thus, television manufacturers and broadcasters worked together for years to create a common technical platform for higher resolution television programming; accounting firms in the United States joined forces to create the powerful FASB standards; and numerous industry groups rushed in the mid-1990s to define standard protocols for Internet commerce.

As with most cases of standard-setting, competitive urges provide much of the force behind these kinds of cooperative ventures. Firms come together to create standards that will enable them to compete against other rivals.[26] Just as political power stems from the ability to set and enforce the laws of the state or the international system, so does market power rest with an ability to set market standards. And sometimes the only way to create these competitive standards is through cooperation.[27]

Creating international rules

At the international level, the generation of rules occurs along largely analogous paths. Norms emerge unseen and often unheralded, prodded by the migration or expansion of groups that carry their local customs along with them. Norms can also develop along the lines of "epistemic communities," groups of like-minded individuals who come together across national lines to pursue a common agenda.[28] International law, by contrast, emanates from the same fractious, often torturous, process that characterizes law-making at the national level. It emerges from a seemingly endless stream of conferences and working groups; of draft conventions and corridor politicking.

Finally, at the international level, standards arise either through the formal channels of an international organization or through the less formal but perhaps more forceful mechanism of transnational private actors. The European Union, for instance, could be described as a massive

---

[26] This rivalry is particularly obvious in the race to develop standards for desktop computing. See, for instance, Kimberly Caisse, "Industry: NC vs. Net PC issue stresses platform," *Computer Reseller News*, September 1, 1997, pp. 121,123; and Michael Borrus and John Zysman, "Wintelism and the changing terms of global competition: prototype of the future?" BRIE Working Paper 96B (Berkeley: Berkeley Roundtable on the International Economy, February 1997).

[27] A similar dynamic characterizes successful cartels, which are essentially a set of private rules for market behavior. See Debora L. Spar, *The Cooperative Edge: The Internal Politics of International Cartels* (Ithaca: Cornell University Press, 1994).

[28] According to some scholars, shifting norms with regard to environmental protection, trade in services and human rights can be traced empirically to the coalescence of these transnational groups. Literature along these lines includes Peter Haas, *Saving the Mediterranean: The Politics of International Economic Cooperation* (New York: Columbia University Press, 1994); Haas, "Introduction: Epistemic communities and international policy coordination," *International Organization* 46 (Winter 1992); Kathryn Sikkink, "Human rights, principled issue-networks and sovereignty in Latin America," *International Organization* 47 (Summer 1993); and William Drake and Kalypso Nicolaidis, "Ideas, interests and institutionalization: trade in services and the Uruguay Round," *International Organization*, Vol. 46, No. 1 (Winter 1992) pp. 37-100.

exercise in standard setting, typified by the thousands of technical specifications issued by the Brussels-based Commission. Note, though, that even in their most official manifestation, standards at the international level tend to derive from standards that already exist at the national level. In practice, this means that the "winners" of a domestic rivalry can often impose their standards on the broader international market – either through the marketplace itself, or through careful maneuvering within international standard-setting agencies. Rupert Murdoch's BSkyB, for example, created the standard for satellite TV and conditional access systems in the United Kingdom and then exported these standards through careful lobbying with the European Commission.[29] The venue may change, therefore, but the game remains the same. Those with power tend to create the rules, and the generation of rules bestows further power upon their creators.

Enforcement

To be effective, rules must be enforced. Definitionally, we can consider enforcement as *the means or mechanisms by which the subjects of a rule are persuaded or forced to comply.* Enforcement is the proverbial slap on the face or hand, a signal to the offender that a rule has been broken and that the offense carries costs. Sometimes this signal is violent, but usually it is not. Like rules themselves, enforcement can come from various avenues and manifest itself in very different forms.

Once again, we can consider six broad categories of enforcement. Enforcement can occur at the hands of society, the state, or private actors. It can apply to the rules of nations or of the international system.

Enforcement by society

In society, enforcement occurs through deeply ingrained rites and practices. Societies enforce their rules by teaching them to children, embedding them in the everyday rituals of interaction, and ostracizing those who stray. At the societal level, rules are enforced through repetition and persuasion rather than force. Consider again *guanxi*, one of the strongest examples of a societally-based business norm. *Guanxi* is enforced through habit and punished by exclusion. If one reneges on a personal contract, or neglects an established relationship, he or she will be punished – not necessarily by the state, but by members of the relevant community. Subsequent deals will not materialize, favors once granted may be withdrawn.

A similar process marks the enforcement of international norms. By the time they have bubbled up to the international systems, most norms have already been embedded both in domestic society and in national law. Thus while we can identify international norms of business – such as repugnance to slavery or, perhaps, a general distaste for child labor – such norms do not usually have an independent means of enforcement.[30]

---

[29]See Debora Spar and Paula Zakaria, *BSkyB*, Harvard Business School Case 9-798-077; and Helen Burton, "Digital broadcasting in the United Kingdom," *Computer and Telecommunications Law Review*, vol. 1. 1997, pp. 33-42.

[30] In the case of international sanctions against South Africa's apartheid regime, it appears that both paths of enforcement were at work. See Audie Klotz, *Norms in International Relations: The Struggle against Apartheid* (Ithaca: Cornell University Press, 1995).

Recent developments in international relations theory also suggest the possibility that norms generated at the international level can subsequently make their way back to the national level. See Martha Finnemore, *National Interests in International Society* (Ithaca: Cornell University Press, 1996); and David Strang and Patricia

Enforcement by the state

When rules take the form of laws, the only entity with the power to enforce them is the state. Laws may be sanctioned, of course, by the norms of society and societies may do their part to uphold the laws that govern them. Laws against murder and incest, for example, are clearly enforced by society as well as by the state. But ultimately the power of law rests with enforcement by the state.

States enforce their laws through a variety of means and with varying degrees of vigor. At some level, enforcement by the state is always a matter of force. Indeed, it is the control over the legitimate use of force that defines the state in most instances and separates it from other societal actors.[31] This basic connection applies in all states, from the most pacifist and legalistic ones to the most violent and dictatorial. Everywhere, the state's control rests ultimately on its control of force; and the power of the law stems from ultimate control by the state. This connection may be attenuated by divisions of power and legal systems; it may be softened by ideological commitment or societal support. But it exists in all states.

The connection between force and law is most obvious in dictatorial or authoritarian regimes, where laws are often little more than the wishes of the leader, and the leader's hold on power stems from his control of the military forces. Such was the case in Idi Amin's Uganda or in the stream of military groups that have ruled Burma since 1962. It also describes Stalin's Russia, Qaddafi's Libya, and Saddam Hussein's Iraq.[32] In all these systems, leadership rests partially on a legitimacy derived through ideology, but mostly on a basic control over the military resources of the state. Enforcement is thus bundled directly with law, and both emanate from the central power of the leadership.

In these systems, enforcement becomes a simple function of the leader's desire. When Idi Amin wanted to seize the property of Indians living in Uganda, he simply did it. Though he cloaked the seizure in a legal document, the law was far less important than the physical enforcement of it.[33] Similarly, when Burma's SLORC decided to open the country to foreign investment, it opened quickly and decisively – and provided military coverage for investments, such as the Yadana natural gas pipeline, that might be subject to attack from disaffected local groups.[34] The impact on foreign firms in these two cases was dramatically different, but the process was equally simple and predictable. Enforcement followed the leadership's interests. Doing business under such circumstances may be unsavory or even immoral, but it is also relatively straightforward. To understand the likely pattern of enforcement, foreign firms need only to look at the leadership's preferences.

In democratic states, the relationship between law creation and enforcement is somewhat more complicated. Generally, policies in democratic states are enforced clearly and consistently. Yet there are also instances in which even highly democratic and legalistic countries will allow for

---

Mei Yin Chang, "The International Labor Organization and the welfare state: International effects on national welfare spending, 1960-80, "*International Organization* 47 (Spring 1993). For a review of this literature, see Jeffrey T. Chekel, "The constructivist turn in international relations theory," *World Politics* 50 (January 1998), pp. 324-48.

[31] The relationship between coercion and state power lies at the historical core of political philosophy. Classic treatments include F. A. Hayek, *The Constitution of Liberty* (Chicago, 1960); Nicolo Machiavelli, *The Prince*, translated by Leo Paul S. de Alvarez (Irving, Texas: University of Dallas Press, 1980); and John Stuart Mill, *Essays on Politics and Society*, edited by J.M. Robson (Toronto: University of Toronto Press, 1977). Hayek is one of the few theorists to suggest that governments can be divorced – through law – from their coercive role.

[32] The distinction between the first group of countries and the second fits broadly with Kirkpatrick's well-known distinction between dictatorships and authoritarian regimes. See Jeane J. Kirkpatrick, *Dictatorships and Double Standards* (Washington, DC: American Enterprise Institute, 1980).

[33]Formally, expulsion occurred under the terms of the 1972 Expulsion of Asians Presidential Decree.

[34] See Lane LaMure and Debora Spar, *The Burma Pipeline*, Harvard Business School Case 9-797-149.

significant gaps in enforcement. U.S. prohibitions against third-country exports to Cuba, for example, are "on the books," but rarely enforced. (As of early 1998, only two cases had actually been filed.[35]) The U.S. Foreign Corrupt Practices Act, which delineates acceptable conduct for U.S. firms operating in foreign countries, has a similarly spotty record. While most U.S. firms are clearly aware of the law (and many claim vociferously to be in full compliance with it), the number of prosecutions is remarkably small.[36] As with other laws, such as tax provisions or speed limits, firms may play a guessing game in practice, weighing the costs of compliance against the likelihood of getting caught in violation.

There are also instances in which the various agencies of the state simply have little interest in enforcing their own laws. These may be laws passed to appease particular interest groups, or rules created in response to external pressure, or rules made by a part of the government to which the enforcing agency is opposed. Chinese police forces and courts, for example, have shown only a lacklustre resolve to enforce compliance with China's intellectual property laws. Formally, China offers full protection to both intellectual and physical property. It has laws and legal procedures which claim to protect copyrights, trademarks, and patented technologies. Yet numerous Western companies have encountered basic difficulties in preserving the sanctity of their property. Disney, for instance, has discovered a tide of counterfeit merchandise and Microsoft has suffered from widespread piracy of its popular software. In both of these cases, the firm's problems lay not with the letter of the law but rather with a disinterest in the law's enforcement.

Enforcing international law

At the international level, the enforcement of law becomes an even more precarious and unpredictable endeavor. Recall that in the international system law emerges only at the behest of member states. Its enforcement thus rests always with their approval. States must enforce international law since there is no independent force that adheres to the international system or any of its myriad institutions.[37] Indeed it is the very lack of authority within the international system that has led many scholars to characterize it as anarchy and to doubt the prospects for enforceable international law.[38]

Yet international law does exist, as described above, and it is quite frequently enforced. How? Typically, enforcement comes through the same channels employed for national law, with perhaps some extra bumps and twists along the way. States enforce the international laws they have agreed to, and generally abide by the decisions of the international institutions they support. Sometimes, of course, they try to wriggle free. Germany sought a "health" exemption to EU regulation that would have lowered restrictions on the import of non-German beer; France successfully lobbied to have audiovisual products exempted from the GATT in 1993 as part of a "cultural exception"; and Canada insisted that its own cultural industries be protected from NAFTA's

---

[35] See Merrill Goozner, "U.S. law fails to scare Canada firms out of Cuba," *Chicago Tribune*, June 16, 1997, p. 4; Peter Morton, "Canada still won't budge," *Financial Post*, January 8, 1998, p. 5; and U.S. Department of State, Daily Press Briefing, October 13, 1997.

[36] See James R. Hines, "Forbidden payment: foreign bribery and American business after 1977," Kennedy School of Government Faculty Research Working Paper: R95-25 (Cambridge, MA: Kennedy School of Government, 1995).

[37] One might argue that United Nations forces have at least the potential to exert an independent force for compliance with international law. Recall, though, that U.N. forces exist only through the cooperation of member states. They are indeed composed of national military forces "loaned" to the U.N. for pre-specified periods of time and to perform pre-approved tasks.

[38] See Hoffmann, *The State of War*; Kratochwil, *Rules, Norms and Decisions*; Bull, *The Anarchical Society*; and Inis Claude, *Power and International Relations* (New York: Random House, 1962).

free trade rules. Given the extent of international regulations, however, such exceptions are relatively rare. They are also, for the most part, legally in compliance with the laws they attempt to bend; states seek exemptions rather than directly violate the terms of an agreement. This itself is evidence of a significant degree of compliance.

In some cases, international institutions can also wield a power (if not a force) of their own, particularly with regard to small or poorly-endowed states. The International Monetary Fund, for example, is renowned for its ability to impose harsh fiscal medicine on countries seeking its assistance or advice. This power of the IMF is not military, of course, but financial. It is the power to deny its resources to those who choose not to comply with its rules. Ultimately, though, the capacity to enforce its policies still lies within the confines and political system of the nation state. Ironically, only states can enforce international law.[39]

For firms, the implications of this relationship are two-fold. First, that international law is a force to be reckoned with and watched. When states adhere to international arrangements such as the North American Free Trade Agreement (NAFTA), the European Union, or the World Trade Organization, they create laws that can fundamentally alter the environment for trading and investing firms. The second implication, though, is that these laws do not reach full force until and unless they are enforced by the member states. Simply joining an institution or signing a convention is not sufficient; states must undertake to enforce compliance.[40]

Private enforcement

Because the state looms so large in the field of enforcement, private entities would not seem to have much of a role to play. And yet they do. Just as private groups can create rules, they can also enforce them, both at the national and international levels.

At the national level, firms and private groups enforce a large and growing body of rules. Sometimes they enforce the rules of the state or community, acting in effect as hired guns of law enforcement. Private security forces are an obvious example of this relationship; so are private

---

[39] A related but somewhat more controversial proposition is that only states can be subject to international law. This notion takes on a particular relevance in areas such as international human rights law, where states are signatories to international conventions, yet other actors (particularly multinational corporations) are likely to engage in the kinds of behavior forbidden under treaty. While there is considerable debate on the topic, most international legal scholars seem to agree that corporations cannot be held in violation of international law unless the state explicitly forbids a practice (such as child labor) under its own national law. The standard treatment here is Louis Henkin, *Constitutionalism, Democracy, and Foreign Affairs* (New York: Columbia University Press, 1990). With particular relevance to the applicability of international human rights law to multinational corporations, see Henkin, "How business behaves: human rights," (Mimeo, Columbia University, 1997). Related general works include Abram Chayes and Antonia Handler Chayes, *The New Sovereignty* (Cambridge: Harvard University Press, 1995) and Anne-Marie Slaughter, "International law in a world of liberal states," *European Journal of International Law* 6, no. 4 (1995).

[40] In political science, the relationship between states and the international institutions they form has spawned a huge literature, most of which falls broadly under the term "regime." The standard account of regimes and regime formation is Stephen Krasner, ed., *International Regimes* (Ithaca: Cornell University Press, 1983). Works that focus particularly on state compliance with these regimes (and with international law more generally) include Peter Gourevitch, "Squaring the circle: the domestic sources of international cooperation," *International Organization* 50 (Spring 1996); Peter Cowhey, "International telecommunications regime: the political roots of regimes for high technology," *International Organization* 44 (Spring 1990); and Judith Goldstein, "International law and domestic institutions: reconciling North American 'unfair trade' laws," *International Organization* 50 (Autumn 1996). For the classic treatment of state enforcement and international law, see also Hans J. Morgenthau, *Politics Among Nations* (New York: Alfred A. Knopf, fifth edition, 1978) pp. 277-314.

communities.[41] Less dramatic but more widespread is the gradual expansion of professional service firms into realms of enforcement formerly considered the sole province of the state. In the United States and elsewhere, accounting firms police companies' compliance with various provisions of tax and securities law; credit rating agencies report on commercial banks' compliance with capital adequacy standards;[42] and lawyers offer adjudication services that essentially replicate, for a fee, the combined functions of judge and jury.[43]

In all of these cases, private actors help to enforce what governments have already created. In other cases, though, the private sector acts more independently, enforcing the rules of its own creation. The American Medical Association (AMA) and American Bar Association (ABA), for instance, write the rules of their profession and then enforce them: if a doctor commits malpractice or a lawyer engages in unethical conduct, it is the AMA or ABA that bars them from practice. The state is not wholly absent, since it retains the ultimate ability to punish the offender with jail or criminal sanctions. But much of the process, and the bulk of enforcement, remains in private hands.

Increasingly, technology also offers firms the means for independent enforcement. When Rupert Murdoch's BSkyB encountered piracy of its satellite broadcasting service, the company used technology, rather than traditional means of law enforcement, to stymie the pirates. Through its News Datacom subsidiary, Murdoch's News Corporation pioneered a set-top system for encryption and subscriber management that made Sky's broadcasts far more difficult for non-subscribers to decipher.[44] Similar enforcement techniques abound on the Internet, a sphere that (in its formative years at least) has remained tantalizingly beyond the reach of national governments.[45]

A final method of private enforcement comes from an unlikely but increasingly potent source. As business has spread across borders, it has carried in its wake a host of non-governmental organizations and activist groups. Greenpeace and its kin, as mentioned earlier, have a growing ability to generate rules that carry weight across the international system. They can also enforce these rules, albeit through unconventional means. If a firm (or other entity) engages in behavior that these groups deem offensive, they spring into action, mobilizing grassroots networks to highlight the offending practice and throw a spotlight of scorn upon the offending party. Media groups are often eager to join the fracas, which increases pressure and publicity on the target of the NGO's attack.

---

[41] See for example, "It's a small town after all," *Economist*, November 25, 1995, p. 337.

[42] Capital adequacy rates were initially developed by bank regulators, who established specific standards that banks were expected – though not forced – to meet. Over time, though, private groups essentially took over the examining and reporting function. See Ethan B. Kapstein, *Governing the Global Economy: International Finance and the State* (Cambridge: Harvard University Press, 1994); and Raymond Vernon, Debora L. Spar, and Glenn Tobin, *Iron Triangles and Revolving Doors* (New York: Praeger Publishers, 1991), pp. 129-157.

[43] See Irvin E. Richter, "For those who'd rather resolve than litigate," *New Jersey Law Journal*, February 28, 1991, p. 70.

[44] Spar and Zakaria, *BSkyB*; Barry Fox, "Murdoch's cryptic vision for global TV," *New Scientist*, September 11, 1993, p. 20; and "Murdoch's News Datacom at cutting edge of digital broadcasting," *Jerusalem Post*, October 21, 1996, p. 3.

[45] IBM, for instance, launched an ambitious infoMarket Rights Management project in 1996, using a series of advanced technologies to give copyright holders effective control over the dissemination of their works. Other firms like Infringatek offer investigative services to find and punish online violations of intellectual property rights; and several organizations, such as the Business Software Alliance, the Software Publishers' Association, the Association of American Publishers, and the Copyright Clearance Center, have floated their own efforts to license and monitor the use of intellectual property in cyberspace. While most of these groups work with at least the implicit approval of national governments, they are distinctly private organizations, controlling private means of enforcement.

Often, this pressure is sufficient for the firm to retreat from the offending practice or policy. Shell, as described above, backed away from plans to scuttle its offshore Brent Spar oil platform; and Arco and Texaco beat hasty retreats from proposed oil developments in Burma. In all these instances, it seems fair to assert that private actors – non-governmental organizations, activist groups, and the media – enforced the rules that they had helped to create. It is not enforcement in the conventional sense of courts and police forces, but it is enforcement nevertheless: the parties whose behavior the rules sought to guide or control were compelled, eventually, to comply.

Note that in all of these later instances private enforcement stretches far across national borders. Indeed, the enforcement – of property rights, or environmental standards, or labor conditions – is explicitly directed in these cases at the international level, and at activities which by their very nature transcend the traditional boundaries of the state. Rules are being created and enforced, at the international level, by non-state actors. This is a fairly dramatic development, and one which is likely to accelerate along with the pace of globalization.[46]

Implications

Together, the descriptions above lead to a multi-tiered matrix: rules take the form of norms, laws or standards; they exist at either the national or international level; they are generated and enforced by society, by the state, or by private actors. This matrix is reproduced in the diagram below.

Figure 3: Anatomy of Rules

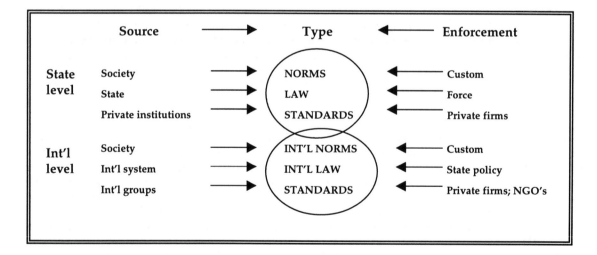

Note that this matrix is a framework for analysis rather than a blueprint for action. It is a tool for understanding the political environment in which firms operate, not a means for determining specific managerial responses. This last step can only be done on the ground and on a case-by-case basis.

---

[46] For an excellent account of these developments and their impact on traditional notions of state power, see Philip Cerny, "Globalization and the changing logic of collective action," *International Organization* 49 (Autumn 1995), pp. 595-625. See also Susan Strange, *The Retreat of the State* (Cambridge: Cambridge University Press, 1996).

There is, therefore, no easy roadmap for responding to the political situation of a target country; no way to put rules into a formula capable of delivering hard answers or particular strategies. There are, however, several broad guidelines that emerge from a focus on rules and which managers can use to shape and inform their own more specific responses.

Analysis: surveying and assessment

The first guideline is evident from the preceding discussion. When managers are trading or investing across borders, they should pay particular heed to the rules that are likely to confront them. They need to survey the political landscape at both the national and international level, carefully scrutinizing the norms, laws and standards that prevail.

This surveying process must be done on the ground and over time. Before embarking on a foreign venture, managers can certainly begin their analysis at home. They can hire lawyers or political consultants and read research reports on their target market. But ultimately, understanding the rules that prevail in the market will involve *being* in that market for some period of time and interacting with relevant decision-makers. Depending on the type of business venture being contemplated, this interaction could involve a whole range of players: from national leaders, party officials, and opposition candidates to local authorities, regulatory officials, and concerned activist groups. With all these groups, it is critical for the firm to decipher how decisions are being made and by whom. They need to get inside the mind of the state, and discover where it is heading.

As the contours of the political landscape become clearer, managers should then push their analysis towards the specific implication for their own venture. How do the rules of country X affect the potential customer base for firm Y's products? How do the rules affect the supply links that the company will need to establish? What is their impact on the company's competitors and on the overall terms of competition?

Managers should, in other words, first make a broad map of a country's political landscape and then superimpose it upon their own commercial interests. This analysis should yield a more precise view of where the risks lie in a target market and how competitive positioning might best be achieved.

Central to the mapping process are two analytical tasks. First, managers must decide, at a general level, whether the rules of a given country are favorable or unfavorable to their proposed venture. And then they must determine where the specific risks to their business lie.

This first piece is relatively straightforward. Once managers understand the rules that prevail in their target market, they simply need to ask themselves whether these rules favor the kind of business they are contemplating or push against it. Do the power brokers and decision-makers actually want the firm's business or not? Are the rules set up to encourage certain kinds of activity or to constrain them? *Is the environment, in other words, favorable, unfavorable or uncertain?* This categorization then frames a set of possible responses.

Favorable conditions

When the rules of a target market coincide with a firm's objectives, the firm will naturally find itself in a rather advantageous position. Since its own business goals will tend to be aligned with the political agenda of the state (or a powerful segment within the state), it can be relatively confident that few political obstacles will be put in its way. If its business model creates natural allies within the country, the firm may even be able to reap whatever additional favors these allies are capable of delivering.

Such political advantage can be a powerful source of market advantage as well. When the Austrian company Lenzing invested in Indonesia in 1978, for example, Suharto's government was so pleased to have a firm that could spur industrial growth and help conserve foreign exchange that it gave Lenzing a wide array of economic benefits. For the next fifteen years, the rayon manufacturer enjoyed prohibitively high tariffs on imported rayon and duty-free access to imported inputs – all due to concessions that the government offered. Lenzing's business at the time was wholly complementary to the country's objectives and thus the firm was able not only to flourish under a conducive set of rules, but also to use the rule-making power of the state to further enhance its competitive position.

Unfavorable conditions

When the rules of a market run against a firm's business model, of course, the picture is less rosy. In these circumstances, the firm must decide whether to leave the market entirely, change its business model, or try to change the rules that it faces. All of these options are possible at different times. All can be wise business strategies under different circumstances.

Consider, for example, the situation that faced Honeywell when it entered the Russian market for residential heating controls in 1991. At that time, the rules of the market ran directly counter to Honeywell's business model. There were no real market prices for energy in Russia, and thus no demand for the energy conservation that Honeywell offered. Furthermore, the natural customers for Honeywell (residential dwellers and apartment managers) had no incentive to save energy since they still received their standard allotment of oil according to Russia's central planning system. With this system in place, the rules of Russia clearly mitigated against Honeywell's business. What the firm did, though, was to *change its business model to meet the rules it found*. It made money through the sale of equipment and received additional funding from the European Bank for Reconstruction and Development, an international agency that had a clear interest in conserving Russian energy and easing the path of firms such as Honeywell.

In other cases, firms can also work to change rules that run contrary to their business model. This is a risky strategy, and can absorb considerable amounts of managerial time. It can also be highly effective. When Toys "R" Us was contemplating entry into the Japanese market, for instance, it gradually realized that all the rules of Japanese retail – both formal and informal – were hostile to its interests. There were formal laws which hampered the creation of large stores (and Toys "R" Us runs only large, warehouse-type stores) and informal structures throughout the retail sector that made it extremely difficult for manufacturers to sell directly to retailers (the core of the chain's buying strategy). But rather than walking away from such a complicated set of obstacles, Toys "R" Us actively worked to change the rules. It won the support of the United States Trade Representative, which pressured Japan's Ministry of International Trade and Industry not to impose some of the prohibitions against large stores that could have been imposed. Then Toys "R" Us won over several of Japan's leading toy manufacturers by quietly threatening to reduce their sales in its U.S. stores. The result was a major expansion of Toys "R" Us in Japan and a distinctive weakening of the rules that had been in place.

Finally, even when rules appear to be permanently unfavorable to a firm's interests, it still may be possible to carve out a strategy, finding some means to enter the market while avoiding its rules. Such opportunities are rare and often risky, but they do exist. When Rupert Murdoch could find no way to enter the British broadcasting market, he turned instead to satellite television, broadcasting into Britain from a satellite legally registered in Luxembourg. His company, BSkyB, literally went around and above an unfavorable political environment. Likewise, when Network Associates, a provider of Internet security software, was forbidden from exporting its encryption software outside the United States, the company published its software code, enabled a Swiss firm to reproduce its product, and then contracted with this firm to supply Network Associates' customers outside the United States. As was the case with BSkyB, the company did not violate the law. It simply went around it.

Uncertain conditions

Some of the most interesting business strategies emerge when the rules of the game are uncertain or changing, when firms can't quite tell whether the political climate of a target market is conducive or not to their prospective venture. Under these conditions, the politically savvy response is often to hedge the situation as much as possible, finding some means of entering the market while protecting against its risks.

When Conoco invested in the chaotic Russian oil market, for instance, it designed a number of innovative responses to the risks it faced. It brought several international agencies into its deal as equity partners; it broke the investment into discrete phases; and, to lessen the likelihood that Russian authorities would be able to exploit any piece of the company's investment, Conoco constructed all of the necessary infrastructure on its own.

In a very different way, Dole, the U.S.-based fruit producer, also hedged the uncertainties it faced in the changing European market. In the early 1990s, when the nations of the European Community were struggling to construct a common policy with regard to banana imports, Dole hedged its position as a U.S. producer by investing in areas (such as the former European colonies) that were likely to receive preferential treatment under the new policy. By contrast, Chiquita Brands (another U.S.-based banana producer) simply assumed that the new rules of Europe would be open and liberal. When the Europeans passed a highly restrictive set of rules, therefore, Dole was relatively secure but Chiquita suffered serious setbacks.

Specification of risk

This notion of hedging relates closely to the second analytical task inherent in the framework of rules. As they map the political landscape of a given market onto their own business plans, managers should continually identify the risks that this matching entails. That is, they must specify the risks of a country, not in the aggregate, but for their own business objectives. And then they must find some means for avoiding or managing these risks.

In many treatments of risk, political risk is portrayed as a discrete probability, a tendency that can be captured at the national level and even reduced to quantitative measurement. Political risk services, for instance, often rank countries, giving Turkey, say, a risk factor of 6.5 and Argentina a 5.2.[47] The framework of rules, by contrast, suggests a very different approach to political risk. It suggests that risk can not be described as adhering across a particular country, but must instead be viewed with regard to a specific commercial venture. Thus, firms investing or trading in Turkey should be concerned less with the overall risks of Turkey than with the specific obstacles or opportunities that Turkey presents to their own project. They must understand the precise risks Turkey poses to them (of volatile taxation policy in their sector; or labor unrest at their plant; or extortion by a well-connected competitor) and then calculate how best to handle these risks within the confines of their own business objectives.

---

[47] For more on the use of formal models of political risk analysis, see Debora Spar, *Note on Political Risk Analysis*, Harvard Business School Case 9-798-022.

Considering foreign ventures along these lines will often reveal innovative approaches to political situations and political risk. Note, for example, how the large Japanese automakers responded to threats of further U.S. protectionism in the mid-1980s. Fearing that the United States would impose tariffs or quotas on Japanese auto imports, firms such as Honda and Toyota invested directly in the United States, thereby rendering any subsequent protectionism less harmful. Foreign investment in this case was not just a commercial decision, but a powerful way to hedge the risks of political change.

Similarly, when Lenzing (the Austrian rayon manufacturer) decided to expand its operations in Indonesia in 1994, it hedged the possibility of political unrest by bringing a new partner – the International Finance Corporation – into the deal. With the IFC on board, Lenzing essentially bought security against the possibility of either expropriation or a change in its own political status. It created a political hedge against political risk – and a hedge that fit neatly with its own business objectives.

Changing the rules

A final implication of a rules-based analysis is that firms, under many circumstances, have the ability to shape the rules that surround them, to bend them toward their interests and deflect potential threats. In all countries, rules are susceptible to influence by a wide range of agents and interests. There will be paths through which firms can shape the formation of these rules, and routes through which they can affect their formation. What will vary from one country to the next are the precise paths and routes through which this influence can best be exerted. In countries with highly developed institutions and strong legal frameworks, the routes to influence will generally be defined by the formal structure of the state and its policies. In the United States, for instance, firms can shape the rules either by lobbying Congress, or by arguing before a variety of federal agencies, or by participating in the private organizations that set particular standards. These measures may be time-consuming. They may be awkward. And firms may see them as a waste of managerial effort. But the results are often difficult to deny. If firms want to influence the rules that affect them, they have to interact with the political structures that create and enforce these rules.

In countries with less formal or sophisticated political structures, the routes to influence are murkier. They are likely to entail a greater reliance on personal relationships, and on links to power that may not be immediately discernible. In Indonesia, for example, power resided for decades in the web of personal and familial ties that surrounded President Suharto. Influencing the rules meant finding the appropriate strand of this web and convincing the relevant power broker to support a particular cause, or law, or policy.

Finally, even at the international level, there is often ample opportunity for firms to change the rules that confront them. They can do this either by working through their own governments, convincing their home state to represent their interests in international negotiations, or by venturing directly to international organizations and standard-setting bodies. When Pfizer wanted stronger international protection of intellectual property, for instance, it worked with both the U.S. government and the World Intellectual Property Organization, ultimately managing to add a whole new range of intellectual property issues to the policy agenda of the GATT (General Agreement on Tariffs and Trade). When Rupert Murdoch's BSkyB wanted to ensure its position as the dominant provider of pay television in the United Kingdom, it skated adroitly through the British regulatory system and then had its technical standard formally endorsed by an international consortium attached to the European Commission.

It is true that influencing the rules is a high-stakes game. It involves time, energy, and money that the firm may not be willing to expend. It also puts companies into the uncomfortable position of asking managers to perform tasks for which they may be unprepared or even ill suited. Not all firms will want to play this game, and not all should. Yet even the most reluctant should be well aware of the rules that surround them and well attuned to the process by which these rules are created and enforced. They should understand how deeply the rules of any market can affect the terms of business that prevail there, and how firms can use these rules to shape their own competitive strategy. They need to understand that in business, as in politics, power often lies with those that make the rules.

Part III

RULES OF THE INTERNATIONAL LEVEL

Regarding NAFTA

In the aftermath of World War II, the countries of the industrialized world engaged in an unprecedented round of institution-building. Convinced that the horrors of the war were due in part to the isolationist economic policies of the 1930s, they launched a series of institutions designed to prevent such policies from ever again holding sway over the world's economies. At the center of this institutional framework was the GATT (General Agreement on Tariffs and Trade), a broad and overarching organization with an explicit mandate to reduce tariff barriers and thus expand global flows of trade. Its sister organizations, the International Monetary Fund (IMF) and World Bank, were more formal in structure and narrow in scope. The IMF sought to provide a stable structure for international monetary cooperation, while the World Bank was charged with providing funds for war-ravaged economies to rebuild themselves.[1]

For the next several decades, these global institutions proved remarkably successful in delivering the benefits foreseen by their creators. Under the auspices of eight successive GATT rounds, tariffs tumbled to historic lows, falling from pre-war levels of up to 60% to developed-country averages of only about 4%.[2] Accordingly, global trade flows exploded. Between 1950 and 1975, for example, the volume of world trade increased by 500% — more than twice the growth rate of global output.[3] Capital flows grew more slowly at first, but then also expanded dramatically. During the latter half of the 1980s, foreign direct investment (FDI) flows grew at an average of 24% annually, exceeding $200 billion by 1990.[4] While the bulk of this economic interaction remained, as it began, within the more developed countries, the World Bank and IMF nevertheless also played a crucial role in channeling funds to the less developed world and supervising the means of their use.

Not surprisingly, all of the institutions of the post-war system had their critics. Marxists regarded the entire system as but a "rich man's club," a tool for perpetuating the dominance of the

---

[1] For more information, see Lakshmi Gopalan, David Moss, and Lou Wells "International Institutions," HBS Case N9-796-116.

[2] Richard N. Gardner, "The Bretton Woods-GATT System After Fifty Years: A Balance Sheet of Success and Failure," in Orin Kirshner, ed., *The Bretton Woods-GATT System: Retrospect and Prospect after 50 Years*. (New York: M. E. Sharpe, 1996), p. 197.

[3] Harlan Cleveland, "The 'Informatization' of World Affairs," in *Ibid.*, 295.

[4] *World Investment Report 1994*. (New York: United Nations, 1994), Table I.4, 12.

Research Associate Elizabeth Stein prepared this case under the supervision of Professor Debora Spar as the basis for class discussion rather than to illustrate either effective or ineffective handling of an administrative situation. It is based on research originally conducted by Brett Kidd and Vivian Moran, MBA Class of 1996.

wealthy against the impotence of the poor. Many in the developing world resented the intrusions of the World Bank and the IMF into their domestic economies; and even in the developed world, observers periodically railed against the tyranny — and endless talk — of the Geneva-based GATT bureaucracy. Yet, for the most part, these criticisms were overwhelmed by strong support for the achievements of the GATT and its sister institutions. Indeed, in the eyes of most analysts, the institutions of the post-war system had succeeded admirably in meeting their goals. They had expanded world trade and capital flows, extended market mechanisms throughout the world, and created a climate in which international businesses, and individual countries, could all thrive. The system, quite simply, had worked.

It worked so well, in fact, that by the mid-1980s a second generation of institutions was beginning to emerge across the international landscape. Like the GATT and the IMF, these new institutions were created on the premise that economic integration *between* their members could increase absolute rates of growth *within* their members' separate states. As in the GATT and IMF, again, the role of institutions was to design, monitor, and enforce the process of integration — to establish the new rules of the game and ensure all members played by them. In a significant departure from the post-war pattern, however, these new institutions were explicitly regional, rather than global. Instead of expanding integration piecemeal across the far-flung countries of the world, they strove for a deeper and more complete integration among a cluster of neighboring states. The logic of this movement was straightforward: in exchange for limiting the number of their members, regional groups could create strong cross-national institutions and more competitive local economies. Merely by being smaller and composed of more similar states, they could expedite negotiations that often lingered for years, or even decades, at the international level. And in the process, they might even hasten the development of global institutions, since liberalization within any regional group was likely to spawn imitation by any outside country that wanted to join the club.

The first of the regional trade arrangements was the European Community (EC). Though launched as early as 1957 with the signing of the Treaty of Rome, the EC did not really gather significant momentum until 1985, when its members agreed to speed and expand the scope of European integration. Dismayed by Europe's relatively dismal economic performance during the 1970s and early 1980s, they decided, in effect, to eliminate economic and financial borders within Europe. By 1992, the target date for Europe's single market, the 12 member states pledged to remove all border controls on the movement of goods, people, and capital within the EC and to coordinate their monetary and exchange rate policies. To implement this dramatic program, the member nations also agreed to create an infrastructure of EC institutions: a court, a parliament, a council of ministers, and a cadre of roughly 16,000 bureaucrats.

Once these institutions and policies were in place, supporters of the single market expected it to generate enhanced trade flows, and thence growth, across Europe. Projections for this growth were considerable. One influential study, for example, concluded that integration within the Community would add an average of 4.5% to the EC's GDP, improve the balance of payments by roughly 1% of GDP, deflate prices by 6.1%, and reduce unemployment by about 1.5%.[5]

Regardless of the accuracy of these projections, the very promise of a single market ignited a fascination with regional institutions in the mid-1980s and early 1990s. During this time, several wholly new institutions were launched, including the Asia-Pacific Economic Cooperation forum (APEC), the European Economic Area (EEA), and the Southern Cone Common Market (MERCOSUR). Others, like the Andean Pact, Caribean Community (CARICOM), and Gulf

---

[5] Paolo Cecchini, *The European Challenge 1992: The Benefits of a Single Market.* (Brookfield, Vermont: Gower, 1988), pp. 97-98.

Cooperation Council (GCC), had existed prior to the formation of the single market, but were reactivated by the thought of a "Fortress Europe" and the possibility that global economic institutions might be surpassed by regional ones. In the short-term, few of these regional associations achieved anything close to the level of commitment and institutionalization already apparent in Europe. But one group, the North Americans, did.

On December 17, 1992, leaders of the United States, Canada, and Mexico signed the North American Free Trade Agreement, or NAFTA. Set to be launched in January of 1994, NAFTA eliminated all tariffs among its three member countries, creating as a result the largest free trade zone in the world.[6] Building on the U.S.-Canada Free Trade Agreement of 1988, NAFTA both widened and deepened the economic integration of North America: widened by the addition of Mexico's 93 million people; and deepened by the scope of activities now subject to the regional arrangement. In addition to the elimination of all North American tariffs, NAFTA provided for a phased reduction of non-tariff barriers and a gradual convergence of economic regulation across the members' borders. The treaty's provisions also covered investment rights and intellectual property protection. It was supplemented further by a series of "side agreements" dealing with import surges, labor conditions, and environmental standards.

Projections of NAFTA's impact were as varied as the projectors themselves. Estimates ranged from the Institute of International Economics' sunny prediction of a net gain of 130,000 new U.S. jobs,[7] to former California governor Edmund G. Brown, Jr.'s charge that 800,000 Mexican farming families would be driven off communal lands, causing 700,000 additional illegal migrants to flood north, "[depressing] wages on both sides of the border by rapidly increasing the surplus of labor."[8] Estimates of NAFTA's political and commercial impact were no more certain. Some analysts saw the agreement as a stepping stone towards enhanced trade and prosperity throughout the Americas. U.S. Labor Secretary Robert Reich, for instance, endorsed the Agreement with the assertion that "Market expansion is a positive-sum game in which all parties stand to gain."[9] Others saw it just as distinctly as a movement away from global free trade and towards U.S.-dominated protectionism. From London, the *Financial Times* warned that "Nafta could... become a weapon of regionalised trade war. In the face of the EC's 'Fortress Europe', Nafta would then draw the ring fence for 'Fortress America'."[10]

Meanwhile, even as analysts debated NAFTA's purported effects, businesses were scrambling to discover just what the newly-minted institution meant for them. Presumably, all firms doing business in Canada, Mexico, or the United States would be influenced to some extent by the broad economic, political, and commercial forces unleashed by NAFTA. Just how these forces would manifest themselves, however, and how they would affect the competitive environments of specific industries and firms remained to be seen.

The three "caselets" presented below describe events that surrounded three different North American firms as NAFTA came into being. The caselets are neither wholly idiosyncratic nor fully

---

[6]Officially, NAFTA is bigger than the European Community, since its 385 million consumers outnumber Europe's 360 million.

[7] Gary Clyde Hufbauer and Jeffrey J. Schott, *North American Free Trade: Issues and Recommendations.* (Washington, DC: Institute for International Economics, 1992), pp. 55-56. Hufbauer and Schott also conclude that U.S. wage levels would be essentially unchanged.

[8] Edmund G. Brown, Jr., "Free Trade Fetish: Things Have Changed Since David Ricardo's Time," *The Washington Post,* September 14, 1992, p. A15.

[9] Testimony of Labor Secretary Robert D. Reich before the Ways and Means Committee, United States House of Representatives, September 14, 1993.

[10] David Dodwell, "When the Talk Turns to Trade: Mexico, Canada and the US are Set to Clinch a NAFTA Deal," *Financial Times,* July 9, 1992, p. 18.

representative. They simply describe three different firms, from three different industries and three different countries, trying to determine how best to respond to the changes wrought by NAFTA.

Case One: Iowa Beef Processors

Initially, Robert Peterson, the Chairman, President, and CEO of Iowa Beef Processssors (IBP) had greeted NAFTA with great enthusiasim. With 1994 export revenues of $1.5 billion, IBP was already the twenty-sixth largest exporter in the United States, and the largest processor of beef and pork products in the world. Over the past decade, Peterson had seen his company's exports soar and he was anxious to maintain this momentum. For 1995, IBP was projecting export revenues to reach $1.8 billion, a 20% increase from 1994 and four times the amount it had shipped a decade ago. The passage of NAFTA, Peterson figured, could only help IBP achieve this growth.

With these optimistic expectations, IBP moved quickly into the expanded North American market. In 1994 the company purchased Lakeside Farm Industries, the second largest meat processing firm in Canada. It also began exploring joint venture possibilities with Grupo Gigante, Mexico's third largest supermarket chain. These two ventures were IBP's first non-marketing investments outside of the United States.

To Peterson and his colleagues at IBP, these movements into Mexico and Canada were a natural response to NAFTA — a way of gaining the economies of scale inherent in an expanded market. With access to 121 million potential customers and a plentiful supply of livestock, the Canadian and Mexican operations could give IBP the size and increased cash flows that it needed to fund and support its growth. Others in the industry, however, regarded IBP's actions in a wholly different light: as manipulative, unfair, and possibly even illegal. In the wake of NAFTA, these groups began to fight.

The protests came largely from the U.S. ranching community, producers of the livestock bought by IBP and its competitors. For the ranchers, the early warning signs of NAFTA had been ominous. Indeed, in the months following NAFTA's passage, many small farmers and ranchers had seen cattle prices plummet to 20-year lows. Between 1993 and 1994 alone, cattle prices had dropped 35%. There was a 50% increase in the percentage of commercial farmers on the brink of bankruptcy or foreclosure. While most experts, including those at the National Cattlemen's Association, attributed falling prices to a cyclical oversupply of livestock, rising corn prices, the devalued peso, and a severe drought in Mexico, many ranchers placed the blame squarely on NAFTA, citing NAFTA's abolishment of tariffs and import quotas on Mexican cattle as the reason for their dire situation. As evidence, they pointed to the 92% increase of Mexican beef imports in 1995, and the resulting loss to U.S. producers of an estimated $90 million.

To make matters even worse for the ranchers, the apparent source of their ill-fortune — low-priced Mexican livestock — was also the source of IBP's growing profits. Thus, the ranchers began in 1994 to mobilize against IBP and its competitors, charging them with collusive practices and calling for congressional investigations into their business operations. Despite a recent U.S. Department of Agriculture (USDA) study which had concluded that meat processors were not acting collusively, arguments advanced by the National Family Farm Coalition, the American Farm Bureau Federation, and other rancher organizations began in 1995 to resonate throughout the U.S. political system. Dan Glickman, the U.S. Secretary of Agriculture, created a commission to study the meat processors and directed the USDA's antitrust organization, the Packers and Stockyard Administration, to investigate allegations that IBP had manipulated the Chicago

Mercantile Exchange's futures market. Meanwhile, a bipartisan group of congressional representatives, including Senate Minority Leader Tom Daschle, was urging remedial action. At a press conference Daschle stated emphatically that "Something is wrong ...when packers make record profits and producers take a huge loss. Something is wrong when three firms control over 80% of the livestock market."[11] Explicitly, many local farmers blamed NAFTA for their woes: "NAFTA," explained one Montana rancher, is "a terrible thing that's been done to us. We're taking the brunt of this thing. It's benefiting the packers, the feeders and the banks and it's hurting the producers, the consumers and the taxpayers."[12] These sentiments quickly made their way into presidential politics, where the anti-NAFTA rhetoric of Pat Buchanan and Ross Perot continued to highlight the plight of U.S. ranchers and point the finger of blame at IBP and its competitors.

Peterson was well-aware of the political power that farmers wielded. A clear majority of representatives in Congress, including every Senator, was backed in part by agricultural interests. The meat processing industry had felt the power of these interests before. At the turn of the century, high levels of concentration in the meatpacking industry had become the target of "trust-busting" producers. The result was the 1921 Packers and Stockyards Act which broke up the dominant players and imposed a tight regulatory framework on the raisers and packers of livestock — a chilling precedent for Peterson in his current situation. Another more recent precedent lay in the anti-NAFTA lobbying efforts of Florida farmers, who had persuaded Congress to pass legislation that significantly curtailed the import of Mexican-grown tomatoes. If similar legislation were imposed on Mexican cattle imports, IBP would surely find itself in a much more hostile and less viable commercial environment.

Personally, Peterson remained convinced that an unlikely combination of market phenomena was to blame for the crash in U.S. cattle prices, and that IBP and NAFTA had simply become convenient targets for the ranchers' blame. He could not, however, ignore the ranchers' political protests against North American free trade and those who benefited from it. In this environment, the strategic response of IBP to NAFTA had, ironically, become an anti-NAFTA argument.

Case Two: Magna International[13]

At the time of NAFTA's passage, Magna International was just beginning to recover from the worst period in the company's history. After years of rapid growth, the company had been badly hit by the general downturn in the North American auto market; in 1990 it lost $C224 million, more than it had earned in the previous ten years combined. In the wake of these losses, Magna had drastically restructured both its financial and operational activities. As a result, by the end of 1992, recovery at the Canadian auto parts manufacturer seemed well underway, and management was determined to avoid any further strategic mistakes.

Magna International had been founded in 1954 by Frank Stronach, an Austrian tool and die maker who launched the company with a C$2000 bank overdraft. For the next three decades, the company grew at an exceptional pace, eventually developing a reputation as one of North

---

[11] "Panel to Look into Effects of Consolidation of Meatpacking Industry," *Gannett News Service*, February 14, 1996.

[12] Rose Fryer, "Promise of NAFTA Turns To 'Shafta,' Ranchers Say NAFTA Blamed for Low Cattle Prices," *The Salt Lake Tribune*, December 24, 1995, p. F1.

[13] This caselet is an abridged version of Tony Frost and Ann Frost, "Magna International and the North American Free Trade Agreement," in Paul Beamish and C. Patrick Woodcock (eds.), *Strategic Management 4th edition*. (Toronto: J. Irwin, 1996).

America's premier suppliers of automotive systems and components. By 1992, its 68 plants were producing over 5000 different parts — the broadest range of any independent supplier in the industry — employed 15,000 people, and generated over $C2.4 billion in sales.

With four separate product divisions (interiors, metal stamping, trim, and engines), Magna positioned itself as a full-line supplier to the automotive industry. The vast bulk of its business came from supplying integrated modules and systems to original equipment manufacturers (OEMs). Critical to this strategy were both an emphasis on product innovation and a careful targeting of OEM product lines. As Dennis Bausch, Magna's Senior Vice President of Marketing and Strategic Planning, explained:

> It's the old 80:20 rule. In North America, the top 10 selling vehicles account for about 25% of total automobile production. What we try to do is pick those winners. Right now, 50% of our sales come from parts we produce for the 10 best sellers.

To maintain these "best sellers," Magna worked closely with its OEM customers, coordinating just-in-time delivery and locating its plants as close as possible to those of the OEMs.

NAFTA was by no means the first institution to affect Magna's relations with these crucial customers. Indeed, U.S.-Canadian trade in autos and auto parts had long been shaped by the dictates of formal treaties: first by the 1965 U.S.-Canadian Auto Pact, and then by the 1988 U.S.-Canadian Free Trade Agreement. Though different in degree, both of these treaties had essentially required the U.S. Big Three auto firms to produce or source locally in order to gain access to the Canadian market. As the largest Canadian-based supplier, Magna had generally benefited from these accords.

The addition of Mexico to the U.S.-Canada Free Trade Agreement introduced a fundamentally new dynamic to the North American auto industry. During the negotiations for NAFTA, the key objective of the Big Three was to gain improved access to the Mexican consumer market, then the world's fastest growing market for automobiles. The subsequent treaty ensured this access through three key provisions: (1) an immediate halving of Mexico's 20% tariff on autos and light trucks and a 10 year phase out of the remaining tariff; (2) a 10 year phase out of Mexico's requirement that vehicles sold in Mexico contain 36% domestic content; and (3) an immediate reduction in Mexico's trade balancing requirement from $2 of automotive exports for every dollar's worth of imports, to 80 cents, and to zero by 2004. The automotive industry hailed this last provision as "the single most significant accomplishment of the NAFTA automotive negotiations."

The gradual phase out of tariff and non-tariff barriers was designed to ensure that the budding Mexican parts industry would not be wiped out by immediate exposure to international competition, a central objective of the Mexican negotiators. Still, analysts were predicting that up to 75% of Mexican parts companies might be forced to exit the market.[14] Faced with this prospect, many Mexican suppliers were scrambling to form alliances with their U.S. and Canadian counterparts.

The terms of NAFTA's transition also reflected one of the Big Three's major priorities, namely to ensure that foreign producers could not use Mexico as a simple export platform to the U.S. market. The gradual phase out clearly benefited producers with established Mexican facilities, primarily Chrysler, Ford, and General Motors, as well as Nissan and Volkswagen, since new

---

[14]Kay G. Husbands, "Strategic Alliances in the Mexican Auto Parts Industry," International Motor Vehicle Program Working Paper, Massachusetts Institute of Technology, 1993.

entrants were required to establish sourcing relationships with Mexican suppliers just as the established OEMs had done. NAFTA ensured that there were no "late mover advantages" conferred on companies such as Toyota and Honda that had yet to establish Mexican production facilities. North American parts suppliers also stood to gain by several NAFTA provisions, especially the increase in the North American content requirement from 50% to 62% over an eight year period. Japanese producers, who were on record as calling the auto provisions of the agreement "a giant step in the wrong direction," were expected to have the most difficulty meeting the new content requirements.

For firms such as Magna, however, NAFTA seemed in general like a good deal. Magna had strong relations with Big Three plants throughout the United States and Canada, and even a new stamping facility in Mexico, established to supply Volkswagen's plant in Puebla. Still, Fred Jaekel, President and Chief Operating Officer of Magna's stamping and assembly division, was not sure how best to respond to the treaty's passage. Mexico's low wage costs tempted him to boost production there, but he was also wary of moving too far from his OEMs and of problems Magna had already faced in finding skilled employees in Mexico and preventing costly downtime on its equipment. Jaekel also knew that Mexican steel makers were unable to provide the automotive grade steel necessary for most of his stamping operations, a situation that not even NAFTA was likely to change in the near future. Finally, there were the added costs and difficulties associated with Mexico's notoriously poor infrastructure. The shipment of supplies into and out of Mexico could increase both Magna's transportation costs and the likelihood of damaged goods.

Fundamentally, Jaekel's strategy depended on predicting what the OEMs would do as a result of NAFTA. Would they relocate existing capacity to Mexico or simply add capacity there? Which models were they likely to produce in Mexico, and in what volumes?

Already, the Big Three had announced several impending investments in Mexico. Rumors in the trade also suggested that foreign parts suppliers might invest up to $4.2 billion in Mexico by 1996. Industry analysts also pointed to the potential migration of small car production from Canada and the United States to Mexico. Finally, NAFTA would almost certainly force non-U.S. auto producers such as Toyota and Mercedes to increase the extent of their North American production — and Mexico clearly offered the lowest-wage site for any further investment.

Jaekel knew of all these developments. But he still wasn't sure what they meant for the U.S.-based OEMs, or for Magna. If there was one thing Magna had learned from its recent difficulties, however, it was that all investment plans needed to be focussed, strategic, and in line with the best use of company resources.

Case Three: Sony's Nuevo Laredo Plants

Since 1994, Sony's plants at Nuevo Laredo had been the happy beneficiaries of both the passage of NAFTA and the subsequent crash of the Mexican peso. As the peso tumbled (losing nearly two-thirds of its value between February, 1994 and December, 1995) and inflation soared, Sony found that the relative cost of its key Mexican input — labor — had tumbled as well. Since the bulk of its Mexican production was exported outside of Mexico, these lower costs translated almost immediately into higher profits.

Sony had first invested in North America in 1972, when a rising yen and heightened protectionism in the United States compelled the firm to open its first television manufacturing plant in San Diego. By the mid-1980s San Diego had become the core of Sony's North American operations, producing over 1 million high-end Trinitron color television sets a year. To support this core, Sony had also moved aggressively into Mexico, establishing a series of maquiladora plants to produce the Trinitron's most labor-intensive components.[15] It also pioneered a flexible strategy of straddling the U.S.-Mexican border. It kept a small staff of designers and engineers at San Diego, along with a high-technology factory and a workforce of about 2,000. Just across the border, Sony's Tijuana subsidiary, Video Tec de Mexico, oversaw several production facilities and an additional labor force of 4,000 lower-wage workers. Using the twin plants, Sony provided North America with both television sets and computer monitors. Constant communication across the border allowed Sony's management to react quickly to market conditions, shorten the time between design and store shelves, and reduce costs.

As a result of this relationship, Video Tec had become an increasingly important part of Sony's global strategy. But the passage of NAFTA made it critical. Under the terms of the treaty, "North American" products could eventually be traded, free of tariffs, across the NAFTA region. To qualify for this treatment, however, all of a product's key components, including materials and labor, had to be wholly North American in origin. This stringent requirement fell particularly heavily on foreign-based producers of manufactured items such as cars, computers, and television sets. In the past, many of these producers had imported components from abroad, reassembled them in Mexico or the United States, and then sold them as local manufactures. Under NAFTA, this import-and-assembly strategy no longer made sense. Instead, for all non-North American firms, NAFTA nearly forced a strategy of local investment. Without this investment, plants such as Sony's San Diego facility — primarily a design and assembly operation — would fall below NAFTA's local content requirement and thus see their production subject to tariffs. Well aware of this logic, Asian firms had poured money into Mexico in the early 1990s, transforming the border city of Tijuana into one of the world's largest centers of television production.

As these factories multiplied across the U.S.-Mexican border, the increased presence of Asian managers highlighted the vast differences between Japanese and Mexican work styles. For the most part, the Japanese had tried to adapt to the local culture, hiring managers such as Francisco Solis, the Mexican vice president who oversaw the 2,400 workers at Sony's Nuevo Laredo plants. Most of the Japanese companies had also stopped insisting that their Mexican employees wear uniforms and attend early morning exercises — traditional Japanese practices that had never proven particularly popular with the Mexican workforce.

Still, just as its Mexican production was becoming more important and profitable for Sony, the company was also encountering labor problems at several of its Mexican sites. Shortly after the company fired a number of workers at Nuevo Laredo, four human rights groups filed a complaint with the U.S. National Administrative Office (NAO), one of several agencies created under the auspices of NAFTA. The origins of the NAO were complex, and its powers unclear. Established by a side agreement to the NAFTA treaty, the agency was a response to concerns, particularly on the part of U.S. labor, that U.S. and Canadian jobs would flee to Mexico's cheaper wages and laxer regulatory environment. To prevent the more egregious aspects of this migration, the three member states formed a trilateral labor commission consisting of the top labor officials of each country and supported by three separate National Administrative Offices. Officially, both the Commission and the separate NAOs had authority to monitor the enforcement of existing labor law and to apply sanctions in cases of violation.

The charge against Sony was one of the first to come before the NAO. The petitioning groups charged that Sony had fired its workers, not for poor performance, but rather because they had been trying to organize an alternative slate of candidates to run against candidates from CTM,

---

[15] Maquiladoras are foreign-owned plants located along the U.S.-Mexican border. Inputs for production are imported tariff free; all output is exported.

Mexico's most powerful union, in the plant's union election. The groups claimed that after workers called a work stoppage to protest what they saw as a fixed union election, Sony used police violence to suppress the workers involved. For the U.S. NAO, the question was whether the Mexican government had failed to enforce its own labor laws, but the charges echoing through the press highlighted Sony's role in the affair. Both Sony management and officers from CTM denied any wrongdoing. Jose Maria Gonzalez, the regional CTM boss, claimed that his union had merely exercised its right to expel "troublemakers." "We do not need agitators here," he stated. "We have a magnificent relationship with Sony. Our main priority is to protect the investment climate and guarantee job stability."

In the past, Solis had been able to settle labor disputes by dealing either with regional CTM bosses such as Gonzalez, or with the (usually sympathetic) Mexican government. But he had no relations with the newly-created Commission, nor any sense of how it would resolve labor disputes such as Sony's. Early reports were encouraging, albeit ambiguous. Claiming that the Mexican government had been unable to answer key legal questions, the U.S. NAO concluded that, "it remains unclear whether... the workers have any viable recourse against improper union actions." Solis also had reports, however, that U.S. Labor Secretary Robert Reich had taken a particular interest in the Nuevo Laredo case. Solis wasn't sure how to approach the situation or how to avoid future complications in any of Sony's other Mexican plants.

Exhibit 1   Key Provisions of the North American Free Trade Agreement

- **Tariffs and Other Trade Barriers:** NAFTA provides for the elimination of all tariffs on goods qualifying as North American under its rules of origin. For most goods, duties will be eliminated immediately or phased out over five to ten years. For some sensitive items, tariffs will be phased out over 15 years. All other prohibitions and quantitative restrictions such as quotas and import licenses will be eliminated.

- **Rules of Origin:** Rules of origin are necessary to ensure that NAFTA benefits are accorded only to goods produced in North America. The rules specify that goods originate in North America if they are wholly North American. Goods containing nonregional materials are also considered North American if the nonregional materials are sufficiently transformed in the NAFTA region so as to undergo a change in tariff classification. In some cases, goods must include a specified percentage of North American content.

- **Agriculture:** Mexico's import licenses will be eliminated immediately, and each country's tariffs on all farm products will be phased out over a 15-year period.

- **Automotive Goods:** At the end of eight years, 62.5% of a car's value must be made in North America for it to qualify for duty-free treatment.

- **Financial Services:** U.S. and Canadian financial service and brokerage firms will be allowed to set up wholly-owned subsidiaries in Mexico for the first time in 50 years. Over a six-year transition period, market share will be limited.

- **Government Procurement:** The agreement opens a significant portion of government contracts in each NAFTA country to suppliers from the other NAFTA countries in goods, services, and construction. Over ten years, Mexico will eliminate its current reserve of practically all government contracts for Mexican companies.

- **Intellectual Property Rights:** Each country will provide adequate and effective protection of intellectual property rights on the basis of national treatment and will provide effective enforcement of these rights against infringement.

- **Telecommunications:** NAFTA provides U.S. and Canadian firms with nondiscriminatory access to Mexico's public telephone network and removes all investment restrictions by 1995.

- **Trucking:** U.S., Canadian, and Mexican trucking companies will be allowed to carry international cargo across borders.

Source: Adapted from Phyllis Dininio and Helen Shapiro, "North American Free Trade Agreement — Free For Whom?," HBS Case 792-049.

Exhibit 2   Composition of North American Trade, 1990

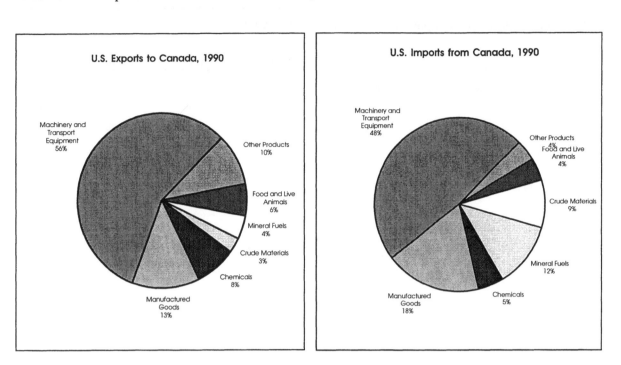

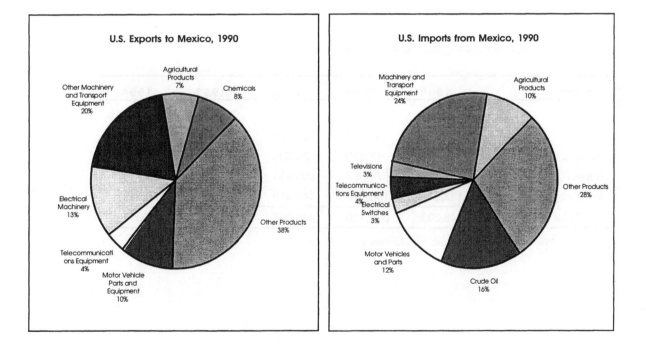

Source: U.S. Department of Commerce, Offices of Mexico and Canada.

Exhibit 3   Scale and Concentration in the U.S. Meat Industry

Size Distribution of Companies and Plants, 1974–1988

	1974	1979	1984	1988
Share of commercial cattle slaughtered by:				
Four largest companies	21%	28%	37%	57%
Eight largest companies	31%	39%	46%	66%
Twelve largest companies	37%	44%	53%	70%
Number of plants slaughtering over 50,000 annually		153	136	106
Share of commercial slaughter in plants of over 50,000 per annum		78%	83%	90%

Source: U.S. Department of Agriculture.

Exhibit 4   Sales of Passenger Cars in Mexico, 1990-1994

Company	1990	1991	1992	1993	1994
Chrysler	52,503	64,681	83,675	59,614	54,247
Ford	51,412	56,460	68,323	52,807	50,285
General Motors	31,298	42,970	50,835	51,267	63,667
Nissan	79,945	79,353	100,051	83,358	98,784
Volkswagen	133,645	148,646	142,419	151,697	148,109
Total Sales	348,803	392,110	445,303	398,743	415,092

Source: *Ward's Automotive Yearbook*, various issues.

Exhibit 5 Cost of Auto Assembly, United States and Mexico, 1992

	United States	Mexico
Labor[a]	$700	$140
Parts and subassemblies	7,750	8,000
Component shipping costs	75	600[b]
Finishing vehicle shipping	225	400
Inventory costs	20	40
Total	$8,770	$9,180

[a]Assumes 20 hours of labor per U.S.-made car; 30 hours per Mexican-made car. All figures in U.S. dollars.

[b]Assumes stampings shipped from the United States.

Source: U.S. Congress, Office of Technology Assessment, *U.S. Mexico Trade: Pulling Together or Pulling Apart?*, ITE-545 (Washington, D.C.: U.S. Government Printing Office, October 1992), p. 145.

Exhibit 6 Cost of Wiring Harness, United States and Mexico, 1992

Assembly cost (40 minutes): Mexico (Maquiladora plant)[a]	$1-$2
Added shipping costs for Mexican assembly	$7
Extra inventory costs for Mexican production	$.50
Assembly cost (40 minutes): United States:	
Big Three internal supplier (@ $35/hour)	$23
Unionized supplier (@ $26/hour)	$17
Nonunion supplier (@ $18/hour)	$12
Mexican cost advantage	$2.50–$14.50

Source: U.S. Congress, Office of Technology Assessment, *U.S. Mexico Trade: Pulling Together or Pulling Apart?*, ITE-545 (Washington, D.C.: U.S. Government Printing Office, October 1992), p. 147 .

Exhibit 7   Growth of Mexico's Maquiladora Sector

	Number	Employees ('000)	Added Value (US$ millions)
1984	672	200	1,160
1988	1,396	369	2,316
1992	2,075	506	4,844
1993	2,114	542	5,540
1994ᴱ	2,085	579	5,952

Note: E = estimate

Source: INEGI, *Estadica de la Maquiladora de Exportación*, various issues.

Union Carbide's Bhopal Plant (A)

Just after midnight on December 3, 1984, methyl isocyanate gas began leaking from a Union Carbide plant in Bhopal, India. By the time the leak was finally sealed, 10,000 gallons of the highly toxic gas had sprayed into the atmosphere, forming a deadly cloud that covered 25 square miles and killed or injured over 100,000 people. It was the worst industrial accident in history.

In the aftermath of the tragedy, Bhopal became a symbol of corporate negligence and risk. Around the world, public interest groups clamored for increased regulation of potentially hazardous industrial processes, and governments responded with a series of measures directed particularly at the chemicals industry. For firms in these industries, Bhopal was a turning point, highlighting the risk of industrial malfunction and the high cost of falling under public scrutiny. It also underscored the difficulties of conducting arms-length transactions in distant countries, for despite popular perceptions, the U.S.-based Union Carbide Corporation had never directly controlled the daily operations of the Bhopal plant. Rather, Bhopal was a joint venture between Union Carbide, the Indian government, and a number of private Indian companies. All of the plant's workers and managers were Indian nationals, and the Indian government had overseen the plant's design and construction in 1973.

Nevertheless, the brunt of the public outcry—and legal liability—fell on Union Carbide. In the months after the accident, plaintiffs in the United States and India filed tens of thousands of lawsuits. Investors responded by dumping Union Carbide shares, driving the company's market value down by $832 million in the first week after the tragedy. A decade later, both Union Carbide and the town of Bhopal were still reeling from the effects of the leak.

Below are three excerpts describing various aspects of the tragedy at Bhopal. The first is a general description of what occurred the night of December 3, focusing on the residents of Bhopal and the immediate causes of the leak. The second, from a *Business Week* article, describes the effect on Union Carbide and how its management responded to the initial news of the tragedy. The third excerpt is from the key U.S. court decision on the Bhopal case. In it, the judge describes why Union Carbide must stand trial in Indian, rather than United States, court.

* * * * *

Suzanne Hull, MBA 1993, and Research Associate Julia Kou prepared this case under the supervision of Professor Debora L. Spar as the basis for class discussion rather than to illustrate either effective or ineffective handling of an administrative situation.

Excerpt 1: From "It was like breathing fire..." *Newsweek*, December 17, 1984[1]

It was an unseasonably cold night in Central India. In the shanty towns of Bhopal, thousands of poor families were asleep. At a nearby railway station, a scattering of people waited for early-morning trains. Suddenly, at the local Union Carbide plant, a maintenance worker spotted a problem. A storage tank holding methyl isocyanate (MIC), a chemical used in making pesticides, was showing a dangerously high pressure reading. The worker summoned his boss. The supervisor put out an alert. But it was already too late. A noxious white gas had started seeping from the tank and spreading with the northwesterly winds. At the Bijoy Hotel near the railroad, sociologist Swapan Saha, 33, woke up with a terrible pain in his chest. "It was both a burning and a suffocating sensation, " he said. "It was like breathing fire."

Wrapping a damp towel around his nose and mouth, Saha went outside to investigate. Scores of victims lay dead on the train-station platform. "I thought at first there must have been a gigantic railway accident," he recalled. Then he noticed a pall of white smoke on the ground, and an acrid smell in the air. People were running helter-skelter, retching, vomiting and defecating uncontrollably. Many collapsed and died. Dogs, cows and buffaloes were also on the ground, shuddering in death throes. Saha made his way to the railway office, only to find the station master slumped over his desk. For a moment, he thought that an atom bomb had hit Bhopal. Staggering back to the hotel, half blind himself by now, he sat down to write a farewell letter to his wife.

Saha lived, but thousands of others did not escape. For days the body count ticked upward— from 300 to 1,000 to more than 2,500—in the worst industrial accident in history. Across Bhopal, hospitals and mortuaries filled to overflowing. Muslims were buried four and five to a grave, and Hindu funeral pyres burned round the clock. As many as 100,000 survivors may be left with permanent disabilities: blindness, sterility, kidney and liver infections, tuberculosis and brain damage. There were fears that a cholera epidemic could strike. Breaking off a campaign swing through southern India, Prime Minister Rajiv Gandhi rushed to Bhopal. Local officials ordered a full-scale judicial inquiry—and demanded that Union Carbide compensate victims of the disaster.

As a precaution, Union Carbide stopped production and distribution of methyl isocyanate at a plant similar to the Bhopal factory in Institute, West Virginia. But it deflected questions about what caused the mishap until it could complete an internal investigation. The prospects of staggering lawsuits helped drive down the company's stock and forced officials to deny rumors that Union Carbide might have to declare bankruptcy. When Warren Anderson, the chairman of the firm, flew to Bhopal to talk about relief, local authorities arrested him on charges of criminal negligence. Later they released him. Union Carbide offered emergency relief, but refused to discuss outright compensation.

Most of Bhopal was asleep when disaster struck. After the leak started, as many as 200,000 people ran through the city streets, coughing, screaming, and calling out to each other. At about 2 a.m., the pesticide factory's siren went off. Thinking a fire had broken out, hundreds rushed toward the plant—straight into the path of the deadly gas. The train station was littered with the bodies of railroad employees and red-uniformed porters. The junction was paralyzed for 20 hours, making it impossible for survivors to flee by train. Those wealthy enough to own cars gathered their families and tried to escape. But many drivers were blinded by the gas, and there were scores of accidents.

City of Corpses The next morning it looked like a neutron bomb had struck. Buildings were undamaged. But humans and animals littered the low ground, turning hilly Bhopal into a city of corpses. Outside the mortuaries, bodies lay in piles. Those of Muslims were piled on top of each other in hurriedly dug graves. At night the city glowed with the flames of funeral pyres, so many

---

that the local cremation grounds ran out of wood. A fresh supply had to be shipped in overnight before as many as 70 pyres could proceed with Hindu rituals.

The city's hospitals came under siege. Hordes of sufferers, many still vomiting, crowded the emergency rooms. The worst off were old people, children, and the poorest shanty town inhabitants. Many of them were chronically ill from malnutrition even before suffering the effects of the methyl isocyanate. Many doctors had also been exposed to the gas and were unable to work. Medical students and policemen had to be brought in from neighboring towns to help out. What the victims needed most, said one harried doctor, were massive doses of antibiotics and vitamins. But some of the more inexperienced volunteers treated them with anything at hand—glucose, painkillers, even stomach pills. One house painter named Salim arrived at a hospital with ulcerated eyes and burning pains in his stomach. A medical worker gave him a handful of high-potency antacid tablets.

"Keep Calm" Rumors spread like brush fire. One day after the disaster, a blanket of early-morning fog caused people to speculate that another gas leak had taken place. Policemen had to take to the streets in cars to stop everyone from panicking. "Keep calm," they called out through their loudspeakers. "There has been no new leak." There was another report that all the milk and vegetables in the food shops had been contaminated. In the end, that also turned out to be false. However, a local official rekindled fear when he told townspeople to wash their vegetables carefully.

The roots of the Bhopal disaster traced back from almost 20 years. In the mid-1960s, India was in the midst of its "Green Revolution"—the central government's plan to eliminate chronic food shortages. Increased production of pesticides and fertilizers was a vital element of this project. So when Union Carbide approached New Delhi about building a pesticide plant, the authorities were receptive. A feasibility plan for the Bhopal factory was finished in 1969. Three years later both parties signed a letter of intent. In 1975 the Indian government granted Union Carbide a license to manufacture pesticides. The company was set up with 51 percent majority ownership by Union Carbide, with the other 49 percent in the hands of private Indian companies and individuals.

Cronyism In those days the surrounding area was not densely populated. Bhopal is the capital of Madhya Pradesh state: 900,000 people live there now. But Union Carbide built its factory on the outskirts of the city. Even in 1975, M.N. Buch, a local official in charge of public services, foresaw that the railroad and the plant would attract more people. He tried to get the plant moved beyond city limits, citing a law requiring that factories manufacturing dangerous substances be built at least 15 miles from population centers. But nothing happened. Buch was removed to another post: soon afterward Union Carbide donated $2,500 to the city for a park. In the following years, more than 100,000 people moved into northeast Bhopal, most of them settling in the shanty towns of Jayaprakash Nagar and Kali Parade.

As time passed, strong ties grew between Union Carbide and the local political establishment. The pattern of apparent cronyism developed in part because Union Carbide was obligated to hire local management and employees. A well-known local official in the Congress (I) Party, Indira Gandhi's political vehicle, became the plant's lawyer. The former police chief of Madhya Pradesh got a contract to protect the plant. A nephew of the state's former education minister was hired to handle public relations. And the brother-in-law of the deputy chief secretary of the state of Madhya Pradesh took a high-level job at the factory. Lavish parties for local dignitaries were often thrown at Union Carbide's luxurious guest house in the Shyamala Hills. In 1983, when the Congress (I) Party held a regional conference in Bhopal, VIP's were put up at the guest house.

Because of these cozy ties, some labor leaders and environmental groups charged [that] numerous early-warning signals at the plant went unheeded. On Dec. 24, 1978, a huge fire started in the plant's naphtha-storage area, sending a cloud of billowing black smoke over the city. "Nobody in Bhopal slept that night," one local resident recalled. Then on Dec. 26, 1981, a worker named Ashraf died from a leak of phosgene gas inside the factory. A supervisor said Ashraf had collapsed after he "removed his gas mask." But the company gave no explanation for the seepage itself. Fifteen days later, another phosgene leak left as many as 24 people severely ill, including a number of local residents. . . .

Until 1980, the Union Carbide plant imported methyl isocyanate. Then, in accordance with India's industrial self-sufficiency policy, it started manufacturing the chemical on the premises. The process was highly dangerous. Carbon monoxide, itself highly toxic, was mixed with chlorine to form deadly phosgene gas. Phosgene was then combined with methylamine to produce methyl isocyanate. It was in turn used to make Sevin Carbaryl, a pesticide effective on as many as 100 different crops and some 180 types of insects. At Union Carbide plants in America, Sevin is made with U.S. technology. But the process used in Bhopal was researched and developed by an Indian research team. The Indian product was also known for its extra strength: it could kill insects, mites and nematodes at the same time, and required only 24 hours of spraying.

Experts were still unsure what caused the massive gas leak. It happened in one of three storage tanks, each holding some 40 tons of MIC, which were lodged partially underground in the Union Carbide complex. A sharp change in temperature, impurities inside the tank or even a minuscule crack could have caused a rapid buildup in pressure. But the real problem came as the gas began to seep into the air. The MIC should have passed through a "vent scrubber," a small chimney-like protuberance filled with caustic-soda solution, which renders the gas harmless. But this time the vent scrubber failed to work. Nor did the Bhopal plant have other safety devices, common in many U.S. plants, that would have alerted workers to the pressure buildup sooner.

As it was, the needle on the tank's pressure gauge had inched up well beyond the danger level before the night-shift worker noticed it and notified his supervisor. The chemical has a very low boiling point. So by the time it started leaking out, it had turned from liquid to gas. MIC is so powerful that it must be let into the atmosphere in less than 2 parts per 100 million in order not to cause harm. During the accident, it escaped much faster than that. According to union officials, at least five tons of MIC seeped out in 30 minutes before the tank was sealed. The effects of the chemical on human beings resemble those of nerve gas. When inhaled, it reacts with water in the lungs, often choking the victim to death instantaneously. It can be just as lethal when absorbed through the skin. . . .

* * * * *

Excerpt 2: From "Union Carbide fights for its life," *Business Week*, December 24, 1984[2]

Five days after Bhopal's crisis started, it slowly, agonizingly began to abate. The poisonous cloud of methyl isocyanate gas, which leaked from a pesticide plant on the outskirts of the Indian city had long since dispersed. The death toll topped 2,000 and tens of thousands more were suffering— but the number of deaths each day was declining for the first time since the tragic leak occurred on Monday, Dec. 3. "The worst is over," an Indian doctor said.

Across the globe, the worst was just beginning for Union Carbide Corp. which owns 51% of the plant. "My first reaction was disbelief," said Carbide Chairman and Chief Executive Warren M. Anderson, who learned of the accident early Monday morning when reports put the death count at 36. "As the day went on, and that number crept up and up, I almost felt that if I'd go back to sleep and wake up all this would disappear. It's a shattering experience." On Thursday, Carbide employees around the world stopped simultaneously for a moment of silence. At headquarters in Danbury, Conn. the tribute came during lunch hour in the normally cacophonous cafeteria. "The only sound was a few people weeping," recalls one employee.

---

[2]Reproduced from December 24, 1984, issue of *Business Week* by special permission, copyright © 1984 by McGraw-Hill, Inc.

Class action   On another level, too, the company has been badly shaken. The damage claims are sure to be enormous, and it is even conceivable that Carbide, America's 35th largest industrial corporation, could be driven into bankruptcy court.

The lethal gas released in India swept through an area inhabited by 200,000 people. As many as 100,000 required medical treatment. Survivors may suffer partial blindness and lung or liver damage—and long-term effects of exposure to the gas are unknown. Many in India, which ordered a criminal investigation of the incident, demanded compensation on the scale of U.S. awards. Five American attorneys, including Melvin M. Belli, filed a class action seeking $15 billion in damages. Many more suits are expected. "If a U.S. court accepts them, it could put Union Carbide out of business," speculates a London-based international claims expert.

From the start, the company, which enjoys a relatively good reputation in safety matters, put on a brave face. Said Jackson Browning, Carbide's director of safety, health, and environmental affairs: "The Bhopal tragedy is without precedent. But it is believed that, considering both the insurance and other resources available, the financial structure of Union Carbide is not threatened in any way." Anderson, a 63-year-old lawyer who joined Carbide in 1945, spoke to the press less than 24 hours after his return from a three-day trip to the subcontinent. "I met with [other Carbide executives] for an hour and a half before coming here," he said, "and in our judgment we will be a viable company."

Many outsiders weren't so sure. The company's stock dropped precipitously, wiping out 27%, or almost $1 billion, of its market value—in part because Carbide refused to disclose the amount of insurance it carried. That raised questions about the adequacy of its coverage at no more than $200 million. If the bill for Bhopal goes much higher, the No. 3 U.S. chemical maker would be forced to find other means to cover claims. And it might well have difficulty selling assets, even at book value. Two-thirds of them are related to petrochemicals, industrial gases, metals, and carbon products - all businesses plagued with overcapacity.

Carbide denies that it will seek bankruptcy court protection. But even if it does not the company is certain to be hurt. The experience of Swiss pharmaceutical maker F. Hoffmann-La Roche & Co. is a chilling example. One Saturday in July, 1976, a chemical reactor at its plant near Seveso, Italy, blew a safety valve, spraying poisonous dioxin over the town. Eight years later, the cleanup is just ending. Five company managers were sentenced to jail, and the company has paid out some $130 million to settle claims resulting from the damages—most, if not all, covered by its insurance. But no one died at Seveso. Nor, as yet, have any long-term health effects come to light. Yet the company did suffer a temporary loss of sales in Italy, and for a time a boycott of its products was threatened. "It tarnished our image," a company official concedes.

Threats and bombs   No one knows precisely what happened at Bhopal—whether the leak was caused by equipment failure or human error, for example. Anderson stressed that Union Carbide India Ltd., "operated as a separate company," although he defended the Indian managers of the plant. "Under the best of circumstances to find out what went wrong is not easy," he added. "When you complicate that with all the furor, you are talking weeks to sort this out."

But Carbide has already been hit on the periphery. In West Germany and Australia, protesters threatened the company, ignited gasoline bombs at Carbide facilities, or spray-painted the words "poison killers" and "swine" on its buildings. Anderson concedes that Bhopal will stain Carbide for a long time. "We have a stigma," he says. "We can't avoid it."

For the time being, there is no way to estimate how much financial damage Carbide will suffer. That is likely to turn in part on where the lawsuits are heard. Belli's filing quickly made clear that despite substantial legal hurdles, lawyers for the victims, and perhaps even the Indian government, will fight to get American courts to hear the cases.

That could expose Carbide to stunning judgments. U.S. juries routinely make awards in amounts unfathomable in India. A Rand Institute study of U.S. suits for asbestos exposure, for example, found that companies spent $101,000 to resolve each claim. At that rate, even by conservative estimates of the Bhopal devastation, Carbide and its insurers could be looking at a legal bill above $5 billion, about equal to the company's net worth.

Just as important, both the Belli suit and a second filed by different lawyers in New York on Dec. 11 lodge claims against the parent—not the Indian subsidiary—because there would be substantial difficulties in getting a U.S. court to consider a suit against an Indian company. In any event, the monumental potential liability would almost certainly exhaust the entire value of Union Carbide India.

Weak spots   Already some outsiders are speculating that the Carbide defense could have weak spots. For one thing, other chemical companies contend that pesticides similar to those produced by Carbide in India can be made without large stockpiles of methyl isocyanate. Japan's Sumitomo Chemical Co. produces such pesticides with other chemical reactions. Mitsubishi Chemical Industries Ltd. uses a continuous process that consumes methyl isocyanate as fast as it is made.

Anderson, however, denies that the technology and equipment used in Carbide's non-U.S. locations are in any way inferior to those used in the U.S. The alternative processes, the company says, create different safety problems, including much more hazardous waste. He also asserts that, in terms of equipment, safety, and skilled personnel, there was "nothing left to be desired" at the Bhopal plant.

Evidence that Carbide knew of various safety problems at Bhopal, however, has surfaced. Two years ago, Carbide inspectors from the U.S. found 10 major deficiencies at the plant. Carbide declares that the Indian subsidiary said in June that nearly all had been fixed. The company conceded that American safety experts had not returned to Bhopal. Yet Anderson states flatly: "There's no criminal responsibility here."

* * * * *

Excerpt 3: From In Re: Union Carbide Corporation Gas Plant Disaster

*The sections below come from a decision handed down by a U.S. court of appeals on January 14, 1987.[3] In accordance with a previous court order, the plaintiffs in the case included all those who had filed claims against Union Carbide with regard to the disaster at Bhopal. The defendant was Union Carbide. In an earlier case brought to district court in New York,[4] Union Carbide had sought to dismiss the claims against it on grounds of **forum non conveniens**—that the New York court was an inconvenient and thus improper site for the case. The judge had decided in favor of Union Carbide; the plaintiffs appealed; and thus the case went to the court of appeals. What follows is the appeals court's rationale for upholding the original decision.*

The accident occurred on the night of December 2-3, 1984, when winds blew the deadly gas from the plant operated by Union Carbide India Limited (UCIL) into densely occupied parts of the city of Bhopal. UCIL is incorporated under the laws of India. Fifty and nine-tenths percent of its stock is owned by Union Carbide Corporation (UCC), 22% is owned or controlled by the government of India, and the balance is held by approximately 23,500 Indian citizens. The stock is publicly traded on the Bombay Stock Exchange. The company is engaged in the manufacture of a variety of products, including chemicals, plastics, fertilizers and insecticides, at 14 plants in India and employs over 9,000 Indian citizens. It is managed and operated entirely by Indians in India.

---

[3]For official records, the case is listed as 809 F.2d 195 (2nd Cir. 1987).
[4]634 F. Supp. 842.

Four days after the Bhopal accident, on December 7, 1984, the first of some 145 purported class actions in federal district courts in the United States was commenced on behalf of victims of the disaster. On January 2, 1985, the Judicial Panel on Multidistrict Litigation assigned the actions to the Southern District of New York where they became the subject of a consolidated complaint filed on June 28, 1985.

In the meantime, on March 29, 1985, India enacted the Bhopal Gas Leak Disaster (Processing of Claims) Act, granting to its government, the Union of India (UOI), the exclusive right to represent the victims of India or elsewhere. Thereupon the UOI filed a complaint in the Southern District of New York on behalf of all victims of the Bhopal disaster, similar to the purported class action complaints already filed by individuals in the United States. The UOI's decision to bring suit in the United States was attributed to the fact that, although numerous lawsuits (by now, some 6,500) had been instituted by victims in India against UCIL, the Indian courts did not have jurisdiction over UCC, the parent company, which is a defendant in the United States actions...

By order dated April 25, 1985, [U.S. District Court] Judge John F. Keenan appointed a three-person Executive Committee to represent all plaintiffs in the pre-trial proceedings. It consisted of two lawyers representing the individual plaintiffs and one representing the UOI. On July 31, 1985, UCC moved to dismiss the complaints on grounds of *forum non conveniens*, the plaintiffs' lack of standing to bring the actions in the United States, and their purported attorneys' lack of authority to represent them. After several months of discovery,[5] the individual plaintiffs and the UOI opposed UCC's motion. After hearing argument on January 3, 1986, the district court granted the motion, dismissing the lawsuits before it on condition that UCC:

1. consent to the jurisdiction of the courts of India and continue to waive defenses based on the statute of limitations,

2. agree to satisfy any judgment rendered by an Indian court against it and upheld on appeal, provided the judgment and affirmance "comport with the minimal requirements of due process," and,

3. be subject to discovery under the Federal Rules of Civil Procedure of the United States.

On June 12, 1986, UCC accepted these conditions subject to its right to appeal them; and on June 24, 1986, the district court entered its order of dismissal. In September 1986 the UOI, acting pursuant to its authority under the Bhopal Act, brought suit on behalf of all claimants against UCC in the District Court of Bhopal, where many individual suits by victims of the disaster were then pending.

[Simultaneously, as described above, the UOI also appealed the U.S. district court's order of dismissal. Below, the appeals court responds to this appeal.]

As the district court found, the record shows that the private interests of the respective parties weigh heavily in favor of dismissal on grounds of *forum non conveniens*. The many witnesses and sources of proof are almost entirely located in India, where the accident occurred, and could not be compelled to appear for trial in the United States. The Bhopal plant at the time of the accident was operated by some 193 Indian nationals, including the managers of seven operating units employed by the Agricultural Products Division of UCIL, who reported to Indian Works Managers in Bhopal. The plant was maintained by seven functional departments employing over 200 more Indian nationals. UCIL kept at the plant daily, weekly and monthly records of plant operations and records of

---

[5]"Discovery" refers to the process by which documents and other relevant information are discovered and disclosed prior to a trial.

maintenance as well as records of the plant's Quality Control, Purchasing and Stores branches, all operated by Indian employees. The great majority of documents bearing on the design, safety, start-up and operation of the plant, as well as the safety training of the plant's employees, is located in India. Proof to be offered at trial would be derived from interviews of these witnesses in India and study of the records located there to determine whether the accident was caused by negligence on the part of the management or employees in the operation of the plant, by fault in its design, or by sabotage. In short, India has greater ease of access to the proof than does the United States.

The plaintiffs seek to prove that the accident was caused by negligence on the part of UCC in originally contributing to the design of the plant and its provision for storage of excessive amounts of the gas at the plant. As Judge Keenan found, however, UCC's participation was limited and its involvement in plant operations terminated long before the accident. Under 1973 agreements negotiated at arm's length with UCIL, UCC did provide a summary "process design package" for construction of the plant and the services of some of its technicians to monitor the progress of UCIL in detailing the design and erecting the plant. However, the UOI controlled the terms of the agreements and precluded UCC from exercising any authority to "detail design, erect and commission the plant," which was done independently over the period from 1972 to 1980 by UCIL process design engineers who supervised, among many others, some 55 to 60 Indian engineers employed by the Bombay engineering firm of Humphreys and Glasgow. The preliminary process design information furnished by UCC could not have been used to construct the plant. Construction required the detailed process design and engineering data prepared by hundreds of Indian engineers, process designers and sub-contractors. During the ten years spent constructing the plant, its design and configuration underwent many changes.

The vital parts of the Bhopal plant, including its storage tank, monitoring instrumentation, and vent gas scrubber, were manufactured by Indians in India. Although some 40 UCIL employees were given some safety training at UCC's plant in West Virginia, they represented a small fraction of the Bhopal plant's employees. The vast majority of plant employees were selected and trained by UCIL in Bhopal. The manual for start-up of the Bhopal plant was prepared by Indians employed by UCIL.

In short, the plant has been constructed and managed by Indians in India. No Americans were employed at the plant at the time of the accident. In the five years from 1980 to 1984, although more than 1,000 Indians were employed at the plant, only one American was employed there and he left in 1982. No Americans visited the plant for more than one year prior to the accident, and during the 5-year period before the accident the communications between the plant and the United States were almost non-existent.

The vast majority of material witnesses and documentary proof bearing on causation of and liability for the accident is located in India, not the United States, and would be more accessible to an Indian court than to a United States court. The records are almost entirely in Hindi or other Indian languages, understandable to an Indian court without translation. The witnesses for the most part do not speak English but Indian languages understood by an Indian court but not by an American court. These witnesses could be required to appear in an Indian court but not in a court of the United States. Lastly, Judge Keenan properly concluded that an Indian court would be in a better position to direct and supervise a viewing of the Bhopal plant, which was sealed after the accident. Such a viewing could be of help to a court in determining liability issues.

After a thorough review, the district court concluded that the public interest concerns, like the private ones, also weigh heavily in favor of India as the situs for trial and disposition of the cases. The accident and all relevant events occurred in India. The victims, over 200,000 in number, are citizens of India and located there. The witnesses are almost entirely Indian citizens. The Union of India has a greater interest than does the United States in facilitating the trial and adjudication of the victims' claims. **Despite the contentions of plaintiffs and amici[6] that it would be in the public interest to avoid a "double standard" by requiring an American parent corporation (UCC) to submit to the jurisdiction of American courts, India has a stronger countervailing interest in adjudicating the claims in its courts according to its standards rather than having American values and standards of care imposed upon it.[7]**

India's interest is increased by the fact that it has for years treated UCIL as an Indian national, subjecting it to intensive regulations and governmental supervision of the construction, development and operation of the Bhopal plant, its emissions, water and air pollution, and safety precautions. Numerous Indian government officials have regularly conducted on-site inspections of the plant and approved its machinery and equipment, including its facilities for storage of the lethal methyl isocyanate gas that escaped and caused the disaster giving rise to the claims. Thus India has considered the plant to be an Indian one and the disaster to be an Indian problem. It therefore has a deep interest in ensuring compliance with its safety standards. Moreover, plaintiffs have conceded that in view of India's strong interest and its greater contacts with the plant, its operations, its employees, and the victims of the accident, the law of India, as the place where the tort occurred, will undoubtedly govern. In contrast, the American interests are relatively minor.

Having made the foregoing findings, Judge Keenan dismissed the actions against UCC on grounds of *forum non conveniens* upon the conditions indicated above, after obtaining UCC's consent to those conditions subject to its right to appeal the order...

Upon argument of the appeal, UCC also took the position that the district court's order requiring it to satisfy any Indian court judgment was unfair unless some method were provided, such as continued availability of the district court as a forum, to ensure that any denial of due process by the Indian courts could be remedied promptly by the federal court here rather than delay resolution of the issue until termination of the Indian court proceedings and appeal, which might take several years. UCC's argument in this respect was based on the sudden issuance by the Indian court in Bhopal of a temporary order freezing all of UCC's assets, which could have caused it irreparable injury if it had been continued indefinitely,[8] and by the conflict of interest posed by the UOI's position in the Indian courts where, since the UOI would appear both as a plaintiff and a defendant, it might as a plaintiff voluntarily dismiss its claims against itself as a defendant or, as a co-defendant with UCC, be tempted to shed all blame upon UCC even though the UOI had in fact been responsible for supervision, regulation and safety of UCIL's Bhopal plant.

Having reviewed Judge Keenan's detailed decision, in which he thoroughly considered the comparative adequacy of the forums and the public and private interests involved, we are satisfied that there was no abuse of discretion in his granting dismissal of the action...Practically all relevant factors demonstrate that transfer of the cases to India for trial and adjudication is both fair and just to the parties.

Plaintiffs' principal contentions in favor of retention of the cases by the district court are that deference to the plaintiffs' choice of forum has been inadequate, that the Indian courts are insufficiently equipped for the task, that UCC has its principal place of business here, that the most probative evidence regarding negligence and causation is to be found here, that federal courts are much better equipped through experience and procedures to handle such complex actions efficiently than are Indian courts, and that a transfer of the cases to India will jeopardize a $350 million settlement being negotiated by plaintiffs' counsel. All of these arguments, however, must be rejected.

---

[6]"Friends of the court," or those with interests affected by the litigation.

[7]Emphasis added by casewriter.

[8]The Indian court's temporary restraining order has since been dissolved upon UCC's agreement to maintain sufficient assets to satisfy a judgment rendered against it in India.

Little or no deference can be paid to the plaintiffs' choice of a United States forum when all but a few of the 200,000 plaintiffs are Indian citizens located in India who, according to the UOI, have revoked the authorizations of American counsel to represent them here and have substituted the UOI, which now prefers Indian courts. The finding of our district court, after exhaustive analysis of the evidence, that the Indian courts provided a reasonably adequate alternative forum cannot be labelled clearly erroneous or an abuse of discretion.

The emphasis placed by plaintiffs on UCC's having its domicile here, where personal jurisdiction over it exists, is robbed of significance by its consent to Indian jurisdiction. Plaintiffs' contention that the most crucial and probative evidence is located in the United States is simply not in accord with the record or the district court's findings. Although basic design programs were prepared in the United States and some assistance furnished to UCIL at the outset of the 10-year period during which the Bhopal plant was constructed, the proof bearing on the issues to be tried is almost entirely located in India. This includes the principal witnesses and documents bearing on the development and construction of the plant, the detailed designs, the implementation of plans, the operation and regulation of the plant, its safety precautions, the facts with respect to the accident itself, and the deaths and injuries attributable to the accident.

Although the plaintiffs' American counsel may at one time have been close to reaching a $350 million settlement of the cases, no such settlement was ever finalized. No draft joint stipulation in writing or settlement agreement appears to have been prepared, much less approved by the parties. Most important, the UOI, which is itself a plaintiff and states that it now represents the Indian plaintiffs formerly represented by American counsel, is firmly opposed to the $350 million "settlement" as inadequate. . . .[9]

UCC contends that Indian courts, while providing an adequate alternative forum, do not observe due process standards that would be required as a matter of course in this country. As evidence of this apprehension it points to the haste with which the Indian court in Bhopal issued a temporary order freezing its assets throughout the world and the possibility of serious prejudice to it if the UOI is permitted to have the double and conflicting status of both plaintiff and co-defendant in the Indian court proceedings. It argues that we should protect it against such denial of due process by authorizing Judge Keenan to retain the authority, after *forum non conveniens* dismissal of the cases here, to monitor the Indian court proceedings and be available on call to rectify in some undefined way any abuses of UCC's right to due process as they might occur in India.

UCC's proposed remedy is not only impractical but evidences an abysmal ignorance of basic jurisdictional principles so much so that it borders on the frivolous. The district court's jurisdiction is limited to proceedings before it in this country. Once it dismisses those proceedings on grounds of *forum non conveniens* it ceases to have any further jurisdiction over the matter unless and until a proceeding may someday be brought to enforce here a final and conclusive Indian money judgment. Nor could we, even if we attempted to retain some sort of supervisory jurisdiction, impose our due process requirements upon Indian courts, which are governed by their laws, not ours. The concept of shared jurisdictions is both illusory and unrealistic. The parties cannot simultaneously submit to both jurisdictions the resolution of the pre-trial and trial issues when there is only one consolidated case pending in one court. Any denial by the Indian courts of due process can be raised by UCC as a defense to the plaintiffs' later attempt to enforce a resulting judgment against UCC in this country. . . .[10]

---

[9]Several of the court's determinations have not been reproduced here.

[10]Emphasis added by casewriter.

Exhibit 1   Map of India

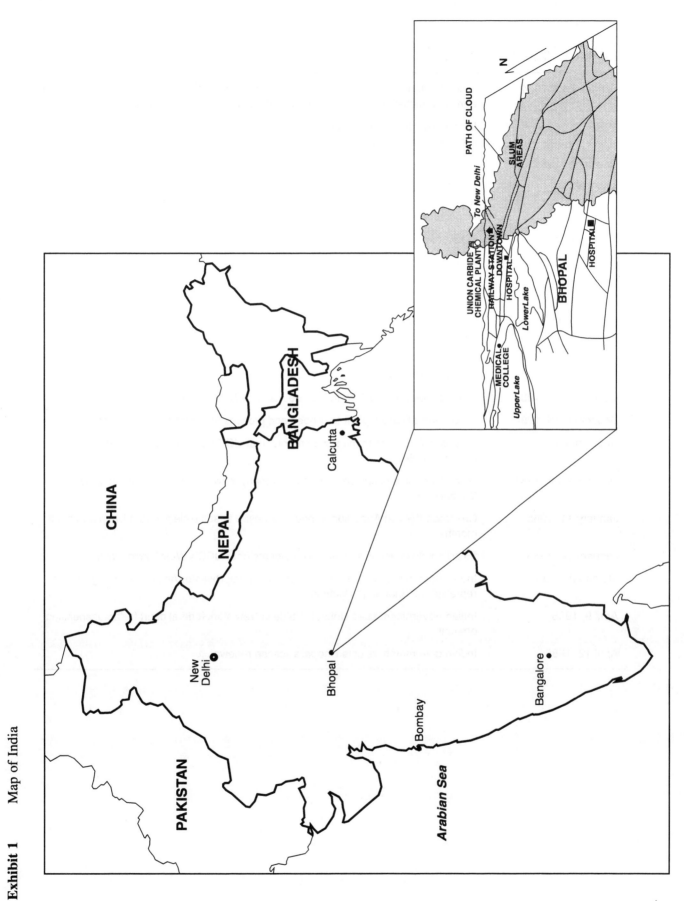

Exhibit 2   Time Line of Events

February 15, 1974	Union Carbide Corp. (UCC) announces plans for construction of a multi-million dollar agricultural chemicals plant in Bhopal. Scheduled for completion in 1976.
1975	Indian government grants Union Carbide India Limited (UCIL) a license to manufacture pesticides.
December 1981	A phosgene gas leak at the UCIL plant kills one worker and injures 24 others.
May 1982	UCIL's three company inspectors discover ten potentially major safety deficiencies, as well as a number of other irregularities at the Bhopal plant. Local government inspectors, however, continue to give the plant routine approval.
November 1984	Maintenance engineer on each shift eliminated.
December 3, 1984	Poisonous methyl isocyanate leak in Bhopal kills 2,500 people and injures 100,000 others.
December 5, 1984	Investors dump 6 million UCC shares on the market.
December 9, 1984	Warren Anderson (Union Carbide Chairman) leaves for India. $1 million in aid donated to victims. Union Carbide announces plans to set up orphanage.
December 11, 1984	Union Carbide confirms that an earlier UCIL inspection had turned up chemical-tank problems at Bhopal.
December 12, 1984	Class action lawsuits filed in U.S. courts on behalf of victims.
December 13, 1984	Indian officials allow plant to reopen and process the remaining methyl isocyanate.
December 17, 1984	*Chemical Engineering* magazine reports that UCC had tried to sell Bhopal plant earlier in 1984.
December 24, 1984	Union Carbide stockholders sue the company in two separate actions related to Bhopal leak.
January 11, 1985	Chairman Warren Anderson announces desire to settle claims from Bhopal within 6 months.
January 30, 1985	$3 billion class-action suit filed by residents near UCC's West Virginia plant.
March 29, 1985	Indian government passes the Bhopal Gas Leak Disaster Act, empowering itself to represent all Bhopal gas victims.
April 9, 1985	Indian government sues Union Carbide in New York federal court for an unspecified amount.
April 12, 1985	Indian government rejects Bhopal's license renewal.

Exhibit 3   Union Carbide Corporation—Selected Financial Data, 1982-1994 (in US$ millions except per share figures)

	1982	1983	1984	1985[a]	1986[b]	1987	1988	1989	1990[c]	1991	1992	1993	1994
Net sales	9,061	9,001	9,508	6,390	6,343	6,914	8,324	8,744	5,238	4,877	4,872	4,640	4,865
Cost of sales	6,687	6,581	6,702	4,607	4,354	4,788	5,480	5,875	3,876	3,770	3,750	3,589	3,673
Research and development expense	240	245	265	181	148	159	159	181	157	157	155	139	136
Selling, administrative and other expenses	1,249	1,243	1,221	725	729	764	807	924	466	408	383	340	290
Depreciation	426	477	507	470	453	463	473	498	278	287	293	276	274
Interest on long-term and short-term debt	236	252	300	243	529	311	300	304	269	228	146	70	80
Other income (expense), net	162	(120)	77	(1,076)	77	(50)	(1)	(84)	n/a	n/a	n/a	n/a	n/a
Pre-tax income (loss) from continuing operations	385	82	590	(912)	207	379	1,104	878	365	(147)	178	227	471
Provision (credit) for income taxes	58	(10)	227	(599)	64	121	415	284	130	(50)	45	78	137
Income (loss) from continuing operations	310	79	323	(503)	130	232	662	573	188	(116)	119	165	389
Income (loss) from discontinued operations	—	—	—	(96)	5	—	—	—	120	107	67	—	—
Net income (loss)	310	79	323	(581)	496	232	662	573	308	(28)	(187)	58	379
Net income (loss) per share	4.47	1.13	4.59	(2.78)	4.78	1.76	4.88	4.07	2.19	(0.22)	(1.46)	0.36	2.44
Total assets	10,616	10,295	10,518	9,670	7,571	7,892	8,441	8,546	7,389	6,826	4,941	4,689	5,028
Long-term debt	2,428	2,387	2,362	1,713	3,057	2,863	2,295	2,080	2,058	1,160	1,113	931	899
Total capital	8,305	7,999	7,962	7,062	4,877	4,998	5,178	5,724	5,338	4,694	2,710	2,395	2,479
UCC stockholders' equity	5,159	4,929	4,924	4,019	1,006	1,247	1,836	2,383	2,373	2,239	1,238	1,428	1,509
Total debt/total capital	33.9%	34.0%	33.7%	38.7%	72.1%	63.6%	53.2%	47.8%	54.0%	52.0%	54.3%	40.3%	38.2%
Common shares outstanding (thousands)	70,153	70,465	70,450	202,821	127,695	132,248	137,602	141,578	125,674	127,607	132,865	150,548	144,412
Number of employees	103,229	99,506	98,366	52,117	50,292	43,119	43,992	45,987	17,722	16,705	15,075	13,051	12,004

Source: Union Carbide Corporation annual reports.

[a] A major restructuring program began in August 1985, when UCC began selling off a total of six business segments: films-packaging, metals, battery products, home and automotive products, specialty polymers and composites, and agricultural products.
[b] Amounts for 1985 reflect a three-for-one stock split effected as a two-for-one stock dividend in March 1986.
[c] Effective July 1, 1989, Union Carbide Corporation became a holding company. The predecessor company changed its name from "Union Carbide Corp." to "Union Carbide Chemicals & Plastics Company Inc." UCC&P was a wholly owned subsidiary of the holding company. Beginning in 1990, the consolidated financial statements no longer included an entry for "Other income."

Exhibit 4   Union Carbide Corporation: Industry Segment Results, 1982-1989 (in US$ millions)

	1982	1983	1984	1985	1986	1987	1988	1989
Sales								
Petrochemicals[a]	2,609	2,551	2,636	—	—	—	—	—
Industrial Gases	1,405	1,361	1,522	1,580	1,560	1,872	2,076	2,349
Metals and Carbon Products[b]	1,107	1,024	977	571	570	619	723	782
Consumer Products[c]	1,933	1,895	1,907	—	—	—	—	—
Specialties and Services[a]	2,007	2,170	2,466	732	772	98	—	—
Chemicals and Plastics	—	—	—	3,507	3,441	4,325	5,525	5,613
TOTAL UCC Consolidated	9,061	9,001	9,508	6,390	6,343	6,914	8,324	8,744
Identifiable Assets								
Petrochemicals[a]	3,268	2,934	2,862	—	—	—	—	—
Industrial Gases	1,710	1,864	1,840	1,977	1,849	2,490	2,599	2,771
Metals and Carbon Products[b]	1,641	1,431	1,351	898	718	829	814	815
Consumer Products[c]	1,408	1,360	1,346	—	—	—	—	—
Specialties and Services[a]	2,174	2,327	2,820	1,043	1,038	533	674	521
Chemicals and Plastics	—	—	—	3,186	3,198	3,506	3,995	4,068
Inter-segment eliminations	(78)	(59)	(92)	(13)	(10)	—	—	—
TOTAL UCC Consolidated	10,123	9,857	10,127	7,091	6,793	7,358	8,082	8,175
Operating Profit (Loss)[d]								
Petrochemicals[a]	(39)	71	222	—	—	—	—	—
Industrial Gases	176	204	258	222	276	237	230	222
Metals and Carbon Products[b]	79	(14)	31	(146)	49	20	46	44
Consumer Products[c]	223	217	226	—	—	—	—	—
Specialties and Services[a]	200	202	238	(181)	(3)	(14)	—	—
Chemicals and Plastics	—	—	—	(142)	472	534	1,204	1,003
Inter-segment eliminations	18	(2)	(2)	(6)	(3)	—	—	—
TOTAL UCC Consolidated	657	678	973	(253)	791	777	1,480	1,269

Source: Union Carbide Corporation annual reports.

a Certain Petrochemicals-related subsidiaries and plastics-related Specialties subsidiaries were reclassified into the Chemicals and Plastics division. Remaining businesses in Petrochemicals and Specialties & Services were discontinued in 1987.
b The Metals business was sold in 1985.
c The Consumer Products division was sold in 1985.
d Operating profits cannot be derived directly from **Exhibit 3** since they include unusual charges not included in the consolidated financial statements.

Exhibit 5   Union Carbide Corporation: Geographic Segment Results, 1982-1994 (in US$ millions)

	1982	1983	1984	1985	1986	1987	1988	1989	1990	1991	1992	1993[a]	1994
Sales													
United States and Puerto Rico	6,051	6,189	6,766	4,691	4,555	4,778	5,758	5,793	3,827	3,530	3,529	3,443	3,535
Canada	553	551	521	313	241	298	429	463	192	158	137	130	136
Europe	856	850	871	646	747	876	929	1,053	594	550	550	454	474
Latin America	714	557	573	476	519	638	777	961	187	200	222	241	218
Asia Pacific and Other	887	854	777	264	281	324	431	474	438	439	434	372	502
TOTAL UCC Consolidated	9,061	9,001	9,508	6,390	6,343	6,914	8,324	8,744	5,238	4,877	4,872	4,640	4,865
Operating Profit													
United States and Puerto Rico	369	416	677	(329)	599	567	1,142	917	556	89	275	299	433
Canada	(23)	11	11	(78)	47	57	113	106	19	(22)	(14)	(53)	14
Europe	94	66	76	39	42	30	61	73	14	4	13	18	12
Latin America	107	105	132	101	98	106	142	144	10	13	8	6	16
Asia Pacific and Other	92	82	79	20	8	16	22	29	24	27	30	28	74[b]
Inter-segment eliminations	18	(2)	(2)	(6)	(3)	1	-	-	1	11	4	(1)	2
TOTAL UCC Consolidated	657	678	973	(253)	791	777	1,480	1,269	624	122	316	297	551
Identifiable Assets													
United States and Puerto Rico	7,319	7,150	7,552	5,153	4,835	4,709	5,507	5,707	3,826	3,712	3,575	3,579	3,777
Canada	814	925	875	639	628	618	770	803	508	361	367	263	259
Europe	807	719	711	733	879	1,238	1,228	1,406	347	351	316	255	305
Latin America	799	728	781	701	758	776	822	940	132	140	151	140	203
Asia Pacific and Other	778	749	683	276	251	426	409	333	274	317	213	210	272
Inter-segment eliminations	(394)	(414)	(475)	(411)	(558)	(409)	(654)	(1,014)	(99)	(120)	(53)	(28)	(7)
TOTAL UCC Consolidated	10,123	9,857	10,127	7,091	6,793	7,358	8,082	8,175	4,988	4,761	4,569	4,419	4,809

Source: Union Carbide Corporation annual reports.

[a] Due to the merger between Union Carbide Corp. and Union Carbide Chemicals & Plastics Inc. in 1993, operating profit was calculated on a total consolidated basis.

[b] Includes an $81 million gain on the sale of a manufacturing facility and distribution terminal in Hong Kong and a $24 million charge from the write-down and sale of the corporation's stockholding in Union Carbide India Limited.

Exhibit 6   Market Share Price of Union Carbide Stock, 1982-1994

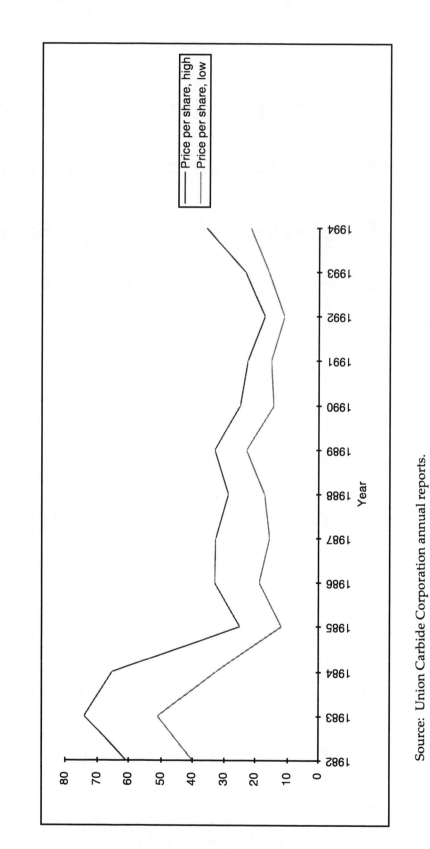

Source: Union Carbide Corporation annual reports.

Exhibit 7   Top 40 Industrial Corporations in 1984, Ranked by Sales

Rank	Company (Headquarters)	Sales (US$ millions)	Industry
1	Exxon (New York, NY)	90,854	Petroleum
2	General Motors (Detroit, MI)	83,890	Automotive
3	Mobil (New York, NY)	56,047	Petroleum
4	Ford Motor (Dearborn, MI)	52,366	Automotive
5	Texaco (Harrison, NY)	47,334	Petroleum
6	International Business Machines (Armonk, NY)	45,937	Information processing
7	E.I. du Pont de Nemours (Wilmington, DE)	35,915	Chemicals
8	American Telephone & Telegraph (New York, NY)	33,188	Telecommunications
9	General Electric (Fairfield, CT)	27,947	Diversified
10	Standard Oil (Indiana) (Chicago, IL)	26,949	Petroleum
11	Chevron (San Francisco, CA)	26,798	Petroleum
12	Atlantic Richfield (Los Angeles, CA)	24,686	Petroleum
13	Shell Oil (Houston, TX)	20,701	Petroleum
14	Chrysler (Highland Park, MI)	19,573	Automotive
15	U.S. Steel (Pittsburgh, PA)	18,274	Diversified
16	United Technologies (Hartford, CT)	16,332	Diversified
17	Philips Petroleum (Bartlesville, OK)	15,537	Petroleum
18	Occidental Petroleum (Los Angeles, CA)	15,373	Petroleum
19	Tenneco (Houston, TX)	14,779	Petroleum
20	Sun (Radnor, PA)	14,466	Petroleum
21	ITT (New York, NY)	14,001	Diversified
22	Procter & Gamble (Cincinnati, OH)	12,946	Consumer & food products
23	R.J. Reynolds Industries (Winston-Salem, NC)	11,902	Tobacco
24	Standard Oil (Ohio) (Cleveland, OH)	11,692	Petroleum
25	Dow Chemical (Midland, MI)	11,418	Chemicals
26	Allied (Morris Township, NJ)	10,864	Aerospace & automotive parts
27	Unocal (Los Angeles, CA)	10,838	Petroleum
28	Eastman Kodak (Rochester, NY)	10,600	Imaging
29	Boeing (Seattle, WA)	10,354	Aerospace
30	Westinghouse Electric (Pittsburgh, PA)	10,265	Diversified
31	Goodyear Tire & Rubber (Akron, OH)	10,241	Tires & rubber products
32	Philip Morris (New York, NY)	10,138	Tobacco
33	Dart & Kraft (Northbrook, IL)	9,759	Food & consumer products
34	McDonnell Douglas (St. Louis, MO)	9,663	Aerospace
35	Union Carbide (Danbury, CT)	9,508	Chemicals
36	Beatrice Foods (Chicago, IL)	9,327	Food & consumer products
37	Rockwell International (Pittsburgh, PA)	9,322	Aerospace & electronics
38	Xerox (Stamford, CT)	8,971	Imaging
39	General Foods (Rye Brook, NY)	8,600	Food products & services
40	PepsiCo (Purchase, NY)	8,428	Beverages and food products & services

Source: Adapted from *Fortune*, April 29, 1985, p. 266.

The Burma Pipeline

Politics often bubbles to the surface in the oil business. . . .[1]

In early 1997, John Imle, president of Unocal Corporation, was confident about his firm's prospects in the emerging markets of Southeast Asia. With over 30 years of experience in the region, Unocal had already established successful energy production facilities in Thailand, the Philippines, and Indonesia and was continuously exploring for new resource extraction opportunities. Anticipating that significant increases in energy demand would accompany the rapid economic growth and development occurring throughout the region, the company had recently added Burma to its growing list of Southeast Asian partners. As he considered Unocal's first large-scale project in the country, Imle was optimistic that this new relationship would generate large returns and future business opportunities.

Structured as an investment consortium including the French oil company Total, Unocal, and the national energy companies of Thailand and Burma, the $1.2 billion project revolved around the construction of a 416-mile pipeline to transport natural gas from the offshore Yadana ("treasure" in Burmese) gas field into both countries. Once completed in mid-1998, the project would yield an estimated 650 million cubic feet of natural gas per day (mmcf/d) and over $400 million in annual revenue well into the twenty-first century.[2] In hopes of extending this good fortune, Unocal and its French co-investor had also signed a second agreement with the Burmese government to explore an additional 4,427 square mile block around the Yadana field.[3] With pipeline construction nearly complete and promising exploration contracts on the horizon, Unocal was well-poised to continue its expansion into the emerging markets of Southeast Asia.

Increasingly, though, Yadana and Unocal had become a source of controversy, not only in Burma and Thailand, but in North America and Europe as well. Defense of the pipeline against attacks from anti-government guerrilla forces was reportedly exacerbating refugee problems along the Burma-Thai border; exiled Burmese groups were suing Unocal for alleged human rights abuses incurred in the ongoing construction of the project; U.S. labor unions were calling for investigations into Unocal's involvement with the Burmese government, a supposed conduit for drug money laundering; non-governmental organizations in Thailand and the United States were protesting the pipeline's environmental impact; and U.S. consumer boycotts were successfully pressuring several prominent firms to withdraw business operations from Burma. Even the U.S. government had recently become involved, imposing sanctions on investment in Burma to protest the ruling military junta's repression of pro-democracy movements. Imle knew that the Burma pipeline had enormous

---

Lane T. La Mure (Ph.D. candidate, Harvard University) prepared this case under the supervision of Professor Debora Spar as the basis for class discussion rather than to illustrate either effective or ineffective handling of an administrative situation.

resource and profit potential for his firm. He also knew that the project could easily become a public relations nightmare and a liability for Unocal.

Unocal

Founded in 1890, the Union Oil Company of California (Unocal) was the product of a merger between three California oil companies: Sespe Oil, Torrey Canyon Oil, and Hardison and Stewart Oil. The partnership was fragile until 1894, when Lyman Stewart assumed control of the small company and guided its steady expansion until his retirement in 1914. Replacing his father as company president, Will Stewart expanded Unocal's refining capacity and holdings of local service stations, boosting the company's annual sales to $90 million by the end of the 1930s. Over the next several decades, the corporation continued to grow, despite two takeover attempts, a number of failed exploration ventures, and a series of public relations disasters associated with a large oil spill off the California coast in 1969. When oil shocks convulsed Western markets in the 1970s, Unocal invested substantial sums in the research and development of alternative energy resources. It also continued an aggressive global search for traditional oil reserves.[4]

This joint strategy paid off handsomely in the 1980s. The company entered the decade with sizable oil and gas holdings and a very strong financial position. In 1985, these assets enabled the firm to survive a hostile takeover attempt by the infamous raider T. Boone Pickens. The defense, however, forced Unocal to increase its debt holdings from $1.2 billion to $5.3 billion. CEO Richard Stegemeier responded by closing Unocal's unprofitable production and refining facilities, selling real estate properties that did not hold oil or gas, and rebuilding reserves that had dwindled in the aftermath of the takeover bid.[5] Aggressive restructuring continued under CEO Roger Beach, who assumed office in mid-1994 and led Unocal in selling its low return refining and marketing assets, buying back $1.2 billion in debt and company stock, and streamlining business divisions for international energy projects.[6]

By 1997, the company was tightly reorganized and poised again for aggressive expansion. With a growth strategy focused explicitly on overseas operations, Unocal no longer considered itself "a U.S. company with foreign operations, but a global energy company with strong U.S. operations."[7] As such, it remained heavily engaged in exploration projects, seeking to expand its growing reserves, extraction capacity, and profits. In 1997, with company stock averaging $40 a share, Unocal described itself as the world's largest publicly traded, independent energy resource company, ranking first in production, reserves, and private geothermal energy output.[8]

Between 1995 and 1996, Unocal's holdings of foreign oil and gas reserves as a percentage of its total reserves increased by 25 percent. In 1996, the company's exploration and development yielded more than 268 million BOE (barrels of oil equivalent) in new reserves, 94 percent of which were in foreign projects. Eighty-seven percent of the new reserves were in Asia (113 million BOE in Thailand, 73 million BOE in Burma, and 46 million BOE in Indonesia), where the company anticipated significant growth opportunities.[9] Accordingly, in early 1997, Unocal opened a "twin corporate headquarters" in Kuala Lumpur, Malaysia.

With this base, Unocal made Southeast Asia the center of its global focus. It was a logical and compelling choice. Along with many of its competitors, the company anticipated that the region's emerging economies would continue to grow at a projected 7 percent a year, generating higher standards of living, increased energy consumption, and the continued development of vast, unexploited resources. With over 30 years of experience in the region, Unocal already operated six oil and gas fields in Indonesia, two major geothermal projects in the Philippines, an exploration project in Vietnam, and several large natural gas facilities in Thailand.[10] In early 1993, it had added to this regional portfolio by signing a production sharing contract with the Burmese government.

Burma[11]

Slightly smaller in size than Texas, Burma lies at the heart of Southeast Asia. Situated in a predominantly tropical climate, the country possesses vast natural resources, including coal, natural gas, petroleum, timber, copper, tin, zinc, precious stones, and opium. The economy is mixed, with private activity prevailing in agriculture and light industry, while the state maintains control in energy, foreign trade, and heavy industry. The country's 47 million inhabitants include over 135 separate ethnic groups and mountain tribes, many of which speak languages other than the official Burmese.[12]

Modern Burma boasts a checkered and tumultuous past. In 1948, national hero Aung San led Burma to independence after more than a century of British colonial rule, establishing a parliamentary democracy and open elections. Just over a decade later, in March 1962, General Ne Win and the armed forces staged a coup d'etat that overthrew the ruling democracy and implemented instead a distinctive national ideology and plan of action termed "The Burmese Way to Socialism." In 1974, the military drafted the national constitution, effectively codifying its control over the country. Under the "Burmese Way," the country moved from an outright military dictatorship to a more subtle constitutional dictatorship. The military fused governmental powers in the creation of a unitary state, allowing a single political party (the Burma Socialist Programme Party) to run the regime-controlled legislature (the People's Assembly). Despite the trappings of institutional autonomy, Burma remained a totalitarian society, run by the military in line with its own interests.[13] Although he formally ceded power in 1981, the eccentric Ne Win was widely thought to exert significant influence over subsequent military leaders and policies.[14]

By 1988, twenty-six years of Ne Win's "Burmese Way to Socialism" had brought the economy to a standstill. Buried under nearly three decades of incompetent administration and unsuccessful centralized economic planning, Burma was on the brink of bankruptcy, with chronic shortages of essential goods and brewing discontent over ineffective government policies. In March of 1988, when riot police shot a student outside a Rangoon teahouse, economic frustration exploded into social unrest. Throughout the capital and other parts of the country, student and citizen protests erupted, sparking demands for democracy and change. Daw Aung San Suu Kyi, daughter of the celebrated independence hero Aung San, quickly emerged as the leader of the National League for Democracy (NLD) and mounted a powerful campaign against the suddenly besieged military government.[15]

In September 1988, after five months of political protest and organized demonstrations, a group of military leaders banned the country's only existing political party and established a "temporary" ruling junta, organized under the Orwellian acronym of SLORC (State Law and Order Restoration Council). In the ensuing crackdown, an estimated ten thousand citizens were killed and thousands imprisoned. The SLORC closed universities, banned public gatherings, established strict curfews, and sought to reinstate totalitarian control over the once peaceful society.[16] In an effort to destroy any remaining opposition, the junta confined Aung San Suu Kyi to house arrest and imprisoned or killed several of her followers. Despite these brutal efforts and sustained repression, however, support for the democracy movement remained strong.

When legislative elections were finally held in May of 1990, the National League for Democracy won an overwhelming 80 percent of the seats, leaving the military's favored party in the minority. The embarrassed SLORC promptly nullified the results, promising to hold new elections only when the military and Burma's 135 recognized ethnic minorities approved a new national constitution. Now a Nobel Peace Prize laureate, Aung San Suu Kyi remained defiant and under house arrest, refusing to participate with the SLORC in the drafting of a non-democratic constitution.

The country's economic outlook was equally tenuous. Since 1988, the SLORC's rule had brought little in the way of economic prosperity. The government's four-year plan (1992-1996) to boost agricultural output had produced disappointing results and efforts to increase exports of the country's abundant commodities, such as rice and teak, had faltered badly.[17] By December 1996, poor economic conditions and frustration over the lack of promised elections threatened to ignite another cycle of social unrest and bloody crackdown. In response to spiraling food prices and a depreciating currency (kyat), students and farmers took to the streets in protest. Once again, the SLORC closed universities and arrested several hundred citizens.[18] In public pronouncements, the ruling junta reaffirmed its commitment to "annihilate any internal elements who [were] trying to disrupt the country."[19]

Yet somehow, in the midst of this turmoil and repression, foreign direct investment (FDI) in Burma was steadily increasing. Between 1990 and 1995, FDI grew from $286 million to $1.3 billion; by 1996, this figure was projected to reach nearly $3.8 billion. Singapore accounted for the largest percentage of Burma's FDI, followed by the United Kingdom, Thailand, France, Malaysia, and the United States.[20] Nearly half of the investments were in the oil and gas sectors, followed by hotels and tourism, fisheries, real estate, mining, and manufacturing. Having signed production and/or exploration agreements with Unocal, Total, Texaco, Premiere Oil, Nippon Oil, and ARCO (Atlantic Richfield Co.), the ruling junta was optimistic that its vast and unexploited reserves of natural gas and oil would lead to economic salvation.

Natural Gas

Natural gas, a simple hydrocarbon typically found in porous underground reservoirs, generally consists of methane, ethane, propane, butane, pentane, and associated impurities, such as nitrogen, carbon dioxide, and hydrogen sulfide.[21] Like oil, gas originates in organic shale, the byproduct of millions of years of pressurized heat chemically transforming the remains of prehistoric plants and animals into modern fossil fuels. Accordingly, gas deposits exist in both associated (mixed with oil) and non-associated (isolated from oil) forms. By virtue of its chemical composition, natural gas combustion produces comparatively lower levels of carbon dioxide and sulfur emissions than do other fossil fuels, such as oil or coal.

The production and transportation of natural gas occurs in three basic stages. First, the gas is gathered from well bores in small diameter pipelines for simple separations of water, formation sediments, and condensate (liquid hydrocarbons similar to crude oil). Second, inert gases or vapor pressures that do not meet pipeline specifications are removed. Third, the gas is pressurized and transported via pipeline to market. In areas where large reserves exist beyond pipeline distance from a ready market, the gas may be liquefied at -161 degrees Celsius and transported by oceangoing tanker. In its final form, natural gas is generally used to produce heat or electricity for industrial and residential purposes.[22]

As of January 1990, worldwide proven natural gas reserves measured 132,897 billion cubic meters (885,980 million "barrels" equivalent), compared to a global reserve of 988,425 million barrels of oil.[23] Approximately 70% of the world's natural gas was held in Eastern Europe and the Middle East, with the remaining reserves scattered across Africa, Asia, Latin America, North America, and Western Europe.[24] Although natural gas production had grown steadily since World War II, consumption was still concentrated in just three regions: North America, Europe, and the Far East. Several prominent studies, however, predicted significant changes in these consumption patterns.

As of 1997, most energy forecasts suggested that the production and consumption of oil and gas would continue to increase between 1996 and 2015, establishing several prominent trends. First, many predicted that advances in extraction and transportation infrastructure would move the gas industry from a regional market to a global one, dramatically expanding trade and output. Second, as gas production around the world increased, the three top consuming regions would meet their rising demands with imports from emerging markets, particularly the Middle East, Latin America, Africa, and the former Soviet Union. Third, as these patterns manifest themselves, gas would gain significant market share over competing fossil fuels (coal and oil), with power generation and industrial output driving appreciable demand growth in every region of the world.[25] As a result, by 2015, worldwide natural gas demand was projected to grow by more than 76 percent over 1996 levels.[26] These demand increases were expected to be especially large in developing countries, where progress and modernization depended on access to energy.

Asia's soaring economies typified many of these trends. Political and economic liberalization, coupled with average annual GDP growth rates of 7 percent, led to the widespread belief that overall gas demand in Asia would grow at 7.5 percent a year between 1995 and 2010. Although the region was largely self-sufficient in 1995, the emergence of these trends meant that as much as 40 percent of liquefied natural gas (LNG) in the region would need to be imported. [27] Not surprisingly, publication of these forecasts had brought about intensified exploration efforts across Asia and a concomitant boom in the development of the region's natural gas infrastructure.[28] Armed with similar projections, Unocal considered Southeast Asia and Burma's Yadana Project a critical part of its growth strategy.

The Yadana Project[29]

Holding 5 trillion cubic feet of reserves, the Yadana natural gas field was located in 150 feet of water in the Andaman Sea, approximately 43 miles off the coast of Burma. Originally discovered by the state-owned Myanma Oil and Gas Enterprise (MOGE) in 1982, Yadana remained unexploited for over a decade. It was not until 1992, after a mature gas market began to emerge in Thailand, that Total signed a production-sharing agreement with the Burmese government. Scouring for additional reserves in Southeast Asia, Unocal immediately recognized the project's potential. As company president John Imle noted, "It involves the development of a known, abundant natural gas field, using off-the-shelf technology and serving a market with rapidly expanding demand. There are no technological or economic hurdles to developing the Yadana field."[30] Accordingly, in early 1993, Unocal readily accepted Total's invitation to join a development consortium.

With Total as the project operator, the pipeline was scheduled to commence operation in mid-1998. For 30 years thereafter, a set of four offshore platforms would produce approximately 525 million cubic feet of natural gas per day (mmcf/d), most of which would flow through a 416-mile pipeline to the Ratchaburi power plant in Thailand. In addition to meeting part of Thailand's 120 percent projected increase in electrical power demand, the pipeline would also double Burma's natural gas production, providing it with 125 mmcf/d for power projects near the capital city of Rangoon. The $1.2 billion project was sponsored by four co-venturers: subsidiaries of Unocal (28.26%) and the Paris-based Total Corporation (31.24%), Thailand's PTT Exploration & Production Public Co. Ltd (25.5%), and Burma's MOGE (15%). In February 1995, the four companies signed a 30-year sales contract for the supply of natural gas to Thailand's Petroleum Authority and a separate sales agreement extending natural gas to Burma. In February 1997, Total, Unocal, and MOGE signed an additional production-sharing contract for a 4,427 square mile area near the Yadana field that could also be accessed by the pipeline project.

The pipeline to Ratchaburi was planned in three sections. Thirty-six inches in diameter and composed of 5,000 four and a half ton lengths of pipe, the line's first section began at the offshore platform complex and extended 215 miles along the ocean floor to Daminseik, a small coastal village in Burma. Installation was slated to begin in mid-1997. The second section, started in late 1996, included a pipeline center, pressure stations, and a metering facility. Extending through Burma's Tenasserim region, it ran 39 miles from landfall at Daminseik to the Burma-Thai border and was completed in May of 1997. The third section, to be developed by the Petroleum Authority of Thailand in late 1997, extended 161 miles from Ban-I-Tong, on the Burma-Thai border, to Ratchaburi (just outside Bangkok). In July 1998, the entire project would become operational.

Even before the pipeline was built, Unocal and Total had recognized the sensitivities that might surround it. Accordingly, the four consortium members had pledged themselves to monitor and evaluate the full impact of their construction activities. They started in May of 1994, by hiring teams of specialists to select the most environmentally responsible path for the onshore pipeline route. This portion of the project would cut a temporary 13 meter wide path, as well as a permanent 4 meter wide access road, from Daminseik across the neck of Burma to Bon-I-Tong, traveling through a forested region dotted with rural villages. According to Unocal representatives, the route that was ultimately selected minimized contact with vulnerable populations and vegetation. It traversed through some deciduous and evergreen forests, avoiding nearby rainforests and villages. Much of the area had already been subjected to previous slash-and-burn farming and logging by local inhabitants. The additional environmental impact of the project would therefore be minimal. Teams of contract specialists performed similar evaluations for the offshore and coastal portions of the pipeline, claiming to provide "the most comprehensive regional environmental review of the area ever conducted."[31]

In addition to these environmental surveys, the consortium undertook a variety of community development initiatives in the thirteen Burmese villages located near the pipeline's planned route. After establishing village communications committees to assess the needs of people living in the area, the companies implemented a three-year, $6 million socioeconomic development program. The initiative provided nineteen doctors to an area which had none, offered free medical services to the 35,000 local inhabitants, renovated nearby hospitals, planned seven health centers, built and furnished six new schools, established several farming projects, undertook efforts to develop local infrastructure, and waived gas transportation charges to meet the energy requirements of the affected villages. As one of Unocal's general manager's noted, "We remain fully committed to supporting these projects. Not only will they build the local economy and provide people with greater job opportunities, but they promote long-term economic self-sufficiency for the people in this region."[32]

To construct the pipeline, the Yadana consortium employed two thousand local workers at higher than prevailing market wages. They also established the tuition-free Yadana Technical School in Rangoon, training 74 Burmese nationals to begin pipeline monitoring and maintenance in March 1998. As a matter of policy, all participants promised strict adherence to the fair treatment of workers, local inhabitants, and the environment. Throughout Unocal's involvement in the pipeline, the board of directors conducted periodic reviews, concluding that ". . . from moral, ethical, economic and human development perspectives, the Yadana project represents a significant opportunity to bring sustainable, long-term benefits to the people of Myanmar."[33]

As of late 1997, the Yadana Project was well underway. A temporary Burmese base camp had been built, the onshore portion of the pipeline had been completed, and offshore platform construction had advanced into its final stages. Further exploration was already underway in offshore areas near the Yadana gas field, and similar developments were occurring nearby. U.S.-based Texaco, Britain's Premier Oil, and Nippon Oil of Japan were jointly constructing a natural gas extraction facility to access Burma's offshore Yetagun gas field, and ARCO, which had already entered a production sharing agreement with the Burmese government, had begun drilling in the Bay of Bengal. Amidst all of this activity and excitement, however, the Yadana project had become mired in controversy and confusion. None of the problems stemmed directly from the project or the contractual arrangements that had created it. Yet the controversy that emerged around Yadana quickly became serious enough to put Unocal's involvement in the project—and the firm's reputation—into serious jeopardy.

Endless Controversy

Ever since the project's inception in 1992, Unocal's involvement in Burma had made headline news. As the largest U.S. investor in Burma, constructing the country's largest foreign investment and infrastructure project, the company had been widely criticized by a broad coalition of human rights groups, environmental organizations, and consumer advocates. Repeatedly, Unocal reiterated its commitment to the region and its adherence to widely accepted codes of conduct. But by 1997, the criticisms had reached a fever point. They focused, in particular, on four critical aspects of the Yadana project: pipeline security, human rights, drugs, and environmental impact.

Pipeline Security[34]

In March 1995, five Burmese members of a Yadana survey team had been killed by anti-SLORC forces operating in the area. Subsequent attacks on Total's base camp reportedly occurred on two other occasions, injuring six project workers.[35] In response, and to fend off further attacks, the SLORC allegedly sent 4,000 troops to patrol the pipeline construction area.[36] North of the pipeline route, an additional 100,000 troops engaged in eliminating the remaining jungle strongholds of the Karen National Union (KNU), a predominantly Christian ethnic group that had been fighting for autonomy from the government since 1949. When a faction of the KNU vowed to destroy the pipeline, the SLORC launched one of its most aggressive military offensives of the past decade, driving 15,000 refugees into bordering Thailand.[37] With 90,000 Burmese already taking shelter along the border, Thai officials began repatriating thousands of unarmed men, women, and children back to the neighboring zone of conflict in February 1997. Aid workers and rebel leaders feared that continued repatriation would allow the SLORC to complete its drive toward total annihilation of the Karen ethnic community.[38]

By March 1997, for the first time since World War II, the Burmese government controlled most of the Burma-Thai border and the critical area surrounding the pipeline corridor. Notably, however, the SLORC still faced several pockets of resistance, and most of the previously signed cease-fire agreements with ethnic insurgents were near collapse.[39] In an effort to solidify their control of the area, SLORC authorities were thought to be planning continued offensives against any remaining KNU strongholds near the Yadana project. Rebel groups within Burma and protesters in the United States partially blamed Unocal for many of the ensuing events, claiming that security for the pipeline project had provoked the SLORC's onslaught.[40] Opponents argued that "the pipeline [had] effectively furthered SLORC economic as well as military agendas in Southern Burma, as the contract [was] being used to legitimize SLORC military activities throughout the entire Tenasserim region."[41]

In response, officials at Total denied that the two subsequent attacks had occurred, noting only that "the government has told us that they will make the area safe."[42] Similarly, Unocal cited its policy of political neutrality and suggested that "the general vicinity of the pipeline has not been the scene of ethnic conflict reported elsewhere in the region." In a 1995 discussion with anti-SLORC activists, Imle had also expressed his concern that guerrilla threats against the project would incite the SLORC to more violence: "Let's be reasonable about this. What I'm saying is that if you threaten the pipeline, there's going to be more military. If forced labor goes hand-in-glove with the military, yes, there will be more forced labor. For every threat to the pipeline, there will be a reaction."[43] In the provision of security for the Yadana project, however, SLORC military forces were allegedly committing atrocious human rights violations.

Human Rights

Reports of the SLORC's human rights abuses were not new. In fact, since its takeover in 1988, the SLORC had been repeatedly condemned by the international community for its disregard of human rights and prolonged confinement of Aung San Suu Kyi. As of 1997, hundreds of political prisoners remained in detention or awaited sentencing without due process of law. Basic rights in most countries--such as freedom of speech, press, association, and religion--were regularly denied Burmese citizens. Under the SLORC's iron-fisted rule, the government allegedly relied on the forced displacement of Burmese village populations, arbitrary seizure for forced labor, extrajudicial execution, kidnapping, torture, arbitrary arrest, and other means of physical repression.[44] According to critics of the SLORC and Unocal, such abuses had regularly occurred in the construction and defense of the Yadana pipeline project.

Opponents of Yadana primarily focused their criticisms on three related claims. First, they claimed that the SLORC was forcing villagers in the region to serve as unpaid porters and laborers for military and infrastructure projects related to pipeline security. For example, several human rights groups credibly reported that thousands of men, women, and children were being forced to build the Ye-Tavoy Railway, which they said would be used for transporting SLORC security battalions and military supplies to the pipeline area. Poorly treated workers routinely lacked access to adequate healthcare, housing, nutrition, or clean water.[45] Second, critics argued that the forced portering contributed to additional, systematic human rights abuses. Beyond widespread confirmation by several non-governmental organizations operating along the Burma-Thailand border, Yozo Yokota, the United Nations Special Rapporteur for Burma, reported that "arbitrary killings, beatings, rapes, and confiscation of property by the SLORC [were] most commonly occurring in the border areas where the Army [was] engaged in military operations or regional development projects."[46] Finally, opponents claimed that in early 1992, the SLORC had destroyed or forcibly relocated several villages to clear the pipeline route.[47]

In addition to publicizing reports of these abuses, critics of Yadana argued that Unocal and Total were liable for the atrocities being committed: "Since the pipeline project [was] the direct cause of troops moving through the area, it [was] also the indirect cause of the corresponding increase in portering and associated abuses."[48] Two class-action lawsuits filed in United States federal court made precisely this argument.

In September 1996, the National Coalition Government of Burma (NCGB) and the Federation of Trade Unions of Burma filed a lawsuit against Unocal and Total. The NCGB, which consisted of exiled parliamentary members originally elected in 1990, alleged that Unocal's use of SLORC security forces had resulted in the systematic destruction and relocation of villages, the widespread use of forced labor, and a series of human rights atrocities, including murder and rape. For example, the suit claimed that in their efforts to relocate one village, SLORC soldiers kicked and beat a woman, causing her to fall into a fire with her month-old baby. By the time she and her husband reached a hospital, the baby had died from an infected head wound. The suit sought an undisclosed amount in monetary damages and an injunction against Unocal's participation in the pipeline project.

In a second lawsuit against Unocal, Total, and the SLORC, fifteen plaintiffs representing the people of Burma also sought undisclosed monetary compensation for alleged physical abuses by the military.[49] Using the nineteenth century Alien Tort Claims Act to sue multinational companies in U.S. courts for actions outside the United States which violated international law, the suit argued that Unocal and Total should have foreseen the human rights abuses that were caused by their associated security forces. While a federal judge in the case dismissed the claims against the SLORC and the state-owned MOGE, he allowed the suit to proceed against the oil companies.[50]

As they fought their legal battles, Unocal and Total vehemently denied any wrongdoing. Unocal said that the lawsuits were "false, irresponsible, and frivolous."[51] President Imle explained the company's position: "We believe the lawsuits are politically motivated. We believe they are totally without merit. And we plan to defend ourselves to the fullest extent possible. But those suits are not going to affect our business."[52] The companies also used satellite photography to argue that no villages had been destroyed or relocated in the construction of the pipeline route. Unocal and Total stated that all landowners were fairly compensated for acquired lands and that pipeline workers were paid above market wages, as formalized under signed agreements. Throughout construction of the project, both Unocal and Total voiced a strong commitment to the fair treatment of workers and villagers living in the area affected by the Yadana pipeline. In addition, Imle noted that while the SLORC may have used forced labor to build the Ye Tavoy, the railroad remained incomplete and far from operational. He also claimed that Unocal protests to the SLORC had actually decreased human rights abuses, with the government agreeing to curb the use of forced labor in railway construction.[53]

Drugs

In addition to human rights concerns, critics of the regime also alleged that the SLORC profited from an illicit narcotics trade that flourished in isolated regions of northern Burma. Not only did the country produce an estimated 60 percent of the heroin consumed in the United States, but critics claimed that the ruling junta was instrumental in drug production and trafficking. The U.S. Assistant Secretary of State for International Narcotics concluded that drug traffickers were among the top financial backers of infrastructure projects in Burma, easily laundering money in SLORC-controlled banks.[54] More importantly, a 1996 investigation by Geopolitical Drugwatch in Paris suggested that the MOGE, Unocal's Burmese partner in the Yadana Pipeline, was "the main channel for laundering the revenues of heroin produced and exported under the control of the Burmese Army."[55] These allegations spurred small groups of Unocal shareholders and members of the U.S.-based Oil, Chemical, and Atomic Workers International Union (OCAW) to submit a shareholder resolution demanding an independent investigation into the MOGE and its drug-related activities.[56]

Unocal issued a strong public response to the charges, calling them "an unfounded and reckless attempt to smear Unocal and its thousands of honest, dedicated employees. The allegation that any Unocal executive would ever condone drug money laundering is totally untrue and outrageous."[57] While Imle acknowledged the illegal drug problem in Burma, he questioned the credentials of Geopolitical Drugwatch and denied any allegation that the SLORC was responsible for drug money laundering.[58] The company also petitioned the Securities and Exchange Commission to legally exclude the resolution from its proxy statement, claiming that it would violate the Myanmar Official Secrets Act, which "makes it illegal for any person, for purposes prejudicial to the safety or interests of the State to obtain, publish or communicate to any other person information which might be directly or indirectly useful to an enemy."[59] Ultimately, the resolution was overwhelmingly defeated by a shareholder vote of 19 to 1.

Environmental Impact

Despite the early-stage evaluations that the investment consortium had conducted, international environmental groups had also lined up to attack the Yadana project. Seizing on offshore drilling as essentially detrimental, they argued that the drilling process produced toxic muds that could de-oxygenate the water and kill bottom dwelling marine life. Drilling also generated large quantities of toxic brine, which could damage fish and marine life in the area.[60] Above the water, critics claimed, daily emissions from offshore drilling rigs were equally harmful, producing waste equivalent to 7,000 cars driving fifty miles.[61]

The bulk of the environmentalists' concern, however, centered on the environmental impact of the onshore pipeline. Even with the carefully chosen route from Daminseik to Ratchaburi, groups such as the Earth Rights Network, the International Rivers Network, and Greenpeace claimed that construction of Yadana would result in "destruction to wetlands and mangrove ecosystems, forest clearing, fragmentation of habitat and disruption of biological corridors, establishment of logging concessions, and increased poaching of endangered species."[62] Critics also worried that the project could damage the Tenasserim watershed and a wildlife area protected by the Karen, which contained tigers, rhinoceros, elephants, and other protected species. Most importantly, perhaps, environmental groups asserted that the opaque operations of the SLORC, coupled with an apparent lack of environmental regulation, would give Unocal and Total free reign in destroying and polluting Burma's fragile ecosystem. As one report noted, "the environmental costs of [the] Yadana natural gas development scheme may be enormous. Without adequate mechanisms for protection, marine life and wildlife as well as human populations are at risk."[63] While they conceded that both companies had conducted environmental evaluations, opponents noted that neither company had publicly released the findings.

On the Thai side of the border, environmental opposition was even stronger. As designed, the pipeline would cut through a pristine watershed zone and a series of national parks and wildlife sanctuaries which formed the largest conservation area in mainland Asia. In the process, it would allegedly destroy large tracts of undisturbed forest and almost certainly affect the 120 species of land mammals (45 of which were considered threatened in Thailand and 15 of which were internationally classified as threatened) living in the area. The pipeline would also cause severe soil erosion, which could threaten regional villages with large landslides. Even more dramatically, the pipeline's planned route crossed two active geological faults, raising the possibility of gas leakage or a major explosion in the event of renewed seismic activity. According to regional ethnic leaders, "If the pipeline was damaged, natural gas made up of between 80-95 percent methane would leak and cause extensive damage, not only to people living in the vicinity but also to wildlife and other natural resources."[64] Opponents noted that between 1983 and 1988, Thai officials had recorded earthquake epicenters near the project site six times, registering between 4.1 and 5.8 on the Richter scale.[65] Although the National Environment Board of Thailand had conducted environmental impact and seismic evaluations of the pipeline route, critics suggested that the studies ignored the project's effects on wildlife and forest ecology.

The Free Burma Coalition

Taken by themselves, each of the criticisms against Yadana was fairly significant, and each was voiced by activist groups with their own levers, and levels, of influence. What made these criticisms particularly powerful, however, was the ability of the various groups to coordinate their opposition and present a united front against the Yadana pipeline. Until the mid-1990s, such concerted protests were relatively rare. Environmental groups focused on their set of problems and pressure points, human rights groups on their own network of information and influence, and so on. But the advent of the Internet changed these standard patterns. Suddenly activist groups were able to join forces and exchange information with unprecedented ease. Grassroots connections, long the backbone of activism, became, quite literally, electrified.

Given the breadth of activist interest in Burma, coalition occurred rapidly. In the early 1990s, the Free Burma Coalition was formed, a diverse mix of high school, university, environmental, human rights, religious, and labor organizations, which soon comprised one of the world's largest single student movements. Modeled after the anti-apartheid movement in South Africa, the Free Burma Coalition had two explicit objectives: "1) To weaken the grip of the State Law and Order Restoration Council (SLORC) by cutting its substantial flow of foreign currency provided by multinational corporations such as Total, Unocal, Texaco, and ARCO among others; and 2) To strengthen the position of the democratic forces within Burma by building up an international movement calling for the end of totalitarian rule under [the] SLORC."[66] In pursuit of these objectives, the coalition organized peaceful protests, publicized consumer boycotts, and lobbied for federal sanctions as well as state and local selective purchasing laws.

A logical focal point for all of these activities was Unocal, Burma's largest U.S. foreign investor. The Coalition sponsored consumer boycotts and writing campaigns, urging members to send letters and mutilated gas credit cards to company CEO Roger Beach. Opponents also took more direct action. In one demonstration at a Unocal shipping terminal in Los Angeles, for example, several protesters from the Free Burma Coalition were arrested after chaining themselves to company trucks and storage tanks.[67] Eventually, the group's influence began to spread. In addition to Unocal, opponents also targeted Texaco and ARCO, protesting outside shareholder meetings, organizing consumer boycotts and letter writing campaigns, proposing shareholder resolutions demanding withdrawal from Burma, and urging investors to sell their holdings of company stock.[68] By early 1997, the Free Burma Coalition could claim at least partial responsibility for the withdrawal of several U.S. companies from Burma, including Apple Computers, Eastman-Kodak, Eddie Bauer, Hewlett-Packard, J. Crew, Levi-Strauss, Liz Claiborne, Motorola, PepsiCo, Walt Disney, and Wente Vineyards.

The Coalition also pressured city councils and state legislatures to adopt selective purchasing laws. By early 1997, 13 cities, including New York City and San Francisco, and the state of Massachusetts had passed laws barring government agencies from purchasing goods or services from any company that maintained operations in Burma. Several other states, such as Texas and Connecticut, were considering similar legislation.[69] Organizers hoped that the laws would encourage firms to remove operations and foreign exchange from the country. Although the legality of the selective purchasing laws remained under dispute, their mere passage pointed to an increasingly powerful consumer voice and activist presence.

Eventually, the influence of the Burma protesters reached the national level. In July 1996, the U.S. Congress passed the Cohen-Feinstein amendment to the Foreign Operations Appropriations Act of 1997, requiring a ban on new U.S. investment in Burma if the Clinton Administration determined that the SLORC had harmed Aung San Suu Kyi or engaged in "large-scale repression" of its democratic opposition. Referring to the SLORC as "an ugly acronym for an ugly government," Secretary of State Madeleine Albright suggested that the conditions for the investment ban had been met in early 1997, as the junta continued to disrupt NLD gatherings and restrict Suu Kyi's freedom of movement.[70] In May of 1997, President Clinton formally imposed sanctions, arguing that "the actions and policies of the SLORC regime constitute an extraordinary and unusual threat to the security and stability of the region, and therefore to the national security and foreign policy of the United States."[71] This followed similar actions by the European Union, which stripped the country of its preferential trade status to condemn the use of "slave labor" practices.[72]

Response

Meanwhile, of course, Unocal had not sat idly by. As early as 1992, it had started to lobby aggressively—in Washington, in Burma, and at the state level. In 1996, company representatives journeyed to Washington to demonstrate Unocal's efforts to help the 35,000 Burmese villagers living along the pipeline route. The company's representatives pointed out that the project partners had hired doctors, immunized over 1,000 children, undertaken different farming projects, rebuilt clinics and schools, and enhanced local water and electricity infrastructure. As company president Imle asserted, "We are proud of the Yadana project because it does what current government policy fails to do: improve the lives of others. It is an outstanding model of responsible economic development that can make a difference to the people of Myanmar and Thailand. For the first time in many villagers' lives, our project brings hope and the chance of a better way of life. . . . To those who ask how we can remain in Myanmar, we respond, 'How can we ever justify leaving?'"[73]

Unocal also contributed to, and participated in, several groups with interests in Southeast Asia. One of them, the Asia-Pacific Exchange Foundation, was attacked for sponsoring trips to the pipeline project site for House majority whip Tom DeLay and three other members of Congress.[74] Responding to criticism of this relationship, the company claimed that it had "every right to support an organization that encourages a balanced view of foreign policy issues and supports educational endeavors pertaining to Asia. Asia is the future. It certainly is an important part of Unocal's strategy."[75] The company also worked with the National Foreign Trade Council to create USA Engage, a coalition that included 600 companies and claimed former U.S. trade representative Clayton Yeutter as one of its spokespersons. The purpose of the organization was to demonstrate the harmful effects of international sanctions on American corporate sales and profits.[76] USA Engage argued that unilateral sanctions generally hurt local populations and U.S. corporations, exerting little pressure on target governments.[77] Unocal also sought to increase the interest of policy groups and think-tanks on the issue of sanctions. The company and the investment consortium held briefings and site visits for European, Asian, and American reporters, two non-governmental organizations, several U.S. Congress members, and State Department officials.

On announcement of the U.S. sanctions, CEO Roger Beach responded ". . .We are terribly disappointed because we feel that engaging in other infrastructure projects for Myanmar at this time would be very beneficial to the development of the economy of Myanmar."[78] A company spokesman similarly noted that "These sanctions are going to do nothing to speed change in Burma, but they are going to speed up the departure of U.S. companies."[79] Although Unocal decided to forego two additional Burmese exploration possibilities in compliance with the sanctions, the firm remained focused on Asia: "The Administration's action will not change the company's long-term strategic direction of developing major energy-related projects throughout this region."[80]

Imle felt particularly strongly about the sanctions, as he had been an vocal opponent throughout the lobbying process. While he understood the rationale behind the consumer boycott movements and U.S. government sanctions, he questioned whether any of these efforts would touch the well-entrenched SLORC. He also believed that if Unocal pulled out of the project, any number of European or Asian oil companies would probably take its place. Imle's explicit goal for Unocal and Burma was constructive engagement of the SLORC: "If Washington wants to influence the future of Myanmar, it must make it possible for U.S. companies to increase their investment, not reduce it. That would strengthen American influence by speeding the transfer of U.S. business principles, fair labor practices, health and safety and environmental standards and technologies."[81]

Activists in the Free Burma Coalition, however, praised the sanctions as moving the Burmese people one step closer to democracy. Robert E. Wages, president of OCAW, argued that "The decision [to impose sanctions] reflect[ed] a major victory in the struggle to make multinational corporations accountable for their actions at home and abroad."[82] While noting that Unocal had agreed to abandon exploration efforts in two offshore areas, opponents vowed to continue pressuring Unocal and Total to "withdraw their shares in the gas pipeline project. We ask that all corporations not engage in any business in Burma until a democratic government is in place. Foreign revenue only lines the pockets of SLORC officials and helps keep the brutal regime in power."[83]

As he thought about the Yadana pipeline, Imle considered several issues. While the lucrative project formed a critical component of Unocal's global focus, it continued to pose several problems. In recent months, the brutal SLORC had responded to civil protests by tightening its grip and arresting pro-democracy supporters. These actions had revved up activity on the Internet and within the Coalition, as activists re-affirmed their commitment to the anti-Yadana campaign. In the foreseeable future, at least, human rights and environmental concerns would continue to play a prominent role in the pipeline project—and thus, in Unocal's plans for expansion across Asia.

Exhibit 1   Regional Map

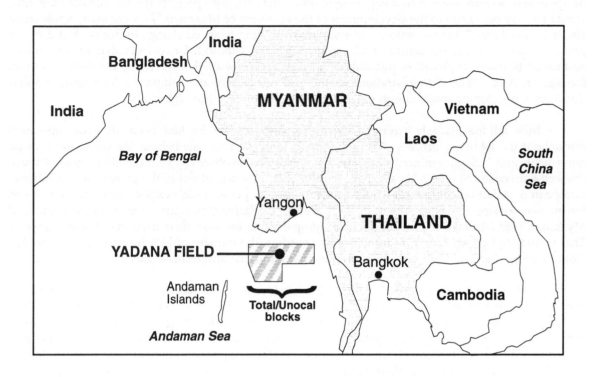

Exhibit 2   Map with Pipeline Route

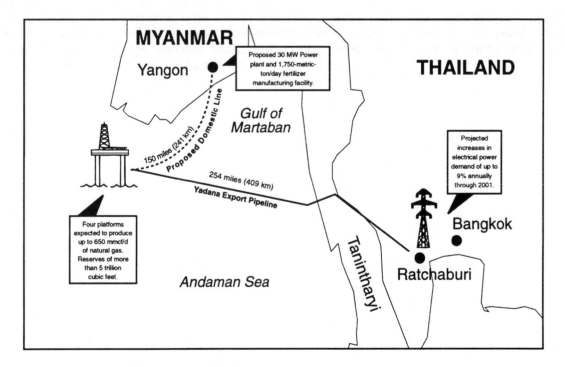

Source: Unocal, Yadana Project, November 1995

Exhibit 3   Top 15 Oil Companies by Total Assets, 1993 (thousand US$)

Rank	Company	Total Assets	Total Revenues	Net Income	Annual Natural Gas Production (bcf)[a]	Natural Gas Reserves (bcf)
1	Exxon Corp.	84,145,000	111,211,000	5,280,000	1,583.0	25,816.0
2	Mobil Corp.	40,585,000	63,975,000	2,084,000	1,665.0	16,959.0
3	Chevron Corp.	34,736,000	37,082,000	1,265,000	902.0	7,741.0
4	Amoco Corp.	28,486,000	28,617,000	1,820,000	1,487.0	17,650.0
5	Shell Oil Co.	26,851,000	21,092,000	781,000	553.0	5,199.0
6	Texaco Inc.	26,626,000	34,071,000	1,068,000	748.0	5,970.0
7	ARCO	23,894,000	19,183,000	269,000	449.0	8,005.0
8	Occidental Petroleum	17,230,000	8,544,000	283,000	238.0	2,136.0
9	British Petroleum (USA)	14,864,000	15,714,000	1,461,000	—	—
10	Conoco Inc.	11,938,000	15,771,000	812,000	481.0	3,680.0
11	Enron Corp.	11,504,315	8,003,393	332,522	262.2	1,772.2
12	Phillips Petroleum	10,868,000	12,545,000	243,000	509.0	6,069.0
13	USX Marathon	10,806,000	11,962,000	(29,000)	317.0	3,748.0
14	Coastal Corp.	10,277,000	10,136,100	115,800	122.0	925.5
15	Unocal Corp.	9,254,000	8,344,000	213,000	623.0	6,632.0

Source: *Oil and Gas Journal Databook*, (Tulsa, Oklahoma: Pennwell Books, 1995) pp. 8-9.

[a]bcf=billion cubic feet

Exhibit 4   Unocal Corporation Consolidated Balance Sheets, 1992-1995[a] (thousand US$)

	1995	1994	1993	1992
Cash	94,000	148,000	205,000	157,000
Receivables	920,000	897,000	877,000	1,039,000
Inventories	360,000	341,000	326,000	326,000
Other current assets	202,000	142,000	170,000	138,000
Total current assets	1,576,000	1,528,000	1,578,000	1,660,000
Net PP&E	7,109,000	6,823,000	7,175,000	6,896,000
Investments and adv. to subs	1,101,000	895,000	847,000	788,000
Deferred charges	25,000	30,000	30,000	NA
Deposits and other assets	80,000	61,000	76,000	108,000
Total assets	9,891,000	9,337,000	9,706,000	9,452,000
Accounts payable	804,000	688,000	735,000	712,000
Current long term debt	NA	NA	54,000	151,000
Accrued expenses	285,000	313,000	300,000	391,000
Other current liabilities	227,000	256,000	107,000	182,000
Total current liabilities	1,316,000	1,257,000	1,196,000	1,436,000
Deferred charges/inc	1,340,000	1,182,000	1,461,000	1,339,000
Long term debt	3,698,000	3,461,000	3,468,000	3,546,000
Other long term liabilities	607,000	622,000	NA	NA
Total liabilities	6,961,000	6,522,000	6,125,000	6,321,000
Preferred stock	513,000	513,000	513,000	513,000
Common stock, net	247,000	244,000	241,000	241,000
Capital surplus	319,000	237,000	163,000	149,000
Retained earnings	1,874,000	1,847,000	2,230,000	2,234,000
Treasury stock	NA	NA	452,000	NA
Other equities	(23,000)	(26,000)	(18,000)	(6,000)
Total shareholders' equity	2,930,000	2,815,000	3,581,000	3,131,000
Total liabilities and net worth	9,891,000	9,337,000	9,706,000	9,452,000

Source: Unocal Corporation Annual Reports, 1993-1996.

[a]All statements from December 31.

Exhibit 5 Unocal Corporation Consolidated Statements of Income, 1992-1995[a] (thousand US$)

	1995	1994	1993	1992
Net sales	8,133,000	7,797,000	8,077,000	9,887,000
Cost of goods sold	4,993,000	5,694,000	5,813,000	7,428,000
Gross profit	3,140,000	2,103,000	2,264,000	2,459,000
R&D expenditures	199,000	200,000	164,000	238,000
SG&A	1,457,000	555,000	489,000	703,000
Depreciation and Amortization	1,022,000	947,000	963,000	964,000
Non-operating Income	292,000	168,000	267,000	174,000
Interest expense	291,000	275,000	304,000	379,000
Income before tax	463,000	294,000	611,000	349,000
Provision for income tax	203,000	170,000	268,000	153,000
Extraordinary items and disc. ops.	NA	(277,000)	(130,000)	24,000
Net Income	260,000	(153,000)	213,000	220,000
Shares outstanding	247,310	244,199	241,324	240,671
Share price[b]	27.625	27.625	28.0625	24.6875

Source: Unocal Corporation Annual Reports, 1993-1996.

[a]All statements from December 31.

[b]Average of annual high and low.

Exhibit 6 Unocal Sales and Earnings Data by Category, 1992-1996 (million US$)

	1996	1995	1994	1993	1992
Crude oil and condensate	2,495	1,964	1,996	1,928	2,270
Natural gas	1,482	1,031	1,109	1,104	1,033
Agricultural products	514	486	373	319	292
Geothermal	131	120	135	145	197
Natural gas liquids	95	97	96	101	116
Petroleum products	16	84	89	458	1,236
Minerals	97	95	79	62	80
Consumer excise tax	—	—	5	87	283
Other	161	58	95	134	427
Total	4,991	3,935	3,977	4,338	5,934
Operating revenues	110	176	141	137	164
Other revenues	227	278	154	255	149
Total revenues from continuing operations	5,328	4,389	4,272	4,730	6,247
Discontinued operations	4,271	4,036	3,693	3,614	3,814
Total revenues	9,599	8,425	7,965	8,344	10,061

Source: Unocal Corporation, 1996 Annual Report.

Note: Total revenues include 'Nonoperating income,' which is excluded from Net sales under **Exhibit 6.**

Exhibit 7 Annual Economic Indicators for Burma, 1991-1996

	1996	1995	1994	1993	1992	1991
GDP at current prices (Kyat bn)	751.8	613.2	473.1	360.3	294.4	186.8
Real GDP growth (%)	5.5	9.8	7.5	6.0	9.7	(0.6)
Consumer price inflation (%)	16.2	25.2	24.1	31.8	21.9	32.3
Population (m)	47.0	46.2	45.4	44.6	43.7	42.7
Exports ($ m)	820.0	750.0	810.0	696.0	590.7	430.6
Imports ($ m)	2,300.0	2,010.0	1,497.0	1,302.0	1,010.2	842.3
Current account ($ m)	(806)	(603)	(173)	(194)	(204)	(344)
Reserves excluding gold ($ m)	200.0	561.1	422.0	302.9	280.1	258.4
Total external debt ($ m)	NA	6,988	6,502	5,730	5,327	4,853
Debt-service ratio (%)	NA	51.5	51.4	39.8	42.8	50.9
Official exchange rate (av.) Kyat:$	5.87	5.67	5.97	6.16	6.10	6.28

Source: Adapted from Economist Intelligence Unit, *EIU Country Report: Myanmar,* fourth quarter 1996 and first quarter 1997.

Exhibit 8 1996 Foreign Direct Investment in Burma by Country of Origin

Country	Rank	Number of Enterprises	Total Approved Investment (US$millions)
Singapore	1	50	1,158.85
United Kingdom	2	25	1,011.16
Thailand	3	33	946.16
France	4	2	466.37
Malaysia	5	16	446.27
United States	6	15	243.57
The Netherlands	7	5	237.85
Japan	8	11	183.42
Austria	9	1	71.50
Hong Kong	10	17	64.44
Republic of Korea	11	9	60.59
Australia	12	10	39.00
Canada	13	9	32.53
Indonesia	14	2	21.00
China	15	6	15.95
Total		211	4,998.66

Source: Adapted from *Myanview,* January, 1997, p. 11.

Exhibit 9   Foreign Investment in Burma by Sector, April 1996

Sector	Number of Projects	Foreign Capital (US$millions)
Agriculture	1	2.69
Fisheries	15	252.04
Mining	27	319.73
Manufacturing	53	193.53
Oil and Gas	24	1,435.42
Transportation	7	121.22
Hotels and Tourism	34	647.63
Real Estate	6	251.45
Industrial Estate	1	12.00
Others	1	1.67
Total	169	3,237.38

Source: Adapted from *Myanview*, July, 1996, p. 11.

Note: The discrepancy between FDI totals in **Exhibits 9** and **10** reflects a difference between approved and actual investment.

Exhibit 10   World Energy Outlook Projections of Natural Gas Demand (million tons of oil equivalent)

Area	1991	2000	2010
World	1,727	2,020	2,718
OECD	828	964	1,231
OECD North America	516	571	700
OECD Europe	247	313	404
OECD Pacific	65	80	127

Source: OECD, *Natural Gas Transportation: Organisation and Regulation*, (Paris: OECD, 1994), p. 12.

Exhibit 11   Average Annual Growth Rates in Fossil Fuel Demand, 1971-1992

Region	Solids (%)	Oil (%)	Gas (%)
North America and Mexico	2.7	0.6	—
OECD Europe	-.01	-.01	5.4
OECD Pacific	1.8	1.2	12.9
Former Soviet Union	-1.1	1.1	5.7
East Asia	4.7	6.3	17.5
South Asia	5.7	5.3	10.3
China	5.2	5.9	7.3
Middle East	12.3	7.4	8.6
South and Central America	5.0	2.2	6.3
Africa	3.8	4.2	13.3

Source: *Petroleum Economist*, February, 1996, p. 2.

Exhibit 12 Unocal Stock Price, 1993-1997

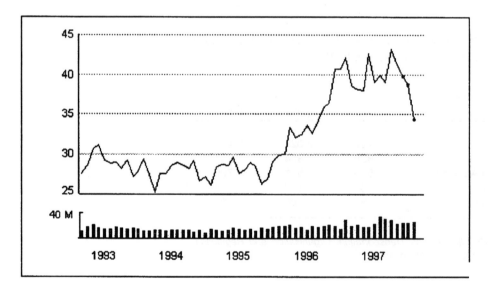

Endnotes

[1]   "Total Shrugs off Burma Politics," *The Financial Times*, July 23, 1996, p. 23.

[2]   Unocal, *The Yadana Project*, November 1995, pp. 4-5.

[3]   Michael Richardson, "Unocal Expands Burma Investment as Others Pull Out Over Rights," *International Herald Tribune*, January 31, 1997, p. 13.

[4]   Fred L. Hartley, *'The Spirit of 76:' The Story of the Union Oil Company of California*, (New York: The Newcomen Society in North America, 1977); Richard J. Stegemeier, *A Century of Spirit: The History of Unocal* (New York: The Newcomen Society of the United States, 1991); Union Oil Company of California, *Sign of the 76: The Fabulous Life and Times of the Union Oil Company of California* (Los Angeles: Union Oil Company of California, 1976).

[5]   Douglas Sun, "Unocal Corporation," *International Directory of Company History*, vol. 4 (Chicago: St. James Press, 1991), pp. 569-571. On Total, Unocal's co-venturer, see William Pitt, "Total Compagnie Francaise des Petroles S.A.," *International Directory of Company History*, vol. 4 (Chicago: St. James Press, 1991), pp. 557-561.

[6]   http://www.unocal.com/newucl/ahead.html.

[7]   Unocal (1995), p. 16.

[8]   Unocal, *Unocal in Myanmar (Burma): The Yadana Project*, March 1997, p. 1. In the energy industry, 'independent' refers to non-governmental and non-vertically integrated.

[9]   PR Newswire, "Unocal Replaces 101% of Worldwide Oil, Gas Production 1996; Foreign Production Replacement at 234%," February 13, 1997.

[10]   Unocal (1997), pp. 25-27.

[11]   On May 27, 1989, the ruling junta decreed that English-language texts should use the term "Myanmar" instead of "Burma" when referring to the country. "Myanmar," meaning fast or strong in Burmese, is the indigenous Burmese name for the country. As the term is neither consistent with its English usage nor accepted by many groups within the country, the name Burma will be used. See Michael Fredholm, *Burma: Ethnicity and Insurgency* (Westport, Connecticut: Praeger, 1993), p. 7.

[12]   U.S. Central Intelligence Agency, *The World Factbook*, September 7, 1995.

[13]   Chi-shad Liang, *Burma's Foreign Relations: Neutralism in Theory and Practice* (New York: Praeger, 1990), p. 43.

[14]   Like many in Burma, Ne Win was extremely superstitious, frequently consulting a personal astrologer to determine economic policy. In 1987, for example, the Burmese currency was reissued in 45 and 90 kyat bills to reflect Ne Win's lucky number 9 (4+5=9). Similarly, the government changed the official name of the country from Burma to Myanmar on May 27, 1989 (2+7=9). Fredholm (1993), pp. 243-246.

[15]   Fredholm (1993), pp. 58-59.

[16]   Fredholm (1993), pp. 64-65.

[17]   Economist Intelligence Unit, *EIU Country Report: Myanmar*, first quarter 1997; *Myanview: A Quarterly Review of Economic and Political Trends in Myanmar*, January 1996, pp. 4-5; July 1996, pp. 10-11; January 1997.

[18]   Economist Intelligence Unit (first quarter 1997).

[19]   Economist Intelligence Unit (first quarter 1997), p. 12.

[20]   See *Myanview* (January 1996), p. 4. Official statistics list Unocal's investment under Total of France and Texaco's under Premier of the United Kingdom, suggesting that the United States may actually be the largest foreign investor in Burma.

[21]   International Energy Agency, *Natural Gas Transportation: Organization and Regulation* (Paris: OECD, 1994), p. 32.

[22]   The author is grateful to Michael Thacher, of Unocal, for technical clarifications on natural gas processing and extraction.

[23]   International Energy Agency, *Natural Gas: Prospects and Policies* (Paris: OECD, 1991), p. 211. Two technical notes: 1) one cubic meter of natural gas under normal pressure contains approximately one-thousandth of the energy of the same volume of crude oil. 2) "Proven reserves are estimated quantities that analysis of geological and engineering data demonstrate with reasonable certainty to be recoverable in future years from known reservoirs under existing economic and operating conditions," Energy Information Administration, *International Energy Outlook 1996* (Washington D.C.: U.S. Department of Energy, May 1996).

[24]   See International Energy Agency (1994), pp. 11 and 31.

[25]   Energy Information Administration (1996); Neil E. Foreman, "Global Production through 2005," *World Oil*, December 1996; International Energy Agency (1991); George Ives, "Operating Companies to Install 18,800 Miles of Lines in 1997," *Pipe Line and Gas Industry*, January 1997; Mostefa A. Ouki, "Pipelines Still to Provide Supply to Remote Markets," *The Petroleum Economist*, February 1996, p. 4: Warren True, "World Pipeline Construction Looks to Remain Robust to Century's Turn," *Oil and Gas Journal*, February 10, 1997.

[26]   Energy Information Administration (1996), p. 35.

[27]   Derek Bamber, "Full Steam Ahead for New Generation of LNG Schemes," *Petroleum Economist*, November 1996, pp. 4-6; International Energy Agency (1996).

[28]   "Natural Gas Spurring Southeast Asian E&P," *Offshore*, February 1997; "Far East .Ê.Ê. Natural Gas Activity Leads Regional Construction Work," *Pipe Line and Gas Industry*, November 1996, pp. 32-36; Peggy Williams, "The Cold Wars," *Hart's Oil and Gas Investor*, February 1997, pp. 33-36.

[29]This section draws heavily from Total, "The Yadana Gas Development," July 1996; and Unocal (1995, 1997).

[30]   John F. Imle, Jr., "Testimony to Senate Banking Committee Hearing on S. 1511," May 22, 1996, p.Ê1.

[31]   Unocal (1995), p. 10. See also Total (1996), p. 11.

32   Unocal Board of Directors, quoted in David Garcia, "Yadana Project Brings Jobs, Services to Villages," *Seventy Six*, First Quarter, 1996, p. 6.

33   Garcia (1996), p. 6.

34   For a very broad discussion of security (e.g., economic, supply, physical, etc.) issues and natural gas, see International Energy Agency, *The IEA Natural Gas Security Study*, (Paris: OECD, 1995).

35   Earth Rights Network and Southeast Asian Information Network, "Total Denial: A Report on the Yadana Pipeline Project in Burma," Chapter 2, http://sunsite.unc.edu/freeburma/docs/totaldenial/td.html, July, 1996. In an interview with the author, consortium members denied that this second attack had occurred.

36   *Periscope Daily Defense News Capsules*, "SLORC Ensures Security for Gas Pipeline Laying," JanuaryÊ30, 1997.

37   Seth Mydans, "In Thai Camps, Fear of Burmese Troops Grows," *New York Times*, March 1, 1997, p.Ê3A.

38   *Periscope Daily Defense News Capsules*, "Economic Gains Driving Burmese Military Offensive," February 28, 1997.

39   Economist Intelligence Unit (first quarter 1997), p. 15.

40   *Periscope Daily Defense News Capsules* (February 28, 1997).

41   Earth Rights Network and Southeast Asian Information Network (1996), Chapter 2.

42   Earth Rights Network and Southeast Asian Information Network (1996), Chapter 2.

43   http://www.irn.org/burma/unocal.html, "Unocal: Making a Killing in Burma."

44   See Amnesty International, "Myanmar: Human Rights Still Denied," November 1994; Human Rights Watch Asia, "Burma/Thailand: The Mon: Persecuted in Burma, Forced Back from Thailand," December 1994; The U.S. Department of State, *Country Reports on Human Rights Practices for 1996* (Washington D.C.: U.S. Government Printing Office, January 1997); The U.S. House of Representatives, "Recent Developments in Burma, Hearing Before the Subcommittee on Asia and the Pacific, September 7, 1995" (Washington D.C.: U.S. Government Printing Office, 1996).

45   Earth Rights Network and Southeast Asian Information Network (1996), Chapter 4.

46   http://www.un.org/rights/. Yokota, Yozo. "Situation of Human Rights in Myanmar." *Human Rights Questions: Human Rights Situations and Reports of Special Rapporteurs and Representatives*, February 1995. Imle suggests that Yokota was not referring to the pipeline region in this quote.

47   Earth Rights Network and Southeast Asian Information Network (1996), Chapter 5.

48   Earth Rights Network and Southeast Asian Information Network (1996), Chapter 4.

49   Ted Bardacke, "Oil Companies are Sued Over Burmese Gas," *Financial Times*, October 4, 1996, p. 9; Nigel Holloway, "Long Arm of the Law," *Far Eastern Economic Review*, September 19, 1996.

[50]   Christian Berthelsen, "Unocal/Burma Suit," City News Service, March 26, 1997. The judged cited sovereign immunity in his decision to drop the suit against the SLORC and MOGE.

[51]   Unocal, "Unocal Statement in Response to Press Release from Law Offices of Cristobal Bonifaz," http://www.unocal.com/newsvws/96html., September 3, 1996.

[52]   *Asiaweek*, "'Sanctions Hurt People:' Unocal Tries to Defend a Controversial Project," February 21, 1997, p. 24.

[53]   Personal communication with John Imle, August 12, 1997.

[54]   PR Newswire, "According to OCAW Unocal Tries to Block Union Request for an Investigation of Link to Burmese Heroin Trade," February 27, 1997. See also Christopher Cox, *Chasing the Dragon: Into the Heart of the Golden Triangle* (New York: Henry Holt and Co., 1996).

[55]   Quoted in Jim Lobe, "Burma-U.S.: SLORC may be in Albright's Sights," Interpress Service, December 20, 1996.

[56]   PR Newswire, "SEC Accepts Retired Oil Worker's Shareholder Resolution to Investigate Unocal's Links to Drug Money Laundering; OCAW President Expects Further Roadblocks from Unocal," March 20, 1997.

[57]   Unocal, "Unocal Responds to OCAW Allegations Concerning Yadana Project in Myanmar," http://www.unocal.com/newsvws/96html, December 23, 1996.

[58]   Personal communication with John Imle, August 12, 1997.

[59]   PR Newswire (February 27, 1997).

[60]   http://www.irn.org/burma/total.html. and http://www.irn.org/burma/unocal.html.

[61]   Earth Rights Network and Southeast Asian Information Network (1996), Chapter 7.

[62]   http://www.irn.org/burma/unocal.html.

[63]   Earth Rights Network and Southeast Asian Information Network (1996), Chapter 7.

[64]   *The Bangkok Post*, "Burma Gas Deal Seen as Threat to Thailand's Forests," March 12, 1995, p. 4.

[65]   Burma News Network, "Ecological Disaster (TERRA): The Yadana Pipeline Route Controversy," http://www-uvi.eunet.fr/asia/euro-burma/total, January 1, 1997.

[66]   http://danenet.wicip.org/fbc/mission.html.

[67]   *Reuters Financial Service*, "Protesters in Los Angeles Against Burma Pipeline," December 12, 1996.

[68]   David Chance, "Political, Environmental Groups Target Texaco," *The Reuter Business Report*, MayÊ11, 1997; Jim Lobe, "U.S.-Burma: Sanctions Campaign Keeps Rolling," Interpress Service, May 15, 1997.

[69]   Veronica Smith, "Burma Boycott Movement Fells Biggest Prize Yet: Pepsi," Agence France Presse, January 30, 1997.

[70]   Economist Intelligence Unit (first quarter 1997), pp. 6-7; Interpress Service, "Burma-U.S.: PepsiCo's Pullout Leaves Focus on Oil Companies," January 28, 1997.

[71]   http://www.usia.gov/regional/ea/burma/invsanc.html, "Clinton Message to Congress on Burma Sanctions," May 20, 1997.

[72]   Kimberley Music, "U.S. Wavers on Myanmar Investment Ban as EU Punishes Slave Labor Practices," *The Oil Daily*, December 19, 1996, p. 3.

[73]   Imle, "Testimony" (1996).

[74]   U.P.I., "Congressional Trip Criticized," March 14, 1997.

[75]   Quoted in Ed Timms and Susan Feeney, "Foes of Burma Regime Question DeLay's Visit Sponsor, Lawmaker's Spokesman Deny Impropriety," *The Dallas Morning News*, March 14, 1997, p. 1A.

[76]   Paul Magnusson, "A Troubling Barrage of Trade Sanctions From All Across America," *Business Week*, February 14, 1997, p. 59.

[77]   Imle, "Testimony," (1996), p. 7; "A Case for Investment in Burma," *International Herald Tribune*, February 6, 1997; "Keep Door Open in Myanmar," *Journal of Commerce*, February 28, 1997; National Association of Manufacturers, *A Catalog of New U.S. Unilateral Economic Sanctions for Foreign Policy Purposes 1993-1996*, March 1997.

[78]*Oil and Gas Journal*, April 28, 1997, p. 2.

[79]   Tim Shorrock, "Rights, Drugs Issues Spark Ban on Myanmar; US Prohibits Investment, Citing Concern Over Illegal Narcotics Trade," *Journal of Commerce* April 23, 1997, p. 1A.

[80]   http://www.usia.gov/regional/ea/burma/invsanc.html, May 20, 1997.

[81]   John Imle, Jr. "Keep Door Open in Myanmar," *Journal of Commerce*, February 28, 1997.

[82]   *Oil and Gas Journal*, April 28, 1997, p. 2.

[83]   http://www.irn.org/burma/unocal.html

Hitting the Wall: Nike and International Labor Practices

Moore: Twelve year olds working in [Indonesian] factories? That's O.K. with you?
Knight: They're not 12-year-olds working in factories... the minimum age is 14.
Moore: How about 14 then? Does that bother you?
Knight: No.

— Phil Knight, Nike CEO, talking to Director Michael Moore in a
scene from documentary film *The Big One*, 1997.

*Nike is raising the minimum age of footwear factory workers to 18... Nike has zero
tolerance for underage workers.* [1]

— Phil Knight, 1998

In 1997, Nguyen Thi Thu Phuong died while making sneakers. As she was trimming
synthetic soles in a Nike contracting factory, a co-worker's machine broke, spraying metal parts
across the factory floor and into Phuong's heart. The 23 year-old Vietnamese woman died instantly.[2]

Although it may have been the most dramatic, Phuong's death was hardly the first
misfortune to hit Nike's far-flung manufacturing empire. Indeed, in the 1980s and 1990s, the
corporation had been plagued by a series of labor incidents and public relations nightmares:
underage workers in Indonesian plants, allegations of coerced overtime in China, dangerous working
conditions in Vietnam. For a while, the stories had been largely confined to labor circles and activist
publications. By the time of Phuong's death, however, labor conditions at Nike had hit the

---

[1] "Nike CEO Phil Knight Announces New Labor Initiatives," *PR Newswire*, May 12, 1998.
[2] Tim Larimer, "Sneaker Gulag: Are Asian Workers Really Exploited?" *Time International*, May 11, 1998, p. 30.

---

*Research Associate Jennifer L. Burns prepared this case from published sources under the supervision of Professor Debora L.
Spar as the basis for class discussion rather than to illustrate either effective or ineffective handling of an administrative
situation. This case was based on a paper written by Class of 1999 MBA students Skardon Baker and Dan Connolly.*

mainstream. Stories of reported abuse at Nike plants had been carried in publications such as *Time* and *Business Week* and students from major universities such as Duke and Brown had organized boycotts of Nike products. Even Doonesbury had joined the fray, with a series of cartoons that linked the company to underage and exploited Asian workers. Before these attacks, Nike had been widely regarded as one of the world's coolest and most successful companies. Now Nike, the company of Michael Jordan and Tiger Woods; Nike, the sign of the swoosh and athletic prowess, was increasingly becoming known as the company of labor abuse. And its initial response — "We don't make shoes" — was becoming harder and harder to sustain.[3]

Nike, Inc.

Based in Beaverton, Oregon, Nike had been a corporate success story for more than three decades. It was a sneaker company, but one armed with an inimitable attitude, phenomenal growth, and the apparent ability to dictate fashion trends to some of the world's most influential consumers. In the 1970s, Nike had first begun to capture the attention of both trend-setting teenagers and financial observers. Selling a combination of basic footwear and street-smart athleticism, Nike pushed its revenues from a 1972 level of $60,000 to a startling $49 million in just ten years.[4] It went public in 1980 and then astounded Wall Street in the mid-1990s as annual growth stayed resolutely in the double digits and revenues soared to over $9 billion. By 1998, Nike controlled over 40% of the $14.7 billion U.S. athletic footwear market. It was also a growing force in the $64 billion sports apparel market, selling a wide range of sport-inspired gear to consumers around the globe.[5]

What differentiated Nike from its competitors was not so much its shoes as its strategy. Like Reebok and adidas and New Balance, Nike sold a fairly wide range of athletic footwear to a fairly wide range of consumers: men and women, athletes and non-athletes, in markets around the world. Its strategy, though, was path-breaking, the product of a relatively simple idea that CEO Phil Knight had first concocted in 1962 while still a student at Stanford Business School. The formula had two main prongs. First, the company would shave costs by outsourcing *all* manufacturing. There would be no in-house production, no dedicated manufacturing lines. Rather all product would be made by independent contracting factories, creating one of the world's first "virtual" corporations — a manufacturing firm with no physical assets. Then, the money saved through outsourcing would be poured into marketing. In particular, Knight focussed from the start on celebrity endorsements, using high-profile athletes to establish an invincible brand identity around the Nike name. While other firms had used celebrity endorsements in the past, Nike took the practice to new heights, emblazoning the Nike logo across athletes such as Michael Jordan and Tiger Woods, and letting their very celebrity represent the Nike image. "To see name athletes wearing Nike shoes," Knight insisted, "was more convincing than anything we could say about them."[6] With the help of the "swoosh," a distinctive and instantly recognizable logo, Nike became by the 1990s one of the world's best known brands, as well as a global symbol of athleticism and urban cool.

But within this success story lay a central irony that would only become apparent in the late 1990s. While the *marketing* of Nike's products was based on selling a high profile fashion item to affluent Americans who only wished they could "Just Do It" as well as Woods or Jordan, the *manufacture* of these sneakers was based on an arms-length and often uneasy relationship with low-

---

[3] The quote is from Martha Benson, Nike's regional spokeswoman in Asia. See Larimer, p. 30.

[4] David B. Yoffie, *Nike: A (Condensed)*, HBS Case 391-238 (Boston: HBS Press, 1991), p. 1.

[5] Both figures are for retail sales. *Footwear 1999*, (North Palm Beach; Athletic Footwear Association, 1999), introduction; Dana Eisman Cohen and Sabina McBride, *Athletic Footwear Outlook 1999*, (New York: Donaldson, Lufkin & Jenrette, 1998), p. 3.

[6] Yoffie, p. 6.

paid, non-American workers. For according to Knight's original plan, not only would Nike outsource, but it would outsource specifically to low cost parts of the world.

Nike signed its first contracts with Japanese manufacturers but eventually shifted its supply base to firms in South Korea and Taiwan, where costs were lower and production reliable. In 1982, 86% of Nike sneakers came from one of these two countries and Nike had established a large network of suppliers in both nations. But as South Korea and Taiwan grew richer, costs rose and Nike began to urge its suppliers to move their operations to new, lower cost regions. Eager to remain in the company's good graces, most manufacturers rapidly complied, moving their relatively inexpensive plants to China or Indonesia. By 1990, these countries had largely replaced South Korea and Taiwan as the core of Nike's global network. Indonesia, in particular, had become a critical location, with six factories that supplied Nike and a booming, enthusiastic footwear industry.[7]

Taking Care of Business

At first, Indonesia seemed an ideal location for Nike. Wages were low, the workforce was docile, and an authoritarian government was yearning for foreign direct investment. There were unions in the country and occasional hints of activism, but the Suharto government clearly was more interested in wooing investors than in acceding to any union demands. So wages stayed low and labor demands were minimal. In 1991, the daily minimum wage in Indonesia's capital city was barely $1, compared to a typical daily wage of $24.40 in South Korea[8] and a U.S. hourly wage in athletic shoe manufacturing of about $8.[9] For firms like Nike, this differential was key: according to a reporter for the *Far Eastern Economic Review*, shoes coming out of China and Indonesia cost roughly 50% less than those sourced from Taiwan and South Korea.[10]

Just as Nike was settling into its Indonesian operations, though, a rare wave of labor unrest swept across the country. Strikes, which had been virtually nonexistent in the 1980s, began to occur with increasing frequency; according to government figures, there were 112 strikes in 1991,[11] a sharp increase from the 19 reported in 1989.[12] A series of polemical articles about foreign companies' labor abuses also appeared in Indonesian newspapers, triggering unprecedented demands from factory workers and empowering a small but potent band of labor organizers.

The source of these strikes and articles was mysterious. Some claimed that the Indonesian government was itself behind the movement, trying to convince an increasingly suspicious international community of the country's commitment to freedom of speech and labor rights. Others saw the hand of outside organizers, who had come to Indonesia solely to unionize its work force and embarrass its foreign investors. And still others saw the outbursts as random eruptions, cracks in the authoritarian veneer which quickly took on a life of their own. In any case, though, the unrest occurred just around the time of Nike's expansion into Indonesia. In 1991 the Asian-American Free Labor Association (AAFLI, a branch of the AFL-CIO) published a highly critical report on foreign companies in Indonesia. Later that year, a group of Indonesian labor economists at the Institut Teknology Bandung (ITB), issued a similar report, documenting abusive practices in Indonesian

---

[7] Philip M. Rosenzweig and Pam Woo, *International Sourcing in Footwear: Nike and Reebok,* HBS Case 394-189 (Boston: HBS Press, 1994), pp. 2 - 5.

[8] Elliot B. Smith, "K-Swiss in Korea," *California Business,* October 1991, p. 77.

[9] Rosenzweig and Woo, p. 3.

[10] Mark Clifford, "Pain in Pusan," *Far Eastern Economic Review,* November 5, 1992, p. 59.

[11] Suhaini Aznam, "The Toll of Low Wages," *Far Eastern Economic Review,* April 2, 1992, p. 50.

[12] Margot Cohen, "Union of Problems: Government Faces Growing Criticism on Labour Relations," *Far Eastern Economic Review,* August 26, 1993, p. 23.

factories and tracing them to foreign owners. In the midst of this stream of criticism was a labor organizer with a deep-seated dislike for Nike and a determination to shape its global practices. His name was Jeff Ballinger.

The Role of Jeff Ballinger

A labor activist since high school, Ballinger felt passionately that any company had a significant obligation towards even its lowliest workers. He was particularly concerned about the stubborn gap between wage rates in developed and developing worlds, and about the opportunities this gap created for rich Western companies to exploit low-wage, politically repressed labor pools. In 1988, Ballinger was assigned to run the AAFLI office in Indonesia, and was charged with investigating labor conditions in Indonesian plants and studying minimum wage compliance by overseas American companies. In the course of his research Ballinger interviewed workers at hundreds of factories and documented widespread worker dissatisfaction with labor conditions.

Before long, Nike emerged as a key target. Ballinger believed that Nike's policy of competing on the basis of cost fostered and even encouraged contractors to mistreat their workers in pursuit of unrealistic production quotas. Although Indonesia had worker protection legislation in place, widespread corruption made the laws essentially useless. While the government employed 700 labor inspectors, Ballinger found that out of 17,000 violations reported in 1988, only 12 prosecutions were ever made. Bribery took care of the rest.[13] Nike contractors, in particular, he believed, were regularly flouting Indonesian labor laws and paying below-subsistence wages that did not enable workers to meet their daily requirements for food and other necessities. And to top matters off, he found Nike's attitude in the face of these labor practices galling: "It was right around the time that the swoosh started appearing on everything and everyone," Ballinger remembered. "Maybe it was the swagger that did it."[14]

What also "did it," though, was Ballinger's own strategic calculation — a carefully crafted policy of "one country-one company." Ballinger knew that his work would be effective only if it was carefully focussed. And if his goal was to draw worldwide attention to the exploitation of third-world factory workers by rich U.S. companies, then Nike made a nearly ideal target. The arithmetic was simple. The same marketing and branding power that drove Nike's bottom line could also be used to drive moral outrage against the exploitation of Asian workers. After the publication of his AAFLI report, Ballinger set out to transform Nike's competitive strength into a strategic vulnerability.

For several years he worked at the fringes of the activist world, operating out of his in-laws' basement and publishing his own newsletter on Nike's practices. For the most part, no one really noticed. But then, in the early 1990s Ballinger's arguments coincided with the strikes that swept across Indonesia and the newfound interest of media groups. Suddenly his stories were big news and both the Indonesian government and U.S. firms had begun to pay attention.

Early Changes

The first party to respond to criticism from Ballinger and other activists was the government itself. In January 1992 Indonesia raised the official minimum daily wage from 2100 rupiah to 2500 rupiah (US$1.24). According to outside observers, the new wage still was not nearly enough: it only provided 70% of a worker's required minimal physical need (as determined by the Indonesian government) and was further diluted by the way in which many factories distributed wages and

---

[13] Interview with casewriter, Cambridge, MA, July 6, 1999.
[14] Ibid.

benefits.[15] The increased wage also had no impact on "training wages," which were lower than the minimum wage and often paid long after the training period had expired. Many factories, moreover, either ignored the new wage regulations or successfully petitioned the government for exemption. Still, the government's actions at least demonstrated some willingness to respond. The critics took note of this movement and continued their strikes and media attacks.

Despite the criticism, Nike insisted that labor conditions in its contractors' factories were not — could not — be Nike's concern or its responsibility. And even if labor violations did exist in Nike's contracting factories, stated the company's general manager in Jakarta, "I don't know that I need to know."[16] Nike's company line on the issue was clear and stubborn: without an inhouse manufacturing facility, the company simply could not be held responsible for the actions of independent contractors.

Realizing the severity of the labor issue, though, Nike did ask Dusty Kidd, a newly-hired member of its public relations department, to draft a series of regulations for its contractors. In 1992, these regulations were composed into a Code of Conduct and Memorandum of Understanding and attached to the new contracts sent to Nike contractors. In the Memorandum, Nike addressed seven different aspects of working conditions, including safety standards, environmental regulation and worker insurance. It required its suppliers to certify they were following all applicable rules and regulations and outlined general principles of honesty, respect, and non-discrimination.

Meanwhile, other shoe companies had been facing similar problems. Reebok, a chief competitor of Nike, also sourced heavily from Indonesia and South Korea. Like Nike, it too had been the subject of activist pressure and unflattering media. But unlike Nike, Reebok had moved aggressively into the human rights arena. In 1988, it created the Reebok Human Rights Award, bestowed each year on youthful contributors to the cause of human rights, and in 1990 it adopted a formal human rights policy.[17] When activists accused the company of violating workers' rights in Indonesia, Reebok responded with a far-reaching set of guidelines, one that spoke the explicit language of human rights, set forth specific standards for the company's contractors and promised to audit these contractors to ensure their compliance.[18] It was a big step for an American manufacturer and considerably farther than Nike had been willing to go.

Into the Spotlight

By 1992, criticism of Nike's labor practices had begun to seep outside of Indonesia. In the August issue of *Harper's* magazine, Ballinger published an annotated pay-stub from an Indonesian factory, making the soon-to-be famous comparison between workers' wages and Michael Jordan's endorsement contract. He noted that at the wage rates shown on the pay stub, it would take an Indonesian worker 44, 492 years to make the equivalent of Jordan's endorsement contract.[19] Then the Portland *Oregonian*, Nike's hometown newspaper, ran a series of critical articles during the course of the 1992 Barcelona Olympics. Also at the Olympics, a small band of protestors materialized and handed out leaflets that charged Nike with exploitation of factory workers. The first mainstream coverage of the issue came in July 1993, when CBS interviewed Indonesian workers who revealed that they were paid just 19¢ an hour. Women workers could only leave the company barracks on

---

[15]A factory, for example, could pay a base wage lower than 2500 rupiah, but bring total compensation up to legal levels by the addition of a food allowance and incentive payments (see Aznam, p. 50).

[16] Adam Schwarz, "Running a Business," *Far Eastern Economic Review,* June 20, 1991, p. 16.

[17] Rosenzweig and Woo, p. 7.

[18] Ibid., pp. 16-17.

[19] Jeff Ballinger, "The New Free-Trade Heel," *Harper's Magazine,* August 1992, p. 64.

Sunday, and needed a special letter of permission from management to do so. Nike responded somewhat more forcefully to this next round of allegations, hiring accounting firm Ernst & Young to conduct formal audits of its overseas factories. However, because Ernst & Young was paid by Nike to perform these audits, activists questioned their objectivity from the start. Public criticism of Nike's labor practices continued to mount.

Then suddenly, in 1996, the issue of foreign labor abuse acquired a name and a face: it was Kathie Lee Gifford, a popular daytime talk show host. In April human rights activists revealed that a line of clothing endorsed by Gifford had been manufactured by child labor in Honduras. Rather than denying the connection Gifford instantly rallied to the cause. When she appeared on television, crying and apologetic, a wave of media coverage erupted. Or as Ballinger recalls, "That's when my phone really started ringing."[20] Although Nike was not directly involved in the Gifford scandal, it quickly emerged as a symbol of worker exploitation and a high-profile media scapegoat.

Child labor was the first area of concern. In July, *Life* magazine ran a story about child labor in Pakistan, and published a photo of a 12 year old boy stitching a Nike soccer ball.[21] Then Gifford herself publicly called upon fellow celebrities such as Michael Jordan to investigate the conditions under which their endorsed products were made and to take action if need be. Jordan brushed away suggestions that he was personally responsible for conditions in Nike factories, leaving responsibility to the company itself. When Nike refused to let Reverend Jesse Jackson tour one of its Indonesian factories the media jumped all over the story, noting by contrast that Reebok had recently flown an executive to Indonesia just to give Jackson a tour.

At this point, even some pro-business observers began to jump on the bandwagon. As an editorial in *Business Week* cautioned: "Too few executives understand that the clamor for ethical sourcing isn't going to disappear with the wave of a magic press release. They have protested, disingenuously, that conditions at factories run by subcontractors are beyond their control... Such attitudes won't wash anymore. As the industry gropes for solutions," the editorial concluded, "Nike will be a key company to watch."[22]

The View From Washington

Before long, the spotlight on the labor issue extended all the way to Washington. Sensing a hot issue, several senators and representatives jumped into the action and began to suggest legislative solutions to the issue of overseas labor abuse. Representative George Miller (D-CA) launched a campaign aimed at retailers that would mandate the use of "No Sweat" labels to guarantee that no exploited or child labor had been employed in the production of a garment. "Parents," he proclaimed, "have a right to know that the toys and clothes they buy for their children are not made by exploited children." To enforce such guarantees, Miller added, "I think Congress is going to have to step in."[23]

On the heels of this public outcry, President Clinton convened a Presidential task force to study the issue, calling on leaders in the apparel and footwear industries to join and help develop acceptable labor standards for foreign factories. Known as the Apparel Industry Partnership (AIP), the coalition, which also included members of the activist, labor, and religious communities, was

---

[20] Casewriter interview.

[21] Nike's vigorous protests stopped the magazine from running the photo on its cover. Nike convincingly argued that the photo was staged, because the ball was inflated so that the Nike "swoosh" was clearly visible. In fact, soccer balls are stitched while deflated. However, the company did admit it had inadvertently relied on child labor during its first months of production in Pakistan.

[22] Mark L. Clifford, "Commentary: Keep the Heat on Sweatshops," *Business Week*, December 23, 1996, p. 90.

[23] "Honduran Child Labor Described," *The Boston Globe*, May 30, 1996, p. 13.

meant to be a model collaboration between industry and its most outspoken critics, brokered by the U.S. government. Nike was the first company to join.

In order to supplement its hiring of Ernst & Young, in October 1996 Nike also established a Labor Practices Department, headed by former public relations executive Dusty Kidd. In a press release, Knight announced the formation of the new department and praised Nike's recent initiatives regarding fair labor practices, such as participation in Clinton's AIP, membership in the organization Business for Social Responsibility, and an ongoing dialogue with concerned non-governmental organizations (NGOs). "Every year we continue to raise the bar," said Knight. "First by having Ernst & Young audits, and now with a group of Nike employees whose sole focus will be to help make things better for workers who make Nike products. In labor practices as in sport, we at Nike believe 'There is No Finish Line.'"[24] And indeed he was right, for the anti-Nike campaign was just getting started.

The Hotseat

As far as public relations were concerned, 1997 was even worse for Nike than 1996. Much as Ballinger had anticipated, Nike's giant marketing machine was easily turned against itself and in a climate awash with anti-Nike sentiment, any of Nike's attempts at self promotion became easy targets. In 1997 the company began expanding its chain of giant retail stores, only to find that each newly opened Niketown came with an instant protest rally, complete with shouting spectators, sign waving picketers, and police barricades. Knowing a good story when they saw it, reporters eagerly dragged Nike's celebrity endorsers into the fracas. Michael Jordan was pelted with questions about Nike at press conferences intended to celebrate his athletic performance, and football great Jerry Rice was hounded to the point of visible agitation when he arrived at the grand opening of a new Niketown in San Francisco.[25]

Perhaps one of the clearest indicators that Nike was in trouble came in May 1997, when Doonesbury, the popular comic strip, devoted a full week to Nike's labor issues. In 1,500 newspapers, millions of readers watched as Kim, Mike Doonesbury's wife, returned to Vietnam and found a long-lost cousin laboring in dismal conditions at a Nike factory. The strips traced Kim's growing involvement in the activist movement and the corrupt factory manager's attempts to deceive her about true working conditions in Nike contracting factories. In Doonesbury, Nike had reached an unfortunate cultural milestone. As one media critic noted: "It's sort of like getting in Jay Leno's monologue. It means your perceived flaws have reached a critical mass, and everyone feels free to pick on you."[26] The appearance of the Doonesbury strips also marked the movement of anti-Nike sentiment from the fringes of American life to the mainstream. Once the pet cause of leftist activists, Nike bashing had become America's newest spectator sport.

Even some of the company's natural friends took a dim view of its actions. The *Wall Street Journal* ran an opinion piece alleging that "Nike Lets Critics Kick it Around." The writer argued that Nike had been "its own worst enemy" and that its public relations efforts had only made the problem worse. According to the writer, had Nike acknowledged its wrongdoing early on and then presented economic facts that showed the true situation of the workers, the crisis would have fizzled.[27] Instead it had simply gathered steam. Even more trouble loomed ahead with the anticipated release of *The*

---

[24] "Nike Establishes Labor Practices Department," *PR Newswire*, October 2, 1996.

[25] "Protestors Swipe at the Swoosh, Catch Nike's Jerry Rice Off Guard," *The Portland Oregonian*, Feburary 21, 1997, p. C1.

[26] Jeff Manning, "Doonesbury Could Put Legs on Nike Controversy," *The Portland Oregonian*, May 25, 1997, p. D01.

[27] Greg Rushford, "Nike Lets Critics Kick it Around," *The Wall Street Journal*, May 12, 1997, p. A14.

Big One, a documentary film by Michael Moore that was widely expected to be highly critical of Nike's labor practices.

Damage Control

Late in 1996 the company decided to turn to outside sources, hiring Andrew Young, the respected civil rights leader and former mayor of Atlanta, to conduct an independent evaluation of its Code of Conduct. In January 1997, Knight granted Young's newly-formed GoodWorks International firm "blanket authority … to go anywhere, see anything, and talk with anybody in the Nike family about this issue."[28]

Shortly thereafter Young went to Asia, visited Nike suppliers and returned to issue a formal report. On the day the report was released, Nike took out full-page advertisements in major newspapers that highlighted one of Young's main conclusions: "It is my sincere belief that Nike is doing a good job... But Nike can and should do better."[29] Young did not give Nike carte blanche with regard to labor practices. Indeed, he made a number of recommendations, urging Nike to improve their systems for reporting workers' grievances, to publicize their Code more widely and explain it more clearly, and to implement cultural awareness and language training programs for expatriate managers. Young also stated that third party monitoring of factories was necessary, but agreed that it was not appropriate for Nike's NGO critics to fulfill that function.

Rather than calming Nike's critics, though, Young's report had precisely the opposite effect. Critics were outraged by the report's research methodology and conclusions, and unimpressed by Young's participation. They argued that Young had failed to address the issue of factory wages, which was for many observers the crux of the issue, and had spent only 10 days interviewing workers. During these interviews, moreover, Young had relied on translators provided by Nike, a major lapse in accepted human rights research technique. Finally, critics also noted that the report was filled with photos and used a large, showy typeface, an unusual format for a research report.

From the start, Nike executives had argued in vain that they were the target of an uninformed media campaign, pointing out that although Nike was being vigorously monitored by activists and the media, no one was monitoring the monitors. This point was forcefully made by the publication of a five page *New Republic* article in which writer Stephen Glass blasted the Young report for factual inaccuracies and deception, and summed up: "This was a public relations problem, and the world's largest sneaker company did what it does best: it purchased a celebrity endorsement."[30] Glass's claims were echoed by several other media outlets that also decried Nike's disingenuousness and Young's ineptitude. However, within months a major scandal erupted at the *New Republic* when it was discovered that most of Glass's articles were nearly fictional. Apparently, Glass routinely quoted individuals with whom he had never spoken or who did not even exist, and relied upon statistics and information from organizations he invented himself.

---

[28] Andrew Young, *Report: The Nike Code of Conduct*, (GoodWorks International, LLC, 1997) p. 27.

[29] Young, p. 59.

[30] Stephen Glass, "The Young and the Feckless," *The New Republic*, September 8, 1997, p. 22.

The Issue of Wages

In the public debate, the question of labor conditions was largely couched in the language of human rights. It was about child labor, or slave labor, or workers who toiled in unsafe or inhumane environments. Buried beneath these already contentious issues, though, was an even more contentious one: wages. According to many labor activists, workers in the developing world were simply being paid too little — too little to compensate for their efforts, too little compared to the final price of the good they produced, too little, even, to live on. To many business economists, though, such arguments were moot at best and veiled protectionism at worst. Wages, they maintained, were simply set by market forces: by definition, wages could not be too low, and there was nothing firms could or should do to affect wage rates. As the debate over labor conditions evolved, the argument over wages had become progressively more heated.

Initially, Nike sought to defuse the wage issue simply by ignoring it, or by reiterating the argument that this piece of the labor situation was too far beyond their control. In the Young Report, therefore, the issue of wages was explicitly set aside. As Young explained in his introduction: "I was not asked by Nike to address compensation and 'cost of living' issues which some in the human rights and NGO community had hoped would be a part of this report." Then he went on: "Are workers in developing countries paid far less than U.S. workers? Of course they are. Are their standards of living painfully low by U.S. standards? Of course they are. This is a blanket criticism that can be leveled at almost every U.S. company that manufactures abroad... But it is not reasonable to argue that any one particular U.S. company should be forced to pay U.S. wages abroad while its direct competitors do not."[31] It was a standard argument, and one that found strong support even among many pro-labor economists. In the heat of public debate, however, it registered only as self-serving.

The issue of wages emerged again in the spring of 1997, when Nike arranged for students at Dartmouth's Amos Tuck School of Business to conduct a detailed survey on "the suitability of wages and benefits paid to its Vietnamese and Indonesian contract factory workers."[32] Completed in November 1997, the students' *Survey of Vietnamese and Indonesian Domestic Expenditure Levels* was a 45 page written study with approximately 50 pages of attached data. The authors surveyed both workers and residents of the areas in which the factories were located to determine typical spending patterns and the cost of basic necessities.

In Vietnam, the students found that "The factory workers, after incurring essential expenditures, can generate a significant amount of discretionary income."[33] This discretionary income was often used by workers to purchase special items such as bicycles or wedding gifts for family members. In Indonesia, results varied with worker demographics. While 91% of workers reported being able to support themselves individually, only 49% reported being able to also support their dependents. Regardless of demographic status, 82% of workers surveyed in Indonesia either saved wages or contributed each month to their families.[34]

Additionally, the survey found that most workers were not the primary wage earners in their households. Rather, in Vietnam at least, factory wages were generally earned by young men or women and served "to *augment* aggregate household income, with the primary occupation of the

---

[31] Young, p. 9-11.

[32] Derek Calzini, Shawna Huffman, Jake Odden, Steve Tran, and Jean Tsai, *Nike, Inc: Survey of Vietnamese and Indonesian Domestic Expenditure Levels*, November 3, 1997, Field Study in International Business (Dartmouth, NH: The Amos Tuck School, 1997), p. 5.

[33] Ibid., p. 8.

[34] Ibid., p. 9.

household parents being farming or shopkeeping."[35] The same was often true in Indonesia. For instance, in one Indonesian household the students visited, a family of six had used one daughter's minimum wage from a Nike factory to purchase luxury items such as leather couches and a king sized bed.[36] While workers in both countries managed to save wages for future expenditure, the authors found that Indonesians typically put their wages in a bank, while Vietnamese workers were more likely to hold their savings in the form of rice or cows.

Economically, data such as these supported the view that companies such as Nike were actually furthering progress in the developing countries, providing jobs and wages to people who formerly had neither. In the public view, however, the social comparison was unavoidable. According to the Tuck study, the average worker in a Vietnamese Nike factory made about $1.67 per day. A pair of Penny Hardaway basketball sneakers retailed at $150. The criticism continued to mount.

In November there was even more bad news. A disgruntled Nike employee leaked excerpts of an internal Ernst & Young report that uncovered serious health and safety issues in a factory outside of Ho Chi Minh City. According to the Ernst & Young report, a majority of workers suffered from a respiratory ailment caused by poor ventilation and exposure to toxic chemicals. The plant did not have proper safety equipment and training, and workers were forced to work 15 more hours than allowed by law. But according to spokesman Vada Manager the problems no longer existed: "This shows our system of monitoring works. We have uncovered these issues clearly before anyone else, and we have moved fairly expeditiously to correct them."[37] Once again, the denial only made the criticism worse.

Hitting the Wall

Fiscal Year 1998

Until the spring of 1997, Nike sneakers were still selling like hotcakes. The company's stock price had hit $76 and futures orders reached a record high. Despite the storm of criticism lobbied against it, Nike seemed invincible.

Just a year later, however, the situation was drastically different. As Knight admitted to stockholders, Nike's fiscal year 1998 "produced considerable pain." In the third quarter 1998, the company was beset by weak demand and retail oversupply, triggered in part by the Asian currency crisis. Earnings fell 69%, the company's first loss in 13 years. In response, Knight announced significant restructuring charges and the layoff of 1,600 workers.[38]

Much the same dynamic that drove labor criticism drove the 1998 downturn: Nike became a victim of its own popularity. Remarked one analyst: "When I was growing up, we used to say that rooting for the Yankees is like rooting for U.S. Steel. Today, rooting for Nike is like rooting for Microsoft."[39] The company asserted that criticism of Nike's labor practices had nothing to do with the downturn. But it was clear that Nike was suffering from a serious image problem. For whatever

---

[35] Ibid., p. 31.

[36] Ibid., p. 44.

[37] Tunku Varadarajan, "Nike Audit Uncovers Health Hazards at Factory," *The Times of London*, November 10, 1997, p. 52.

[38] Nike Corporation, *Annual Report 1998*, (Nike, Inc.: Beaverton, OR) p. 1, 17-30.

[39] Quoted in Patricia Sellers, "Four Reasons Nike's Not Cool," *Fortune*, March 30, 1998, p. 26.

reasons, Americans were sick of the swoosh. Although Nike billed its shoes as high performance athletic gear, it was well known that 80% of its shoes were sold for fashion purposes. And fashion was a notoriously fickle patron. Competing sneaker manufacturers, particularly adidas, were quick to take advantage of the giant's woes. Adidas' three-stripe logo fast replaced Nike's swoosh among the teen trendsetter crowd; rival brands New Balance and Airwalk tripled their advertising budgets and saw sales surge.

To make matters worse, the anti-Nike headlines had trickled down to the nation's campuses, where a newly invigorated activist movement cast Nike as a symbol of corporate greed and exploitation. With its roots deep in the University of Oregon track team (Knight had been a long distance runner for the school), Nike had long treasured its position as supplier to the top athletic universities. Now, just as young consumers were choosing adidas over Nike at the cash register, campus activists rejected Nike's contracts with their schools and demanded all contracts cease until labor practices were rectified. In late 1997, Nike's $7.2 million endorsement deal with the University of North Carolina sparked protests and controversy on campus; in early 1998 an assistant soccer coach at St. John's University, James Keady, publicly quit his job rather than wear the swoosh. "I don't want to be a billboard for a company that would do these things," said Keady. [40]

Before long, the student protests spread to campuses where Nike had no merchandising contracts. Organized and trained by unions such as UNITE! and the AFL-CIO, previously apathetic college students stormed university buildings to protest sweatshop labor and the exploitation of foreign workers. In 1999, activists took over buildings at Duke, Georgetown, the University of Michigan and the University of Wisconsin, and staged sit-ins at countless other colleges and universities. The protests focused mostly on the conditions under which collegiate logo gear was manufactured. Declared Tom Wheatley, a Wisconsin student and national movement leader: "It really is quite sick. Fourteen-year-old girls are working 100-hour weeks and earning poverty-level wages to make my college T-shirts. That's unconscionable."[41] University administrators heeded the student protests, and many began to consider codes of conduct for contract manufacturers.

Saving the Swoosh

Nike's fiscal woes did what hundreds of harsh articles had failed to do: they took some of the bravado out of Phil Knight. In a May 1998 speech to the National Press Club, a humbled Knight admitted that "the Nike product has become synonymous with slave wages, forced overtime, and arbitrary abuse."[42] Knight announced a series of sweeping reforms, including raising the minimum age of all sneaker workers to 18 and apparel workers to 16; adopting U.S. OSHA clean air standards in all its factories; expanding its monitoring program; expanding educational programs for workers; and making micro loans available to workers. Although Nike had been formally addressing labor issues since 1992, Knight's confession marked a turning point in Nike's stance towards its critics. For the first time, he and his company appeared ready to shed their defensive stance, admit labor violations did occur in Nike factories, and refashion themselves as leaders in the effort to reform third world working conditions.

Nike's second step was to get more involved with Washington-based reform efforts. In the summer of 1998, President Clinton's initial task force on labor, the Apparel Industry Partnership (AIP), lay deadlocked over the ever-delicate issues of factory monitoring and wages. Although the

---

[40] William McCall, "Nike's Image Under Attack: Sweatshop Charges Begin to Take a Toll on the Brand's Cachet," *The Buffalo News*, October 23, 1998, p. 5E.

[41] Nancy Cleeland, "Students Give Sweatshop Fight the College Try," *Los Angeles Times*, April 22, 1999, p. C1.

[42] John H. Cushman Jr., "Nike to Step Forward on Plant Conditions," *The San-Diego Union-Tribune*, May 13, 1998, p. A1.

AIP had a tentative proposal, discussion ground to a halt when the task force's union, religious, and corporate members clashed.

While the AIP proclaimed itself as an exemplar of cooperative solution making, it soon became apparent that its members had very different views. One key concept — "independent monitoring" — was highly contentious. To Nike, the hiring of a separate and unrelated multinational firm like Ernst & Young fulfilled any call for independent monitoring. But activists and other critics alleged that if an independent monitor, such as an accounting firm, was hired by a corporation, it thereby automatically lost autonomy and independence. According to such critics, independent monitoring could only be done by an organization that was not on a corporate payroll, such as an NGO or a religious group. The corporations, by contrast, insisted that a combination of internal monitoring and audits by accounting firms was sufficient. Upset at what they saw as corporate intransigence, the task force's union and religious membership abruptly exited the coalition.

The remaining corporate members of the AIP were soon able to cobble together a more definitive agreement, complete with an oversight organization known as the Fair Labor Association (FLA). The FLA was to be a private entity controlled evenly by corporate members and human rights or labor representatives (if they chose to rejoin the coalition). It would support a code of conduct that required its members to pay workers the legal minimum wage or the prevailing local standard, whichever was higher. The minimum age of workers was set at 15, and employees could not be required to work more than 60 hours per week. Companies that joined the Association would be required to comply with these guidelines and to establish internal monitoring systems to enforce them; they would then be audited by certified independent inspectors, such as accounting firms. In the first three years after a company joined, auditors would inspect 30% of a company's factories; later they would inspect 10%. All audits would be confidential.

Nike worked tirelessly to bring other manufacturers into the FLA, but the going was tough. As of August 1999, the only other corporate members were adidas, Liz Claiborne, Reebok, Levi's, L.L. Bean, and Phillips Van Heusen. However, Nike's efforts to foster the FLA hit pay dirt with U.S. colleges and universities. The vocal student anti-sweatshop movement had many administrators scrambling to find a solution, and over 100 colleges and universities eventually signed on. Participants ranged from the large state universities that held Nike contracts to the eight Ivy League schools. The FLA was scheduled to be fully operational by the fall of 2000.

Meanwhile, by 1999 Nike was running extensive training programs for its contractors' factory managers. All managers and supervisors were required to learn the native language of their workers, and received training in cultural differences and acceptable management styles. In addition to 25 employees who would focus solely on corporate responsibility, Nike's 1,000 production employees were explicitly required to devote part of their job to maintaining labor standards. In Vietnam, the company partnered with the National University of Vietnam in a program designed to identify and meet worker needs. It also helped found the Global Alliance, a partnership between the International Youth Foundation, the MacArthur Foundation, the World Bank, and Mattel, that was dedicated to improving the lives of workers in the developing world.

Although Nike's various concessions and new programs were welcomed as a victory by several human rights groups, other observers argued that Nike still failed to deal with the biggest problem, namely wages.[43] Wrote *New York Times* columnist Bob Herbert: "Mr. Knight is like a three-card monte player. You have to keep a close eye on him at all times. The biggest problem with Nike is that its overseas workers make wretched, below-subsistence wages. It's not the minimum age that

---

[43] John H. Cushman, Jr., "Nike Pledges to End Child Labor and Apply U.S. Rules Abroad," *The New York Times,* May 13, 1998, p. D1.

needs raising, it's the minimum wage."[44] Similarly, while some labor leaders accepted the FLA as the best compromise possible, others decried it as sham agreement that simply provided cover for U.S. corporations. A main objection of these critics was that the FLA standards included notification of factories that were to be inspected, a move criticized by some as equivalent to notifying a restaurant when a critic was coming to dine. According to Jeff Ballinger, Nike's original critic, the company's reform record was mixed. Ballinger was confident that Nike had at least removed dangerous chemicals from factories, but otherwise he remained skeptical: "If you present yourself as a fitness company you can't very well go around the globe poisoning people. But on wages, they're still lying through their teeth."[45]

---

[44] Bob Herbert, "Nike Blinks," *The New York Times,* May 21, 1998, p. A33.
[45] Casewriter interview.

Exhibit 1   Nike Inc. Financial History, 1989 – 1999 (in millions of dollars)

Year Ended May 31	1999	1998	1997	1996	1995	1994	1993	1992	1991	1990	1989
Revenues	$8,776.9	$9,553.1	$9,186.5	$6,470.6	$4,760.8	$3,789.7	$3,931.0	$3,405.2	$3,003.6	$2,235.2	$1,710.8
Gross margin	3,283.4	3,487.6	3,683.5	2,563.9	1,895.6	1,488.2	1,544.0	1,316.1	1,153.1	851.1	636.0
Gross margin %	37.4	36.5	40.1	39.6	39.8	39.3	39.3	38.7	38.4	38.1	37.2
Restructuring charge, net	45.1	129.9	--	--	--	--	--	--	--	--	--
Net income	451.4	399.6	795.8	553.2	399.7	298.8	365.0	329.2	287.0	243.0	167.0
Cash flow from operations	961.0	517.5	323.1	339.7	254.9	576.5	265.3	435.8	11.1	127.1	169.4
Price range of common stock											
High	65.500	64.125	76.375	52.063	20.156	18.688	22.563	19.344	13.625	10.375	4.969
Low	31.750	37.750	47.875	19.531	14.063	10.781	13.750	8.781	6.500	4.750	2.891
Cash and equivalents	$ 198.1	$ 108.6	$ 445.4	$ 262.1	$ 216.1	$ 518.8	$ 291.3	$260.1	$119.8	$ 90.4	$85.7
Inventories	1,199.3	1,396.6	1,338.6	931.2	629.7	470.0	593.0	471.2	586.6	309.5	222.9
Working capital	1,818.0	1,828.8	1,964.0	1,259.9	938.4	1,208.4	1,165.2	964.3	662.6	561.6	419.6
Total assets	5,247.7	5,397.4	5,361.2	3,951.6	3,142.7	2,373.8	2,186.3	1,871.7	1,707.2	1,093.4	824.2
Long-term debt	386.1	379.4	296.0	9.6	10.6	12.4	15.0	69.5	30.0	25.9	34.1
Shareholders' equity	3,334.6	3,261.6	3,155.9	2,431.4	1,964.7	1,740.9	1,642.8	1,328.5	1,029.6	781.0	558.6
Year-end stock price	60.938	46.000	57.500	50.188	19.719	14.750	18.125	14.500	9.938	9.813	4.750
Market capitalization	17,202.2	13,201.1	16,633.0	14,416.8	5,635.2	4,318.8	5,499.3	4,379.6	2,993.0	2,942.7	1,417.4
Geographic Revenues:											
United States	$5,042.6	$5,460.0	$5,538.2	$3,964.7	$2,997.9	$2,432.7	$2,528.8	$2,270.9	$2,141.5	$1,755.5	$1,362.2
Europe	2,255.8	2,096.1	1,789.8	1,334.3	980.4	927.3	1,085.7	919.8	664.7	334.3	241.4
Asia/Pacific	844.5	1,253.9	1,241.9	735.1	515.6	283.4	178.2	75.7	56.2	29.3	32.0
Americas (exclusive of U.S.)	634.0	743.1	616.6	436.5	266.9	146.3	138.3	138.8	141.2	116.1	75.2
Total revenues	$8,776.9	$9,553.1	$9,186.5	$6,470.6	$4,760.8	$3,789.7	$3,931.0	$3,405.2	$3,003.6	$2,235.2	$1,710.8

All per common share data has been adjusted to reflect the 2-for-1 stock splits paid October 23, 1996, October 30, 1995 and October 5, 1990. The Company's Class B Common Stock is listed on the New York and Pacific Exchanges and traded under the symbol NKE. At May 31, 1999, there were approximately 170,000 shareholders.

Source: Nike, Inc., *Annual Report 1999.*

Exhibit 2   Estimated Cost Breakdown of an Average Nike Shoe, 1999

$3.37	Labor costs
$3.41	Manufacturer's overhead
$14.60	Materials
$1.12	Profit to factory
$22.50	Factory price to Nike
$45	Wholesale price
$90	Retail price

Source: Jennifer Lin, "Vietnam Gives Nike a Run for Its Money," *The Philadelphia Enquirer,* March 23, 1998, p. 1.

Exhibit 3   Prices of Some Popular Running Shoe Styles in New York City, 1996

	Nike Air Max		New Balance 999		Saucony Grid Shadow	
	Men's	*Women's*	*Men's*	*Women's*	*Men's*	*Women's*
Foot Locker	$140	$135	$124	$105	$85	$85
Paragon Sports	140	135	135	109	70	70
Sports Authority	140	140	101	101	78	78
Super Runners Shop	140	130	125	110	85	85

Source: "Feet Don't Fail...," *The New York Times,* November 3, 1996, Section 13, p. 12.

Exhibit 4   Summary Revenue and Expense Profile of Minimum Wage Workers by Demographic
Type (in Indonesian Rupiah)

	SH	SO	Dorm	MH	MO	Total (weighted)
Number of respondents	67	161	33	21	32	314
Base wages	172,812	172,071	172,197	173,905	172,650	172,424
Total wages	**225,378**	**238,656**	**239,071**	**248,794**	**244,458**	**236,893**
Rent	14,677	40,955	12,121[a]	24,775	56,050	32,838
Food	84,774	95,744	90,455	103,421	128,793	103,020
Transportation	48,984	24,189	7,219	17,471	38,200	28,560
Savings	38,369	41,783	70,303	29,412	49,185	44,154
Contribution to home	22,175	37,594	57,644	25,222	25,089	34,441
Total uses	**208,980**	**240,266**	**237,741**	**200,301**	**297,318**	**243,013**

[a]17 of the 33 respondents were provided free housing by the factory. The remaining 16 paid a subsidized monthly rent of Rp 25,000.

Note: Monthly Wages and Total Uses of wages may not match due to averaging.

Key to demographic type:

SH - Single workers living at home
SO - Single workers living away from home and paying rent
Dorm - Single workers living away from home and living in factory subsidized housing
MH - Married workers living at home
MO - Married workers living away from home

Source: Derek Calzini, Shawna Huffman, Jake Odden, Steve Tran, and Jean Tsai, *Nike, Inc: Survey of Vietnamese and Indonesian Domestic Expenditure Levels,* November 3, 1997, Field Study in International Business (Dartmouth, NH: The Amos Tuck School, 1997), pp. 9-10.

Exhibit 5 Typical "Basket" of Basic Food Expenditures for Indonesian workers (in rupiah)

Rice	800-1,300	per 5 servings
Instant Noodles	300-500	per serving
Eggs	2,800-3,000	per 18 eggs
Tofu	1,500	per 15 servings
Tempe	1,500	per 15 servings
Kancang Pangung	1,500	per 15 servings
Peanuts	2,600	per kilogram
Oil	2,300	per liter
Other "luxury" foods		
Fish	6,000	per kilogram
Chicken	4,500-5,000	per chicken

Source: Derek Calzini, Shawna Huffman, Jake Odden, Steve Tran, and Jean Tsai, *Nike, Inc: Survey of Vietnamese and Indonesian Domestic Expenditure Levels,* November 3, 1997, Field Study in International Business (Dartmouth, NH: The Amos Tuck School, 1997), p. 45.

Exhibit 6   Strikes and Lockouts in Indonesia, 1988 - 1997

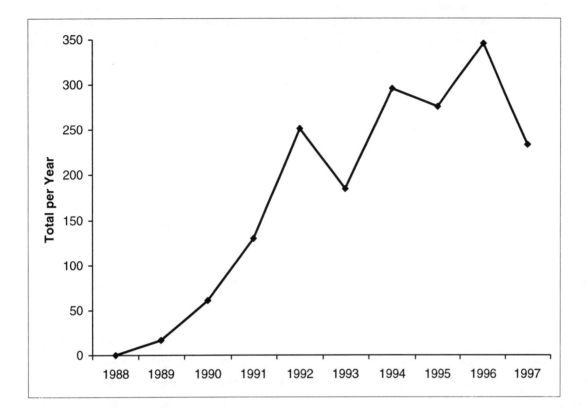

Source: International Labour Office, *Yearbook of Labor Statistics 1998* (Geneva; ILO, 1999), p.1213.

Exhibit 7 Wages and Productivity in Industrialized and Developing Nations (figures in $ per year)

	Average Hours Worked Per Week		Yearly Minimum Wage		Labor Cost Per Worker in Manufacturing		Value Added Per Worker in Manufacturing	
	1980-84	1990-94	1980-84	1990-94	1980-84	1990-94	1980-84	1990-94
North America								
United States	35	34	6,006	8,056[b]	19,103	32,013[b]	47,276	81,353
Canada	32	33	4,974	7,897[b]	17,710	28,346[b]	36,903	60,712
Mexico	--	34	1,002	843	3,772	6,138	17,448	25,991
Europe								
Denmark	--	37	9,170	19,933[b]	16,169	35,615[b]	27,919	49,273
France	39	39	10,815	22,955[b]	16,060	38,900[b]	26,751	61,019[e]
Germany	41	40	[a]	[a]	21,846[d]	63,956[b,d]	--	--
Greece	--	41	--	5,246	6,461	15,899[b]	14,561	30,429
Ireland	41[c]	41[c]	--	--	10,190	25,414[b]	26,510	86,036
Netherlands	40	39	9,074	15,170[b]	18,891	39,865[b]	27,491	56,801
Asia								
China (PRC)	--	--	--	--	472	434[d]	3,061	2,885
Hong Kong	48	46	--	--	4,127	13,539[b]	7,886	19,533
India	48	48	--	408	1,035	1,192	2,108	3,118
Indonesia	--	--	--	241	898	1,008	3,807	5,139
Japan	47	46	3,920	8,327[b]	12,306	40,104[b]	34,456	92,582
South Korea	52	48	--	3,903[b]	3,153	15,819[b]	11,617	40,916
Malaysia	--	--	--	[a]	2,519	3,429	8,454	12,661
Philippines	--	43	--	1,067	1,240	2,459	5,266	9,339
Singapore	--	46	--	--	5,576	21,534[b]	16,442	40,674
Thailand	48	--	--	1,083	2,305	2,705	11,072	19,946

A.) Country has sectoral minimum wage but no minimum wage policy. B.) Data refer to 1995 – 1999. C.) Data refer to hours worked per week in manufacturing. D) Data refer to wage per worker in manufacturing. E.) International Labor Organisation data.

Source: World Bank, *World Development Indicators 1999* (Washington, D.C.; World Bank, 1999), pp.62-64.

Exhibit 8   Indonesia: Wages and Inflation, 1993-97

| | 1993 | | 1994 | | 1995 | | 1996 | | 1997 | |
	Minimum	Maximum	Minimum	Maximum	Minimum	Maximum	Minimum	Maximum	Minimum	Maximum
Monthly wages in manufacturing industry (thousands of rupiah)	196	2,920	207	3,112	238	3,453	241	3,453	439	6,050
Minimum wage regional average[a] (thousands of rupiah)	72		94		112		118		130	
Annual percent change	17.7		30.8		19.5		5.4		10.2	
Consumer price inflation	8.5		9.4		8.0		6.7		57.6	
Exchange rates (average Rp:$)	2,161		2,249		2,342		2,909		10,014	

Source: International Monetary Fund, Economist Intelligence Unit.

Figures are based on periodic surveys of primarily urban-based business establishments and include transportation, meal, and attendance allowances.

[a]Calculated from minimum daily figure for 30 days per month. Increased by 9% to Rp122,000 in 1996 and by 10% to Rp135,000 in 1997.

Exhibit 9 *Life* magazine photo of Pakistani child worker

Source: *Life* Magazine, June 1996, p. 39.

Exhibit 10 Doonesbury Cartoons About Nike

Copyright: Doonesbury © 1997 G. B. Trudeau. Reprinted with Permission of Universal Press Syndicate. All rights reserved.

Exhibit 11 Anti-Nike Activist Materials

Nike, Inc. in Indonesia I

JUST DO IT!

"You know when you need a break. And you know when it's time to take care of yourself, for yourself. Because you know it's never too late to have a life." (Nike advertisement)

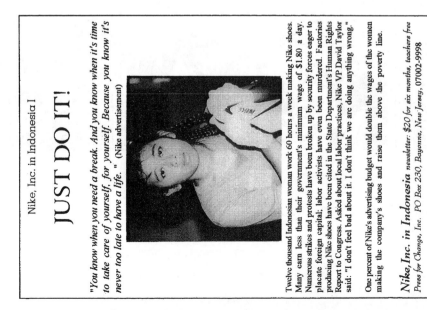

Twelve thousand Indonesian woman work 60 hours a week making Nike shoes. Many earn less than their government's minimum wage of $1.80 a day. Numerous strikes and protests have been broken up by security forces eager to placate foreign capital; labor activists have even been murdered. Factories producing Nike shoes have been cited in the State Department's Human Rights Report to Congress. Asked about local labor practices, Nike VP David Taylor said: "I don't feel bad about it. I don't think we are doing anything wrong."

One percent of Nike's advertising budget would double the wages of the women making the company's shoes and raise them above the poverty line.

Nike, Inc. in Indonesia newsletter: *$20 for six months, teachers free Press for Change, Inc. PO Box 230, Bayonne, New Jersey, 07002-9998*

Source: Jeff Ballinger; http://www.nikeworkers.org [10/29/99]; http://www.corpwatch.org/nike/ [10/29/99].

Part IV

INTERNATIONAL TRADE IN THE AGE OF INFORMATION

Pfizer: Global Protection of Intellectual Property

*The biggest single change in management during my career has been the increase
in time that managers spend dealing with government.*

-Edmund T. Pratt, Jr.
Chairman and Chief Executive Officer
Pfizer Inc.
April 1991

Introduction

In the spring of 1991, top officials at Pfizer were rethinking their strategy for improving protection of the company's intellectual property around the world. Until that time, Pfizer and other members of a coalition of American companies known as the Intellectual Property Committee (IPC) had focused on achieving an intellectual property agreement in the Uruguay Round of the GATT negotiations. Under the leadership of Chairman and Chief Executive Edmund Pratt, Pfizer had been instrumental in transforming intellectual property (a category including primarily patents, copyrights, trademarks, and trade secrets) from a lawyer's specialty into an international trade issue of great concern to governments around the world. The IPC had forged an unusual tripartite coalition among European, Japanese, and United States industry to work with their respective governments to secure global protection for intellectual property through the GATT.

By 1991, however, it was unclear whether an acceptable intellectual property agreement or, indeed, any agreement at all would emerge from the GATT negotiations. Lou Clemente, Pfizer's general counsel, and Lillian Fernandez, the director of International Affairs in Pfizer's Public Affairs Division, along with Pratt, were considering the possibilities.

A Brief History of Pfizer

Based in New York City, Pfizer was a worldwide company with over 40,000 employees, approximately two-thirds of whom were employed outside the United States. Its principal lines of business were pharmaceuticals, which accounted for approximately one-half of its annual sales,

---

Research Associate Michael A. Santoro prepared this case under the supervision of Professor Lynn Sharp Paine as the basis for class discussion rather than to illustrate either effective or ineffective handling of an administrative situation.

as well as hospital products, consumer products, animal health, specialty minerals, and specialty chemicals. These products were available in more than 140 countries. In 1990, Pfizer was ranked eighth worldwide in dollar volume of sales of pharmaceutical and medical products.[1] Of its six principal R&D centers, four were located abroad: in Sandwich, England; Amboise, France; Nagoya, Japan; and Illertissen, Germany. The company had manufacturing facilities in more than 65 countries. Twenty-one production facilities were located in Less Developed Countries (LDCs).

Founded in 1849, Pfizer was until World War II primarily a manufacturer of specialty chemicals and the leading world supplier of citric acid, a product with many industrial uses. Through the production of citric acid, Pfizer developed fermentation skills which were regarded as among the best, if not the best, in the world. During World War II, these skills enabled Pfizer to develop cost-effective methods for the mass production of penicillin. The company focused on manufacturing bulk pharmaceuticals such as penicillin and other antibiotics and sold very few pharmaceuticals under its own label until the mid-1950s. One exception was Terramycin, the first antibiotic to be discovered by Pfizer scientists and the first to be sold under the Pfizer brand name. Introduced in 1950, Terramycin marked the entry of Pfizer into the ranks of research-based companies.

Pfizer's expansion into international markets began after World War II with the sale of bulk pharmaceuticals, most notably antibiotics, to European nations rebuilding under the Marshall Plan. About this time, Pfizer started manufacturing and selling a variety of over-the-counter and ethical (i.e. prescription) drugs under its own label. In the early 1950s, largely to meet worldwide demand for its new antibiotics, particularly Terramycin, the company began setting up distribution and manufacturing facilities in other parts of the world, including Asia and Latin America. Pfizer was the first major U.S. pharmaceutical company to establish operations in many of these countries, though European companies such as Hoechst, Bayer, ICI, Beecham, Sandoz, and Ciba-Geigy were also expanding operations into developing countries at this time.

From a commercial perspective, LDC markets had never accounted for more than 10%-12% of Pfizer's worldwide sales. But Pfizer had chosen to stay in difficult countries like Bangladesh, Nigeria, and India. Over time, and despite the difficulties, some LDCs had nevertheless provided healthy profit pictures. Moreover many executives felt committed to relationships Pfizer had established in these countries. They had high hopes for the future as well. Hopes for the future had also propelled Pfizer into major joint ventures in China in 1989 and Hungary in June 1991 when few other companies were willing to make major commitments.

With the chairmanship of Edmund Pratt beginning in 1972, Pfizer increased its emphasis on developing new and innovative proprietary drugs. During this period, marked by steady increases in research spending, Pfizer became a major pharmaceutical innovator. A 1990 study of pharmaceutical research by leading companies had ranked Pfizer ninth in total research spending,[2] and by 1991, the company had built up a sizable portfolio of new products and drug candidates. Having launched new pharmaceutical products in 37 international markets in major industrialized countries in 1990, Pfizer planned 60 new launches for 1991.[3] To market its

---

1. *Medical Advertising News*, "Top 50 Companies," September 1991.
2. *Medical Advertising News*, "Top 50 Companies," September 1990.
3. Pfizer Annual Report, 1990, p. 2.

products in the United States, Pfizer had hired some 500-600 new salespeople and added an additional sales company, Pratt Pharmaceuticals, named for its chairman.

Table A   International Sales at Pfizer

Region	1990	1989	1988	1987
United States	$3,472.9	$3,096.6	$2,884.2	$2,651.4
Europe	1,503.5	1,190.1	1,176.4	1,051.5
Asia	873.1	876.1	807.5	704.3
Canada/Latin America	419.6	386.2	405.9	399.1
Africa/Middle East	136.9	122.5	111.4	113.5
International	2,933.1	2,574.9	2,501.2	2,268.4
Consolidated	$6,406.0	$5,671.5	$5,385.4	$4,919.8

Source: Pfizer Inc.

During Pratt's tenure, Pfizer's sales rose from $1 billion in 1972 to over $6 billion in 1990 (see **Exhibit 1**). Net income increased from $103.4 million in 1972 to approximately $800 million in 1990. Although it was unclear precisely how much growth was due to products manufactured under patent, Pfizer officials viewed patent protection as critical to corporate strategy. One financial analyst estimated that Pfizer products under patent would generate $4 billion in worldwide sales in 1995 and account for 40% of the firm's revenues.[4]

Like other major pharmaceutical companies, Pfizer's return on equity in 1990 was nearly double that of the median return for *Fortune 500* companies.[5] As it entered 1991, Pfizer had just completed the sale of its citric acid business, once the mainstay of the company. The sale reaffirmed Pfizer's commitment to a strategy of innovation.

The International Pharmaceutical Industry

The international pharmaceutical industry's global sales were estimated at more than $56 billion for 1990.[6] Seventy percent of both production and consumption was concentrated in advanced industrial nations. Companies based in the United States, Japan and Germany accounted for 50% of world production. Of the world's 20 largest firms by worldwide sales in 1990, eleven were based in the United States, two in Switzerland, three in Germany, and three in the United Kingdom.[7] A little over 10% of world production took place in LDCs, mostly in India, Brazil, Mexico, Argentina, Egypt and the Republic of Korea. The largest consumers of pharmaceuticals were the United States, where 21% of the world's pharmaceutical dollars were spent, and Japan, where 14% were spent. LDCs together accounted for approximately 14% of world spending.[8]

---

4. Brian O'Reilly, "Drugmakers Under Attack," *Fortune*, July 29, 1991, p. 60.
5. *Id.* at p. 48.
6. Pharmaceutical Manufacturers Association, 1989-1991 Annual Survey Report, p. 4.
7. "Top 50 Companies," *Medical Advertising News*, September 1991.
8. Unless otherwise noted, all data in this paragraph from Van R. Whiting, Jr., "Mexico's Modernization: Nationalism or Liberalism in Pharmaceuticals," *Business in the Contemporary World*, Spring 1990, p. 45.

Competition was driven by the development of new products and the promotion of existing ones, including brand name products on which patents had expired or never existed. In pharmaceuticals, as in most other knowledge-based industries, the costs of production were a miniscule proportion of the costs of discovering and marketing new products. Drug research required substantial capital and extremely long development time with a substantial risk of failure. Dr. Joseph DiMasi of Tufts University estimated an average cost of $231 million and more than 10 years to bring a new pharmaceutical from the laboratory through the regulatory review process in the United States.[9] Each phase of the lengthy process of bringing a new drug to market—from initial discovery to the development of promising compounds through preclinical and human investigations, to the New Drug Application approval process—was fraught with expense and uncertainty. Industry representatives estimated that 5,000 to 10,000 promising new substances had to be evaluated for each new drug that reached the market.

The costs of research and development were rising at Pfizer and in the rest of the industry. Pfizer had estimated expenditures of $750 million on research and development in 1991, an increase of 17% over 1990. According to the Pharmaceutical Manufacturers Association, U.S. pharmaceutical firms spent $8.2 billion (representing 16.8% of sales) on research and development in 1990, compared with $5.5 billion (15.8% of sales) in 1987.[10] In other research-oriented industries such as those represented by IBM, General Motors, Sony, and AT&T, research expenditures were in the range of 4%-6% of annual sales.

The Importance of the Patent System

Pfizer depended on the patent system to protect and justify its investment in innovation. Granted by governments, patents gave inventors certain exclusive rights to exploit their inventions for a limited period of time. These rights typically included the right to make, use, and sell the product or process covered by the patent. The world's first patent laws dated to 1474 when the Republic of Venice granted 10-year patents to inventors of new devices. According to United States patent law, "whoever invents or discovers any new and useful process, machine, manufacture or composition of matter" was entitled to obtain a patent.[11] The invention had to be novel and not obvious to a person having ordinary skills in the art to which the patent pertained. In return for disclosing the invention to the public in the patent application, the inventor was granted for 17 years the exclusive right to exploit the invention and/or to license it to others for a fee.

In 1991, nearly all the fully industrialized countries had patent systems similar to that of the United States. The period of protection varied, however, and except for the United States and the Philippines which awarded a patent to the first to invent, the other nations of the world awarded a patent to the first to file for it. There were also variations in the scope of a patent and the conditions under which compulsory licenses could be required, as well as differences in the openness or secrecy of the application, the requirements of the application, the period of time needed for approval, and the procedures for challenging a patent. However, not all of these systems had been in place as long as that of the United States. And patents on pharmaceutical

9. Joseph A. DiMasi, "Rising Research and Development Costs for New Drugs in a Cost Containment Environment," paper of Center for the Study of Drug Development, Tufts University, Boston, Mass., 1991.
10. David Rutman, "The Price of Doing R&D Soars," *Chemical Week*, June 13, 1990, p. 48.
11. 35 U.S.C. §101.

products, as distinct from patents on the processes by which they were made, were relatively recent in some industrialized countries (**Exhibit 2**).

Both product and process patents were critical to the research-based segment of the pharmaceutical industry. However, since most drugs could be produced through a variety of processes, product patents were particularly important. Unless the product itself was patented, a competitor could legally produce it using a process different from the patented one. Since the costs of developing and marketing drugs were so high relative to the costs of copying and selling them, pharmaceutical companies sought the protection of both product and process patents. Only with both could they achieve an adequate return on their investments and generate resources to subsidize research and development of additional new drugs.

The social justification for patent protection was rooted in several ideas. One was promoting innovation. The United States Constitution, for example, provided for a system of copyrights and patents to "encourage the progress of science and the useful arts."[12] A period of exclusivity provided inventors an opportunity to recoup and profit from their investment in expensive and time-consuming research. By limiting the duration of the patent, governments attempted to achieve an appropriate balance between the social benefits of increased innovation and the increased costs to consumers of patented products.

Sometimes patents were justified as the inventor's "natural right" or proper reward for inventive activity. According to this view associated with the seventeenth-century English philosopher John Locke, the inventor acquired exclusive rights to an invention by virtue of having labored to produce it. Other members of society were morally obligated to recognize the rights of authors and inventors by not copying their creative works without their permission. Still others saw the inventor's rights as a *quid pro quo* for disclosing an invention to the public. One Pfizer executive saw patents as resting on the principles of liberal democracy and reflecting a "social contract among citizens, government, and innovators." In his view, countries like Canada abrogated this social contract when they passed laws taking away intellectual property rights.

Patent Protection at Pfizer

Under Pratt's leadership, Pfizer was aggressive in protecting and defending its pharmaceutical patents. The company employed some 35 patent attorneys and agents in-house, while relying on outside counsel for patent litigation. Pfizer, said Pratt, "probably spent more than its competitors on defending its patents." Although the costs and benefits of this policy could not be measured precisely, Pratt explained that it was something the company had to do "to discourage others from stealing its intellectual property." To be sure, Pfizer had achieved some dramatic and profitable victories in patent litigation in the pharmaceutical area as well as in the medical device area, another of Pfizer's businesses heavily dependent on patents. In 1983, for example, the company won a judgment for $56 million in a patent infringement suit involving doxycycline, an orally administered antibiotic. Similarly, in 1989, Pfizer's subsidiary Shiley recovered $53 million in damages in a suit related to blood oxygenators.

Lou Clemente, Pfizer's general counsel, first became involved in patent issues as counsel to the Pfizer International subsidiaries in the early 1960s. "My initial exposure to international

---

12. U.S. Constitution, Art. I, §8.

patent protection issues was through enforcement. I would hear from one of our marketing people that our proprietary products were being copied and manufactured in Europe. In one case a manufacturer was not only copying our product but also counterfeiting Pfizer's name on the product. For the most part, the law in these European countries respected patent rights, and eventually, in some cases after very long and expensive legal proceedings, we were able to shut down these illegal operations by obtaining injunctions."

Not all of these enforcement actions went smoothly for Pfizer, however. "Italy was a particularly difficult place to enforce patent rights," said Clemente, "because there was a law which prohibited pharmaceutical patents. Eventually, this law was declared unconstitutional, and we were able to stop the Italian companies that were stealing our technology."

In the 1970s, having solved their patent enforcement problems in Europe, Pfizer's efforts turned to the LDCs. These markets had by then become important for Pfizer, and lack of patent protection had emerged as a problem in countries such as Mexico, Brazil, Argentina, and India. Gone were the days when lack of infrastructure and technical know-how had protected Pfizer's patents in LDC's. Said Pratt: "We were beginning to notice that we were losing market share dramatically because our intellectual property rights were not being respected in these countries."

Intellectual Property Protection in LDCs

Pfizer and other multinational pharmaceutical companies saw serious deficiencies in the intellectual property protection available in many LDCs. Some declined to grant any protection at all for new chemical and pharmaceutical products. Others offered patent protection for the processes used to produce new drugs, but not for the products themselves (**Exhibit 2**).

Another problem in LDCs was the inadequate duration of patents. This was especially important in the case of drugs which, because of lengthy regulatory reviews, could take many years to reach the market. For example, India, which recognized process but not product patents, granted protection for only five years. Along with other countries, India also required that patented products be produced locally and provided, under certain conditions, for compulsory licensing to local producers willing to pay a fee as determined by the government. Even in countries with patent laws, enforcement and penalties for infringement were often inadequate.

Pfizer's experience in Argentina illustrated many of the problems. Even before Pfizer received the approval of the Argentine government to sell the antiarthritic drug Feldene, a generic competitor was manufacturing and selling it. By the time Pfizer was able to bring the drug to market, it faced six competitors manufacturing Feldene without paying any royalties to Pfizer.

The availability of patent protection also influenced strategic decisions of the firm's international division. For years the company had debated whether or not to shut down the manufacturing facilities in India. "The Indian government was forcing us to license our products to local companies," said Pratt, "and the government was also controlling prices." Although other pharmaceutical companies faced with similar erosion in market share shut down many of their international operations, Pfizer, Pratt said, was determined to "hang in there."

The Indian operations had been unprofitable for many years. Pratt continued, "We had a large investment in plant and equipment, but we were not making any profit. Fortunately, we were doing well in our other operations so it didn't affect our overall performance dramatically. Still, there were some within the company who argued that we should shut down the operations and take a write-off. I was not one of those people. For one thing, over 2,000 members of the Pfizer family worked there. We had a responsibility to them and to the community that they were based in, which really needed our products. And there was always the possibility that the situation would turn around, and India remained a very large potential market for us."

Initial Efforts at Changing the World Intellectual Property Environment

Pfizer's initial efforts, in the late seventies and early eighties, at changing the intellectual property climate were aimed at persuasion. Clemente recalled that "we went everywhere trying to press our position, including the World Bank. We tried to get the State Department interested in the issue, but they were security-oriented rather than business-oriented at this time." Clemente continued, "We were convinced that providing incentives for invention was truly a good thing for developing countries. We tried to persuade leaders of developing countries of this point of view. We tried to enlist the aid of the U.S. Embassies. All of our efforts at persuasion were fruitless." Pratt explained, "Developing countries told us they were too young, too weak, and too poor to have strong patent laws. But my answer to that was that the United States was a developing country when it wrote patent protection right into the Constitution in 1789!"

Pfizer had a particularly difficult time within the World Intellectual Property Organization (WIPO), one of the fifteen "specialized agencies" of the United Nations. WIPO, headquartered in Geneva, was established in 1967 to administer various multilateral treaties dealing with the legal and administrative aspects of intellectual property. The most important of these treaties were the Paris Convention for the Protection of Industrial Property adopted in 1883 (The "Paris Convention") and the Berne convention for the Protection of Literary and Artistic Work adopted in 1886 (The "Berne Convention"). In 1991, 101 nations were parties to the Paris Convention (**Exhibit 3**) and 84 nations were parties to the Berne Convention.

The Paris Convention required each contracting state to grant the same patent protection to nationals of other contracting states as it granted to its own nationals. The Convention also provided for the right of priority, whereby after a patent application was filed in one country, the applicant had 12 months to file for a patent in any of the other contracting states without losing priority. The Paris Convention specified the conditions under which each contracting state could provide by law for compulsory licensing or, in rare instances, the revocation of a patent (unjustified failure to work a patent, for example). Finally, as to matters not covered by the Convention, each contracting state was free to legislate to, for example, exclude certain fields of technology, or fix the duration of patents. There were no specific enforcement mechanisms or dispute resolution procedures under the Paris Convention.

Since the Paris Convention specifically allowed many of the practices Pfizer sought to change, Pfizer approached WIPO to attempt to change the Convention. But Pfizer made no progress at WIPO. "Our approach to WIPO was a disaster," recalled Clemente. "As a UN organization, WIPO works by majority, and, simply put, there were more of them than us. Our experience with WIPO was the last straw in our attempt to operate by persuasion."

Networks of Influence

After the disastrous experience with WIPO, Pfizer sought other avenues for securing adequate patent protection. Under the leadership of Pratt, this effort extended throughout the Pfizer organization and engaged individuals and companies inside and outside the industry. For instance, during the WIPO debate, Barry MacTaggart, then Chairman and CEO of Pfizer International, published in the *New York Times* an op-ed piece entitled "Stealing from the Mind" **Exhibit 4**). This article reflected a considered decision to take a tough, open position and to name countries with bad patent protection, despite the risk of incurring their displeasure. Public statements like this by company leaders, as well as internal memos directed to key executives and managers, conveyed the message that intellectual property should be treated as a priority issue. The operating plans and budgets developed annually for each operating division also emphasized the importance of public affairs, including intellectual property protection, and identified specific objectives to be accomplished.

As a result, country managers in problem countries such as Mexico, Brazil, Korea, Argentina, Indonesia, Taiwan, Thailand, and India worked to build a consensus in favor of intellectual property protection through involvement with local business, professional, academic, and government groups. This was sometimes easier for expatriates than for local nationals more likely to face special pressures from their governments. Several hundred Pfizer executives around the world spoke up for intellectual property protection through the trade associations and business organizations with which they were affiliated.

Pfizer executives played key roles in many leading business groups. For example, Gerald Laubach, then president of Pfizer Inc., sat on the board of the *Pharmaceutical Manufacturers Association (PMA)*, as well as on President Reagan's *Council on Competitiveness*. Pratt headed up the *Business Roundtable* of 200 CEOs. Besides his involvement in many legal groups, Clemente was active with the New York-based *U.S. Council for International Business*, along with Mike Hodin, Pfizer's vice president-Public Affairs. Clemente chaired the council's Intellectual Property Committee while Hodin headed up its EC Committee. Pfizer executives were also involved with the *National Foreign Trade Council* and the *U.S. Chamber of Commerce*.

Overseas, Pfizer International's president, Bob Neimeth, was chair of the Trade Committee of the *Business and Industry Advisory Committee (BIAC) to the OECD*. His predecessor, MacTaggart, was involved with the *U.S.-India Business Council* of U.S.-based companies with interests in India. Pfizer's vice president of Public Affairs in Japan worked closely with the Japan Pharmaceutical Manufacturers Association (*JPMA*). Other Pfizer executives were involved with similar Business Councils linked to other countries such as Mexico, Brazil, Thailand, Turkey. Still others excutives worked with sister PMA organizations in the United Kingdom, France, Germany and other countries.

Early on, Pfizer established links with key organizations such as the EC Committee of the *American Chamber of Commerce in Belgium*. More than just a committee, the group served as a principal contact with the EC from 1985. Pfizer also built connections to think tanks and the academic community connected to leading universities in OECD countries to strengthen the intellectual foundation for its political efforts.

Through this complex network of organizations and relationships, Pfizer worked the intellectual property issue and built interest and support for its position from the early 1980's onward. A number of the organizations issued reports and papers which provided guidance to government officials in the United States and abroad.

Pratt's Role in Forming the IPC

Pratt, himself, was well-placed to promote intellectual property protection at the highest levels of the U.S. government. Appointed by President Carter to the Advisory Committee on Trade and Policy Negotiations (ACTPN) in 1979, Pratt became the organization's chairman in 1981. This group of private sector leaders was charged with reviewing and reporting to Congress on the policies of the United States Trade Representative's (USTR) office, but their primary purpose was to advise the USTR on trade matters.

For six years, Pratt led this committee in pursuing an aggressive trade agenda. He worked on expanding market access for the service sector and on foreign investment. He also promoted intellectual property protection. As head of ACTPN, Pratt was at the forefront of a revolution in thinking about trade and investment. He and others dissolved the conceptual boundaries that had previously separated these two issue areas and supported institutional structures to reflect the new insights. In the early eighties, the USTR created a new position for an Assistant USTR for International Investment and Intellectual Property. Working with the new Assistant and the USTR, Pfizer and the PMA developed a position paper directed to the White House staff which eventually resulted in a Presidential statement on the importance of intellectual property to the United States and led to important changes in Sections 301, 303, and 501 of the U.S. trade law.[13]

Pfizer was not the only company worried about its intellectual property. Other pharmaceutical companies, as well as copyright-based industries such as software, publishing, movie, and sound recordings, were becoming increasingly concerned. In the 1980s, the press began to report that counterfeit copies of luxury goods such as $3,500 Cartier watches could be bought for $20 in countries with weak intellectual property laws such as Korea. It was estimated that software vendors lost $500 million annually in overseas sales because of inadequate intellectual property protection. Annual losses in the agrichemical industry were estimated at $200 million. The most alarming study came from the U.S. International Trade Commission which estimated that inadequate intellectual property protection cost U.S. firms between $43 and $61 billion in 1986 alone.[14]

In the early 1980s, Pratt and IBM Chairman John Opel, who chaired the intellectual property task force of ACTPN, pressed their concerns with William Brock, the U.S. Trade Representative. They circulated proposals for improving intellectual property protection to the USTR, to the President, and to trade officials, and argued vigorously for including intellectual property on the agenda of the upcoming round of the GATT negotiations (the "Uruguay Round"). The General Agreement on Tariffs and Trade (the GATT) was a multilateral agreement adhered to after World War II by the United States and 22 other nations. By 1990, there were 96 "contracting parties" or members of GATT (**Exhibit 5**). Aimed at expanding and liberalizing world trade, the GATT governed many of the trade relations between these nations, and included rules about quantitative trade restrictions and subsidies, as well as antidumping provisions. An important feature of the GATT was the intermittent series of trade negotiation

---

13. See text below, "Changes in U.S. Trade Law."
14. Jacques J. Gorlin, "Yo, ho, ho, and a Gucci Bag," *World Paper*, March 1989, p. 2.

rounds. From 1947 through 1980, there had been seven such rounds, culminating in the Tokyo Round from 1973 to 1979. The Uruguay Round was the eighth GATT round.

Pratt explained the strategy of addressing intellectual property issues through the GATT: "Unlike in WIPO, we thought we could achieve real leverage through GATT. Many of the countries lacking intellectual property protection at least had important trading relations with the United States and the rest of the developed world. Moreover, through GATT we could forge intellectual property standards that were supported by dispute resolution and enforcement mechanisms, both of which were lacking in WIPO."

According to Pratt, it was not hard to persuade U.S. officials that something should be done to stop the theft of U.S. companies' intellectual property. But getting intellectual property on the GATT agenda posed some difficulty. Traditionally, the GATT negotiations had covered the reduction of trade barriers such as tariffs and subsidies. Many, including some GATT officials, did not believe the GATT was an appropriate vehicle for prescribing national standards for intellectual property protection. Border controls against counterfeit goods, a subject under discussion by a GATT Working Group established at the end of the Tokyo Round in 1979, were one thing. Standards for intellectual property protection, like those sought by ACTPN, were quite another. Moreover, Article XX (d) of the GATT specifically left intellectual property protection to the discretion of the contracting nations, provided their laws were not discriminatorily applied against other nations, or otherwise in conflict with GATT. Opponents of GATT norms on intellectual property also argued that WIPO was the appropriate forum for this discussion. But Pratt and others countered that even if not all intellectual property issues were within the purview of GATT, surely some were. Hence the phrase "Trade-Related Aspects of Intellectual Property Rights" (TRIPS) was coined to describe the new GATT subject.

In 1985 Clayton Yeutter became the U.S. Trade Representative. Although Yeutter favored the proposal, he knew that getting intellectual property on the GATT agenda would require the support of the other industrialized countries. He advised Pratt and Opel to get the word out to their counterparts in the rest of the world so that they, in turn, could pressure their governments to include intellectual property in the negotiations. In March 1986, Pratt and Opel mobilized a group of CEOs from 13 companies in diverse industries such as movies, computers and pharmaceuticals to form the Intellectual Property Committee (IPC).[15] Financed by its members, the IPC undertook to provide private sector input, to monitor the trade negotiations, and to forge alliances with European and Japanese industry in support of better intellectual property protection. Each member company appointed an intellectual property specialist and a trade or government relations specialist to work with the IPC.

The IPC provided a unique opportunity for collaboration between trade and patent experts. In some member companies, specialists from the two areas had never before communicated. The IPC also brought together specialists from various areas of intellectual property—copyright, patent, trademark, and others. As a consultant to the IPC noted, "Once brought together, copyright-based companies and patent-based companies realized that they had been facing the same pirates."

---

15. The thirteen members of the IPC were: Pfizer, IBM, Merck, General Electric, Du Pont, Warner Communications, Hewlett-Packard, Bristol-Myers, FMC Corporation, General Motors, Johnson & Johnson, Monsanto, and Rockwell International.

By the summer of 1986, IPC members were talking to their counterparts and to government in Europe and Japan. Building on the network of relationships already in place, the IPC forged a tripartite coalition among the IPC, the European Union of Industrial and Employers' Confederations (UNICE), and the Keidanren, a private federation of economic organizations in Japan. Although the Europeans and Japanese were at first skeptical of the GATT proposal as well as the effectiveness and authority of the IPC, all recognized the need for global protection for intellectual property.

The Tripartite Coalition at Work

The tripartite coalition's members succeeded in convincing their governments that intellectual property should be on the agenda for the GATT negotiations, and the Ministerial Declaration kicking off the Round included intellectual property as a subject of negotiation. As chairman of ACTPN and as official adviser to the USTR, Pratt attended the opening meeting of the Uruguay Round at Punta del Este in September 1986.

From September 1986 through June 1988, the negotiators became mired in debate over the competency of the GATT negotiating group and the scope of the negotiations. The IPC took advantage of this hiatus to develop a tripartite consensus on the substance of the minimum standards to be negotiated and to create a document the negotiators could use as a guide. In November 1986, IPC, UNICE, and Keidanren members met in Brussels to begin this work. The result appeared in June 1988: a 100-page report detailing the minimum standards for an acceptable TRIPS agreement. This document, the "Basic Framework," (summarized in **Exhibit 6**) addressed six categories of intellectual property: patents, copyrights, semiconductor chips, trademarks, industrial designs and trade secrets.

Several areas of difference had to be overcome to achieve the "Basic Framework." One particularly thorny issue was copyright protection for computer programs. Representatives of the Keidanren wanted to treat computer programs as a special category with distinctive principles that would permit "decompilation" (a sort of reverse engineering), rather than fully protecting programs as literary works under copyright. Concerned about opening the door to diluted copyright protection modelled on Japanese law, UNICE and IPC representatives opposed such an approach. On this issue, the IPC and UNICE prevailed and the "Basic Framework" accorded computer programs the same copyright protections as literary works.

Trade secret protection was another area requiring resolution. In the United States, case law and state statutes protected certain types of secret business information. European Community states had more-or-less similar protection for trade secrets. Japan, however, had no such system, and the Keidanren initially resisted including trade secrets in the "Basic Framework." In the end, however, the IPC and UNICE prevailed and the "Basic Framework" contained a section on proprietary information. After the release of the "Basic Framework," Japan for the first time in its history passed a trade secret law based on U.S. and German models.

Not all areas of conflict were capable of being resolved. Long-standing disputes over patent law threatened to unravel the coalition. Europe and Japan were particularly concerned about the basic rule of priority. In the United States, unlike in Europe, Japan, and almost every other nation in the world, patents were awarded to the first to invent rather than the first to file a patent application. While Americans argued that the first-to-invent system favored the individual, the Japanese thought it rendered patent rights unduly uncertain. At any time, someone might come forward to challenge the validity of a patent on the grounds of an earlier invention date. Moreover, the Japanese thought their system of public disclosure of patent applications preferable to the American system of keeping applications secret. Under the Japanese system, they said, it was easier to identify and resolve disputes before a patent was granted.

Adding insult to injury from the European and Japanese perspective was American bias in favor of U.S.-based inventive activity. Under U.S. patent law, an inventor who had worked abroad could not establish a date of invention any earlier than the date of first filing a patent application abroad.[16] Hence European and Japanese inventors who had done their inventive work outside the United States felt discriminated against when they filed patent applications or became involved in patent litigation in the United States because they were assigned priority dates based on when they first applied for a patent rather than when they conceived the invention, the priority date assigned to inventors working in the United States.

The Europeans and Japanese were also unhappy with Section 337 of the U.S. trade law which was used to penalize allegedly unfair competitive practices including patent infringement. They believed that foreign patent defendants brought before the U.S. International Trade Commission, which was not a court, received less favorable treatment than domestic defendants who had to be sued in a federal court where they could, among other things, file counterclaims.[17]

Feelings about these and other issues ran high during the negotiations, but in the end the parties agreed that it was not necessary to resolve everything. As several IPC member companies explained, "The breakthrough came when we all realized that it was not our objective to harmonize intellectual property standards through the GATT negotiations. Rather, we only needed to agree on minimum standards for all GATT nations to follow. Harmonization could proceed through WIPO."

The "Basic Framework" was a unique collaboration among the United States, European, and Japanese business communities. According to John A. Young, president and chief executive officer of Hewlett-Packard Company, the "Basic Framework" was "unprecedented . . . the first time that the international business community has jointly developed a document of this magnitude and such substantive detail for presentation to our government negotiators."[18]

While the U.S. government text closely followed the coalition's position, Clemente believed that "the European governments were less willing to adopt these views. Instead, they chose to emphasize the differences between the United States and Europe. The Japanese government was even less responsive to the document. In the Japanese culture there is a much different relationship between government and business. In Japan, it is the government which decides what is best for Japan and for Japanese business." Pratt added, "We have had Japanese businessmen visit us, and ask us to describe our lobbying techniques and to explain how we are able to exert so much influence over the government."

---

16. 35 U.S.C. secs. 104, 119.
17. In 1989, a Dutch company obtained a ruling from a GATT dispute panel that Section 337 violated GATT principles of national treatment. *Financial Times*, January 30, 1989.
18. Intellectual Property Committee Press Release, June 14, 1988.

Challenges to the Coalition's Views

Shortly after her appointment in 1987 as director of International Affairs at Pfizer, Lillian Fernandez, a former Congressional staffer in Washington, was challenged to defend the coalition's views. Arthur Dunkel, the Secretary-General of GATT, was unhappy with the inclusion of intellectual property on the Uruguay Round agenda. He was particularly upset about the implications for pharmaceuticals. He spoke frequently about the importance of access to health care in developing countries, the high costs of drugs, and the sovereignty of nations to regulate cost and access to drugs. Fernandez described one memorable occasion:

> When he finished his speech, there was total silence as people at the table looked at me to respond. Three years working on Capitol Hill prepared me for dealing with sticky situations. I calmly explained to Mr. Dunkel that granting patent protection was not the same thing as eliminating price controls for drugs and that many nations in Europe had both patent protection and price controls. I also said that it was inappropriate to single out drugs for the problems of medical access in developing countries, and that it was the lack of a health care delivery system that was the problem. Finally, I asked him to consider whether stealing drugs was any more acceptable than stealing food. We certainly don't condone stealing food as a means of dealing with the hunger problem.

Changes in U.S. Trade Law

While intellectual property protection was being discussed in the GATT negotiations, Congress was strengthening the hand of U.S. negotiators. In 1984, Congress had passed important trade legislation which for the first time authorized the U.S. government—on its own and without a showing of injury by the industry—to take retaliatory action against countries failing to give adequate protection to intellectual property (Section 301). The Trade and Tariff Act of 1984 had also called on the USTR to report on the barriers to trade in countries throughout the world (Section 303), and authorized the President to consider the adequacy of intellectual property protection in deciding whether a developing country should be granted tariff preferences under the U.S. Generalized System of Preferences (Section 501).

The 1988 Omnibus Trade and Competitiveness Act pushed the USTR further toward implementing this legislation. It introduced a process for identifying offending countries and pressuring them to improve intellectual property protection. Under the provision known as "Special 301," the USTR was required each year to identify foreign states denying intellectual property protection to U.S. firms and to designate the most important as "Priority Foreign Countries."[19] Within 30 days of identifying "Priority Foreign Countries," the USTR was to begin an investigation to determine whether the foreign practices violated U.S. rights under a trade agreement or were "unreasonable" or "discriminatory."

In May 1989, the USTR declined to name any "Priority Foreign Countries" under Special 301. Instead, the USTR placed 17 countries on a "Watch List" and 8 others on a "Priority Watch List." The Priority Watch List included Brazil, India, Mexico, Peoples Republic of China,

---

19. 19 U.S.C §2242, *et seq.*

Republic of Korea, Saudi Arabia, Taiwan, and Thailand.[20] In November 1989, citing progress made in these countries, the USTR moved Saudi Arabia, Korea, and Taiwan from the Priority Watch List to the Watch List. Mexico was removed from both lists in January 1990 in recognition of its announced plan to strengthen patents.

In April 1991, because of inadequate protection of pharmaceutical patents, the USTR for the first time named three nations—India, China, and Thailand—as "Priority Foreign Countries" under Special 301. According to U.S. figures, all three countries had significant trade surpluses with the United States in 1990. India's annual trade surplus was some $700 million; Thailand's $2.7 billion; and China's $11 billion. Three trading partners—the European Community, Brazil, and Australia—were placed on the Priority Watch List" and 23 others were placed on the "Watch List."

The U.S. Applies Trade "Leverage"

These changes in U.S. trade law increased the leverage available to U.S. officials negotiating intellectual property standards with offending nations. Many, including Clemente, believed that pressure created by possible retaliation under section 301 of the 1984 trade legislation had led to the 1986 bilateral agreement on intellectual property between the United States and Korea.

Leverage was also brought to bear in negotiations with Mexico. When Mexican President Salinas came to Washington in June 1990 to discuss a free trade agreement, U.S. officials were well prepared. IPC members and others had lobbied hard to convince Congress and the Administration of the importance of intellectual property protection. Salinas was advised that it would be necessary for Mexico to pass an adequate intellectual property law as a prerequisite for a trade agreement.

Pfizer and the pharmaceutical industry regarded Mexico's initial proposal as inadequate: it did not include protection for drugs in the "pipeline," those already patented elsewhere but not yet marketed in Mexico. In 1991 the Pharmaceutical Manufacturers Association (PMA) said they would not enthusiastically support "fast-track" authorization for Bush to negotiate a free trade agreement with Mexico unless intellectual property protection met higher standards, including "pipeline" protection.[21]

In June 1991, Mexico passed a new patent law which Pratt described as truly world class. Under the new law, pharmaceutical companies could obtain 20 year patents on new drugs including those patented in other countries but not yet launched in Mexico. Compulsory licensing was limited to exceptional circumstances and would not be granted if the patented product, or products made from the patented process, were being imported into Mexico. A PMA official called the new law "an outstanding achievement for any country, let alone a developing country such as Mexico."[22]

---

20. The original "Watch List" included: Argentina, Canada, Chile, Colombia, Egypt, Greece, Indonesia, Italy, Japan, Malaysia, Pakistan, the Philippines, Portugal, Spain, Turkey, Venezuela, and Yugoslavia.
21. In general, under the "fast-track" procedure, the President was required to present a draft of a trade agreement he intended to sign 90 days before doing so. Congress could either accept or reject the legislation implementing the trade agreement in its entirety, without any amendments.
22. Linda Diebel, "U.S. Again Beats Drum for Cultural Free Trade," *Toronto Star*, May 25, 1991, p. D1.

The United States was less successful in applying leverage in other countries. For example, Canada's Bill C-22, passed in 1987, gave 20-year exclusive patent protection only to pharmaceuticals researched and discovered in Canada. Otherwise, compulsory licenses were readily available to generic companies willing to pay a royalty fee (typically 4%) to the patent holder. Companies intending to manufacture for export were entitled to exercise the license immediately, while those intending to manufacture for the Canadian market had to wait seven years from the date of regulatory approval. (Companies wishing to import the drug had to wait 10 years to exercise the license.) In addition, an innovator's rights could be further restricted if Canada's Patented Medicine Prices Review Board found the price of a patented drug excessive.

Unhappy with Bill C-22, the PMA, the IPC, and others vowed to press for more stringent patent protection in Canada as talks for an expanded U.S.-Mexico-Canada free trade agreement progressed in 1991. To counter concern that expanded patent protection would increase drug prices, the PMA pointed to a recent report showing that consumer drug prices did not increase as a result of Bill C-22. But debate about the impact on drug prices continued. An official of a Canadian generic drug manufacturer criticized the report for looking at average prices rather than focusing on the price of new drugs.[23]

The United States also encountered resistance in Brazil. Six months after placing Brazil on the Special 301 "Priority Watch List" in May 1989, the United States levied 100 percent tariffs on $39 million of imports from Brazil in retaliation for pirating U.S. drug patents. Rather than yield to U.S. pressure, however, Brazil in 1990 filed a GATT complaint against the United States, citing its enforcement of Special 301. The complaint was later abandoned by Brazil in the context of negotiations with the United States over the reform of Brazil's patent laws.[24]

Thailand was another country attempting to withstand U.S. trade pressure even though the United States accounted for nearly 25% of its export market. In 1990, unhappy with Thailand's progress on patent protection for pharmaceuticals, the PMA successfully urged the U.S. government to revoke Thailand's benefits under the U.S. Generalized System of Preferences, which allowed exports from many developing countries to enter the United States duty free.

Thailand's experience illustrated the conflicts facing LDC governments confronted with U.S. trade pressure. In May 1988, the eight-and-a-half-year-old Thai government was toppled by a no-confidence vote after it introduced in the National Assembly a compromise bill on patents.[25] Politicians in the Philippines faced similar political dissatisfaction when the Philippine Congress declined to pass a bill removing patent protection from drug products.[26] Mexico's new patent law also met with domestic criticism when it was passed in 1991.[27]

The LDCs' Point of View

Developing countries regarded the decision to give pharmaceuticals patent protection as a matter of national sovereignty. Accordingly, they viewed international efforts to pressure them

---

23. *Ibid.*
24. Interview with USTR official.
25. "New Thai patent legislation only meets part of PMA's request," *Financial Times*, September 1, 1989.
26. Ramon Isberto, "Philippines: Senate not likely to remove drug patents," *Inter Press Service*, Manila, May 18, 1991.
27. Henry Ricks, "Mexico shores up intellectual property control," *Reuters*, Mexico City, July 4, 1991.

into recognizing patents on pharmaceuticals as an unwarranted infringement on their right to self-determination. In both GATT and WIPO negotiations, many took the position that nations were free to exclude or limit patent protection in particular areas, such as pharmaceuticals, on grounds of public interest, public health, nutrition, national development, or social security. These nations defended their power to compel patentholders who did not manufacture their inventions within the nation's borders to license their patents to competing domestic manufacturers for reasonable royalties.

A Chinese official explained his personal views on the difficulties facing developing countries. "Intellectual property protection has everything to do with a country's level of development—its resources, science, technology, and industry. Some African countries cannot afford even an office, let alone the training in law, foreign languages, and technical fields required of patent officials." He described the background of China's patent law.

China's patent law was adopted in 1984, but a patent law in China could not have been imagined before 1979. In those days knowledge was in the public domain. It would have been wrong to grant a patent. Nowadays, the work of intellectuals is more respected and people realize that creative labor is integral to economic development. But many people still look at things the old way and believe it is all right to copy others. We must educate people to understand what a patent is and why it is important for science and industry, and we need to encourage inventive activity in our institutions and universities. Without the right attitudes, patent protection has no basis.

We also need resources to establish more patent offices and to train patent examiners and court officials. Since the implementation of the patent law in 1985, 2000 cases have been brought and 1000 cases decided in Chinese courts. One-hundred seventeen thousand patent applications have been filed in this period, but we only have 400 patent examiners in China. We also lack resources for research and development. We can't yet afford to provide an advanced level of protection. The developed countries need to be realistic. They cannot expect too much in a short time, and they should recognize the progress we have made over the past six years. We are now working on a revision of our patent law and have outlined a program for a transitional period for the next ten years or so. We have an active and positive attitude toward protecting intellectual property and will get it over time.

Pharmaceuticals are currently excluded from our patent law, along with foods, beverages, scientific discoveries, rules and methods for mental activities, methods for diagnosing and treating disease, and plant and animal varieties. We didn't include pharmaceuticals because we were concerned that prices would be too high. We weren't really sure what would happen. We have studied countries like Japan, Italy, and India to see the effects of protecting pharmaceuticals. We want to see more experiences of countries. In the long run, the fields of intellectual property protection will get broader and broader, but we must do it gradually in a country like China. If we set a task that is impossible to achieve, we can't get anywhere. This is realistic.

Gradualism was also the watchword among Latin American pharmaceutical manufacturers, too. An official of the Latin American Association of Pharmaceutical Industries (ALIFAR), predicted that product protection for pharmaceuticals would be a reality in five to ten years. "In the meantime," she explained, "protection is not possible because of poor economic conditions in Latin America. It is impossible for us to invest in research because we have no resources, and it is very important for public administrators to buy medicine for the social security system at affordable prices."

Nevertheless, she thought U.S. pressure would force changes in the law. "We accept that there will be changes, but the issue is how. We want to be able to obtain licenses. We want to limit the absolute right of intellectual property. For example, we think the patent law of Canada is a good system. There, people can obtain an automatic license for pharmaceuticals and pay royalties."

Argentina, the headquarters of ALIFAR, was itself waging a difficult battle to sustain local production of drugs. In 1989, Argentine manufacturers controlled 54 percent of a $1.5 billion market. According to a researcher with the Economic Commission for Latin America and the Caribbean, it was the only Latin American nation where more than 15% of the pharmaceutical market was controlled by domestic producers financed with local capital.[28] Despite such a significant pharmaceutical manufacturing segment, Argentina still had a $250 million deficit in international trade in pharmaceuticals.

Under Argentine law, patents were recognized only on processes, not on final products. Local manufacturers thus competed with multinational drug manufacturers by developing alternative processes for manufacturing drugs produced under process patents. In early 1989, the Argentine government signed an agreement with the local pharmaceutical companies to encourage the growth of the pharmaceutical sector. Domestic drug manufacturers agreed to contribute three percent from sales revenues to a "medical assistance fund" to benefit the medical needs of the seven million Argentines thought to be living in conditions of extreme poverty. And in November 1990, facing increased pressure from the United States to change its patent law, Argentine drug manufacturers went on the offensive by taking out a full-page advertisement in the *New York Times*. They argued that Argentina's patent policy was a necessary short-term solution to make drugs affordable to Argentines living in and near poverty. See **Exhibit 7**. Other voices within Argentina questioned this view and favored a development strategy oriented to international trade with recognition of intellectual property in all areas of economic activity.[29]

India, another opponent of stronger intellectual property protection, had recently assessed the 1970 revisions of its previously strict and comprehensive patent law. The revisions had aimed to encourage domestic production and reasonable prices. The new law granted patent protection to processes only—and not to pharmaceutical products—for a period of five years. Moreover, it allowed the Indian government, three years after a patent was granted, to require a patentholder to license its patent to another company if the patentholder was not manufacturing the product in India and selling it at a reasonable price. A report of the Indian National Working Group on Patent Laws concluded that as a result of the 1970 law, Indian drug prices went from among the

---

28. Gustavo Capdevila, "Argentina: Defies U.S. Over Local Pharmaceutical Protection," *Inter Press Service*, Buenos Aires, March 30, 1989.

29. Fundacion de Investigaciones Economicas Latino Americanas (FIEL), "Protection of Intellectual Property Rights, The Case of the Pharmaceutical Industry in Argentina," Buenos Aires, 1990.

highest in the world to among the lowest in 1991, and that the Indian pharmaceutical industry had benefitted to the point where India was nearly self-sufficient in the manufacture of bulk pharmaceuticals.[30] The *Calcutta Business Standard*, however, reported that "The Indian Patents Act has retarded the development of new drugs in India" and that "the number of applications for patents in general and for pharmaceuticals, food and agrochemicals in particular, is falling year after year."[31]

Pfizer, too, had undertaken to improve health care in the LDCs. In Gambia, Pfizer participated in a program to improve the distribution of pharmaceuticals. Beginning in the mid-1970s, Pfizer worked closely with Brazilian officials to launch a major demonstration project to combat schistosomiasis, a parasitic disease prevalent in Brazil. The firm also prepared multimedia materials to distribute throughout Asia and Latin America to highlight the role sanitation and drugs play in the control of hookworm and roundworm infestations. In addition, Pfizer, in a program sponsored by the World Health Organization (WHO), trained scientists from LDCs in chemical and microbiological control.

The IPC Responds

Acting on behalf of the pharmaceutical companies located within their borders, the governments of the developed nations pressured the LDCs to strengthen their patent protection laws. For example, in 1989, Carla Hills, the USTR, supported linking U.S. help with Brazil's $120 billion debt to Brazil's cooperation on patent protection. She commented: "I think it is fundamentally wrong for Brazil not to protect intellectual property. And it hurts their national interest because investors all around the world will not want to go into Brazil if they believe their intellectual property—their rights in software, books, recordings, patents—are stolen."[32]

The IPC also attempted to convince developing nations to institute patent protection. Such protection, the IPC argued, would encourage pharmaceutical companies to develop new products for their markets, spur the development of local innovation and industry, and encourage multinational corporations to locate manufacturing facilities within their borders. A report commissioned by Pfizer and the PMA concluded that "there is a causal linkage between economic modernization and the presence of efficient property rights, including intellectual property rights."[33] The report recommended that "protecting intellectual property should be a public policy goal of developing countries seeking sustained economic growth."

As for the effect on consumer prices, industry argued that competition among patented products would insure a measure of control. In any event, since 90% of the 250 items on the World Health Organization's Essential Drugs list were off patent, recognition of patents on new products would have little effect on the price of most drugs used in developing countries. Industry also pointed to Eastern European countries such as Poland and Czechoslovakia where the first steps toward privatization and the creation of conditions favorable to democratic capitalism had included good patent laws for pharmaceuticals.

---

30. Robert Weissman, "Prelude to a new colonialism," *The Nation*, March 18, 1991, p. 336.
31. Suresh Thakur Desai, "India Patents Act-II: Acting as a Bar to Innovation," *Calcutta Business Standard*, November 22, 1990.
32. Terry Atlas, "Hills backs using Brazil debt in bargaining on patents," *Chicago Tribune*, April 12, 1989, p. B3.
33. Richard T. Rapp and Richard T. Rozek, "Benefits and Costs of Intellectual Property Protection in Developing Countries," Working Paper #3, National Economic Research Associates, Inc., June 1990.

Developing country officials, however, were not entirely persuaded. The ALIFAR official, for example, commented, "It is not enough to protect intellectual property in general, there must be better economic conditions in order to induce foreign companies to invest. Their main objective is to export goods to improve the balance of trade." She doubted that intellectual property protection would help the local pharmaceutical industry. "With protection, it will be very difficult for Latin American producers to compete because they will be unable to get licenses. It is not in the interests of foreign companies to give licenses."

Other advocates for the LDCs' position remained concerned about issues of national sovereignty. They argued that it should be their decision whether or not to give broad patent protection, not a mandate forced upon them as a condition of participation in the world trade markets. They pointed out that the United States, in the early stages of its development, had not honored copyrights granted by other nations and that some other industrialized nations like Japan had only fairly recently recognized product patents on pharmaceuticals.[34]

Pratt saw the issue less in terms of sovereignty and more in terms of reciprocity: not "an eye for an eye," but "an eye for a tooth," as he explained. The fact remained that the United States was a very important market for developing countries. In return for access to that market, Pratt thought developing countries should be expected to respect U.S. companies' intellectual property. Pratt believed the U.S. government should assert its own sovereignty by limiting or denying access to U.S. markets to countries that inadequately protected intellectual property.

Brussels: December 1990

When the coalition's "Basic Framework" was released in June 1988, Pratt and others at Pfizer had high hopes for a strong TRIPS agreement. But by late 1990, the prospects had dimmed. At the ministerial meeting in Brussels in the winter of 1990 it became apparent that the Europeans were unwilling to negotiate hard for an acceptable TRIPS accord. The document that emerged from the meeting was not what the IPC or Pfizer had hoped for.

IPC members had various explanations for the European attitudes. Some noted the Europeans' protective tendencies toward former colonies and their reluctance to use bilateral instruments like U.S. 301. Indeed, Europeans generally preferred multilateral approaches and were critical of the United States' use of 301 as they had been critical of the U.S.-Korea agreement of 1986 which had provided preferential treatment for the United States. Other IPC members noted the Europeans' desire to "play the middle" between the United States and the Third World and to appear more reasonable than the United States. The fact that EC members, Spain, Portugal, and Greece, did not yet have adequate protection made the issue somewhat awkward for EC officials.

Moreover, European government officials seemed much less responsive than their American counterparts to the needs of business. As Pratt pointed out, ". . . the U.S. government's Advisory Committee on Trade [and Policy] Negotiations . . . has no European

---

34. Rajan Dhanjee and Lawrence Boisson de Chazournes, "Trade Related Aspects of Intellectual Property Rights (TRIPS): Objectives, Approaches and Basic Principles of the GATT and of Intellectual Property Conventions," *Journal of World Trade*, October 1990, p. 5.

counterpart."[35] In addition, European patent lawyers were loathe to see their technical specialty turned into a political issue handled at the senior executive level.

Recognizing the paramount importance the Europeans (particularly the French) placed on achieving an acceptable agriculture agreement in the Uruguay Round, some feared the European negotiators might be willing to bargain away TRIPS in exchange for a watered-down agriculture agreement. Coincidentally, many of the nations accused of having weak intellectual property protection, Argentina, *e.g.*, were in the best position to profit from a reduction of agricultural subsidies in the European Community.

Brussels was also the occasion of unnecessary misunderstanding between the industry coalition and their various governments. For example, industry and the negotiators disagreed about including the "moral rights" of authors in the negotiations. In many jurisdictions, the author of a literary work had an explicit and legally inalienable "moral right" to control the interpretation of that work. Industry wanted to avoid the issue and to steer clear of any linkage to WIPO and the Berne Convention and to focus, instead, on minimum standards. The negotiators, on the other hand, accepted the idea that the Berne Convention established the starting point for negotiations. In the end, an acceptable compromise appears to have been worked out. But industry representatives from both sides of the Atlantic felt the dispute had been an unnecessary excursion into a wholly "philosophical debate."

Pfizer and the IPC were concerned about several issues that had emerged as topics of heated debate. The question of how much "pipeline" protection would be adequate had yet to be resolved. In addition, the Brussels draft had contained a provision on "international exhaustion" of patent rights favored by the LDC's. The tripartite coalition was opposed to the concept of international exhaustion which would have meant that once a patent-holder or licensee put products on the market in a given country, the patent-holder could exercise no further control over the flow of those goods anywhere in the world. Thus, drugs sold with the consent of the patent-holder in a country with low drug prices (because of price controls, for example) could be bought and shipped to markets with higher prices where they might compete directly with the patent-holder's higher priced products.

After the worrisome experience of Brussels in December 1990, the IPC determined to lobby the European and Japanese negotiators directly, making it clear that the IPC would oppose Congressional ratification of a weak TRIPs agreement. Others suggested that stronger messages be sent to the Europeans, including letting it be known that the IPC was considering supporting bilateral negotiations on the model of the earlier negotiation with Korea. As one of the IPC members suggested, "we need to make the Europeans understand that they are not the only game in town."

European governments and European industry were not in perfect accord on the terms of an acceptable TRIPS agreement. As one UNICE official explained, "European governments want to get as many LDCs as possible committed to the GATT system. They would rather have a general GATT instrument on intellectual property than a Code among fewer countries. And they are willing to trade off certain property rights in order to achieve this. Originally, industry planned to work first for a Code, and then seek full integration of intellectual property principles

---

35. Edmund T. Pratt, Jr., "European Business Must Speak Up for GATT Progress," *Wall Street Journal* (Eur. ed.), January 8, 1991.

into the GATT system. But the governments do not want this." Unlike the amendment of GATT, the adoption of a "Code" did not require the unanimous consent of the GATT contracting parties. However, a "Code" essentially functioned as a separate agreement which bound only those nations that ratified it. Still, the IPC thought a code would allow for meaningful agreement without going for the lowest common denominator.

A UNICE official believed that European Commission officials, in contrast to European national government officials, were strong supporters of European industry's position. In his view, cooperation between United States industry and government had been rather close, though he was not convinced that the United States government had followed industry's recommendations in the end. The Japanese government, he thought, had done what its industry wanted. He nevertheless commented on the high level of American business involvement in public policy making. "American business people and companies are much more active in public affairs at home and abroad than European companies."

Even as the IPC was debating strategies for bringing the Europeans back in line, Clemente was beginning to feel uneasy about the projected course of events. In Clemente's view and that of other IPC members, a bad TRIPS agreement was worse than no TRIPS agreement. "Enshrining a bad TRIPS into a treaty would only make it harder to pursue better terms in bilateral and trilateral negotiations, such as the upcoming free trade discussions with Mexico and Canada." Clemente urged that the IPC use its resources to explore other avenues and identify other pressure points. He also suggested it might be time to increase bilateral pressures such as those created through Special 301. One IPC member suggested the United States should defer forgiveness of loans to Latin American countries until they agreed to adequate intellectual property protection.

Fernandez was more optimistic about the possibility of obtaining an acceptable TRIPS agreement. "At the end of the day," said Fernandez, "the negotiators know that they will have to come to Congress for approval of the agreement. Without a strong TRIPS provision, there will be strong opposition in Congress."

Conclusion

Pfizer and other members of the IPC had managed to exert great influence over the international trade agenda during the 1980s and into the 1990s. Pratt's exceptional level of involvement in public policy making had earned him a very favorable reputation among American trade officials. A UNICE official remarked that the tripartite cooperation among Japanese, European, and United States industry was unique in his memory. "This was the first time that industry from the three areas worked so closely together for a common objective."

But as the negotiations for the Uruguay Round were coming to a close, it was not clear what the outcome would be. The GATT working group on intellectual property had yet to resolve any of the issues being debated. There was no consensus on dispute resolution, subject matter exclusions, minimum patent term, compulsory licensing, transitional periods, or any of the other issues that divided the LDCs and the industrialized countries.

The "Basic Framework" had not addressed a number of issues that had emerged as important to various parties, issues such as "pipeline" protection important to the pharmaceutical industry; protection for "appellations of origin" important to European wine producers; and "international exhaustion" of intellectual property rights sought by the LDCs. Some agencies of the U.S. government, particularly the Department of Defense, NASA, and the Department of Health and Human Services, wanted the TRIPS agreement to include a broad "government use" provision giving the government a right to use patented inventions. Industry, on the other hand, was concerned that broad language would be interpreted inappropriately in developing countries.

It was unclear whether the United States would achieve its objectives in the negotiations. Speaking before Congress in 1991 U.S. Trade Representative (USTR) Carla Hills described the U.S. position on TRIPS.

> Our four basic objectives in these negotiations are to obtain adequate standards of protection that each signatory country must embody in its law in patents, copyrights, trademarks, trade secrets and semiconductor layout design; secondly, effective enforcement provisions that specify how rights holders should be able to enforce their rights internally and at the border; thirdly, a GATT dispute settlement mechanism for intellectual property disputes arising under the agreement; and finally, the right under international law to apply trade sanctions when another country fails to live up to its obligation under the agreement.[36]

Pratt acknowledged the possibility that the best that could be hoped for was a strong "Code" among some GATT members that would gradually come to include all the contracting parties of GATT. He summarized his feelings about the multilateral approach in GATT:

> It was very ambitious of us to imagine that we could achieve an acceptable TRIPS agreement in GATT. When GATT was formed just after World War II, there were only 23 nations involved. Now there are 96, all of whom must agree to any new proposal. Naturally, this is going to make it very difficult to agree on any strong TRIPS provisions. But working through GATT has allowed us to make tremendous progress. We have put intellectual property protection on the world agenda. We have clarified what a good patent agreement must contain. We have used the momentum of GATT to help forge bilateral intellectual property agreements with the Koreans, the Chinese, the Russians, and with Eastern Europe. Perhaps most important, we have shown how international business can initiate and help shape public policy . . . and that in our interdependent world industry in the United States, Japan and Europe can overcome their differences to mold a unified public policy response.

In the midst of this uncertainty, Pratt, Clemente, and Fernandez were considering what sort of TRIPS agreement Pfizer would be willing to support. The IPC was assessing how to improve the prospects for an acceptable TRIPS agreement as well as alternative approaches to securing intellectual property protection around the world.

---

36. Testimony of Carla Hills, United States Trade Representative, Hearing of the Intellectual Property and Judicial Administration Subcommittee of the House Judicial Committee, May 15, 1991 ("Hills Testimony").

Exhibit 1 Financial Summary, Pfizer, Inc. and Subsidiary Companies (millions of dollars, except per-share data)

	1990	1989	1988	1987	1986	1985	1984	1983	1982	1981	1980
Net sales	$6,406.0	$5,671.5	$5,385.4	$4,919.8	$4,476.0	$4,024.5	$3,875.9	$3,764.7	$3,496.0	$3,280.9	$3,054.3
Operating costs and expenses:											
Cost of goods sold	2,259.4	2,062.3	2,020.1	1,986.9	1,720.4	1,545.7	1,528.4	1,548.4	1,554.3	1,567.8	1,463.7
Marketing, distribution, and administrative expenses	2,452.7	2,109.8	1,880.9	1,681.1	1,465.3	1,313.2	1,252.6	1,227.0	1,132.7	1,019.6	941.6
Research and development expenses	640.1	531.2	472.5	401.0	335.5	286.7	254.8	229.5	199.4	178.6	161.6
Income from operations	1,053.8	968.2	1,011.9	940.8	954.8	878.9	840.1	760.0	609.6	514.9	487.4
Interest income (expense)—net	61.2	78.8	99.4	60.1	47.1	30.7	2.2	(16.0)	(33.0)	(62.6)	(53.5)
Other income (deductions)—net	(11.7)	(130.5)	(7.5)	9.9	(37.0)	(28.2)	(28.4)	(41.4)	(26.3)	(10.0)	(22.4)
Nonoperating income (deductions)—net	49.5	(51.7)	91.9	70.0	10.1	2.5	(26.2)	(57.4)	(59.3)	(72.6)	(75.9)
Income from continuing operations before provision for taxes on income and minority interest	1,103.3	916.5	1,103.8	1,010.8	964.9	881.4	813.9	702.6	550.3	442.3	411.5
Provision for taxes on income	297.9	231.3	309.4	317.3	300.7	296.4	296.2	248.4	208.6	160.1	149.5
Income from continuing operations before minority interests	805.4	685.2	794.4	693.5	664.2	585.0	517.7	454.2	341.7	282.2	262.0
Minority interests	4.2	4.1	3.1	3.3	4.2	5.3	6.3	5.8	5.4	5.7	7.1
Income from continuing operations	801.2	681.1	791.3	690.2	660.0	579.7	511.4	448.4	336.3	276.5	254.9
Loss from discontinued operations—net of taxes	--	--	--	--	--	--	--	--	--	(52.4)	--
Net income	$ 801.2	$ 681.1	$ 791.3	$ 690.2	$ 660.0	$ 579.7	$ 511.4	$ 448.4	$ 336.3	$ 224.1	$ 254.9
Effective tax rate	27.0%	25.2%	28.0%	31.4%	31.2%	33.6%	36.4%	35.4%	37.9%	36.2%	36.3%
Depreciation	$ 199.9	$ 184.3	$ 176.8	$ 162.0	$ 147.1	$ 129.5	$ 127.3	$ 114.9	$ 110.2	$ 96.9	$ 87.2
Capital additions	547.5	456.5	343.7	258.3	196.1	195.8	182.7	241.8	271.7	290.9	163.9
Cash dividends paid	396.7	364.0	330.1	296.8	269.7	241.2	211.2	183.7	139.8	118.5	105.7
As of December 31:											
Working capital	$1,319.0	$1,593.2	$1,750.5	$2,144.1	$1,728.8	$1,708.7	$1,363.9	$1,217.3	$1,117.8	$1,147.9	$1,089.3
Property, plant, and equipment—net of accumulated depreciation	2,109.8	1,784.1	1,655.1	1,505.9	1,351.5	1,268.5	1,161.7	1,163.3	1,138.5	1,006.7	830.4
Total assets	9,052.0	8,324.8	7,593.2	6,872.3	5,178.5	4,458.7	4,035.7	3,915.8	3,748.0	3,643.1	3,358.6
Long-term debt	193.3	190.6	226.9	248.9	285.4	323.5	341.7	487.4	520.5	691.5	584.9
Long-term capital[a]	5,665.8	5,062.1	4,865.9	4,471.2	3,926.1	3,453.4	2,939.6	2,781.3	2,635.8	2,505.6	2,243.2
Shareholders' equity	5,092.0	4,535.8	4,301.1	3,882.4	3,415.2	2,927.3	2,495.5	2,188.2	1,996.6	1,716.3	1,579.5
Common Share Data											
Earnings per common share:											
Continuing operations	$ 4.77	$ 4.04	$ 4.70	$ 4.08	$ 3.90	$ 3.44	$ 3.06	$ 2.70	$ 2.11	$ 1.79	$ 1.70
Discontinued operations	--	--	--	--	--	--	--	--	--	(.33)	--
Net	4.77	4.04	4.70	4.08	3.90	3.44	3.06	2.70	2.11	1.46	1.70
Cash dividends paid per common share	2.40	2.20	2.00	1.80	1.64	1.48	1.32	1.16	.92	.80	.72
Shareholders' equity per common share	30.84	27.44	26.00	23.60	20.70	17.87	15.30	13.52	12.70	11.21	10.52
Weighted average number of common and common share equivalents outstanding used to compute earnings per common share (thousands)	168,576	169,696	169,424	170,563	170,796	170,556	169,644	168,555	162,973	157,700	149,223
Number of employees (thousands)	42.5	42.1	40.9	40.7	40.0	39.2	39.2	40.9	40.6	42.0	41.6
Net sales per employee (thousands of dollars)	151	135	132	121	112	103	99	92	86	78	73

Source: Pfizer Inc. Annual Report, 1990

[a]Defined as long-term debt, deferred taxes on income, minority interests, and shareholders' equity

Exhibit 2   Status of Patent Protection in OECD and Latin American Nations

| | OECD | | | Latin America | |
Nation	Process Patent (year of adoption if relatively recent)	Product Patent (year of adoption if relatively recent)	Nation	Process Patent	Product Patent
Australia	Yes	Yes	Argentina	Yes	No
Austria	Yes	Yes (1987)	Bolivia	Yes	No
Belgium	Yes	Yes	Brazil	No	No
Canada	Yes	Yes (1983)	Chile	Yes	Yes
Denmark	Yes	Yes (1983)	Columbia	Yes	No
England	Yes	Yes (1949)	Costa Rica	Yes	No
Finland	Yes	(1995)	Cuba	Yes	No
France	Yes	Yes (1960)	Dominican Republic	Yes	Yes
Germany	Yes	Yes (1968)	Ecuador	Yes	No
Greece	Yes	(1992)	El Salvador	Yes	Yes
Holland	Yes	Yes (1978)	Guatemala	Yes	No
Iceland	Yes	No	Honduras	Yes	No
Ireland	Yes	Yes	Jamaica	Yes	Yes
Italy	Yes (1978)	Yes	Mexico	Yes	Yes
Japan	Yes (1965)	Yes (1976)	Nicaragua	Yes	No
Norway	Yes	(1992)	Panama	Yes	Yes
Portugal	Yes	(1992)	Paraguay	Yes	No
Spain	Yes	(1992)	Trinidad and Tobago	Yes	Yes
Sweden	Yes	Yes (1978)	Uruguay	Yes	No
Switzerland	Yes	Yes (1977)	Venezuela	Yes	No
Turkey	No	No			
United States	Yes	Yes			

Source: ALIFAR 1991

Exhibit 3   Members of the Paris Convention

Algeria, Argentina, Australia, Austria, Bahamas, Bangladesh, Barbados, Belgium, Benin, Brazil, Bulgaria, Burkina Faso, Burundi, Cameroon, Canada, Central African Republic, Chad, China, Congo, Côte d'Ivoire, Cuba, Cyprus, Czechoslovakia, Democratic People's Republic of Korea, Denmark, Dominican Republic, Egypt, Finland, France, Gabon, Germany, Ghana, Greece, Guinea, Guinea-Bissau, Haiti, Holy See, Hungary, Iceland, Indonesia, Iran (Islamic Republic of), Iraq, Ireland, Israel, Italy, Japan, Jordan, Kenya, Lebanon, Lesotho, Libya, Liechtenstein, Luxembourg, Madagascar, Malawi, Malaysia, Mali, Malta, Mauritania, Mauritius, Mexico, Monaco, Mongolia, Morocco, Netherlands, New Zealand, Niger, Nigeria, Norway, Philippines, Poland, Portugal, Republic of Korea, Romania, Rwanda, San Marino, Senegal, South Africa, Soviet Union, Spain, Sri Lanka, Sudan, Suriname, Swaziland, Sweden, Switzerland, Syria, Togo, Trinidad and Tobago, Tunisia, Turkey, Uganda, United Kingdom, United Republic of Tanzania, United States of America, Uruguay, Vietnam, Yugoslavia, Zaire, Zambia, Zimbabwe.

Source: WIPO 1990

Exhibit 4   "Stealing From The Mind," *The New York Times*, Friday, July 9, 1982

In recent days many people have been shocked that Japanese businessmen might have stolen computer secrets from I.B.M. The allegations are the latest twist in the tense worldwide struggle for technological supremacy, but few businessmen, especially those involved in high-technology, research-based industries, can be very surprised.

Their inventions have been "legally" taken in country after country by governments' violation of intellectual-property rights, especially patents. It has been going on for some time, and it is getting worse. Through political and legal dealings, many governments, including Brazil, Canada, Mexico, India, Taiwan, South Korea, Italy, and Spain, to name a few, have provided their domestic companies with ways to make and sell products that under proper enforcement and honorable treatment of patents would be considered the property of the inventors. And now the United Nations, through its World Intellectual Property Organization, is trying to grab high-technology inventions for underdeveloped countries.

As more and more countries yearn for industrialization, it is ironic that less and less respect is given those laws and principles that have attended industrialization in the last hundred years. This is nowhere more true than in the area of patent protection for high technology, where learning how to manufacture a product requires enormous resources but actually manufacturing it turns out to be quite simple. It is in acquiring the knowledge to make new products—computers, pharmaceuticals, telecommunications equipment, chemicals and others—that American companies have been so good. And it is this knowledge that is being stolen by the denial of patent rights.

For example, India has denied Pfizer the right to exercise its own patent covering doxycycline, an antibiotic used widely around the world. It reserves to Indian companies the right to manufacture and sell that drug, even though the result has been that far less of it is available in India than is needed. Another illustration is Canada's compulsory licensing law, which has obliged Smith, Kline & French to grant patent rights on its antiulcer drug, Tagamet, to a local company that invested nothing in its research and development. The royalty in such a transaction is a meager 4 percent.

Patents are a vital stimulus to technological innovation and a vital part of doing business. In 1883, Western nations met in Paris to write a treaty that firmly conferred international legitimacy on intellectual-property rights— patents and trademarks—and asserted their critical relations to technological innovation. The thought then, which is still valid, was that the enormous human and financial costs attending technological innovation are worth the risks only if the invention is protected from duplication for a period of years in which the inventor can reasonably hope to recoup his costs. Under this arrangement, the inventor is then free to disseminate the technology.

Many developing countries, and some that are clearly developed, do not respect this arrangement. In many cases, however, their laws give the impression that they do, thereby encouraging inventors to place their products on the market. Once a product is on the market, the information issued with a patent makes it easy to steal the technology unless its protection is enforced.

The irony is that by eroding patent protection, governments are likely to accomplish the opposite of their professed intentions. They may appear to benefit from the inventions they take, but these gains are made at the expense of the system that nourishes industrial creativity.

What's more, the revisions to the Paris treaty being considered by delegates to the United Nations organization would confer international legitimacy on the abrogation of patents. The principle the World Intellectual Property Organization seeks to introduce would enable a nation to deny the inventor the protection of a patent or, worse still, prevent him from exercising his own invention if the product is not made from scratch in that nation.

So far, the United States has opposed such a theft of American technology. Unfortunately, European nations have failed to insist on the respect of these principles of international law and of the international economic system. Canada, Australia and New Zealand have gone even further and argue that for these purposes their nations should be considered developing countries! The competition for world markets and international business is becoming ever more tense, and that is the very reason the United States should insist more than ever that the principle underlying the international economic system be respected and upheld.

Barry MacTaggart is chairman and president of Pfizer International Inc.

© 1982 by The New York Times Company. Reprinted by permission.

Exhibit 5

Contracting Parties to the GATT (96)

Antigua and Barbuda	Ghana	Niger
Argentina	Greece	Nigeria
Australia	Guyana	Norway
Austria	Haiti	Pakistan
Bangladesh	Hong Kong	Peru
Barbados	Hungary	Philippines
Belgium	Iceland	Poland
Belize	India	Portugal
Benin	Indonesia	Romania
Botswana	Ireland	Rwanda
Brazil	Israel	Senegal
Burkina Faso	Italy	Sierra Leone
Burundi	Jamaica	Singapore
Cameroon	Japan	South Africa
Canada	Kenya	Spain
Central African Republic	Korea, Republic of	Sri Lanka
Chad	Kuwait	Suriname
Chile	Lesotho	Sweden
Colombia	Luxembourg	Switzerland
Congo	Madagascar	Tanzania
Côte d'Ivoire	Malawi	Thailand
Cuba	Malaysia	Togo
Cyprus	Maldives	Trinidad and Tobago
Czechoslovakia	Malta	Turkey
Denmark	Mauritania	Uganda
Dominican Republic	Mauritius	United Kingdom
Egypt	Mexico	United States of America
Finland	Morocco	Uruguay
France	Mayanmar	Yugoslavia
Gabon	Netherlands	Zaire
Gambia	New Zealand	Zambia
Germany, Federal Republic	Nicaragua	Zimbabwe

Acceded provisionally

Countries to whose territories the GATT has been applied and which now, as independent states, maintain a de facto application of the GATT pending final decisions as to their future commercial policy (28).

Algeria	Guinea-Bissau	St. Vincent and the Grenadines
Angola	Kampuchea	São Tomé and Principe
Bahamas	Kinbati	Seychelles
Bahrain	Mali	Solomon Islands
Brunei Darussalam	Mozambique	Swaziland
Cape Verde	Papua New Guinea	Tonga
Dominica	Qatar	Yuvalu
Equatorial Guinea	St. Christopher and Nevis	United Arab Emirates
Fiji	St. Lucia	Yemen, Democratic
Grenada		

Source: Gatt Director-General

Exhibit 6   The Basic Framework's Fundamental Principles of Patent Protection

Rights Resulting From A Patent

1. A patent shall provide the right to exclude others from the manufacture, use or sale of the patented invention and, in the case of a patented process, the ability to exclude others from the use or sale of the direct product thereof, during the patent term.

Patentability

2. A patent shall be granted for any new, industrially applicable and unobvious devices, products and processes without discrimination as to subject matter, conditions for application, grant or maintenance in force of a patent.

The Patent Term

3. The term of a patent generally shall be 20 years from filing.

Working and Compulsory Licensing

4. A patent shall not be revoked because of nonworking.

5. Compulsory licenses because of nonworking shall be granted only to permit local manufacture. Where justified legal, technical or commercial reasons make it impractical to carry out the invention locally, importation authorized by the patentee which meets local needs shall be deemed to satisfy the requirements for working.

6. Neither exclusive nor sole compulsory licenses shall be granted.

7. Compulsory licensing provisions shall not discriminate against particular classes of subject matter.

8. If a compulsory license is granted, the patentee shall be fully compensated.

9. If a compulsory license is granted, the compulsory licensee is entitled only to immunity from suit under the patent.

Voluntary Licensing

10. Voluntary licensing shall not be discouraged by governments by imposing on the parties to license agreements, terms or conditions which are unreasonable or discriminatory.

Patent Enforcement

11. Nondiscriminatory and equitable civil procedures and remedies shall be available for effective patent enforcement. Remedies shall include preliminary and final injunctions as well as monetary awards adequate to compensate patentees fully and serve as an effective infringement deterrent.

12. Fair, reasonable and effective court procedures shall be available for ascertaining the facts of infringement.

Transition Rules

13. Transition rules shall be developed in connection with these fundamental principles.

Source: "Basic Framework of GATT Provisions on Intellectual Property," Intellectual Property Committee, Keidanren, and UNICE (June 1988), pp. 32-33.

Exhibit 7

Should Multinational Pharmaceutical Manufacturers Be Permitted to Monopolize Production and Sales of Life-Saving Drugs in Poor Countries?

The suggested retail price of a leading brand anti-ulcer drug in the United States is $55.15.[a] The same branded drug in Argentina costs $19.63. A popular anti-arthritis drug sells in the U.S. at a suggested retail price of $169.84.[a] In Argentina, the same branded drug sells for only $35.08. These are only two examples among literally hundreds where the price of pharmaceuticals in the U.S. is dramatically higher than in Argentina.

The reason for the price difference is competition. In Argentina, where the per capita income is only $2,300 (versus $16,497 in the U.S.), this competition has kept prices within reach of average Argentine citizens, and within reach of an overburdened and virtually bankrupt Argentine healthcare system for the aged and poor.

The competition comes from Argentine drug manufacturers who have long produced, under Argentine law, drugs to meet local needs at prices local people can afford. The drugs are identical to those produced by multinational drug manufacturers.

Today, the U.S. Pharmaceutical Manufacturers Association (PMA), representing many major multinational drug producers, is lobbying for swift introduction of restrictive patents. If they succeed at GATT, or succeed by exerting pressure in bi-lateral negotiations, the PMA's multinational companies will have an effective monopoly on pharmaceutical production and sales in Argentina. Drug prices will skyrocket. The strains on the healthcare system will be even more acute—similar action in other countries has bankrupted healthcare systems. People who need the drugs won't be able to afford them, and Argentine unemployment will increase.

Our position is this.

The multinational drug manufacturers are entitled to receive some recognition for the products they invent. However, they should not be permitted to monopolize health markets through the use of restrictive patents. Nor should they be allowed to kill Argentina's infant pharmaceutical industry.

The Government of Argentina has agreed with the U.S. Government that a draft bill will be introduced in Argentina's Congress before September 1991. The bill will address the question of intellectual property rights on pharmaceuticals. This is a significant and positive move towards bringing Argentina into line with the international trading community. But Argentina, like many other countries which have attempted to introduce similar major changes, needs time to make a transition.

The PMA should not be allowed to monopolize pharmaceutical manufacturing and distribution in Argentina. Our country and people cannot afford it.

We are being reasonable. We expect the PMA to do the same.

C.I.L.F.A.

[a]Source: *Physician's Desk Reference*

Centro Industrial de Laboratorios Farmaceuticos Argentinos

Esmeralda 130-5° plso, 1035 - Buenos Aires, Republica Argentina

---

Being There:
Sony Corporation and Columbia Pictures

"America is to entertainment what South Africa is to gold and Saudi Arabia is to oil."

— The Economist, 1989

On September 24, 1989, Sony Corporation, the Japanese electronics giant, bid $3.4 billion in cash for Columbia Pictures Entertainment Inc. It was the highest bid ever by a Japanese company for any U.S. property. Three days later, Columbia approved the deal, and Coca-Cola Co., which owned 49% of the studio, sold its shares to Sony. (After the 1987 film *Ishtar* released by Columbia had lost $25 million, Coke lost its zest for the movie business.) In addition to the cash price, the Japanese electronics giant assumed nearly $2 billion in debt and contractual obligations. In return, Sony gained access to Columbia's library of over 2,700 movies and 23,000 television episodes, including more than 260 series.

On both sides of the Pacific, the deal attracted a great deal of attention, not only for the amount of money concerned but also for the precedents being set. In acquiring Columbia, Sony was diversifying far from its core electronics business. It was also establishing itself as a major multinational player, one of a small number of firms who controlled technologies at all ends of the rapidly expanding markets for information and entertainment services. Most dramatically, though, with Columbia Pictures Sony had bought more than a large U.S. corporation. It had purchased a chunk of American culture, and possibly even of American influence.

Sony Corporation

The Sony Corporation was founded as the Tokyo Tsushin Kogyo (Tokyo Telecommunications Engineering Corporation) in 1946 by Akio Morita and Masaru Ibuka to invent and develop new consumer products for Japan's post war economy. With just $500 in borrowed capital, the company set up shop in a burned-out room and turned out their first

Research Associate Julia Kou prepared this case under the supervision of Professor Debora Spar as the basis for class discussion rather than to illustrate either effective or ineffective handling of an administrative situation.

commercial product—a rice cooker. The cookers barely broke even, but within a few years, the fledgling company had begun to prosper from new electronic products, particularly a tape recorder that Ibuka had modeled after an American model and marketed by translating into Japanese a U.S. military pamphlet entitled *Nine Hundred and Ninety-Nine Uses of the Tape Recorder*.[1] The company's real break-through, though, occurred after 1953 when Ibuka acquired a patent license for transistors, tiny capacitors developed by Bell Laboratories that could be used in place of clumsier vacuum tubes. Morita and Ibuka began mass production of transistor radios in 1954, and dubbed their new product Sony, after *sonus*, the Latin word for sound. Soon thereafter, the pair renamed their company Sony.

From its inception, Sony stood apart from more established rivals such as Matsushita, Toshiba, and Hitachi. Sony was a young company by Japanese standards, and was never part of the sprawling *keiretsu* system that defined and surrounded the other firms. It lacked a strong domestic base, as well as the huge sales and distribution networks that supported the others. Early in his career, Morita approached some of Japan's major trading houses to see if they would assist him in selling the company's new radios abroad. But he quickly backed away when he sensed that the giant firms did not share his own fervor for technology or philosophy of business. Instead, Sony chose to remain an upstart and adopt rebel ways, competing on the basis of technological innovation and pushing aggressively into overseas markets. While its competitors were slowly expanding their domestic operations, Sony specifically targeted the lucrative U.S. market for consumer electronics. In 1960, it was one of the first Japanese firms to open an office in the United States; in 1961 it was the first to list shares on the New York Stock Exchange. Throughout this period, it followed an explicit strategy of "succeed first in the U.S. market, bring back the reputation to Japan, then spread out to Europe and other countries."[2]

For the most part, the strategy worked. Internationally and at home, Sony continued to prosper from technological advances that set industry standards for a wide range of products. In 1968, it developed a sophisticated color-television technology that led to the enormously successful Trinitron, and to the virtual explosion of the color television market. In 1979, it launched the now-legendary Walkman, a lightweight tape player and headsets that changed the way people listened to music and spawned a generation of competitors. And in the 1980s it joined with the Dutch electronics firm Philips to pioneer compact disk (CD) technology and lead yet another revolution in music.

Sony's only significant failure came in the early 1980s, when its Betamax format VCR lost out to the technologically inferior VHS. Sony had developed the video cassette recorder as early as 1975, but quickly encountered resistance from motion picture studios—particularly the Walt Disney Company and Universal Pictures—that protested that the new machine would encourage widespread copyright infringement of movies and television programs. Litigation between Sony and the studios dragged on for years, but by the time the matter reached the U.S. Supreme Court, the proliferation of VCRs had already made any legal restrictions on private video copying nearly impossible to enforce. In the interim, however, Sony's competitor JVC had developed a separate VCR formula, VHS, which permitted an additional three hours of playing time and was

---

1. See "Sony Corporation," *International Directory of Company Histories* (Detroit, MI: St. James Press, 1994), Vol. II, p. 101.
2. Cited in Thomas W. Malnight and Michael Y. Yoshino, "Sony Corporation: Globalization," HBS Case No. 391-071. The case contains an excellent and elaborate description of Sony's development and its focus on a global strategy.

incompatible with Sony's Betamax. While Sony was fighting its legal battles with the studios, JVC had launched an intensive marketing campaign and convinced Hollywood to start releasing movies in VHS. Unlike Sony, JVC also aggressively licensed its technology to other manufacturers to build an installed base of VHS machines, and priced its machines below Betamax. Although Betamax was generally considered the superior format, VHS soon became the industry standard, and Sony lost its initial position in the lucrative VCR market. It also learned, painfully, that technological innovation alone could not insure dominance in the entertainment market. Instead, it needed to think more strategically about the match between its entertainment hardware and the products—music, movies, and programs—they employed. Thus began Sony's preoccupation with finding compatible software in whatever formats it developed.

In January 1988 this search led Sony to purchase CBS Records, the world's largest record company, for $2 billion. Apparently, the acquisition was the brainchild of Sony's new CEO, Norio Ohga, a former opera singer who was particularly committed to the company's new "software strategy."[3] With CBS, Sony purchased one of the "five majors" of the international record business, and a tremendous stock of music that it could now offer on its increasingly popular CDs. Technologically, the deal was also a natural, since Sony had been producing phonograph records in a joint venture with CBS since 1968. Just one year after the acquisition, CBS Records already accounted for 16% of Sony's total sales.[4]

With CBS on board, Sony had forged one key link in the vertically-integrated entertainment chain. But the company was not content to stop there. Instead, a number of forces seemed to be pushing it to invest even more dramatically in the U.S. entertainment business. After years of skyrocketing growth, worldwide sales of consumer electronics had flattened, increasing at an annual rate of only 2 percent. Consequently, many Japanese consumer electronics firms had already begun diversifying into industries such as semiconductors, robotics, and heavy machinery. In addition, since 1985 the value of the yen had risen strongly against the dollar, inducing many Japanese firms to buy U.S. properties at bargain prices. A wave of protectionism heightened the temptation for high profile firms like Sony to replace their exports to the United States with investment directly in the U.S. market.

On technological grounds, moreover, investing in the entertainment industry once again offered some intriguing synergies. Owning a motion picture studio, for instance, would allow Sony to provide movies and television shows for the millions of color TVs and VCRs it manufactured. Potentially, it would also enable the company to promote new technologies such as 8-millimeter cameras, viewers, and associated equipment. With its own extensive film library, Sony would have a ready supply of 8mm. films and could thus avoid the bottleneck that had ultimately killed Betamax. Finally, Sony's sophisticated video-making equipment also could be used to cut production costs by about 25%, adding valuable profits to Columbia's bottom line. Overall, it was an attractive vision, and one that the company adopted wholeheartedly after its purchase of CBS Records. As founder Morita explained: "After we acquired CBS Records, I thought, 'Now we have become the largest maker of music software in the world. And Sony is the largest video hardware company. So why don't we have video software?' Ever since, my mind has been set on making an acquisition in video software."[5]

---

3. "Sony's Big-Picture Strategy," *U.S. News and World Report*, October 9, 1989, p. 36.
4. "Sony's Hollywood," *Tokyo Business Today*, December 1989, p. 17.
5. Quoted in "Japan Invades Hollywood," *Newsweek*, October 9, 1989, p. 66.

Very quickly, Sony began looking—and bidding—in earnest. It offered $1.1 billion in cash and stock for MGM/UA Communications, but withdrew from the deal when MGM/UA majority shareholder Kirk Kerkorian insisted on buying back the famous MGM name and logo. Reportedly, it also seriously considered acquiring Paramount Communications, Inc., an entertainment and publishing conglomerate, but made no official offer. Then, late in 1988, it set its sights on Columbia Pictures.

Columbia Pictures Entertainment Inc.

Founded in 1918 as the CBC Film Sales Company, Columbia Pictures was a major player in the international entertainment industry. Since the 1930s, Columbia had been among the leading American producers of feature-length films, turning out such classics as *It Happened One Night* and *On the Waterfront,* in addition to a stream of highly successful "B", or lower budget, films. When the advent of television first threatened the motion picture industry in the late 1940s, Columbia had also been the first major studio to react, creating a subsidiary to produce directly for television programs such as *Rin Tin Tin* and *Father Knows Best.* Throughout the 1950s and 60s, it maintained its dual focus on movies and television, benefitting doubly from the ability to rebroadcast its movie hits for a one-time home audience.

Late in the 1960s, the studio produced a string of successes that seemed likely to ensure its position as an industry leader. *Guess Who's Coming to Dinner, To Sir With Love,* and *Divorce American Style* all became instant classics. Columbia's 1969 film, *Easy Rider,* starring Peter Fonda, Dennis Hopper, and Jack Nicholson, became a virtual phenomenon. But immediately after these successes, the studio ran into trouble. A dearth of box office hits led to $82 million in losses between 1970 and 1973, and the subsequent replacement of long-time CEO Abe Schneider by Alan Hirschfield, a former investment banker. To head its ailing motion picture division, Columbia hired David Begelman, a talent agent who in 1977 was found to have misappropriated roughly $60,000 in corporate funds. Begelman left Columbia in 1978, as did Hirschfield.

For the next several years, the studio floundered, lacking any apparent managerial direction, and narrowly avoiding a hostile takeover bid from Kirk Kerkorian. Then, in 1982, the Coca-Cola company bought 49% of Columbia Pictures for $750 million. Under Coca-Cola's leadership, the studio began slowly to change. Together with CBS and Home Box Office it started a new venture, Tri-Star Pictures, which quickly found success with popular films such as *Rambo* and *The Natural.* It also purchased the Loews Theater Chain and re-assumed the video distribution of its own films.[6]

But still Columbia's troubles persisted. Even though its television shows and Loews theaters were extremely popular, its continued unlucky streak at the movies had offset any major profits during the 1980s. In fact, when Sony first began to look at Columbia Pictures in 1988, the studio remained heavily laden with $1.4 billion in debt despite an increasing share of box office receipts. It had spent millions wooing big-name stars such as Cher and Michael Douglas, but had not made enough from their fame to improve the studio's bottom-line performance. High budget

---

6. This section draws heavily on information provided in "Columbia Pictures Entertainment, Inc.," *International Directory of Company Histories,* Vol. IV, p. 136.

flops such as *Winter People* and *Lock-Up*, a lackluster Sylvester Stallone prison film, had only made matters worse.

Thus in November 1988, Coca-Cola began looking for partners.   One of the first to approach was Michael Schulhof, vice-chairman of Sony Corp. of America, who sat down with Columbia President Victor Kaufman in Columbia's corporate dining room to discuss the possibility of a joint venture. A string of meetings followed, and new players, such as Walter Yetnikoff, head of CBS Records, were invited to join. By the spring of 1989 the negotiations came down to two people: Schulhof and Herbert Allen, a member of both Columbia's and Coca-Cola's boards. Sony enlisted the services of Skadden, Arps, the merger law firm, and the Blackstone Group, a takeover adviser. It also sought the support and advice of Hollywood powers such as superagent Michael Ovitz.[7]

The summer of 1989 recorded Hollywood's biggest season ever, but Columbia did not share in the success. *Ghostbusters II* was regarded as a failure, doing only half as well as the original, and *When Harry Met Sally*, which was a success, owed the bulk of the receipts to Rob Reiner's Castle Rock Entertainment. Meanwhile, the high-profile *Casualties of War*, starring Michael J. Fox, cost the studio $25 million but fizzled at the box office. By the end of the summer, Columbia had only received a meager 14% of total box office receipts.

This weak performance only heightened Coca-Cola's desire to remove itself from the movie business. Meanwhile, the dollar was slowly strengthening against the yen, making Columbia more expensive to any Japanese buyer, and Sony more anxious to buy quickly. When Australian Christopher Skase outbid Rupert Murdoch for MGM/UA Communications in September, the pressure increased even more. As one insider explained, "The number of Hollywood brand names suddenly got rather skimpy. It was time to move or to watch the film show start without them."[8]

And so on September 24, Sony moved. In an early morning phone conversation, Schulhof offered Allen $27 per share. Three days later, Columbia approved the deal, and Sony purchased the studio. After the acquisition, Sony immediately offered $200 million for the Guber-Peters Entertainment Co., an independent film company run by the producers Peter Guber and Jon Peters, best known for producing the smash hits *Batman* and *Rain Man*. Time Warner Inc., now Sony's main U.S. nemesis, reacted quickly, arguing that the "dynamic duo" had already signed an agreement to work exclusively for Warner Brothers until 1994. A bitter legal fight ensued, with Warner accusing Sony of "violating American business ethics" and Sony charging Warner of "an anti-Japanese bias."[9] Industry insiders also joined the increasingly nasty fray, arguing that Sony's high-priced bidding revealed its naivete about the entertainment industry. Warner Chairman Steve Ross, for instance, publicly gloated that "if Morita knew what he was getting himself into, he wouldn't have touched those guys with a 10-foot pole."[10] Sony executives, however, were sanguine, seeing the Guber-Peters deal as a way of covering their own vulnerability: a lack of familiarity with the software of entertainment. In the end, they gave Warner somewhere between $300 and $500 million in assets (the exact terms of the deal were never released) to secure the

---

7. See "Japan Invades Hollywood," p. 65.
8. Quoted in "When Columbia Met Sony . . . A Love Story," *Business Week*, October 9, 1989, p. 44.
9. See Paul Farhi and Steven Mufson, "Lights! Camera! Contract! Sony's Pursuit of Guber, Peters Produces a Mega-Million Dollar Gamble," *Washington Post*, December 17, 1989, p. H-1.
10. ibid.

---

release of Guber and Peters. Then, armed with its own dynamic duo, Sony entered the movie business.

The U.S. Entertainment Industry

When Sony bought Columbia, it joined what was by any account a booming industry. The entertainment business was exploding overseas, and American-made movies, TV shows, and music were popular with audiences worldwide. In 1988, the entertainment industry brought America $5.5 billion in foreign earnings, making it the country's second largest net export after aerospace. American programs constituted as much as 40% of the 125,000 hours of programming aired in 1989 on TV stations in the European Community.[11]

Exports of U.S. movies and television shows, moreover, had helped to implant a seemingly indelible American image on global viewing patterns. The soap opera *Dallas*, for instance, was a cultural icon of sorts, airing for 11 years in 99 countries and becoming the most popular drama in history. In the People's Republic of China, an estimated 200 million people tuned in each Sunday evening at 6:30 to watch Walt Disney Co.'s half-hour show, *Mickey and Donald*.[12] In Japan, Hollywood's output usually captured about half of all box office receipts. This pattern of U.S. dominance showed no signs of diminishing in the late 1980s. On the contrary, even as other U.S. industries were suffering under an onslaught of foreign competition, entertainment exports were on the rise. According to the Motion Picture Association of America, Hollywood exported $4.4 billion in film and TV shows in 1988, a 33% increase over 1987.

American dominance in the entertainment industry was bolstered by the continued inability of any would-be competitors to break out of their own domestic markets. Despite years of efforts and a handful of successes, few non-U.S. firms had ever been able to market movies or television programs to a global audience. This inability stemmed from some simple yet deep-seated obstacles. First, the size and scope of the U.S. entertainment infrastructure overwhelmed that of any of its competitors. Launched in the immediate aftermath of World War I, the U.S. industry had grabbed—and held on to—all the advantages of moving first. U.S. films had defined the media, and established genres such as Westerns and horror films that quickly drew an international audience. Once established, the U.S. studios had also rapidly expanded and diversified, gaining in the process a way to cover the costs of their inevitable flops and a means of increasing the profits on their successes. Box office duds, even expensive ones, could be compensated by a few big hits, and the hits could yield even bigger returns in the secondary markets—television, cable, home video, etc.—that the studios also controlled. This security enabled Hollywood to spend much more lavishly than any of its foreign rivals.

The U.S. studios also undoubtedly benefitted from the global acceptance of English as a first or second language. Whereas French, or German, or Italian film-makers had to translate or dub their movies to sell them to the lucrative English-speaking audiences, U.S. producers could make films in their own language, and assume that most of their potential audience would accept

---

11. "Invasion of the Studio Snatchers," *Business Week*, October 16, 1989, p. 53.
12. Disney later pulled the program in 1990 because it generated extraordinary demand for counterfeit Disney consumer products.

them as is.[13] As a result, non-English speaking audiences grew comfortable with dubbing and subtitles, while American audiences almost universally rejected these intrusions and the foreign films that employed them.

Finally, and most intangibly, American movies and American culture had simply been accepted by vast sections of the world's population. Whether it was the diversity of the American experience, the exuberance, or the underlying emphasis on individual freedom and potential, U.S. films won a global approval that foreign competitors had not even been able to approach. In the eyes of many foreign viewers, movies and television were Hollywood, and Hollywood was America.

In the face of these seemingly permanent obstacles, foreign broadcasters had turned to licensing and distribution, purchasing U.S. programs for re-broadcast in their own markets. But by the 1980s, many foreign media firms had grown restless with this arrangement. To be a global player in the entertainment industry, they realized, you had to be in the U.S. market. And to get into that market, you had to invest directly in the U.S. entertainment business. Or as Michael Bornemann, president of Germany's Bertelsmann Music Group, explained, "America is the cultural heart of the world. If you want to be a global player in the entertainment business, you have to be in the United States."[14]

And thus, late in the 1980's, foreign buyers descended on the Hollywood studios. The Australian Rupert Murdoch came first, purchasing Twentieth Century Fox for roughly $575 million. Then in 1989, Sony stunned the industry with its purchase of Columbia. Others followed quickly in Sony's wake. In June 1990, Pioneer LDC Inc., a unit of Japan's Pioneer Electronic Corp., invested $60 million in Carolco Pictures (producer of *Rambo* and *Terminator*) in exchange for a 10% stake in the company. In November, Disney formed a partnership with Japanese institutional investors, including Yamaichi Securities and Fuji Bank, to provide $600 million in film financing for its studios. The following month, Matsushita Electrical Industrial Co., the world's largest consumer electronics firm, acquired MCA Inc. for $6.1 billion. And in October 1991, Toshiba and C. Itoh & Co., Ltd. each invested $500 million into a joint venture with Time Warner.

For the studio heads, the acquisitions and investments were timely. The buyers, especially the Japanese, offered large amounts of financial backing without, they promised, any significant managerial change. Like Sony's management, moreover, Hollywood executives were also intrigued by the marketing and technological prospects that could emerge from a merger of Hollywood's software and Japan's hardware. Others in the United States, however, were considerably less pleased, finding in the string of acquisitions evidence of a "Japanese invasion" into the soul of America.

---

13. Four English-speaking countries—the United States, Canada, Britain, and Australia—accounted for 80% of all money spent on television programming worldwide. See Paul Farhi, "Star of Stage and Screen," *Washington Post*, November 5, 1989, p. H-1.
14. Quoted in Farhi, "Star of Stage and Screen."

Backlash

In retrospect, Sony's purchase of Columbia came at an extremely awkward time. Since the dollar began its decline in 1985, foreign firms had been slowly acquiring corporate assets in the United States. While initially these purchases drew little public notice, the eventual weight of the acquisitions became by 1988 a subject of serious concern.

Not surprisingly, the brunt of attention fell on the Japanese. Since Japan began its much-vaunted export drive, U.S. firms had seen their market shares decline in a number of mature industries such as automobiles and steel. Then innovations like Sony's Trinitron and VCR technologies had virtually eliminated U.S. firms from the lucrative consumer electronics market. For many Americans, Japanese foreign direct investment in the U.S. market was but the next step in the "Japanese invasion"—and a step too far.

In 1988, anti-Japanese sentiment was running particularly high in the United States. Just one year earlier, the U.S. government had revealed that Toshiba had sold submarine-quieting technology to the Soviet Union, violating the accepted norms of CoCom, an international organization that regulated the transfer of technology to the Soviet bloc. The revelation of the "Toshiba affair," as it was soon dubbed, created a flurry of activity in Washington, as representatives rushed to introduce bills that would ban the sale of Toshiba products in the United States and help U.S. firms struggling to compete against Japanese rivals. At one point, a band of representatives even smashed Toshiba products in a widely-publicized event on the steps of Capitol Hill. Even as Japan's export policies were coming under increased scrutiny, moreover, Japanese firms were quietly increasing their purchases of U.S. assets. In 1988 alone, Japanese interests bought $6.5 billion worth of American real estate and a $13 billion stake in various companies. In highly publicized transactions, real estate mogul Minora Isutani bought California's famed Pebble Beach golf course, and Mitsubishi Estate Co. bought a controlling stake in the Rockefeller Group, the company that owned New York City's Rockefeller Center, Radio City Music Hall, and the Rockettes.

Against this backdrop, Sony's purchase of Columbia was not warmly received. One week after the deal was signed, *Newsweek*'s cover story, "Japan Invades Hollywood," featured Columbia's trademark Lady Liberty draped in a kimono. Stories such as "Invasion of the Studio Snatchers" and "The Selling of U.S. Media" echoed a common fear of Japanese take-over and cultural imperialism. "It's not bad for the movie business and it's not bad for Columbia," claimed David Geffen, chief executive of the Geffen Co., an independent record and film company, "but I wonder if it's bad for America . . . [A] giant part of the education of young people in this country comes from film and TV and someone should be paying attention to what's going on."[15] Other articles worried aloud that Sony's "synergy" would allow it eventually to control a vertically-integrated multimedia chain that no American firm could even touch, much less rival.[16] Still others painted the acquisition as a fundamental blow to the independent spirit of U.S. film-making. As one article in the *Los Angeles Times* lamented:

---

15. Paul Farhi, Stuart Auerbach, and Mark Potts, "Report of Bid by Sony Raise Questions," *Washington Post*, September 27, 1989, p. B-1.
16. See Neil Gross, "Japan's Hollywood: More Ominous Than it Seems," *Business Week*, October 15, 1990, p. 115.

The simple presumptions about equality and justice as fundamentals of American society and as dramatized by the movies have had a powerful impact all over the world. And the freedom of the American screen to be critical of American society when it has fallen short of its own ideals has been watched with envy by audiences—and filmmakers—even in nominally democratic countries where the screen is guarded more circumspectly.

The freedom of the American film to deal with social and political issues here or abroad has been one of its glories (an infrequent glory, maybe, in a medium designed to divert and entertain, but a glory when it happens). This is not to say that things will inevitably change. But all the foreign buyouts are predicated on profits and the bottom line—in considerations of which chance-taking and daring departures from the norm are anathema.

Individual filmmakers or stars with clout may be able to buck the bottom-line mentality. But the fact that Akira Kurosawa, Japan's greatest filmmaker, had to look to the United States rather than to his own industry to be able to make "Kagemusha," "Ran," and "Dreams" does not invite confidence.

And that old devil, the well-known chilling effect, is a presently incalculable consequence of all the takeovers. How will it play in Peoria is no longer the relevant geographic question.

It is a new day in Hollywood, and no mistake.[17]

On Capitol Hill, similar sentiments surrounded the Sony deal. An alarmed Representative Edward J. Markey (D-Mass), head of the House telecommunications subcommittee, ominously warned that the Sony deal "ought to trigger a discussion of larger issues."[18] Unless U.S. corporate managers planned for long-term growth, he argued, they were bound to fall behind the Japanese, who had strategies to control worldwide distribution in electronics and entertainment. Rep. Markey also feared that Sony would package its library of Columbia films with its own HDTV sets, establishing a *de facto* national standard for HDTV and circumventing the elaborate federal efforts to do so.

Building on these concerns, Rep. Leon Panetta (D-Monterey, Calif.) introduced legislation to limit foreign ownership in the cultural and entertainment industries. Defending his proposal, Panetta stressed, "We must continue to safeguard against several real and disturbing possibilities. It is increasingly apparent that our cultural industries, particularly the entertainment and motion picture industries, are in danger of being dominated by foreign owners. It seems to me that this phenomenon is not healthy for America, nor would it be accepted by any other nation."[19]

---

17. Charles Champlin, "The Film Industry Is Not Just Another Business," *Los Angeles Times*, November 28, 1990, p. F-1.

18. Quoted in "Invasion of the Studio Snatchers," p. 54.

19. Quoted in Kara Glover, "Analysts Say Bill to Limit Foreign Ownership of Hollywood Doomed," *Los Angeles Business Journal*, October 21, 1991, p. 6.

Behind Panetta's fears and some Hollywood objections lay an increasingly important anomaly in federal regulation. Under prevailing policy, U.S. television networks were prohibited from owning production studios. Originally, the law was intended to promote competition in the film industry, keeping the powerful networks (ABC, CBS, and NBC) from exerting undue influence on the smaller and more numerous production houses. But, with consolidation and then foreign investment in the studios, many insiders argued that the rules had become obsolete, and even anti-competitive. As CBS Chairman Laurence A. Tisch complained in a letter to the chairman of the Federal Communications Commission, "A continuation of U.S. regulations protecting foreign-owned mega-studios from the competition of American-owned networks . . . is ludicrous."[20]

To make matters even worse, Sony's founder and chairman, Akio Morita, had just co-authored a controversial book, *The Japan that Can Say No*, which dealt at great length with the shortcomings of the American political and economic system.[21] Bootleg translations of the book, along with Morita's other activities,[22] raised concern about Sony's acquisition of Columbia, even though Morita said he had "no intention to interfere with Columbia's management."[23]

Ultimately, whether or not Sony intended to re-orient Columbia Pictures became the dividing line of opinion. Those who expected Sony to change the company substantially worried that the changes would be detrimental: they would inject a Japanese flavor into an all-American industry and impose Sony's vertically-integrated empire on the U.S. entertainment industry. Those who expected a hands-off approach, however, saw the investment as purely a financial transaction and thus found little cause for concern. As one industry expert professed, "Sony isn't going to order anyone to bring in a Japanese director or a Japanese scenery person just because it's a Japanese company. They're businessmen. They're not stupid."[24]

After the Buyout Wave

In the aftermath of the acquisition the fervor that had initially surrounded the deal began to abate. Bills to halt the "Japanese invasion" languished in Congress as investment flows into the United States declined precipitously.[25] With time, the great question mark in the Sony-Columbia Pictures deal drifted from "Is it bad for the United States?" to "Was it wrong for Sony?"

The two years immediately following the acquisition were tough ones for Sony. In both 1990 and 1991, the Japanese firm sank roughly $500 million into Columbia, and watched annual overhead for expenses like salaries and talent contracts rise by nearly 50%. Determined not to interfere with the creative and intuitive art of movie-making, Sony executives gave free reign to

20. Cited in John Burgess, "TV Networks Wave Nationalistic Flag," *Washington Post*, October 4, 1990, P. E-1.
21. Morita collaborated with Shintaro Ishihara, a fiercely nationalistic member of parliament who pushed such ideas as the remilitarization of Japan.
22. Morita served as vice-chairman of the Federation of Economic Organization (Keidanren), the organization that more than any other spoke on behalf of the collective interests of Japanese big business.
23. Quoted in "Why Sony is Plugging Into Columbia," *Business Week*, October 16, 1989, p. 58.
24. Kenji Katani, quoted in "Invasion of the Studio Snatchers," p. 54.
25. According to the International Monetary Fund, Japanese direct investment in the United States fell from $17.4 billion in 1990 to $5.2 billion in 1991.

Jon Peters and Peter Guber, who went on a wild and highly-publicized spending spree. In 1990, Columbia Pictures Entertainment earned more than $200 million in operating profits but suffered negative cash flow, thanks to the intricacies of entertainment bookkeeping which allowed a studio to count movie production costs as an asset, rather than as an expense. Under the industry's idiosyncratic accounting conventions, a film studio could report big profits yet have no cash—which was exactly what happened with Columbia.

Meanwhile, Sony was also plagued by personnel problems in the highest ranks of management. Chairman Morita, 70, underwent open-heart surgery in the summer of 1990, just as CEO Norio Ohga was recovering from a heart attack. Acknowledging frictions between its conservative hardware division in Park Ridge, N.J. and its brash new software businesses, Sony also reorganized its U.S. operation. CBS Records and Columbia Pictures were renamed Sony Music Entertainment and Sony Pictures and, along with Sony Electronics Publishing, were grouped together under a newly-created subsidiary, Sony Software Corporation. Around the same time, three top executives abruptly departed Sony's software operations. High-flying producer Jon Peters left Sony Pictures in May 1991; in September, Walter Yetnikoff unexpectedly resigned as chairman of Sony Music; and in October, Frank Price, CEO of Sony Pictures, agreed to step down. Profits also continued their decline, and in 1991 the combined cash flow of Sony Pictures and Sony Music turned negative. Then, just when Sony thought the bad news could not get any worse, it released *Hudson Hawk*, a $50 million film starring Bruce Willis that opened to scathing reviews and lost about $35 million in the United States. Headlines such as the *Wall Street Journal's* "Hudson Hawk seen as Dead Duck," did little to boost Sony's image as a producer of high quality and popular films.

Matters improved somewhat in 1992, when Columbia and Tri-Star Pictures released four winners in a row: *A League of Their Own, Universal Soldier, Mo' Money,* and *Single White Female.* But simultaneously, Columbia's profitable TV production unit was faltering. The market for syndicated reruns, such as *Designing Women*, had deteriorated, and Columbia had few pioneering new offerings. In the third quarter of 1992 alone, Sony Corp. announced a 37% decline in operating income. Financially, it seemed that Sony's new software business was doing little more than draining funds from its parent company.

An even bigger problem, however, lay with Sony's synergies—or lack thereof. From the start, Sony had purchased Columbia, not so much to make money in the movie business, but to secure and expand its hardware operations. But as of 1994, the benefits of the software-hardware link were not yet evident. The new technologies that Sony had hoped to promote through its in-house libraries—especially 8 mm. cameras and audiodisks—had not fared particularly well with consumers. Nor had Sony succeeded in marketing one entertainment medium through another. It tried most spectacularly to make cross-marketing work in its 1993 film *Last Action Hero*, a $60 million action extravaganza starring Arnold Schwarzenegger that sported a soundtrack by Sony recording artists and prominently featured two new Sony consumer electronics products. *Last Action Hero* was presented in theaters with a sophisticated new Sony sound system and footage from the film was used to produce an interactive video game. The film, unfortunately, bombed at the box office, negating all of Sony's much-hyped tie-ins and confirming critics' perception that Sony had grossly overpaid for Columbia and its management team. Critics of Sony's high-priced acquisition received further ammunition early in 1994, when Sony Music Entertainment (Japan) announced that it would lend $660 million to its ailing motion picture business. Soon thereafter, Hollywood erupted in rumors about the impending sale of Columbia Pictures.

Beyond the company's immediate financial woes, moreover, some analysts argued that Sony's strategic vision was simply misplaced. As a powerhouse in hardware and a leader of technological innovation, Sony lost its edge and its competitive advantage when it ventured to the very different worlds of music and movie-making. Pointing, for instance, to the troubles Sony inherited when Michael Jackson, one of its leading stars, was accused of sexual abuse, one commentator quipped, "Wouldn't it have been easier to stick at home making Walkmans?"[26] Critics also charged that Sony had overestimated the potential of software as a driver for the hardware business. Vertical integration, the critics insisted, was irrelevant in the entertainment industry. Good software would eventually be converted into all the hardware formats; and good hardware would always drive conversion of the desired software. Or as one analyst debunking the synergy theory explained, "It's like saying that people who own a restaurant must also own a huge ranch. Studios are not that profitable. So why take the gamble?"[27] In addition, the critics argued, even if a company could potentially use software to push its hardware sales, Sony's share of the film market was still far too small for it ever to make or break a particular format. Even conversion of the entire Columbia Pictures library into 8mm. film, for instance, would not by itself alter the fate of 8mm. viewing technology if consumers decided that they did not need the new technology. Similarly, analysts scoffed at the idea that Sony—or any company—could market its products by including them in high-profile films. As one insider put it, "I don't think there's ever been a can of Coke sold because it appeared in a movie."[28]

Others, however, insisted that the strategy was sound and the synergies, at least over the long run, abundant. As Sony's Schulhof explained, "In the late 1970s we began to recognize the need to take Sony beyond hardware. Through our experience with Betamax, we discovered that the compelling motivation for the purchase of hardware is software."[29] And thus Sony maintained that it was merely playing out Morita's long-term vision of vertical integration. By this logic, even if Columbia Pictures was not making money, it was making pictures that would ensure Sony a leading position in the next-generation market for entertainment. Accordingly, Sony was investing widely in related fields such as electronic publishing, interactive multimedia, and video games. The company also spent heavily on the development of HDTV, hoping to build a library of HDTV software and work backwards from the software to establish the hardware standard.

Until around 1994, Sony's defense of its strategy was painted as just that: the defense of an acquisition that U.S. analysts roundly criticized as foolhardy. But, then, another wave of consolidation and diversification hit the entertainment business. This time, it was telecommunications companies that flooded Hollywood, rushing to combine their growing cable distribution systems with the studios' ready library of programming. The rush was made particularly acute by technological advances which promised to allow 500-channel service and link home computers and televisions along a seamless "information highway." Viewing this development, even the most cynical observers began to re-consider the wisdom—and value—of Sony's investment in Columbia. "Suddenly, the Japanese don't look so stupid paying what they did for the studios," admitted one.[30]

26. Bill Emmott, "How Japan Got Mugged in Hollywood," *New York Times*," November 26, 1993, p. A35.
27. Benjamin Stein, quoted in "Will Sony Make it in Hollywood?" *Fortune*, September 9, 1991, p. 162.
28. Quoted in "Last Action Hero—Or First $60 Million Commercial?" *Business Week*, April 12, 1993.
29. Quoted in "Will Sony Make it in Hollywood?" p. 162.
30. Quoted in James Bates, "Japanese-led Studios Seek TV Links," *Los Angeles Times*, October 22, 1993, p. D-1.

For the time being, however, Sony seemed to have no interest in selling Columbia Pictures, even at a profit. Instead the company seemed content to wait, and possibly even to deepen its investment through its own alliances with telecommunications studios. As CEO Ohga aptly described Sony's long-term outlook, "Those who have the assets have power."[31]

31. Quoted in Takeshi Matsuzaka, "Pictures Flop Soaks up Sony Cash," *Nikkei Weekly*, February 28, 1994, p. 8.

Exhibit 1   Sony Corporation: Consolidated Financial Results, 1986-1994 (billions of yen)

	1986	1987[a]	1988	1989	1990	1991	1992	1993	1994
Net sales and revenue	1,474	619	1,588	2,201	2,945	3,691	3,929	3,993	3,734
Cost of sales	1,087	452	1,147	1,475	1,938	2,506	2,838	2,929	2,756
SG&A	345	148	380	566	712	888	911	938	878
Operating income	42	19	61	160	295	297	180	126	100
Other income and expenses	42	6	11	5	(68)	(33)	(25)	(34)	2
Income before taxes[b]	84	26	72	166	227	265	216	93	102
Taxes	49	16	41	95	127	152	96	57	87
Net income[c]	41	13	37	72	103	117	120	36	15
Current assets	974	922	1,143	1,434	2,202	2,234	2,358	2,110	2,024
Investments and advances	115	115	102	113	337	214	232	257	298
Property, plant, and equipment	333	343	454	545	868	1,047	1,217	1,138	1,049
Other assets	28	31	246	273	963	1,108	1,104	1,025	898
Total assets	1,450	1,411	1,945	2,365	4,370	4,602	4,911	4,530	4,270
Current liabilities	628	587	1,003	1,119	1,996	2,105	2,052	1,743	1,408
Long-term liabilities	215	215	284	319	927	1,000	1,243	1,273	1,437
Minority interest			12	15	17	21	79	86	96
Equity	606	609	646	912	1,430	1,476	1,537	1,428	1,330
Exchange rate (¥/US$)	162	146	125	132	157	141	133	116	103

Source: Sony Corporation annual reports.

[a] Five months' results.
[b] Pre-tax income in 1992 includes $62 billion gain on subsidiary sale of stock.
[c] Net income includes investments in and transactions with affiliated companies.

Note: Numbers may not add due to rounding.

Exhibit 2   Sony Corporation: Business Segment Results 1986-1994 (billions of yen)

	1986	1987[a]	1988	1989	1990	1991	1992	1993	1994
Sales by Area:									
Japan	450	212	538	731	869	1,024	1,058	1,028	1,024
United States	435	165	434	586	858	1,055	1,119	1,216	1,154
Europe	315	146	351	498	715	1,018	1,080	1,040	833
Other areas	251	86	232	330	437	598	672	709	723
Sales by Product Group:									
Video equipment	481	189	451	573	744	908	896	828	669
Televisions	332	129	315	342	446	882	948	928	841
Audio equipment	415	190	479	561	722	552	593	634	618
Other products	225	102	271	329	420	619	713	772	817
Records			39	340	455	476	450	447	462
Movies					93[b]	258	329	385	328

Source: Sony Corporation annual reports.

[a] Five months' results.
[b] Four months' results.

Note: Numbers may not add due to rounding.

Exhibit 3   Columbia Pictures Inc.: Financial Results 1986-1989 (US$ thousands)

	1986	1987	1988[a]	1989
Revenues	$1,354,989	$1,065,987	$ 217,024	$1,615,724
Operating income	226,811	45,285	(134,411)	147,582
Net income	101,957	50,656	(104,629)	21,749
Current assets		572,156	1,034,542	786,663
Total assets	2,770,713	3,457,143	3,422,913	3,564,864
Current liabilities	733,747	934,309	817,075	586,818
Long-term debt	93,201	916,031	1,042,040	1,313,819
Equity	1,331,019	1,046,000	1,041,791	1,060,683
Revenues				
Theatrical	551,429	430,065	95,398	755,891
Television	759,429	593,784	89,580	620,086
Exhibition			27,455	235,386
Other	44,029	42,138	4,591	4,361
Operating Income				
Theatrical	26,809	27,482	(23,427)	26,440
Television	239,563	154,063	4,960	155,655
Exhibition			4,759	32,860
Other	(8,096)	(6,642)	7,316	3,475
Corporate overhead	(31,465)	(29,618)	(14,019)	(70,848)
Film inventory write-down			(114,000)	
Restructuring provision		(100,000)		
Capital Expenditure				
Theatrical	3,833	3,822	344	6,050
Television	752	2,524	404	1,103
Exhibition			2,565	34,360
Other	476	907	72	-
Corporate	4,424	2,648	519	11,512
Sales by Geographic Area				
United States & Canada	1,162,601	956,119	176,730	1,299,313
Europe & Africa	105,577	66,636	29,152	210,954
Pacific	51,154	30,194	8,250	64,896
Latin America	35,657	13,038	2,892	40,561

Source: Columbia Pictures annual reports.

[a]For period December 18, 1987 to February 29, 1988.

Exhibit 4   Sales of Consumer Electronic Products in the United States (US$ millions)

Product	1985	1986	1987	1988	1989	1990
Video, total	**11,142**	**12,226**	**12,290**	**11,896**	**11,846**	**11,905**
Color TV	5,565	6,040	6,303	6,277	6,530	6,376
Monochrome TV	328	373	341	236	156	132
Projection TV	488	529	527	529	478	626
VCR decks	4,738	3,978	3,442	2,848	2,625	2,439
Camcorders	NA	1,280	1,651	1,972	2,007	2,260
Laserdisc players	23	26	26	34	50	72
Audio, total	**6,784**	**7,660**	**8,164**	**8,526**	**8,585**	**8,733**
Audio systems	1,372	1,370	1,048	1,225	1,217	1,270
Audio components	1,132	1,358	1,715	1,854	1,871	1,935
Portable audio equipment	1,140	1,389	1,469	1,547	1,595	1,645
Home radios	379	408	409	377	379	360
Autosound equipment	2,761	3,135	3,523	3,523	3,523	3,523
Other Products, total	**1,325**	**1,535**	**2,129**	**2,150**	**2,136**	**2,176**
Blank audio cassettes	270	300	375	367	384	376
Blank videocassettes	1,055	1,235	1,006	936	923	948
Accessories	NA	NA	748	847	829	852

Source: Electronics Industries Association, *Consumer Electronics in Review 1991*, p. 9.

Exhibit 5   Typical Life Cycle of a Successful U.S. Film

Time Period	Release
First 3 months	U.S. theater exhibition
After 3 months (sometimes sooner)	Foreign theater exhibition
6-9 months	U.S. home video and pay-per-view
9-12 months	Foreign home video
1-2 years	U.S. cable television
2-5 years	U.S. network television
3 years	Foreign television
6 years	U.S. television syndication

Source: Standard & Poor's Industry Surveys, "Leisure-Time," September 1, 1988, p. 1.
        Reprinted by permission of Standard & Poor's, a division of McGraw-Hill Inc.

Exhibit 6   Profile of the U.S. Motion Picture Industry

Year	Box Office ($ billion)[a]	Admission (billions)	Average Ticket Price ($)	Number of Screens[b]
1986	3.78	1.02	3.71	22,765
1987	4.25	1.09	3.91	23,555
1988	4.46	1.09	4.11	23,234
1989	5.03	1.13	4.45	23,132
1990	5.02	1.06	4.23	23,689
1991	4.80	1.14	4.21	24,570
1992	4.87	1.17	4.15	25,105
1993	5.15	1.24	4.14	25,737

Source: Motion Picture Association of America.

[a] United States and Canada.
[b] United States only.

Exhibit 7   U.S. Box Office Market Shares

Distributor	1986	1987	1988	1989	1990	1991	1992	1993
Columbia/Tri-Star	17%	11%	9%	16%	14%	20%	19%	18%
Disney	10	14	19	14	16	14	19	16
Twentieth Century-Fox	8	9	12	7	13	12	14	11
MGM/UA	4	4	10	6	3	2	1	2
Orion[a]	7	10	7	4	6	9	-	-
Paramount	22	20	15	14	15	12	10	9
Universal	9	7	10	17	13	11	12	14
Warner Bros.	12	12	11	17	13	14	20	19
Others	11	13	7	5	7	6	5	11

Source: Standard & Poors' Industry Surveys, "Leisure Time," various years.

[a] Orion Pictures Corp. filed for bankruptcy under Chapter 11 in October 1992.

Exhibit 8   Top Worldwide Markets for U.S. Theatrical Films[a]

Country	1986	1987	1988	1989	1990	1991	1992
United States	1,165	1,246	1,414	1,780	1,829	1,848	2,010
Japan	103	138	142	202	237	201	165
Canada	87	97	125	153	148	134	130
Germany	65	98	101	118	175	142	162
France	99	101	99	128	164	137	141
United Kingdom & Ireland	49	73	90	115	144	121	127
Italy	65	70	73	85	117	75	65
Spain	48	49	68	95	110	107	123
Australia	27	32	45	74	70	63	67
Sweden	17	24	27	39	48	30	32
Rest of world	239	252	250	340	435	416	418
Total	1,963	2,180	2,434	3,127	3,479	3,274	3,440

Source: Motion Picture Export Association of America data published in *Variety*.

[a] Represents U.S. dollar value (in millions) of theatrical rentals of Motion Picture Export Association of America members (MPEA), which account for an estimated 90-98% of worldwide movie rental distributed by U.S. companies.

Note: Numbers may not add due to rounding.

Exhibit 9   U.S. Movie Hits, 1988-1990

1988		1989		1990	
Movie (Distributor)	Box Office Receipts (US$ million)	Movie (Distributor)	Box Office Receipts (US$ million)	Movie (Distributor)	Box Office Receipts (US$ million)
Rain Man (MGM/UA)	172.1	Batman (Warner)	251.2	Home Alone (Fox)	285.0
Roger Rabbit (Disney)	154.1	Indiana Jones and Last Crusade (Paramount)	197.2	Ghost (Paramount)	217.4
Coming to America (Paramount)	128.2	Lethal Weapon 2 (Warner)	147.2	Dances with Wolves (Orion)	184.0
Big (Fox)	113.5	Look Who's Talking (Tri-Star)	138.1	Pretty Woman (Disney)	178.4
Twins (Universal)	110.3	Honey, I Shrunk the Kids (Disney)	130.2	Teenage Mutant Ninja Turtles (New Line)	133.2
Crocodile Dundee II (Paramount)	109.3	Back to the Future II (Universal)	116.4	Hunt for Red October (Paramount)	120.7
Die Hard (Fox)	80.7	Ghostbusters II (Columbia)	112.5	Total Recall (Tri-Star)	118.3
Naked Gun (Paramount)	78.0	Driving Miss Daisy (Warner)	106.6	Die Hard 2 (Fox)	115.3
Cocktail (Disney)	78.0	Parenthood (Universal)	95.4	Dick Tracy (Disney)	103.7
Beetlejuice (Warner)	73.0	Dead Poet's Society (Disney)	94.3	Kindergarten Cop (Universal)	90.8

Source: Standard & Poor's Industry Surveys, "Leisure Time," March 14, 1991, p. L34; and November 12, 1992, p. L6.

Notes: Box office results are for the United States and Canada.
Movies are grouped based on the year in which they first appeared in theaters; all receipts were not necessarily collected in that year.

Exhibit 10   Comparative Company Analysis, 1988-1993

	1988	1989	1990	1991	1992	1993
Revenues (US$ million)						
Disney Company	3,438	4,594	5,844	6,182	7,504	8,529
Matsushita Electric	38,552	41,699	37,753	46,804	56,015	60,826
News Corp.	4,355	6,397	6,720	8,587	7,811	7,482
Paramount Communications	3,056	3,392	3,869	3,895	4,265	4,031
Sony Corp.	11,450	16,252	18,343	25,649	29,439	34,422
Time Warner	4,507	7,642	11,517	21,021	6,309	6,581
Net Income (US$ million)						
Disney Company	522	703	824	637	817	300
Matsushita Electric	1,303	1,617	1,482	1,836	999	331
News Corp.	336	403	217	252	407	605
Paramount Communications	385	12	259	122	213	128
Sony Corp.	294	549	655	829	903	313
Time Warner	289	(256)	(227)	(99)	86	(221)
Return on Assets (%)						
Disney Company	13.8	14.1	12.8	8.8	9.6	3.7
Matsushita Electric	4.8	5.6	4.8	4.7	2.9	1.4
News Corp.	6.8	12.9	5.4	1.3	4.6	5.5
Paramount Communications	9.9	29.4	4.8	3.0	5.1	1.9
Sony Corp.	3.8	5.0	6.3	4.2	4.1	2.0
Time Warner	8.2	7.8	2.0	2.1	2.7	0.9
Return on Equity (%)						
Disney Company	28.3	29.8	27.1	18.3	21.1	6.4
Matsushita Electric	7.4	8.6	8.2	8.1	3.9	1.1
News Corp.	12.9	30.6	6.9	(4.7)	6.5	7.9
Paramount Communications	18.4	64.6	7.0	3.2	6.7	1.5
Sony Corp.	6.0	11.1	11.3	8.2	8.1	2.4
Time Warner	23.2	(18.8)	(67.1)	(192.2)	(24.2)	(20.7)
Earnings Per Share (US$)						
Disney Company	0.95	1.28	1.50	1.20	1.52	0.55
Matsushita Electric	0.67	0.76	0.68	0.83	0.46	0.16
News Corp.	2.17	2.57	1.56	1.73	2.27	1.62
Paramount Communications	3.21	0.09	2.16	1.03	1.79	0.63
Sony Corp.	1.15	1.83	1.95	2.03	2.20	0.79
Time Warner	1.25	(1.09)	(3.42)	(2.40)	(1.46)	(0.90)

Source: Company annual reports and Worldscope.

BSkyB

People watch bucketfuls of tv in this country. It's cold, it's rainy, the weather's miserable outside. There's nothing else to do really...

--British television executive

Early in 1983 Rupert Murdoch's News Corporation bought a floundering British company called Satellite Television and renamed it Sky. Though scorned at the time by industry analysts and media barons, Sky quickly became an undeniable powerhouse in British television. It pioneered the development of the British satellite broadcasting industry, handily defeating the better connected, better capitalized consortium that was designed to destroy it. It wrested control of viewing rights to some of Britain's most coveted programming, including coverage of the country's Premier League soccer.[1] It won a series of regulatory challenges to its growing market presence and had even begun, in less than a decade, to threaten the position of the indomitable BBC (British Broadcasting Corporation). By 1997, Murdoch's Sky was the most profitable broadcaster in the United Kingdom and one of Britain's top 20 corporations.[2]

Yet, just as Sky was buttressing its place in the British market, the rules of the game began to shift again. In Britain as elsewhere the fundamental nature of broadcasting was changing. Analogue transmission was giving way to digital formats and the Internet, satellite, video-on-demand and narrowcasting all promised to overwhelm the role of traditional broadcasters and television stations. To some observers, it was a situation ripe for Sky and the industry-defying brashness that defined Murdoch's career. Others felt it was the beginning of the end. Sky had prospered in large part by writing the rules of its own game. What would happen to its power as the rules began to change?

Rupert Murdoch and the Creation of Newscorp

Sky from the start was the brainchild of Rupert Murdoch. Already one of the most influential men in British media, Murdoch had built his improbable empire from an Australian newspaper started by his father. After consolidating his father's assets, Murdoch created *The Australian* in the mid-1960s, the nation's first serious national newspaper. He then diversified into television, acquiring stations in Australia, New Zealand, and Hong Kong. In 1968 Murdoch began to expand northwards as well, purchasing *News of the World*, a British tabloid. During the 1970s, Murdoch

---

[1] Called football in Britain.
[2] See Mathew Horsman, "Sky: the inside story," *The Guardian*, November 10, 1997, p. 4.

Professor Debora Spar and Paula Zakaria, MBA 1997, prepared this case as the basis for class discussion rather than to illustrate either effective or ineffective handling of an administrative situation.

continued his push, acquiring both additional tabloid (or lower-market) papers such as the *National Star* and the *New York Post,* and higher-end papers such as the *Village Voice* and *New York* magazine. By the end of the 1980s, Murdoch's News Corporation owned the *Times* and *Sunday Times* in Britain; the *Boston Herald* and *Chicago Sun Times* in the United States, and Hong Kong's *South China Morning Post*. And those were only the highest profile publications. News Corporation had also purchased the Twentieth Century Fox film studio and Metromedia television stations, combining their assets to create Fox Broadcasting, the fourth national television network in the United States.

Television in Britain

Before Sky, the British television industry had evolved in a slow and rather predictable fashion. For most of this time, the market was dominated by the venerable BBC, an institution respected in Britain and around the world for its high quality programming and technical leadership. As was the pattern across most of Europe, the BBC was government-run and financed. Funding for the broadcasts came from the proceeds of a £89.50 license fee paid annually by all British television owners regardless of their viewing preferences. In 1996, the license fee, and thus the BBC's "revenue," came to £1.8 billion. In return for these proceeds, the BBC was expected to serve a public mission, informing and elevating the British public in addition to entertaining them. The BBC was also required to comply with government standards for content and distribution. In general, both viewers and the government regarded the system as a success. With a staff of thousands of writers, directors, producers and reporters, the BBC was roundly seen as a national treasure, an integral part of Britain's cultural heritage and a high-profile mouthpiece to the world. Or as one industry insider described its role: "Television provided a public service for the good of the people. The broadcasters and the government were quite certain they knew what was best for the masses."[3]

Eventually, though, some of the masses began to protest against the BBC's monopoly over British television. In 1954 the government complied with requests for an expanded variety of programming and allowed for the creation of an independent, advertising-sponsored channel, named Independent Television (ITV). In 1981 a second channel, Channel 4, was added as well. Though free of the BBC's public service mandate, the new channels were still closely linked to the British government and its various regulatory agencies. ITV was essentially a conglomerate of private, regional stations, financed by commercial advertising but still under strict regulation by an Independent Broadcasting Authority (IBA).[4] The IBA, in turn, owned Channel 4, which was funded by taxes on the ITVs and devoted to minority audiences and niche programming.

The competition that emerged from this structure was limited and unthreatening. The ITVs and BBC competed for market share but not funding; the regionally-based ITVs rarely competed for the same advertising revenue; and the BBC, with its massive staff and license fee, retained its traditional pre-eminence in expensive, high quality programming.

The advent of cable television did little to affect this basic structure. In 1984 the Cable and Broadcasting Act allocated cable franchises to petitioning firms, but restricted the provision of cable television only to those regions where geography made terrestrial broadcasting (the traditional ground-based tower system) impossible. As a result, cable "passed by" less than one percent of

---

[3] Personal interview, London, July 1997.
[4] Pankaj Ghemawat, "British Satellite Broadcasting Versus Sky Television," Harvard Business School Case 9-794-031.

Britain's television households in 1985. In the United States, by contrast, 36% of households subscribed to cable in that same year.[5]

For the next decade, cable expanded only slowly. Restricted by their geographical limits and without an obvious source for programming, cable companies had little competitive advantage against the far better entrenched BBC and ITVs. So they continued to lay cable and offer their services, but without seeing any significant growth in their market penetration. By 1994, a decade after the Cable and Broadcast Act, only 650,000 British homes were connected to any form of cable.[6]

This was the world of British television --- quiet, staid, high quality and comfortable. Until Rupert Murdoch came along.

Sky Takes Off

In the early 1980s, satellite television in Britain was even less developed than cable. Technologically, satellite broadcasts had been possible since the late 1960s, when scientists first succeeded in launching data transmission satellites into stationary orbit. Essentially, these are transmitters that hover exactly 22,300 miles above earth -- the point at which their revolution precisely matches the earth's rotation. From this point, the satellite's transmission can consistently reach a specified region of the earth – the satellite's "footprint" -- 24 hours a day.

In an effort to extend and control the commercial use of satellites, a multilateral organization known as the World Administrative Radio Council had parsed out the world's known satellite space in 1977. Each of the participating countries received five channels on existing broadcast satellites at that time, plus a certain amount of space for future satellites. While most European governments wrestled with the allocation of these channels, Britain moved particularly slowly. By the mid-1980s, the British government had still not allocated its channels to any domestic broadcaster. The BBC had declined the government's initial approach, protesting that they did not have the funds to support the additional programming and sales effort that a satellite channel would require, much less the resources to build and launch a dedicated satellite.

And thus the field was wide open in 1981, when an independent producer named Brian Haynes launched Satellite Television plc (SATV). Rather than petitioning for a piece of Britain's allocated space, Haynes persuaded the European Space Agency to allow him to rent space on an underutilized telecommunications satellite whose footprint included most of Europe and England. Because this was a communications satellite rather than a broadcast satellite, it was not covered by any of Britain's broadcast regulations.

Haynes's vision was to emulate American satellite pioneers Ted Turner (of CNN) and Jerry Levin (of HBO). Like them, he intended to transmit programming via satellite to cable stations, which would then redistribute the shows to individual households. Eventually, Haynes hoped, the development of smaller and cheaper receiving dishes would enable him to bypass the cable operators and transmit directly to his customers' homes. But in the meantime Haynes quickly found himself in a treacherous position. With only a small budget behind him, he could not afford to make or buy the programming that might lure subscribers or cable operators to his new channel. And without a solid subscriber base, he could not earn sufficient revenues to fund his operations or his programming. Repeatedly, Haynes was forced to search for new investors. It was on one of those searches that he discovered Rupert Murdoch's News Corporation.

---

[5] From Willis Emmons and David Grossman, "Note on Cable Television Regulation," Harvard Business School Case 9-391-022.
[6] "Survey of Cable TV and Satellite Broadcasting," *Financial Times*, October 6, 1993, p. 4.

In 1983, News Corp. paid £10 million for a majority interest in SATV. Rapidly, News coined the new name Sky and replaced Haynes and his management team with television executives skilled in the programming side of the business.[7]   For the next four years, Sky broadcast a news and entertainment channel to subscribers in 20 European countries. The channel broadcast 18 hours a day and reached over 10 million households via local cable systems.[8]   Total investment over the four years was £40 million.

It wasn't until 1986, five years after Haynes's SATV and a decade after Britain had obtained satellite broadcasting capacity, that British broadcasters at last grew interested in satellite television. In April of that year, the IBA publicly invited applicants to lease three of the country's five government-owned satellite transmitters. Sky, the only applicant with experience in satellite television, lost out to a hastly-assembled consortium called British Satellite Broadcasting (BSB). BSB was a high-powered group with ambitious plans. It included two of the country's ITVs (Granada and Anglia Television) plus Pearson, a diversified information and entertainment company, Richard Branson's Virgin Records and Amstrad a marketer and distributor of consumer electronics. Together the consortium aimed to provide Britain's first direct-to-home satellite channel. To maintain the non-commercial image built by the BBC, BSB planned to earn its revenues from subscription rather than advertisement. Its transmission standard would be based on D-MAC, a technologically ambitious standard that the European Union had recently endorsed for all government-owned broadcast satellites. Unlike older transmission standards, D-MAC would be compatible with the long-awaited high definition television (HDTV). By employing a D-MAC-based system, BSB planned to leapfrog existing transmission standards and position itself to dominate the next generation of television broadcast in Britain. It also planned to sell cutting-edge "squarials," small square receiving dishes that would epitomize the company's technological prowess. Start-up costs for the venture were estimated at half a billion dollars for a three channel service. Amid great fanfare, BSB predicted a launch date of October 1989.

As BSB hired some of the country's top managers and television programmers, Sky scrambled unceremoniously to relaunch its own satellite service. On June 8, 1988, Murdoch announced that Sky, too, would soon offer a direct-to-home (DTH) satellite service, complete with its own small receiving dishes and popular new programming. To transmit the DTH channels, Sky would lease four transmitters on a new Astra communications satellite. Unlike BSB, Sky would employ an older transmission standard, dubbed PAL.

Compared with BSB's lofty ambitions, Sky's was nearly an old-fashioned plan. PAL was considered an inferior technical standard and would never be compatible with HDTV transmission. Sky's dishes were also lower-tech than those proposed by BSB, and its satellite provider was barely a player in the European satellite industry. By the late 1980s, nearly all of Europe's satellites were high powered, national direct broadcast systems similar to that which the British government had allocated to BSB. Astra, by contrast, was launched by Societe Europeene des Satellites (SES), a small private company based in Luxembourg. It was only a medium-powered satellite by emerging standards -- but it was private, foreign, and officially a communications, rather than a broadcast, satellite. Britain's regulators had no jurisdiction over anything transmitted from Luxembourg's satellite space.

Murdoch made his break from the British regulators transparent and loud. With Sky's DTH service, he proclaimed, "We are seeing the dawn of an age of freedom for viewing and freedom for advertising. Broadcasting in this country has for too long been the preserve of the old Establishment that has been elitist in its thinking and in its approach to programming."[9] He vowed to begin broadcasting in February 1989, only six months after the announcement of Sky's plans -- and eight months prior to BSB's launch.

---

[7] William Shawcross, *Murdoch* (New York: Simon & Schuster, 1992) p. 207.
[8] Ghemawat, p. 3.
[9] Shawcross, p. 343.

Once the dual announcements had been made, the rivals raced to acquire precious programming rights. Not surprisingly, both headed straight to Hollywood, hoping to lock in the British distribution of popular U.S. films. After an expensive bidding war, Sky paid a reported £270 million to acquire the rights to films from Orion, Touchstone, Warner Brothers, and News Corp's own Twentieth Century Fox. BSB negotiated a £550 million deal for the rights to movies from Paramount, Universal, MGM/United Artists and Columbia Pictures.[10] As part of his negotiations, Murdoch agreed to what would become a critical arrangement. Because Sky's footprint spread across the European continent, its broadcast could be received outside the United Kingdom. To preserve their viewing rights in Europe, the studios thus insisted that Murdoch encrypt their films, restricting Sky's viewership to paying subscribers. In response, Murdoch shifted from an advertising-based business plan (his original intent) to a subscription-based plan. He also rushed to acquire the requisite technologies: a means to encrypt and de-scramble Sky's broadcasts and to manage a complicated mix of subscriber preferences.

Sky launched its new service as promised, in February of 1989. It then began a blitzkreig sales effort with a direct marketing organization and over 1000 salespeople. After failing to sell its home receivers at retail outlets, the company literally went door-to door, with an initial deal that included free subscription to Sky's movie channel, installation of the dish and receiver and free maintenance.[11] BSB, meanwhile, was slowing down, dragged by technical problems with the untested D-MAC format. When BSB finally launched in April 1990, Sky was already in 1.1 million households; approximately 600,000 via satellite dishes and the remainder through cable.[12]

By this point, BSB was already the second most expensive British start up in history, topped only by the Channel Tunnel. Launched with $700 million, the consortium had raised an additional $1.5 billion at the start of 1990. Under the terms of the debt covenant, the group needed to sign half a million subscribers by December in order to receive the next infusion of capital. And Sky was already capturing the market.

BSB fought Sky on two simultaneous fronts: with subscribers and with the British regulatory authorities. In a highly public campaign, BSB charged that Sky had circumvented British regulation through "technological wizardry," using its perch above Luxembourg to exempt its programming from British regulation.[13] The consortium also urged that the existing Broadcasting Act of 1981 be expanded to include cable and satellite broadcasters; if it were, then the Australian-born Murdoch, whose News Corp already owned two of Britain's largest national newspapers, would be in violation of British laws prohibiting foreign ownership of television and cross-ownership, by anyone, of newspapers and television.

By October, it had become clear that BSB had lost both the regulatory and the subscriber battles. With only 120,000 household subscribers, the consortium was roughly half a million short of its goal and losing £8 million a week.[14] The critical last tranche of financing would be withheld. Meanwhile, when Margaret Thatcher's government passed the Broadcasting Act of 1990, Sky emerged unscathed. The law extended ownership rules to terrestrial television broadcasters and to satellite broadcasters who employed high powered satellites. Medium powered satellites like Astra's, however, were not covered under the new regulation. Late in October, BSB and Sky began formal negotiations. In November, the two companies merged to form BSkyB. With a 50% share of the new company, News Corp was clearly the controlling force. Sky had won.

In the aftermath of the deal, controversy swept through the British broadcasting industry. The chairman of the IBA, who only learned about the merger an hour before its signing, declared the

[10]Shawcross, p. 345; Ghemawat, p. 8; and "The battle of Britain is taking its toll on the media barons," *Business Week*, February 5, 1990, pp. 38-9.
[11] Richard Lander, "The satellite war; low tech against high tech," *The Independent*, March 25, 1990, p. 10.
[12] Ghemawat, p. 9.
[13] Shawcross, p. 382.
[14] Shawcross, p. 383; "How BSB was Koed," *The Economist*, November 10, 1990, p. 79.

deal "illegal and brutal." Canceling the BSB's formal contract to transmit, he proclaimed, "It is clear to the IBA that the completion of the merger, for which the IBA's consent was neither obtained nor sought, gave rise to a serious breach of BSB's program contract."[15] Echoing these sentiments, the Labour party's broadcasting spokesperson asserted that "This merger is a skyjack. We are totally opposed to a satellite monopoly, particularly when controlled by a non-EC national."[16] The Office of Fair Trade, Britain's anti-monopoly watchdog, declared its intention to investigate whether having a single satellite provider was anti-competitive.[17] Even the usually pro-business *Economist* joined the anti-Murdoch fray, calling the deal a "Wapping in the Air," and referring to Murdoch's previous success in breaking the once-powerful British printing union.[18]

Yet Murdoch and his new BSkyB remained largely unaffected by the uproar. Under the terms of the 1990 Broadcasting Act, the IBA was to be replaced by a new regulatory agency, the Independent Television Commission (ITC). During the transition, the IBA was effectively a lame duck. So threats from that direction carried little weight. More importantly, Thatcher's government remained strongly supportive of the Act and of Murdoch. Thatcher herself defended the need to introduce more competition into the staid world of British broadcasting. She acknowledged having a conversation with Murdoch two days before the announcement of BSkyB, but insisted that no "specifics" had been discussed.[19] A member of Thatcher's cabinet was perhaps more forthcoming in describing the government's response. "Once the merger happened," he explained, "the choice was between no satellite company and the merged company. We could have stopped Sky by amending the Broadcast Act to keep News Corp out of satellite or we could have made it illegal to advertise on satellite. If we had done that we would have finished up with no satellite television and we would have irritated Murdoch, the worst of all outcomes. He was our friend and he supported us. We owed him for Wapping and for his support. And, Murdoch was people we could not bully. Look at the *Sun*. Look at the *Times*. We needed his political support."[20]

In the end, no formal proceedings were brought against the merger and BSkyB set out to establish itself as Europe's leading provider of satellite television.

BSkyB Takes Off

The next several years were extremely busy for the newly formed company. It consolidated its operations, substantially expanded program offerings, grew its subscriber base, and pioneered cutting edge computer systems. With Murdoch turning his energies to other corners of his empire, the management of BSkyB fell increasingly to Sam Chisholm, a former managing director at Australia's Nine Network, who had been appointed chief executive late in 1990. Chisholm came to Sky with a reputation for legendary programming instincts and a ruthless managerial style. As one associate described him: "Chisholm came out of a truly competitive television environment. The whole of his strategy was that if any piece of programming looked like it might have value at any time in the future, you should buy it and grow it or buy it and kill it."[21] When Chisholm came on board, BSkyB was losing £5 million a week.[22] Murdoch hired his fellow Australian to turn the network around. While moving rapidly on all fronts, Chisholm concentrated on two key aspects of BSkyB's strategy: controlling content and controlling access.

---

[15] "UK: The marketing story," *Marketing*, November 8, 1990. (Reprinted from Reuter Textline.)
[16] Ibid.
[17] Andy Fry and Mat Toor, "Sky's the limit for satellite TV," *Marketing*, November 8, 1990.
[18] "Broadcasting: Wapping in the air," *The Economist*, November 10, 1990, p. 72.
[19] Georgina Henry, "UK: Prime Minister knew of satellite TV merger," *The Guardian*, November 12, 1990. (Reprinted from Reuter Textline.)
[20] Case writer interview, London, July, 1997.
[21] Quoted in Mathew Horsman, "Rupert's Sam missile," *The Guardian*, November 10, 1997, p. 2.
[22] Estimates of these losses vary considerably. The £5 million figure is from "The gambler's last throw," *The Economist*, March 9, 1996, p.68. Horsman claims losses of £14 million in "Sky: the inside story: he barks and bites," *The Guardian*, November 10, 1997, p. 4.

Controlling Content

In April 1991 BSkyB was formally relaunched, complete now with five channels of programming: Sky One, Sky News, The Movie Channel, Sky Movies Plus, and Sky Sports. Before year end, four more channels were added: The Children's Channel, MTV, Screensport, and Lifestyle. Unlike the first five, Sky did not own the content of these latter channels. It merely bought the rights to them, and transmitted them from the Astra satellite, free of charge, to Sky subscribers.

Chisholm and his negotiators also returned to Hollywood where, as the sole satellite provider in Britain, they were now in a better bargaining position. After a year of discussion, Sony, Columbia Pictures, Warner Brothers and Disney's Touchstone all agreed to improved terms for Sky: by the end of the year, BSkyB controlled the British rights to more than 90% of Hollywood's first run movies. Reportedly, the five-year deals cost Sky well over a billion dollars. It was widely rumored in the industry that Sky had convinced the studios to link licensing fees to subscriber levels, thereby deferring payments while pre-empting their competitors from buying future film rights away from Sky.

With movies in its pocket, Sky turned next to sports. Early in 1992, the company bought the exclusive rights to Cricket's World Cup. Almost at once, sales of its satellite dishes doubled to 100,000 a month.[23] In May, Sky announced a £304 million deal for the exclusive rights to televise all games of Britain's Premier League soccer (a 22 member group of the country's best teams) for four years. Previously, these rights had been held by the ITVs, which generally paid roughly £55 million for the same contract. Now, if soccer fans wanted to see their games, they had to subscribe to Sky. Satellite dish sales skyrocketed and subscribers grew by 30% in 1992. "Soccer," as Murdoch later modestly described it, "was very important to BSkyB."[24]

In September of 1992, Sky Sports became a premium channel, meaning that subscribers had to pay an extra fee above the basic package. Meanwhile, News Corp continued to acquire sporting rights. By the end of 1996, BSkyB owned the rights to the Ruby League, the Football League (the three levels of Britsh soccer below the Premier League), Britain's overseas cricket tours, and Ryder Cup golf. Each year, because of Sky's aggressive bidding, the price of these rights soared higher. By 1996, when Sky rebid for the Premier League's four year contract the bill came to £670 million.

As BSkyB expanded its program content, its product offerings grew increasingly complicated. In 1990, it had provided all subscribers with the same basic channels for a flat fee. By 1996, subscribers could choose from a wide range of choices, picking (and paying) for what they wanted to see. From its original three channels, Sky now had thirty "basic" channels, six premium channels, and a smattering of pay-per-view events. To manage this increased complexity, the company relied on a increasingly sophisticated system of conditional access.

Controlling Access

Pioneered largely by Sky, a conditional access system is the brains of a home satellite system. So long as a satellite service derives its revenues primarily from advertising, conditional access is not really a concern. The company can simply broadcast its programs "free to air," and not worry about the precise number or identity of its viewers. When a system is based on subscriber revenues, however, the identity of these viewers becomes critical: those who watch must pay. When a system offers, like Sky, a wide and diverse menu of programming, each viewer must be able to choose precisely what he or she wants; each must receive precisely what they've ordered; and each must pay what they owe. Managing this system thus becomes a critical part of the channel's business strategy.

---

[23] "Who pays wins," *The Economist*, May 23, 1992, p. 64.
[24] "How the Fox Network grabbed the football from mighty CBS," *Wall Street Journal*, December 20, 1993, pp. B1, B6.

Sky first developed a conditional access system early in 1990, when its arrangements with the Hollywood studios forced the company to encrypt its programming and rely on a subscription-based business model. To develop the encryption software, Sky approached Adi Shamir, a mathematician at the Weizmann Institute of Science in Israel and also a founder of RSA Data Security, a leader in digital security software. Together with Yeda Research and Development, the company through which the Weizmann Institute commercialized its technologies, News formed News Data Security Products. Through a somewhat complex trading relationship, News then created a subsidiary, News Datacom, to receive exclusive license to NDSP's encryption technology and focus wholly on encryption and subscriber management. In July, 1992, News bought out all other shareholders. In December of that year Stephen Barden, formerly general manager at BSkyB, was brought in as CEO.[25]

Essentially, Sky's conditional access system consisted of two integrated parts -- a set-top box and a subscriber management system. The subscriber management system functions somewhat like a credit card processing center. It receives orders from new customers; processes change requests or specific choices from existing customers; and keeps track of payment. Every day, customized computer programs process thousands of requests and changes. As these requests are processed, a customer service center codes the information and sends it to a broadcast receiver. The receiver then sends a scrambled signal to the "smart card" installed in each customer's set top box. Though the card looks like a simple credit card, it actually contains a powerful microprocessor which contains the code necessary to unscramble the particular channels ordered by a subscriber. The card thus "tells" the set top box which portions of the satellite transmission to receive and decipher.[26]

Technologically, the system created and installed by News Datacom is extremely sophisticated. It employs cutting edge encryption algorithms to manage what its engineers claim to be pirate-proof digital broadcasting systems. It enables BSkyB to match precisely its viewers' preferences and payments, and to control access to its valuable program rights. It also gives the company an inordinately powerful competitive edge. Once subscribers are hooked into the Sky system, switching is difficult and relatively unlikely. Since the receiving dish is installed to face only the Astra satellite, it can not pick up signals from other transmitters. If it is moved, it will no longer receive Sky. Similarly, Sky's payment and conditional access system only processes Sky's subscriptions. To receive other encrypted signals, Sky viewers would need to install a second set top box, as well as a second satellite. A possible choice -- but not a likely one.

Not surprisingly, then, most would-be competitors to Sky decided in the early- and mid-1990s to piggyback on Sky's existing infrastructure rather than compete against it. Along with MTV and the Children's Channel, VH1, Nickelodeon, the Family Channel and Bravo all eventually added their own content to Sky's programming. As of 1997, BSkyB was still the only satellite television company in Britain. Approximately 15% of Britain's households subscribed to some package of Sky's programming, and many more bought Sky channels through cable distributors. In June of 1996, BSkyB's revenues crossed the billion pound mark for the first time. Its profits that year were more than £300 million. As CEO Chisholm summarized the company's position "subscribers are switching on to Sky in record numbers. . . BSkyB is now extremely well positioned to capitalize on the introduction of digital television and the significant benefits that will flow from this new technology."[27] Other observers, however, were less sanguine. Reviewing the digital landscape, one member of the European Parliament worried that Sky's clear dominance threatened the very "democracy and culture" of Europe. "Whoever controls the decoder controls the gateway, and rules governing access by broadcasters to the decoder will determine what goes on the set. There is fear that Sky's stranglehold will continue into the digital age."[28]

---

[25] Barry Fox, "Murdoch's cryptic vision for global TV," *New Scientist*, September 11, 1993, p. 20; William Lewis, "TV smart cards," *Financial Times*, May 2, 1996, p. 12.
[26] See "Murdoch's News Datacom at cutting edge of digital broadcasting," *Jerusalem Post*, October 21, 1996, p. 3.
[27] "The Sky's the limit for BSkyB," *New Media Age*, March 6, 1997, pp. 10-11.
[28] David Brown, "Watch with big brother," *The Scotsman*, December 4, 1996, pp. 39-40.

Challenges

Murdoch and Sky seemed invincible. But then, late in the 1990s, rapid developments in the British broadcasting industry raised a number of new and unforeseen challenges. Three in particular threatened to encroach upon Sky's well-embedded market position: the growing reach and ambition of Britain's cable companies; the advent of digital transmission formats; and the changing nature of regulation in Britain.

Cable Competition

As described earlier, the cable television industry in Britain had grown more slowly and conservatively than it had elsewhere. Hampered by geographical restrictions, outpowered by the BBC and then Sky, British cable companies had never developed an independent source of programming or a dedicated subscriber base. Instead, they leased proprietary content from BSkyB or elsewhere and simply delivered it across their direct-to-home cable network. This arrangement essentially robbed the companies of any competitive advantage or market flexibility. They were forced to buy content at whatever price -- and Sky, more often than not, was setting the prices. Reportedly, Sky refused to permit any of the cable companies to purchase discrete blocks of desired programming. Instead, they had to purchase pre-bundled packages, where popular premium shows (sports, news) came together with less broadly attractive programming. Because Sky had the content, it generally did not suffer much negotiation about the price. It set prices, and the cable companies had little choice but to accept. Typically, Sky charged the cable providers 59% of the retail price paid by Sky's own subscribers. Commenting on this pricing structure, one cable executive complained, "My typical cost of sales is 65%. If I am paying 59% to Sky, where do I make my money? I still have to pay to transmit. They are a brutal monopolist."[29]

Throughout the 1990s, the cable companies endeavored to compete with this "brutal monopolist" not through programming or pricing, but on the basis of differentiated service. Technologically, Britain's is the Rolls Royce of cable systems. It employs a highly sophisticated broadband cable infrastructure, capable of carrying not just television signals but also phone communication and high speed Internet connections. The system can also be converted to a digital format easily and inexpensively. Thus, Britain's leading cable operators had positioned themselves as multiple providers. To their subscribers they offered not just television programming but *both* cable and telephone service for a low combined rate. As the Director General of one cable firm explained his long term strategy: "In the short term we are gaining market share by providing good prices. In the long term we can compete on services because our existing technology will allow us to provide all kinds of interactive services such as banking and shopping. Satellite technology simply cannot provide the kind of interactivity that we can."[30]

Going Digital

If cable's boasts had occurred against a backdrop of constant technology, their threat might well have been limited. But in 1995 and 1996, the advent of digital technologies was suddenly calling into question the very notion of broadcasting and the shape of Britain's existing regulatory environment.

Technically, digital television (like all digital applications) involves the transmission of data in a simple binary form. In analogue transmissions, data is sent from the source to the recipient as a wave, with a fair amount of information redundancy required to reproduce the transmitted image accurately. In digital transmission, by contrast, the data is encoded in a binary language using ones

---

[29] Case writer interview with cable company executive, London, June, 1997.
[30] Case writer interview with cable company executive, London, June, 1997.

and zeroes, with no information redundancy whatsoever. These digits are then reconfigured (into an image or sound) at the receiving site. Commercially, the beauty of digital formats is that they allow for a greater clarity of reproduction: digital compact discs have a clearer sound than vinyl LPs; digital television provides a sharper and more accurate picture. More importantly, perhaps, techniques for digital compression dramatically increase the carrying capacity of nearly all transmission media (often referred to simply as "pipes"). With digital signals transmitted in a compressed form, television frequencies, for example, can carry five to six, even ten times as many channels as they could in the analogue world. So can radio frequencies, short wave radio frequencies and even old-fashioned fiber optic cables. The much-lauded "500 channel universe" was entirely a creation of digital compression: by squeezing television (and other) signals into ever-narrower bands of data, digital compression vastly multiplied the potential distribution of movies, news, television programming. Of anything, indeed, that could be converted into a electronic stream of binary digits.

In the United States, the focus of the "Digital Revolution" in the 1990s was largely the Internet. In Britain, by contrast, the television and media markets received the lion's share of attention. And BSkyB was a central figure. Before the move to digital, Britain's television spectrum supported five traditional analogue channels: three BBC channels, Channel 4, and ITV. All were standard terrestrial broadcasters: they used television towers to send analogue signals "free to air" to any viewer equipped with a receiving aerial. Digital compression meant that these five analogue channels could carry instead 36 digital channels. To receive the new (and presumably improved) digital picture, customers would need either a new digital television set, or a set top box that could convert the digital signal for their older analogue set. Cable companies could also convert (quite easily) to digital formats, expanding their capacity to over 150 channels. And satellite had basically the same expansive potential.

The question, of course, was who would fill these expanded digital "pipes," and with what. In the summer of 1996, the British Parliament published the Broadcast Act of 1996, setting forth its plans for the allocation of digital terrestrial licenses. The core of the policy was the creation of six "multiplexes," frequency channels capable of transmitting between three and six digital channels. Two of the multiplexes would be reserved for existing analogue stations (one for the BBC; the other for services of Channels 3 and 4). The remainder would be awarded as 12-year licenses to interested applicants. Digital service from these channels was expected to commence in July 1998.[31]

In the eyes of many observers, the allocation of the multiplexes would at last create some competition for both BBC and BSkyB. By creating whole new avenues for distribution, the digital channels could break Sky's stranglehold on the pay TV market and bring new blood into what had become again a fairly staid and stable industry. The opportunity, as one observer asserted, "was to exploit the cultural richness of television as a mass medium and to give a much needed boost to media diversity in Britain."[32]

But Murdoch, not surprisingly, had other plans. When British regulatory agencies first trumpeted their plans for a new 36-channel digital universe, Murdoch countered with a far more ambitious agenda. In August 1995 he first announced his intention to launch 120 digital channels from a new digitally-equipped satellite. One year later he pushed the ante up, promising to deliver 200 digital channels from the end of 1997, with an eventual total of 500.[33]

Further complicating the picture (and Sky's position) was the related issue of set top boxes. All of the plans for digital television -- be it cable, terrestrial, satellite or even wireless -- involved set top boxes. It was the boxes that would control access to multiple offerings, descrambling the channels that viewers had chosen and paid to receive. It was the boxes that would be the brains for a

---

[31] For more on the details of the 1996 Act, see Helen Burton, "Digital broadcasting in the United Kingdom," *Computer and Telecommunications Law Review*, vol 1, 1997, pp. 33-42.
[32] "A brave new world: a brave new decision," *The Guardian*, April 14, 1997, p. 4.
[33] See Stephen Barden, "Let's get digital," *The Independent*, December 8, 1996.

multiple channel, pay-per-view world. And Sky, through its News Datacom subsidiary, was the only company in Britain that owned the rights to set top boxes. It was also the only company that already had an installed base of set top boxes: its existing 3.5 million direct-to-home subscribers.[34]

On the surface, then, BSkyB appeared to be entering the digital age from an unassailably strong position. It had the programming; it had the channel potential; it had the boxes. It also, as of May, 1997, had a bid to become one of Britain's new digital multiplex providers.[35] Together with two of the country's most powerful ITVs, Carlton and Granada, Sky formed a new consortium, British Digital Broadcasting (BDB), to launch a proposed digital terrestrial service. With a planned investment of £300 million, BDB would target a mass television audience with a combined menu of sports, movies, and news programming -- content that the three participating firms already controlled. In its bid, BDB asked to be considered either for all three available multiplexes or for one. Their only major competitor was Digital Television Network (DTN), an unlikely consortium of International Cable Tel, a U.S. cable operator, and United News and Media, a British broadcaster.[36] Unlike BDB, DTN had no existing access to broad market programming. Instead, it proposed to serve a highly segmented minority subscriber base and offer a variety of two-way communications services such as shopping and information retrieval. If BDB was the old guard, DTN was clearly the long shot. And few in 1996 had much confidence in its long term prospects. BDB was thus the front runner in the bid for Britain's digital multiplexes.

Obviously, then, the threat to Sky did not come from the digital technologies themselves. On the contrary, the move to digital left Sky, if anything, in an even stronger competitive position. The threat came from the regulatory changes that the technology had created.

The Regulators

Traditionally, television in Britain has fallen under the overlapping jurisdiction of three regulatory agencies. The primary agency is the Independent Television Commission (ITC), which oversees and licenses all commercial television services, including terrestrial, cable and satellite.[37] Its central function is to ensure fair competition among broadcasters and hold them to agreed standards for program and advertising content. If a broadcaster violates the regulatory norms of the ITC, the agency has the ability to revoke or alter the broadcast license. The second regulator, the Office of Fair Trade (OFT), has a broader mandate. As Britain's overarching watchdog of competition, it has authority to discipline television broadcasters for unfair or anti-competitive. The third regulator, OFTEL (Office of Telecommunications), is not even officially related to the television industry. Yet because its bailiwick covers all of Britain's telecommunications industry, and because telephone and cable in Britain share a common wiring system, OFTEL's authority frequently laps into the field of television. Indeed, since the advent of cable television, many within the television industry have regarded OFTEL as a more powerful regulator than either the ITC or the OFT.

In the mid-1990s, each of these regulatory bodies was reviewing, at some level, complaints against BSkyB's entrenched market position. In December of 1995, a rash of complaints from cable operators compelled OFT to conduct a formal review of BSkyB's conduct in the pay television market. OFT reviewed Sky's exclusive rights to sports and movie programming, its conditional access system and its control over most of the available transponder space. In December 1996 it concluded that although Sky had a leadership position in all elements of its pay television business, its leadership did not constitute an abuse of power.[38] Six months later, following another round of

---

[34] "Sky's the limit," *New Media Age*, March 6, 1997, p. 10.
[35] Keith Weir, "UK media heavyweights team up for TV fight," *European Business Report* May 2, 1997. (Reprinted from Reuter Textline.)
[36] "Aerial combat," *The Economist*, May 24, 1997, pp. 63-4.
[37] The ITC effectively replaced the IBA as of January 1990.
[38] See Office of Fair Trading, "The Director General's Review of BSkyB's Position in the Wholesale Pay TV Market," London, December, 1996.

complaints from the cable companies, ITC agreed to conduct a similar investigation of Sky. The European Commission, meanwhile, had responded to the advent of digital technologies with the publication of an Advanced Television Standards Directive. A long and often highly technical document, the Directive sought to lay the framework for the development of digital television in Europe. It stressed the importance of inter-operability of standards, allowing consumers to "receive all their digital TV through one box."[39] It also was quite explicit on the topic of set top boxes. It required that, in the digital environment, conditional access services would have to be available to all broadcasters on a "fair and reasonable basis." As interpreted, this meant that all broadcasters would have to have equal access to a set top box, even if they did not own the box or its conditional access software.

Behind this rather complicated technological provision lay a key strategic demand -- and months of political maneuvering. Much of BSkyB's power at this point lay in its network of set top boxes. So long as Sky controlled the boxes, it wielded leverage over both its customers and its competitors. Customers needed Sky boxes to receive Sky's popular content and competitors needed to piggyback on Sky's infrastructure if they wanted to reach its ever-expanding base of subscribers. For years, many in the British television industry (and particularly the BBC and cable operators) had bristled against the competitive position embedded in Sky's boxes. They hoped to use the advent of digital technologies (and the corresponding wave of new regulation) to break what they saw as Sky's unfair stranglehold over British television. Accordingly, many in Britain (and Europe as well) began to advocate the development of a "common interface," a plug-in conditional access system that would enable a variety of broadcasters to share a common set top box. Sky, of course, disagreed. Arguing that a common interface simply did not make sense either commercially or technologically, Sky joined a European-wide industry forum, the DVB (Digital Video Broadcasting Project) to reconsider the issues surrounding digital transmission and conditional access. After several years of discussion, the group, which was composed primarily of engineers, proposed a set of digital television standards that rejected a common interface in favor of a "Simulcrypt" option. With Simulcrypt, broadcasters would incorporate encryption data into their transmissions and then allow a decoder (presumably an existing one) to receive and descramble their signal. DVB also agreed to work towards a common interface, but did not suggest making such an interface mandatory.[40] These standards, proposed to the European Commission, were eventually incorporated into the Advanced Television Standards Directive.

To Sky, the Commission's decision merely reinforced the reasonableness of its own position and the commercial impossibility of trying to squeeze various smart cards and payment systems into one already-complicated box. Others in the industry, however, saw the Directive as yet another political victory for Sky, evidence of its power even in Brussels and in the impending world of digital television.

Under the terms of the Directive, Sky (and other conditional access providers in Europe) would have to offer all digital broadcasters non-discriminatory access to their systems. They also were required to keep accounts for their access services separate from their other businesses, and to refrain from prohibiting equipment manufacturers from including common interface systems in their boxes. In Britain, responsibility for implementing the Directive fell to OFTEL, which rapidly declared its intent to defend the availability of access on a "fair and reasonable basis."[41] How this provision would translate to commercial reality, however, remained unclear.

---

[39] "TV Standards Directive Signals Digital TV Lift-off Towards Information Society," Press Release, Commission of the European Communities, July 25, 1995.
[40] See Burton, p. 39.
[41] OFTEL Review of Conditional Access Systems, December 1996.

The Summer of '97

In April of 1997, Britain's ITC began reviewing proposals for the digital multiplexes. With only DTN and BDB in the running, the industry concurred that BDB was the only possible choice. Sky would thus receive a platform for digital terrestrial broadcasts.

Its rivals, particularly the cable companies, were lobbying vigorously for someone to clip Sky's wings. But OFT was moving slowly and OFTEL was largely preoccupied with parallel developments in the telecommunications sector. A formal regulatory check on Sky seemed highly unlikely. Then something unusual happened. Late in the spring, British authorities made a formal request to the Competition Directorate of the European Commission, asking for an inquiry into Sky's participation in the BDB consortium. Two aspects of the request were noteworthy. First, that the regulators were directly targeting Sky. And second that they asked the Commission for an inquiry *before* choosing a bid winner. Although this violated standard policy, the Commission agreed to review Sky's position.

Defining what competition meant in a rapidly developing industry was not easy. In general, policy-makers within the Directorate appreciated the advantages of scale in capital-intensive industries such as telephony, television, telecommunications and computing. After decades of watching the separate European nations protect their own small and often uncompetitive "national champions," the general view in the EU was to allow strong European firms to grow unfettered and to resist taking any regulatory actions that might stifle competition or innovation. At the same time, however, the Competition Directorate wanted to prevent any single dominant player from controlling its market -- particularly if that market lay at the intersection of any of the new or converging industries.[42] On June 3 Karel Van Miert, the EU's Commissioner for Competition formally announced his discomfort with the BDB bid. "There is a problem so far as the pay TV business is concerned," he asserted, "because there could be an enhancement of an already-dominant position."[43] Two weeks later, the ITC announced that it would only consider the BDB bid if BSkyB relinquished its equity stake in the consortium. Sky was out.

Within the week, BDB structured a new deal. Sky withdrew from the consortium with £75 million and a five year contract for the supply of programming to the new venture. According to Morgan Stanley's estimates, the programming contract would provide Sky with roughly £300 million a year in incremental operating profits.

Meanwhile, Sky was also active on the technology front. It consolidated News Datacom and its subscriber management system into a new company, NDS, and purchased Digi-Media Vision, a firm with cutting edge technologies for video compression and multiplexing. Soon thereafter, the company demonstrated a prototype of a new digital set top box, one that could simultaneously employ several different scrambling systems.[44] Together with Matsushita, British Telecom (BT) and Midland Bank, Sky also formed British Interactive Broadcasting, a novel and ambitious interactive venture. According to the company's plans, BIB would manufacture set top boxes capable of interactive services. Using either phone lines or television connections, BIB boxes would enable customers to shop on line, conduct bank transactions, and so forth. To attract these customers, the new venture planned to spend £600 million to subsidize the retail price of the new digital set top box.[45] BIB was expected to launch in the summer of 1998.

The market, however, had reacted sharply to news of Sky's forced withdrawal from the BDB consortium. By August of 1997, BSkyB's stock was at a one year low, having lost more than a billion

---

[42] Case writer interview, Brussels, July 1997.
[43] "EU raises doubts on digital TV license bid," *Financial Times*, June 4, 1997.
[44] Junko Yoshida, "Mogul maneuvers for digital tv presence on a grand scale," *Electronic Engineering Times*, June 16, 1997.
[45] "Battle of the boxes," *The Economist*, October 4, 1997, p. 73.

dollars of market value since the ITC announcement. The Premier League, the jewel of Sky's sporting empire, had also indicated its interest in severing links with Sky and broadcasting its own events. And several Hollywood studios had recently mentioned that, in the impending 500-channel universe, they might begin to sell their pay-per-view rights to an overlapping set of television providers.

Sky, it appeared, was at a crossroads. In June its long-time head Sam Chisholm resigned, citing health concerns. Many in the industry murmured, however, that his departure had far more to do with the arrival of Elisabeth Murdoch, Rupert's 27-year old daughter and heir apparent at Sky. Industry analysts clamored that the end of Sky was near, that the EU had at last broken its stranglehold on Britain's pay television market, and that changing technologies would soon eliminate any vestiges of its competitive advantage. But BSkyB had heard many of these predictions before.

Exhibit 1   Satellite and Broadband Cable Development in the United Kingdom, 1989-1996

	1989	1990	1991	1992	1993	1994	1995	1996
Total TV Homes (000s)	21,214	21,518	22,007	22,046	22,145	22,303	22,412	23,436
Direct to Home Satellite								
DTH	497	1,278	1,734	2,097	2,477	2,754	3,138	3,566
Penetration (%)	2.3	5.9	7.9	9.5	11.2	12.3	14.0	15.2
Broadband Cable								
Homes Passed	557	828	1,016	1,567	2,327	3,336	4,968	7,157
Homes Connected (TV)	87	149	192	331	473	708	1,044	1,523
Penetration (%)	15.6	18.0	18.9	21.1	20.3	21.2	21.0	21.3

Source: Office of Fair Trading, "The Director General's Review of BSkyB's Position in the Wholesale Pay TV Market," London, December,1996, p. 25; Andrew Bailes, "The UK Cable and Satellite Market," *Financial Times Telecoms and Media Publishing: An FT Marketing Brief*, London, 1997, p. 67.

Exhibit 2 Market Share of Total Viewer Hours in the British Television Market, 1992-1996

	1992	1993	1994	1995	1996
(Percentage of Total Viewer Hours)					
Terrestrial					
BBC1	33.7	32.7	32.4	32.1	32.5
BBC2	10.5	10.3	10.6	11.2	11.6
ITV	40.8	39.9	39.5	37.2	35.1
Channel 4	10.1	11.0	10.7	11.0	10.8
Total Terrestrial	95.1	93.9	93.2	91.5	89.9
BSkyB					
Sky One	1.1	1.4	1.1	1.2	1.3
Sky News	.3	.3	.2	.4	.3
Sky Sports	.5	.6	.7	.9	1.0
Movie Channel	.5	.6	.7	.8	.8
Sky Movies	.9	.9	.8	.9	.9
Nickelodeon/ Paramount			.2	.4	.5
Total BSkyB	3.3	3.8	3.7	4.6	4.8
Other					
Discovery/TLC	.2	.2	.3		
Eurosport	.3	.3			
MTV	.2	.3	.3	.2	.2
Children's Channel	.2	.2	.1	.2	.2
TNT and Cartoon	.4	.6	.8		
UK Gold		.6	.6	.6	.6
Total Other	.4	1.1	1.6	2.1	2.4

Source: Toby Syfret, "UK Trends in Multi Channel Audiences and Advertising Revenue," *Financial Times Media and Telecoms: An FT Marketing Brief*, London, 1997, p. 38.

Exhibit 3 Pay Television Channels Available in Britain, 1996

Channel	Owner	Description	% Share of Pay TV Audience
Encrypted Basic Channels			
Sky One	BSkyB	Entertainment	14
Sky News	BSkyB	News	3
Sky Travel	BSkyB	Travel	<1
Sky Soap	BSkyB	Entertainment	<1
QVC	QVC/BSkyB	Home Shopping	na
MTV	Viacom	Music	2
VH-1	Viacom	Music	2
Nickelodeon	Viacom/BSkyB	Children's	4
Children's Channel	Flextech/Pearson	Children's	2
Bravo	Flextech	Entertainment	1
Family Channel	IFE/Flextech	Entertainment	1
Discovery/Learning	Discovery	Documentary	4
CMT Europe	Consortium	Country Music	<1
UK Gold	Consortium	Entertainment	6
UK Living	Consortium	Women's Lifestyle	3
History Channel	A & E/BSkyB	Entertainment	na
Paramount Channel	Viacom/BSkyB	Entertainment	<1
EBN	Tel. Inc/Dow Jones	Business News	<1
Sci-Fi Channel	Viacom	Entertainment	na
Encrypted Premium Channels			
Sky Movies	BSkyB	Films	9
The Movie Channel	BSkyB	Films	8
Sky Movies Gold	BSkyB	Films	2
Sky Sports	BSkyB	Sports	na
Sky Sports 2	BSkyB	Sports	13
Sky Sports Gold	BSkyB	Sports	<1
Disney Channel	Disney	Entertainment	3
The Racing Channel	SIS	Sports	na
The Adult Channel	Graff PPV	Adult	na
Playboy	Playboy/BSkyB	Adult	na
Fantasy Channel	Northern and Shell	Adult	na
JSTV	NA	Japanese	na
Chinese Channel	Pacific/Shaw	Chinese	na
ZeeTV	Zee TV	Asian	na
Free-to-Air Channels			
TNT	Turner	Entertainment	1
Cartoon Network	Turner	Children's	7
CNN	Turner	News	na
CNE	NA	Chinese	na
Eurosport	TFI/Canal+/ESON	Sports	2

Source: Office of Fair Trading, "The Director General's Review of BSkyB's Position in the Wholesale Pay TV Market," London, December,1996, pp. 141-42.

Exhibit 4   Cable Only Channels in Britain, 1996

Channel	Owner	Description
Basic Channels		
The Parliament	Consortium	Parliament
Performance	Daily Mail	Arts
Travel	Landmark	Travel
Identity	Black Ent.	West Indian
Asia Net	NA	Asian
Channel One	Daily Mail	Regional
Live TV	Mirror Group	Regional/Gossip
The Box	TCI	Music
Euronews	France TV/RAI	News
Channel Guide	Picture Apps	Programme Listings
MBC	Private	Middle East
Landscape Channel	Landscape	Music
Vision	NA	Christian
NBC Superchannel	NBC/Marcucci	Entertainment
Selec TV	Carlton	Education
Worldnet	NA	Entertainment
Mid Extension	Jones Cable	Education
Bloomberg TV	Private	Information
Premium Channels		
Namaste	NA	Asian
HVC	Graff PPV	Movies

Source: Office of Fair Trade, "The Director General's Review of BSkyB's Position in the Wholesale
Pay TV Market," London, December, 1996, p. 142.

Exhibit 5   BSkyB Financial Highlights, 1992-1996

(£ Millions)

	1992	1993	1994	1995	1996
Revenue					
DTH Subscribers	154	263	407	582	728
Cable	19	33	48	75	122
Advertising	44	64	78	92	110
Other	16	20	17	29	49
Total Revenue	233	380	550	778	1,008
Operating Expenses	280	318	380	533	693
Operating Profit	(47)	62	170	245	315

Source: BSkyB Annual Reports

Exhibit 6   BSkyB Direct To Home Prices, 1991-1996 (£)

	1991	1992	1993	1994	1995	1996
Multi Channel				6.99	9.99	10.99
Sky Sports			5.99	11.99	14.99	15.99
One Movie Channel	9.99	11.99	11.99	11.99	14.99	15.99
Two Movie Channels	14.99	16.99	16.99	16.99	19.99	21.99
One Movie Channel and Sky Sports			16.98	16.99	19.99	21.99
Two Movie Channels and Sky Sports			19.98	19.99	22.99	24.99

Source: Office of Fair Trading, "The Director General's Review of BSkyB's Position in the Wholesale Pay TV Market," London, December, 1996, p. 32.

The Internet promises to be the site of a commercial revolution. Rules can make it happen.

RULING THE NET

by Debora Spar and
Jeffrey J. Bussgang

Ever since the Internet burst into the public realm, it has held aloft the promise of a commercial revolution. The promise is of a radical new world of business – a friction-free arena where millions of buyers and sellers complete their transactions cheaply, instantaneously, and anonymously. Cut free from layers of middlemen, companies will be able to sell their products directly to their customers; consumers will be able to customize products, interact with the companies that supply them, and conduct business from the comfort of their own homes. By bringing companies and customers together, the Internet thus promises to widen markets, increase efficiencies, and lower costs. Those are radical promises, and on their strength thousands of companies have already joined a massive scramble to cyberspace.

For many of those companies, however, the Internet has yet to deliver on its promises. Although doing business in cyberspace may be novel and exhilarating, it can also be frustrating, confusing, and even unprofitable. Whereas for some companies on-line commerce is a natural outgrowth of their business, for others – particularly in information-intensive industries such as software, publishing, and financial services – moving into cyberspace is a difficult endeavor. The problems these companies face have little to do with a lack of technology or imagination. They stem instead from a lack of rules.

Why, in the midst of such a critical transformation, should managers pause to consider anything so mundane as rules? The answer is that rules are critical to commerce. Without the order that rules create, business cannot be conducted.

At the moment, there are few rules in cyberspace. The legal status of electronic copyright is still vague, as are the legal and practical issues surrounding on-line exchange and "electronic cash." There is also limited authority to enforce rules on the Internet and little capacity to punish those who violate the norms of on-line conduct. Although

Debora Spar is an associate professor at the Harvard Business School in Boston, Massachusetts, and Jeffrey J. Bussgang is director of transaction products at Open Market in Cambridge, Massachusetts.

PHOTO BY TONY RINALDO

these problems have been well documented, they persist nevertheless. And until they are solved, cyberspace will remain a frontier town – a land of opportunities, to be sure, but also one of tremendous risks.

In surveying this frontier, it is important to realize that the current lack of rules does not necessarily mean that governments will send in the cavalry or that companies will walk away in despair, leaving the Internet to the hackers and the chat lines. Instead, it simply means that companies need to think carefully before making any headlong leaps into cyberspace. Rather than just posting pages on the World Wide Web, for instance, companies may want to move more selectively, clustering themselves into on-line communities where rules pre-

nities will also shift the balance of power between business and government toward business. That evolution will occur not because of the power of particular companies, or because business is opposed by nature to an open Internet or a free flow of information. Rather, commerce will move toward on-line communities simply because companies need a basic infrastructure of rules to survive.

This vision of Internet commerce is a less radical one than that embraced by many Internet proponents, and a far cry from the friction-free world of open and unregulated commerce espoused by such figures as Bill Gates. But it takes into account the realities facing most companies today. In our view, the commercial promise of the Internet is still vast, but it does not lie in the unmanaged reaches of cy-

Like early automobile drivers, early users of the Internet devised their own rules of the road.

Don't change the subject

:-)

vail and commerce can proceed. Auto parts suppliers, for example, might band together in an exclusive network serving only the auto industry, whereas investment management firms might want to

berspace. Nor does it come solely from the Internet's technical ability to facilitate transactions and reduce costs. Instead, the promise lies in the ability of companies to form well-defined communities that will protect their property and promote their own interests. It lies in the potential of other companies to construct these communities, to intermediate their commerce, and to guard their members. The commercial promise of the Internet, in short, requires rules for its fulfillment. And the companies that stand to reap the greatest profits in cyberspace are the pioneers who will write, support, and enforce the new rules of the emerging frontier.

Until rules are established and enforced, cyberspace will remain a frontier town.

sell their services only where distribution is limited and payment ensured.

These sorts of on-line communities will create a very different form of electronic commerce from the one envisioned today by many Internet adherents. The communities will not be open to all; they will increasingly charge customers for their services; and they will not permit information to flow across seamless borders. They will change the current spirit of the Internet and bring order and management to the Net's unruly tangle. By writing the rules for commercial transactions, on-line commu-

The Rules of Exchange

When the Internet was first developed in the 1960s, it was governed by clear codes of conduct and working norms of behavior. Developed by a community of like-minded scientists, the rules were rarely written down or even explicit, but they did not have to be, because travelers on the Net could easily observe them. Just as early automobile drivers informally devised rules of the road, so too did early Internet users develop their own norms of behavior. They created symbols to express emotions such as happiness [:-)] and unhappiness [:-(]. They created some explicit rules, such as Don't change the subject and Read the FAQ [frequently-asked-questions] file, and they even created a language of sorts with terms such as *flame* and *spam*. Despite its outward image as an untamed realm of hackers, the early Net was in fact a rule-bound, orderly community. The rules, however, evolved to serve the interests of a particular community – researchers in academia and in the U.S. Department of Defense, who had no desire to profit from their on-line activities.

search questions that had previously bound users together. They were also largely unfamiliar with many of the Internet's specific protocols. Cyberspace for the newbies was simply an adventure – an opportunity to meet people, gain information, and perhaps re-create some sense of small-town intimacy and immediacy. But many newcomers also came to cyberspace for profit, to explore the Net's potential, and to stake a claim in a technology that promised to revolutionize the nature of transactions. As a result, the Internet's new business district – the ".com domain" – quickly swelled to become the largest sector of the Net.

Dramatic levels of growth and a radical shift in the Internet's population of users make necessary a new set of on-line rules. Yet because the Net lacks

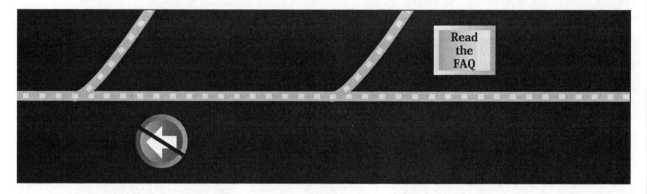

For roughly 20 years, that community flourished. But in the early 1990s, the community's rules and values were suddenly attacked by hordes of "newbies," new users who had scrambled on-line. Whereas the Internet in the early 1980s consisted of only about 25 linked networks, it had grown by 1995 to include more than 44,000 networks extending to 160 countries and including 26,000 registered commercial entities. Somewhere between 40 million and 50 million computers were connected to Internet hosts in 1995, and that number was growing by an estimated 10% to 20% per month.

The entrance of the newbies did more than just increase the sheer numbers on the Internet; it led to a fundamental change in the Net's culture. Arriving on-line largely through new commercial services and Internet access providers, these new users were riding a wave of privatization that began with the emergence of commercial service providers in 1989 and continued when the Internet was officially opened to commercial ventures in 1990. The newbies had little interest in the re-

any central authority or organizing structure, rules are emerging piecemeal, pulled and prodded by the often conflicting interests of business, governmental agencies, and traditional Net users. In general, the governmental agencies and traditional users have been more explicit than businesses in describing how they want rules to evolve. The U.S. government, for example, has focused largely on safeguarding defense-related access and regulating

The Net's rules are emerging piecemeal, pulled and prodded by business, governmental agencies, and traditional users.

access to pornography. Traditional users have lobbied vociferously for open communications, universal access, and a ban on government intervention of any sort. The business community, by contrast, has been relatively quiet. Rather than thinking abstractly about rules, most companies have concentrated on the more immediate tasks of getting on-line and claiming a stake in cyberspace.

That focus is shortsighted because it overlooks the greatest potential for companies on the Internet: the opportunity not only to master the game of electronic commerce but also to create the rules of the game. In particular, companies can influence the creation of rules in three distinct areas: property rights, means of exchange, and enforcement.

Property Rights

All economic systems are based fundamentally on a shared understanding of property rights. Developed over decades or even centuries, property rights clarify the basis of ownership and exchange. They provide a consistent way of defining who owns what and how possessions can be transferred from one owner to another. Property rights reduce the costs of exchange by clarifying ownership and providing a means for punishing thieves; thus they define not only possession but also theft.

In modern market economies, property rights also provide the incentives that drive growth. If property is communal or property rights are ill defined, no one in the community has much incentive to produce anything more than he or she can consume. What creates the incentive and impels progress is a system that defines private property and enables its owners to make use of it for their own benefit. Without the ability to garner the returns from one's property, there is no incentive to invest in specialization or technology or even to put in a hard day's work. To generate such investments, communities create and preserve rules of private property.[1] And as economies evolve, so too must the rules.

The connection between property rights and commerce applies with full force to the Internet. The advent of electronic commerce does not eliminate business's basic need for an infrastructure to clarify ownership and allow owners to reap economic rewards. But at the moment, online property rights are imprecisely defined; the Net remains a virtual free-for-all where information is seen as a public good and ownership is up for grabs.

Understandably, then, companies that deal in the business of information are approaching the Net with caution. The Recording Industry Association of America, for instance, held back because it was worried that its products might be changed or misrepresented on-line. Likewise, the Smithsonian Institution has limited the electronic reproduction of its artistic works; as a spokesperson told the *New York Times*, the institution reasons that "at least for now...cyberspace is a chaotic wild west frontier full of highway bandits and subject to only the roughest kind of vigilante justice."

There is one fairly obvious way to solve the problem of property rights on the Internet: the creation of law by central governments. In cyberspace, that law would probably come from an extension of existing copyright law. Because copyright provides for the commercialization of intangible products – intellectual property – the extension of copyright law into cyberspace would seem to make sense. By guaranteeing the rights of intellectual property owners, copyright law should allow information-based companies to move more confidently onto the Internet. Accordingly, lawmakers in Washington, D.C., have recently begun to tinker with copyright law. In September 1995, a group convened by the White House's Information Infrastructure Task Force recommended changing the 1976 copyright law to explicitly include transmission as a form of distribution. The group also endorsed a "fair use" provision that would limit any noncommercial use of intellectual property that nevertheless damages the legal owner of the property.

If enacted as law, these provisions will do a lot to protect the property of companies that transact in cyberspace. But they won't do nearly enough. First, copyright is already one of the most intricate and esoteric areas of law. Courts vary widely in their interpretation of existing statutes and even in their understanding of a given law's intent. The extension of those laws into a new realm of commerce is almost sure to create ambiguity and uncertainty, leaving courts and litigants to fumble toward new definitions of private property and property rights. Second, because the laws are national, they will have little influence on the Internet's international transactions. Thus, even if the laws stop a company based

> **Copyright laws are no help to companies searching for on-line thieves.**

UNDER PENALTY OF LAW THIS TAG NOT TO BE REMOVED EXCEPT BY THE CONSUMER

in Cincinnati from covertly downloading a competitor's software, textbook, or database, they may not stop that company from routing the material through a computer in Thailand or the Netherlands. Finally, even if the laws were applied at the global level (and there is some talk of doing so under the new World Trade Organization), they still would not provide the means for businesses to determine if their information has been altered or copied in cyberspace. The laws also offer no solution to the thorny problems involved in tracing online violations. Even if a company suspects that its product has been stolen, how can it find the thief, especially if the transactions have been routed through multiple sites and untraceable user IDs?

Again, there are measures that governments can take to fill those gaps. They can establish a central registration point for user IDs, as France initially did with its innovative Minitel service. They can use central crime-fighting units, as the United States did in directing a raid by the FBI on on-line pornography and in tracking down Kevin Mitnick, the credit card hacker. But such forays are likely to be limited both by the diffuse structure of the Internet and by the antigovernment sentiment that still prevails within it.

Meanwhile, the door is open for private companies to move directly into the rule-making business. Although companies cannot write the rules of intellectual property rights, they can establish rule-bound areas of the Internet– "virtual communities" in which rules are enforced. In those areas, companies can perform the functions that governments are not yet capable of fulfilling. For a fee or by contract, they can protect the rights of on-line property. Just as merchants in medieval times developed the customs and practices that eventually became commercial law in Europe, so can contemporary companies and entrepreneurs create the rules of electronic commerce.

Consider, for example, the services provided by America Online. AOL sells access to the Internet. It gives users an easy way to enter cyberspace and a new forum in which to advertise products or disseminate ideas. When new subscribers join AOL, though, they get much more than a pathway to the Net. They get a well-regulated, well-maintained road. AOL offers a user-friendly environment and direct access to commercial services. In return, it regulates all users and demands that they comply with explicit rules. Likewise, when a content provider signs on with AOL, it does not simply transmit its information into the vast reaches of the Internet. Rather, it provides its content – news stories, photographs, flight schedules – directly to AOL, which then redistributes the content to its own subscribers, a discrete and identifiable customer base. By intermediating the transaction, AOL converts the Internet from an open, lawless realm into a secure community where access is controlled and rules are enforced. As a result, AOL can assure its content providers that their sales will be controlled, identified, and reimbursed. In effect, AOL creates and enforces the property rights of its customers. Even without a well-defined legal infrastructure, AOL is writing the rules of commerce.

Means of Exchange

Rules for commercial transactions constitute a second area ripe for private intervention. In most economic systems, currency of one form or another is used as payment in transactions. Typically, currency is issued by a central government that retains a monopoly over its creation and backs it with fractional reserves of precious metals or other countries' currencies. Even when the currency is not directly backed by a tangible asset, a government's management of its supply can create value based on confidence (that the government will always accept it as a store of value) and scarcity (because there is never quite enough to go around).

In contrast to the rules of property rights, which must change to meet the demands of electronic commerce, the rules governing currency could probably function quite well for electronic exchange. Even in cyberspace, customers can order goods priced in dollars, charge them to a credit card, and let banks intermediate the financial transaction. There is nothing intrinsic about the Internet that demands new means of exchange. There are no technical obstacles to routing and recording even nontraditional transactions through established routes; nor are there demands for new levels of financial oversight or regulation.

Instead, the impetus for change stems from the instantaneous and intangible nature of electronic transactions. If electronic purchases become commonplace, they are likely to include such "micro-transactions" as buying one article from the *Atlantic Monthly* or browsing through the *New York Times* for three minutes. The cost of processing those services by credit card would overwhelm the price of the service itself; such costs could doom small on-line entrepreneurs from the start. If payment could take place instantly, however, then the costs of transacting would plummet and commercial activity could flourish. As an added benefit, electronic exchange could, like cash transactions, allow buyers and sellers to maintain their anonymity. With a wallet full of "E-cash," buyers could purchase items quickly and anonymously in cyberspace. Without having to rely on credit cards, bank tellers, and checkbooks, they could save both time and money. This is the radical vision of Internet commerce – fast, cheap, and anonymous.

Technologically, the creation of electronic money depends on the issuance of an anonymous electronic note. An institution would sell electronic money to its customers, coding the E-cash onto a wallet-

**Purchase item
VISA** (enter account number)

**Purchase item
Checking Account**
(deduct amount)

**Purchase item
E-CASH** (enter account number)

Consumers could save time and money by using E-cash rather than credit cards, bank tellers, or checkbooks.

sized card or transmitting it directly to another on-line merchant. It would debit the disbursed E-money, plus a small transaction fee, from customers' regular bank accounts. For this process to work, the electronic transfers must remain anonymous and secure, and transaction fees must be kept low. In the past, similar requirements were met by the agencies of a central government. Governments printed currency, allowed it to circulate anonymously, punished those who stole or copied it, and covered their expenses through taxation. On the Internet, however, there is no central authority to establish the means of exchange. And national governments have little interest in taking on the problem, because E-cash raises a host of troubling law-enforcement questions. For example, would E-cash expand the possibilities for tax evasion and money laundering? And how would governments track the assets of individuals or the trading balances of states? If E-cash proliferates, many aspects of economic activity will likely escape the scrutiny of government agencies; thus they have little incentive to play any role in its creation.

For private companies, by contrast, the incentives are vast. First, there is the cost-cutting potential of electronic payment. Banks in particular have a considerable interest in cutting the costs of intermediate transactions and moving directly to electronic payment systems. Several institutions, such as Citibank and Wells Fargo, already employ proprietary software systems that allow customers to do

their banking on-line. As banks and other financial-service institutions increasingly compete on the basis of transactions rather than relationships, these payment systems will become critical to their success.

But the real breakthrough will come when electronic payment systems are pushed into the broader reaches of cyberspace. Eventually, the value of E-cash, like the value of any currency, will be determined by the market's demand for it. For demand to increase, the currency will have to be widely accepted. In the past, governments ensured this acceptance simply by proclaiming their currency legal tender. In the future, the game will be inherently more competitive. Companies that establish the most accessible and secure means of exchange will capture the market of all those seeking to conduct electronic transactions. And success in this game will breed more success, because a currency's acceptance by some users will increase its attractiveness to others.

Not surprisingly, then, the race to develop the means of secure electronic exchange has become one of the most spirited competitions in cyberspace, with start-ups such as DigiCash and Cyber-Cash taking on established players such as Visa and MasterCard. To some extent, it is a race of technology: Winning will entail the refinement of encryption algorithms – which scramble electronic signals and allow access through mathematically encoded digital signatures – as well as the development of secure "electronic wallets." The race, however, is also about rules, because technology alone cannot support a full-fledged system of electronic exchange. If payment systems are to proliferate along the Internet, some trusted entity will have to oversee and regulate their use. The issue goes beyond the widely publicized threat of credit card theft. The question is, Can large companies attain the confidence necessary to conduct business over the Internet? Even with major leaps in encryption technology, few institutions are likely to feel sufficiently comfortable with the Internet's open architecture to entrust it with millions of dollars' worth of transactions. Performing commercial transactions in a private electronic network is a far cry from allowing them to occur in the blatant public spaces of the Internet.

If companies are to push their financial transactions into the broader reaches of the Net, they will need some means of recourse. At a minimum, they will need to know that some identifiable, credible entity is backing the security of their transactions and preventing widespread fraud and abuse. Historically, governments have served in that role, but private companies will have to do so on the Internet. Financial institutions, with their combination of trusted brand-name and risk-management experience, are particularly well suited for this role. Yet the attributes of those institutions could also eventually adhere to any other trusted entity – the local telephone company, a utility, a local newspaper. In any case, the entity managing an exchange system would also need to bundle its means of exchange with rules of security and enforcement.

Security and Enforcement

Security and enforcement pose the most obvious problems for Internet commerce. They also create the most tantalizing opportunities for new business development. Before any E-cash changes hands, and indeed before any real financial transaction occurs on-line, the parties to an exchange must have confidence that their transaction is secure. That is, they must know that the buyers or sellers are really who they claim to be, that the information being exchanged cannot be stolen or altered en route, and that the payment being offered is real.

These levels of security do not yet exist broadly on the Internet. Instead, as information travels through the network, it passes through many computers and sorters and is thus exposed to a host of possible points and paths of interception. Although the Electronic Communications Privacy Act of 1986 specifically forbids eavesdropping on electronic transmissions, laws of that kind are extraordinarily difficult to enforce because no policing agency controls the points of access. This basic lack of control is a major impediment to the growth of electronic commerce.

The need to guarantee information integrity presents a second security problem. Once information is put on-line, its creators can do little to ensure that it will not be altered electronically. Thus hospitals worry about patients' records being changed, and authors and publishers are concerned that their views might be misrepresented. Moreover, just as the nature of the Internet makes it difficult to detect the theft of information, its current structure also makes it virtually impossible to trace tampering. Anyone can operate on-line under a false name. A *New Yorker* cartoon makes the point: A dog, sitting at a computer keyboard, turns to his canine companion and remarks, "On the Internet, nobody knows you're a dog." As the Internet grows, security problems are likely to mount. In 1990, the federally funded Computer Emergency Response Team reported 130 break-ins on the Internet. According to an article in *Technology Review*, that number grew to 1,300 in 1993 and 2,300 in 1994.

Usually break-ins, like tampering, fraud, and theft, are considered to be within the purview of governmental agencies. But on the Internet, governments have not yet defined precisely what constitutes theft, nor have they established the institutions to trace or apprehend thieves. So the field is wide open to private development. The most obvious opportunity lies with the technologies of electronic security. Theoretically, cutting-edge technologies such as encryption and fire walls can solve security problems by fully protecting on-line transmissions. (Fire walls protect a company's internal network from outside users by establishing physical filters between networks.) Neither technology has been perfected or widely deployed, but many industry insiders believe that within a year or two, both will be powerful enough to guarantee the security of transactions. And the companies that reach perfection first will generate a new current of enthusiasm for commercial activity on the Net. At the moment, the leader in digital-security software

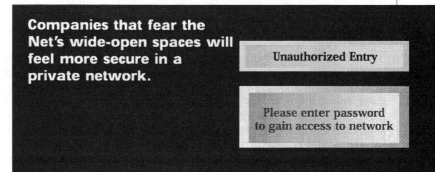

Companies that fear the Net's wide-open spaces will feel more secure in a private network.

Unauthorized Entry

Please enter password to gain access to network

is RSA Data Security, which has already licensed its encryption algorithms to major Net players such as IBM and Netscape. Other companies, such as Verisign and Microsoft, have also joined the race.

Meanwhile, there is another race going on, a race less obvious in some respects but ultimately more important. The development of secure technologies is absolutely critical to the expansion of Internet commerce, but it is not sufficient. To facilitate the expansion of electronic commerce, even the most sophisticated technologies will have to be embedded in broader, more secure networks. And those networks, along with their security systems, will have to be managed by some trusted intermediary. Enter again private companies, making rules and managing virtual communities.

On-line communities are necessary because individual security precautions have only a limited value on the Net. Value lies, instead, in a wider,

If the Internet is a lawless frontier, then service providers are the new marshals in town.

protected community of users, who can communicate among themselves confidentially and thus confidently. The value of the community is created by the entities that run and manage it. They are the ones who determine its size, choose its members, implement security provisions, and punish violators. If the Internet is a lawless frontier, then these service providers are the new marshals in town. Unlike the old marshals, though, they are also constructing the towns and then marketing them by bragging about the local security and clientele. Wyatt Earp would have drooled.

Communities and Commerce

For on-line communities to form, content providers need to feel confident about whom they are dealing with, how their material is being used, and how they are receiving payment. What they need, in short, is an entity to transform the anonymity and anarchy of the Internet into a market with identifiable customers and recordable transactions. That entity would manage a corner of the Internet where explicit rules and norms would prevail.

Early forms of management entities already exist in such Internet service providers as UUnet, PSINet, and Bolt Beranek & Newman. But the services they make available are still minimal, limited largely to granting their users a means of access to the Internet and some tools for navigating it. What these providers could offer (and presumably soon will) are the value-added services associated with rules and rule making. They could, for instance, provide secure transaction services, limit access to certain groups, or cluster their users into communities linked by similar interests or needs.

Such communities already exist on-line in the form of chat groups and bulletin boards. But their rapid proliferation has undermined some of the Net's early sense of community and begun to raise concerns among some users about the risks of association with unknown, untraceable parties. Some users, especially old-time hackers and technophiles, will probably want to remain in the vast, anonymous realm of the open Web. But others – parents who want their children reading the *Encyclopaedia Britannica* but not *Hustler*, researchers who tire of their professional discussions being interrupted by outsiders, technophobic shoppers who love L.L. Bean but hate keyboards – will probably prefer to exchange the adventure of cyberspace for a more regulated and predictable community. Service providers can fill this need by creating customized, managed communities in cyberspace and setting their own standards for on-line exchange.

To set and maintain those standards, service providers will need to employ many of the technologies described earlier. They will need, for example, an accurate means of tracking who is online and what those people are doing. That way, any content provider can learn who is making use of its product and, more important, can be paid for its "microsales" to those users. Armed with the appropriate tracking and billing technologies, the service provider would perform the crucial functions of intermediation: It would track customers, bill them, and pay content providers. It would also guarantee that violators of the rules would be punished, most likely by expulsion from the community.

Microsoft Network is one example of this trend toward on-line communities. Originally conceived as another proprietary on-line service, MSN has recently been repositioned as an Internet community with well-ordered rules and value-added services. Other on-line services, such as AOL, Prodigy, and CompuServe, are similarly reinventing themselves as full-service Internet communities. And they are not alone. Time Warner's popular Pathfinder site – which offers rich content from across the media giant's empire – requires users to register, tracks their subsequent usage, and plans soon to offer accompanying transaction services. Several other telecommunication and media companies have also announced plans to launch their own communities on the Internet.

While the shift toward communities of commerce is most evident in consumer-oriented services, the logic of communities extends even further than that. A computer manufacturer could easily create an Internet community with its key distributors, just as a large clothing company might reap the benefits of establishing a secure transaction infrastructure with its suppliers. Universities could choose to distribute their course catalogs only within their own corners of the Internet, and banks could dedicate separate, secure lines for their own internal transactions. The recent interest in using the Internet as an intracompany business tool – an "Intranet" – is yet another variation on those themes.

In all these examples, the companies managing the on-line transactions of their users would have created privately ruled communities, just as developers in some urban areas have built private "towns," complete with strict rules, security forces, and gates to keep outsiders away. To build these communities, service providers would employ encryption, fire walls, and other evolving technologies to control access in the same way as developers control it in physical communities.

This vision – of walls and guards and tracked activities – is precisely opposed to the open market and universal access approved of by most Internet proponents. It is also seemingly at odds with the democracy that mass electronic communication is thought to foster. But although private towns may well undermine the broad goals of an open, egalitarian society, managed virtual communities do not restrict the prospects for free, open communication. They merely divide the realms of activity, just as most people already divide their own activities into private and public spheres. Moreover, by establishing limited, ordered communities, service providers have the potential to increase dramatically the number of people who venture on-line. For despite the terrific growth in Internet use, many people still find cyberspace too noisy, too anarchic, and too cumbersome for their purposes. By restricting the on-line options, fine-tuning the offerings to match a select group of users, and offering some means of recourse in case of fraud or abuse, service providers can develop the kinds of managed communities that will draw new users on-line and increase the productivity of those already there.

Most important, though, service providers can create an environment conducive to commerce. As long as the Internet remains an open, unregulated space, companies from information-intensive industries such as publishing, software, and financial services are unlikely to shift large segments of their business on-line. They may advertise or encourage chat groups to discuss their products, but they probably will not sell them directly through cyberspace. To make the final leap, they – and presumably all content providers – need systems of property rights and exchange, as well as a means of enforcement. Central governments are not now in a position to make or enforce the needed rules, and the Internet as a whole has no controlling body. Individual companies or entrepreneurs are likely to develop the technological means for implementing rules – encryption, fire walls, tracking systems, and so on – but only if they have some prospect of reaping the benefits from their investment or innovation. Service providers can facilitate the development of a

Commerce will migrate to areas where rules prevail and responsibility can be assigned.

market by purchasing or licensing the technologies from their creators and then using them to create a commercial space that would bring together buyers, sellers, browsers, and advertisers in a regulated, orderly community.

In the long run, the Internet will not transform business into a friction-free realm in which millions of anonymous buyers and sellers meet for one-shot, instantaneous transactions. Nor will the Net remain unregulated and uncensored. Portions of the Net may stay that way, but they will not be busy with commerce. Rather, commerce will migrate to areas where rules prevail and responsibility can be assigned. Some of those areas probably will appear unorganized, and transactions within them will take place faster and more cheaply than in the physical world. But increased speed and reduced costs will not lead to the disappearance of rules, communities, or intermediaries. On the contrary, the real move to electronic commerce will demand several layers of intermediaries to form new communities and support new rules. Electronic commerce requires those changes, which will also provide companies with the greatest opportunity for profit. In cyberspace, the real power will lie with those who make the rules.

1. The argument of this section draws extensively on the work and writings of Douglass C. North. See, in particular, North, *Structure and Change in Economic History* (New York: W.W. Norton & Company, 1981); and North and Robert P. Thomas, *The Rise of the Western World: A New Economic History* (Cambridge: Cambridge University Press, 1973).

Reprint 96309   To place an order, call 1-800-545-7685.

Network Associates: Securing the Internet

If privacy is outlawed, only outlaws will have privacy.

— Phil Zimmermann, designer of Pretty Good Privacy software

This is the revenge of people who couldn't go to Woodstock because they had too much trigonometry homework.

— Stewart Baker, general counsel, National Security Agency[1]

On March 20, 1998, Network Associates, Inc., (NAI) announced that it would begin selling its popular Pretty Good Privacy computer encryption software through a Dutch subsidiary. It was a simple announcement of a commercial relationship, yet it caught the worlds of business and politics by surprise. In 1998, computer encryption was a strictly regulated technology in the United States. Because of its military links and its potential threat to national security, encryption software was treated as a munition and U.S. firms were forbidden from exporting so-called "strong" encryption without a special license. NAI, a leader in the market for strong encryption products, had not applied for this license.

Instead, arguing that their international product was not subject to U.S. controls, NAI had contracted with a Swiss computer company to sell a product that was "functionally equivalent" to its Pretty Good Privacy. Under this arrangement, NAI customers outside the United States could purchase the Swiss software and expect it to be fully compatible with NAI's own U.S. version. Technically, there was no violation of U.S. export law, since no product was being exported. According to NAI executives, there had not even been any assistance provided to the Swiss firm.

---

[1] Steven Levy, "The Cypherpunks Vs. Uncle Sam," *The New York Times Magazine*, June 12, 1994, p. 70.

Research Associate Jennifer L. Burns prepared this case under the supervision of Professor Debora L. Spar as the basis for class discussion rather than to illustrate either effective or ineffective handling of an administrative situation. This case is based on original papers written by Class of 1998 MBA students Angelina Ornelas, Vickie Pisowicz, John Applegate, Ken Gonzalez, and Mark Weinberg, and was written with the assistance of the HBS California Research Center.

Rather, the Swiss company had simply relied upon public information, including previously published versions of the Pretty Good Privacy source code.[2]

Officially, then, no exports had occurred, and NAI had not violated the letter of U.S. law. Yet the intent of the firm's actions was clear. Immediately after NAI's announcement, the U.S. government launched its own rebuttal. Charging that "This [action] flies in the face of our policy," the Commerce Department opened a formal investigation into the company's activities.[3] The potential ramifications of this move were serious.

In openly flouting the spirit – if not the law – of U.S. encryption export policy, NAI assumed an explicit risk of censure. If the Commerce Department found NAI to be in violation of U.S. export law, it could impose a range of civil penalties ranging from fines to placement on the government's "denied persons list." In this last case, NAI would be prevented from exporting any products at all.[4] Investors were not unaware of such risks: the day NAI announced its decision, its stock price fell by 7%.[5] Executives at NAI, however, were unperturbed. They knew the risks of their decision and were prepared to accept them. This was a company well-accustomed to taking risks and moving quickly.

Background: A Fast Mover

Not even a year old, NAI was already a rising star in the U.S. software industry. Created in December 1997 by the merger of McAfee Associates and Network General Co., NAI instantly became the world's tenth largest independent software company, specializing in the emerging field of network security and management. From the start, CEO Bill Larson made bold purchases a centerpiece of NAI's growth strategy, and the new company quickly gained attention from its rapid-fire spate of acquisitions.

Immediately following the initial $1.3 billion merger, NAI bought Pretty Good Privacy, Inc., Magic Solutions, and Helix, all recognized leaders in various aspects of network security and management. In the first half of 1998, NAI made an acquisition nearly every month, purchasing such high profile companies as Trusted Information Systems, Inc., Dr. Solomon's Group, and Cyber Media. This dizzying pace only excited investors. Although NAI posted a large net loss for the third quarter of 1998, it simultaneously outperformed analysts' earnings estimates and saw its stock price rise 3.9%, to $36.25.[6] Listed on the Nasdaq (NETA), as of January 1999, NAI employed about 2,400 people worldwide and had a market value of well over $6 billion.

Like many other Internet-related firms, NAI had soared to prominence on the back of the "information revolution" and the prospect of a multi-billion dollar market for electronic commerce (e-commerce). Like many, it saw in the Internet a vast new market for both retail and business trade, and a vast opportunity to profit from servicing and facilitating this trade. The excitement was palpable in Silicon Valley, and NAI was eager to be among the first ranks of the Internet pioneers.

What distinguished NAI's strategy, though, was a careful focus on a critical corner of the

---

[2] David Bank, "Network Associates Will Use Dutch Unit to Circumvent Encryption Export Rules," *The Wall Street Journal*, March 20, 1998, p. B7.

[3] Undersecretary of Commerce William Reinsch, quoted in John Shinal, "Network Associates' Encryption Plans Draw Criticism," *Bloomberg Financial Newswire*, March 20, 1998.

[4] Casewriter interview with Bruce Kutz, Bureau of Export Administration, U.S. Department of Commerce, Washington, D.C., October 6, 1998.

[5] Shinal.

[6] "Network Associates Inc. Operating Results Exceed Forecasts Despite Net Loss," *The Wall Street Journal*, October 20, 1998, p.B2.

Internet market. In the late 1990s projections for online commerce ranged from $6 billion to $130 billion by the year 2000.[7] One of the unknowns which accounted for this wide range, and one of the factors driving these estimates, was the provision of security. For despite all the excitement that surrounded the Internet, despite the predictions and buzz of new markets, many users remained worried about the inherent unruliness of cyberspace and the dangers of transmitting valuable information across it.[8]

Consumers, for instance, hesitated to reveal their credit card numbers or personal information to anonymous web sites and retailers; businesses worried about the theft or misuse of confidential information. Indeed, according to a survey published in March of 1998, 86% of consumers did not shop online due to security concerns.[9] Similar fears were pushing business users to rely on mail or messenger services for their more delicate transactions.[10]

It was these concerns that formed the core of NAI's business. NAI's strategy, in fact, was to create the software products that could guarantee the security of Net transactions and then to sell and service these products across a wide range of customers and functions. Already, the company's acquisitions had given it a very strong foothold in this market and, more importantly, a reputation for delivering the top-notch products that wary Internet users demanded. NAI's purchase of Trusted Information Systems, Inc., for instance, gave it a leadership position in both firewall construction and authentication tools, two key pieces of any network security system. (Firewalls are programs that secure internal networks from Internet intruders by establishing a virtual barrier around the system. Authentication tools are programs that assign and enforce password controls.) With the acquisition of Dr. Solomon's, the company cemented its dominant position in the market for virus protection, which was based on the use of anti-virus programs to scan for and eliminate potentially harmful viruses. The only thing missing from this suite of security products was encryption – the tool which, in many respects, was the core element of any data security program.[11]

Conceptually, encryption software is a simple product. It hides any message by scrambling (or encrypting) it, replacing each letter or number with another. The message is then de-scrambled (or "de-crypted") by the receiver, who holds the same code book as the sender. It is a basic kind of secrecy, with the complexity determined by the intricacy of the code and the means by which it is transmitted to its users.

In the 1990s, the preferred means for encrypting computer data and transmissions was through the use of so-called "public key" cryptography. With this system, each user's "key" is actually a mathematical algorithm consisting of two interlocking parts: a public key and a private key. The public key is a code that must be distributed to any potential communicant, commonly by posting on a web site. Messages encrypted with this public key can only be decrypted with the private key, a related algorithm known only to the recipient. The beauty of public key cryptography is that there is no "master key" that must be shared and protected from outsiders, only a set of single, private keys.

---

[7] See for instance Computer Industry Forecasts (Cloverdale, CA: Data Analysis Group) Third Quarter, 1998, pp. 92–127; *The Forrester Report*, vol. 4, no. 6 (Cambridge, MA: Forrester Research, Inc., 1997); and Clint Willis, "Future Shop: Does Amazon.com Really Matter?" *Forbes*, April 6, 1998, p. 55.

[8] George Anders, "Click and Buy: Why – and Where – Internet Commerce is Succeeding," *The Wall Street Journal*, December 7, 1998, p. R4. For a review of other concerns, see Debora L. Spar and Jeffrey J. Bussgang, "Ruling the Net," *Harvard Business Review*, May/June 1996, p. 125.

[9] Heather Green, Catherine Yang, and Paul C. Judge, "A Little Privacy Please," *Business Week*, March 16, 1998, p. 98.

[10] Kristian Chronister, "Purchasers Predict Rise in Net-based Buying – But Legal Questions and Security Concerns Still Pose Problems," *Electronic Buyers News*, August 4, 1997, (www.techweb.com. Section: Online @EBN).

[11] Rutrell Yasin, "The Next Level," *Internet Week*, January 26, 1998, p. 47.

For public key cryptography to work, though, the public part of the code must be unbreakable. Mathematically, this means that it must consist of an algorithm long enough and complicated enough to resist attack by sophisticated hackers and powerful computers. For years, the government had maintained that its Data Encryption Standard (DES), which employed a 56-bit algorithm, was complex enough to guarantee security. These claims were debunked in June 1997, when thousands of computers working in tandem deciphered a DES message. A year later, a computer built by the Electronic Freedom Frontier cracked a DES-protected message in less than three days. The break-ins demonstrated that 56-bit algorithms were no longer adequate in the face of increasing computer power.[12] From that point on, it became clear that to ensure privacy, computer users would have to rely on more sophisticated encryption with longer bit lengths. This so-called "strong" encryption relied on 128-bit algorithms and, in 1998 could not be cracked by any known technology. The most popular strong encryption program was Pretty Good Privacy, a program that had been created and widely distributed by Phil Zimmermann, a legend in the encryption community. It was also the product that NAI bought in 1997 when it purchased PGP from Zimmermann.

In 1998, the global market for encryption software products was growing rapidly. Indeed, some NAI officials estimated the market could even reach $5 billion by 2001.[13] And because e-commerce was still in its infancy, there was no established leader in the market for encryption software. NAI could easily become this leader. It had a well developed strategy, an established brand name, relevant business experience, and a range of complementary products to offer. What it did not have, except under limited circumstances, was permission to sell Pretty Good Privacy outside the United States.

U.S. Encryption Policy

History: From Caesar to the Soviets

Because it was originally created as a military device, encryption had long fallen within the province of governments. Military commanders used encryption to protect their communications and governments often piggy-backed upon this technology to protect their own diplomatic messages. The first documented use of encryption occurred as early as 50-60 BC, when Julius Caesar sent messages to his far-flung forces using encryption that encoded messages by simply shifting the letters of the alphabet a fixed amount.[14] In the 1790s, Thomas Jefferson took encryption technology a few steps further with his invention of a wheel cipher to encrypt text. This was re-invented in several later forms and used in World War II by the United States Navy as the Strip Cipher, M-138-A.[15]

It was during the post-war period that encryption first came to rely on relatively sophisticated technology. It was also during this period that the U.S. government began to treat encryption as an integral part of the country's national security system. As the technology developed from ciphers to computers, encryption quickly fell under the purview of the United States' expanding national security agencies. The Central Intelligence Agency (CIA) and Federal Bureau of Investigation (FBI) had a deep concern for its use and development, and the National Security Agency (NSA) took the lead in its creation. For many years, in fact, the NSA employed the vast

---

[12] For a complete history of efforts to break DES, go to http://www.eff.org/DEScracker/.

[13] Angelina Ornelas and Vickie Pisowicz, interview with John Calles, Network Associates Chief of Technical Securities, April 23, 1998.

[14]David Kahn, *The Codebreakers* (New York: The Macmillan Company, 1967) p. 83.

[15]Kahn, pp. 192, 325.

majority of America's known encryption experts. In this climate, not surprisingly, all encryption technologies were classified as "munitions" and regulated by the Department of State. Exports were strictly forbidden.

So long as encryption remained an esoteric technology of America's security elite, no one in the broader public cared very much about the policies that surrounded it. But the advent of the Internet changed all that. Nearly overnight, encryption shifted from a purely military commodity to one with a broad and profitable market reach. And thus, suddenly, long-standing security concerns were at odds with new commercial demands. The government still wanted to regulate encryption and prevent its export to hostile states and individuals. But firms such as NAI were eager to break into the lucrative encryption market and determined not to cede this market to their less-constrained European competitors. For several years, the debate between these two interests raged on, becoming over time a major facet of U.S. policy towards the Internet and the commercial development of cyberspace.

Encryption Policy in the 1990s

Like many products designed for the Internet, encryption software was almost inherently international. To work, the encryption algorithm had to be applied at both ends of any communication. So if a bank or a multinational corporation wanted to secure the transfer of information among its branches or subdivisions, it needed to apply the same software across its global network. In the early 1990s, however, U.S. firms were explicitly forbidden from selling encryption software outside the United States, or even from allowing any of their domestic customers to use the software overseas. As a result, major U.S. companies such as America Online, Netscape Communications, and Microsoft Corporation often had to partner with foreign software providers to ensure the security their customers demanded.[16] To U.S. software firms, this represented an ironic transfer of technology, and an unfortunate loss of business. To the U.S. national security agencies, however, there was more at stake than market share or profits.

While not denying the commercial potential of encryption technologies, the national security agencies argued that security concerns had to take precedence in the formation of national policy. Without some means of access to electronic communication, national security could easily be compromised. Terrorists could plot far from the government's ability to hear; subversive groups could exchange information about bomb-making or chemical weapons; money launderers or tax evaders would have whole new realms in which to maneuver.

One FBI agent made the following analogy to illustrate the fears of his agency: "O.K., someone kidnaps one of your kids and they are holding your kid in this fortress up in the Bronx. Now, we have probable cause that your child is inside this fortress. We have a search warrant. But for some reason, we cannot get in there... And there are guys in there, *laughing* at us. That's what the basis of this issue really is – we've got a situation now where a technology has become so sophisticated that the whole notion of a legal process is at stake here!"[17] While none of the agencies wanted to stem the Internet's growth or strangle its free spirit, they did want at least to preserve the tools of enforcement that had existed before the Net sprang to life.[18]

The first step in this direction was the infamous "Clipper Chip" proposal, set forth by the Clinton administration in 1993. This proposal stated that all new computers would be required to contain a special piece of encryption circuitry, designed by the NSA, whose key would be held by the

---

[16] Edmund L. Andrews, "U.S. Restrictions Give European Encryption a Boost," *The New York Times*, April 7, 1997, p. D1.

[17] Levy, p. 48.

[18] Casewriter interview with Bruce Kutz, Washington, D.C., October 10, 1998.

U.S. government. With the proper warrant, law enforcement investigators would be able to use this key to override any encryption software.

Opposition to Clipper was swift, loud and unyielding. Almost immediately, a motley group of computer programmers, privacy advocates, corporate strategists, and politicians coalesced to voice their disapproval and prevent Clipper from becoming policy. In keeping with the somewhat libertarian culture of the Internet, the debate relied on highly politicized language. The administration was characterized in Orwellian terms while opponents styled themselves as freedom fighters. Response at times verged on the hysterical: "The war is upon us," wrote one activist in 1994. "Clinton and Gore folks have shown themselves to be enthusiastic supporters of Big Brother."[19] Echoed John Perry Barlow, Vice-Chairman of the Electronic Frontier Foundation: "Clipper is a last ditch attempt... to establish imperial control over cyberspace."[20]

A second stream of protest was less heated and less obvious, but perhaps more influential. It came from commercial interests which were quick to point out that strong encryption was already available around the world. While U.S. firms dominated most areas of the computer industry, they already faced stiff competition in the field of encryption from firms and individuals based out of Russia, Israel, and other countries. Given that lawbreakers could easily obtain strong encryption from these sources, opponents argued, encryption export regulation was only hurting U.S. businesses and doing nothing to prevent the catastrophes that government agencies predicted.

In the end, the supporters of Clipper backed down, cowed by the combined lobbying force of commercial interests and hard-core Internet activists. The Clinton Administration retreated from its support of the Clipper Chip, but continued to search for some other means to address the concerns voiced by the CIA and FBI.

Key Management and Congressional Forays

In 1996, after extensive conversations with industry representatives, the administration settled on a softer and less overt approach. It announced the launch of a new Key Management Infrastructure (KMI), under which the regulation of commercial encryption products was transferred from the Department of State's munitions list to the Department of Commerce's dual use list. This meant that encryption technology was no longer officially viewed as a weapon. In addition, the Administration created a license exemption that allowed encryption products of any strength to be exported freely as long as they had key-escrow accounts that the government could access. Practically, this meant that private keys were not truly private, but rather were accessible to a central administrator who could turn them over to law enforcement agencies. Finally, KMI allowed a two-year liberalization period during which companies could export 56-bit keys, provided they began to develop software with key-escrow as a standard feature.[21]

While the license exemption, liberalization period, and key recovery scheme all eased the prohibition on exporting, they also all required a substantial amount of paperwork. Before any encryption product could be exported, the Commerce Department had to determine that it had a key recovery system in place. This meant that exporting firms had to submit their plans to the Commerce Department and wait for its formal approval. Companies exporting 56-bit encryption products also had to submit progress reports to the Commerce Department every six months.

---

[19] Levy, p. 46.

[20] John Perry Barlow, "Jackboots on the Infobahn," *Wired*, April 2, 1994, p. 40.

[21] William Reinsch, "Testimony Before the House Subcommittee on Telecommunications, Trade, and Consumer Protection," September 4, 1997, (www.bxa.doc.gov/press/97/warhsenc.htm).

The new regulations also created the beginnings of a third party system for key-licensing. Although KMI did not demand that the government hold the keys for any key recovery system, it did mandate the licensing and approval of the independent key holders. In practice, this provision meant a further round of forms and approvals for companies that exported encryption products. Because KMI required the development of key recovery systems in all new software, it also was perceived by some observers as a stealthy launch of domestic encryption controls.[22]

Meanwhile, encryption policy remained a hotly contested issue within the halls of Congress. Urged on by a host of disparate groups, various bills began to wend their way through the legislative process. In 1997 alone, seven new bills involving encryption technology regulation were introduced in Congress, but by year's end none had been signed into law. Encryption policy was also the subject of two lawsuits filed on First Amendment grounds by computer science professors who had been forced to remove encryption source code from course websites.[23]

The progress of one bill, the Security and Freedom through Encryption (SAFE) Act, demonstrated the ability of various government and private interests to affect policy. Originally supported by industry and privacy advocates because it called for a full removal of export controls, SAFE soon succumbed to the fierce lobbying of law enforcement agencies. In September of 1997, the bill's original pro-export position was threatened by the proposed Oxley-Manton amendment, which called for domestic controls on encryption and a strengthening of export controls. When private sector groups predictably opposed this addition, SAFE was instead amended with the Markey-White amendment, which reiterated a commitment to loosening export controls and protecting domestic encryption from regulation, but also called for the establishment of a National Electronic Technologies (NET) Center, an organization devoted to assisting law enforcement agencies gain access to commercial encryption systems.[24] Although SAFE soon stalled on the floor of the House, the NET idea did gain some currency and was part of a later "E-Privacy" act introduced in May 1998 by Senators Ashcroft and Leahy. The E-Privacy act mixed loosening controls with an expanded government bureaucracy, and consequently met with a lukewarm response from both sides of the debate.[25] At the end of 1998, Congress still had not passed any definitive legislation regarding encryption.

Enter Network Associates

Most companies headquartered in California's Silicon Valley were listening attentively to the din emanating from Washington, D.C. But some were more impatient than others. As executives at NAI surveyed the encryption landscape, one conclusion seemed clear. Unless they acted quickly, they risked losing a huge opportunity. Two other computer companies, Sun Microsystems and RSA Data Security, Inc., had made previous attempts to collaborate with overseas partners, but had

---

[22] Kenneth Mendelson, Stephen T. Walker, and Joan D. Winston, "The Evolution of Recent Cryptographic Policy in the United States," Steve Walker and Associates Publications, 1998 (www.stevewalker.com/top.html), p. 8. Until that point, encryption software sold within the United States had largely escaped the radar screen of regulators and national security agencies.

[23] Laurie Flynn, "Two Encryption Cases Cast Shadow on Academia," *The New York Times on the Web*, May 3, 1998, http://www.nyt.com/library/tech/98/05/cyber/articles/03encrypt.html.

[24] Mendelson, Walker, and Winston, pp. 12-13.

[25] Jeri Clausing, "New Encryption Legislation Billed As a Compromise," *The New York Times on the Web*, May 13, 1998, http://www.nyt.com/library/tech/98/05/cyber/articles/13encrypt.html.

quickly retreated in the face of Commerce Department investigations.[26] NAI executives were confident that they could avoid these regulatory obstacles and still secure the business opportunities that encryption so obviously presented.

NAI's Decision

When NAI purchased Pretty Good Privacy in 1997, it was well aware of the software's political risks. After all, the program's designer, Phil Zimmermann, had been the subject of a three year government investigation after he posted the 128-bit encryption software on his Internet home page. Although Zimmermann wasn't selling his product, the government alleged that he had violated the export law because his program could be downloaded from anywhere in the world. Zimmermann approached his actions from an entirely different perspective, seeing the posting of Pretty Good Privacy (PGP) as "a human rights issue." Like many of the computer programmers who had rallied to defeat Clipper, Zimmermann viewed computers and the Internet as a channel for free speech and a route to personal freedom. Perhaps because of these high-minded themes, Zimmermann – and PGP – had become well-known icons among the Internet community.[27]

In 1996, the government closed its investigation of Zimmermann without calling for prosecution. With the pressure of indictment lifted, Zimmermann, who had little business experience, was happy to sell his product to NAI, provided that he could still retain some influence on the technology. NAI employed him as a cryptographic consultant and rapidly hatched plans to market PGP as a commercial product.

Much of their plan emerged naturally. Due to Zimmermann's generosity with his program, PGP was already widely distributed and well-regarded. Indeed, in the seven years that PGP had been freely available as "shareware," it had become established in Europe and the United States as the strong encryption standard of choice. Any computer user with an intermediate level of computer knowledge could download PGP from sites around the world and use it to encrypt messages.

What NAI brought to this pirate software network was a brand name and the promise of concomitant services. As NAI executive Peter Watkins recalled, "we looked at the multimillion unit installed base of PGP users in Europe and thought, 'isn't it a shame that these people have never been able to pay us for the software?'" The company was not at all concerned that PGP's earlier availability might undercut sales. To the contrary, executives realized that piracy had, in effect, built their installed base. NAI estimated that over 90% of current PGP users were businesses that did not want to use illegally obtained software. Thus a simple phone call would be sufficient to convince these new customers to pay a royalty fee. [28]

Outside the United States, however, the business model grew murkier. To make PGP commercially viable, NAI had to be able to export it – and allow its customers to use it – outside the United States. Yet U.S. law still made these sales exceedingly complicated. Upon reviewing the regulations, NAI strategists discerned several possibilities. Exporting 128-bit encryption without a license or a corresponding key recovery system was prohibited. So was assisting foreign nationals in developing strong encryption. But NAI's freedom of speech was protected by the first amendment, and while this protection might not extend to web postings, it did clearly cover books. Thus, as NAI strategists understood the regulations, it was perfectly legal for anyone to publish encryption codes

---

[26] Bank, p. B7. Sun and RSA had attempted to develop encryption software in collaboration with programmers in Russia and China. Not surprisingly, given the historic animosity between those countries and the United States, these attempts were quickly challenged by the Commerce Department.

[27] Casewriter interview with Phil Zimmermann, Santa Clara, CA, November 11, 1998.

[28] Casewriter interview with Peter Watkins, General Manager and Vice President, Net Tools Secure Division, Santa Clara, CA, November 11, 1998.

in "human readable form."[29] In fact, Zimmermann had published the source code through MIT Press in 1995, and subsequent publications had been issued by Pretty Good Privacy, Inc. Given the legality of publishing the code, company strategists thought the regulations could not forbid one further step of adding basic formatting that made a book readable by computer scanners. Believing it was operating clearly within the confines of the law, NAI published a book of PGP code in 1997.

Not long after, cn Labs of Switzerland, a small group of cryptography students working under a computer science professor in Rapperswil, developed what Watkins termed the "functional equivalent of PGP." As Watkins explained, this software was developed "with no assistance from us, in any way, shape, or form." In return for a small royalty, cn Labs agreed to an exclusive license with NAI. The Swiss company would develop a European version of PGP which would be completely compatible with the PGP sold in the U.S. market.[30]

While NAI didn't quite know how cn Labs had developed the software in question, the company had a definite plan for marketing and selling it. PGP (or its Swiss equivalent) would be shipped from Ireland and billed through NAI's Amsterdam subsidiary. cn Labs, an organization that employed no U.S. citizens, would be responsible for technical support, training, and sales. "We executed this strategy real fast," Watkins admitted, noting that such speed was a characteristic of NAI's initial strategy. The arrangement, though, served several obvious purposes. Now, a U.S. corporation could purchase PGP and then refer its foreign subsidiaries to the product made by cn Labs. The technology would be perfectly compatible, the United States government would not be able to access any encrypted messages, and there were no forms to fill out. NAI, as Watkins described, had put itself in the business of "taking away paper headaches."

Risky Business

With the Dutch release of PGP, Network Associates appeared to have skated adroitly through the twists, turns, and inconsistencies of U.S. regulation. But there remained the question of consequences. To executives at NAI, their decision followed a sensible analysis of business risk. When they bought PGP they reasoned that the risk was "manageable." And when they developed their export strategy, they took a rational chance. As Watkins recalls: "I asked myself, 'Am I going to go to jail? Well, probably not. OK.'"[31] NAI executives firmly believed that they were operating well within the sphere of law.

Pushing this calculation was increasing evidence that the Clinton Administration was beginning to favor the views of industry over those of the FBI and NSA. In 1996, for example, a National Research Council study commissioned by Congress had recommended that export controls be significantly relaxed.[32] Then in 1997, the movement of jurisdiction from the State Department to the Department of Commerce had placed encryption in a more business friendly environment. Even more recently, official statements had begun to underscore the need for cooperation and dialogue in this area, rather than rules and restrictions. In a March letter, Vice President Al Gore had indicated that the administration would not push for domestic encryption controls, and spoke of the need to "pursue a good faith dialogue over the coming months between industry and law enforcement,

---

[29] Casewriter interview with Kelly Blough, Director of Government Relations and Export Policy, Santa Clara, CA, November 11, 1998.

[30] Casewriter interview with Watkins, Santa Clara, CA, November 11, 1998.

[31] Casewriter interview with Watkins, Santa Clara, CA, November 11, 1998.

[32] Mendelson, Walker, Winston, p. 5.

which can produce cooperative solutions."[33] Later that month, only days before NAI announced its move, this emphasis on dialogue was seconded by the FBI. An FBI representative assured the Senate Judiciary Committee that "we are all looking at this point not to impose mandatory legislation and will work cooperatively with industry to find whatever solutions are available."[34]

Overall, then, NAI was sanguine about the ultimate outcome of its decision. Indeed, NAI executives had even sent the Commerce Department a press release a few days before they publicly announced their European move, and took the lack of response as a positive sign. Only later did the company learn that the officials it had faxed were out of the office at the time, and had learned of the company's decision through the news media. NAI's Director of Government Relations and Export Policy, Kelly Blough, reflected: "In retrospect, we probably shouldn't have been as public as we were."[35] From the beginning, NAI had been prepared for an investigation, and retained copies of all its correspondence with cn Labs. The company remained convinced that its actions were fully in compliance with U.S. law.

Denouement

As NAI had suspected, the Department of Commerce was not deaf to the pleas of industry and had been working on more permissive regulations throughout 1997. In the words of one insider, the regulations were delayed by "an interagency morass."[36] Perhaps NAI's moves helped break this impasse, for in May of 1998 Commerce announced that there would be "forthcoming regulations."

The details came in September, 1998, and represented a breathtaking change in government policy. Under the new rules, 56-bit encryption could be exported anywhere except seven "terrorist" countries (Cuba, Iran, Iraq, North Korea, Libya, Syria, Sudan) after a one time technical review, with no requirement for the development of key recovery systems. Encryption above 56-bit could be sold to foreign corporations only with a key recovery system, but companies were not required to register a third party key-holder with the government. In the most startling departure from past policy, the government announced: "Very strong encryption with any key length (with or without key recovery) will now be permitted for export under license exemption, to several industry sectors. For example, U.S. companies will be able to export very strong encryption for use between their headquarters and their foreign subsidiaries worldwide except the seven terrorist countries."[37] Under this policy, NAI would be permitted to sell Pretty Good Privacy from its California headquarters to the defined industry sectors of insurance, health/medical, on-line merchants, and banking.

It appeared that the U.S. government had capitulated in the face of widespread opposition. Officials at Commerce defended their decision on the grounds that they had succeeded in changing the emerging encryption architecture. They also noted that strong encryption sales were only permitted to industries where there was already an established level of trust and government regulation. Further, many of the changes had been proposed by those within government who had come to agree with the software industry's logic. A few days before the new regulations were announced, the President's Export Council Subcommittee on Encryption released a brief report that

---

[33] Jeri Clausing, "Gore Letter Seems to Soften Stance on Encryption," *The New York Times on the Web*, March 5, 1998, http://www.nyt.com/library/tech/98/03/cyber/articles/05encrypt.html.

[34] Jeri Clausing, "FBI Halts its Push for Encryption Access Legislation," *The New York Times on the Web*, March 18, 1998, http://www.nyt.com/library/tech/98/03/cyber/articles/18encrypt.html.

[35] Casewriter interview with Blough, Santa Clara, CA, November 11, 1998.

[36] Casewriter interview with Kutz, Washington, D.C., October 6, 1998.

[37] The White House, Office of the Press Secretary, "Administration Updates Encryption Policy," press release, September 16, 1998 (http://207.96.11.93/press/98/EncryptionWH.htm).

described the many faults of current U.S. policy and admitted that "the adverse impact of controls on U.S. industry is palpable." The report noted that U.S. companies were losing ground in the encryption market, and that this "foreshadows a weakening of the U.S. position as a leader in electronic commerce generally."[38] In the calculus of national security versus national profitability, the market appeared to have won.

Meanwhile, other firms were beginning to hover. In September 1998 yet another Silicon Valley startup, TriStrata Inc., generated headlines and enthusiasm to match those surrounding NAI. To a large extent, the fanfare that greeted TriStrata was due to its star-studded cast of executives and directors. Tom Perkins, founder of the famed venture capital firm Kleiner Perkins Caufield and Byers, served as a director. The company's Chairman, M.M. Atalla, had designed the security system of PIN numbers used in 80% of bank ATMs worldwide. And Paul Wahl, TriStrata's President and CEO, had been wooed from the chief executive slot of SAP America, a subsidiary of the world's largest producer of business software. Wahl's step down from head of a multibillion dollar international subsidiary to run an unknown startup drew interest and comment in the business press. But Wahl saw a gap in the market for secure information and management products, and felt that he and Atalla could combine to make a world class product. The company had offered its first product in the fall of 1997, and was preparing to begin large scale sales in 1999. With a contract to provide security for accounting firm PricewaterhouseCoopers LLP already in hand, its future looked bright.

TriStrata saw itself as a secure information management company with a particular focus on encryption software. Unlike NAI, though, and indeed unlike nearly everyone else in the field of encryption, TriStrata had chosen not to build its security systems around public key cryptography. Instead, the new firm used a wholly different method, based on the Vernam cipher, a method first developed in 1917. Also known as the "one-time pad," this cipher is essentially a long string (or "pad") of random numbers. Pieces of the string are used to encrypt messages; once used, the random numbers must be discarded – hence the phrase "one-time pad."[39] The idea of using the Vernam cipher was highly controversial within the encryption community. Although reliance on random data could create a "theoretically unbreakable" encryption code, conventional wisdom held that the use of random numbers required too much computer power and was impractical for everyday use.[40] TriStrata, however, advertised itself as having developed a new method of encryption based on, but not identical to, the one-time pad. Enrolled clients would receive a large block of data, from which random numbers would be generated to encrypt messages. Once a series of numbers had been used, it would automatically be discarded.

This different technology led to a different perspective on U.S. government regulation. Even under the stricter KMI regulations, TriStrata's secure information management would have been approved for export, because centralized access (similar to a master encryption key) was included as a standard product feature. Because TriStrata's system depended on a continuous stream of shared random numbers, users were not required to have individual keys, and hence there was no need for key approval.

The validity of the security TriStrata offered was immediately questioned by prominent cryptographers and the computer industry press.[41] Reactions ranged from skepticism about TriStrata's "randomness" to outright scorn for the company. Cryptographer Bruce Schneier was

---

[38] The President's Export Council Subcommittee on Encryption, "Findings of the President's Export Council Subcommittee on Encryption," September 18, 1998 (http://209.122.145.150/PresidentsExportCouncil/PECSENC/pecsenc1.htm).

[39] Dan Backman, "TriStrata: A Giant Step in Enterprise Security," *Network Computing*, August 15, 1998, p. 29.

[40] "Internet: TriStrata Promises the Crypto Moon," *Computer Wire: Network Briefing*, September 9, 1998.

[41] "'Unbreakable' Crypto Sows Industry Strife," *PC Week*, October 12, 1998, p. 35.

blunt: "These guys have no clue."[42] But according to TriStrata executives, the strength of security was not their main focus. Much as NAI had taken a chance with the probability of government investigation, TriStrata's security program took a chance with the extremely limited probability that a hacker could crack its security. Instead, the company focused most of its energy on providing an integrated security system that could encrypt messages faster than public key cryptography and without the need for a system of public and private keys. As Atalla argued: "I am a good cryptographer, but I don't think it's worth a damn.... The goal is to have a system that works."[43] TriStrata's system also provided a firewall for intranets and a central server that tracked all encryption activity within an organization. In terms of performance, preliminary reviews indicated that TriStrata's technology was exceptional: a file that PGP took more than 130 seconds to encrypt could be protected by TriStrata's software in 18 seconds.[44]

Because TriStrata's product was fundamentally compatible with the government's interest in access, it was granted unrestricted export rights. This easy agreement with government regulation both sprung from and reinforced TriStrata's philosophy that corporations could work with the evolving regulatory structure and design a product that would satisfy both consumers and their governments. In the words of Atalla, "we see where the laws should be heading... and we take them there."[45]

---

[42] Don Clark, "TriStrata Security to Launch Software for Protecting Computer Information," *The Wall Street Journal*, September 8, 1998, p. B6.

[43] casewriter interview with M.M. Atalla, Redwood Shores, CA, November 12, 1998.

[44] Backman, p. 28.

[45] casewriter interview with Atalla, Redwood Shores, CA, November 12, 1998.

Exhibit 1a. Network Associates' Consolidated Balance Sheet

December 31,	1997	1996
(in thousands, except per share data)		
Assets		
Current assets:		
Cash and cash equivalents	$ 123,494	$ 125,141
Marketable securities	123,882	134,029
Accounts receivable	125,284	77,391
Prepaid expenses, taxes and other	57,612	31,420
Total current assets	430,272	367,981
Marketable securities	109,184	46,483
Fixed assets, net	28,570	28,363
Deferred taxes	16,173	12,088
Intangible and other assets	17,732	2,841
Total assets	$601,931	$457,756
Liabilities		
Current liabilities:		
Accounts payable	$18,439	$33,552
Accrued liabilities	141,083	36,360
Deferred revenue	69,464	51,398
Total current liabilities	228,986	121,310
Deferred revenue and taxes, less current portion	13,186	7,523
Total liabilities	242,172	128,833
Stockholders' equity		
Preferred stock and common stock	699	666
Additional paid-in capital	191,047	139,263
Other	(54)	514
Retained earnings	168,067	188,480
Total stockholders' equity	359,759	328,923
Total liabilities and stockholders' equity	$601,931	$457,756

Source: Based on Network Associates, *Annual Report 1997.*

Exhibit 1b. Network Associates' Statement of Operations

Years Ended December 31	1997	1996	1995
(in thousands, except per share data)			
Net revenue:			
Product	$510,770	$343,940	$252,231
Services and support	101,423	77,854	26,679
Total revenue	612,193	421,794	278,910
Cost of revenue:			
Product	77,669	57,550	37,873
Services and support	30,547	19,363	10,849
Total cost of revenue	108,216	76,913	48,722
Operating costs and expenses:			
Research and development	85,021	52,244	36,771
Marketing and sales	181,017	122,638	92,295
General and administrative	43,060	30,315	20,134
Amortization of intangibles	858	3,169	1,356
Acquisition and other related costs	175,800	30,669	19,936
Total operating costs and expenses	485,756	239,035	170,492
Income from operations	18,221	105,846	59,696
Interest and other income, net	14,743	9,548	8,799
Income before provision for income taxes	32,964	115,394	68,495
Provision for income taxes	61,320	51,284	26,154
Net income (loss)	$ (28,356)	$ 64,110	$ 42,341
Net income (loss) per share—basic	$ (0.41)	$ 0.97	$ 0.67

Source: Based on Network Associates, *Annual Report 1997.*

Exhibit 2. Encryption: How it Works

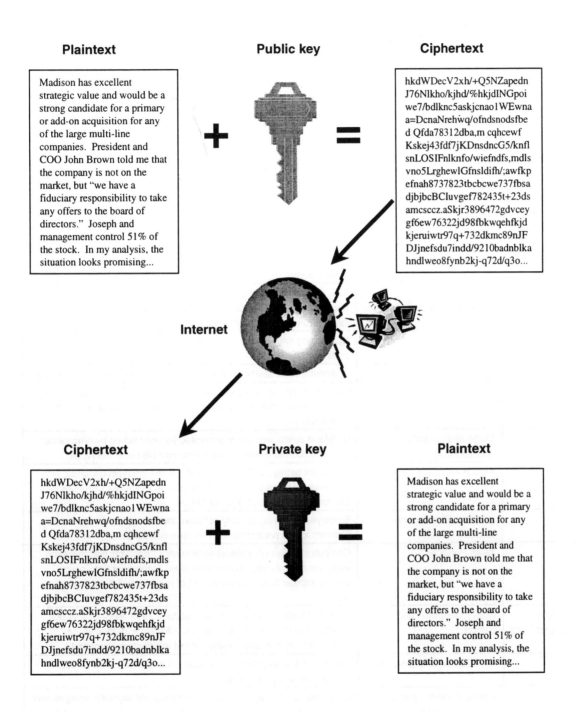

Exhibit 3. The Fears of Government: Cases Involving Encryption in Crime and Terrorism, 1994-1997

Terrorism	Aum Shinri Kyo (Supreme Truth)	March 20, 1995. Cult bombs Tokyo subway with nerve gas. Authorities uncover encrypted information on cult's computer detailing plans of mass destruction.
	Bolivian Terrorists	Military sting operation captures Bolivian terrorists who had assassinated four U.S. Marines. Utilized decryption assistance from AccessData Corporation of Orem, Utah.
	Ramsey Yousef	Bombed World Trade Center in 1994. Bombed Manila Air airliner in 1995. FBI seized laptop computer and finds encrypted files.
	New York Subway Bomber	1995—Authorities decrypt information on bomber's computer. Use information against bomber during trial.
	James Dalton Bell	Bell sends encrypted messages to associates to persuade them to kill government employees. Authorities find terrorism plans on computer, decrypt messages to other parties following Bell's capture.
Organized Crime	Dutch organized crime	Used palmtop computers with encryption technology to monitor unmarked police vehicles.
	Multi-site gambling enterprise	Bookmaker operating multiple sites encodes information on customers and bets using encryption technologies. Authorities eventually break code and retrieve four years of records. Bookmaker pleads guilty.
	Theft, fraud, and embezzlement of funds	U.S. defense contractor embezzled in Germany. Crooks store encrypted financial records. Authorities break code and use information in obtaining confession.
	National drug ring	Dallas drug ring dealing in Ecstasy uses encryption technology to protect address book.
	Cali cartel	Communication devices seized in 1995 that made use of encryption.
	Italian Mafia	Head of Italian police's crime and technology center, Maria Christina Ascents, claims that Mafia use of encryption hinders government investigations.
	Drugs and possible counterfeiting	Maryland police encounter encrypted file maintained by drug dealer. Possible counterfeiting involved, however file never decrypted.
Espionage	Aldrich Ames spy case	CIA agent betrays U.S. government. Ames encrypts computer files. Government breaks code with help from AccessData Corporation. Evidence used in case against Ames.
	Insider theft of proprietary software	Employee steals proprietary software that cost $1 million to develop. Planned to use product to start his own company.
	Kevin Poulson	Computer hacker commits several crimes. Encrypts files including evidence compiled against his enemies. Department of Energy supercomputer breaks code at cost of hundreds of thousands of dollars.
Pedophiles and Child Pornographers	Child molestation and suicide	Senator Charles Grassley testifies at June 1997 hearings that boy commits suicide after being molested. Personal organizer may contain information about molester but information encrypted.
	International pedophile ring	Priest in U.K. distributes pornography over Internet. Authorities decrypt computer messages.
	Child pornography and possible corporate espionage	California man engages in both distributing pornographic images over the Internet and corporate espionage. Computer files encrypted using Pretty Good Privacy. Files never recovered.

Source: Denning and Baugh, Cases Involving Encryption and Crime and Terrorism, http://www.cs.georgetown.edu/~denning/crypto/cases.html.

Exhibit 4. Guidelines for Preparing Encryption License Applications

The Bureau of Export Administration
Guidelines for Preparing Encryption License Applications

For all license applications (i.e. technology transfers, hardware and/or software development, manufacturing arrangements, or resale/transfer of encryption items), the following information (if not included on the completed BXA Form 748P) will facilitate an expeditious review by the agencies:

1. Identify the class of end user such as U.S. wholly-owned or controlled entity (50% or greater ownership), bank, financial institution or government agency. If the ultimate consignee is a financial institution, identify if the end user is lawfully obligated to maintain records of the data secured with the exported encryption item and, if so, identify the laws/regulations mandating the recordkeeping.

2. Identify and describe the encryption items to be exported, to include the cryptographic capabilities (i.e., encryption algorithms and key lengths) of each encryption item.

3. Describe in detail the intended end use of each encryption item.

In addition to above:

A. If your application involves only **technology transfers, hardware and/or software development, or manufacturing arrangements**, the following information will facilitate an expeditious review by the agencies:

1. Identify and describe any products to be developed with the exported encryption items, to include the cryptographic capabilities (i.e., encryption algorithms and key lengths) of each developed product. Identify the envisioned class of end user (i.e., U.S. subsidiaries, banks/financial institutions, or governments) for each developed product and identify, if possible, whether the product will support recovery of plain text.

2. Identify the form in which the export will be executed (i.e., via magnetic media, hard copy technical drawings or documentation).

3. Explain the manufacturing/development process.

4. Explain the disposition of: 1) the encryption items subject to this license application; and 2) the finished products (e.g., "returned to the U.S.", "for resale in a specific country", or "sold as part of an encryption licensing arrangement (ELA)". If sold as part of an ELA, the license may be subject to semi-annual reporting requirements.

B. If your application involves only the **resale/transfer of encryption items only**, the following information will facilitate an expeditious review by the agencies:

5. Identify, by license number, any previous licenses received for the same or similar encryption item. If similar, identify the differences in the cryptographic functionality and, if applicable, the differences in the intended end use of the encryption item as opposed to a previously approved license.

6. If applicable, describe any technical safeguards that prevent the encryption items from being used for purposes other than the stated end use. If possible, describe how the encryption item will support recovery of plain text.

Please see our fact sheet for additional information on license applications involving the "deemed export" of encryption technology by foreign nationals or call Bernie Kritzer at (202) 482-0894.

Source: http://www.bxa.doc.gov/factsheets/encguide.htm

Exhibit 5.   Licensing Practices for Encryption Items

The Bureau of
Export Administration
Licensing Practices for Encryption Items

Encryption license applications are reviewed on a **case-by-case basis** to determine whether the export or reexport is consistent with U.S. national security and foreign policy interests, and licensing decisions are made based on the merits of each individual application. The purpose of this handout is to make the review process more transparent to exporters of encryption products. *It is informational only, and does not have any regulatory effect, nor does it guarantee a particular outcome from the review process.*

Encryption items and classes of end users that generally have been given **favorable consideration** in licensing review, subject to appropriate conditions:

1) Certain 40-bit encryption software, which are not eligible for the mass market provisions of License Exception TSU (see Supplement 6 to Part 742 of the EAR), and certain 40-bit encryption hardware, being exported to most end users;

2) Certain 56-bit encryption commodities/software being exported to U.S. subsidiaries or to "financial institutions";

3) Certain encryption commodities/software that implement the Secure Electronic Transactions (SET) protocol or other "financial-specific," products being exported to most end users to secure electronic commerce transactions/communications;

4) Certain 128-bit encryption commodities/software that have a recovery feature, being exported to U.S. subsidiaries, "financial institutions", or to certain (commercial) foreign end users;

5) Certain 128--bit encryption commodities/software for "home banking" purposes as long as the product is limited to bank/client communications/transactions and does not allow client-to-client communications/transactions.

6) Certain 128-bit general purpose encryption commodities/software being exported to "financial institutions" for inter/intra banking, provided the manufacturer of the exported product has an approved KMI Commitment Plan;

7) Certain 128-bit general purpose encryption commodities/software being exported to U.S. subsidiaries, provided the product allows for recovery of the plaintext.

REMEMBER: Products, end-uses, destinations, and classes of end users are all factors taken into account in the case-by-case review of license applications.

Source: http:www.bxa.doc.gov/factsheets/licguide.htm

Exhibit 6.   U.S. Encryption Legislation Current and Pending in 1997

TITLE	SPONSOR	OBJECTIVE
E-Privacy Act	Sen. Ashcroft (R)	- abolishes key requirement for export and domestic use, except for U.S. government employees, provided similar product in public domain or available from foreign supplier -sets penalties for criminal use of encryption -establishes National Electronic Technologies Center (NET) to study / monitor encryption
Encrypted Communications Privacy Act of 1997	Sen. Leahy (D)	- permits export of any encryption that is in public domain or available from foreign source -sets penalties for criminal use of encryption
Secure Public Networks Act	Sen. McCain (R)	-prohibits domestic key recovery requirement -sets penalties for criminal use of encryption, legal procedures for retrieval of keys - key escrow and Commerce Dep. review required to export encryption greater than 56-bits
Promotion of Commerce On-Line in the Digital Era (Pro-CODE) Act of 1997	Sen. Burns (R)	- prohibits domestic restrictions on encryption -permits export of any encryption that is in public domain or available from foreign source - establishes Information Security Board to study encryption
Security and Freedom Through Encryption (SAFE)	Rep. Goodlatte (R)	- establishes NET center to study / monitor encryption technology -permits unrestricted export of encryption - amendments prohibiting encryption export added during legislative review process
Communications Privacy and Consumer Empowerment Act	Rep. Markey (D)	-prohibits development of domestic controls on encryption
Computer Security Enhancement Act of 1997	Rep. Sensenbrenner (R)	- requires National Institute of Standards and Technology to study computer security, but forbids NIST to develop restrictions on encryption

Source: THOMAS http://www.loc.gov

Exhibit 7   NAI's Public Face

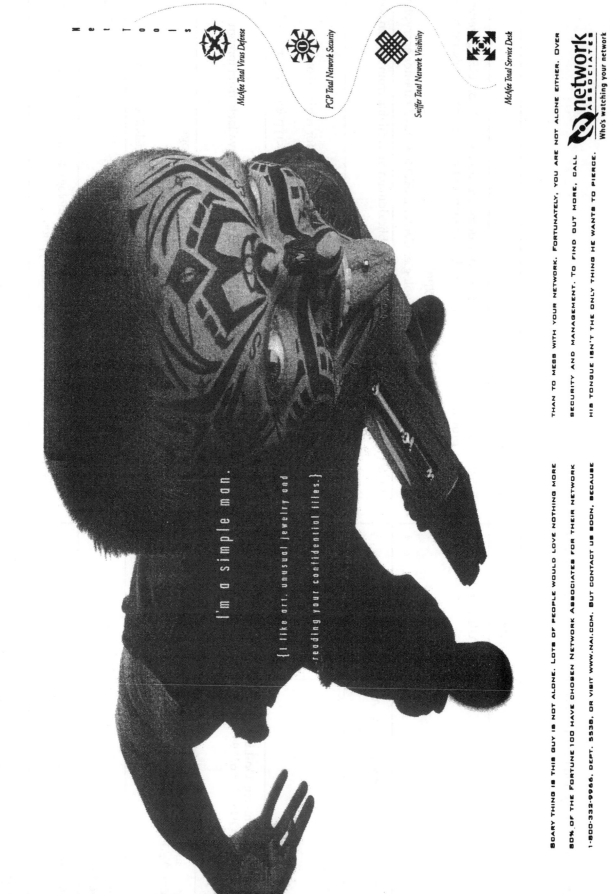

Source: Network Associates, Inc.

Singapore's Trade in Services

You see the beautiful lotus flower that is Singapore? We want to pick the flower. But, instead of putting it in a vase, we take the whole root and plant it here. Then it can really blossom.[1]

—Zhang Xinsheng, Mayor of Suzhou

In the [future], Singapore must overcome our lack of resources by harnessing economic space outside the country. We must create products and services that are not bound by traditional concepts of space and constraints.[2]

—Philip Yeo, Chairman, Singapore Economic Development Board

In 1994, Singaporean construction crews began clearing the land around Wuxi, an industrial city 150 kilometers west of Shanghai in Jiangsu province. Covering 82.3 square kilometers, the land they plowed would become a new city of sorts, a planned conglomeration of factories, business hotels, shops, and apartments that would comprise the Wuxi-Singapore Industrial Park and its sister development, the Wuxi National New and Hi-Tech Industrial Zone. The landlord of both developments was Wuxi-Singapore Industrial Holdings, a joint venture between the Wuxi state authorities, a cluster of Singaporean companies, and the Salim Group of Indonesia. With an explicit focus on high technology manufacturing, the Wuxi National Park, as the developments were usually called, would eventually accommodate 115 industrial tenants, the majority of them foreign investors. Development and management services for the Wuxi Park would be provided by a newly created firm, the Wuxi-Singapore Industrial Park Investment Company (WSIP). Another Singaporean joint venture, Wuxi International Management Services, would market the park to potential tenants.

---

[1] *Wall Street Journal*, September 15, 1994.
[2] *Economic Development Board Yearbook, 1992/93.*

Research Associates Julia Kou and Laura Bures prepared this case under the supervision of Professor Debora Spar as the basis for class discussion rather than to illustrate either effective or ineffective handling of an administrative situation.

As development proceeded at Wuxi, construction was also underway just 60 kilometers down the road at Suzhou, where a Singaporean consortium was leading the effort to create another new town, the Singapore-Suzhou Township. At a projected cost of $30 billion, Suzhou was even more ambitious in design than Wuxi. Praised by Chinese President Jiang Zemin as a "pioneering model for cooperation between China and Singapore and a new step in the country's economic reform,"[3] Suzhou was to be an outpost of Singapore in China, managed by a core of Singaporean firms and replicating Singapore's methods and modes of administration. With a full range of industrial, residential, and commercial holdings, the 70- square-kilometer township would eventually support a population of 600,000 and provide employment for 360,000.

While Wuxi and Suzhou were among Singapore's most ambitious overseas projects, they were by no means the only ones. On the contrary, the two Chinese townships were part of an expanding ring of industrial parks and export zones, all managed by Singaporean firms and boasting many of Singapore's famed business amenities: skilled labor, top-notch infrastructure, and predictable rules of law and administration. In many ways, Singapore's industrial parks were the logical culmination of its carefully-crafted development strategy. For decades, Singapore's Economic Development Board (EDB) had positioned the country as a global service center, a safe and secure base for companies doing business in Asia. To attract foreign investors, the Singaporean government had removed virtually all restrictions on flows of goods and capital and invested heavily in both its human and physical infrastructures. As the investors came and the economy grew, the tiny island nation had rapidly become a commercial and financial hub for all of Southeast Asia.

But, increasingly, Singapore's prospects for growth were being clouded by one of the few forces beyond the control of its government. With only 637 square kilometers and three million people, the country was simply running out of room to grow. To keep the economy expanding at its customary pace, therefore, Singapore's leaders had to find some means of obtaining resources and generating wealth beyond the island's own border. The solution they proposed, and the solution that led directly to the construction crews at Wuxi and Suzhou, was for Singapore to "go regional."

Enunciated first by Singapore's patriarch, Lee Kuan Yew, going regional essentially meant exporting Singapore's investment infrastructure to other countries of the region. Under this approach, the EDB encouraged local firms to develop a "second wing" on Singapore's economy, redistributing their lower-end operations elsewhere in Asia while upgrading the functions that remained in Singapore. The only problem with this strategy, though, was that it still relied on resources that Singapore lacked. Because the country had focused for so long on attracting and providing for foreign corporations, it simply did not have a great number of home-grown firms. In particular, it lacked the large-scale manufacturing firms which would be the most logical companies to take advantage of cheaper wage rates and larger markets abroad. And so, from the very start of Singapore's regional drive, Prime Minister Goh Chok Tong had decided that Singapore would invest abroad in the same areas it had developed so successfully at home: infrastructure, efficiency, governance, and marketing. Rather than develop new firms and new competencies, it would retain its position as a service provider, easing the way for other countries' firms to expand their business in Asia. To implement this rather intriguing strategy, Singapore entered the industrial parks business.

The idea behind the parks was straightforward. Under the supervision of the EDB, Singaporean firms would develop a string of overseas enclaves to replicate the business environment that, physically, could no longer expand in Singapore. In these enclaves, which planners saw as eventually rimming the southern Asian region, foreign firms would feel comfortable and secure, and

---

[3]Xinhua News Agency, January 14, 1995.

Singaporean firms would expand their own business by providing the services—such as construction, administration, and marketing—to ensure the necessary levels of stability and security. Singapore's firms, in other words, would specialize almost entirely in services. And Singapore, together with its parks, would become the ultimate service economy.

Singapore: A Brief History of Investment and Growth[4]

In the first three decades of its independence, Singapore had attained a remarkable level of growth, wealth, and stability. With GDP growth rates that averaged 9% a year from 1965 to 1995, the island nation had rapidly transformed itself from a center of *entrepôt* trade to a highly diversified, modern economy. By the 1990s, Singapore's economic growth had spawned a large and increasingly prosperous professional and middle class, and a population that was literate, well-employed, and decently housed. In 1996, per capita GDP was expected to exceed $28,400, putting Singapore on par with the United States.[5]

Throughout this period of tremendous growth, the bulk of Singapore's development—from building physical infrastructure to maintaining social order and calculating the optimal number of engineering graduates—came under the purview of the People's Action Party (PAP). Led by Prime Minister Lee Kuan Yew and Goh Keng Swee, the country's first finance minister, the PAP implemented a unique form of "democratic socialism" that ranged from "direct participation in the industry to the supply of infrastructure facilities by statutory authorities, and to laying down clear guidelines to the private sector as to what they could and should do."[6] The public sector was extensive by design and government-run companies straddled nearly every industrial sector, from defense to food processing, steel to semiconductors, and banking to property development. To fund such massive and widespread investment, the government relied on its compulsory social-security savings fund, the Central Provident Fund, which extracted substantial contributions, ranging from 10% to 40%, from the combined salaries of all employees and employers. In addition to these domestic savings, the government also began to court capital inflows from foreign firms in the 1960s, wooing investors with tax holidays, financial assistance, and research and development support. Led by the EDB, it also began to enact domestic policies that were likely to increase Singapore's attractiveness to foreign firms. The government invested heavily, for instance, in primary and technical education and struck a cooperative pact with the nascent unions, whose power had already been largely broken by Lee Kuan Yew and the PAP. The EDB then widely publicized its government's actions abroad, underscoring Singapore's ability to ensure foreign firms of a low-cost, low-risk environment and a compliant and well-educated labor pool. Before long, these enticements succeeded in drawing scores of foreign investors to Singapore, especially since most other developing countries in the 1960s were busily crafting strategies to restrict the reach of multinational corporations.

Initially, Singapore attracted mostly labor-intensive firms, particularly those in textiles, garments, and ship repair. During the 1970s, however, with development well underway, the EDB began to prod investors to shift toward higher-technology and capital-intensive industries. In 1973, the National Wages Council[7] allowed wages to rise at an accelerated pace to force the

---

[4]For an excellent and extensive account of Singapore's history and development, see Edward Prewitt and Forest L. Reinhardt, "Singapore," HBS Case 9-793-096.

[5] *Times Newspapers Limited,* November 3, 1995.

[6]*Business Times,* May 27, 1995, p. 2.

[7]The National Wages Council was formed in 1972 with tripartite representation from government, employers, and labor.

creation of more skilled positions, while firms were given special incentives to upgrade their manufacturing processes and increase productivity. In 1979, in a policy that became known as the Second Industrial Revolution, the National Wages Council raised wages by an average of 20% and chose twelve sectors—including computer software, precision engineering, and electronic instruments—for special promotion. Singaporean workers were retrained, and the government restructured its educational system to focus more intensively on engineering, science, and vocational training.

Meanwhile, the EDB continued to streamline and enhance its investment program. It developed an innovative "one-stop" service that promised to meet potential investors at the airport, guide them to a possible investment site, and guarantee their venture a quick start-up date. Along the way, the investor would encounter a full range of pleasant and efficient services: an excellent airline, a top-rated airport, impeccable public transportation, and so on. The country's macroeconomic policies reflected this same pro-business stance, with no foreign exchange controls, no restrictions on the repatriation of capital or the remittance of funds, and no taxes on interest income from foreign currency deposits. The base corporate tax rate was only 27%, and nearly all economic sectors were open to foreign investment. The handful of exceptions were in basic infrastructural services such as power, telecommunications, and port operations, all of which were run by various arms of the Singaporean government and constituted an integral part of its strategy to create a hospitable environment for investment.[8] The country's legal system, patterned after that of the British and rigorously enforced, reassured Western businesses that their contracts and disputes could be settled in a familiar fashion. Finally, Singapore's infamous commitment to cleanliness and order made the city-state a safe and pleasant living environment for Western executives.

And thus, spurred by these enticements and inducements, the investors came. And when Singapore moved up the value chain, they generally followed. By the late 1970s, foreign investment flows into Singapore regularly topped $1 billion a year, and capital-intensive industries, such as computer components and peripherals, had become the mainstay of the country's burgeoning industrial sector.

By the late 1980s, however, Singapore's development strategy was showing signs of losing steam. Part of the problem, ironically, was a direct result of the country's success. Because the Singaporean model had worked so well, it had spawned imitators all across Asia, most notably in Malaysia, Thailand, and the emerging markets of China and India. For these countries, Singapore represented a particularly powerful example, since it had achieved its growth in a relatively short period of time and without sacrificing either political or social stability. For Singapore, however, its attractiveness to its giant neighbors was a threat as much as a compliment. With populations of roughly one billion a piece, China and India had markets whose sheer size could overwhelm Singapore and attract the lion's share of future trade and investment in Asia. Commenting on this threat in 1993, Singapore's Minister of Information and Industry warned that the imitators might be able to improve upon Singapore's success, noting that "after all, they have more clever people than we have, lots of land, and abundant national resources."[9]

For Singapore, the biggest risk lay with the potential loss of investors. The country had grown, after all, largely by opening its borders to foreign firms and their capital. If these foreigners

[8] The Singaporean government was wholly responsible for power, water, and gas services (through the Public Utilities Board), telecommunications (through Singapore Telcom), port operations (through the Port of Singapore Authority), and the development of industrial estates and housing (through the Jurong Town Corporation and the Housing Development Board).
[9] Brigadier General George Yeo, speech to the Singapore International Chamber of Commerce, quoted in the *Straits Times*, June 5, 1993, p. 36.

left, or even if new firms just stopped coming, Singapore's economic growth would be bound to falter. Facing this possibility, Singapore's leaders began to concentrate on developing programs to entice investors to stay. Because Singapore clearly could not compete with its larger neighbors in terms of costs or space or market size, these programs instead sought to leverage the island's existing strengths in infrastructure and communications, establishing Singapore as a global center for investment and services.

With programs like "Information Technology 2000" and "International Business Hub 2000," the government pledged to make Singapore a world leader in logistics and business communications and to link all homes, offices, schools, and factories in a sophisticated computer network. At the same time, though, the EDB also began to craft the programs that would allow Singapore to meet its emerging competitors head-on. Central to these programs was Lee Kuan Yew's notion of regionalization, which promised not only to differentiate Singapore from the larger markets of China, India, and Indonesia, but also to allow Singaporeans to enter these markets themselves, taking their skills, their services, and their foreign investors with them.

The Regionalization Drive

Like most things in Singapore, the regionalization drive was part of a carefully-conceived strategy. It began with the recognition that Singapore's future growth depended in large part on the simultaneous growth and development of its neighbors, particularly China, India, and the ASEAN nations. To drive this growth and insure a place within it, the Singaporean government made a basic commitment to support outward foreign direct investment, both from Singaporean firms and from foreign firms with bases and relationships in Singapore. While the bulk of the investment was to be private, the EDB would retain its historical task of coordination and facilitation. In addition, the Singaporean government pledged to invest up to $15 billion of its own reserves in Asian projects. For all projects, both private and public, the EDB proposed a four-step approach for potential inventors: (1) analyze the market potential of selected Asian cities; (2) assemble appropriate business partners; (3) forge linkages back to Singapore; and (4) refine the political instruments—such as bilateral government commissions—to smooth the investment. The EDB also created a host of financial incentives, such as tax exemptions, fixed rate financing, and training grants. By 1994, all elements of the regionalization drive were in place and many Singaporean firms, particularly those in traditional service sectors such as construction, had rushed to take advantage of the EDB's support and inducements. During the first half of 1994, 44 Singaporean firms secured nearly $415 million worth of contracts and subcontracts in Southeast Asia.[10]

While some of these firms had entered into independent deals with outside firms or municipalities, most of their contracts were linked to the real core of Singapore's regionalization drive: the industrial parks. Conceptually, the industrial parks were hardly a new idea. Rather, they drew on several decades of experience in Asia with export processing zones, areas specifically prepared and reserved for foreign investors. In these zones, or parks as they were quickly dubbed, the local government would concentrate all the resources and supporting facilities that foreign firms in a less-developed economy were likely to demand. Special tax rates were usually offered, technological resources were clustered nearby, and materials and goods could generally pass through the zones without paying local tariffs. The zones also customarily boasted the best physical infrastructure in the local area and offered investors additional amenities such as schools, apartments, clubs, and recreational areas. In exchange for these attractions, the foreign investors

---

[10]*Business Times*, March 29, 1995, p. 20.

who located in the industrial zones were expected to produce the exports, capital inflows, and technological spillovers that the local economy could not generate by itself.

The first and most well-known industrial park was Singapore's Jurong Industrial Estate, established in 1961 with an industrial-residential-recreational complex, Japanese and Chinese gardens, and Asia's only open-air aviary. After Jurong, Singapore opened four additional industrial parks and succeeded in wooing to them such major multinationals as Hewlett Packard, Texas Instruments, and Apple Computers. Shortly afterwards, neighboring countries adopted the industrial park strategies. Malaysia began to establish Free Trade Zones in 1971; Taiwan constructed three Export Processing Zones between 1965 and 1970; South Korea built a Free Export Zone in Masan in 1971 and another in Iri a few years later; and Hong Kong organized the Hong Kong Industrial Estates Corporation in 1977.

Amidst all this imitation, officials at the EDB began to realize by the mid-1980s that the success of their industrial parks had created an exportable advantage for Singapore. Thus, even before Singapore launched its formal regionalization drive, Singaporeans had gone into the industrial parks business, developing elsewhere in Asia the same kinds of export zones that had proven so successful in attracting investors to Singapore.

The Batam Park

The first of these parks was created in January 1991, when Singaporean and Indonesian officials presided at the opening of Batam Industrial Park, a 5-square-kilometer site in the center of Batam, an Indonesian island located only 20 kilometers southeast of Singapore. Designed to support light industries such as electronics, printing, and packaging, the Batam Park was owned and managed by the Batamindo Investment Corporation (BIC), a consortium of Singaporean and Indonesian firms which also owned the Park's design and management company, Batamindo Industrial Management (BIM). On the Indonesian side, the majority shareholders of the consortium were the Salim Group, the world's largest Chinese-owned conglomerate, and Bimantara, an Indonesian conglomerate controlled by Bambang Trihatmodjo, son of Indonesia's President Suharto. On the Singaporean side, 30% ownership was held by Singapore Technologies Industrial Corporation, a government-linked corporation, and 10% by Jurong Environmental Engineering.

More than just an industrial area, Batam was also the first product of Singapore's ambitious "Growth Triangle" strategy. Conceived in 1990 by an agreement between the Indonesian and Singaporean governments, the Growth Triangle was explicitly designed to blend together the two countries' very different patterns of factor endowments and comparative advantage. Indonesia brought the land and labor, Singapore the infrastructure and administrative skills. Thus, for all practical purposes, Batam functioned as a separate, self-contained municipality in Indonesia. An independent utility center ensured the Park's residents of a reliable source of water, electricity and power, while a dedicated communications tower and microwave transmission system were constructed and jointly operated by Singapore Telecom International, Telkom of Indonesia, and BIC. To ensure the Park's investors of a stable and predictable investment climate, BIM offered a one-stop approval center modeled after the EDB's operations in Singapore. BIM also recruited and trained workers (mostly female immigrants from the neighboring island of Java) to staff the Park's factories. It handled applications for business licenses and work permits, provided 24-hour security services, and maintained living quarters for the Park's workers—all of course, for additional management fees. A commercial center within the Park housed a bank, training services, management consultancy, restaurants, a medical center, supermarkets, a post office, convenience stores, a mosque and a church. A BIM subsidiary, Batamindo Shipping and Warehousing, provided cargo services and warehousing facilities.

Between 1991 and 1993, construction and marketing efforts had attracted roughly $119 million worth of foreign investment to the Batam Park; by 1996, the Park counted 79 multinational companies as its residents, and included assembly operations for firms such as Smith Corona, Philips, Sumitomo, and Sanyo Energy.[11] The Indonesian government, meanwhile, had warmly embraced the industrial park concept and supported the development of seven neighboring parks on Batam Island alone. Despite this enthusiasm, however, the parks had not yet created the business climate that their backers had envisioned. While Batamindo in particular had witnessed a tremendous improvement in basic infrastructure, parts of the Park still resembled a building site more than a viable city. Low labor productivity, high turnover, and corruption, common problems for foreign investors throughout Indonesia, plagued firms at Batamindo as well, despite BIM's ongoing efforts to buffer its tenants from external influences. Moreover, because the Batam Park had developed so quickly and attracted such a high-profile list of investors, it also had the highest wages in Indonesia by 1994 and some of the nation's most rapidly escalating land prices.

Extending the Model: Bangalore

Undeterred by these concerns, Singapore's EDB began to discuss in 1993 the possibilities for developing a second overseas park, this one in Bangalore, the emerging center of India's high technology sector.

After initial discussions between Indian Prime Minister P.V. Narasimha Rao and Singaporean Prime Minister Goh, Philip Yeo of the EDB led a delegation to Bangalore in July 1993. Their agreed-upon aim was to create a one-stop Information Technology (IT) park that integrated advanced manufacturing, design and development, training, showroom, office, recreation, and residential activities in one location. The park would thus add the business and physical infrastructure to Bangalore's existing technological base; already, the city boasted one-third of India's large pool of software professionals and was home to electronics and software giants such as Texas Instruments, Motorola, Hewlett Packard, and IBM. What the park would offer to the next line of foreign investors was a means to access the growing cluster of low-wage Indian software developers and other related professionals without having to wade through India's notoriously inefficient bureaucracy or suffer with its notoriously poor infrastructure. Instead, as in the Batam Park, the Bangalore Information Technology Park promised investors a tempting combination of Singaporean services and Indian cost advantages.

Organizationally and politically, the Bangalore Park was structured much like its Indonesian predecessor. The park was established as a joint venture between Singapore's Information Technology Park Investment Pte. Ltd. (ITPI) (40%), India's Tata Industries Ltd. (40%), and Karnataka Industrial Areas Development Board (20%), the investment arm of the local Karnataka government. ITPI was a consortium of six Singaporean firms assembled solely to oversee the development of Bangalore Park. Its members included the publicly-listed L&M Group Investments Ltd; RSP Architects Planners and Engineers (Pte) Ltd, Singapore's largest architectural and building consultancy firm; Singapore Technologies Industrial Corporation, a defense-related, government-linked firm held by Singapore Technologies; Sembawang Construction, held in part by Temasek, the government's largest non-defense diversified holding company; Technology Parks, a subsidiary of Jurong Town Corporation; and Parameswara Holdings, the investment division of the

---

[11] *Fortune*, March 4, 1996.

Singapore Indian Chamber of Commerce and Industry. Tata Industries, meanwhile, was an investment company owned by the Tata Group, one of India's largest and most influential companies. Under the joint venture agreement establishing the Bangalore Park, Tata's obligations included gaining all the necessary approvals from the Indian government and central bank for foreign equity participation, assisting in foreign currency and equity transactions, and assisting in domestic marketing and sales.

With an estimated construction cost of S$670 million, the 0.26-square-kilometer Bangalore Park was to be located in Whitefield, an eastern suburb of Bangalore City. Phase I of the project was slated to open by the second quarter of 1996 and Phase II a year later.

Even while construction was still underway, the publicity surrounding the park generated both commercial and political reaction. Spurred by the prospect of increased investment, commercial rents in Bangalore increased 50% in the first six months of 1994, while residential rates rose 30% over their 1993 levels. In February 1994, militant farmers in the region began to protest publicly against foreign computer firms in Bangalore, claiming multinationals impinged upon India's sovereignty and that computer firms, in particular, reduced demand for the labor-intensive jobs upon which India's overpopulated economy so critically depended. After KFC, America's fried chicken fast-food chain, opened an outlet in Bangalore in June 1995, demonstrators succeeded in temporarily closing the restaurant's doors on the grounds that KFC used excessive levels of certain food additives in its fare. Another outlet in New Delhi, which opened in November, was ordered closed three weeks after opening due to similar complaints. Though the closure was overturned by the high court of Karnataka state, it was believed that the two incidents were politically motivated by the BJP, India's main opposition party, which aimed to drive out multinational corporations in "unimportant sectors."[12] In addition, an Indian farmers' forum vowed to fight KFC and other multinational firms "tooth and nail" to prevent their entry into the Indian market.[13] In early February 1996, the KFC in Bangalore was ransacked for the second time by farmers protesting the presence of multinationals, which they claimed were subverting Indian cultural traditions and ruining millions of farmers.

Neither the protests nor the rising rents, however, diminished planners' expectations for the Bangalore Park. On the contrary, they only underscored the benefits that the planners fully expected the Park to offer investors: a safe, predictable, and well-serviced entry into one of the world's largest and most dynamic emerging markets.

Singapore and China

If developing a safe haven for investors was an attractive proposition in India, it was an even more enticing prospect in China—a country whose economy was growing at unprecedented rates in the early 1990s and whose leaders were particularly attracted to the Singaporean model of growth and governance. With a population of 1.2 billion and an economy expanding at over 10% a year, China since 1990 had captured the interests of the world's multinational firms, nearly all of which saw a dramatic potential in entering the world's largest market.

But especially for western firms, entering China still entailed a tremendous amount of risk and uncertainty. The currency remained unconvertible, the political leanings of the country's aging

---

[12] *Agence France Presse,* December 4, 1995.
[13] *Agence France Presse,* February 4, 1996.

communist leadership were unclear, and business relied heavily on *guanxi*, a hazy network of personal ties and commitments that few outsiders were competent to master.

This combination of political uncertainty and commercial opportunity created a nearly perfect fit for Singapore's regional strategy. China had land, physical resources, and a labor pool that Singapore lacked. Singapore had the capital, technology, and development track that China sought. Investors wanted to enter China but worried about the risks they would encounter. Singaporeans felt confident about their ability to master China's risks but did not have sufficient home-grown firms to make much of a dent in the vast Chinese market. So the idea of Singaporean-run investment enclaves—already tempting in Indonesia and India—was particularly well-suited to the Chinese context.

What made the fit even more powerful was the Chinese government's quiet embrace of Singapore's unique mode of governance. While the island's brand of "democratic socialism" held uncomfortable overtones for many more liberal states, it struck a strongly responsive chord with China's communist party leaders. Recognizing the economic disasters that communism had brought to China, the nation's leadership was slowly coming to accept the tenets of market capitalism, taking seriously Deng Xiaoping's 1978 proclamation that "To get rich is glorious!" But even while moving cautiously towards the market, China's leaders were reluctant to loosen their grip on the country's political system. Instead, they wanted a blend of liberalization and control, allowing just enough freedom for economic growth to occur without diminishing the extent of their own power.

In Singapore, China's leaders saw a viable example of this blend. Thus, when Deng Xiaoping conducted his famous tour of China's southern cities in 1992, he commented repeatedly on the lessons of Singapore, noting that, "Singapore enjoys good social order and is well-managed. We should tap on their experience and learn how to manage better than them."[14] Deng's "southern lectures" spawned a series of Chinese delegations to Singapore, each trying to capture the island's winning formula of managing a growing economy through a tight-knit partnership between the public and private sectors. The Chinese also wanted to understand how Singapore had prevented its foreign investors from introducing "undesirable elements" into local society and how the government had maintained crime-free streets and a population that respected authority. One mayor of a small Chinese town had even reportedly spent his time in Singapore examining the island's methods for rubbish removal.[15]

It was precisely this type of emulation that both fed Singapore's fear of China and drove its interest in the Chinese market. In 1992, Singaporeans invested $990 million in 742 Chinese projects, making them the country's fifth largest foreign investors.[16] Likewise, of the 150 foreign investment projects that EDB coordinated in 1993, 52% went to China.[17]

The real push into China, however, focused on the creation of industrial parks, since it was the parks that promised to exploit the full synergies between China, Singapore, and foreign investors. In the parks, Singaporean and Chinese officials could, in effect, recreate the investment advantages of Singapore directly in China. In this context, the Wuxi and Suzhou Industrial Parks were conceived.

---

[14]*South China Morning Post*, May 31, 1995.

[15]From a speech by Singapore's Brigadier General George Yeo, printed in the *Straits Times*, June 5, 1993, p. 36.

[16]The four largest sources of investment in China were Hong Kong, Taiwan, Japan and the United States. See *Business Times*, January 14, 1994, p. 2.

[17]Singapore Economic Development Board, Press release, December 21, 1994.

The Singapore-Suzhou Township

The idea of developing a "Singapore II" in China was born in stages. In October 1992, Mayor Zhang Xinsheng, mayor of Suzhou, invited Singapore's Deputy Prime Minister, Ong Teng Cheong, to visit his city and discuss the prospect for joint undertakings. The following spring, Mr. Ong then revisited China with Lee Kuan Yew, completing the customary business circuit of Beijing, Shanghai, Pudong, and Shandong, with additional side trips to Suzhou and Wuxi. During that trip, Chinese and Singaporean officials agreed that Singapore would develop an industrial township somewhere in China.

During the next several months, various Chinese mayors took their turn at "pitching" their cities to Singapore's EDB. All were impressive, but Mayor Zhang's Suzhou stood out above the rest. Known locally for its scenic bridges and waterways, Suzhou was located in Jiangsu province, directly at the center of China's burgeoning economic growth. Fourth among China's coastal cities in terms of industrial output, Suzhou derived 60% of its revenues from its 15,000 private or "township" enterprises. Suzhou's residents were among the wealthiest in the region, with an annual per capita income in 1992 of roughly $970. The city's traditional industries included textiles and machinery, and a skilled labor pool, earning approximately $58 a month, was readily available. The city's infrastructure was also above average. Rail and river connections linked Suzhou to the international airport and seaport in Shanghai, as well as to 10 other major cities such as Beijing, Tianjin, Hangzhou, and Nanjing.

Reviewing these attractions, the EDB chose Suzhou in 1992 as the site of its first industrial park. Working closely with the local government, it then began to structure the terms of the park's development. To lead the project, the EDB chose the Keppel Group, a government-linked corporation and former ship repairing agency that had grown to become one of Singapore's largest and most diversified conglomerates. With Keppel at the helm, the Singapore-Suzhou Townships Development Pte. Ltd. (SSTD) was incorporated in Singapore in September 1993 with authorized capital of $300 million and a mandate to garner all the necessary expertise and financing for the project.

The 20 members of the SSTD included property developers, engineering firms, and investment-holding companies. All but two of the participants were government-linked companies based in Singapore. To oversee the park's physical construction, SSTD formed a joint venture with the Suzhou Industrial Park Investment Company, a newly-formed enterprise composed of Jiangsu and Suzhou state-owned enterprises. The resulting joint venture company, the China-Singapore Suzhou Industrial Park Development Company (CSSD), was constituted with 65% Singaporean capital and 35% Chinese (see **Figure A**).

Figure A Organizational Structure of the Singapore-Suzhou Township

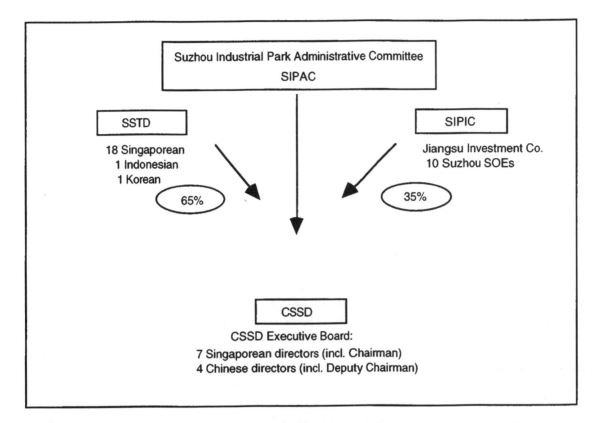

On February 26, 1994, the Singapore-Suzhou Township was formalized through two agreements between the two governments and their agencies and a third agreement with the private sector. The major premises of the agreements were as follows:

- The governments of the Republic of Singapore and the People's Republic of China pledged support for the township. Each side agreed to appoint a Deputy Prime Minister or Vice Premier to jointly chair a PRC-Singapore Joint Steering Council, responsible for all major issues relating to the adaptation of Singapore economic and public administration experience in the Suzhou Township. The Suzhou Industrial Park Authority Commission (SIPAC), comprising Jiangsu and Suzhou officials, held ultimate authority over township policies and terms for investors.

- Jurong Town Corporation (JTC), representing agencies of the Singapore government and the Suzhou municipal government, agreed to adapt Singapore's economic and public administrative expertise to Suzhou. Chinese personnel would be sent to Singapore for training and Singaporean officials would be posted to Suzhou to assist. A Coordinating Council, headed by Chinese Vice Premier Li Langqing and Singaporean Deputy Prime Minister Lee Hsien Loong (Lee Kuan Yew's eldest son), was formed to oversee the broader issues of how to transfer Singapore's governance style to Suzhou. The Joint Working Committee, co-chaired by JTC Chairman Wong Hung Kim and Suzhou Mayor Zhang, would supervise specific projects.

- The Suzhou Township was declared an Economic Trade and Development Zone, making it the fourth EDZ in greater Suzhou. SSTD and the Suzhou municipal government agreed to key commercial terms available to foreign investors. These included land price, tenure of land-use rights, preferential policies, investment activities, and provision of basic infrastructure.

Located in eastern Suzhou, the Suzhou Township would integrate industrial facilities with residential, commercial, and recreational components for both workers and nonworkers. It also enclosed Jinji Lake to allow for a range of tourist facilities. To facilitate this construction, roughly 20,000 households would be relocated during the development's three phases. The infrastructure for the park—factories, power plants, water and sewage facilities, warehousing, and residential units—would all be constructed by the various members of SSTD.

In addition to this massive physical development, the government of Singapore also pledged to transfer to its Chinese counterparts the "software" of economic and public administrations—that is, to pass on its own experience in urban planning, environmental management, building design, and construction. Although officials from both sides stressed that China could not directly adopt Singaporean methods of administration, they also agreed that the EDB would oversee the development in Suzhou of certain basic administrative systems: an investment approval process, tax incentives, and transparent legal rules. In the process, Singapore would in effect be selling to China its greatest competitive advantage: its legal and commercial infrastructure. Commenting on this relationship, one foreign broker in 1993 predicted that "Suzhou will be marketed as a little piece of Singapore, next door to Shanghai. The one place in China where you can rely on the phones and you don't have to bribe officials."[18]

As of March 1996, CSSD had signed agreements with 56 investors for a total committed investment of $1.8 billion.[19]

The Wuxi-Singapore Industrial Park

Launched in December 1993, the Wuxi-Singapore Industrial Park resembled quite closely its neighbor in Suzhou. Again, local authorities held a minority position (30%) in the controlling joint venture; again, the bulk of the physical development would fall to Singapore's government-linked corporations. Wuxi was smaller than Suzhou, with expected employment of only 10,000. It also targeted only high-technology industries, differentiating itself not only from Suzhou but also from other large-scale industrial parks such as Pudong, a massive development on the outskirts of Shanghai. The Wuxi Park also included a third major equity holder, the Salim Group of Indonesia.

Extending Singapore's one-stop-shopping concept, the park's developer, Wuxi-Singapore Industrial Park Investment Co. (WSIP), promised (for an additional fee) to handle all the initial legwork for its investors. It would recruit workers, apply for the firm's business license, submit tenders for contractors, and so on. It would also set the terms of employment for a company's labor force, using a formula pioneered at Batam that bound workers to a company for two years at a recommended wage level of $44 per month. For another fee, the Port of Singapore Authority would provide all investors in Wuxi with transport, warehousing, and logistical support services.

---

[18]Quoted in "Lee can do," *The Economist*, August 21, 1993, p. 52.
[19] *Fortune*, March 4, 1996.

As of March 1996, 32 tenants, including Murata, Sumitomo Electric, and Seagate Technology had agreed to invest in Wuxi, and a $100 million third phase of development was underway.[20]

Bolstered by these developments, Singapore's EDB continued to explore further expansions into China. In May 1995 Prime Minister Goh led a record 72-member delegation to several Chinese cities, including Wuhan, Chongqing, Chengdu, and Shanghai. During the course of the trip, Mr. Goh proposed to develop a township near Shanghai, with the Singapore Housing Development Board providing the "software" on town management and maintenance. In the wake of Goh's visit, Singaporean companies announced another flurry of deals, committing to invest $1.1 billion in new Chinese projects.

Singapore-led consortia were also developing an industrial park and a beach resort in Bintan, Indonesia as well as marine and petroleum complexes in Indonesia's Karimun Islands. Further plans were underway for a $250 million Vietnam-Singapore Industrial Park outside Ho Chi Minh City and another township development in Myanmar.

Elsewhere in Asia, the evidence of Singapore's regionalization drive was beginning to raise some quiet concerns. Noting that Singapore's success had come at the expense of its own local enterprises, some experts worried that an expansion of the industrial parks would impede the growth of domestic Asian entrepreneurs. More dramatically, others argued that Singapore's development efforts in neighboring countries were akin to colonization. Philip Yeo, head of the EDB, dismissed these criticisms. "It's hard for a nation of three million," he argued, "to colonize China, India, and Vietnam."[21]

---

[20] *Business Times*, March 5, 1996.
[21]*Business Times*, October 29, 1994, p. 4.

Exhibit 1   Map of South and South-East Asia

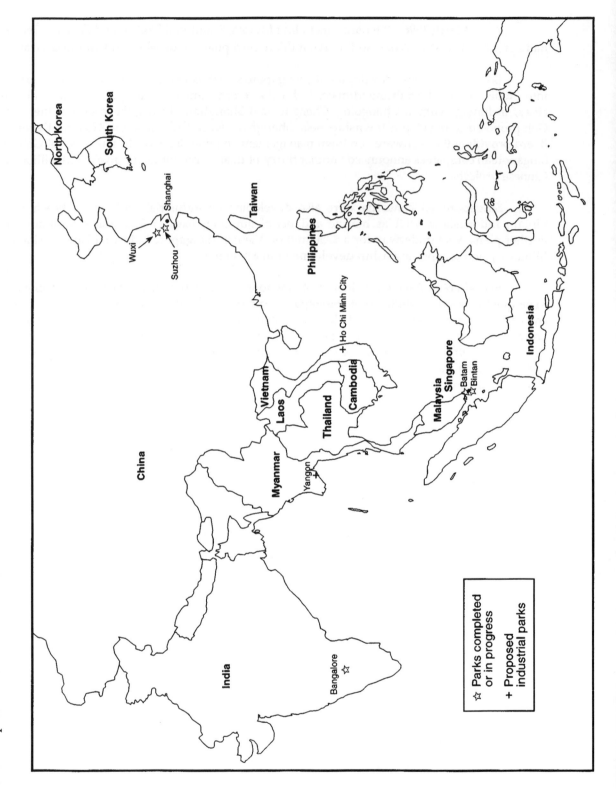

Exhibit 2   Singapore's Balance of Payments, 1965-1994
(US$ millions)

	1965	1970	1975	1980	1985	1990	1991	1992	1993	1994
Current account	(59)	(572)	(584)	(1,563)	(4)	2,095	3,992	3,748	2,039	11,950
Trade balance	(248)	(855)	(2,030)	(2,970)	(1,508)	(4,718)	(3,791)	(5,782)	(8,065)	2,106
Merchandise exports	918	1,447	5,481	19,430	22,854	51,095	57,156	62,068	71,959	98,689
Merchandise imports	(1,166)	(2,302)	(7,511)	(22,400)	(24,362)	(55,812)	(60,948)	(67,850)	(80,025)	(96,583)
Services, net^a	215	291	1,450	1,944	1,086	6,142	6,958	8,563	9,244	10,014
Credit	323	556	2,416	4,856	5,062	15,439	16,821	18,794	20,879	22,983
Debit	(108)	(265)	(966)	(2,912)	(3,976)	(9,297)	(9,863)	(10,231)	(11,635)	(12,969)
Income, net	NA	NA	35	(429)	631	1,114	1,324	1,563	1,557	607
Credit	NA	NA	380	953	1,814	6,469	7,464	8,407	9,091	8,429
Debit	NA	NA	(345)	(1,382)	(1,183)	(5,355)	(6,140)	(6,844)	(7,534)	(7,822)
Private transfers, net	(12)	(21)	(39)	(104)	(205)	(274)	(340)	(405)	(482)	(778)^c
Official transfers, net	(14)	13	—	(3)	(8)	(169)	(159)	(190)	(215)	NA
Capital account										
Direct investment, net	16	93	254	1,138	809	4,005	4,444	5,982	6,062	3,411
Into Singapore	NA	NA	292	1,236	1,047	5,575	4,888	6,730	6,829	5,588
Abroad	NA	NA	(38)	(98)	(238)	(1,570)	(444)	(748)	(767)	(2,177)
Portfolio investment, net	—	—	(2)	13	175	(1,140)	(802)	(819)	(944)	785
Other long-term capital^b	2	47	328	432	34	(1,156)	(1,521)	(244)	(891)	(2,408)
Short-term capital, net	20	33	NA	NA	(319)	2,949	(1,187)	641	5,225	NA
Reserves, net	5	(185)	(407)	(663)	(1,337)	(5,431)	(4,198)	(6,100)	(7,578)	(4,736)
Errors and omissions	16	584	411	643	642	(1,322)	(728)	(3,208)	(3,913)	(9,001)

Source: International Monetary Fund, *Balance of Payments Yearbook*, various issues; *International Financial Statistics Yearbook*, various issues.

^aFigures for 1965 and 1970 combine net services and net income.

^bData for 1975, 1980, and 1994 include short-term capital.

^cCurrent transfers, net.

Note: Numbers may not add due to rounding.

Exhibit 3 Singapore's Gross Domestic Product by Industry, 1965-1994 (in per cent)

	1965	1970	1975	1980	1985	1990	1991	1992	1993	1994
Manufacturing	15.1	24.8	26.1	29.5	23.6	28.8	28.6	26.5	27.5	28.2
Construction	5.9	9.5	8.8	7.1	10.6	5.3	6.1	6.4	7.4	7.1
Commerce	27.6	22.0	21.0	18.9	17.0	17.9	17.5	16.3	17.8	17.6
Transport & communications	11.3	7.3	9.0	12.0	13.4	14.2	14.3	14.1	12.1	14.5
Finance & business	13.7	16.9	20.4	20.5	27.3	26.0	27.4	24.6	28.8	26.6
Others	26.4	19.5	14.7	12.0	8.1	7.8	6.1	12.1	6.4	6.0
GDP (in current S$ millions)	4,411	10,592	12,910	25,091	35,138	66,175	73,038	79,083	89,006	98,446
GDP (in 1985 S$ millions)	5,069	12,172	14,836	28,833	35,138	57,272	61,081	64,771	71,212	78,765

Source: Singapore Ministry of Trade and Commerce, *Economic Survey of Singapore*, various issues.

Exhibit 4 Foreign Direct Investment Inflows to Selected Asian Countries, 1981-1992 (US$ millions)

Country	1981-1985	1986-1990	1991	1992
	(Annual Average)			
China	850	2,853	4,366	11,156
Hong Kong	576	1,945	538	1,918
India	59	182	145	140
Indonesia	236	599	1,482	1,774
Korea, Republic of	117	676	1,116	550
Malaysia	1,083	1,126	3,998	4,469
Pakistan	77	175	257	349
Philippines	63	493	544	228
Singapore	1,349	3,247	4,395	5,635
Sri Lanka	42	40	48	123
Taiwan	189	987	1,271	879
Thailand	279	1,188	2,014	2,116
Vietnam	6	6	32	—

Source: Adapted from *World Investment Report 1994*, p. 71.

Exhibit 5 Singapore's Total Direct Investment Abroad, 1993 (S$ billions)

Country	Total Amount of Direct Investment
Malaysia	4.7
Hong Kong	4.0
Netherlands Antilles	2.8
United States	1.8
New Zealand	1.5
Cayman Islands	0.8
Belgium	0.5
Indonesia	0.5
Netherlands	0.5
China	0.4
Exchange rate: S$:US$ (1993 average)	1.63

Source: Adapted from Economic Intelligence Unit, *Country Report 4th Quarter 1994*.

Exhibit 6   Comparative Regional Data

	Hong Kong	China	Japan	South Korea	Taiwan	Viet Nam	Indonesia	Malaysia	Singapore	India
Social Indicators										
Population (mil)	5.5	1,203.0	125.5	45.6	21.5	74.4	203.6	19.7	2.9	936.5
Life expectancy (years)	80	68	79	71	75.5	66	61	69.5	76	59
Infant mortality rate per 1,000	5.8	52.1	4.3	20.9	5.6	44.6	65	24.7	5.7	76.3
Adult literacy (%)[a]	77	78	99	96	86	88	82	78	89	52
Unemployment rate (%), 1994	1.9	2.7[b]	2.9	2.0	1.6	20	3.0[c]	2.9	2.6	NA
Persons per physician, 1990	919	809	610	1,070	831	2,916	7,030	2,590	820	2,460
Access to electricity, 1992 (% households)	100	67	NA	100	NA	15	26	84	100	82[d]
Production										
Total GNP (US$bil), 1994	136.1	508.2	2,527.4	508.3	257	83.5	619.4	166.8	57	1,253.9
Per capita GNP (US$), 1994	24,530	2,500 (est.)	20,200	11,270	12,070	1,140	3,090	8,650	19,940	1,360
As a percent of GDP:										
Agriculture	0	27	2	8	3.5	36	19	15.8	0	32
Industry	23	34	42	45	41.4	21	40	44.2	38	27
of which:										
Manufacturing	16	NA	26	26	32.9	NA	21	30.1	28	17
Services	77	38	56	47	55.1	NA	40	40.0	62	40

Source: Asian Development Bank, *Key Indicators of Developing Asian and Pacific Countries 1994*; Far Eastern Economic Review, *Asia 1995 Yearbook*; Central Intelligence Agency, *The World Factbook 1995*.

a Latest available.
b Unemployment rate refers only to urban areas; underemployment figures not included.
c Underemployment figures not included.
d Villages with access to electricity as a percent of total villages.

Exhibit 7   GDP Growth in Asia, 1994

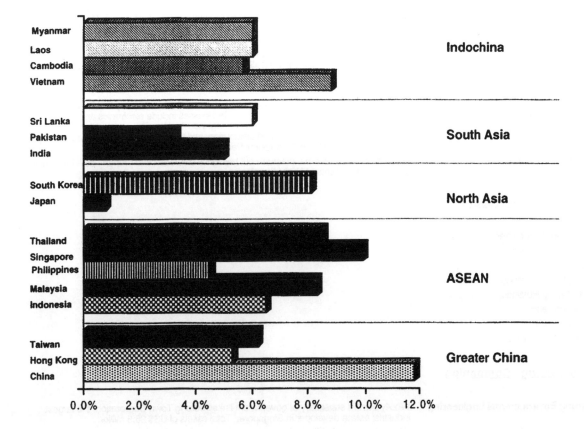

Source: Data compiled from the Economist Intelligence Unit, *Business Asia,* various issues.

Exhibit 8   Selected Shareholders of Singapore Suzhou Township Development Pte Ltd.

Diversified Conglomerates

Keppel Corporation

Leader of the consortium. One of Singapore's largest and most diversified conglomerates with total assets of US$ 7 billion. Operates through the Asia Pacific in ship repair, property, engineering, banking and financial services, transportation and telecommunications.

KMP

A flagship of the Salim Group of Indonesia, with assets over US$ 560 million. Involved in property investment and development, manufacturing, food processing, agrotechnology and investment holding.

Samsung Electronics

A division of South Korea's Samsung Corp. with total sales of US$10.8 billion in 1993. Became the 20th shareholder of SSTD after it announced plans for a $ 34 million joint venture to manufacture refrigerators, microwaves and washing machines. Next planned venture will be a $23 million manufacturing plant for semiconductors.

Sembawang Corp

A GLC conglomerate with total assets of US$ 850 million. Engaged in construction, property development, steel fabrication, process and environmental engineering, ship repair, and rig-building.

Singapore Technologies Industrial Corp Ltd (STIC)

A division of Singapore Technologies, a government-linked company that began as Singapore's defense manufacturer. Core businesses include electronics and information technology, precision engineering, industrial leasing, construction and development, food processing and distribution, and travel and leisure. Prior industrial park projects included the Batam Industrial Park and Bintan Industrial Estate.

Wing Tai Holdings

Started as a garment manufacturer but has since diversified into property development and trading. Total assets of US$ 850 million.

Property Developers

Centrepoint Properties
City Developments
DBS Land
Liang Court Holdings
Lum Chang Holdings
Pidemco Land
Singapore Land
Straits Steamship Land

Engineering Companies

Jurong Environmental Engineering

Wholly-owned subsidiary of government-linked Jurong Town Corporation, the largest industrial estate developer in Singapore. Total assets of US$ 26.5 million.

Sum Cheong Corporation

Wholly-owned subsidiary of Hong Kong's publicly listed Sum Cheong International Limited. Total assets of US$ 140 million.

Investment Holding Companies & Others

NTUC Co-operatives
Shing Kwan Investments
SLF International
Temasek Holdings
Technology Parks Pte Ltd

Source: Singapore Economic Development Board

Exhibit 9   Foreign Investment Business License Application Procedure in Wuxi, China

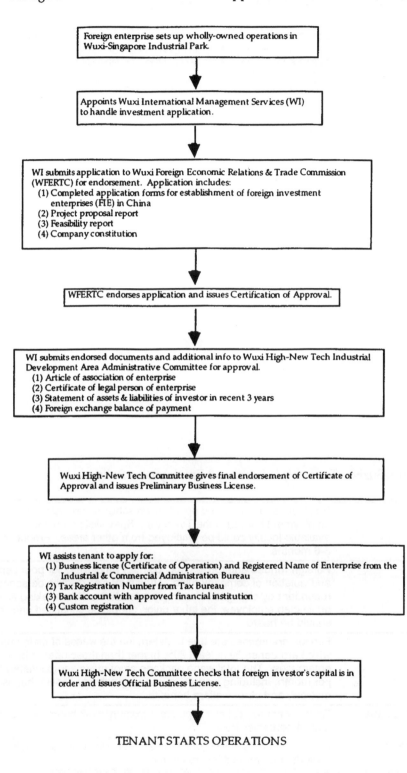

Source: Wuxi International Management Services Pte Ltd.

Exhibit 10   Tax Incentives for the Singapore-Suzhou Township

Investment	Foreign investors who reinvest profits would obtain a 40% rebate on income tax.
	Those who reinvest profits in an export-oriented or high-technology enterprise in operation for 5 years or more would obtain a full rebate of the income tax paid on the amount reinvested.
Local Income Tax	Foreign-funded enterprises would be exempted from local income tax up to the end of year 2000.
Repatriation of Profits	Foreign investors may repatriate profits abroad free of the 10% withholding tax.
Custom Duty and Value-Added Tax	Foreign-funded enterprises may import for their own use building materials, production and management facilities, production fuel, raw materials, spare parts, reasonable amount of vehicles (excluding cars), and articles for office use without paying custom duty and value-added tax.
	Unless otherwise noted by state regulations, products manufactured within the Township for export would be exempted from export tax and value-added tax.
	Machinery, equipment, and other building materials required for construction of infrastructure in the Township are exempted from custom duty and value-added tax.
	Foreign investors who bring into the country personal articles for setting up homes are exempted from custom duty and value-added tax.
Property Tax	Foreign-funded enterprises which purchase for their own use newly constructed buildings are exempted from property tax for 5 years from the date of completion of construction or the date of purchase.

Source: Singapore-Suzhou Township Development

Exhibit 11   Singapore-Suzhou Township's Labor and Employment Policies

• Employment	Employees may be hired openly from schools and institutes, or through an employment bureau in the Township. Specialist personnel who are not available locally could be employed from other areas. Probation period of 3-6 months.
• Dismissal	Foreign-funded enterprises may dismiss employees for poor performance and violation of company rules. They may also dismiss personnel made redundant by changes in business operations. When taking action against an employee, the labor union should be consulted and an appeal should be heard.
• Wage	Foreign enterprises are free to determine the wages of their employees which are generally at least 20% higher than those offered by local enterprises. The total wage package amounts to approximately US$ 100 per month, including insurance, housing subsidy, festive bonuses, medical, and other welfare benefits.
• Work Hours and Leave	Government regulations stipulate maximum work hours of 8 hours per day and 44 hours per week.
• Employee Insurance	Foreign enterprises will contribute 25% of each Chinese employee's wage towards a retirement insurance fund.

Source: Singapore-Suzhou Township Development

Exhibit 12 Financial Summary of Selected Government-Linked Companies, 1992-1994 (in S$ millions)

	Keppel Corp			Straits Steamship Land			Wing Tai Holdings			Sembawang Corp		
	1992	1993	1994	1992	1993	1994	1992	1993	1994	1992	1993	1994
Sales	1,682	1,559	1,529	87	68	59	162	192	202	708	666	1,104
Cost of goods sold	1,400	1,275	1,230	55	37	22	135	166	194	587	567	988
Operating income	242	239	257	21	21	22	24	20	2	92	76	71
Net income	145	165	188	26	29	36	9	10	12	94	92	80
Total assets	6,076	7,913	11,173	1,914	1,850	2,125	1,163	1,154	1,267	1,307	1,355	1,957
Current liabilities	2,658	4,180	6,809	48	27	174	177	128	204	464	411	651
Long-term debt	572	565	324	358	357	201	498	583	516	44	46	83
Common equity	1,573	1,817	2,171	1,085	1,112	1,387	349	307	425	758	851	917
Earnings per share (S$)	0.24	0.30	0.35	0.06	0.07	0.08	0.03	0.04	0.04	0.32	0.37	0.39

Source: Company annual reports

Exhibit 13 Shareholders of Selected Government-Linked Companies

Company	Current Shares	Shareholders	Major Shareholders (%)
Keppel Corporation Ltd.	478,271,489	4,644	Temasek Holdings, Ltd., (32.52%)
Straits Steamship Land	451,374,611	4,960	Temasek Holdings, Ltd., (52.27%)
Wing Tai Holdings Ltd.	387,201,500	3,904	Wing Sun Development, (53.17%), (Jointly)
Sembawang Corporation Ltd.	221,578,000	3,399	Temasek Holdings (Pte) Ltd., (39.1%)
			HSBC (Singapore) Nominees Ltd., (12.36%)
			DBS Nominees Pte Ltd., (10.59%)
			Chase Manhattan (Singapore) Nom., (9.89%)

Source: Company annual reports